WineWise

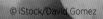

SECOND EDITION

WineWise

YOUR COMPLETE GUIDE TO UNDERSTANDING, SELECTING, AND ENJOYING WINE

Steven Kolpan, Brian H. Smith, and Michael A. Weiss

THE CULINARY INSTITUTE OF AMERICA

Houghton Mifflin Harcourt
Boston • New York • 2014

The Culinary Institute of America:

President	Dr. Tim Ryan '77, CMC
Provost	Mark Erickson '77, CMC
Director of Publishing	Nathalie Fischer
Editorial Assistant	Laura Monroe '12

For information about permission to reproduce selections from this book, write to Permissions, Houghton Mifflin Harcourt Publishing Company, 215 Park Avenue South, New York, New York 10003.

www.hmhco.com

Library of Congress Cataloging-in-Publication Data

Kolpan, Steven.
Winewise : your complete guide to understanding, selecting, and enjoying wine / Steven Kolpan, Brian H. Smith, and Michael A. Weiss, The Culinary Institute of America.— Revised edition.
      pages cm
ISBN 978-0-544-33462-5 (cloth); 978-0-544-33257-7 (ebook)
1. Wine and wine making—Popular works. I. Smith, Brian H. II. Weiss, Michael A.
III. Title. IV. Title: Wine wise.
TP548.K5785 2014
663'.2—dc23
                    2014016316

Book design by Vertigo Design NYC

Printed in China
TOP 10 9 8 7 6 5 4 3 2 1

STEVEN KOLPAN

For my loving family, my dearest friends, my students, my community.

BRIAN H. SMITH

For my wife, Polly, who helps me believe.

MICHAEL A. WEISS

For my teacher Thinley Norbu Rinpoche, our sangha, my wife, Jenny, brother, Richard, and friends. For anyone who has experienced generosity through wine, may you be equally generous to others.

Contents

1

PALATE PLEASURE

ENJOYING WINE

TODAY IN THE UNITED STATES WINE HAS SURPASSED BEER AND SPIRITS AS THE ALCOHOLIC BEVERAGE OF CHOICE FOR Americans who drink. Not only that, but as of late 2011, the United States is the number-one consumer of wine in the world. Obviously, more people are enjoying wine than ever before in their homes, at parties and other social events, or when dining out. We have found that many wine drinkers want more information, both about the wines they enjoy drinking and about wines they haven't tried yet. We've written this book with exactly these folks—you, our readers—in mind. In contemporary society, information can be power, so a heightened awareness about wines will make you a smarter wine consumer, a more wine-knowledgeable host or guest, and a wine-savvy restaurant customer. And with this new information comes the *fun* of wine, because you don't have to indulge in an intellectual exercise every time you open a bottle. You will be WineWise!

In this chapter we concentrate on basic information that will help you to understand why wine comes in so many different styles and flavors, the different ways that people enjoy wine, why some wines cost more than others, and what the label on the bottle can tell you about the wine. Instead of a separate chapter on winemaking, we decided to weave winemaking comments into this and other chapters, concentrating on the effect of winemaking decisions on the style of the wine without spending too much time on technical details. Subsequent chapters will introduce you to some of our favorite wines from the prominent wine-producing areas of the world, help you to get a handle on pairing wine with a wide variety of foods, and give you some insider tips on what you need to know to enjoy wine at home or in a restaurant. The final section of *WineWise* includes a buying guide for specific wines at various price points. Equipped with all this information, you will be ready to enjoy all that the glorious world of wine has to offer.

A question of style

WE'VE ALREADY SUGGESTED THAT THERE are three key opportunities to enjoy wine: at home, in a social setting (such as a party), or in a restaurant. We could also add that there are three other fun/functional uses for wine:

as an aperitif—a drink before dinner

as a drink in a social group or intimate setting, as formal or informal as you like, outdoors or indoors

as an accompaniment to a meal

With just these considerations, you can easily see that the style of any chosen wine will vary according to its purpose. For example, we appreciate a drink before dinner if it is light and simple and relatively low in alcohol, something that excites the appetite, as opposed to something that is full, heavy, and immediately satisfying; save that wine for dinner.

Different skin-contact time will result in lighter or darker degrees of pigmentation, as shown by these rosé wines.

So wine is made in many different styles to meet our various needs. To begin with, there are three basic styles of wine:

still—without bubbles

sparkling—with bubbles

fortified—with added alcohol

WINEMAKING

FERMENTATION

Strangely enough, both the bubbles and the alcohol in wine come from the same place—fermentation. The process of fermentation depends on the presence of yeasts. Some winemakers use yeasts that are naturally present on the skin of the grapes, while others add a specific type of purchased yeast that has been isolated in a laboratory. As soon as the yeasts meet the sugar in grape juice, they start converting that sugar into alcohol and carbon dioxide. If the carbon dioxide is allowed to drift off into the atmosphere, the wine will be still—without bubbles. If the carbon dioxide is retained, the wine will be sparkling (see page 3 for how this is done).

The level of alcohol in a wine depends on how much sugar was originally present in the grape juice and on how much of the sugar is converted. If all of the sugar is converted, the wine will contain approximately 12% to 15% alcohol (in other words, 12% to 15% of the liquid contents of the bottle is alcohol). The wine will also be described as "dry," meaning not sweet, without residual sugar. But not all wine regions are the same. Some have cool climates, others are warmer. In general, a cool-climate vineyard site will produce grapes with lower sugar levels, creating wines that will have lower alcohol (anywhere from about 8% to 12%). These wines will also have higher acidity, a distinctly crisp, clean feel, with a refreshing, pleasantly sour taste in the mouth (think lemon or grapefruit). In contrast, warmer places produce grapes with higher sugars and lower acidity, leaving the possibility of higher alcohol and a softer,

WHAT IS THAT NAME?

Most wine labels include a name of the wine. Increasingly, for most consumers all around the globe, the most common name on the label is simply the grape variety. So, if Cabernet Sauvignon grapes were used to make the wine, Cabernet Sauvignon will be the name of the wine on the label. For many European wines, the traditional practice is to name the wine for its place, such as Chianti in Italy, or Bordeaux in France. When a European wine uses a place name, it means that by law and by tradition only certain grape types can be used to make the wine. Throughout our chapters on the wines of Europe, many of which use place-name labels, we will indicate which grape types are used in which places.

ALEXANDER VALLEY VINEYARDS

CABERNET SAUVIGNON
ALEXANDER VALLEY
Estate Grown & Bottled
SONOMA COUNTY   *Vintage* 2012
ESTABLISHED 1962   WETZEL FAMILY ESTATE

A typical varietal label showing Cabernet Sauvignon as the grape variety. Courtesy of Alexander Valley Vineyards.

smoother sensation in the mouth (think a blackberry-flavored milkshake).

If the winemaker chooses to stop the yeasts from completing their work, there will be residual sugar left in the wine, creating anything from a lightly sweet taste to a very sweet one. Within our three basic styles (still, sparkling, and fortified), then, there are three subcategories of dryness/sweetness:

- dry—no or very little sweetness
- lightly sweet—sometimes called off-dry
- very sweet, dessert-like

COLOR

To keep the pattern of threes going, it is well known that wine comes in three main colors:

- white
- red
- rosé

We would have to add that there are many variations of color within those three, from very pale white to deep, inky purple.

You might think that the color of the grapes determines the color of the wine, but this is not always true. What is true is that red wine can only be made from red grapes, since the red color is extracted from the grape skins during the winemaking process. Similarly, white grapes can only produce white wine. But since almost all grapes have clear (or "white") juice, it is possible to squeeze white juice out of red grapes to make white wine. This also means that the winemaker can control the rate of color extraction from red grapes to produce a wine with only a small amount of pink color—a rosé wine. Rosé can also be made by blending a lot of white wine with a little bit of red.

These are the basics of winemaking, at least for producing still wines. To visualize a matrix of possibilities that offers many permutations of wine style, from a pale white, lightly sweet still wine to a dry rosé sparkling wine to a deep purple, very sweet fortified wine, read on.

BUBBLES IN THE BOTTLE

The Champagne method, or *methode champenoise* (now also used in places other than Champagne), requires that grapes be harvested by variety (as the finished sparkling wine may be the product of one grape or several), and that the juice of each grape variety is fermented separately, then blended. But these "base wines" are all still, not sparkling. The still wines—either a blend or the product of one grape variety—may be adjusted with older wines from other vintages to fit the "house style" of the producer. That house style is bottled along with a small amount of extra sugar and yeast inside each bottle, and the bottle is closed with a cap (like a beer cap) or temporary cork. The bottles are laid down horizontally in the cellar and left to rest, during which time the yeasts and sugar create a second fermentation inside that bottle, which causes carbon dioxide to be trapped in the wine. The trapped carbon dioxide produces millions of bubbles inside the very same bottle that the consumer eventually opens, pours, and enjoys.

In addition to producing bubbles, the second fermentation in the bottle also means that there is yeast sediment left in each bottle that has to be removed, but not before the winemaker allows the wine to take on the yeast flavors and aromas. If the bottle is left for a long time with the yeast "lees" (the spent yeast cells) inside the bottle, the yeasts will eventually break down and create enzymes and amino acids that have the effect of producing a rich texture in the wine. That process takes at least one year. In the Champagne region, the minimum period for this is 15 months, but many producers there leave their premium wines in this aging stage for three years or sometimes much longer.

To remove the yeast sediment from the bottle after aging, the bottles are periodically agitated by hand or mechanically to drive the sediment into the neck of the bottle with the bottle becoming inverted over time.

The inverted bottles then pass through a freezing solution that creates a plug of ice in the neck of the bottle. That plug contains all of the yeast sediment. When the bottle is turned upright, the cap is removed and the yeast pellet is expelled from the bottle. Immediately, more wine is added to replace the wine lost in the plug, and the winemaker may also take the opportunity to add a small amount of sugar solution (known as "*dosage*") to adjust the final dryness/sweetness of the wine. Finally, a traditional sparkling wine cork is inserted.

THE SPIRIT IN THE BOTTLE

A wine is described as "fortified" when extra-high-proof spirit is added to the wine. If the spirit is added to the wine after the fermentation is complete, there will be no remaining sugar in the newly fortified wine, making a finished product that is dry in taste, not sweet. Typical products of this type are the Fino and dry Oloroso Sherries of Spain (see page 242). To make a sweet fortified wine, the spirit is added very soon after the wine's fermentation has begun. The addition of the high-alcohol spirit halts the fermentation, leaving residual sugar in the wine. The Port wines of Portugal are a fine example (see page 256). Some sweet, fortified Sherries are also made by initially

Yeast sediment collects on the lower side of the horizontal bottle after the second fermentation. Frederic Handengue: CIVC.

The explosive nature of disgorging by hand.

creating a dry Sherry, and then adding concentrated, reduced grape juice as a sweetener. This is true of many Sherries labeled "Cream."

BODY

With one more threesome, we can round out the basic vocabulary of wine. Depending on where the grapes are grown and what winemaking methods are used, the wine will be:

light-bodied

medium-bodied

full-bodied, or heavy

This means that our impression of the "weight" of the wine in the mouth ranges from light (think lemonade) to medium (orange juice) to full (tomato juice) to very full (root beer float or chocolate milkshake). Light-bodied wines are usually associated with cool-climate areas and straightforward winemaking using stainless-steel vats and little or no aging. To get to the full-bodied version, you need to put the wine through a rigorous body-building process, a sort of enhanced steroid program with oak aging and malolactic fermentation. We have further comments on these practices on page 7.

The price to pay

EVEN THE MOST CURSORY GLANCE around a wine shop will reveal that a standard 750 milliliter (25.4 ounce) bottle of wine can carry a price lower than $5.99 or higher than $599. Is the second bottle really at least a hundred times better? We think the answer is a resounding NO! What makes the difference? What makes one bottle cost more than another?

The actual cost of producing a bottle of dry, still wine can be as little as 50 cents and rarely exceeds $30. So how do we get to $599 or more? There are three main considerations in the pricing of wine:

costs of production

availability versus scarcity

what the market will bear

COSTS OF PRODUCTION

All winemakers incur costs, but some incur higher costs than others. Those who have higher costs believe that they are producing a higher-quality wine. How does this work? Winemaking includes a series of decisions, and each one of those decisions will impact the style of the wine, the quality, and the price. Many of those decisions include incurring higher costs of materials and pursuing a more labor-intensive path. For every decision there are winemakers who defend this methodology, arguing that there is a discernible increase in quality (often true). At the same time, there are winemakers who belittle these arguments and claim that their faster, less expensive, more mechanized methods result in wines that are just as good (not so much).

IN THE VINEYARD

These decisions go back to the very beginning of a vineyard and carry on through to the bottling and even the marketing of the wine. First, the grower must choose which grape to plant and where to plant it. The very best wines are usually produced from *Vitis vinifera* grapes. *Vitis vinifera*, when translated from the Greek, means "vines to make wine." Vinifera includes the usual suspects: Chardonnay, Sauvignon Blanc, Merlot, Cabernet Sauvignon, and on and on (for a discussion of the major vinifera grapes, see Chapters 2 and 3).

In California, the cost of vineyard land can run anywhere between $35,000 and $350,000 per acre, depending on whether it is already planted and whether it is deemed to be a premium and desirable site. For example, a flat, valley-floor strip of land with rich, fertile soils is cheaper and easier to plant and maintain than a rocky hillside plot with good exposure to the sun and protection from winds, but many people would claim that the hillside plot will produce better wine.

A steep hillside vineyard is harder to work, necessitating more manual labor.

Vine density is an important consideration in producing wine. Planting a vineyard with wide spacing of 8 to 10 feet (2.42 to 3 meters) between the vines and between the rows makes for easier and more cost-effective mechanized maintenance and harvesting. A spacing ratio of 3.3 feet by 3.3 feet (1 meter by 1 meter) will provide up to four times as many vines in the same amount of land. Though there may be more vines per acre, each plant is "programmed" by pruning to produce fewer grapes per vine. This requires more hand labor, which can be far more expensive than using machines in the vineyard.

And so it goes. Some vineyard owners pay a team of 20 pickers to go through the vineyard several times over a period of three or four weeks, hand-harvesting only those bunches that are visibly ripe into small plastic trays so that precious juice is not lost under the weight of too many bunches of grapes. Other producers swear that a mechanical harvester with a single operator can do just as good a job in 24 hours. The cost differential is enormous.

One of the highest costs in wine production comes in the form of strict selection of grape material before or at harvest time to ensure that only the finest fruit is made into wine. By going through the vineyard three to four weeks before harvesting and removing the weaker or poorer clusters of grapes, some producers maintain that they will produce better wine. This practice is known as a "green harvest." What they are doing is lowering their yield, picking only the healthiest grapes, and harvesting perhaps 2 tons per acre (5 tons per hectare) rather than 5 tons per acre (12.5 tons per hectare).

After the grapes have been picked, some producers will pay workers to sort bunches of grapes, removing any unripe or moldy fruit as it moves along a conveyor belt or "sorting table" prior to entering the winemaking process. Grapes that are afforded the extra-special care and attention described above will command higher prices. Napa Valley premium Cabernet Sauvignon grapes have been fetching more than $5,000 per ton, Merlot as much as $3,400. Less highly regarded sites in California may command as little as $400 per ton for the same varietals.

Effect on Style. Wineries that produce a limited amount of wine in a labor-intensive process from premium land claim that they are producing a more

Tending the vineyard by hand, removing unwanted leaves and unripe bunches.

hand-crafted wine that has more intense or more complex flavors that are characteristic of the place the grapes were grown, the "*terroir*." Such wines cost more to make and will be priced accordingly.

COSTS AT THE WINERY

Most producers today use stainless-steel tanks for most if not all of their fermentation needs. But stainless-steel fermentation tanks are like coffee-makers—you can buy the basic model, or you can get the version with all the bells and whistles. The more expensive models provide the winemaker with greater control, especially temperature control, and temperature can make or break a successful fermentation. It can even dictate the style of the wine. A wine produced by a long, slow, cool fermentation will give the consumer a lot of fresh, forward fruit character, with a clean mouthfeel. But using that technology costs more, and the wines will be priced accordingly.

Malolactic Fermentation. There are other choices as well. Most winemakers agree that consumers will enjoy certain wines more if the wine is put through a process called "malolactic fermentation." This is particularly true of almost all red wines, some whites (such as Chardonnay), especially those aged in barrels, and just a few sparkling and rosé wines. By introducing a friendly type of bacteria to the wine—a strain of lactobacillus, the active culture found in yogurt—the winemaker can convert a harsh form of acid (malic, the acid in green apples) into a softer one (lactic, the acid in milk), providing a richer, smoother feeling on the tongue. But all of this takes time and costs money.

Oak. Then there is the wood debate. For centuries, winemakers used wooden barrels to store wine, and that practice gradually evolved into purposely leaving wine in barrels to age. Current consumer preference favors a noticeable wood character in certain styles of wine, especially Chardonnay and many red wines. How that wood character is achieved is part of the cost equation. For a long time, the preferred type of wood for aging wine has been oak. Placing the wine in a brand-new oak barrel (which costs as much as $950 for a barrel that holds about 60 gallons [225 liters]) is far more expensive than leaving the wine in a stainless-steel tank that has been temporarily lined with rough-cut oak staves. The oak stave immersion method is in turn more expensive than stirring oak chips into the stainless-steel vat. Is there a difference? Purists maintain that the flavors and effects achieved from a real wooden barrel are far cleaner and more balanced than the effects of oak staves or oak chips. Certainly, a wine aged in a real oak barrel will cost more.

Barrel aging takes time, and that means that the wine is still at the winery, not on the wine store shelves or on a restaurant's wine list. Following barrel aging, some producers will insist on keeping the wine at the winery after bottling, allowing the wine to rest, giving the various characteristics of the wine a chance to marry and become a more harmonious whole. As we all know, time is money, and wines held back by the producer will cost more.

High-tech stainless-steel tanks with integrated refrigeration keep everything under control in modern wineries.

There is still an important place for barrel aging at many wineries.

OAK: WHAT THE WINEMAKER WANTS

The primary effect of an oak barrel on wine is to add to its flavor profile because the liquid helps to pull flavoring components from the barrel. The most obvious flavor is often described as vanilla, because the sap of oak contains vanillin.

Vanillin is found in the sap of European oaks, so that when wine is stored in oak barrels, the vanillin is leached from the oak staves into the wine. Whether it comes across to you as vanilla or butterscotch or caramel doesn't really matter—it all has the same effect of giving the wine that desired flavor and making the wine seem just a tiny bit sweet. It will also soften the texture of the wine, since the vanillin gives the impression of a smooth, syrupy consistency. In the case of white wines, that same consistency can be enhanced by leaving the wine on the lees (expired yeast cells) in the barrel—what the French call "sur lie." As the yeast cells break down they release enzymes that contribute to a richer feel in the mouth.

If the wine stays in the barrel for too long, however, it may take on what we believe to be negative characteristics—too much wood flavor, which will overpower the wine's natural flavors, and too much tannin, a compound that masks the vanilla effect and leaves a drying sensation and bitter taste on the tongue. We have sampled far too many wines that taste mostly of wood. We would prefer to see winemakers use wood in the same way that a painter uses a frame. The job of the frame is to set off the picture, to enhance it. If the frame enters the picture, there is something wrong!

Clarification. As with almost all beverages today, we expect wines to be clear and free of haze. But fermentation is a messy process that creates all kinds of debris that can remain suspended in the wine. So the winemaker has to decide if the wine should be clarified or stabilized using additives or machinery, both of which speed up the clarification process. Or should the wine simply sit at the winery, allowing time and gravity to slowly achieve what humans and machinery can speed up? Critics of mechanical or chemical clarification charge that such processes strip the wine of its essential flavors and characteristics and that the wine will be better if left alone. Even though the machinery for clarification and stabilization is expensive, it is less expensive than keeping the wine at the winery. Anything that prevents the wine from reaching the consumer increases the cost.

Xtreme wines, xtreme costs

THERE ARE BIZARRE LENGTHS THAT some winemakers go to in order to produce something extraordinary. This is particularly true in the production of sweet and sparkling wines.

OH SO SWEET

It is fairly easy to produce a simple, lightly sweet wine by stopping the fermentation before all of the sugars have been converted to alcohol. This leaves residual sugar in the wine, making the wine taste sweet. But to produce a very sweet, dessert-style wine, extreme steps are often taken. Grapes can be left to hang on the vine for an extended period of time until they dehydrate and become raisins, or until they are attacked by a specific type of mold, which also causes the grapes to dehydrate. As these grapes lose water, their sugar content is concentrated in smaller quantities of

liquid, making them extremely sweet. The mold is called *Botrytis cinerea* or "noble rot." It is considered a beneficial mold and is highly prized by producers of sweet wines—there is no carryover of moldy flavors to the wines. Because of the dehydration factor, these remarkably sweet wines are produced in very limited quantities, which in turn makes them very expensive, sometimes as much as $100 or more per half bottle (375 milliliters [12.7 ounces]).

As if the above were not extreme enough, winemakers in areas susceptible to freezing temperatures, such as Canada and Germany, have taken matters one step further, allowing grapes to stay on the vine well past the regular picking date until they are frozen by the first very cold spell. The frozen grapes are harvested and pressed, producing minuscule quantities of very sweet juice that leaves behind most of the grape's water content as ice. Once again, these measures result in very highly priced wines. The sweet "Icewines" produced along these lines can easily cost from $75 to more than $100 per half bottle.

The beginning of botrytis on a ripe bunch of Riesling grapes.

Riesling grapes that have frozen on the vine and will be made into Icewine.

of trapping carbon dioxide gas in the original stainless-steel fermentation tank and then bottling the wine under pressure so as not to lose the gas. Using the tank method creates a very different style and quality of wine, with much bigger bubbles that fade more easily; this wine should be sold at a much lower price point.

So why are some wines more expensive?

IT ALL COMES DOWN TO whether the winemaking methods tend more toward mass production or small-batch nurturing. If the grapes are of a fashionable variety (such as Merlot), from a premium region (say, Napa), and from a prized plot of land (such as Three Palms Vineyard), the wine will be considerably more expensive than a Merlot wine from Macedonia.

And if the winemaker seeks to retain a level of individuality in the wine by keeping small batches separate, careful monitoring of the fermentation process, skillful blending, the use of wood, aging, or a combination of all or some of these approaches, those wines will also be higher-priced.

AVAILABILITY VERSUS SCARCITY

In any market, certain goods are in limited supply, and because they are rare but in demand, those goods can command high prices. In some instances output is artificially limited to keep prices high. In the case of wines, certain items are in short supply simply because it is impossible to produce any more. For example, the 2.5 acre (1 hectare) vineyard of Les Caillerets in the village of Meursault in Burgundy, France, will produce only about

BUBBLING OVER

Many people still see sparkling wine as a luxury item, and much of that image is connected to price. The most expensive sparkling wines in the world continue to come from the Champagne region of France, commanding retail prices from about $35 to more than $250 per bottle. But there are reasons why Champagne and some other sparkling wines can be so expensive. As with any wine, very good wine comes from the highest-quality grapes, most often grown on premium vineyard sites, and those grapes command high prices. But in the case of great sparkling wine, the winemaking process is very long and demands a very high level of skill (see pages 3–4).

The Champagne method takes time, skill, and labor, including aging of the wine once it's in the bottle. Aging helps to add quality to the finished wine, but it also ties up the producer's cash, and that adds up to a more expensive bottle of wine. That's why some bottles of sparkling wine cost more than others. At the other end of the spetrum is the relatively inexpensive method

FONDÉE EN 1869

CHEVALIER-MONTRACHET
GRAND CRU
Appellation Contrôlée

Vinifié, Élevé et Mis en bouteilles par

LOUIS JADOT
F 21200 - FRANCE

IMPORTED BY
KOBRAND CORPORATION
NEW YORK, N.Y.

KOBRAND
Wines · Spirits

WHITE BURGUNDY
TABLE WINE
750 ml/ALC. BY VOL. 13,5%

PRODUCE OF FRANCE

The Chevalier-Montrachet vineyard produces very little wine made from Chardonnay grapes at a very high price. Courtesy of Kobrand Corporation.

555 cases (6,660 bottles) of wine each year for the entire world market. For that reason alone it is in limited supply and will be priced accordingly.

Similarly, certain Champagnes from specific vineyard sites are available in very small quantities. Or some Champagnes are made in limited supply because they are aged for an extended period of time after the second fermentation in the bottle and the producer does not want to commit a large segment of production to such long aging.

As we pointed out earlier, Icewines and botrytis-affected sweet wines are, by their very nature, in limited supply and expensive. So it is the limited resources of grapes or juice that will create a product of limited availability but one that is in high demand and carries a high price.

WHAT THE MARKET WILL BEAR

There are wines that are in relatively plentiful supply but are still high-priced. Those wines are not rare, but they have earned a reputation for being consistently very good. The best examples of these wines come from the Bordeaux region of France. The reputation for great wines from

this region has been well established since the eighteenth century, so much so that modern wine collectors continue to be willing to spend large sums of money to acquire them. A case in point is the wine from Chateau Mouton Rothschild. The chateau produces around 34,000 cases of wine each year from an estate of 195 acres (79 hectares). That's a lot of wine, but the price per bottle on release is almost always well over $1,000. A well-earned reputation for consistently high quality can justify higher prices.

The same can be said for what have become known as boutique or "cult" wines from producers all around the world, such as Screaming Eagle Cabernet Sauvignon from California or Hill of Grace Shiraz from Australia. Their reputation for quality means that they can charge a retail price of more than $500 per bottle for their wines (and considerably more on a restaurant wine list) and the market will bear it.

Of course, if a wine receives a very high rating in the wine press, usually based on a 100-point scale, the price of that wine may almost automatically increase. A wine that receives a score of 95/100 is likely to sell for more—sometimes far more—than a wine that receives a score of 90/100 or (perish the thought) an 80 or 85. We are not fans of wine scores, and we find that when we taste the highest-rated wines we often don't agree that the wine is "all that." Alternately, we find ourselves enjoying many less expensive wines that receive far more humble scores. Our *WineWise* tip: learn to *trust your own palate* and be confident that just because a wine critic may not like the wine that you in fact love, you are not wrong. Enjoying wine on your own terms is simply a matter of personal taste, not a report card.

Sometimes even the bottle itself adds tremendous cost to the wine. Bottles with flowers etched into the glass, bottles dipped in gold paint and with an ace of spades as its logo, bottles created by and signed by famous artists, and on and on, will add to the price of the wine, even if what's in the bottle does always not merit that inflated price.

BRANDS VERSUS TERROIR WINES

Over the last two to three decades there has been a proliferation of branded wines in the marketplace. During the 1900s, place-named wines ruled the wine market, either from Europe or from New World producers who lazily "borrowed" a European place name, such as Chablis or Champagne, to market their wines. But in the twenty-first century, New World winemakers have realized that their wines don't need the cachet of a European name to be successful, and the branding of wines is seen as a viable way of capturing and maintaining loyal fans.

Some of the most successful brands to date in the United States include Sutter Home, Barefoot, Woodbridge, and Menage a Trois from California, and the range of Australian wines offered under the [yellow tail]® label. There are many other successful and recognizable brands, including Red Bicyclette from France and Ecco Domani from Italy. What do these brands offer? A surefire recipe for success—reliable quality, affordable prices, a consistent profile jam-packed with ripe, fruit-driven flavors, and smooth texture. There are no surprises in these wines, and that is exactly what millions of us want, all around the world. Such cookie-cutter wines are possible in a world where multinational corporations own vast tracts of vineyard land in sunny, flat areas where huge quantities of ripe grapes can be ensured every year.

In contrast, *terroir* wines originate from smaller plots of land in more challenging climates that create noticeable differences in the wines from year to year. They are also more likely to include non-fruit aromas and flavors, such as "wet rock "or "moist undergrowth," that are not appealing to everybody.

Is one "better" than the other? Is fast food better than a meal prepared with love from fresh, seasonal ingredients? Both meals will stop hunger, but only one will be nutritious and soul-satisfying. Sometimes we crave salty, fatty French fries, but sometimes we want an elegant meal over candlelight. Branded wines and *terroir*-driven wines are different concepts, different approaches. Branded wines can be and usually are of good quality. They have to be in such a competitive market. Without that quality they simply wouldn't survive. A branded wine should provide good quality at a good price, be fun to drink, and work well with your food. A *terroir*-driven wine should create a very different experience, and hopefully a memorable one.

THE IMPORTANCE OF PLACE

You may have noticed that we've made several references to the concept that where the grapes are grown is an important consideration in the quality of the wine. This concept is reflected in current labeling practices that include an indication of place on the label. In the wine world, the term *"appellation"* has come to mean a defined, named geographic area dedicated to growing grapes for wine production. Some appellations are considered to be premium areas for producing certain kinds of wines, and many appellations, especially in the Old World (Europe) have become associated with one or more specific grape varieties.

How the appellation system works

ALL WINE-PRODUCING NATIONS OF THE world have appellation systems, and there are common characteristics to all of them. Appellations range from very small in area to very large. In many cases, smaller appellations can be found inside larger ones, just like those Russian dolls where the larger dolls have smaller dolls inside them. One general rule about the size of an appellation is that smaller appellations usually command higher prices for their wines. For the name of an appellation to be used on a wine label, most of the grapes must come from that region. Most nations have adopted legislation requiring that a minimum of anywhere from 85% to 100% of all grapes used to make the wine must come from any place named on a label. Another common characteristic of appellation systems is that existing county or state names, such as Sonoma County or California, can be used as an indication of the origin of the grapes.

Two good examples of how the appellation system works can be found in the wine areas of Bordeaux and Sonoma.

The Bordeaux Appellations

1. You start with France, a national appellation.

2. Inside France is Bordeaux, a regional appellation.

3. Inside Bordeaux are several district appellations, one of which is Haut-Medoc.

4. Inside Haut-Medoc are six villages, each an appellation in its own right. They are St-Estephe, Pauillac, St-Julien, Margaux, Listrac, and Moulis.

5. If all the grapes used to make the wine came from vineyards within one of these villages, the label will include a phrase such as "*Appellation Pauillac Protegee.*"

The Sonoma Appellations

1. You start with California, a state appellation.

2. Inside California is North Coast, a regional appellation.

3. Inside North Coast is Sonoma County, a county appellation.

4. Inside Sonoma County is the Russian River Valley appellation.

5. Inside the Russian River Valley are two sub-appellations: Chalk Hill and Green Valley.

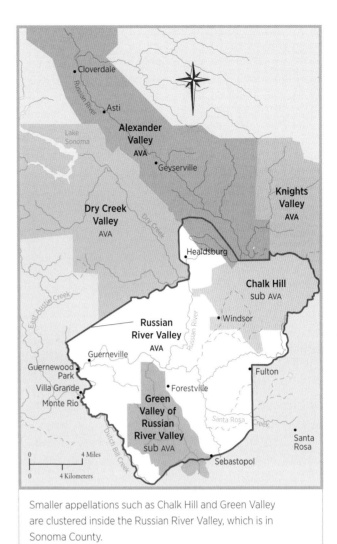

Smaller appellations such as Chalk Hill and Green Valley are clustered inside the Russian River Valley, which is in Sonoma County.

6. If more than 85% of the grapes used to make the wine came from vineyards in the Chalk Hill area, the label can include the name "Chalk Hill."

ASSOCIATING PLACE WITH GRAPE

As mentioned before, some appellations in Europe become specifically associated with one or more grape varieties, both because certain areas have a long history of sticking with a particular grape variety or varieties, and also because the appellation laws in Europe often require that a specific grape variety or varieties *must* be used to make the wine if the place name appears on the label. For

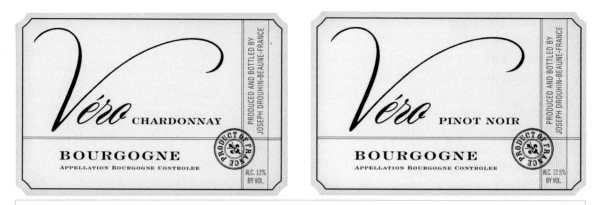

Joseph Drouhin's Vero bottlings of white and red Burgundy labels also identify the grape variety as Chardonnay and Pinot Noir, respectively.

example, white wine from the Burgundy region of France is made from Chardonnay only—the winemakers have no choice. Red wine from Burgundy in France is Pinot Noir. Case closed! In contrast, New World wine areas (just about everywhere outside of Europe) have no laws that dictate what grape must be used in any appellation. Even so, some New World areas have become recognized as masters at producing wines from one particular grape—for example, Napa Valley in California is closely identified with Cabernet Sauvignon, while the Willamette Valley in Oregon is Pinot Noir country.

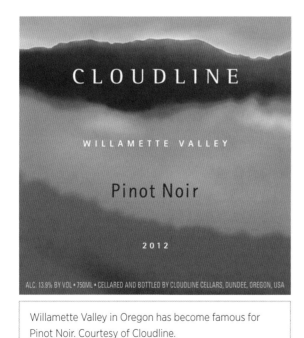

Willamette Valley in Oregon has become famous for Pinot Noir. Courtesy of Cloudline.

Closures

WE THINK IT'S IMPORTANT TO include some comments here on bottle closures. We are happy to report that we fully support the move by many producers to use screwcaps to close the bottle instead of corks, and we strongly encourage consumers of all stripes to accept them. Screwcaps are not a sign of inferior quality. In fact, in many ways, a screwcap could denote a wine of higher quality since the screwcap is impervious to bacteria and mold, and provides an almost completely airtight closure. Corks have been notorious for becoming infected with bacteria or for not fitting properly and allowing air to seep into the bottle, both of which will spoil the wine. You've heard the term "corked" wine? That's a wine that is spoiled by a type of mold (TCA) that can spread through the cork into the bottle, and TCA doesn't know the difference between a $5 bottle of wine and a $500 bottle. A wine sealed with a screwcap can't be "corked" simply because there is no cork.

This is not to say that we see a day when all wines will be stoppered with screwcaps, but especially for those wines that are consumed within four or five years of production, we believe that screwcaps are the way to go.

Choosing wine

ONE THING WE WANT TO emphasize up front is that most of the wines we buy for personal use are under $20 a bottle, in many cases under $15. How do we do that? By venturing off the beaten path to lesser-known wine areas and by experimenting with lesser-known grape types. If you know, for example, that you really like straightforward, fresh, fruity white wines to enjoy with grilled fish outdoors in the summertime, then we hope you will learn from this book that Albarino from Rias Baixas, Spain, and Moschofilero from Mantinia, Greece, fit that profile, and hope that you will try them.

Most of all, we believe that anyone can learn to taste wine and be his or her own critic. By following some of the simple steps below about tasting wine, and by trying some of our suggestions from the various regional chapters, you can create your own matrix of what it is you like, and why. We would encourage you to find a knowledgeable and reliable wine merchant or store clerk with whom you can discuss your preferences. In a restaurant discuss the style of wines you enjoy with a sommelier or a knowledgeable server, and don't be shy about setting a price point, the amount you're willing to spend on a bottle of wine.

As we mentioned earlier in this chapter, perhaps our biggest word of warning is not to take as gospel everything that wine critics (including us) say about a wine. Most of the time wines are tasted and judged in the absence of food, and we believe very strongly that wine is food and is made to pair with other foods. We also believe that it is impossible to quantify the pleasure that a wine can bring—there are far too many variables such as the climate, your disposition at the moment, the noise level, the company, and whether it's a banquet for 200 at the White House or a lakeside picnic for two.

Tasting and enjoying wine

WE ENCOURAGE YOU TO DEVELOP the "mental habit" of tasting wine. Not that every sip of wine that enters your mouth has to be analyzed and commented on, but you will reap greater pleasure if you take a few minutes to objectively taste a wine before deciding whether you subjectively enjoy it. At the very least, you will get used to the idea that you can taste a wine in a restaurant and confidently accept it, or reject it if you feel it is not right.

All wine books will tell you that there are separate stages to tasting wine—look at it, smell it, taste it. That is true, but you will find the whole exercise easier once you understand that there are connections from one step to the next.

APPEARANCE

We look at wine in the glass mostly to get an idea about the "strength" of the wine. A red or white wine that is relatively pale and translucent will probably be light in all of its characteristics—more delicate aroma, light flavor, an easy presence in the mouth. In contrast, a white wine that shows deeper gold hues or a red wine with deep purple, opaque notes will have a stronger, more assertive aroma and flavor and a tenacious, more powerful presence in the mouth. These are the essential differences between a light-bodied wine and a full-bodied one. When it comes to sparkling wine, you want an enormous quantity of teeny-tiny bubbles that exhibit real persistence in the glass, what is called a good "*perlage*."

AROMAS

In smelling a wine, there are three main aspects to consider: intensity of smell, simplicity versus complexity, and types of smell. Lighter, more

The practice of recognizing aromas can be enhanced by adding fresh ingredients such as fruits or herbs to wine.

delicate aromas usually follow from the visual conclusion that the wine is pale, and will help you to conclude that the wine is light-bodied. A more assertive, more powerful, perhaps earthier aroma will lead you in the direction of a fuller-bodied wine. You will also find that there is generally an association among lighter wines, such as Riesling (white) or Gamay (red), where fruit is the primary noticeable smell, with the earthier notes in the background. In contrast, fuller-bodied wines such as oaked Chardonnay or Cabernet Sauvignon are often accompanied by more powerful aromas, where fruit is complemented (and hopefully not overwhelmed) by wood and mineral, earthy smells.

There are thousands of aromas that you might find in wines, but don't let that worry you. If you are new to this, the easiest way to proceed is to think of categories of smell, rather than specific smells. Is there a floral aroma? Or is it primarily fruit? Or are there vegetal or herbal notes? Those are great starting places, and from there you will find it is not hard to progress at your own speed to breaking those broad categories into smaller ones *if you want to*. Remember, you don't have to. If you are the adventurous type, you might consider whether the floral aroma is delicate and fleeting or heady and perfumed—you can guess where those two different conclusions would lead you. Or you might distinguish between the smell of green, acidic fruits, such as limes, as compared to the rich

ripeness of dark cherries and dark plums. Most of all, aromas in wines should be pleasant; if you detect any unpleasantness when smelling a wine, do not hesitate to send it back in a restaurant or take it back to a wine store. The most objectionable of all smells in wine comes from wines that have been in contact with a tainted cork. Those wines are described as "corked" or "corky," and they smell of a dank, damp basement, paper, or wet, rotting cardboard. Once you come across it, you will never forget it, and you should store that smell away in your memory for future reference and action. Note: screwcap wines are never corked. Just saying.

TASTE

Much of the action of looking at and smelling wine is about impressions, pleasant or otherwise. It is when you place the wine in your mouth that you can make physical conclusions about the taste of the wine. We encourage you to recognize that anybody can taste, since we all have taste buds, and it will help you to remember that taste is a narrow concept. The Western world has traditionally accepted four tastes—sweet, sour, bitter, and salty—and tasting wine becomes much easier when you realize that only three of these are present in wine to any appreciable degree (wine is not really salty).

Sweet, sour, and bitter often show up in wine, singly or in combination, and are the result of components in the wine that came from the grapes. Sugars alert our sweetness-detecting taste buds, most of which are located on the tip of the tongue. The sweet effect is a light, fleeting but pleasant sensation, similar to the initial impact of ice cream or a soda. Acids set the sour-sensing taste buds all a-tingle along the sides of the tongue and will also cause one set of salivary glands at the top of the cheeks to jump to attention. Many people appreciate this bracing sensation as it cleans and refreshes; it is exactly what is meant by "palate cleansing." Phenols, which are bitter compounds, have the greatest effect on the taste buds at the very back of the

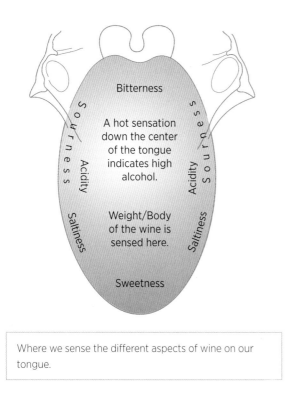

Bitterness

A hot sensation down the center of the tongue indicates high alcohol.

Weight/Body of the wine is sensed here.

Sweetness

Sourness

Sourness

Acidity

Acidity

Saltiness

Saltiness

Where we sense the different aspects of wine on our tongue.

tongue, like the wickedly pleasant thrill of dark chocolate. The most common bitter component in wine is tannin, the same component found in black tea. It also has a drying, astringent effect on the tongue.

Indeed, many of our preferences in tastes can be predicted by the way we drink tea or coffee. If you add cream and sugar, you will probably prefer sweeter tastes and smoother textures in fresh, fruity wines. Espresso drinkers who take their coffee strong and black are more likely to appreciate bitter tastes and the drying effect found in powerful red wines. You can test this out for yourself by experimenting with sugar water, lemon juice, and strong tea to represent sweet, sour, and bitter. You can even see what happens when more than one taste is present by adding some of the lemon juice and then the sugar water to the tea.

The tea will become less bitter with the addition of lemon and sugar and will take on the complexity of all three tastes, just as wine will.

We believe it is useful to recognize the presence or absence of sweet, sour, or bitter tastes. It is different from the highly complex world of attributing perceived "flavors" to wine, such as strawberry, apple, chocolate, or vanilla. Those have much to do with the aromas that were detected at the smelling stage. Initially concentrating on the three tastes is much more useful than pondering whether you detect apple or pear.

Determining the sweetness or lack of sweetness in a wine is very helpful in figuring out how you might use that wine with food (see chapter 14). An absence of sugar sweetness in wine means that all the sugars from the grapes have been converted to alcohol, and the wine is described as "dry" (see "Fermentation," page 2).

The level of acidity in the wine will impact our perception of what is called its "texture." Wines with high levels of acidity seem to be crisp or sharp, like biting into a Granny Smith apple, while wines with lower acidity appear to be softer and smoother, like milk. That perception of texture will also affect our use of the wine and what foods work well with it. Appreciable levels of bitterness in a wine can be an important factor in determining whether we actually like the wine, since the bitter taste is the last one noticed, at the back of the tongue, and stays with us longest.

Once you have mastered the three tastes, it is important to enjoy and savor what the wine offers, and even to see how the wine changes with time. You might even find it is fun to consider and describe the flavors of wines, launching into poetic and flowery descriptions. There's nothing wrong with that as long as you are sincere, and as long as you are enjoying the wine.

Glasses

OUR FINAL WORDS ABOUT ENJOYING wine have to do with glasses. We have used many different vessels in our wine careers and would never deny that circumstances may sometimes dictate that a simple tumbler is the appropriate glass (or even a jelly glass, if that's the only container available). But our experience tells us again and again that a good glass is often invaluable. Our recommendation is for a stemmed glass with a thin lip, as thin as the practical consideration of washing will allow. Try it—it makes a difference.

2

GREAT VINES MAKE GREAT WINES

MAJOR WHITE GRAPES

ITHOUT GRAPES, THERE IS NO WINE. THROUGHOUT THE WORLD, THERE ARE DOZENS, INDEED HUNDREDS, OF WHITE grapes used to make wine. Some of these grapes you've probably heard of—Chardonnay, Sauvignon Blanc, Riesling—but many of them—Albarino, Cortese, Semillon, Rkatsiteli, Assyrtiko, and on and on—may not be so familiar.

We want to take you on a quick worldwide tour of the six major white grapes and their wines. Once you've familiarized yourself with these grapes, you'll begin to become WineWise about most of the white wines you're likely to encounter, buy, and enjoy.

In later chapters we'll mention some of the "minor" white grapes—fruits that make great wine but are closely identified with more specific wine regions and countries.

So get ready to learn a few things about some of the best-known white wine grapes in the world. It should come as no surprise to our readers that we'll begin with the grape that makes the wine drunk 'round the world . . . Chardonnay.

Chardonnay

CHARDONNAY: THE PROFILE

Chardonnay rules. The grape that growers, winemakers, and wine drinkers love, Chardonnay grows just about everywhere in the modern wine world. Unless forbidden by law to appear in the vineyards of a particular wine region of the Old World (such as in Bordeaux, France), Chardonnay vines show up in both cool and warm climates and in both the Northern and Southern Hemispheres. As much a brand—the accepted "vanilla" of wine—as it is a grape, Chardonnay defines whether a wine region has "arrived," whether it is part of the global club, and if it is to be taken seriously. Likewise, if we're at a party on planet Earth and have a glass of white wine, most of us assume that the wine is Chardonnay unless specified otherwise. The appeal of the familiar is strong, and Chardonnay has become our default white.

Many people believe that Chardonnay is "the grape that tastes like oak," and that's understandable because more often than not Chardonnay is fermented and/or aged in oak barrels, or exposed to oak chips. Unfortunately, some of the wines made from Chardonnay, including some expensive ones, are overoaked, which throws off the balance of flavors in the wines. These days, however, we taste far fewer wines that are reminiscent of lumber and far more that taste like fruit.

A well-made Chardonnay should contain flavors of apples and citrus and can be anywhere from light, crisp, and green/underripe when the grapes are grown in a cool climate to rich in tropical fruit notes such as pineapple and mango when the grapes come from warmer growing regions. When oak is added to the equation, the wine takes on both sweet vanilla and buttered toast flavors. Note that not all Chardonnay-based wines are oak-aged or oak-fermented, especially those from cooler climates, and some of these wines, redolent

Chardonnay grapes. © iStock/David Gomez.

with refreshing acidity, are gaining in popularity, especially when paired with food.

Obviously, one of Chardonnay's charms is its wide range of styles. Another charm is that you can find drinkable Chardonnay for under $10, extraordinary Chardonnay for well over $100, and a solid representation at every price in between those extremes. There is a style and price to please every potential Chardonnay consumer. No wonder it has become the most popular single varietal—white or red—in the world.

Grape growers and winemakers love working with Chardonnay for several reasons. First, the vine grows in varied climates and soils, and even though classic Chardonnay-based wines are made from cool-climate grapes, such as those that grow in Burgundy, France, or the Russian River Valley of California, acceptable wine is produced from grapes that grow in warm wine regions, too. Chardonnay grapes grow best in stony soils rich in calcium, but they will do just fine in far more fertile soils.

Second, Chardonnay's yield in the vineyard—measured in tons per acre—is pretty flexible. As usual, the best wines begin with low-yielding vines, but quite drinkable Chardonnay can be produced from ripe grapes grown in relative abundance.

A "varietal" label. Chardonnay produced by the Benziger Family Winery, from fruit harvested in the Carneros district of California. Courtesy of Kobrand Corporation.

Third, Chardonnay grapes produce a base wine that is fairly neutral and needs the signature of the winemaker to create a style for the finished wine. Unlike other fine wines that are highly regarded for their raw materials (grapes) and non-interventionist winemaking techniques, successful Chardonnay needs the hand of the winemaker.

There are artisanal Chardonnay winemakers whose signature is unique and whose wines can be quite rare and expensive. More often, however, Chardonnay is the cash cow for a wine producer, and to meet consumer expectation, the signature of that producer becomes more of a rubber stamp than an autograph. While the best Chardonnay producers achieve balance and quality in their wines through a delicate touch and restraint, far too many Chardonnay producers pull out all the technical stops and end up with a manipulated wine geared to please the palates of a mass audience.

Sure, there has been some resistance to the universal acceptance of Chardonnay as the quintessential white wine, most notably the short-lived "ABC" (Anything But Chardonnay) fad that never became a real movement. Just protesting the ubiquitous Chardonnay by drinking other varietals puts the focus on its power in the marketplace and diminishes the attractive flavor profiles of other grapes. True, Riesling (see page 27) or Sauvignon Blanc (see page 24) may be the anti-Chardonnay, but each of these varietals has a lot more to offer as delicious white wine than as a protest drink.

We could go on and on about the glut of mediocre Chardonnay in the marketplace, but that would be too easy, too obvious. More important, dissing Chardonnay obscures the fact that this grape can—and does—produce some of the world's best white wines.

We should drink the wines we like and the wines we can afford. If, for example, you've found a $7 Chardonnay from Australia that you really enjoy, then that is a great wine for you to share with friends anytime at lunch or dinner. Expensive fine white Burgundy from France (by law, 100% Chardonnay, though the name of the grape does not appear on the label) is a special-occasion treat that will expose you to another world of Chardonnay. There is just so much Chardonnay available from so many different countries, in so many different styles, and at so many different price points. Let's take a look at some of the places that make delicious and distinctive Chardonnay.

FRANCE

Burgundy (see page 174) is considered the ancestral home of fine Old World Chardonnay. The thing to remember about Burgundy is that virtually all of its white wines with geographical names (the name of the place, not the grape, appears on the label) are 100% Chardonnay, and some of them—even the most affordable ones—can be delicious, even memorable. The three most important major subregions within Burgundy for fine Chardonnay are Chablis (see page 175), for crisp, green-fruit, high-acid, mineral-laden, often unoaked Chardonnay grown in a very cool climate and chalk/limestone soils; Cote de Beaune (see page 177), for rich, complex, balanced wine—oaked, but restrained—with perhaps white pepper and floral aromatics; and Macon (see page 179), which can produce warmer-climate, medium-bodied Chardonnays, some of them simple, several of them with pleasing mineral flavors and complexity.

A "place-name" label. Puligny-Montrachet is a village in Burgundy, France, known for the high quality of its Chardonnay grapes. A white wine from Puligny-Montrachet is—by law—100% Chardonnay, even though the name of the grape does not appear on the label. Courtesy of Kobrand Corporation.

Chardonnay is one of only three legal grapes in the Champagne region of France (see page 152) and the only white grape allowed in this famous sparkling wine. The only other grapes allowed in Champagne are Pinot Noir and Pinot Meunier, both red varietals. What Chardonnay does for Champagne is provide lightness and delicacy, as well as bracing acidity, especially because Champagne is the coldest grape-growing region in all of France.

Chardonnay grows in many other wine regions of France, particularly in southern France, where warm weather and high yields in the vineyards most often result in drinkable, affordable, but not particularly memorable wines.

THE UNITED STATES AND CANADA

Chances are you've tasted several California Chardonnays (see Chapter 4), and you've liked some better than others. With about 100,000 acres (40,000 hectares) of Chardonnay planted, more than any other varietal, California grows this grape all over the state, from the coolest vineyard sites to the warmest. California has adopted the rich, oaky, vanilla style of Chardonnay as its signature, though there are some "leaner, greener" exceptions.

Wines whose labels read simply "California" Chardonnay can be produced from grapes grown anywhere in the state, and most often the source of the fruit in these wines is the warm Central Valley. These wines tend to be full-blown, rich, ripe, and oaky, with mature, ripe fruits in the background. Because the grapes are sourced in such warm conditions, these wines often lack the refreshing snap of acidity that cool weather brings. You can easily buy a Chardonnay labeled "California" for under $10 in your wine shop or supermarket. When served chilled with broiled fish, roast chicken, or grilled vegetables, these wines will usually do their job: provide a suitable accompaniment to food.

If you are looking for Chardonnay of higher quality (at a higher price), wines produced from grapes grown in the cooler growing regions of California can be good to exquisite. Prices start at about $14, but it is not uncommon to pay $35 or more for very fine Chardonnay from places such as Napa Valley, Carneros, Sonoma Coast, Russian River Valley, Edna Valley, Santa Maria Valley, Santa Barbara County, Sta. Rita Hills, and Santa Lucia Highlands.

New York State (see page 110) produces fine Chardonnay in the Finger Lakes, Hudson River Region, and Long Island, which feature cooler climates than the vast majority of California's cooler growing regions. Chardonnay from the Finger Lakes does not rely on oak to define its style, as the ripe grapes maintain their refreshing fruit acids, and the finished wines can display a lovely balance of flavors. Chardonnay from cool-climate Long Island can also be impressive, the style a bit oakier than the Finger Lakes but with balance and zesty fruit. A small amount of very good, high-acid, cool-climate Chardonnay is also produced in Hudson River Region vineyards and wineries.

Cakebread
Cellars

NAPA VALLEY

Chardonnay

ALCOHOL 14.3% BY VOLUME

The Cakebread family makes wine in Napa Valley, California. Cakebread Chardonnay is consistently one of the most popular wines served in upscale restaurants. Courtesy of Kobrand Corporation.

In the Pacific Northwest, Washington State (see page 100) produces a wide variety of Chardonnay styles, but Washington concentrates on Riesling as the white wine flagship for the state. Washington is the largest producer of Riesling wines in the nation. In Oregon (see page 106), some very good cool-weather Chardonnay is grown and produced, but Chardonnay takes a backseat to Oregon's premier red varietal, Pinot Noir, and its premier white, Pinot Gris.

Chardonnay, from drinkable to extraordinarily good, is made in many states, from Texas to Rhode Island, Virginia to Michigan. In addition, Canada (see page 278) produces some fine Chardonnay wines, some of them from single vineyards. Canada's primary Chardonnay region is the Niagara Peninsula in Ontario; secondary is the Okanagan Valley in British Columbia.

THE SOUTHERN HEMISPHERE

In South America, Argentina (see page 120) makes Chardonnay, but the majority of the wines that have reached the U.S. export market have so far been inexpensive, quite drinkable, but not memorable. Chile (see page 116), however, is beginning to show some promise in producing high-quality Chardonnay, especially from grapes grown in the cool-climate Casablanca region. These wines are inexpensive to moderately expensive and deliver delicious, ripe, balanced flavors without a preponderance of oak.

Chardonnay from South Africa (see page 138) can be a mixed bag. Depending on the producer, the wines can be easy-drinking or deep and complex. The best growers and winemakers in South Africa are making some lovely wines at affordable prices, and many are available in the U.S. market.

New Zealand (see page 134) has made its reputation in the export market for its extraordinarily popular Sauvignon Blanc but actually produces some very fine Chardonnay. Chardonnay from the wine regions of Gisborne and Hawke's Bay, both located on the North Island of the country, are well known, with Gisborne Chardonnay featuring flavors akin

Good, affordable Chardonnay is made both in Chile and Argentina.

to peaches and melon, while Hawke's Bay Chardonnay displays more citrus flavors—grapefruit and lime. Chardonnay produced from South Island fruit often comes from the Marlborough wine region, which produces juicy, tropical-fruit-driven wines with fresh, crisp flavors.

Australia (see page 126) produces rivers of Chardonnay, where the varietal is second only to Shiraz in acres planted. Much of Australia's Chardonnay is produced from grapes grown in the gigantic "South Eastern Australia" region, which takes in more than 90% of the vineyards in the entire country. Chardonnay labeled as "South Eastern Australia" should be inexpensive—usually under $10—and easily drinkable, featuring lots of tropical fruit flavors. In addition to mass-produced Chardonnay, Australia also produces some very elegant Chardonnay wines from smaller wine districts, such as the Limestone Coast, Clare Valley, Orange, and the Adelaide Hills.

THE REST OF THE WORLD

Chardonnay grows in just about any country that makes wine. Italy has grown Chardonnay successfully for decades, as has Spain. Portugal grows a little Chardonnay, and so do Germany, Austria, and Switzerland. Greece and Eastern Europe grow quite a bit of Chardonnay, and the new wine regions of China do, too. Chardonnay is everywhere.

Sauvignon Blanc

SAUVIGNON BLANC: THE PROFILE

Like the rest of the white varietals in the wine universe, Sauvignon Blanc lives in the shadow of Chardonnay. For years Sauvignon Blanc seemed poised to make its move as the next big white, but at least for now it must settle for the fact that

it has earned near-universal respect as a strong supporting player on the world wine stage.

Think "green." Sauvignon Blanc at its best exhibits refreshingly high acidity with flavors and aromas of green apples, green grapes, green herbs, and perhaps just a bit of green bell pepper. Lime, kiwi, green honeydew melon, and tropical fruits such as guava, papaya, and passion fruit make some Sauvignon Blanc–based wines, especially those from New Zealand and South Africa, smell and taste like a fruit salad in a glass, poured over calcium-rich stones.

The flavors of Sauvignon Blanc can shift in both subtle and dramatic ways, depending on where the grapes are grown. Let's survey the world of this "green" varietal.

FRANCE

Classic Old World Sauvignon Blanc, from the Loire Valley of France (see page 160), is chiefly represented by the wines Sancerre and Pouilly Fumé. These wines exhibit a high degree of minerality—chalk, limestone, and the brininess of the sea and seashells. The flavors and aromas of citrus fruits, especially lemon and grapefruit,

Sauvignon Blanc grapes. © iStock/David Gomez.

Sancerre is a village in the Loire Valley of France. A white wine labeled "Sancerre" must—according to French wine laws—be made from 100% Sauvignon Blanc grapes. Courtesy of Kobrand Corporation.

St. Supery is a well-known and respected Napa Valley wine producer. Label design by Jeanne Greco; courtesy of St. Supery.

as well as subtle vegetal notes of grass and herbs are prominent in Loire Valley Sauvignon Blanc.

In Bordeaux, France (see page 165), Sauvignon Blanc is often blended with another grape, Semillon (see page 168), to produce a distinctive style of white wine. These wines tend to be medium-bodied and more restrained in their acidity and fruit flavors. The classic medium- to full-bodied versions of these Bordeaux blends come from the districts of Graves (see page 169). White wines from Bordeaux labeled as "Entre-Deux-Mers" (see page 168) or simply "Bordeaux" tend to be more about the straightforward, crisp flavors of Sauvignon Blanc and are lighter wines meant for early drinking.

THE UNITED STATES: CALIFORNIA

In California, where Sauvignon Blanc is the second most important white varietal—Chardonnay, of course, is first—you may find Sauvignon Blanc labeled once in a while as "Fumé Blanc." In the late 1960s, Robert Mondavi coined this name for a style of Sauvignon Blanc that is sometimes richer and fuller than a wine labeled "Sauvignon Blanc." Some people prefer the more "sophisticated" Fumé Blanc style, while others much prefer the "wild" style of Sauvignon Blanc, and

some wine drinkers enjoy both styles, depending on the food they are pairing with the wine.

Sauvignon Blanc from the North Coast of California—Napa, Sonoma, and Mendocino counties—is the antithesis of the Chardonnay produced in the same region. Rather than the rich, oaky, vanilla flavors of Chardonnay that can overwhelm simpler foods, the refreshing, straightforward fruity flavors of Sauvignon Blanc are just the thing for fish—from ceviche to grilled tuna with tomatillo salsa—or a fresh goat cheese, tapas-style appetizers, or chilled gazpacho. California Sauvignon Blanc has emerged as a food-friendly wine, gaining more space on restaurant wine lists and more adherents among American wine drinkers.

NEW ZEALAND

For years, and until quite recently, classic Sauvignon Blanc was defined by the wines of the Loire Valley of France, such as Sancerre. The name of the grape—Sauvignon Blanc—has never appeared on the labels of these wines. In an increasingly varietal-conscious world, these wines have begun to lose their status as classic Sauvignon Blanc, and there are many wines and wine-producing nations ready to take their place, chief among them New Zealand.

New Zealand Sauvignon Blanc, with its distinct style, is often described as a "fruit salad in a glass."

New Zealand Sauvignon Blanc has, especially for many younger wine drinkers, become the classic expression of this varietal. Full of tart lime and tropical aromas and flavors, with grace notes of minerals, grass, and herbs, New Zealand Sauvignon Blanc is pure pleasure, an uncomplicated and fun wine—not a wine to exercise wine expertise on, but a wine to enjoy with myriad tasty dishes. A great accompaniment to spicy foods, especially Asian and Latin American flavors, this wine is like a squeeze of fresh lime juice, awakening and brightening flavors throughout the meal. Once you start to enjoy New Zealand Sauvignon Blanc, it can quickly become a favorite.

The best examples of this popular white are sourced from grapes grown in the vineyards of the Marlborough region, located at the northern tip of New Zealand's South Island. Also look for Sauvignon Blanc from Martinborough on the North Island. The wines are affordable, with many good wines priced well under $15, and some of the best available for between $15 and $25.

New Zealand Sauvignon Blanc is consumer-friendly in another way, too. Just about all of the New Zealand wines you will find in the U.S. market feature screwcaps, not corks, as closures, making New Zealand Sauvignon Blanc a perfect wine for the dinner table or the picnic basket.

SOUTH AFRICA

South Africa's best white wine is its Sauvignon Blanc. When sourced from low-yielding vineyards in the cooler regions, especially Stellenbosch, the wines can be incomparable. With thirst-quenching acidity, a healthy dose of minerality, and green, tropical fruits in the mix, the wines are more fruit-driven than the wines of the Loire Valley, but a bit more restrained in their exuberance, and they can be slightly fuller-bodied than the wines of New Zealand.

OTHER COUNTRIES

Australia produces a wide range of Sauvignon Blanc wines, from simple summer sippers to more complex wines. With Australian Sauvignon Blanc you usually get what you pay for, and it is easy to find wines for under $10, but even the most expensive and best wines are under $25.

Chile produces some delightful Sauvignon Blanc, with lots of forward fruit on the palate, balanced by a vein of mouthwatering acidity, especially from grapes grown in the cool Casablanca and Leyda regions. Sauvignon Blanc from Chile tends to be a bargain-priced gem.

Although perhaps a bit hard to find, Sauvignon Blanc from the Friuli–Venezia Giulia region of Italy is worth the search. Often just labeled as "Sauvignon," these moderately expensive wines can be some of the most elegant examples of Sauvignon Blanc produced anywhere in the world, with a grassy background and subtle fruit acids that refresh the palate.

In Greece, Sauvignon Blanc is increasingly used in blends with another high-acid grape, the indigenous varietal Assyrtiko.

SAUVIGNON BLANC: OTHER STYLES

As we noted earlier, in Bordeaux, France, Sauvignon Blanc is often blended with Semillon to produce an elegant dry white. However, the blend is also responsible for one of the most famous sweet wines in the world, Sauternes (see page 169). Sauternes is based on a heavy percentage (most often 75% to 95%) of botrytis-affected Semillon, with just a bit of Sauvignon Blanc for its refreshing acidity.

Sauvignon Blanc can also make a sweet wine on its own when produced from **late harvest** grapes. Late harvest Sauvignon Blanc is a fairly rare wine, but several New World winemakers continue to produce this style.

Riesling

RIESLING: THE PROFILE

While Chardonnay may get all the glory, many wine lovers believe that Riesling is the finest grape and makes the greatest white wine in the world. For the uninitiated, Riesling is perhaps the most misunderstood varietal, because so many people still believe that Riesling wines must be sweet. This is just not true. The truth is that Riesling can produce extraordinary wines in every style, from bone-dry to incredibly sweet.

Depending on where Riesling is grown, the flavor profile of the varietal can be as varied as its many vineyard sites. High acid is a hallmark of Riesling, with citrus—lemon, lime, grapefruit—and peach and pear flavors. On the nose and on the palate Riesling is rich with minerals, from slate to quartz, and even the faint smell (though not the flavor) of gasoline or diesel fuel. It is impossible to make a general statement about Riesling's flavor profile, as there are so many styles of Riesling in the bottle, and those styles change from vineyard to vineyard, region to region, and country to country.

Riesling grapes. © instamatics/Getty Images.

For Riesling to achieve its full potential as one of the world's great varietals, it needs cold weather. Riesling is also extremely sensitive to the soil types of vineyard sites, absorbing the suggestion of mineral flavors. When the climate and soil are right, Riesling is perhaps the most *terroir*-expressive of all white varietals.

The vein of acidity that runs through fine Riesling will emphasize the green fruit flavors in the drier styles and cut the unctuous sweetness of the syrupy type. In all styles, the magic of great Riesling is that it is mouthwatering and refreshing because of the acidity that defines the varietal. While most Riesling wines are drunk young to celebrate their fresh, green flavors, the high level of acidity that refreshes these young wines also helps to preserve the wine; it is not uncommon to drink Rieslings that are more than 10 years old.

With food, great dry to semi-dry Rieslings can become magical wines. Riesling is a perfect match with grilled fish accompanied by fruit salsas, or spicy Mexican, Cajun, Thai, or Vietnamese food. Most of us love a rich dish, such as duck confit, with a medium- to full-bodied red, but try the confit with an exquisite Riesling, and the contrast of the fatty duck with the acid of the Riesling will create a perfect marriage on the palate: a luscious fruit glaze that will make the dish—and the wine—come alive.

We can't stress enough that fine Riesling is a product of its environment: climate and soil define the character of the varietal. Sure, you can grow Riesling in a warm climate, but it will taste flabby and flat. Grow it in rich, fertile soils, and you lose the minerality that Riesling lovers crave in their favorite wine. Luckily, there are still plenty of sites that are ideal for growing great Riesling, and wonderful wines from around the world—most of them with varietal labels—are currently available at reasonable prices.

While Chardonnay still rules the marketplace, Riesling is making a run (along with Sauvignon Blanc) for a distinguished second or third place in the hearts and minds of wine consumers. Let's explore the Riesling world.

GERMANY

In Germany (see page 265), Riesling is the most important varietal, the grape by which overall German wine quality is judged.

One of the classic growing regions for Riesling in Germany is the Mosel (formerly Mosel-Saar-Ruwer), named for the Mosel River. The Mosel features dramatically steep vineyards on south-facing slopes covered in slate stones, within a cold climate moderated by the warming effect of the sun's rays off the rivers. Mosel Rieslings are very high in acid, with citrus and green fruit flavors, and tend to be light- to medium-bodied. Traditionally, these wines are bottled in green-tinted flutes (the elegant, elongated 750 milliliter [25.4 ounce] bottle), reflecting their "green" style.

The other classic Riesling regions in Germany are located near or within the confines

German wine labels can be difficult to decipher, but German Riesling is easy to love. JJ Prum is an established, quality-driven producer.

of the Rhine River Valley and are represented by the Rheingau, Rheinhessen, and Pfalz zones. Of the three regions, the Rheingau is best known for the quality of its Riesling wines, with Pfalz Riesling a close second. The three Rhine regions are considerably warmer than the Mosel and so produce wines that are richer, riper, fuller-bodied, and somewhat lower in acidity than wines from the Mosel, and the Rhine wines tend to be more full-bodied. Traditionally, wines from these regions are bottled in brown-tinted flutes, reflecting the warmer, earthier, richer style of the Rhine.

It was not so long ago that Germany was having a tough time in the U.S. market with Riesling, even though the wines can be extraordinary. Today, German wines are gaining serious traction in the United States, as wine consumers "discover" Riesling—in all its forms—as an extraordinary accompaniment to food, from appetizers through dessert.

WINEWISE TIP: If you're looking for crisp, refreshing low-alcohol white wines—just the thing on a warm day spent outdoors in the sunshine—German Rieslings are often between 8.5% and 11% alcohol, a lot lower than many other whites that clock in at 13% to 15% alcohol.

FRANCE

Alsace (see page 157), which borders Germany, is home to a particularly French style of Riesling—full-bodied, dry, and higher in alcohol than most German Rieslings. Alsace Riesling enjoys cool enough weather to ramp up acidity in the grapes, but also many days of sunshine along the eastern side of the Vosges Mountains, so the grapes ripen fully. Alsace Riesling at its best can age well for years in the bottle, while the simpler wines are enjoyable in their youth—within two to five years of vintage. Riesling from Alsace is a wonderful match with flavorful fish dishes, but also with semi-soft cheeses or white meats such as poultry or smoked pork.

Because of the German historical and cultural influence in this part of France, Alsace wines are labeled with the name of the varietal, making them accessible to the U.S. market. Alsace wines are bottled in the same elongated "flute" bottles as German wines. Expect to pay between $20 and $50 per bottle for fine Alsace Riesling.

There are sweet versions of Riesling produced in Alsace. Look for the label terms "*Vendange Tardive*" (late harvest, which can be anywhere from dry to semi-sweet to quite sweet) or "*Selection de Grains Nobles*" (botrytis-affected, which produces lusciously sweet wines). These relatively rare wines will be more expensive than dry Alsace Rieslings. As with the best Rieslings of Germany, Alsace wines, even when produced in a sweet style, feature a serious vein of acidity that refreshes the palate.

AUSTRIA

Close by the banks of the Danube River, Austria grows Riesling grapes that translate into some very elegant wines. One of the best wine regions in Austria for Riesling is Wachau, west of Vienna, which owes its cooling breezes to the Danube, and where the vineyards are planted on steep slopes.

Austria produces Riesling in as many styles and quality levels as Germany, but in the export market it has earned a reputation mostly for its bone-dry Riesling wines. In the U.S. market, Austrian Riesling can be hard to find and expensive—$25 and up—especially "Smaragd," the highest-quality wines from the Wachau region. These are fruit- and mineral-driven wines that, like the best wines of Germany and Alsace, can pair with hearty, rich foods, and are certainly ageworthy.

THE UNITED STATES AND CANADA

With the exception of high-quality Riesling made by a literal handful of artisanal winemakers in cooler pockets of the state, if California wineries stopped producing Riesling tomorrow, nobody would notice. The Golden State is just too warm to produce fine Riesling wines on anywhere approaching a commercial basis, especially when the coolest regions are wed to the far more profitable Chardonnay.

So if California is not big on Riesling, where else in the United States is Riesling a star? Washington State (see page 100) is the number-one producer of Riesling in the United States. The total spectrum of styles, from dry to very sweet Rieslings, are produced here. Washington produces some stellar examples of Riesling, but the wines can just as often lack both the inspiring acidity and minerality of classic Riesling. These wines are fine as picnic wines with simple foods and are usually priced as easy-to-sip bargains. The good news is that many Washington producers see Riesling as an achievable challenge, are working hard to produce better wines, and they are succeeding. Also in the Pacific Northwest, a minuscule amount of fresh, crisp, fruit-driven Riesling is produced in the state of Idaho, from vineyards planted along the Snake River, and it is very good.

New York State's Finger Lakes region produces some extraordinary Riesling in several styles, from dry to sweet. Konstantin Frank was a pioneering winemaker and passionate advocate for quality wines from the Finger Lakes.

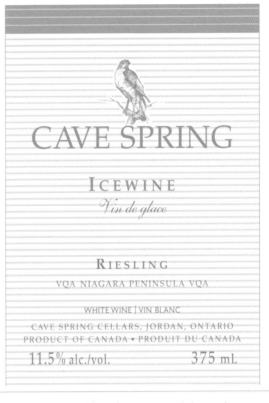

Icewine, produced from frozen grapes, is intensely sweet. Cave Spring is a major quality-driven producer in Ontario, Canada. The nation is the number-one producer of Icewine in the world. Courtesy of Cave Spring Cellars.

Travel cross-country and arrive at Riesling central: the Finger Lakes region of New York State (see page 110). Here, you will find some ultra-fine Riesling wines, made from grapes grown on the stony banks of Cayuga, Keuka, and Seneca lakes. The climate is cold and snowy, with just enough sunshine and reflected warmth from the rivers to produce high-acid, "green" wines—from truly dry to very sweet—that are similar to the style of Germany's Mosel. Finger Lakes Rieslings, which sell for about $12 and up, represent good value for great wines.

Canada, with its cold climate, produces some lovely low-alcohol Riesling wines in several styles, from bone-dry to sweet to its specialty, Icewine, especially from Riesling grapes grown on the Niagara Peninsula of Ontario. Enjoyable and refreshing when drunk young, we've tasted Canadian Riesling that was a decade old and still lively on the palate.

AUSTRALIA

Most Australian Riesling is produced for early consumption and immediate enjoyment, with a select few able to improve over time in the bottle. Crisp and refreshing, Riesling from Australia tends to be lighter on the palate, with lime, ripe peaches, and tropical fruits in the background. Many of the wines have a bit of spice—nutmeg and ginger—that balances the luscious fruit flavors. Nearly all of the wines use screwcaps to preserve those fresh flavors.

Australia's Rieslings are accessible, food-friendly, and priced to sell. Australian producers are, for the most part, making and marketing wines that will work with a simple grilled fish or the spicy flavors of Thailand, Cambodia, or Korea. The wines are good values, with some bottles priced less than $10, most in the low 'teens, and very few priced more than $20.

Gewurztraminer

GEWURZTRAMINER: THE PROFILE

In the world of fine white wine, there is life beyond Chardonnay. If you want that life to include vibrant spices, honeysuckle and rose petal scents, and the unmistakable aroma of lychees, then you may want to give Gewurztraminer a try (say it five times fast: guh-VERTZ-tra-meener).

Gewurztraminer is not for the faint-hearted white-wine drinker, one who looks for subtlety and nuance in every sip. No, Gewurztraminer—both the grape and the wine—is anything but subtle, with its sexy, seductive, perfumed aromatics and its allspice, clove, and cardamom flavors. Fine Gewurztraminer is wine for the sensualist who revels in the wine's voluptuous full body and its fruit-and-spice exoticism.

Gewurztraminer grapes. © iStock/Murphy Shewchuk.

Hogue produces an affordable off-dry Gewurztraminer in the Columbia Valley of Washington State. Courtesy of Hogue Cellars.

The best Gewurztraminer vineyard sites are located in cool-weather regions and rely on low yields in those vineyards to amplify the natural appealing gifts that nature has bestowed upon the Gewurztraminer grape. If grape yields in the vineyard are too high, the finished wine will lack the perfume and power that Gewurztraminer lovers crave. With all the caveats inherent in growing the best examples of Gewurztraminer, it is no wonder that there is no wine region in the world where it is the most-planted varietal. Gewurztraminer is not a cash cow, like Chardonnay. The good Gewurztraminer grower must be committed to the varietal and treat it carefully, even lovingly.

Classic Old World Gewurztraminer is a dry wine, with forward flavors of heady fruit and spice, intermingled and in balance. Alsace, France, is considered the definitive growing region for this style of Gewurztraminer.

New World Gewurztraminer is made in several different styles. It is hard to find wine as dry as the Gewurztraminer produced in Alsace, though a few producers do produce a classic style. Most Gewurztraminer produced in the New World lacks the depth of minerality and spice of the Alsace style, but these fruitier versions can be quite attractive.

Let's take a quick peek at the world of Gewurztraminer—the grape and the wine.

FRANCE

If you've already read the section on Riesling in this chapter, then you might be familiar with Alsace (see page 157). Alsace is home to the classic Gewurztraminer: full-bodied, intensely aromatic, and most often dry (although we've noticed a consumer-driven trend toward sweetness among some producers). Alsace has the ideal growing conditions for the pale pink Gewurztraminer grape: cool weather and lots of sunshine.

Great Alsace Gewurztraminer can age well for years. The simpler wines can be enjoyed in their youth, which means about three to five years after the vintage date. Like so many white wines from Alsace, Gewurztraminer behaves kind of like "a red wine in drag," meaning that while it creates a great match with more complex, richer fish dishes, it also works beautifully not just with white meats—poultry and pork—but also with unusual pairings for a white wine, such as duck and game. Alsace Gewurztraminer is an ideal choice for smoked fish, smoked white meats, and charcuterie, as well as semi-soft and moderately aged cheeses.

Gewurztraminer, much like its Alsatian partner, Riesling, sports a varietal label, making it an easy choice for American wine consumers. As is the usual practice in Alsace, Gewurztraminer is bottled in elongated "flute" bottles. Like Alsace Riesling, prices for good "Gewurz" hover in the $20 to $40 range, and there are rare and expensive sweet versions of Alsace Gewurztraminer produced, too.

GERMANY

Alsace used to be part of Germany before it was part of France, and Alsace was where the Germans specialized in Gewurztraminer. Today, Gewurztraminer grows mostly in the *anbaugebiete* (wine regions) of Pfalz and Baden. Pfalz Gewurztraminer is rarely as dramatic a wine as its Alsatian counterpart; it is fruitier but less spicy. Baden, which is separated from Alsace by the Rhine River, produces some very elegant, full-bodied Gewurztraminer wines.

AUSTRIA

Here the grape is more likely to be called Traminer, and the wines tend to be less "*gewurz*" (spicy), except perhaps in the wine region of Steiermark, where the wines are both floral and full of spice. Other wine regions produce mostly sweet versions.

ITALY

The Alto Adige region (officially a bilingual area, with Italian and German spoken, and formerly part of Austria) is the birthplace of this grape. Here it is called Traminer Aromatico (Italian) or Gewurztraminer (German). Most of it grows around the town of Tramin, and the wines tend to be medium-bodied, floral but not very spicy in the nose and on the palate. We rarely see Gewurztraminer from Italy in the U.S. market, but we should.

THE UNITED STATES AND CANADA

In 1986, there were about 4,000 acres (1,600 hectares) of Gewurztraminer in the United States, but today there are fewer than 2,000 acres (800 hectares) under vine. The reason? Gewurztraminer, which needs a cool climate, is expensive to grow and labor-intensive to cultivate, and it almost never brings nearly as much money per ton of grapes as cool-climate Chardonnay (or even Sauvignon Blanc). In California, Gewurztraminer is planted in the cooler parts of Mendocino County, the Russian River Valley, and Monterey. The wines are mostly off-dry, with a few truly dry wines, especially from the Anderson Valley in Mendocino. The Finger Lakes and Long Island wine regions of New York State produce a very small amount of fine Gewurztraminer, as do Washington State and Oregon.

Canada does not specialize in Gewurztraminer, at least so far, but there are several good examples planted and produced in the Okanagan Valley of British Columbia, including a small selection of some very exciting Icewines.

Pinot Grigio/Pinot Gris

PINOT GRIGIO/PINOT GRIS: THE PROFILE

Currently, Pinot Grigio is the single most popular imported varietal-labeled wine in the United States. Sometimes we wonder why. Great Pinot Grigio is produced in several different countries, but rarely. Most often and unfortunately, Pinot Grigio is just a decent quaff that quenches the thirst and doesn't offend food. Maybe that's what most of us want—a wine that is drinkable and inoffensive, a wine that does not challenge us. The popularity of Pinot Grigio is the engine that feeds its mass acceptance, making it an inclusive wine, one that almost everyone can agree on and enjoy.

Pinot Grigio, most closely identified with Italy, is not really an Italian grape. The grape is Pinot Gris (the "gray" Pinot), found most prominently in Alsace, France. In the vineyard, it is hard to tell if the grape is Pinot Gris or Pinot Noir until after

Sutter Home Winery in California makes a value-driven, consumer-friendly, semi-sweet version of Gewurztraminer that is just great with spicy foods.

Danzante is a value brand of Pinot Grigio from northeast Italy that is popular in the United States. Courtesy of Danzante.

Pinot Grigio/Pinot Gris grapes. © iStock/funstickers.

color-changing *veraison*, as the leaves and grape shapes are identical. Pinot Gris is a variant of the Pinot Noir grape (as is Pinot Blanc).

At its best, Pinot Gris should be a full-bodied white wine, exhibiting spice, honey, honeysuckle, and nuttiness on the nose and tropical flavors on the palate, with just a touch of minerality. To achieve such concentration of flavor, fine Pinot Gris relies on low yields in the vineyard.

While Pinot Gris will always have its small number of admirers, it was not until the intro-duction of the label "Pinot Grigio" that this grape found its place in the sun and on so many dining tables around the world, but especially in the United States.

Maybe we just like saying "Pinot Grigio," a lovely phrase, almost sensual, but now nearly devoid of meaning. When we order Pinot Grigio in a restaurant or buy it in a shop, unless we have a favorite that we stick with, there's no telling what the wine will taste like. Fine Pinot Grigio is dry, but jam-packed with tropical fruits—mango, papaya, and pineapple—and has a long, complex,

rich finish. We've sampled bargain Pinot Grigio that tastes watery; moderate-priced Pinot Grigio that tastes like wine, sometimes pretty good food-friendly wine, but shows no truly distinctive varietal character; expensive Pinot Grigio that evokes the grape but has no sense of place (no *terroir*); and overpriced Pinot Grigio that was . . . well, overpriced and not terribly interesting.

Due to its popularity, you can easily find varietal-labeled Pinot Grigio just about anywhere. So, what countries and regions produce some of the best examples of this wine?

FRANCE

We think Pinot Gris from Alsace defines the wine made from this varietal, but if you like a lighter, more neutral style of Pinot Gris/Pinot Grigio, Alsace Pinot Gris is not for you. However, if you enjoy a full-bodied, assertive white wine without a lot of oak overtones that can pair beautifully with roast chicken or duck as well as grilled tuna or vegetarian lasagna, then you should try this classic wine from the Old World.

ITALY

Of course, most wine drinkers look to Italy for high-quality Pinot Grigio, even though the grape is indeed a French interloper. There are several quality producers in northeast Italy, particularly in the bilingual (Italian/German) province of Alto Adige, which borders Austria, that make clean, Alpine-crisp wines. In the Friuli–Venezia Giulia province of Italy, which borders Slovenia (part of the former Yugoslavia), Pinot Grigio tends to be richer and fuller-bodied. You can expect to pay from $12 to $45 for these wines at retail.

PORER

PINOT GRIGIO

2012

TENUTÆ LAGEDER

SÜDTIROL ALTO ADIGE

Alois Lageder makes fine wines in the Alto Adige region of Italy. Pinot Grigio from his single vineyard, "Porer," is one of the best produced anywhere. Courtesy of Alois Lageder.

Oregon has embraced Pinot Gris as its number-one white grape, eclipsing Chardonnay. The wines can be complex and delicious with a wide variety of foods. King Estate is a large producer of high-quality Oregon wines. Courtesy of King Estate Winery.

THE UNITED STATES

The most important "Cal-Italian" white grape in the Golden State, quite a bit of Pinot Grigio (and a bit of wine labeled "Pinot Gris") is produced in California. Quality ranges from drinkable to excellent, and prices range from inexpensive to too expensive. Go with a producer whose reputation you trust, or ask a knowledgeable retailer or sommelier for a suggestion.

If we choose to drink Pinot Grigio from the United States, our first choice would be a wine from Oregon, where it is most often labeled "Pinot Gris." At their best, the wines are luscious and full-bodied, with mineral and fruit-driven flavors that create a great marriage with a wide range of foods. Pinot Gris is the signature white grape of Oregon, and Oregon is the rare wine region where Pinot Gris vineyard acreage actually exceeds Chardonnay acreage; that's a serious commitment. We think that Oregon Pinot Gris is the benchmark for New World versions of this wine.

Pinot Gris may not be as hip a label choice as Pinot Grigio (even though they mean the same

thing in different languages), but when you taste a fine Oregon Pinot Gris with your dinner, you'll be glad you defied what's popular with your friends in favor of what's happening on your palate.

AUSTRALIA AND NEW ZEALAND

One surefire way to confirm that this grape has "arrived" as one of the world's most popular varietals is to note that Pinot Grigio is one of the varietals in the successful Australian wine brand, [yellow tail]® (which sells more than 8 million cases of wine each year in the United States). But it is not only price-driven brands such as [yellow tail]® that produce Pinot Grigio in the land down under. Artisanal wine producers in both Australia and New Zealand are focusing on Pinot Grigio as a quality varietal, and the wines are slowly beginning to appear in the American market.

The appeal of Pinot Grigio is undeniable, perhaps based on its promise of comfort and reliability. Pinot Grigio—a varietal for the rest of us.

Viognier

VIOGNIER: THE PROFILE

Just when we were comfortable pronouncing Chardonnay as our white wine of choice, along comes Viognier (vee-own-YAY) to make life difficult. Sure, it's inconvenient to learn the name of yet another French varietal, but pronouncing and tasting Viognier—a pleasing aroma of stone fruits is a classic Viognier trait—will be worth the effort.

Viognier is a white grape most closely identified with the northern Rhone Valley of France (see page 183), where it defines the Condrieu appellation, as well as the second-smallest appellation in all of France, Chateau Grillet (only 9 acres [3.5 hectares]). Both Condrieu and Chateau Grillet are quite expensive.

Now Viognier has come to the New World, and with a celebratory vengeance. Plantings of Viognier total more than 3,000 acres (1,200 hectares) in California, and the grape is being grown across the United States.

To thrive, the Viognier grape needs a warm climate; acidity in the finished wine is normally not very high. The best Viognier wines are not oak and alcohol bombs, but subtle wines with several layers of aroma and flavor. A rich wine, Viognier never forgets who brought it to the party: its grapes, not its barrels. You can pair Viognier with the same foods as Chardonnay, but chances are Viognier will give the food a chance to shine, while the Chardonnay might absorb the character of the dish in its own enforced complexity.

Viognier grapes. © iStock/Arina Habich.

Grilled swordfish with peach salsa is a dream dish for Viognier, as are garlic-studded roast chicken and veal schnitzel. We have enjoyed Viognier as our Thanksgiving white wine. Pork roast with apples and pears finds a complementary "sauce" in Viognier.

Viognier is on a roll, appearing with increasing regularity on wine lists and on the shelves of wine retailers. Finding good Viognier is no longer the challenge it once was; you just have to choose the style, region, price, and producers you like.

FRANCE

If you are fortunate enough to taste a Condrieu or the even rarer Chateau Grillet, both produced from Viognier grown in the northern Rhone Valley, by all means do so. These are wines of wondrous depth and structure, with a sensuous, almost lanolin-like oiliness that coats the palate. It is not all that unusual to drink these whites at four to seven years old, but they are especially wonderful to drink when young and fresh.

French IGP (formerly *vin de pays*) producers are making lots of varietal-labeled Viognier in the Pays d'Oc region (see page 149). These wines are good entry-level Viognier, relatively inexpensive whites for the thirsty masses.

Condrieu is a wine district in France's northern Rhone Valley. Jean-Luc Colombo is a prominent artisanal wine producer in the region.

THE UNITED STATES AND THE NEW WORLD

New World Viognier is all about luscious fruit and an appealing, sexy viscosity, a palpable silky texture.

Some of the best American Viogniers have a wondrous perfumed apricot and peach nose and a background of tropical fruit flavors. Good Viognier wines are produced from grapes grown in Washington, Texas, and Virginia, as well as California. These wines sell for between $10 and $25.

We might find the odd bottle of Australian, South African, or New Zealand Viognier, but these are rarities in the American import market. We're more likely to find a blended wine, comprising Viognier, Marsanne, and Roussanne, especially if the wine is produced in Australia.

Viognier can be a good wine for good value or it can be a very expensive wine, but it can be so much more. When you find the right wine with the right food, Viognier can be a wine of dreams, a wine of memories.

California wine producers are making quite a bit of Viognier. Tablas Creek specializes in grapes whose origins are in the Rhone Valley of France, including their Viognier, produced from grapes grown in the Paso Robles wine region of California. The wine is excellent.

3

GREAT VINES MAKE GREAT WINES

MAJOR RED GRAPES

RED GRAPES NOT ONLY MAKE RED WINES BUT ALSO WHITE AND ROSÉ WINES; STILL OR SPARKLING. SOUNDS LIKE magic. But red grapes are all about skin: show a lot of skin and you produce a red wine; a little bit of skin and you get rosé; no skin yields a white.

In the wide world of wine, there are hundreds of different red grapes that produce hundreds of different wines. We're going to start with the basics: six major red grapes that account for so many wines. These grapes often fly solo as the star of a wine (consider Pinot Noir), but sometimes they work and play well together in delicious blended wines (Cabernet Sauvignon/Merlot or Syrah/Grenache blends).

We'll start our survey of the major red grapes with the worldwide ruler of reds, Cabernet Sauvignon . . .

Cabernet Sauvignon

CABERNET SAUVIGNON: THE PROFILE

It seems that Cabernet Sauvignon is everywhere, and that perception is not far from wrong. Almost any recognized wine region that is moderately warm to hot grows Cabernet Sauvignon, and wine drinkers can't seem to get enough of this varietal. Why is it that this grape has captured the hearts, minds, and palates of millions of wine consumers and is now grown on hundreds of thousands of vineyard acres?

For one thing, Cab is always Cab. Wherever you grow it, the varietal makes a wine that is recognizable, true to its varietal character. With vibrant aromas of black cherries, black currants, black plums, black olives, and eucalyptus in a young wine, and hints of cedar and cigar box bouquets as it ages, Cabernet Sauvignon produces reliable, even predictable, full-bodied, in-your-face red wine, with high degrees of both tannins and acidity. Yes, there are differences between New World and Old World Cab, but once you get hooked on this grape, the similarities outshine the differences.

The popularity of Cabernet Sauvignon is both its strength and its weakness. Without the commanding presence of this varietal there simply would not be a successful wine industry and culture in Bordeaux, France, or the Napa Valley of California, or the Maipo Valley of Chile. Cab has put these regions on the world's wine map. But the tremendous popularity of Cabernet Sauvignon has also diminished the important traditional varietals of countries such as Italy and Spain, among others. If there are any grape types that can be accused of "wine imperialism," then the first suspects are Cabernet Sauvignon for red wines and Chardonnay for whites.

Why is Cabernet Sauvignon so successful in the vineyards of so many wine regions and so popular with wine consumers, from the neophyte

Cabernet Sauvignon grapes. © Alistair Berg/Getty Images.

to the auction-quality collector? For grape growers, Cab is a slam dunk; it grows in almost every wine-producing country of the world and adapts well to a wide variety of climates and soils. The grape has a thick skin and is resistant to many of the plant viruses and diseases that plague less hardy varietals.

Cabernet Sauvignon loves oak, especially the assertive spicy vanilla flavors of new oak barrels. The *barriques* used to age Cab are most often about 60 gallons (225 liters), and if all of the barrels are new, the result can be a dramatic, over-the-top, but smooth, sweet black cherry–like wine. Some of the best Cab wines are made using a regimen of new and used barrels to tone down the oak flavors in the finished wine, but the producers of these wines often do so at their peril. Why? Because many of the most influential wine writers and critics who assign numerical scores (such as 92—or, heaven forbid, 82—out of a possible 100 points) seem incapable of evaluating wines that are not loaded up with the overwhelming flavors of new oak.

Sometimes the wine critics get it right when it comes to Cab, but just as often we wonder, "What were they thinking?" when they assign a high score to a wine that tastes like a vanilla-flavored two-by-four. These wines, though they may garner a cult following of well-heeled consumers willing to pay high prices, will not highlight and enhance the flavors and textures of a rare steak or leg of lamb, especially when compared to a Cab (or perhaps another full-bodied red) that exhibits more restraint.

Yet another reason for Cabernet Sauvignon's worldwide success is its ability to work and play well with other grapes. Not all varietals are nearly as sociable. For example, if you want to produce a fine wine made from Pinot Noir or Chardonnay, don't blend with other wines made from different varietals. Conversely, an "anchor wine" made from Cabernet Sauvignon blended with, say, a total of 15% to 25% Merlot and/or Cabernet Franc is a classic mix that started in Bordeaux and made its way around the world. For instance, many esteemed Napa Valley Cabs contain between 5% and 25% Merlot and/or Cabernet Franc.

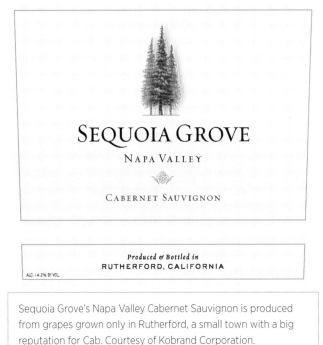

Sequoia Grove's Napa Valley Cabernet Sauvignon is produced from grapes grown only in Rutherford, a small town with a big reputation for Cab. Courtesy of Kobrand Corporation.

John and Doug Shafer make extraordinary Cabernet Sauvignon in the Stags Leap District of Napa Valley, including this delicious and much sought-after Hillside Select bottling.

Cabernet Sauvignon's ability to hook up with other attractive wines takes the creative handcuffs off the winemaker, who can create his or her own style of Cab partially based on the chosen blend. And winemakers are not limited to the classic Bordeaux blending model. In Tuscany, Italy, literally hundreds of "Super Tuscan" wines (see pages 199–201) are based on blends of Cabernet Sauvignon and Sangiovese, the most important traditional grape of the region. In several wine regions of Spain (see pages 224–245), blends of Cab and Tempranillo-based wines are increasingly common. Australia (see page 126) is well known for making a wide range of Cabernet Sauvignon/Shiraz blended wines. The list goes on, but you get the drift.

Because Cabernet Sauvignon is so flexible, there are as many styles of wine as there are winemakers. However, even though the wines vary stylistically, the basic truth is this: Cab is one of the easiest wines to identify, as it exhibits loads of varietal character, whether it is priced at $12 or at $1,200. So why pay the big money for something that is supposedly special? Well, the best wines made primarily from the Cabernet Sauvignon grape display a sense of place, not just varietal character. What you are paying for is the address of the wine, not necessarily the grape that appears on the label. In Bordeaux, you are paying big bucks for the character of the soil and the heralded history of the estate (the *chateau*) on which the grape is grown. In the New World, a "California" Cab should taste decidedly different from a "Napa Valley" Cab, which should taste different from a "Rutherford" Cab (Rutherford is a town within the Napa Valley), and a "single-vineyard Rutherford" Cab should taste even more special than a wine made from grapes grown on more than one Rutherford vineyard or vineyard block. At each heightened level of perceived quality the price goes up, and the difference between the "California" Cab and the single-vineyard Rutherford Cab could easily be far more than $100.

Whatever style and price point you are comfortable with, most Cab is not for the faint-hearted when it comes to pairing with food. Maybe the world's admiration for this varietal is an expression of post-industrial wealth, because Cabernet Sauvignon does not allow us to eat low on the food chain. Rare red meat is what Cab is all about; just look at the wine list in any good steakhouse worth its salt and pepper. Hard cheese such as Parmigiano-Reggiano, full of fat and with just an edge of sweetness, is also a great match for this wine. Try it with a delicate fish dish and you will be suffering through your meal, unless you like the metallic taste that the clash of harsh tannins and omega-3 fatty acids can bring.

Unlike the healthy skepticism tempered with genuine interest in other white wines that some-times greets Chardonnay, Cab is still the king of reds, at least in the American marketplace. Merlot, Pinot Noir, and lately Syrah (all three varietals are discussed later in this chapter) have their boosters and adherents, but the preemi-nent position of Cabernet Sauvignon remains unchallenged. Maybe it's the same reason that some people prefer hard rock to folk music, or love aggressive wall-sized abstract paintings and loathe small quiet landscape watercolors. Some people make football their religion; others love only women's tennis. Cab is bold and brawny and powerful, and its dark, brooding color and complex nature make a statement that appeals to those of us looking for a definition of what a "big red wine" should be. Certainly, there is more to life than Cabernet Sauvignon; however, in every kingdom there are many loyal subjects, but only one king. Cab rules.

FRANCE

The "Left Bank" of Bordeaux (see pages 170–172) is the quintessential classic region for both Cabernet Sauvignon vineyards and some world-famous wines, most often judicious blends of Cabernet Sauvignon, Merlot, and Cabernet Franc, with grace notes sometimes provided by Malbec and Petit Verdot. Outside of Bordeaux, Southwest France grows a lot of Cabernet Sauvignon grapes and produces quite a bit of pretty good wine dominated by the varietal. The Mediterranean provinces of Languedoc and Roussillon (see pages 187–189) in south-central France are awash in high-yielding Cabernet Sauvignon vineyards, where a huge volume of drinkable, varietal-labeled Cab is produced.

Chateau Cordeillan-Bages is a well-known property in Bordeaux, France, located in the Village of Pauillac. The wine is made primarily from Cabernet Sauvignon grapes. Courtesy of Chateau Cordeillan-Bages.

Classic Old World Cabernet Sauvignon—basically, the Bordeaux model—is quite different from the New World wine—basically, the California model (see page 71). We don't get jammy black fruits in the Old World. Instead, we get aromatics of just-ripe blackcurrant, cedar, mushroom dirt, black olive, hints of barnyard, and leather. On the palate, we're likely to taste firm tannins first, with a secondary background of black fruit in young wines, with more fruit, more balanced flavors emerging over time in more mature wines. The best Old World Cab takes patience—years of patience—and that patience will be rewarded.

ITALY

Cabernet Sauvignon has been planted sporadically in the vineyards of Italy for hundreds of years, but today the varietal is planted in the majority of Italy's 20 provinces. Cabernet Sauvignon is sometimes produced as a single-varietal wine or as a Cabernet/Merlot blend, but more often it is blended with wines made from indigenous varietals.

The most heralded blend is Cabernet Sauvignon and Sangiovese, made famous by the much sought-after and often expensive "Super Tuscans." Sangiovese is the backbone of virtually all the traditional wines of Tuscany—Chianti and Brunello di Montalcino, for example—and Cabernet Sauvignon turns out to be a successful partner in many of the region's nontraditional blended wines. Some of these wines are featured prominently on the wine lists of great restaurants and in upscale retail outlets. Some of the most famous examples in which Cabernet Sauvignon dominates the blend include Solaia, Sassicaia, Ornellaia, Excelsus, and Tinscvil.

In Veneto, Lombardy, and Emilia-Romagna, it is easy to find Cab-based wines, often blended with Merlot and Cabernet Franc. Some interesting, delicious wines are now being produced in southern Italy, especially in Sicily, and on the island of Sardinia, where Cabernet Sauvignon is often blended with indigenous varietals.

SPAIN

Cabernet Sauvignon is making its presence known in Spain, often blended with Tempranillo in the wine regions Ribera del Duero and Rioja, among others. In the Penedes region, anchored by Barcelona, the historic and cultural influence of France is expressed in the choice of grapes to make wine, and Cabernet Sauvignon is one of the most important red grapes of the region. It is not uncommon to find varietal Cabernet Sauvignon or a Cabernet Sauvignon/Merlot blend produced in Penedes, but it is just as common to find a Tempranillo/Cabernet Sauvignon blend from this region. Also, the small but prestigious region of Priorat produces Cab-based wines, most often as blends with the indigenous varietals Cariñena (Carignan) and/or Garnacha (Grenache).

THE REST OF THE OLD WORLD

Cabernet Sauvignon grows in just about every wine-producing nation of the Old World, including Portugal, Greece, Bulgaria, Hungary, Romania, and even the warmer parts of Switzerland, Austria, and Germany. Cab is the most important red varietal in the wines of Israel and high-quality blended wines from Lebanon, especially the esteemed Chateau Musar.

THE UNITED STATES: CALIFORNIA

Cabernet Sauvignon is the most widely planted red wine grape in the vineyards of California (Zinfandel is second; see page 55). So much of the Golden State provides a near-perfect match of climate and varietal that Cab has become a no-brainer to grow in the best "artisanal" single vineyards of the Napa Valley, the "industrial" vineyards of the Central Valley, and every peak and valley in between these extremes. These expensive artisanal wines may be produced from

**NAPA VALLEY
RUTHERFORD
CALIFORNIA
2009**

Rubicon

ESTATE BOTTLED
GROWN & PRODUCED BY INGLENOOK, RUTHERFORD, NAPA VALLEY, CALIFORNIA, U.S.A.

Rubicon is a famous and expensive estate-bottled Cabernet Sauvignon–based wine first produced in 1978. Inglenook (formerly Rubicon Estate), perhaps the most historic wine estate in the Napa Valley, is owned by the Coppola family.

vineyards yielding less than 2 tons per acre (5 tons per hectare), while the utilitarian, value-driven industrial wines are produced from vines as big as small trees, yielding close to 15 tons per acre (37.5 tons per hectare). Whichever Cab you choose, and at whatever price point, it still tastes like California Cab, capturing sunshine in a bottle and showing off a jammy, sweet attack of voluptuous black fruit with a dry finish.

If you trade up from the under-$10 Cab to a $30-plus-plus-plus Cab, what you get is an age-worthy wine with deeper concentration of flavor, more subtlety and complexity on the palate and in the nose, and that sense of place (a single vineyard in Sonoma County's Alexander Valley, for example) that some wine consumers are willing to pay for, again and again.

As in Bordeaux, varietal-labeled Cabernet Sauvignon from California will often contain a healthy dose—up to 25%—of Merlot and Cabernet Franc in the finished blend, allowing the individual wine producer to tweak the wine to meet his or her own standards of balance and quality, or just as often to anticipate taste preferences of the American wine consumer.

No one will argue that Cabernet Sauvignon has defined California's red wine industry, just as Chardonnay has defined white wine. The public

has embraced California Cab, from the shelves of supermarkets to the wine lists of the world's most expensive restaurants.

THE REST OF NORTH AMERICA

Cabernet Sauvignon maintains a serious presence in the warmer parts of Washington State's Columbia Valley, such as the Red Mountain and Horse Heaven Hills regions. Cabernet Sauvignon's ability to tough it out in moderately cool weather allows producers to make some attractive wines.

In Oregon, there are about 600 acres (240 hectares) of Cab planted mostly in the Rogue Valley and Umpqua Valley, but Oregon Cabernet Sauvignon lives in the shadow thrown by the state's premier red varietal, Pinot Noir.

New York State's Long Island wine regions grow and produce some lovely Cabernet Sauvignon, but in such small amounts that they rarely leave the New York Metro area. New Mexico, Texas, and Virginia are among other Cab-producing states.

Canada, because of its cold temperatures, produces a lot more Cabernet Franc than Cabernet Sauvignon, but Mexico can produce some drinkable Cabernet Sauvignon, even some very good ones, especially in Baja California's Guadalupe Valley.

SOUTH AMERICA: CHILE AND ARGENTINA

Without Cabernet Sauvignon there probably would be no Chilean wine industry. Chile produces a lot of Cab for the export market, and in the 1990s it developed a reputation for true-to-varietal-type wines at bargain prices. You can still buy Chilean Cab produced from mostly high-yielding vineyards for under $10, but you can also find *terroir*-driven, single-vineyard wines from the Maipo, Colchagua, Aconcagua, and Curico wine regions with high prices to match their pedigree.

Almaviva is consistently one of the finest—and most expensive—Cabernet Sauvignon vines from Chile's Maipo Valley. Courtesy of Viña Almaviva S.A.

In Argentina, there is some varietal Cabernet Sauvignon produced, but Cab is most often reserved for blending with the nation's premier red wine, Malbec. At their best, these wines can exhibit assertive aromatics and complex flavors that make for some ageworthy wines with attractive prices.

AUSTRALIA AND NEW ZEALAND

Shiraz (Australia's name for the Syrah grape) is the showstopper in the vineyards of Australia and enjoys both critical and popular acclaim in the bottle. But Australia produces a lot of full-bodied, jammy Cabernet Sauvignon, too, and just as with Shiraz, it does so at every conceivable price point—from under $10 to over $100, and every price in between these extremes. Cabernet Sauvignon/Shiraz blends are also quite popular and can be delicious.

Wines labeled "South Eastern Australia" are value-driven, consumer-friendly wines, while Cab exhibiting the appellation "South Australia" is likely to kick it up a notch when it comes to quality and price. The best Australian Cabernet Sauvignon originates in the vineyards of the Coonawarra region, followed closely by wines produced from grapes grown in McLaren Vale, Margaret River, or Barossa Valley.

New Zealand produces some lovely Cabs as well as Cabernet Sauvignon/Merlot blends from vineyards in the Hawke's Bay region, located on the southern tip of the nation's North Island.

SOUTH AFRICA

A small number of wine producers in the Stellenbosch region of South Africa make some very fine Cabernet Sauvignon, sometimes blended with Merlot.

Merlot

MERLOT: THE PROFILE

"Cabernet Sauvignon on Prozac" is one of the best definitions we've heard for most of the Merlot-based wines produced in the world today. Merlot is too often turned into a wine that has no rough edges and poses little or no challenge either to the drinker's palate or to his or her food. The Merlot grape is a fabulous blender with Cabernet Sauvignon, but with few notable exceptions—particularly wines produced from grapes grown in the vineyards of Bordeaux's Pomerol and St-Emilion districts, and a small selection of Merlot produced in the United States—this varietal does not often make a compelling wine when left on its own in a bottle.

Merlot is wildly successful around the world, pleasing wine consumers in the Old World, but especially in the New World, and specifically in the United States. Merlot is the ultimate feel-good red, making wines that feature aromas and flavors of ripe, sweet, chocolate-covered black cherries tinged with oaky vanilla overtones, complete with a silky, sexy, voluptuous texture. Most wines made from Merlot are predictable fun and don't require a lot of thought and analysis to enjoy; they're more of a one-night stand than a long-term relationship.

Merlot grapes. © Frank Wing/Getty Images.

Stories of our friends and family members who "don't like red wines" but "*love* Merlot" abound, and with good reason. Most Merlot is completely accessible, from its juicy, rich, sweet flavors and its low levels of tannin and acid to its wide range of price points. While consumer-driven Merlot may not be the greatest match with many foods, it does work well with some and is usually at least inoffensive to others. Most Merlot is a modern miracle of marketing in that it is made with the consumer in mind, and the styles of the finished wines made from this grape fit the parameters of market research and prognostication.

Until the 1980s, Merlot was viewed as a blender, often used to soften the tannins and acids of Cabernet Sauvignon. When Merlot started to become more popular as a stand-alone varietal, the Napa Valley legend Robert Mondavi refused to produce a Merlot because he didn't think it made a very complete wine; he thought of it as kind of "hollow." What we think he meant is that Merlot doesn't often transform into a wine that is well balanced; it lacks what is sometimes called a good "middle palate," the weight and presence of the wine after its initial attack on the tongue and in the mouth. Classic wines display a fine middle

palate, almost like a dotted line across the middle of your tongue. Except in rare cases, Merlot doesn't behave like this.

And yet there is great, fabulous, even otherworldly Merlot produced from relatively thin-skinned grapes grown in the cold clay, gravel, and iron-rich sandstone soils of Pomerol and the sand/limestone/gravel soils of St-Emilion, both located on the "Right Bank" of Bordeaux (see pages 172–173). What is interesting about these wines is that they go against the grain of modern Merlot. They are not "Pow! In your face!" jammy-fruit and big-alcohol bombs, but are medium- to full-bodied wines, more delicate, better balanced, and made to grace our dining tables, especially when we might be enjoying lamb, beef, or cheeses. Ironically, these wines tend to age much longer than the bigger, brawnier Merlot that many of us have come to know and sometimes enjoy.

For the "Merlot Majority," aging is hardly an issue, as we drink most Merlot within a few years of its vintage date. If we stop on the way home at the wine shop or supermarket and pick up a couple of bottles of two-to-three-year-old varietal-labeled Merlot from California or Washington State or Chile or wherever, we'll probably be happily drinking that puppy within the week. In a restaurant, we are likely to order a Merlot that makes us comfortable and content—one we've tasted before and enjoyed. Even if we're trying a

St. Supery is an established producer in California's Napa Valley; the winery produces excellent Merlot. Label design by Rich Wylie; courtesy of St. Supery.

MATANZAS CREEK WINERY

2010 MERLOT
SONOMA COUNTY

ALC. 15.0% BY VOL.

A Sonoma County gem, Matanzas Creek has long been recognized as one of the finest Merlot producers in the United States. Courtesy of Matanzas Creek Winery.

New World Merlot we've never had before, it's unlikely that our first consideration is its age. No, aging Merlot—unless it is a great wine from a great estate—not only is unnecessary, but in most cases it's a bad idea. Unlike Cabernet Sauvignon, the grape with which it is so closely aligned in wine consciousness, Merlot usually lacks the tannins, acids, and overall structure that lead a wine to seriously improve with time.

Merlot competes with Cabernet Sauvignon for being the most-planted red wine grape in the world (each exceeds 700,000 acres [280,000 hectares] worldwide). Because Merlot is so popular, it is planted in almost all of the wine regions of the world except for the absolute coldest places. From Switzerland to Slovenia, from New Zealand to New York, from Austria to Australia, from Argentina to Italy, from South America to South Africa, Merlot is grown just about everywhere. Here are some of the countries and regions you're likely to encounter on the Merlot map.

FRANCE

Merlot is the most planted grape in the Bordeaux region of France (see pages 165–173), and as the world clamors for soft, easy-to-drink reds, its varietal star is ascending here. While it plays a supporting role in the wines from the "Left Bank" of Bordeaux (including the Haut-Medoc and Graves regions), it is the star of the show on the "Right Bank" (Pomerol and St-Emilion) and in the satellite appellations that produce accessible, less-expensive Bordeaux wines.

Merlot is also the most frequently planted red grape in all of France, and its popularity is growing every year. It is grown throughout Provence and the southwest, and in the southern province of Languedoc, among many others. It may be used as the main grape or as a blender in these regions, and many relatively inexpensive French wines with varietal labels are 100% Merlot.

ITALY

Merlot is huge in Italy, with plantings growing exponentially over the last decade or so. The northeastern regions mostly produce wines of no great distinction from vineyards with high yields, but they are easy to drink and affordable.

In the vineyards of Tuscany, Merlot has become an important grape for producing dozens of wines (see pages 199–204). Sometimes Cabernet Sauvignon is blended with Merlot, or with Merlot and Sangiovese, to create the very popular—and oftentimes very expensive—"Super Tuscans."

THE REST OF EUROPE

Merlot is planted in the warmer vineyard sites of Austria, Hungary, Romania, Bulgaria, and Moldova. In these countries the wines produced from the Merlot grape or from Merlot/Cabernet Sauvignon blends are drinkable and affordable. But it is in Switzerland's Italian-speaking Ticino region where Merlot positively dominates, producing some predictable quaffs and a few glorious wines.

THE UNITED STATES: CALIFORNIA

Most of the wines produced from the Merlot grape in California are much like the stereotypical images of Californians themselves: laid-back and mellow. The Golden State produces wines that are fruit-forward with sweet dark-berry flavors, and most often low in acids and tannins. Styles range from light and fruity to massive and complex, but the wines are almost always silky, satiny, and smooth on the palate.

A lot of Merlot is planted in the very warm Central Valley. The wines produced here are simple, easy-to-drink, inexpensive reds that taste like Merlot and work well with a burger, a sandwich, or a slice of pizza; they are not meant to knock your socks, or even one sock, off.

Merlot with more character is derived from the vineyards of California's cooler North Coast wine districts, especially Napa, Sonoma, and Mendocino counties. These wines are darker in color and more concentrated in flavor, and feature ripe-to-overripe fruit flavors in an often full-bodied, even massive high-alcohol wine. Some of these wines, especially those from the Napa Valley, can be very expensive and hard to find. In Sonoma County, the vineyards and wineries of Sonoma Valley, Alexander Valley, and Dry Creek Valley also produce some fine Merlot wines.

OTHER STATES

Washington State has developed quite a reputation for the quality of its Merlot wines, both on the small-producer "boutique" level and the grand scale. Growers in the Columbia Valley and Walla Walla districts have to work hard to make sure all is right in the vineyard and have to pray for winters that are not too frigid. Washington State Merlot is next in line after Chardonnay and Riesling in total acres planted.

L'Ecole No. 41 winery, established in 1983, makes one of Washington's top Merlot wines from its Seven Hills Vineyard in the Walla Walla Valley wine region.

SOUTH AMERICA: CHILE

Merlot is affordable and tastes good to most value-conscious wine consumers, and when you're paying about $10 at retail for a bottle of wine, those are usually the criteria for meeting customer expectations.

AUSTRALIA AND NEW ZEALAND

Although plantings of Merlot are increasing every year in Australia, it is a grape that has yet to really catch on as the basis for varietal-labeled wines (only 4% to 5% of its vineyards are planted with Merlot). Add to this the tradition of blending Shiraz—not Merlot—with Cabernet Sauvignon, and Australia has a bit of a learning curve to get over when it comes to producing Merlot on a large scale. Most of Australia is quite warm—ideal for Cabernet Sauvignon, but not cool enough for Merlot.

New Zealand is cooler than Australia, and the southern tip of the North Island may be an ideal climate to grow Merlot. Indeed, Merlot is New Zealand's third most frequently planted grape (Sauvignon Blanc and Chardonnay are first and second, respectively, making Merlot the most-planted red grape in the nation).

Pinot Noir

PINOT NOIR: THE PROFILE

Pinot Noir is a very finicky grape that defies definition when it comes to style and expectation in the finished wine. Pinot Noir celebrates both its sense of place and the cult of the individual: where it is grown and who is growing it play significant roles in determining the character of the finished wine.

Pinot Noir grapes. © Photodisk/Getty Images.

Growing Pinot Noir is not for everybody. Indeed, people who happily grow Chardonnay, Cabernet Sauvignon, and other less tricky varietals are often petrified by the idea of growing Pinot Noir. It isn't so much that these growers are incapable of doing a good job in the vineyards and the winery; it's that everybody has his or her own opinion on what a "good job" is when it comes to judging wines made from this grape.

More a cliché than a statement of certifiable fact is that the best wines made from Pinot Noir should mimic wines from Burgundy, France, where the grape has been cultivated for at least six hundred years and possibly more than sixteen hundred years. Pinot Noir is celebrated in Burgundy and is by law the only red grape allowed to be grown on its best vineyard sites. The beauty of great red Burgundy wine is also precisely the problem with Pinot Noir: each one tastes different. Each wine might taste wonderful, even seductive, but each seduces differently; one plays off its youthful energy and exuberance to choreograph a lusty dance of desirability, while another relies on its experience and voluptuous maturity to lure us into a garden of delights. When it comes to red Burgundy, one size does not fit all, and to define good Pinot Noir based on the "Burgundy model" is tired and meaningless.

Yet good Pinot Noir is the most food-friendly red wine on the planet. Balanced, with subtle fruits, bracing acidity, and moderate tannins, it is a wine that will pair with a myriad of foods, except for the most intense and the absolute lightest. This is a wine that is comfortable with grilled fish, pasta, roasted vegetables, most red meat dishes, game, poultry, and cheeses. Pinot Noir pairs with Thai, Cambodian, Vietnamese, and Chinese dishes; with many classic Middle Eastern foods; and on and on and on . . .

Of course, the wine world abounds with a lot of Pinot Noir that, if not really bad, certainly needs work. Some are way too light, more like unbalanced rosé than true red wines; others are ponderous, heavy, and overtly alcoholic. Not to evade the question, but it is difficult to describe the ideal Pinot Noir because there are so many different styles available in the marketplace. So likeability becomes a question of very personal

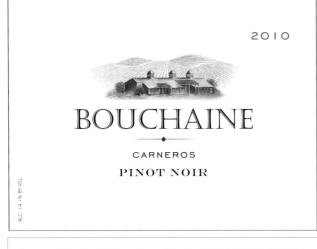

Bouchaine is the oldest continuously operating winery in Carneros, a wine region that traverses both Napa and Sonoma counties and is known for its cool-climate Pinot Noir and Chardonnay.

taste. In describing the ideal Pinot Noir, we're reminded of a quote by Supreme Court Justice Potter Stewart who in 1964 was asked to define obscenity: "I know it when I see it." This quote can be easily adapted to describing the ideal Pinot Noir: "I know it when I taste it."

Still, we want to be helpful to our readers, so when it comes to flavor, let's consider the broad strokes of Pinot Noir. If we can agree that with Pinot Noir you usually get what you pay for—an axiom that is perhaps truer for this varietal than for any other—then we can report some general observations. Bargain-priced Pinot Noir made for early drinking can be charming in its simplicity, tasting of strawberries and, to a lesser extent, cranberries and red raspberries. As you move up the quality ladder, the wines take on more complexity, with a mix of spiced strawberries and black cherries, as well as noticeably higher acidity on the palate. The most complex examples of fine Pinot Noir will demonstrate aromas and tastes of both red and black fruits, but in an earthbound, funky wrap of mushroom, leather, charred wood, smoke, and moist soil. These wines can age from five to 10 years and even longer, and are usually rare and expensive.

Pinot Noir is a thin-skinned grape that traditionally grows best in cool climates, such as one finds in Burgundy and Champagne in France, parts of Germany, Austria, and northeastern Italy.

The Willamette Valley of Oregon and the coolest vineyard sites of Australia and New Zealand show great promise. The cooler growing areas of California—Carneros, Russian River Valley, Anderson Valley, the premier vineyards of Santa Barbara County—are also part of the mix.

Cool weather allows Pinot Noir to develop attractively high levels of acidity, although it can make ideal ripening difficult. Because the grape is light-colored and thin-skinned, tannins are usually soft and subtle. When all of the elements of nature collide successfully, Pinot Noir vineyards can provide the raw material for glorious medium-bodied wines. But these elements strike a delicate balance, and when things go wrong in the vineyard, the result can just as easily be wines that are unpleasant, sometimes with green, unripe flavors, sometimes with flavors of cooked and stewed fruits, overripe and foul.

There is no real consensus about what kind of soil is best for growing Pinot Noir, but most growers agree to disagree over soils rich in either limestone or clay. What almost all growers do agree on is that the soil must be well drained and not overly fertile, to keep yields low.

A very expensive wine from Burgundy, France, made from 100% Pinot Noir grapes. Le Musigny is a *grand cru* vineyard in the village of Chambolle-Musigny and is one of the finest Pinot Noir sites in the world. Courtesy of Kobrand Corporation.

Dutton Estate produces extraordinary single-vineyard, site-specific Pinot Noir in the very cool Russian River Valley in Sonoma County, California. Dutton Estate wines are produced in small quantities and are quite expensive; they are worth every penny. Courtesy of Dutton Estate Winery.

Winemakers have been known to add some Syrah (discussed next in this chapter) or other deeply colored wine to ramp up the color and body of Pinot Noir, but the best wines express their individual *terroir*—their sense of place—without the addition of other wines or the use of technological manipulation. In fact, Pinot Noir is probably the most *terroir*-driven of all red wines (it's Riesling for whites); certainly the Burgundians think so, and we agree.

Burgundy's best vineyard sites (see page 175) are officially rated and government-certified as *premier cru* (first growth) and the even grander *grand cru* (great growth). The wines produced from these vineyards can be moderately to wildly expensive, and many are produced in such small amounts that most of us will never get to taste them even if we could afford them.

Since fine Pinot Noir is so site-dependent, it's time for us to take a quick look at some of the places that grow and produce some of the best examples of this wine.

FRANCE: BURGUNDY AND CHAMPAGNE

In Burgundy, the only red grape planted in the northern subregions of Cote de Nuits and Cote de Beaune (collectively known as Cote d'Or) is Pinot Noir (see pages 179–180). Here, *terroir* carries the day, as wines produced from a small vineyard, or a small part of a larger vineyard, will taste noticeably different from a vineyard site less than a few hundred feet down the road.

There is also a lot of drinkable Pinot Noir from Burgundy that is more affordable than the most prized reds from the Cote d'Or, produced a bit farther south in the Cote Chalonnaise subregion (see page 181). Also don't hesitate to try a wine labeled "Bourgogne" (French for Burgundy), as the best producers make wines from select vineyards in the region that are quite good and quite affordable.

In the Champagne region (see page 152), Pinot Noir is one of only three grapes; the other two are the red Pinot Meunier and the white Chardonnay. These are the only legal grapes in Champagne, and most Champagnes are made from a blend of wines made from varying percentages of these grapes. Champagne is the coldest wine region in all of France, and Pinot Noir ripens just enough to produce a wine that is high in acidity, which meshes beautifully with bubbles to refresh our palates. Since most Champagne is a white sparkling wine, there is very little skin contact—the skin is where all the color is—when Pinot Noir grapes are fermented.

THE REST OF EUROPE

Pinot Noir also grows in Germany (see page 265), where it is known as Spatburgunder, and in Austria (see page 273), where the grape is often called Blauer Burgunder. In Italy (see pages 191–221), where it is sometimes called Pinot Nero, the varietal is grown in Lombardy, where it is an essential constituent of the excellent sparkler Franciacorta. Pinot Noir is also widely planted in the Alto Adige region, where it produces fine still wine.

THE UNITED STATES: CALIFORNIA AND OREGON

California (see page 71) had to navigate a massive learning curve to succeed with Pinot Noir, and even today great California Pinot Noir is a rarity, though a sublime one. The coolest regions—Carneros, which is a shared appellation between Napa and Sonoma counties; the Russian River Valley in Sonoma; the Anderson Valley in Mendocino; the Santa Maria Valley in Santa Barbara; and Mount Harlan in San Benito—are some of the premier growing regions for Pinot Noir.

The knock against California's Pinot Noir has been that the wines lack balance and are too jammy, too alcoholic, too "big," too ripe, too Cabernet-like. California winemakers still produce some of these big wines, but more and more we taste very good Pinot Noir that is made with a gentle touch, with restraint.

Oregon (see page 106) is at the same latitude as Burgundy, and it has developed a well-earned reputation for its Pinot Noir. In particular, the Willamette Valley is one of the greatest places in the entire New World for growing this grape. The best of these wines are delicate but substantive and beautifully balanced. The overwhelming majority of Oregon Pinot Noir winemakers are artisans, producing small amounts of very fine wines. Prices run the gamut from near-bargains to very expensive, and quality runs from good basic varietal character to very special and rare, true to vineyard *terroir* and vintage conditions.

SOUTHERN HEMISPHERE: CHILE, NEW ZEALAND, AUSTRALIA

Pinot Noir seems to have a bright future in the Southern Hemisphere. Chile's coastal Casablanca Valley (see pages 117–118), which is best known for nurturing Chardonnay and Sauvignon Blanc, also provides a good home for Pinot Noir,

New Zealand is making a name for itself with cool-climate Pinot Noir. Grove Mill makes a very good wine in the Marlborough region.

producing very appealing wines that strike a balance between delicacy and juicy ripeness.

Down under, Pinot Noir looks like an up-and-coming star in New Zealand (see page 134). In the Martinborough region, on the southern tip of its North Island, and in Central Otago, on the southern tip of its South Island, cool-climate New Zealand is producing some very exciting and delicious Pinot Noir.

Australia (see page 126) produces a handful of good Pinot Noir wines, but it is still a newcomer here, with the Yarra Valley, located on the outskirts of Melbourne in the state of Victoria, showing real promise. Less than 5% of vineyard plantings in Australia are Pinot Noir, and much of the fruit is utilized quite successfully as part of the blend for Champagne-method sparkling wines.

Syrah/Shiraz

SYRAH/SHIRAZ: THE PROFILE

Syrah and Shiraz are actually the same grape, but with different names. "Syrah" is the Old World (European) name for the grape, while "Shiraz" is definitely a New World moniker, closely identified with, but not limited to, Australia.

There is more Syrah planted in France than anywhere else on earth (about 100,000 acres [40,000 hectares]), and Australia plants at least 70,000 acres (28,000 hectares) of Shiraz, securing second place. The United States is in third place, with about 19,000 acres (7,600 hectares). The popularity of Syrah/Shiraz is growing, and plantings are increasing dramatically worldwide.

In Europe, the classic growing region for Syrah is the northern Rhone Valley of France (see page 183). The most famous Syrah vineyards in the world reside in the Hermitage, Cote-Rotie, St-Joseph, Cornas, and Crozes-Hermitage appellations, all of which give their names to heralded wines. This region is one of the coolest places in the world for growing Syrah, but its heat-retaining slopes, composed of granite soils, help to make ripening of the grape possible.

Syrah/Shiraz grapes. © iStock/barnaby30.

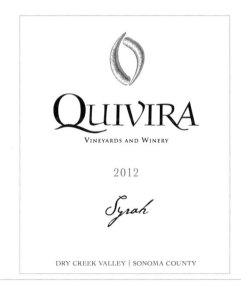

Quivira produces a small amount of single-vineyard Syrah from its own estate in Sonoma County's Dry Creek Valley. The vineyards are certified as biodynamic, and the winery runs on solar power. Courtesy of Quivira Vineyards.

In the New World, the terms "Shiraz" and "Australia" (see page 126) have become synonymous. Original vine cuttings for Shiraz were brought from the Hermitage district of the Rhone Valley to Australia in the nineteenth century, and vineyards are located in various parts of the states of South Australia and New South Wales, with fewer plantings in the cooler states of Victoria and Western Australia. Overall, Australia's vineyards are some of the warmest sites in the world for growing Shiraz.

There are so many different styles of Syrah/Shiraz wines in the market that it is difficult to make any broad generalizations about its flavor and food-friendliness. The wine can be fashioned as a medium-bodied easy sipper that loves to accompany a burger and fries eaten at the beach, or as a massive in-your-face bruiser that needs braised short ribs and creamy mashed potatoes, preferably enjoyed in front of a fireplace during a snowstorm. In between these two extremes is a full gamut of Syrah/Shiraz styles, from sunny simplicity to extraordinarily earthy elegance.

Add to the multiple personalities of Syrah/Shiraz the fact that it is an excellent blending grape with a wide variety of both red and white varietals, and you might be forgiven for thinking that Syrah/Shiraz is just about the ideal wine grape. Actually, there may be no reason for forgiveness, as grape growers, winemakers, and wine consumers have embraced this varietal with wild enthusiasm.

Note: "Petite Sirah" is not Syrah and is not supposed to be Shiraz (though some people have their doubts). Petite Sirah is actually Durif, a grape whose ancestral home is the southern Rhone Valley. Petite Sirah wines, which are almost always big, bold, brawny, and brooding, can be very good, but they also can be over the top in terms of their alcoholic punch. There are some terrific, balanced Petite Sirah wines made in California, where the grape has a long history.

FRANCE: THE RHONE VALLEY AND LANGUEDOC-ROUSSILLON

As we mentioned earlier, the northern Rhone Valley defines classic Old World Syrah. The steep slopes, rich in granite soil, provide just enough sunshine and warmth for full ripening, but not too much. At their best, the Rhone wines made from Syrah are redolent of black fruits, feature complex earthy aromas, have a lovely tannin/acid balance, and offer a kick of cracked black pepper in the nose and in the mouth. Depending on what district the grapes are grown in, the wines can be lighter or darker in color, medium or full in body, with flavors that span from jammy to roasted fruits. Prices are all over the place, starting at around $15 for Crozes-Hermitage and approaching $75 and up for great single-vineyard Cote-Rotie and Hermitage wines.

Unlike the northern Rhone Valley, where Syrah is the *only* red varietal, the southern Rhone Valley plants a lot of Syrah, but as part of a panoply of more than a dozen red grapes found in its vineyards. Here, Syrah is mostly utilized as an important blender, usually taking a backseat to the red grapes Grenache and Mourvedre.

The Languedoc-Roussillon area, the "Midi" of the south of France, actually has twice as many Syrah vines planted as the Rhone Valley. Here, in

Located in the northern Rhone Valley of France, Crozes-Hermitage produces red wines made from 100% Syrah grapes; these can represent solid value for the consumer. Jaboulet is an established wine producer in the Rhone Valley.

addition to a select group of very fine wines made from Syrah and Syrah-based blends, an endless stream of drinkable and affordable varietal-labeled Syrah and Syrah blends are produced from very warm, high-yielding vineyard sites.

THE REST OF EUROPE

We find small patches of Syrah planted all over Italy, where there are some producers making 100% Syrah wines, but many are blended with Italian varietals, especially Sangiovese in Tuscany and Nero d'Avola in Sicily. Several of these Italian wines are sold in the United States. Syrah is planted in the Valais region of Switzerland, and Swiss Syrah can be very tasty, but it is virtually invisible in the U.S. market. Syrah is also grown in Spain, Portugal, and Greece.

THE UNITED STATES: CALIFORNIA AND WASHINGTON STATE

In the United States, we grow the grape and make the wine under either name, Syrah or Shiraz. California (see page 71) has been planting Syrah/Shiraz in earnest since the 1970s with the advent of the "Rhone Rangers," a group of producers

Syrah has become an important wine in Washington State and has garnered much attention. Hogue is a major wine producer in the Columbia Valley; the wines are good values. Courtesy of The Hogue Cellars.

who planted several varietals known to flourish in the Rhone Valley, Syrah chief among them. After a slow start in terms of consumer acceptance, California Syrah/Shiraz is now sought after by wine lovers.

Today, Syrah/Shiraz is being planted in California's best wine-growing regions; the challenge is to find vineyard sites that are not too warm so that the finished wine is not a high-alcohol, full-bodied heady fruit soup. The best California Syrah/Shiraz wines, made from vineyards located in the cooler coastal regions of the Golden State, can be excellent, and tend to follow the Rhone model of Syrah. Wines of restrained, earthy power, they are great with hearty foods.

Washington State (see page 100) has gotten religion when it comes to Syrah/Shiraz. Here, Syrah/Shiraz thrives in the cooler climes of the Columbia Valley, the Walla Walla area, and especially the Yakima Valley. The best wines are deceptively soft and supple, with ripe, even sweet fruit flavors, but with balanced tannins and acidity; wines that are enjoyable now or 10 years from now.

AUSTRALIA

It's as simple as this: without Shiraz, there is no modern Australian wine industry. Australia (see page 126) has been growing Shiraz since the early 1800s, and for most of that time it was considered to be a reliable but undistinguished varietal; the future was all about Cabernet Sauvignon. Ha!

Starting in about 1990, Shiraz came out of its shell, and it came out big time. With an international marketing push and with some very good wines that fit in perfectly with the New World wine drinker's shift from delicate wines to "Pow! Right in the kisser!" wines, people began to fall in love with Shiraz. In addition, you can buy varietal-labeled Shiraz from "Oz" for prices starting at about six or seven bucks per bottle, as well as at every other price point imaginable; whatever the price, the wine is perceived as a very good value. Plus Shiraz fits the new, less formal bistro-style approach to dining that is permeating New World cultures. The Aussies even produce sparkling Shiraz for those of us who are bubbleheads.

Zinfandel

ZINFANDEL: THE PROFILE

When you listen to the 1970s Joni Mitchell song "California" or the Eagles' "Hotel California," do so with a glass of Zinfandel close by. Zinfandel is, if not by fact then at least by legend, California's own wine grape, and California is home to ZAP: Zinfandel Advocates and Producers, a not-for-profit group located in Rough and Ready, California, and solely dedicated to spreading the gospel about Zinfandel through its Zinposium series and its annual ZAP Festival—kind of like Burning Man, but most people keep their clothes on.

So what if Zinfandel and the Italian grape Primitivo have the same DNA? Think of it as California's gift to Italy, even though nobody knows for sure where the grape originated (actually, it's probably Croatia, where it is called Crljenak Kastelanski). However, no one is ever going to convince a wine-stained California Zin lover that the Left Coast is anything less than the spiritual home of its beloved varietal. And no one can deny that whatever the grape's patrimony, it was California that put Zinfandel on the map and a sumptuous wine in the glass.

We need to set the record straight: Zinfandel is a red grape, actually close to black in color. The reason we bring this up is that many of the un-Zinitiated think only of White Zinfandel, which is a pale pink wine, really a semi-dry to semi-sweet light-bodied rosé "cocktail" wine (under $10 and great with spicy pan-Asian flavors), pressed from Zinfandel grapes but with minimal skin contact (the skin is where all the color is).

The beauty of the real thing, however—deep, dark, rich, earthy red Zinfandel wine—begins in the warmer vineyard sites of California. Zin loves heat, and this is one of the few varietals that can actually benefit from a bit of overripening. The best climate combination for Zinfandel is a

Zinfandel grapes. © iStock/David Gomez.

summer filled with really hot days (90°F [32°C] and up) and pretty cool nights (a drop to 40° to 50°F [4.5° to 10°C]), enabling the grower to preserve both high degrees of ripeness and sufficient acidity in the grapes. California has about 50,000 acres (20,000 hectares) of Zinfandel vines planted, and the best vineyards fit this ideal climate profile to a T (or in this case, to a Z).

The other wonderful thing about Zinfandel planted in California is that there are a lot of "old vines." Old-vine Zinfandel, made from grape vines planted in poorer soils and dry-farmed (no drip irrigation), often organically grown, with naturally lower yields, makes for wines of compelling complexity and depth. Sometimes the term "Old Vines" or "Old Vine" will appear on a label, but you should know there is no legal meaning for the term.

If you go to the ZAP website (www.zinfadel .org), you can jump to the Zinfandel Aroma Wheel, which is intriguing because it contains just about every smell known to wine and then some, and allows you to offer up new ones. It is true that, depending on the style of the finished wine, Zin can exhibit a wide variety of aromas: red fruits in a light wine, dried black fruits in a full-bodied version, a hint of black

The label of Sin Zin, produced by Alexander Valley Vineyards, captures the hedonistic pleasure of California Zinfandel. Courtesy of Alexander Valley Vineyards.

Joel Peterson, founder of Ravenswood, makes a wide variety of Zinfandel wines from select California vineyards and at several different price points. Courtesy of Ravenswood.

Since 1969, Paul Draper of Ridge Vineyards has made some of the most elegant California Zinfandels from grapes grown on prized sites in Napa and Sonoma counties, the Santa Cruz Mountains, and Paso Robles. Courtesy of Ridge Vineyards.

pepper in a young Zinfandel, dark chocolate in a mature, Port-style Zin. Confusing? Maybe a little. Basically, what you want to look for in any good glass of Zinfandel is the assertive aromas of fruits—red raspberries, cranberries, strawberries in the lightest versions, black cherries, black plums, even raisins and black figs in the brooding, big Zins. A pleasant smattering of herbs provides some grace notes, as do oak-barrel-inspired spice and vanilla.

Lighter Zins, which in reality are usually at least medium-bodied, are great wines for burgers, pizza, pasta, and roasted or grilled veggies. The big, earthy wines, which, when they are balanced and aged for about five years, are truly Zen Zins, are wonderful with hearty dishes, roasted or braised, as well as beef or pork barbecue. Leg of lamb and a hearty old-vine Zinfandel is such a sensual match, it's practically Zinful.

A good word about the price of Zinfandel wines: you can spend a lot of money on single-vineyard, old-vine, dry-farmed, organically grown Zin from a boutique winery, or you can spend five or six bucks in the supermarket or wine shop on a bottle by a mass-market producer. We have found that with very few exceptions Zin = pleasure no matter the price. There are no other varietals that spring to mind that provide such a democratic and egalitarian wine experience. Maybe the reason that

Zinfandel has become a cult wine in California and elsewhere is that it cuts through all the nonsense of class-based wine snobbery and delivers that pleasure, that fun, at a price that everyone who drinks wine can afford. Don't be afraid to try a Zinfandel that sells for under $10 (and there are many of them); it may just become your favorite "house" wine.

Philosophically, Zinfandel and its place in the world have been summed up beautifully by Joel Peterson, the founder of California's Ravenswood winery, and one of the original ZAP members. When Joel created Ravenswood's tag line, he said a glassful about what Zin should—and should not—be. Taking its place among the greatest statements of all time, right next to $E = mc^2$, "*Cogito, ergo sum*," and "The check is in the mail," is the definitive Zinfandel proclamation: "No Wimpy Wines." When it comes to Zin, that says it all.

While Zinfandel grapes grow in several states, it is California that defines Zinfandel for Americans. Internationally, Italy is by far the most important producer of Zinfandel, but under its Italian name, Primitivo. Australia, Chile, Mexico, and South Africa also produce a small amount of Zin. We applaud the growing of this grape everywhere that it will make good wine, but in our hearts we know that when we want the real thing, we'll be livin' it up at the Hotel California.

ZINFANDEL IN CALIFORNIA

Zinfandel is the second most frequently planted red grape in California (Cabernet Sauvignon is first), and depending on where it is planted and when it was planted, results in the grapes and finished wines can be dramatically different.

Sonoma County grows a lot of Zinfandel, and producers here make some excellent wines, especially in the Dry Creek Valley wine district. Warm days and cool nights give Dry Creek Zin a perfect platform to excel. The slightly warmer Alexander Valley is also a fine place to grow the grape. Sonoma is home to several single-vineyard Zinfandel wines, which display their sense of place with delicious dignity.

The Napa Valley can produce some extraordinary Zinfandel, but here Zin lives in the shadow of Cabernet Sauvignon. Old-vine Zinfandel from Mendocino County vineyards make some of the state's best wines. Paso Robles has some old vines, too, and has made quite a reputation for itself with artisanal Zinfandel from its boulder-strewn soils. In Santa Cruz, Paul Draper of Ridge Vineyards continues to make what many consider to be the finest Zinfandel wines ever produced in the history of the world; these wines really are singular and remarkable.

The Sierra Foothills wine region is synonymous with Zinfandel; more than 80% of the vineyards there are dedicated to the grape. There is quite a bit of old-vine Zin here, and the wines from both small and larger producers can be earthy, complex, and memorable.

In the very warm San Joaquin Valley, quite a bit of Zinfandel is grown, and a lot of it ends up in bargain-brand Zins; some is used for blending into other varietal-labeled wines. But the Lodi area, where the breezes from the delta cool things off, produces some good, small-producer Zin, some of it from old vines.

ITALY

In Italy the grape is called Primitivo, and the wine world didn't take notice of it until 1994, when researchers at the University of California at Davis proved that Primitivo and Zinfandel have the same DNA. Since the DNA discovery, the southern province of Puglia has begun to specialize in Primitivo; most of these wines are quite satisfying and, in the true spirit of Zin, quite affordable.

Grenache

GRENACHE: THE PROFILE

Just a few (hundred) words about Grenache (Garnacha in Spanish). Grenache is one of the most widely planted red grapes in the world, with most of those grapes growing in Spain (at least 225,000 acres [90,000 hectares]) and France (about 125,000 acres [50,000 hectares]). There is quite a bit planted in Italy (where it is sometimes known as Cannonau), and substantial amounts are found in Australia and California (about 6,000 acres [2,400 hectares]).

Chateauneuf-du-Pape, a justifiably famous wine from the southern Rhone Valley of France, can legally be made from as many as 13 different grapes, but the blend is anchored by Grenache.

Grenache grapes. © iStock/Peter Leabo.

Although Grenache is beginning to develop a fine reputation both as a single-varietal wine and as a friendly partner in blended wines, it hasn't always enjoyed its place in the sun. Grenache thrives on hot weather and can achieve very high degrees of sugar in its grape juice (which means it can achieve very high degrees of alcohol as a wine), and it has often been used to give some alcoholic "oomph" to weaker wines. Until recently, the only place that Grenache has received anything close to a full measure of respect is in the southern Rhone Valley, where it is often the anchor of the famous blended wine Chateauneuf-du-Pape (see pages 186–187), among others. But lately things have been looking up for Grenache.

Some very good varietal-label Grenache and blends are being produced from grapes grown in Australia and in California. In Spain (see page 226), where this grape has always been taken for granted as a workhorse, old-vine Garnacha is producing magnificent wines in the Priorat region, even as it continues to be a constituent in the red wines of Rioja, but subservient to the more esteemed Tempranillo grape. In the Navarra region, Garnacha makes some of the loveliest dry rosé wines in the world, just as Grenache does in the Tavel region of the southern Rhone Valley. On the Italian island of Sardinia, Cannonau can produce some delicious, earthy red wines.

Grenache was born to blend with Syrah and another red Rhone resident, Mourvedre. (It is not uncommon to see New World wines labeled as "GSM," which the cognoscenti recognize as a blend of Grenache, Syrah, and Mourvedre.) This blend is also the base for much fine Old World Chateauneuf-du-Pape. These blended wines, whether they are produced in the Old World or the New, can be exciting and soul-satisfying, perfect winter warmers with stews and roasts.

4

LIVING IN THE USA

CALIFORNIA

THERE IS PROBABLY NO BETTER TIME IN HISTORY TO BE AN AMERICAN WINE DRINKER. SO MANY WINES FROM SO MANY wine regions, both established and off the beaten path, are available that it truly is an embarrassment of riches. How to choose from all of the gems that line the shelves of wine shops and supermarkets and jump off the pages of wine lists?

When it comes to wine, most Americans, no matter their political leanings, seem to be of one mind, one heart, one palate. We love our country's wines, and we vote with our wallets and purses for wines produced in the United States. American wine consumers are a patriotic bunch: mostly, we "drink American," while enthusiastically—and increasingly—dabbling with foreign wines from all over the planet. This "global village" approach to enjoying wines from other countries is especially true among "millenials," wine drinkers between 21 and 34 years of age.

Many of us have become "locavores" when it comes to enjoying food and wine, and that's great because all 50 states produce wines for an increasing audience of Americans. Still, there is only one 800-pound gorilla in America's wine cellar that cannot be ignored, and that commanding presence is California . . .

The new American wine culture

THE UNITED STATES IS THE world's number one wine-consuming nation, a position it achieved in late 2011. According to research published by *Wine Spectator* magazine in August 2013, there are, for the first time, an astounding 100 million wine drinkers in the United States; almost one-third of the nation's population. In 2012, wine drinkers in the United States consumed 324 million cases of wine (that's nearly 4 billion bottles!). This rise in consumption represents a true sea change for a country and culture that in the past has been far more identified with beer and spirits. There are some compelling reasons why the United States has risen to the top when it comes to wine consumption, including the following facts:

> There are now far more than 7,000 wineries in the United States, and every state, including Alaska and Hawaii, takes part in that total. Circa 1980, there were about 1,500 wineries; in 1970 there were less than 250. At least 40 of the 50 states have commercial vineyards; the others buy grapes or juice from other states. And wine has become big business in the United States. The wine industry contributes more than $140 billion to the U.S. economy and provides about 500,000 jobs.

As Americans, we seem to love our own wines, but not just the wines of California. Nationwide, we consume about 70% domestic wines. This patriotic percentage would probably be even higher, but the very drinkable, price-attractive wines of Italy, Australia, New Zealand, Argentina, Chile, and even some good bargains from France are also quite popular here, accounting for about 20% to 25% of the total U.S. wine market. Again, millenials drive this part of the market, accounting for about 25% of foreign wine sales in the United States. This demographic, where the locavore movement is so popular, is also far more likely to enjoy American wines not produced in California, but in many other states. By comparison, older "baby boomers," wine drinkers from 55 to 64 years old, only consume about 15% foreign wines and show a decidedly Cali-centric attitude in their domestic wine purchases. Obviously, these percentages, most of which are based on statistics compiled by *Wine Spectator* in 2013, are fluid, but the future of American wine seems poised for growth in many healthy ways.

Wine is perceived as, and has been scientifically proven by physicians and researchers around the world to be, a healthy beverage when consumed with food and in moderation. In the minds of many Americans, wine has become a nearly guilt-free pleasure.

Americans love to dine out in restaurants, and wine is an important part of that dining experience. Traditionally, "wine destination" restaurants are perceived as white-tablecloth venues where prices can be extravagant, but that perception is as dated as an over-the-hill bottle of Merlot. Dining and wine have become a lot more egalitarian, a lot more accessible. Starting in 2004, Olive Garden, the well-known kind-of-Italian restaurant chain, put together a chain-wide wine list of just 38 wines, with 36 of the wines available by the glass, and just about all of them available to taste for free. The result: Olive Garden gives away about 35,000 cases of wine per year but sells nearly 1 million cases per year, making the chain the number-one restaurant venue for wine sales in the entire country. In doing so, Olive Garden (and other wine-savvy restaurateurs and chains) has turned the idea of a "wine destination" restaurant on its ear. You won't find a sommelier at Olive Garden and you won't find detailed wine explanations or even vintage years on their wine lists. You will find a wine list with an average price per bottle of about $30 (as of mid-2013) and well-trained servers who know the broad strokes of the list. Olive

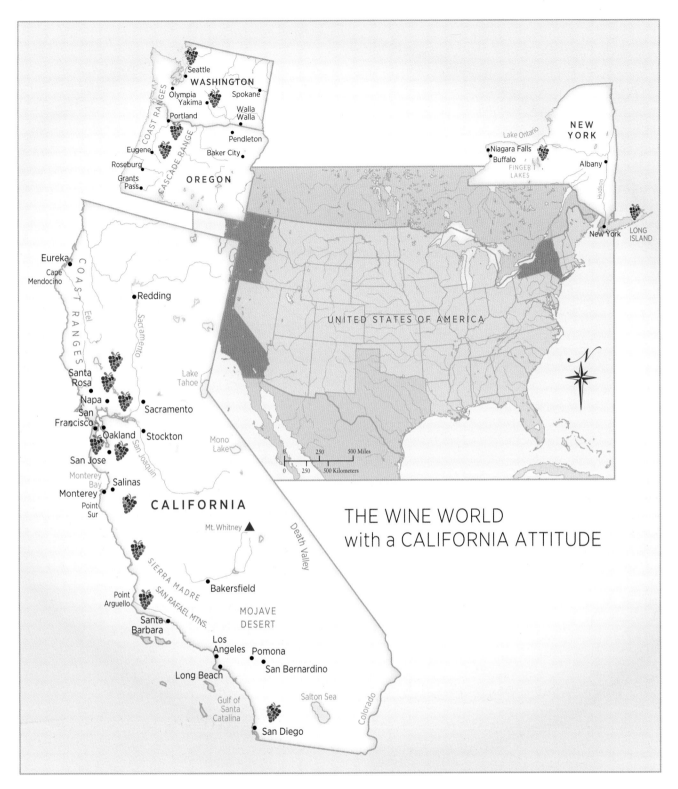

THE WINE WORLD
with a CALIFORNIA ATTITUDE

Garden is just the most obvious example of a huge and welcome revolution in how Americans enjoy wine in restaurants. Clearly, wine has become an integral part of dining out, whether it's to grab a pizza or burger, a bowl of pasta and a salad, or an elaborate and formal multicourse dinner.

Direct shipping of wine, wine clubs, wine tourism, and buying wine from dedicated wine sites on the Internet have revolutionized how Americans buy wine. At least 40 of 50 states allow some form of direct shipments of wine, which allows the consumer to buy directly from an American winery via the Internet. Many web sites, including but not limited to brick-and-mortar stores, offer wines from all over the world, sometimes at dramatic discounts. Wine tourism is a huge industry, and visitors often join wine clubs, allowing them to purchase premium, sought-after wines that are sometimes not available to the general public. There are tasting rooms owned by small producers where the only way you can purchase the wine is in the tasting room or as a member of a club, allowing wines to be shipped to you. This is good marketing by the winery as it creates a strong bond between producer and consumer, who, through tasting with friends and good word-of-mouth, helps that winery to exponentially expand its consumer base.

Over the last 20 years there has been an increase of 40% to 45% in the total wine-drinking population of the United States, driven not only by people traditionally considered to be the American wine drinkers—male, white, middle- or upper-class, middle-aged or older—but also more by women, who now account for close to 65% of the wine purchased in the United States, and by younger wine drinkers. People in their twenties and early thirties love to try a wide variety of wines,

especially what the industry calls "adventure brands," wines with curious and humorous names—Smashed Grapes, Smoking Loon, Plungerhead, 3 Blind Moose, Fat Bastard, Hey Mambo, and, of course, Cat's Pee on a Gooseberry Bush are just some examples among hundreds of such brands. These wines are tasty and fun and are also attractively priced, usually less than $15 per bottle (although a rare bottle of the elegant 2005 Used Automobile Parts is at least 75 bucks!).

Per capita wine consumption has been dropping precipitously in France, Italy, Spain, and Portugal, nations that have been closely identified with wine as their national beverage of choice.

Exports of American wines have grown exponentially and as of 2013 stand at about $1.5 billion per year. About 35% of this wine is sold to the countries that make up the European Union (EU) with Canada at about 30%. In addition, Hong Kong, Japan, and China account for more than $400 million, or more than 25% of total wine exports.

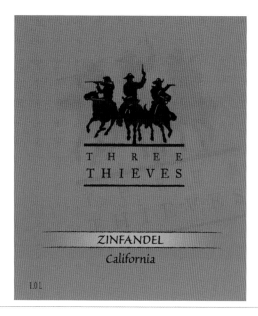

Unusual, often humorous labels that feature animals or tell a story are popular in the U.S. wine market.

Hells Canyon Winery in Idaho makes award-winning wine, including this delicious Cabernet Sauvignon Reserve.

Ironically, our own per capita wine consumption still is quite low, even when compared to the sliding European per capita figures (an average of about 10 gallons [38 liters] per capita in France, Italy, and Spain, but only a little more than 2.5 gallons [9.5 liters per capita] in the United States). However, the combined population of Italy, France, and Spain is about 170 million; the population of the United States is more than 300 million. While we appear to have a growing and dedicated core of wine drinkers, less than 15% of American wine drinkers consume more than 45% of total wine consumed in our country. What this means is that we have a lot of room to grow in both our per capita and total consumption, and since 1996 we have seen steady annual growth in one or both of these metrics.

The United States is developing a measurable and largely home-grown wine culture, and it doesn't stop at increased wine consumption. The Napa Valley, for example, is the hottest tourist destination in California (Disneyland is second; think about it), but it may also surprise you to know that more than 1.6 million people per year visit the vineyards and wineries of Virginia, and the spectacular Biltmore Estate, located in Asheville, North Carolina, is the most-visited winery in the United States. Wineries and vineyards have become tourist destinations, and wine has become a prominent symbol of a sophisticated, relaxed, and enjoyable American lifestyle, both at home and in restaurants. We see wine in our movies (remember *Sideways*?), our literature (and not just in wine books), our colleges (wine courses are immensely popular on campuses throughout the nation), and of course, broadcast, cable, and internet television (note the rise of the Food Network and its various wine-conscious offspring). Wine software (some good, some not so good) abounds, and websites dedicated to wine (again, quality can be very high or very low) are literally innumerable.

There is no doubt that this is wine's moment to shine in America, and it is also the perfect moment for you to become WineWise. This is the best time to be an educated wine consumer because the bounty of quality wines available in the American marketplace has never been greater or more affordable.

This sign, located on Highway 29 in the Napa Valley, is a symbolic gateway to the world of California wine.

The language of the label

THE UNITED STATES IS A great place to start to learn about and enjoy wines, because American wine labels are pretty easy to understand. Knowing what's on the label is critical to knowing what's in the bottle (or box), and once you get the hang of it, reading and decoding wine labels will become second nature, providing an essential first step to becoming an informed wine consumer. So let's jump into the deep end of the wine pool right now and immerse ourselves in learning all about American wine labels.

THE AVA SYSTEM

Every major wine-producing country has a system for naming places where grapes grow to make wine. Some of these places are famous (Napa Valley in the United States, Bordeaux in

The language (and law) of the label: Clos du Val is the wine producer; Napa Valley is where at least 85% of the grapes were grown; Cabernet Sauvignon is the dominant varietal (at least 75%); at least 95% of the grapes were harvested in 2010.

France, and Chianti in Italy are all good examples), but many more are not so well known. These place names, famous or obscure, appear on wine labels and always represent where the grapes for the wine are grown.

Why is this important? Well, the reason some people are willing to pay a lot of money for certain wines has a little bit to do with what grape type the wine is made from, but a lot to do with where those grapes are grown. The "address" of the wine is what separates a world-class white Burgundy from just another French Chardonnay (Chardonnay is the premier white grape for the Burgundy region in France) or a great Napa Valley Cabernet Sauvignon from just another California Cab. Sure, wine drinkers love certain grape varietals, but connoisseurs and wine geeks can make a fetish out of where those grapes are grown.

We're not recommending that you obsess about where the grapes for a particular wine are grown, but the vineyard site—the place from which the finished wine emerges—has a lot to do with the quality of that wine. Certainly, there are artisan winemakers in both famous and not-so-famous wine regions that pour their heart and soul into their wine, and you can taste that passion in the finished product. So much of what the French call *terroir*—the unique qualities that the soil and climate grant to particular vineyards in specific regions—is tied up with the integrity and passion of the grape growers and winemakers of those regions. There are also producers in those same regions that make pretty good to very good wine and trade on the fame of those places. Of course, sometimes the reputation can be blown out of proportion, and it's definitely true that lousy wine can be produced from grapes grown in a famous region.

The reputation of a named wine-growing region—an appellation—is also very important to the commercial success of the wines produced from the vineyards in that region. So, making sure that place name is displayed prominently on the wine label becomes a very important factor in the selling and marketing of that wine. Just having the words "Napa Valley" on a bottle of expensive

Cabernet Sauvignon is an immense advantage to the financial health of any California wine producer.

You should note that in the United States sometimes these named places can be very small districts, with as little as 60 acres (24 hectares) in the entire district (the appellation "Cole Ranch" in Mendocino County), or humongous regions, encompassing parts of several states (the appellation "Lake Erie" takes in parts of New York, Pennsylvania, and Ohio, while the largest wine region in the world, "Upper Mississippi River Valley" takes in parts of Iowa, Illinois, Minnesota, and Wisconsin).

Every country has a different name for its system of naming wine-growing regions, as you'll see when you read about the wines of each of these nations. In the United States, each of these place names is officially and legally registered as part of a system called American Viticultural Areas, or AVAs. Currently, there are more than 215 distinct AVAs in the United States, about 130 of them in wine-behemoth California (about 90% of the wine made in the United States originates in California vineyards). When the name of an AVA appears on a wine label, it means that at least 85% of the grapes used in that wine have been grown in that named AVA. So if a wine is labeled as a 2010 Clos du Val Napa Valley Cabernet Sauvignon (see label on the opposite page; Clos du Val is, in this case, the name of the wine producer), it means that, by federal law, at least 85% of the fruit used in that wine had to be grown in the Napa Valley AVA. The other 15% can be grown anywhere in California.

If a county name appears on a label ("Sonoma County," for example), 75% of the grapes must have been grown in that county. Wines with a "California" appellation on their labels (which must be made from grapes sourced only from vineyards in California), as well as many wines with county appellations, are normally quite drinkable and quite affordable (about $5 to $20).

THE GRAPE NAME

Let's continue decoding the same label—the 2010 Clos du Val Napa Valley Cabernet Sauvignon. We already know that at least 85% of the grapes that make the wine had to grow in vineyards located within the Napa Valley AVA, but what percentage of the wine had to be made from Cabernet Sauvignon grapes? By federal law, the wine must contain at least 75% Cab. The other 25% can be any grapes. So if a wine is labeled with a grape name—a varietal label—the wine must be made from at least 75% of that named varietal.

THE VINTAGE

Same label again: the 2010 Clos du Val Napa Valley Cabernet Sauvignon. What we know so far is that the wine must be made from at least 85% Napa Valley grapes and at least 75% Cabernet Sauvignon. What is the minimum percentage of the grapes that had to be harvested in 2010—the "vintage year"—to make it to the label? The answer is 95%. Up to 5% of the finished wine can be made from grapes from an earlier or (in the case of aging wines before release) later vintage. This 5% gives the winemaker the wiggle room to tweak the wine, adjusting for subtle nuances in color, aroma, or flavor, and to compensate for the "angel's share," which is wine lost to evaporation in the barrel.

Not all wine producers will make their wines using legal minimums of place, grape, and vintage. There are wines that do take to blending (Cabernet Sauvignon and Merlot, for example, are classic blenders), and there are wines that do not (such as Chardonnay and Pinot Noir). Sometimes adding 17% Merlot to a wine labeled "Cabernet Sauvignon" is a good thing, but adding 20% of much cheaper Chenin Blanc to a wine labeled "Chardonnay" is just a way to save money and make a mediocre wine. Quality-minded producers will, for example, produce a 2012 Napa Valley Chardonnay from

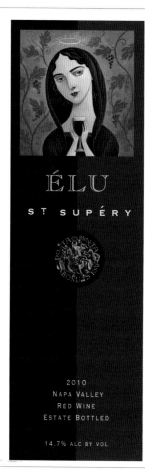

100% Chardonnay grapes grown in the Napa Valley and will probably use 100% of the grapes harvested in 2012 unless they feel strongly that tweaking the vintage with some older or younger wine might improve the finished product.

Also, remember that label laws are *federal minimums* by which all states and producers must abide. Producers in Oregon (see page 106) have chosen to exceed the legal minimums for minimum AVA percentage and/or minimum grape percentage, to call attention to the quality and enhance the marketing of their wines.

OTHER LABEL TERMS YOU MIGHT FIND

Here are some other words and phrases you might find on some wines produced in the United States, and their meanings.

Reserve: About as close to consumer fraud as you can get, this term has almost no legal meaning in this country. "Reserve" can appear on the label of any vintage-dated varietal-labeled wine produced in the United States, including the cheapest wines churned out in mass quantities by any wine producer. This is an outrage that really needs to be addressed, especially to benefit the small group of producers who continue to use the term ethically. A wine that's produced from grapes grown in the best vineyards, that is aged longer in the best oak casks, or has some other special attributes really qualifies as a "reserve" wine. Until a code of conduct for the use of the term is adopted, we think "reserve" should be banished as a label term for wines produced in the United States.

Estate-bottled: "Estate-bottled" is a beautiful and increasingly rare thing, a label phrase with real meaning. What it means is that the producer of the wine (the "estate") has grown the grapes in vineyards that the producer owns or "controls" (as in a long-term lease). In addition, the "estate" must also produce the wine, age the wine, and bottle the wine. Importantly, the producer has not bought any grapes or juice from other growers or suppliers to make the wine. If the name of an AVA (Russian River Valley, for example) appears on a label along with "estate-bottled," as it almost inevitably does, that means that 100% of the grape growing, winemaking, aging, and bottling were undertaken in that named AVA.

Single vineyard: If "single vineyard" appears on a label (for example, "Dutton Ranch," a vineyard located within the Russian River Valley AVA), then 95% of the grapes had to have been harvested from that specific vineyard. The single vineyard does not have to be owned or controlled by the producer; it is perfectly legitimate to purchase grapes for these wines from other growers, some of whom have stellar reputations.

Grown, produced, and bottled: A similar outward sign of quality as "estate-bottled," but with a bit more flexibility for the producer. Grapes are grown, wine is made, and bottling is done by the producer, but without the geographical and percentage limits imposed by "estate-bottled." A wine that is "grown, produced, and bottled" by a Sonoma Valley winemaker can, for example, still source 15% of its grapes outside the Sonoma Valley AVA, as long as that producer grew those grapes. The wine can also be produced, aged, and bottled by the producer outside of (in this case) the Sonoma Valley AVA.

Produced and bottled: This usually means that the producer purchased at least some of the grapes for the wine but made the finished wine and bottled it. Buying grapes is not necessarily a bad thing, and if you buy from famous and highly regarded vineyards (such as Dutton Ranch in the Russian River Valley, mentioned previously, or Sangiacomo Vineyards, who established their reputation in the Carneros AVA and have burnished that reputation with outstanding vineyards in several AVAs within Sonoma County), you will have to wait in line, sometimes for years, to buy those grapes and pay a serious premium when you do. This significantly raises the price of the wine in the bottle. Of course, there are

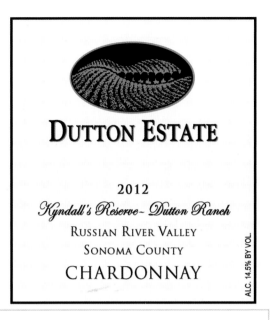

An example of Dutton Estate's single-vineyard wine label, from Dutton Ranch in Sonoma County's Russian River Valley. Courtesy of Dutton Estate Winery.

also producers who buy grapes on the spot market, paying the lowest price possible for grapes or grape juice, and then make and bottle the wine. These wines should be (but aren't always) inexpensive.

Bottled or cellared: These terms could mean anything. The producer may have bought finished wines, maybe blended them for consistency and price advantage, and then bottled or boxed them. We usually avoid these wines, but if we find one or two that work for large gatherings, we never pay more than five or six bucks per bottle, and neither should you. As an example of this kind of wine, "Two Buck Chuck," the line of Charles Shaw branded wines that fly out of Trader Joe's stores across the nation, have a back label that reads "Cellared and Bottled."

Old vines: There is no legal definition for "old vines." If you see this term on a label, the producer wants you to think that the wine in the bottle is somehow special—more complex and elegant, or more rustic and earthy. You see the term "old vine" or "old vines" on several California Zinfandels, and indeed, some of these wines are made from the fruit of vines that are more than 70 or 80 years old. But you are just as likely to find this unrestricted phrase on a bottle of Merlot made from vines that are maybe 20 or 25 years old. Again, the reputation of the producer means a lot when it comes to "old vines," which may or may not really be that "old."

Unfiltered: This means that the wine has not been filtered, or at most has been minimally filtered, before bottling; there is no serious legal standard for "unfiltered." Quite a few winemakers believe that unfiltered wines are better expressions of the finished wine. The idea is that by not stripping the wine of subtle shades of color, desirable aromas, and better flavor, the wine is more of an artisanal product, more "honest." We have found that some unfiltered wines hold true to this ideal, and to filter them would be a mistake. We have also found unfiltered wines that have so little character to begin with that filtering would make them even less interesting. Unfiltered wines are usually red, because most consumers will not readily accept a cloudy white wine, especially one without a stellar reputation.

A NOTE ABOUT GENERIC AND PROPRIETARY LABELS

Now you know how to read a vintage-dated, AVA-named, varietal label, and that should help you to understand the label terminology of more than 90% of the wines produced and sold in the United States. The rest of the wine labels you might run into will fall into two categories: generic labels— a fast-fading, formerly popular category of cheap, manipulated wines often sold in large glass jugs or big five-liter boxes named for famous wine regions of the world (Chablis, Burgundy, etc.) but made from grapes grown in high-yielding, hot-weather vineyards of California. As they make a hasty retreat from the marketplace, the only reason to know about these wines at all is to know enough not to buy them.

But there is another, small category of wines that you will encounter, those with proprietary labels, that you'll want to know about and taste. These wines do not sport varietal labels; they display "fantasy" labels, and are named for real or imagined people, mythological places, or a favorite symbol, phrase, or word chosen by the producer of the wine. Opus One, Insignia, Rubicon, Tribute, Magnificat, Quintessa, Tapestry, The Mariner, Hommage, Cain Five, Mythology, The Spur, and Elu (see label on page 68) are but several of many American reds with proprietary labels. Conundrum, Blancaneaux, and The Whip are just three of the smaller category of whites. These wines can be quite expensive, especially the reds (most are in the $35 to $200 range at retail, far more on wine lists). The whites certainly aren't inexpensive, either (most retail in the $20 to $50 range). The beauty of these wines, especially for the winemaker, is that because they do not sport a varietal label, the 75% minimum for grape type does not apply. For example, Opus One is traditionally almost always produced mostly from Cabernet Sauvignon—at least 75%—but if the winemaker should decide that in a particular vintage a better wine can be produced from 80% Merlot, the finished wine is still Opus One.

You'll find other terms and phrases on a wine label, but they're pretty self-explanatory: alcohol percentage ("13.5% alcohol by volume," for example), how much wine is in the bottle or box (a standard bottle is filled with 750 milliliters of wine, the equivalent of about 25.4 ounces; varietal-labeled boxes tend to house the equivalent of four bottles—a bit more than 100 ounces [3 liters]), and the winery address. Note that the winery address may or may not be located in the same AVA as the vineyards; that's not a problem. Unless the wine is estate-bottled, it is perfectly legal to grow the grapes in one place and produce the wine in another place. Remember, the AVA is all about where the grapes are grown, not necessarily where the finished wine is produced.

So now that we've reviewed the basics of American wine labels, let's move on to the state where most American wine hails from, California.

California: The Garden of Eden?

In 1937, Woody Guthrie, one of America's original singer-songwriters, think the (early) Bob Dylan of his day, penned a song about California entitled "(If You Ain't Got the) Do Re Mi." Guthrie praised California as "a garden of Eden," and then made an astute observation:

> But believe it or not, you won't find it so hot
> If you ain't got the do re mi.

Why do we trot out an old folk song lyric to discuss modern California wines? California is the nation's largest wine producer, and when you see those lush vineyards growing throughout most of the state, you could mistake it for paradise. But it is also true that in California you often get what you pay for, and unless you're willing to part with a big wad of cash—the "do re mi" Woody Guthrie sang about—you just won't get a chance to taste the best that California has to offer.

We're not saying that California doesn't provide some great bargains—or at least good wines at fair prices—but you really have to become WineWise to find these wines. And that means finding producers who consistently maintain a high ratio of quality to price and recognizing the "second labels" of wineries that are best known for expensive or "cult" wines but pay their bills by producing reliable, affordable wines.

In a way, California has done its job of marketing wines produced in "a garden of Eden" almost too well. To make our point, here's our California wine quiz. Don't worry, there are just two questions:

Question 1: *What's the first place you think of when you think of California wines?*

We're guessing that most of our readers answered "Napa Valley." (Please take your pulse and lie down for a moment if you didn't.)

Question 2: *What percentage of all California wines is produced in the Napa Valley?*

a. 75%

b. 50%

c. 30%

d. Less than 5%

Choice (d) is the correct—and, for most people, surprising—answer. Napa, and to a lesser extent Sonoma, seems to have captured the public imagination when it comes to California wines, but both counties together (and Sonoma is twice as large as Napa, with a lot more acres of vineyards) account for less than 15% of the Golden State's wine production. Many of us think that California's best wines *must* come from Napa or Sonoma, but this is wrong, too. While Napa and Sonoma do produce great wines, there are many other places in California—some you've never heard of—that also make impressive wines.

So, where do we find California's best wines (and best bargains)? Let's take a look at some of the things we need to know to make our search successful and fun.

Napa Valley

Cabernet Sauvignon

ALCOHOL 14.2% BY VOLUME

For more than 40 years the Cakebread family has produced some of the finest quality-driven wines in the Napa Valley. Courtesy of Kobrand Corporation.

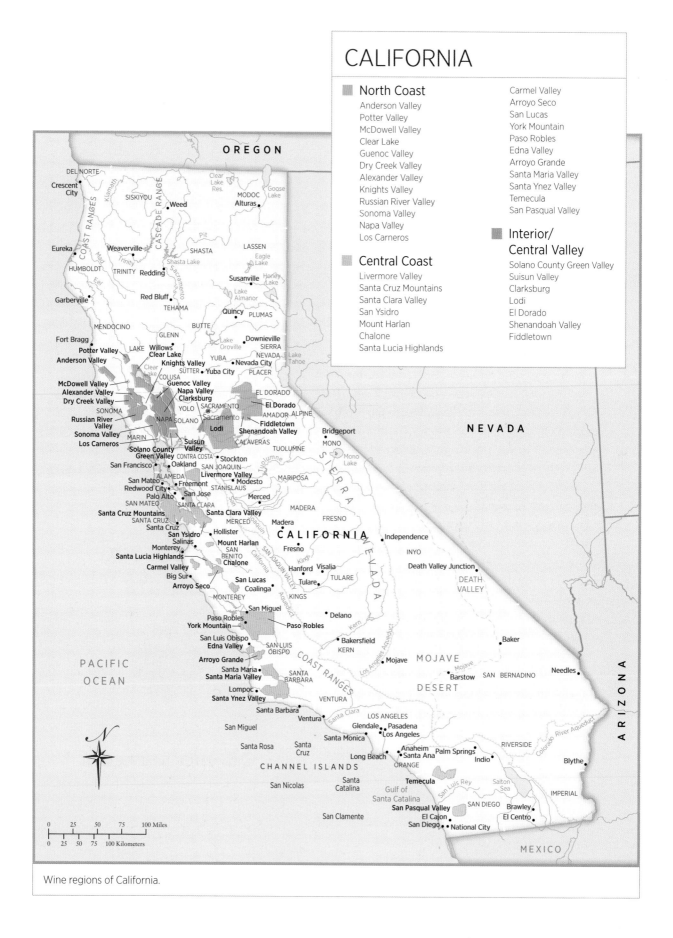

CALIFORNIA

North Coast
Anderson Valley
Potter Valley
McDowell Valley
Clear Lake
Guenoc Valley
Dry Creek Valley
Alexander Valley
Knights Valley
Russian River Valley
Sonoma Valley
Napa Valley
Los Carneros

Central Coast
Livermore Valley
Santa Cruz Mountains
Santa Clara Valley
San Ysidro
Mount Harlan
Chalone
Santa Lucia Highlands

Carmel Valley
Arroyo Seco
San Lucas
York Mountain
Paso Robles
Edna Valley
Arroyo Grande
Santa Maria Valley
Santa Ynez Valley
Temecula
San Pasqual Valley

Interior/ Central Valley
Solano County Green Valley
Suisun Valley
Clarksburg
Lodi
El Dorado
Shenandoah Valley
Fiddletown

Wine regions of California.

Life beyond Chardonnay (and Merlot and Cab)

CALIFORNIA MADE ITS INITIAL REPUTATION for fine wines based on two red grapes and just one white grape, all three of which are grown in the Napa Valley and in Sonoma. The reds are Cabernet Sauvignon and Merlot; the white is Chardonnay. And while it's true that you can find great wines from California by sticking with these three grape types, you will insulate yourself, pay way too much money for wine, and never really experience all that California has to offer the *WineWise* reader.

Believe us: there is life beyond Cabernet, Merlot, and Chardonnay. California produces some excellent whites: Sauvignon Blanc (sometimes labeled as "Fumé Blanc"), Gewurztraminer, and Viognier come to mind. There are also some extraordinary reds: Zinfandel, Pinot Noir, and Syrah (once in a while called Shiraz here), among others. Vineyards are often sited in regions and districts that may not be household AVAs in your house, but they are in ours.

WINEWISE TIP: if you're seeking value in California wine—quality wine at a good price—go off the beaten path, both in terms of wine regions and grape varietals. Look for regions like the Shenandoah Valley, Lake County, Paso Robles, and Lodi, and seek out the often exciting wines made from lesser-known varietals. For whites, try Albarino, Roussanne (and Marsanne/Roussanne blends), Chenin Blanc, and Semillon, among others. For reds, look for Petite Sirah, Grenache, Tempranillo, Sangiovese, and Barbera, just some of the panoply of under-the-radar varietals that will under-promise and over-deliver: the *WineWise* definition of great value in wine.

As is true with wines from all over the world, the reputation of the producer is most often the number-one consideration in choosing a wine from California (or from anywhere else). Some California producers make only wines that are rare and expensive—the "cult" wines that get so much of the attention and the hype in the American wine press. Other producers make high-quality wines that we can enjoy as a daily, integral part of meals. A growing number of California producers make both a small number of flagship wines, which are expensive and hard to find, and wines that are more accessible and affordable, perfect for everyday drinking and enjoying with food.

In the following pages, we're going to introduce you to a gazetteer of California wines, both inordinately expensive and extraordinarily value-driven. Guess which ones excite us more. By now, we hope you realize that while we admire and respect the singular wines that we may taste two or three times during the course of our lives, we absolutely love turning our *WineWise* readers on to good wines that they can afford and enjoy, made by passionate people who want to provide that affordable, enjoyable experience.

WineWise California AVAs

NORTH COAST AVA

The North Coast AVA, which includes Napa, Sonoma, Mendocino, Lake, Marin, and Solano counties, is an appellation of convenience, but one that suggests quality. If a producer makes a wine from 50% Sonoma County grapes, 20% Mendocino County grapes, and 30% Lake County grapes, the AVA on the label will be "North Coast." Or if a wine is made from 70% Lake County grapes and 30% Napa County grapes, the AVA on that label will also read "North Coast." You get the picture: a wine made from any combination of grapes sourced from these counties is rewarded with the North Coast AVA. The North

WHICH AVA SELLS THE WINE?

The North Coast has become a popular AVA associated with high quality by consumers, so sometimes a wine made from 100% Lake County fruit will bear the name "North Coast" instead of the "Lake County" appellation. The reason a producer may choose to label a wine this way involves nothing more than consumer acceptance. "North Coast" is an AVA that strongly resonates with quality-conscious consumers, but "Lake County" may not, at least not yet. Throughout California (and other parts of the world), producers will often opt to label their wines with a larger AVA that has gained the trust of the consumer, even when that producer could label that same wine with a smaller, more specific AVA. This is all perfectly legal. After all, if you grow 100% of your Cabernet Sauvignon grapes in the Chiles Valley District, which is a sub-AVA of the larger Napa Valley AVA, which AVA will you print on your label? Well, if you want to sell your wine at a premium price, "Napa Valley" will be your AVA of choice, at least until "Chiles Valley District" becomes a household name in homes of wine lovers and on restaurant wine lists.

On the other hand, if a smaller AVA has attained fame and widespread consumer acceptance, the producer will definitely choose to use that smaller AVA. For example, the Napa Valley sub-AVAs of Stags Leap District and Rutherford, both of which have a worldwide reputation for great Cabernet Sauvignon, are far more likely to label their wines with "Stags Leap District" or "Rutherford" than with "Napa Valley." But don't be surprised if the famous Napa Valley is mentioned in the text of the market-driven "back label" of these wines, just to make sure that the producers have covered all the bases.

Coast AVA provides assurance to the consumer that the wine is made from grapes grown in what are perceived to be marquee wine-growing areas, and "North Coast" on the label allows the producer to charge a bit more for the wine.

NAPA COUNTY

The best-known AVA in Napa County is Napa Valley. Smaller sub-AVAs of the Napa Valley AVA that you might find on the label include Atlas Peak, Calistoga, Chiles Valley, Coombsville, Diamond Mountain District, Howell Mountain, Carneros (shared with Sonoma County), Mount Veeder, Oak Knoll District, Oakville, Rutherford, Saint Helena, Spring Mountain District, Stags Leap District, Wild Horse Valley, and Yountville.

Less than 100 miles north of San Francisco, the Napa Valley AVA includes almost all of Napa County and has a total of 16 sub-AVAs within it. Each producer in the sub-AVAs is entitled to use either its own AVA name on the label ("Mount Veeder," for example), or the general—and famous—AVA "Napa Valley."

There are about 225,000 acres (90,000 hectares) contained within the Napa Valley AVA, and vineyards cover about 46,000 acres (18,400 hectares) of that area. This is the most expensive agricultural land in the United States, with current prices ranging from about $150,000 to $350,000 per acre, depending on location and if a vineyard is already in place. There are more than 400 wineries within the Napa Valley AVA, even though the total AVA area is only 30 miles long and five miles wide. Nestled between the Mayacamas Mountains to the west and the Vaca Mountains to the east, the Napa Valley, which is shaped like a bowl, benefits from the cool breezes and the moist fog that roll in from San Pablo Bay early in the morning, followed by warm sunshine that pervades the region for several hours per day, and finished by cool evenings. Temperatures can fluctuate up to 20°F throughout the different sub-AVAs, creating appealing microclimates for particular grape varietals.

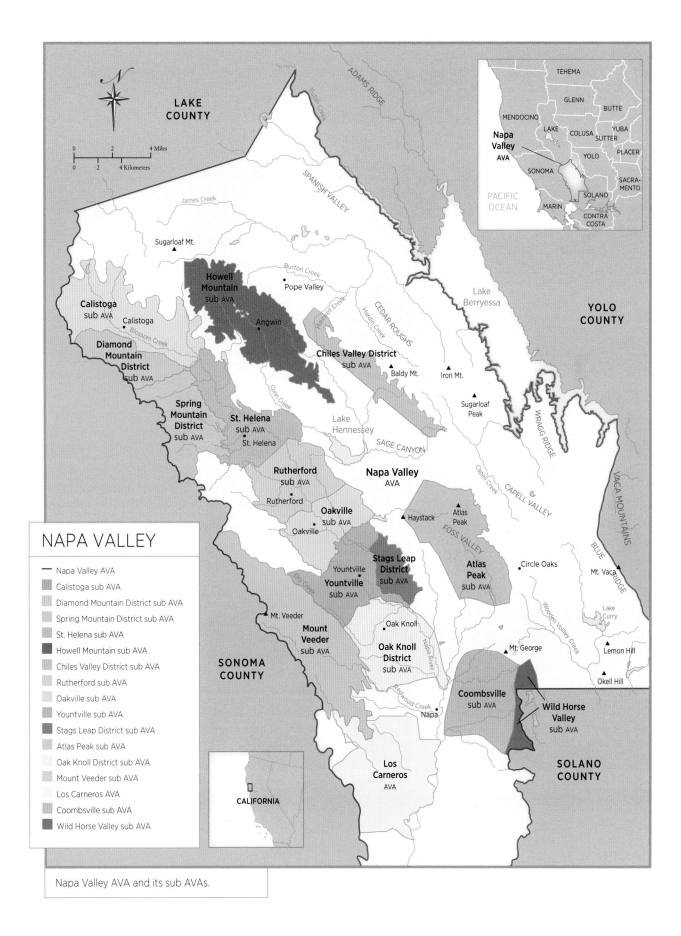

Napa Valley AVA and its sub AVAs.

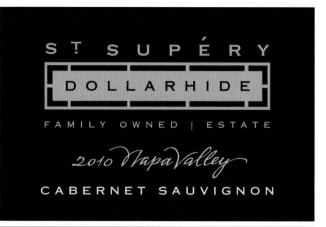

A Sonoma County Sauvignon Blanc, produced by the Benziger Family Winery. This is really good wine at a really fair price—about $15—and should be easy to find. Courtesy of Kobrand Corporation.

An estate-bottled Cabernet Sauvignon produced from the fruit of a single vineyard (Dollarhide) in the Napa Valley. Label design by Jody Hewgill; courtesy of St. Supery.

Speaking of varietals, although there is fine Zinfandel, Merlot, Cabernet Franc, Syrah, Chardonnay, and Sauvignon Blanc produced in the Napa Valley, there is one grape that rules here: Cabernet Sauvignon. Napa Cabs must be included in any list of the world's great wines, which at their best are luscious and fruit-driven, but also complex; accessible when young, but also ageworthy; full-bodied "sunshine in a bottle," but at their best a delicate balance of blackberry and black currant fruit, alcohol, tannin, and acidity.

The Napa Valley is also home to some world-famous Cabernet blends, which feature proprietary labels (see page 70). The original idea for producing these wines was to make a fine wine in the tradition and spirit of Bordeaux, France (see page 165). In Bordeaux, many wines are anchored by Cab, but they are almost always blended with Merlot and Cabernet Franc, among other grapes. The Napa versions, many of which could legally be labeled as Cabernet Sauvignon because they contain more than 75% of that grape, are also often blended with a bit of Merlot and Cabernet Franc. Some of these wines, which are made in relatively small quantities and can sell for far more than $100 per bottle at retail, have become quite famous and find homes on some of the best restaurant wine lists in the United States and beyond.

Although producers in the Napa Valley are not the only folks making these American "Bordeaux blends"—this wine style is produced throughout California and several other states— the concept of these wines originated here, and the Napa Valley proprietary Cab blends continue to define the category. By the way, you may sometimes hear this entire category of reds referred to as "Meritage" wines.

Cabernet Sauvignon and Cabernet blends are closely identified with the Napa Valley AVA, and Napa Valley wine producers get to charge a premium for their address. There are a handful of producers in the Napa Valley known for their Merlot—Duckhorn "Three Palms Vineyard," which sells at retail for just under $100, the justifiably famous Beringer "Bancroft Ranch Howell Mountain" Merlot, which sells for about $60, and the hard-to-find Lewis Cellars Merlot (about 100 cases produced each vintage), which is usually found only on selected wine lists at close to $200, are probably among the most prized. Chappellet is also a fine and time-tested Merlot producer.

Zinfandel is a grape that grows nicely in parts of the Napa Valley and can create a memorable wine. The same is true of Sauvignon Blanc and, to a lesser extent, Chardonnay, which does extremely well in the cool-weather Carneros sub-AVA (see page 79). Still, it is Cabernet Sauvignon that

FAMOUS CABERNET BLENDS OF THE NAPA VALLEY

Some of the most famous proprietary-labeled Cabernet Sauvignon blends in the Napa Valley include the following (sometimes, but not always, expensive) wines, listed in alphabetical order. The names of the wines are followed by the name of their producer.

Affinity Robert Craig

Anthology Conn Creek

Cain Five, Cain Concept, Cain Cuvée Cain

Claret Ramey

Dominus, Napanook Dominus Estate

Dragon's Tooth (actually mostly Malbec) Trefethen

Elu St. Supery

Generations Charles Krug

Hommage Clos Pegase

Howell Mountain Red, The Discussion Duckhorn

Insignia Joseph Phelps

J. Daniel Cuvée Lail Vineyards

Magnificat Franciscan Oakville Estate

Meritage Kirkland Signature (that's Costco!)

Meritage Trinchero

Opus One Robert Mondavi Winery and Baron Philippe de Rothschild partnership

The Oracle Miner Family Vineyards

Oroppas St. Clement

The Poet, M. Coz Cosentino

Profile Merryvale

Proprietary Red Pahlmyer

Quantum Beringer

Quintessa Quintessa Estate

Rebellious Red Sequoia Grove

Rubicon Inglenook

Tapestry Reserve BV (Beaulieu Vineyard)

Terzetto Volker Eisele Family Estate

Trilogy Flora Springs

brought the wine producers of the Napa Valley to the party, and they don't appear to be leaving the festivities with anyone else.

NAPA VALLEY FAVORITES

When it comes to the wines of the Napa Valley, money talks. If you have dollars to burn, you're feeling flush, or you want to celebrate, then navigating the Napa Valley is pretty easy: pay big money, get big wine. It is difficult to find really great values—very good wines at very fair prices—among wines that carry the Napa Valley AVA on their labels. Difficult, but not impossible if you're WineWise. We find that if you focus on some of the old, established names in the Napa Valley, those families and companies that owned their vineyard land and wineries before the modern "gold rush" in the Valley, you just might get some very good wines at very good prices. As we have said before and will say again in these pages, the reputation of the producer is really important in making wine-buying decisions. There are producers making wines that sell for

Opus One—a partnership started by Robert Mondavi and Baron Philippe de Rothschild—has been seen as the flagship for the "Bordeaux blends" of the Napa Valley since its first vintage in 1979.

Chappellet produces very fine Cabernet Sauvignon from its estate vineyards located on Pritchard Hill, one of Napa Valley's best mountainside vineyard sites. The vineyard is farmed organically. Courtesy of Chappellet Winery.

extravagant prices, and their wines are worth it because drinking that wine is a singular, if expensive, experience. If that producer creates a wine that is more consumer-friendly in terms of its price, we'll bet you the price of the bottle that the "bargain" wine will be good, too. Then there are those rare producers—rare especially in the Napa Valley—who pride themselves on making wines that are high in quality but moderate in price.

The following wineries are some of our favorite Napa Valley producers. Please note that some of these producers make second-tier wines with the "California" appellation on the label, but we have included in this list only those wineries that display the Napa Valley AVA on their labels. Most bargains in the Napa Valley are defined as wines under $25, which elsewhere in the world might be considered moderately expensive.

Producers whose wines are mostly expensive but worth it include Acacia, Amusant, Araujo Estate, Artesa, David Arthur, Azalea Springs, BV (Beaulieu Vineyard), Benessere, Beringer, Burgess, Cafaro, Cain, Cakebread, Caymus, Ceja, Chanticleer, Chappellet, Chateau Montelena, Clos du Val, Clos Pegase, Corison, Cosentino, Robert

Craig, Cuvaison, Diamond Creek, Domaine Carneros, Domaine Chandon, Dominus Estate, Downing Family, Duckhorn, Dunn, Dyer, Ehlers, El Molino, Etude, Far Niente, Flora Springs, Robert Foley, Forman, Franciscan, Franus, Frog's Leap, Girard, Grgich Hills, Groth, Hagafen, Hall, Havens, Heitz, The Hess Collection, Inglenook, Jade Mountain, Jarvis, Kuleto Estate, La Jota, Lail, Lamborn, Larkmead, Lewis, Liparita, Livingston-Moffett, Lokoya, Mayacamas, Merryvale, Miner Family, Robert Mondavi Winery, Mumm Cuvee Napa, Newton, Nickel & Nickel, Patz & Hall, Joseph Phelps, Pine Ridge, Plumpjack, Pride Mountain, Provenance, Quintessa, Kent Rasmussen, Rudd, Schramsberg, Selene, Sequoia Grove, Shafer, Signorello, Silver Oak, Robert Sinskey, Sky, Smith-Madrone, Spottswoode, Stag's Leap Wine Cellars, Stags' Leap Winery, Steltzner, Storybook Mountain, Swanson, Philip Togni, Trefethen, Truchard, Turley, Turnbull, Vineyard 7 & 8, Volker Eisele Estate, Voss, Whitehall Lane, York Creek, and ZD Winery, among many others.

Napa Valley producers who offer (relative) bargains include Atlas Peak* (an asterisk indicates wines that are widely available), Beaucanon, Blockheadia,* Buehler, Conn Creek,

Vineyards in Carneros.

Joel Gott,* Green and Red,* Honig,* Charles Krug,* Luna,* Markham,* Louis M. Martini,* Nichelini, Raymond,* Rombauer,* Round Hill,* and Trinchero Family.*

SOME WINEWISE NAPA VALLEY SUB-AVAS

Currently, the Napa Valley AVA contains 16 sub-AVAs within it. We're going to take a look at some of the majors and some of their best-known producers. Read on to find out more about:

CARNEROS, an AVA that is shared with Sonoma County, and is best known for Pinot Noir, Chardonnay, and sparkling wines

OAKVILLE, RUTHERFORD, AND STAGS LEAP DISTRICT, three notable AVAs located on Napa's valley floor, each known primarily for extraordinary Cabernet Sauvignon wines and Cabernet-based "Bordeaux blends"

HOWELL MOUNTAIN AVA, DIAMOND MOUNTAIN DISTRICT AVA, SPRING MOUNTAIN DISTRICT AVA, MOUNT VEEDER AVA, AND ATLAS PEAK AVA, the five "mountain" AVAs within the Napa Valley, all of which are known primarily for great Cab but also produce small amounts of white wines.

The "Cool" Region: Carneros AVA. Officially named "Los Carneros," this area is actually an AVA that is shared by both Napa and Sonoma counties, as it borders the north coast of San Pablo Bay. Carneros is also the coolest sub-AVA within the larger Napa Valley AVA, featuring early afternoon fog and cool air. Because of its cool climate, Carneros is the ideal site to plant Chardonnay and Pinot Noir, two varietals that thrive in cool weather, developing crisp acidity in both the fruit and finished wine. Fine varietal-labeled still wines are made from these grapes, but so are delicious Champagne-method sparkling wines that often use a blend of Pinot Noir and Chardonnay as base wines.

Carneros, officially a sub-AVA of *both* Sonoma Valley (see page 85) and Napa Valley, is home to some of the best Chardonnay and Pinot Noir single-vineyard sites in California (Hyde, Sangiacomo, Red Shoulder Ranch, Leveroni, Stanly Ranch, and Mahoney, among many others). Although Carneros is grower-centric, many resident and non-resident wineries have invested heavily in Carneros vineyards in order to assure great raw material for their wines. Seeing the Carneros AVA on a wine label is an outward sign of quality.

Carneros producers who make Chardonnay and Pinot Noir wines that are expensive and worth it include Acacia, Artesa, Benessere, Beringer,

Bouchaine, Cakebread, Ceja, Cline, Clos du Val, Clos Pegase, B.R. Cohn, Cuvaison, Etude, Franus, Frog's Leap, Havens, Paul Hobbs, Jacuzzi, Kistler, Landmark, Patz and Hall, Joseph Phelps, Kent Rasmussen, Schug, Shafer, Robert Sinskey, Robert Stemmler, St. Francis, Truchard, Voss, and ZD.

Producers of (relative) bargains include Benziger* (an asterisk indicates wines that are widely available), BV (Beaulieu Vineyard),* Buena Vista,* Carneros Creek,* Charles Krug,* Cuvaison,* Frank Family, Rombauer,* Saintsbury "Garnet" Pinot Noir,* Steele/Shooting Star,* and Valley of the Moon.*

In the "beautiful bubbles" category, Domaine Carneros, Domaine Chandon, Domaine Mumm, and Gloria Ferrer offer some pretty good values for some very good Champagne-method wines.

The "Valley Floor": Oakville AVA, Rutherford AVA, and Stags Leap District AVA.

We've grouped these three famous sub-AVAs of the Napa Valley AVA together for two reasons. First, they are located close by each other in the central Napa Valley. Driving on Highway 29, the main drag in the Napa Valley, you'll encounter the towns of Rutherford and Oakville right next to each other, with Rutherford sited north of Oakville. Take a turn to the right off Highway 29 when you're in Oakville and you'll end up on the Silverado Trail and in the Stags Leap District AVA. Together, these three Napa Valley sub-AVAs account for about 13,000 acres (5,200 hectares) of some of the most expensive agricultural real estate in the world, dedicated largely to Cabernet Sauvignon vineyards. Cab made from the grapes grown in these three AVAs is full-bodied, rich, complex, and ageworthy; the best wines age gracefully and can be quite expensive.

Stags Leap District (commonly referred to as "SLD") is the smallest AVA of the three, only 2 square miles (5 square kilometers), half of it (1,500 acres [600 hectares]) planted to vines. Wines produced from SLD fruit are powerful, with firm tannins. This description applies not only to the much-heralded SLD Cabs but also to the Merlot and Petite Sirah wines produced here. The AVA is home to some of the best-known California "cult" Cabs, especially Shafer Hillside Select and three wines from Stag's Leap Wine Cellars: "Fay Vineyards," "Cask 23," and "S.L.V."

The Oakville AVA has about 5,000 acres (2,000 hectares) of vineyards, with the vines planted mostly on the valley floor. Oakville Cabernet Sauvignon at its best is scented with fragrant fresh herbs, especially mint and sage. Coffee and tobacco also come through in the nose of the wine. Balance is achieved on the palate by the taste of black currants and sweet cherries, coupled with a slight astringency provided by tannins. Oakville is home to many heralded wines, none more famous than Opus One, produced in partnership by Robert Mondavi and Baron Philippe Rothschild, one of the first proprietary-labeled "Bordeaux blends." Newer "cult" Cabs from Oakville include Dalla Valle, Harlan Estate, and Screaming Eagle, all of which are hard to obtain

A NOTE ABOUT PRODUCERS

You may notice that throughout this chapter, several California wine producers are listed more than once. That's not a mistake. The same producer can make wines from vineyards all over California, and it is not unusual for that to happen. So don't get confused if you see the same producer's name several times and in several different AVAs, or the wines listed as both relative bargains and expensive. That is the way the California wine industry works: the same producer can create expensive Cabernet Sauvignon from the Napa Valley AVA and Sonoma County's Alexander Valley AVA, as well as a very good $12 Cabernet Sauvignon that just reads "California" on the label.

and seriously overpriced when you do find them ($1,000 at retail for Screaming Eagle, and even more on a wine list? Please!).

The Rutherford AVA is about 7,000 acres (2,340 hectares), most of it Cabernet Sauvignon. At harvest, Cabernet Sauvignon planted in the Rutherford AVA is worth about $30 million; that's just the grapes, not the finished wine. There are about 30 wineries in Rutherford, and at least 26 of them produce Cabernet Sauvignon wines. Rutherford Cab features dramatic tannins that often turn into a decadent sundae of bitter chocolate and black fruits—plums and cherries—on the palate. Herbs, especially mint, are prominent in the nose of Rutherford Cab. Since 1880, when Inglenook was founded by Finnish sea captain Gustave Niebaum, Cabernet Sauvignon has defined Rutherford (the original Inglenook estate is now owned by the family of cinema *auteur* Francis Ford Coppola). This mono-grape identity was further cemented, starting in the early 1900s by BV (Beaulieu Vineyard). Tiny amounts of Merlot, Cabernet Franc, and Zinfandel are also planted in the Rutherford AVA.

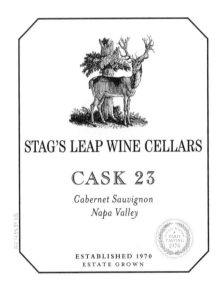

Stag's Leap Wine Cellars Napa Valley Cabernet Sauvignon has been famous since 1976, when it bested the best of Bordeaux in a California-versus-France wine challenge (and did so again 30 years later, in 2006). Courtesy of Stag's Leap Wine Cellars.

There are not many bargains to be found in Stags Leap District, Oakville, or Rutherford, except for the Cabernet-based Rutherford Meritage produced for Costco's Kirkland Signature brand at about $15; Costco is now the largest wine retailer in the United States, and possibly the world, by the way. Most of these wines are going to be expensive to wildly expensive and should be saved for special dinners on special occasions. Here are some well-known producers.

STAGS LEAP DISTRICT AVA: Chimney Rock, Cliff Lede, Clos du Val, Ilsley, Pine Ridge, Regusci, Shafer, Silverado, Robert Sinskey, Stag's Leap Wine Cellars, Stags' Leap Winery, and Steltzner.

OAKVILLE AVA: Cosentino, Dalla Valle, Downing Family, Far Niente, Franciscan, Girard, Groth, Harlan Estate, Miner, Oakville Ranch, Opus One, Pahlmeyer, Plumpjack, Rudd, Screaming Eagle, Silver Oak, Swanson, and Turnbull.

RUTHERFORD AVA: David Arthur, Beaucanon, BV (Beaulieu Vineyard), Cakebread, Caymus, Conn Creek, Frog's Leap, Grgich Hills, Kathryn Hall, Honig, Inglenook, Livingston-Moffett, Peju, Quintessa, Round Hill, Sequoia Grove, Staglin Family, St. Supery, Sullivan, Villa Mt. Eden, Voss, Whitehall Lane, and ZD.

The Magnificent Mountains: Howell Mountain AVA, Diamond Mountain District AVA, Spring Mountain District AVA, Mount Veeder AVA, and Atlas Peak AVA.

We've grouped these five sub-AVAs of the Napa Valley together because the grapes from mountain vineyards express a very different *terroir* than do valley floor vineyards. These five AVAs share high-altitude rocky terrain, soils that don't retain a lot of water, and roots that go deep. You end up tasting a wine with some real complexity and

Vineyards in the Stags Leap District.

structure and a kind of "wild" mountain character that's unpredictable from vintage to vintage. Again, these five mountain AVAs are focused on Cabernet Sauvignon, with a smattering of Cabernet Franc and Zinfandel, and just a bit of Chardonnay and Riesling.

At more than 2,000 feet (610 meters) above sea level, the Howell Mountain AVA escapes the fog that envelops the floor of the Napa Valley, but because of its elevation, this Napa sub-AVA enjoys moderately warm to relatively cool weather even when the sun is shining. Howell Mountain, with only 600 acres (240 hectares) of vineyard planted, is known for two varietals: Cabernet Sauvignon and Zinfandel. Randy Dunn made this AVA famous with his Dunn Howell Mountain Cabernet Sauvignon. Another much sought-after wine is Beringer Howell Mountain Bancroft Ranch Merlot. Storybook Mountain Vineyards makes some of our favorite Zinfandels here.

The Diamond Mountain District AVA covers a rugged 5,000 acres (2,000 hectares) along the Mayacamas mountain range in the northeastern Napa Valley. Diamond Mountain Cab is powerful stuff meant for aging, with an almost chewy texture and assertive tannins. Small artisanal producers have been the rule on Diamond Mountain ever since 1972, when the late Al Brounstein, the founder of Diamond Creek Vineyards, first produced three single-vineyard Cabs ("Red Rock Terrace," "Gravelly Meadow," and "Volcanic Hill").

The Spring Mountain District AVA, with altitudes as high as 2,600 feet (790 meters), is above the fog line of the Napa Valley but gets cool afternoons and warm evenings. Now famous for its Cabernet Sauvignon, Spring Mountain first received attention for its Riesling and Chardonnay wines, and a few producers, including Stony Hill and Smith-Madrone (incredible Riesling), still specialize in elegant whites. Hand-picked mountainside vineyards are small, as is total wine production. Cain Vineyard and Winery produces its "Cain Five" from Spring Mountain fruit and was the first California winery to produce a wine using all five of the classic

Bordeaux red varietals: Cabernet Sauvignon, Merlot, Cabernet Franc, Malbec, and Petit Verdot.

The Mount Veeder AVA is placed atop the highest peak—2,700 feet (825 meters)—of the Mayacamas Mountains. With slopes as steep as 30 degrees, vineyards are difficult to plant and harvest, but that same angle allows for great sun exposure and soil drainage. The finished wines, most of them Cabernet Sauvignon, are distinctively spicy and feature unbridled flavors of wild berries and chewy tannins—wines to last the test of time.

The Atlas Peak AVA is sited high above the stone foothills of the Stags Leap District and across the valley floor from Mount Veeder. Facing west, the vineyards love the direct sunlight afforded them, as well as the cool breezes that envelop the area in the afternoon. The most famous producer here is Atlas Peak Vineyards, founded by Piero Antinori, a legendary wine producer in Tuscany, Italy. Antinori now produces fine wines from these vineyards, but under the Antica label. Storybook Mountain produces a robust Zinfandel here, and this Napa sub-AVA shows a lot of promise with that varietal.

There are almost no bargains to be found in wines labeled with any of these mountainous Napa Valley sub-AVAs, but there are some very fine wines made by these producers if you've got the do re mi—and, in several cases, the patience to find them.

HOWELL MOUNTAIN AVA: Beringer, Robert Craig, Dunn, Robert Foley, Forman, La Jota, Lail, Lamborn Family, Lokoya, and Storybook Mountain.

DIAMOND MOUNTAIN DISTRICT AVA: Azalea Springs, Diamond Creek, Dyer, J-Davies, Lokoya, Reverie, Stonegate, and Von Strasser.

SPRING MOUNTAIN DISTRICT AVA: Beringer, Cain, Fife, Robert Keenan, Newton, Pride Mountain, Smith-Madrone, St. Clement, Stony Hill, Philip Togni, Vineyard 7 & 8, and York Creek.

Spring Mountain District vineyard.

Atlas Peak in the Napa Valley.

MOUNT VEEDER AVA: Chateau Potelle, Robert Craig, Franus, The Hess Collection, Jade Mountain, Mayacamas, Mount Veeder Winery, and Sky Vineyards.

ATLAS PEAK AVA: Antica, Ardente, Atlas Peak Vineyards, Elan, Pahlmeyer, Storybook Mountain, and William Hill.

SONOMA COUNTY

The best-known AVAs in Sonoma County include Sonoma Valley, Russian River Valley, Alexander Valley, Dry Creek Valley, and Carneros (shared with Napa). Other WineWise AVAs you might find on the label are Bennett Valley, Chalk Hill, Fort Ross-Seaview, Green Valley of Russian River Valley, Knights Valley, Northern Sonoma, Pine Mountain-Cloverdale Peak, Rockpile, Sonoma Coast, and Sonoma Mountain.

Sonoma County is twice as large as its neighbor Napa County and has more acres of vines planted than any other single coastal county in California—about 60,000 acres (24,000 hectares). Sonoma is not nearly as showy as Napa, with far fewer millionaire industrialists–turned–wine producers and a lot more multigenerational grape growers and winemakers. The Sonoma culture of tradition and longevity shows in its best wines, produced at more than 200 resident wineries.

If you pushed us against a wall and asked, "Okay, who makes better wines overall, Napa or Sonoma?" we'd have to say it's Sonoma, hands down, with the exception of Cabernet Sauvignon (which can still be very good to excellent in Sonoma). Unlike the Napa Valley, which is Cab-centric, Sonoma County makes very fine wines from a wide variety of varietals, including excellent examples of Pinot Noir, Merlot, Chardonnay, Sauvignon Blanc, and even Gewurztraminer. The quality of the wines can be stellar, and although prices can be quite high and are getting higher, it is still relatively easy to find good values in delicious Sonoma wines if you're WineWise.

Unlike the all-encompassing and more commercially driven appellation "Napa Valley," it is quite common to see "Sonoma County" on these wines. Unless you are a producer with a stellar reputation, if you want to sell a bottle of Napa wine, "Napa County" won't do it, "Napa Valley" will. Not so in Sonoma. You should never shy away from wines with the "Sonoma County" label, which indicates that most of the grapes were picked in the county (at least 75%, but the

St. Francis is one of the benchmark wineries of Sonoma County, known for its high quality. Courtesy of Kobrand Corporation.

best producers work toward 100% Sonoma fruit). Remember, it's a big county with lots and lots of vineyards, so when you purchase the wine of a trusted Sonoma County producer, you're going to get good quality, often at a good price.

Following are some of the best buys in "Sonoma County"–labeled wines. Note that most of these producers also produce wines from more specific AVAs within Sonoma County (for example, Carneros, Alexander Valley, Russian River Valley, etc.); those wines are almost sure to be more expensive than those labeled "Sonoma County." Prices for wines by these producers are especially appealing among the white varietals, with plenty of good-value reds, too.

Sonoma County Favorites. Good producers at good prices are Belvedere, Benziger Family, Blackstone, Chateau St. Jean, Clos du Bois, Gallo Family Vineyards, J. Garcia (for Deadheads and others), Grand Archer, Kenwood, Marietta, Murphy-Goode, Rancho Zabaco, Ravenswood, Sebastiani, Seghesio, Simi, Souverain, St. Francis, Rodney Strong, Taft Street, and Valley of the Moon.

SOME WINEWISE SONOMA COUNTY AVAS

Sonoma County contains 14 AVAs. One of these is the Carneros AVA, which is shared with Napa and which we've already talked about (page 79). Of the remaining AVAs, five are actually sub-AVAs. Also, unlike in Napa, where Cabernet Sauvignon rules, some specific AVAs in Sonoma County have come to be identified with specific varietals. Let's take a look at some of the key AVAs of Sonoma, the grapes they're known for, and some of the best-known producers in each AVA.

Sonoma Valley AVA (Sub-AVAs: Bennett Valley, Carneros, Sonoma Mountain). The Sonoma Valley AVA is justifiably famous as one of the most important places in the history of the northern California wine industry. A large AVA (161 square miles [417 square kilometers]), its weather patterns are so varied that no single varietal dominates. It is easy to find good wines made from Chardonnay, Sauvignon Blanc, Pinot Noir, Merlot, Zinfandel, and Cabernet Sauvignon. The Sonoma Mountain AVA is a sub-AVA of Sonoma Valley, as is cool-climate, quality-driven Carneros. However, due to its reputation and consumer respect and recognition, Carneros is not really considered a "sub-AVA" by producers and wine lovers, even though it legally fits the definition (see page 79). Carneros is kind of its own "brand." Wine quality is high in the Sonoma Valley AVAs and bargains are hard to come by, but there are some worth exploring.

Some of the best-known producers in the Sonoma Valley AVA are Carmenet, B. R. Cohn, Envolve, Gundlach Bundschu, Hanzell, Haywood, Robert Hunter, Kistler, Kunde Estate, Louis M. Martini, Monte Rosso Vineyard, Ravenswood, Sebastiani, Smothers/Remick Ridge, St. Francis, and Joseph Swan; there are many others.

Wine producers in the Sonoma Mountain sub-AVA include Benziger Family Estate, Kenwood's Jack London Ranch, and Laurel Glen.

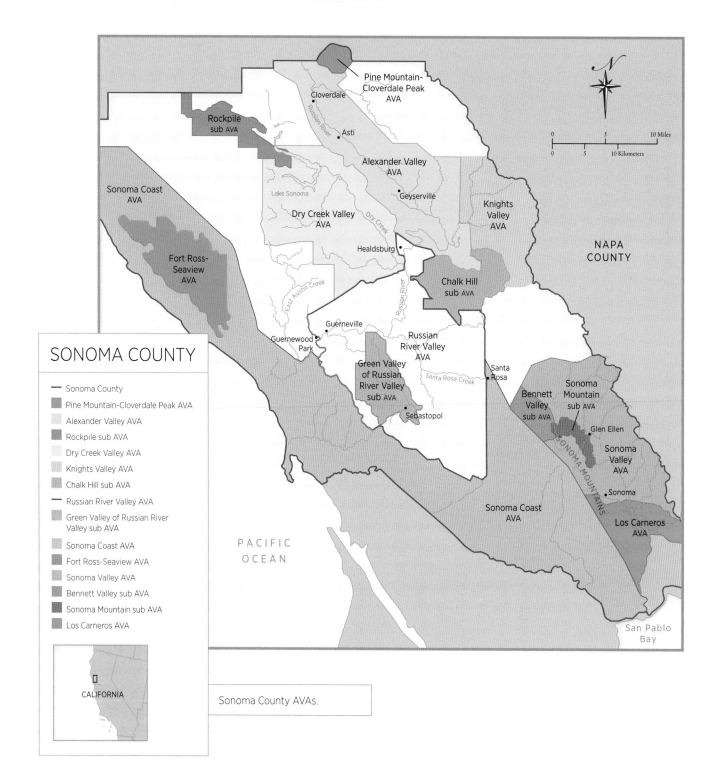

SONOMA COUNTY

- Sonoma County
- Pine Mountain-Cloverdale Peak AVA
- Alexander Valley AVA
- Rockpile sub AVA
- Dry Creek Valley AVA
- Knights Valley AVA
- Chalk Hill sub AVA
- Russian River Valley AVA
- Green Valley of Russian River Valley sub AVA
- Sonoma Coast AVA
- Fort Ross-Seaview AVA
- Sonoma Valley AVA
- Bennett Valley sub AVA
- Sonoma Mountain sub AVA
- Los Carneros AVA

CALIFORNIA

Sonoma County AVAs.

Russian River Valley AVA (Sub-AVAs: Chalk Hill and Green Valley of Russian River Valley).

With more than 16,000 acres (6,400 hectares) of planted vineyards, the Russian River Valley contains close to 20% of the total plantings in Sonoma County. The southern section of the AVA borders the banks of the Russian River and the western section is close to the Pacific Ocean, creating a cool and damp climate, perfect for growing both Chardonnay and Pinot Noir, which account for about 70% of total vineyard plantings in the AVA. Many wine lovers believe that this AVA produces the best *terroir*-driven wines made from these two varietals, and we would agree. Especially where Pinot Noir is concerned, California has had a hard time taming this finicky grape and finessing a delicate finished wine, but Russian River Valley Pinot Noir has gained the respect of the

Sonoma Valley vineyard.

wine world. These wines can be intense, rich, and concentrated, while still delicate and balanced.

In the warmer areas of this AVA, Zinfandel, Merlot, Gewurztraminer, Sauvignon Blanc, and even a bit of Cabernet Sauvignon and Syrah flourish.

Iron Horse, the best-known producer in the Green Valley of Russian River Valley AVA, produces wonderful estate-bottled Chardonnay and Pinot Noir, but it has made its name on several different signature blends of vintage-dated, estate-bottled Champagne-method sparkling wines. These wines are aged four years or more before release, which is but one reason for their complexity and balance.

Russian River Valley wines are uniformly expensive, but their quality often justifies the high price tags.

Some of the best-known producers are:

RUSSIAN RIVER VALLEY AVA: La Crema, Davis Bynum, Davis Family, Dehlinger, Merry Edwards, Gary Farrell, Foppiano, Frei Brothers, Fritz, Gallo, Hanna, Hartford Court, Paul Hobbs, Hook & Ladder, Hop Kiln, J Vineyards, Kenwood, Kistler, Kosta Browne, Lynmar, Martinelli, Martini and Prati, Patz & Hall, Martin Ray, Rochioli, Rutz, Sonoma-Cutrer, Joseph Swan, Taft Street, Topolos, and Williams Selyem.

CHALK HILL SUB-AVA: Albini, Chalk Hill Estate, Chateau Felice, and Rodney Strong.

GREEN VALLEY SUB-AVA: DeLoach, Dutton Estate, Dutton-Goldfield, Emeritus, Iron Horse, Marimar Estate, and Orogeny.

SONOMA COAST AVA

The Sonoma Coast AVA is huge, covering about 500,000 acres (200,000 hectares), and as its name implies, vineyards are planted mostly along the coast of the Pacific Ocean. Encompassing seven sub-AVAs, including the entire Russian River Valley, Carneros, and Sonoma Valley AVAs, Sonoma Coast stretches from the San Pablo Bay to the Mendocino county border. Because of its coastal location, this AVA is known for cool weather, which makes it ideal for Pinot Noir and Chardonnay, and we are seeing some very fine wines bottled with the Sonoma Coast AVA. When the AVA appears on a label it often means that grapes have been sourced within several of its

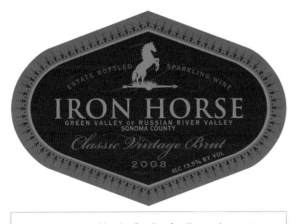

Iron Horse, owned by the Sterling family, produces some of the best estate-bottled, vintage-dated sparkling wines made in California, as well as very fine estate Pinot Noir and Chardonnay, all in the very cool Green Valley, a sub-AVA of the larger Russian River Valley.

constituent sub-AVAs, which, in the right hands, can produce a great wine. Because the sub-AVAs of Sonoma Coast include some of the premier vineyard sites in Sonoma County, we don't find too many examples of producers making a wine from a random hodgepodge of vineyards. Sonoma Coast is a quality-driven AVA, and the wines can be quite expensive. Some of the Sonoma Coast Pinot Noir and Chardonnay producers we like include: Flowers, Freeman, Hirsch, Kistler, Kosta Browne, Kutch, La Follette, Littorai, Martinelli, Patz & Hall, Ramey, Sebastiani, Siduri, and Williams-Selyem, among others.

Alexander Valley AVA and Knights Valley AVA.

The Mendocino County line is the northernmost boundary of Sonoma's Alexander Valley AVA, and its eastern boundary is the Knights Valley AVA. Alexander Valley is a large AVA, with nearly 12,000 acres (4,800 hectares) of vineyards, starring Cabernet Sauvignon and Chardonnay, with Merlot and Zinfandel playing important supporting roles. There are both small and large wine producers in the Alexander Valley. When you see this AVA printed on a wine label, it is an outward sign of quality, a wine worth considering. Although Alexander Valley has its share of expensive wines, relative bargains can still be found, even among estate-bottled wines.

Benziger "Tribute" is a red blend from the Sonoma Mountain AVA, made from grapes grown in certified biodynamic vineyards. Biodynamics is a sustainable farming practice that the Benziger family has adopted for its best wines, with excellent results in both the vineyard and the bottle. Courtesy of Kobrand Corporation.

Buena Vista is considered to be the oldest commercial winery in Sonoma County, having been established by Agoston Haraszthy, a Hungarian immigrant, in 1857.

There are only six resident wineries in the Knights Valley AVA, and only two use the AVA on their labels: Peter Michael and Anakota. Both producers specialize in single-vineyard wines, and the wines are wildly expensive. However, the behemoth winery Beringer owns about 540 acres (218 hectares) in Knights Valley and produces 80,000 cases of a very good Cabernet Sauvignon, as well as Alluvium, a red Bordeaux blend, and Alluvium Blanc, a white blend. All feature the Knights Valley AVA on the label. The Beringer reds sell for about $35, Alluvium Blanc for about $25. Not bad when your neighbor, Sir Peter Michael, has a waiting list of people ready to pay more than a $100 per bottle for his single-vineyard Chardonnays and more than $200 for his his "Les Pavots" red Bordeaux blend.

Some of the best-known producers in the Alexander Valley AVA include deLorimier, Jordan, Lancaster Estate, Ridge, Rodney Strong, Sebastiani, Seghesio, Silver Oak, Simi, Stonestreet, Stuhlmuller, Trentadue, Verite, and Robert Young Estate. Relative bargains in Alexander Valley wines include Alexander Valley Vineyards (including estate-bottled selections), Clos du Bois, Francis Ford Coppola, Frei Brothers, Murphy-Goode, and Windsor.

Dry Creek Valley.

The wines of the Dry Creek Valley AVA sum up the contradictions in the modern California winemaking industry. With dozens of small family-owned vineyards and wineries making fine wines here, the largest landholder and producer in all of Sonoma County—Gallo—is also located in Dry Creek. Healdsburg, the formerly quiet town that anchors Dry Creek, has become increasingly expensive and exclusive as the fortunes of the local wine industry have grown. This AVA has made its reputation on Zinfandel and is considered to be perhaps the finest region for the grape in all of California. Sauvignon Blanc is the stellar white grape here. There are increasing plantings of Syrah and Cabernet Sauvignon in Dry Creek vineyards. Dry Creek Zin is something special and is highly recommended. There are both good values and very expensive boutique wines produced here, but you can't go too far wrong with Dry Creek Zinfandel, no matter the price.

Some of the best-known producers in the Dry Creek AVA include David Coffaro, Dry Creek Vineyard,* (the asterisk indicates a good value), Gary Farrell, Ferrari-Carano, Foppiano,* Frick,* Fritz, Gallo Family Frei Ranch,* Hawley,* Lambert Bridge, Manzanita Creek, Mazzocco, Martin Family, Michel-Schlumberger, Nalle, Pedroncelli,* Peterson, Pezzi-King, Preston, Quivira, A. Rafanelli,* Ridge Lytton Springs, Rued, Sbragia Family, and Seghesio.

ALEXANDER VALLEY VINEYARDS

CABERNET SAUVIGNON
ALEXANDER VALLEY
Estate Grown & Bottled
SONOMA COUNTY   *Vintage:* **2012**
ESTABLISHED 1962   WETZEL FAMILY ESTATE

The Alexander Valley AVA is in Sonoma County. Alexander Valley Vineyards is a leading producer. Courtesy of Alexander Valley Vineyards.

MENDOCINO COUNTY

Although grapes are the second-most-productive cash crop in Mendocino County (marijuana has long held the number-one spot), Mendocino's wines are second to none. Home to many old-vine, dry-farmed organic vineyards, Mendocino produces wines that have a lot of soul, a lot of history. Among reds, Zinfandel is the star in the all-encompassing Mendocino AVA and the Redwood Valley AVA, but some very fine Cabernet Sauvignon is produced in those AVAs, along with Syrah and other red grapes that are originally native to the Rhone Valley of France—Grenache, Mourvedre, Carignan, Petite Sirah. Good examples of Sauvignon Blanc are also produced in Mendocino County, and in the cool-weather Anderson Valley AVA, great Pinot Noir, Chardonnay, Riesling, and Gewurztraminer reign. Also in this AVA you'll find Roederer Estate and Handley, among the best Champagne-method sparkling wine producers in the country.

Organic and sustainable farming has long been a trademark of this region, as championed by many growers and producers, small and large, in Mendocino.

Many of the red wines of Mendocino have great depth of flavor, allowing you to "taste the soil," meaning that the wines have a rustic edge that many other wines lack. Mendocino

Dry Creek
VINEYARD
SOMERS RANCH ZINFANDEL
VINTAGE 2011 · SONOMA COUNTY
DRY CREEK VALLEY
SINGLE VINEYARD SERIES
ALC 14.5% /VOL

The Dry Creek Valley AVA specializes in Zinfandel. This is the label of a fine single-vineyard Zin produced by Dry Creek Vineyard, a quality-driven producer. Courtesy of Dry Creek Vineyard.

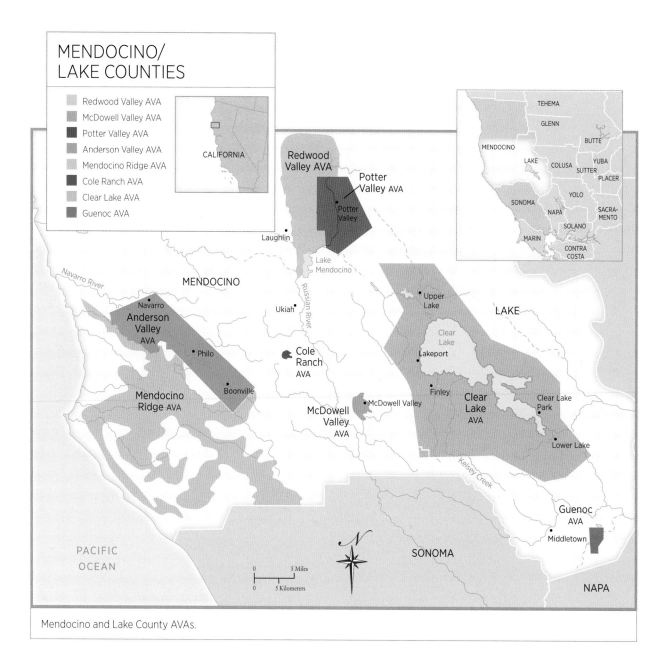

MENDOCINO/ LAKE COUNTIES

- Redwood Valley AVA
- McDowell Valley AVA
- Potter Valley AVA
- Anderson Valley AVA
- Mendocino Ridge AVA
- Cole Ranch AVA
- Clear Lake AVA
- Guenoc AVA

CALIFORNIA

Redwood Valley AVA

Potter Valley AVA

Potter Valley

Laughlin

Navarro River

Lake Mendocino

MENDOCINO

Ukiah

Russian River

Navarro

Anderson Valley AVA

Philo

Cole Ranch AVA

Boonville

Mendocino Ridge AVA

McDowell Valley AVA

McDowell Valley

Upper Lake

Clear Lake

Lakeport

LAKE

Finley

Clear Lake AVA

Clear Lake Park

Lower Lake

Kelsey Creek

PACIFIC OCEAN

0   5 Miles
0   5 Kilometers

N

SONOMA

Guenoc AVA

Middletown

NAPA

TEHEMA

GLENN

BUTTE

MENDOCINO

LAKE   COLUSA   YUBA
SUTTER

PLACER

YOLO

SONOMA

NAPA

SACRA-
MENTO

SOLANO

MARIN

CONTRA
COSTA

Mendocino and Lake County AVAs.

reds are not wimpy. Chardonnay can exhibit great delicacy, the Sauvignon Blanc is lime-juice lovely, the Riesling crisp and complex, the Gewurztraminer spicy and dry. Sparkling wines from the Anderson Valley are some of the best made anywhere in the New World: thirst-quenching and refreshing, but also complex and very food-friendly.

It is amazing to us that the wines of Mendocino still live in the shadow of Napa and Sonoma, but maybe that's a good thing. If the secret were out, Mendocino wines might not continue to be among the best values in fine

California wines, and that would be a shame for *WineWise* readers (and authors). We think that just about any Mendocino wine is worth tasting, many of them several times.

The best-known AVAs in Mendocino County include Mendocino, Anderson Valley, Redwood Valley, and McDowell Valley. Following are some of the best-known producers working in each AVA.

MENDOCINO COUNTY APPELLATION OR MENDOCINO AVA: Blockheadia, Bonterra, Brutocao, Copain, Dendor Patton, Fetzer, Parducci, Steele, and Topel.

French-owned Roederer Estate makes very fine sparkling wines in the cool-climate Anderson Valley of Mendocino County. Courtesy of Maisons Marques & Domaines USA.

ANDERSON VALLEY AVA OR MENDOCINO RIDGE AVA: La Crema, Edmeades, Goldeneye, Greenwood Ridge, Handley* (an asterisk indicates a producer of sparkling wine), Husch, Lazy Creek, Littorai, Londer, Navarro, Roederer Estate,* and Scharffenberger.*

REDWOOD VALLEY AVA: Barra, Frey, Gabrielli, Girasole, Graziano, and Oster.

LAKE COUNTY

The AVAs of Lake County are Benmore Valley, Clear Lake, Guenoc Valley, High Valley, and Red Hills Lake County.

Clear Lake, the largest body of fresh water in California, is located north of Napa and Sonoma and east of Mendocino. The cool Clear Lake AVA, where all but 500 acres of Lake County's 3,800 acres (1,540 hectares) of grapes are planted, is known primarily for the quality of its Sauvignon Blanc. Clear Lake is also the source for fine Cabernet Sauvignon, Cabernet Franc, Merlot, Zinfandel, and Sangiovese.

The biggest player here is Kendall-Jackson Winery and this is where the late Jess Jackson planted his first vineyards. Smaller producers have long been making artisanal wines in the various AVAs within the county. Overall, the scale of production is small; there is only one winery in the Guenoc Valley AVA, for example

(Langtry Estate, which also produces Guenoc wines). However, the "undiscovered" vineyards of Lake County have now been discovered by some of the biggest players in the California wine industry. In 2012, the Gallo winery purchased the much sought-after Snows Vineyard in the Red Hills Lake County AVA, the source of extraordinary Cabernet Sauvignon and Zinfandel grapes; Gallo is perhaps the largest wine company in the world. While the Clear Lake AVA, Red Hills Lake County AVA, or the Lake County appellation appears on more and more bottles of wine, the region is still a feeder of grapes for moderately priced wines that are more likely to carry "North Coast" or "California" as the place of origin on their labels. There are some very good bargains to be had from this region. Wines of good-to-excellent quality at mostly affordable prices; true WineWise choices.

Following are some of the best-known producers that most often will use the Lake County appellation or Clear Lake AVA; some may use the other AVAs of Lake County: Beaver Creek (organic and biodynamic vineyards), Brassfield Estate, Ceago Vinegarden (biodynamic), Guenoc, Langtree, Ployez, Robledo Family, Shooting Star, Steele, and Wildhurst.

Wildhurst makes very good wines that express the soils and climate of Lake County at affordable prices.

CENTRAL COAST

The Central Coast AVA encompasses Alameda, Contra Costa, Monterey, San Benito, San Francisco, San Luis Obispo, San Mateo, Santa Barbara, Santa Clara, and Santa Cruz counties. It would not be unusual to find the name of the county on the labels of many wines as the place of origin, especially in the cases of Contra Costa, Monterey, and Santa Barbara counties. Sub-AVAs of the Central Coast AVA you might find on the label include Arroyo Seco, Edna Valley, Livermore Valley, Monterey, Mt. Harlan, Paso Robles, San Francisco Bay, Santa Cruz Mountains, Santa Lucia Highlands, Santa Maria Valley, Santa Ynez Valley (and its smaller interior AVA the Sta. Rita Hills).

The Central Coast AVA is a huge appellation, with almost 100,000 acres (40,000 hectares) of planted vineyards. With both small and large producers producing both artisanal and industrial wines, it is impossible to make a generalization about this unwieldy AVA.

What we can say is that what is unofficially known as the "North Central Coast" is centered around the AVAs contained in Monterey County, with smaller but important producers in the Santa Cruz Mountains AVA (San Mateo, Santa Clara, San Benito, and Santa Cruz counties) and Livermore Valley AVA (Alameda County), home to Wente Vineyards, the first commercial producer of Chardonnay in California.

California's Central Coast.

Monterey County vineyards supply producers of "fighting varietals"—the name given to varietal-label wines that sell in the $7 to $12 range and "fight" for shelf space in supermarkets and retail shops. Wines made from Monterey County grapes are often blended with wines made from other parts of the state, and so most often the appellation that appears on the label of these relatively inexpensive but quite drinkable wines is "California."

The Monterey AVA is one of those county-wide-and-beyond AVAs, but some smaller AVAs in this part of the North Central Coast have developed a reputation for great wines, mostly whites, with a smattering of extraordinary Pinot Noir, too. The Arroyo Seco AVA is known for Chardonnay, Riesling, and Gewurztraminer; the Chalone AVA for Chardonnay, Pinot Blanc, and Pinot Noir; the Santa Lucia Highlands AVA for high-elevation Chardonnay and Pinot Noir as well as Cabernet Sauvignon and Merlot grown closer to the Salinas Valley floor; and Mt. Harlan for extraordinary single-producer, single-vineyard Pinot Noir.

In the Mt. Harlan AVA, Josh Jensen's Calera winery is home to the Jensen, Mills, Selleck, and Reed vineyards. Singly and as a group, these vineyards may represent the raw material for the best Pinot Noir made in California. What makes these wines so special? We think you can taste Josh Jensen's Pinot passion in his wines. He has gone to great lengths to plant these vineyards at high elevations (more than 2,000 feet above sea level in the Gavilan Mountain range), and found rare-in-California, limestone-rich soils for his wines. Unlike so many very fine California Pinot Noirs, Calera's single-vineyard offerings are not jammy, not even fruit-forward. Instead, from the first sip, the wine achieves a remarkable balance of fruit, tannin, and acidity that can only be described as "Old World" or "Burgundian" (see Burgundy, page 174). These wines cost upward of $65 at retail, but we consider them to be a special-occasion, affordable luxury.

What can be considered the "South Central Coast" comprises the counties of Santa Barbara and San Luis Obispo and has made a reputation for itself not only with the film *Sideways* but also with very fine Pinot Noir and Chardonnay produced from grapes grown in the Santa Maria Valley AVA and Santa Ynez Valley AVA in Santa Barbara County, and the Edna Valley and Arroyo Grande AVAs in San Luis Obispo County. Also in San Luis Obispo you will find the Paso Robles AVA, which still lives in the shadow of Napa and Sonoma, even though it produces wonderful examples of Zinfandel and Cabernet Sauvignon, as well as Syrah, Grenache, Petite Sirah, and several other varietals native to the Rhone Valley of France. The reds of Paso Robles are unique, especially those from vineyards planted on the west side of Highway 101 (rocky, dry soils), and are often great values.

Here are some of the region's best-known producers:

CENTRAL COAST AVA, MONTEREY AVA, SANTA BARBARA COUNTY, SAN LUIS OBISPO COUNTY: Antelope, Au Bon Climat, Beckmen, Bernardus, Bonny Doon, Byron, Calera, Callaway, Chalone, Concannon, David Bruce, Edna Valley Vineyard, Fetzer Five Rivers, Foley, Hitching Post, Jekel, Los Olivos, Meridian, Millbrook, Mirassou, Robert Mondavi Private Selection, Morgan, Fess Parker, Qupe, Scheid, Talbott, Ivan Tamas Estates, and Wente.

ARROYO GRANDE, ARROYO SECO, CHALONE, EDNA VALLEY, LIVERMORE VALLEY, SANTA MARIA, SANTA YNEZ, SANTA LUCIA HIGHLANDS, SANTA CRUZ MOUNTAINS, STA. RITA HILLS, AND MT. HARLAN AVAS: Alban, Andrew Murray, Au Bon Climat, Babcock, Bargetto, Byron, Calera, Cambria, Carmel Road, Chalone Vineyard, Concannon, Claiborne & Churchill, Fiddlehead, Firestone, Thomas Fogarty, Foxen, Gainey, Jaffurs, Justin, Kynsi, Laetitia, Lane Tanner, Mer Soleil, Michaud, Morgan, Ojai, Rancho Sisquoc, Sanford, Santa Cruz Mountain Winery, Saucelito Canyon, Sandhi, Smith and Hook, Steele, Talley, Testarossa, Ventana, Wente, Whitcraft, and Zaca Mesa.

Josh Jensen's Calera Wine Company produces extraordinary estate-bottled wines from single vineyards on the Central Coast, in the Mt. Harlan AVA.

PASO ROBLES AVA: Adelaida, Ancient Peaks, Castoro, Dunning, Eberle, Edmunds St. John, EOS Estate, J. Lohr, L'Aventure, Peachy Canyon, Rabbit Ridge, Ridge, Robert Hall, Roudon-Smith, Saxum, Tablas Creek, Turley, Vina Robles, and Wild Horse.

SIERRA FOOTHILLS AVA AND CALIFORNIA'S INTERIOR

Sierra Foothills. The Sierra Foothills AVA covers seven counties (Amador, El Dorado, Mariposa, Nevada, Placer, Tuolumne, and Yuba) and includes about 180 wineries and close to 6,000 acres (2,400 hectares) of planted vineyards. Soon after the California gold rush, this area became the mother lode for California wine production, but by the time Prohibition hit in 1919, the region's wine industry was little more than a memory. It was revived in the 1970s because of the availability of relatively inexpensive land. The growing conditions are excellent for Zinfandel above all, but also for Cabernet Sauvignon, Merlot, Syrah, and Petite Sirah, as well as some red "Cal-Italians," Sangiovese and Barbera. Whites that do well in the region include Chardonnay and Sauvignon Blanc.

The Amador County appellation is just as likely to appear on a wine produced from this region, especially if it is Zinfandel. There are still hundreds of acres of pre-Prohibition vines planted in the area, and Amador County or

Sierra Foothills Zin is almost always a soulful treat at an affordable price. Many of the wines can be found for under $15, and it is rare to break the $25 barrier unless the wines are sourced from heralded single vineyards (translation: worth the $25-plus price tag).

We highly recommend wines from this region of California for their quality, their earthiness, and their value. Still largely undiscovered—more than 80% of the grapes grown here are sold to producers outside the region—these gems are high on our lists of great and affordable wines.

In the Sierra Foothills AVA, Amador County, and Calaveras County, some of the best-known producers are Amador Foothill, Black Sheep, Boeger, Chatom, Easton, Frogs Tooth, Ironstone, Lava Cap, Madrona, Montevina-Terra d'Oro, Renwood, Sierra Vista, Sobon Estate, St. Amant, and Stevenot.

California's Central Valley. Most often referred to in oversimplified wine-speak as the San Joaquin Valley, this region is best known as *the* source for inexpensive "fighting varietals" and the increasingly shrinking generic-label category ("Chablis," "Burgundy," "Champagne," etc.). Most often, wines from this region, which grows grapes for

The Sierra Foothills, where gold was first discovered during California's gold rush, is the ancestral home of the state's wine industry, with some very good wines from some very old vines. Courtesy of Stevenot Winery.

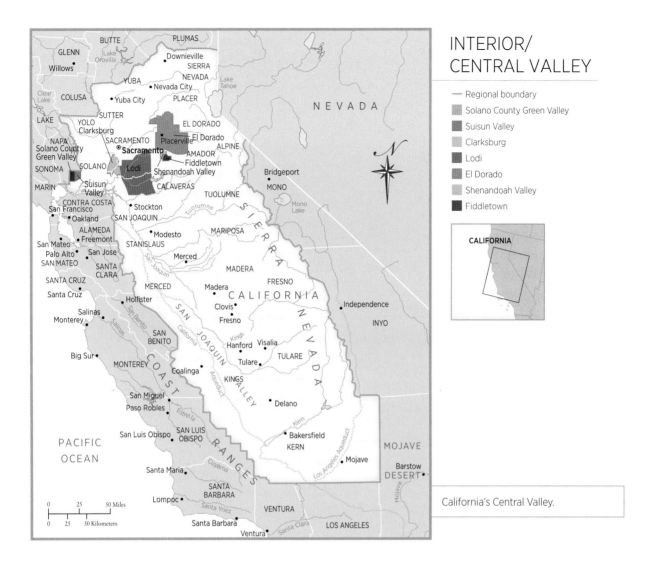

INTERIOR/ CENTRAL VALLEY

- — Regional boundary
- Solano County Green Valley
- Suisun Valley
- Clarksburg
- Lodi
- El Dorado
- Shenandoah Valley
- Fiddletown

CALIFORNIA

California's Central Valley.

close to 70% of the wines produced in the state, will receive the "California" appellation on the label. Two notable exceptions that have become increasingly popular and sought-after in the last 10 years are the Clarksburg AVA and the Lodi AVA.

Clarksburg, with 9,000 acres (3,600 hectares) under vine, is known for excellent Chenin Blanc and Petite Sirah. Clarksburg is home to Bogle, a sixth-generation producer that farms more than 1,200 acres (485 hectares) and is famous for quality wines at very fair prices. We highly recommend Bogle wines and commend the Bogle family for its commitment to excellence and befriending the wine consumer.

The Lodi AVA, in the northernmost part of the San Joaquin Valley, accounts for almost 20% of California's wine production, and benefits from the breezes of cool air provided by the Sacramento River delta. In 1979, Robert Mondavi, who rose to fame in the Napa Valley, returned home to Lodi to produce accessible, affordable, varietal-labeled wines, establishing the value-driven Woodbridge brand. Over the last 20 years or so, Lodi has become an increasingly sought-after AVA, especially for Zinfandel. Famous Zin producers such as Ravenswood, Turley, and Joel Gott produce wines proudly bearing the Lodi AVA on the label. Today, it is easy to find single-vineyard Zinfandel from the Lodi AVA. Prices for these wines are still reasonable, but they are quickly increasing. If you're a *WineWise* reader who loves great Zin and great value, check these wines out now, before the prices go crazy. Here are some of the best-known producers:

Amador County is home to some of the oldest Zinfandel vines in California, and several producers make earthy, brawny Zins. Montevina, owned by the Trinchero family, makes a prime example of the style. Courtesy of Montevina Winery.

The Francis Ford Coppola winery produces an easy-drinking California Pinot Grigio, the "Bianco" in its Rosso & Bianco brand. Courtesy of Francis Ford Coppola Winery.

CLARKSBURG AVA: Bogle, Dancing Coyote, Dry Creek Vineyard, Ehrhardt, Herzog (kosher), and Six Hands.

LODI AVA: Bogle, Borra, Ghost Pines, Gnarly Head, E², Joel Gott, Harmony Wynelands, Herzog (kosher), Jessie's Grove, J. Lohr, Pepperwood Grove/Sebastiani, Ravenswood, Talus, Van Ruiten Family, and Woodbridge by Robert Mondavi.

"CALIFORNIA" WINES

Wines, whether in bottles or boxes, that simply have the word "California" on their label are usually inexpensive wines produced on a moderately large to frighteningly humongous level. The grapes are planted and harvested throughout the state, and wines with the "California" appellation are usually produced using purchased grapes. There are easily hundreds of brands, and sometimes multiple brands might be owned by the same producer (Gallo, the single-largest family-owned winery in the world, owns dozens of separate wine brands—Barefoot, Carlo Rossi, Dancing Bull, Livingston Cellars, Tisdale, The Naked Grape, Turning Leaf, among others—all bearing the "California" appellation).

Wine geeks and wine snobs (for whom there is a special place in hell) often dismiss "California" wines as somehow beneath them, not worth drinking. Much like someone who declares a book or film obscene without reading the book or screening the film, these people show their own ignorance. Admittedly, we are not talking about the world's greatest wines here, but "California" wines serve several useful purposes. They are good entry-level wines for folks who are just getting into wine. They are affordable. And most of the time they are true to their varietal type, so if you have little experience with, say, Sauvignon Blanc or Merlot and you want to find out about them without making a heavy financial commitment, these are good wines for you to enjoy.

As the California wine industry has expanded, an interesting phenomenon has occurred. Quite a few well-known producers in Napa and

Sonoma have started second-label wines with "California" labels. Robert Mondavi, the Napa Valley legend, was among the first to do this, establishing the budget-friendly Woodbridge line of California varietal wines. Sometimes the wines are marketed under their own names, and sometimes they create a fantasy brand. We think that this is a good subcategory for the WineWise consumer. Napa or Sonoma wineries that have established a reputation for quality in their home bases cannot risk putting out an inferior "California" wine, even at a much lower price point. If they do, the bad word of mouth will come back to bite them. These wines, which define the "fighting varietal" category, start at under $7 and rarely exceed $15. So don't make the bonehead move that the truly uninformed wine consumer makes in passing by one of these "California" appellation wines because it's "too cheap." That would not be WineWise.

Obviously, we can't—nor would we want to—list all the "California" wine brands, so we'll limit ourselves to producers we trust. But if you see a "California" wine for seven or eight bucks and something about it calls to you (usually it's a pretty label; that's okay, we've all fallen for those), pick it up and enjoy it. These days, chances are the wine will be better than you expected.

Of the "California" appellation wines, some of the most reliable producers (some of which offer very good bargains) include Antelope Valley, Arrow Creek, Barefoot, Beringer, Blackstone, Bogle, BV Coastal Estates, Canyon Road, Carmenet, Cline,

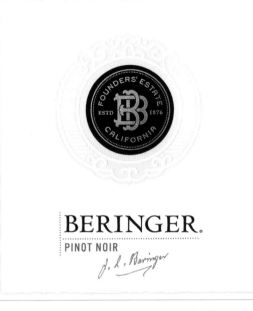

Beringer is a famous name in Napa Valley, but like so many other well-known and respected producers, it also produces a wide variety of "California" wines. About 75% of the state's wines bear the simple "California" appellation, meaning that the grapes are sourced throughout the state.

Coppola Rosso & Bianco, Corbett Canyon, Dancing Bull Zinfandel, Delicato, Echelon, Estancia, Fetzer, Folie a Deux, Forest Glen, Daniel Gehrs, Joel Gott, Herzog, Ironstone, Kendall-Jackson, Marietta Cellars, Meridian, Mirassou, Pepperwood Grove, Quady, Rabbit Ridge, Ravenswood Vintners Blend, Round Hill, Smoking Loon, Sutter Home, Talus, 3 Blind Moose, Toasted Head, Turning Leaf, Vendange, and Woodbridge by Robert Mondavi.

LIVING IN THE USA

WASHINGTON, OREGON, NEW YORK

YOU COULD CHALLENGE YOURSELF TO TASTE EVERY SINGLE WINE PRODUCED IN CALIFORNIA AND NEVER REPEAT YOURSELF for the rest of your life. While it might be fun, you'd be missing out on some of the best wines produced in the United States—the wines of Washington State, Oregon, and New York State.

Life without Riesling, Merlot, and Syrah from Washington, Pinot Noir and Pinot Gris from Oregon, or Riesling and Cabernet Franc from New York is not much of a life for an American wine drinker. These three states have emerged from California's shadow to establish their own identities, their own signatures, their own wines.

While all 50 states produce wine—some of it very good wine— Washington, Oregon, and New York are the three largest wine-producing states after California, and this chapter will focus on the Big Three. We would be remiss, however, not to mention that we have enjoyed some tasty treats from many other states, especially Michigan, Idaho, Texas, New Mexico, Colorado, North Carolina, Virginia, Pennsylvania, and Rhode Island. In several states, the wine industry has been around for a while, but in most states, wine is a new and burgeoning addition to their economic and culinary profiles.

Let's take a tour of the most important wine regions in Washington, Oregon, and New York. Hopefully, our wine-stained prose will get you to try some of these wines or to confirm your appreciation for wines from these states and encourage you to look even farther afield to other states making high-quality wines; we can almost guarantee that once you've tried them, you'll love them. We'll start our excursion in the nation's second-largest vinifera-based wine-producing state, Washington. . . .

Washington

IF YOU THINK THAT ONLY California makes good American wine, you are missing a whole lot. Stylistically, Washington State wines lie somewhere between the exuberant fruitiness of California or Australia and the sometimes reserved, sometimes just-ripe nature of French wines. In other words, Washington State offers the best of both worlds—ripeness and the subtle intrigue of nuanced flavor. Washington State and its wine producers certainly have a good thing going: the history of vineyard development is astounding, and the potential for future expansion is mind-boggling. Even though the rate of growth has slowed from a new winery opening every 11 days in 2000 to every other month today, that rate is still largely unheard of in other parts of the world. As for future growth, imagine this: the current area of planted vineyards in the entire state is about 45,000 acres (18,000 hectares)—but the available area that could be planted in the Columbia Valley, by far Washington's largest AVA, is *11 million* acres (4.5 million hectares).

What does Washington have to support its claim that it is and will continue to be an important producer of premium-quality wines? First and foremost, it has a climate that is conducive to optimal ripening of a number of different grape varieties. Second, it has established an academic/scientific/practical backing for the wine industry in the form of two- and four-year degree programs in viticulture and enology (that's grape growing and winemaking for the rest of us), as well as wine science, to help satisfy the industry's ever-growing need for trained personnel. Third, the Washington Wine Commission is an industry-financed organization that promotes and protects the quality image of Washington wines by creating labeling standards that go beyond the federal government's requirements.

Before we get into the various AVAs and their attributes, let's look at Washington's special labeling provisions, the major grape varieties used, and the climatic advantages that the state's vineyards enjoy.

The sweeping expanse of Columbia Valley vineyards.

WASHINGTON'S LABEL LANGUAGE

PLACE NAMES

If the place name on a Washington wine label is simply the name of the state, then 95% of the grapes must come from that place, as compared to 75% under the federal standard for most states (except California [100%] and Oregon [95%]). If an AVA appears as the place of origin—the Columbia Valley AVA, for example—then 85% of the grapes in the wine had to have been harvested in the named AVA. This is consistent with federal law. The good news in Washington is that no generic-label wines, with their false and phony appellations, such as Burgundy or

Chablis, can be produced in Washington State; Washington's sparkling wines can't be called Champagne. Yes! We like this very much.

RESERVE

In Washington, the meaning of the label term "Reserve" is evolving. According to the Washington Wine Commission, while there are no official rules regarding the use of "reserve," there are some traditional parameters that many producers, especially the best and most high-profile producers, observe. These parameters include: "reserve" wines are produced only in the best vintages; the wines are produced from a rigorous selection of the best grapes and vineyard sites; the wine is produced in small quantities relative to the size of the producer; "reserve" wines sell for a higher price. While none of these voluntary practices carry the rule of law, it is good to see that Washington wine producers recognize that when the consumer sees the word "Reserve" on a wine label there is an expectation of something special, something unique. Let's hope the rest of the American wine industry, particularly in California, also recognizes that expectation and is prepared to do something to give some meaning to the term "Reserve."

MAJOR GRAPE TYPES

Washington is the largest producer of Riesling in the United States (the state's largest winery, Chateau Ste. Michelle, is the largest Riesling producer in the world!). Riesling has become Washington's signature grape, and the wines, from bone-dry to ultra-sweet, can be delicious. Especially in the dry and semi-dry versions, Washington Riesling is a great match for lighter foods, and particularly wonderful with spicy, smoky, and salty dishes, including a wide variety of what might broadly be called "ethnic" cuisines—particularly the vibrant foods of Asia and Latin America. The wines are mostly highly affordable as well, and increasingly easy to find throughout the United States.

Washington Riesling at its best has a floral nose and a clean and pure taste of fruit, especially peach and apricot, tempered by the refreshing acidity of green apple. On the nose and on the palate you might pick up some "minerally" aromatics and flavors that give the wine just a bit of earthiness. The wines are light- to medium-bodied and are the perfect example of an "anti-Chardonnay," as they are fermented in stainless steel, not in small oak barrels, and they are never the alcohol bombs that some clumsily made Chardonnay can be. While the focus in Washington is on the drier styles of Riesling, the sweeter versions, including late harvest wines and the rare Icewine, can be very pleasant, especially as an accompaniment to fruit-based desserts— pies and tarts without gobs of sugar—as well as soft and semi-soft cheeses.

Starting in the mid 1990s, the Riesling movement in Washington State got a boost from a partnership between Chateau Ste. Michelle and Dr. Ernst Loosen, one of the most respected Riesling producers in the world-famous Mosel Valley of Germany. The result of that partnership, "Eroica," is one of the finest New World Rieslings produced anywhere, juicily ripe with a salivating freshness and slight mineral quality. We hope that the other already fine producers of Washington Riesling will continue to respond to the challenge of this new standard. Picture yourself on an Olympic Peninsula waterfront (even in the rain) with fabulous local seafood and glorious local Riesling—ah, life is good!

Overall, Washington's wine production is split pretty evenly between white and red grapes. Riesling and Chardonnay are the leading white grapes of the state and Cabernet Sauvignon and Merlot are the leading reds. Chardonnay from Washington tends to be lighter than its California counterpart, with a more delicate profile, and a light touch of oak. Cabernet Sauvignon and Merlot from Washington are made in the familiar New World style, with lots of fruit up front and tannins in the background. The wines range from complex and expensive to pleasantly drinkable and affordable. Both Washington Merlot and Cabernet Sauvignon wines demonstrate true varietal character, and Merlot is often higher in acidity and better balanced than wines from warmer parts of California.

Rounding out the major white grape varietals planted in Washington are Sauvignon Blanc, Gewurztraminer, Semillon, Pinot Gris, and Viognier. Major red varietals include Syrah and Cabernet Franc, along with a smattering of Lemberger, Malbec, Pinot Noir, and Sangiovese.

WINEWISE TIP: If you ever get the opportunity to sample Washington State Syrah, do not hesitate. It is full-bodied but not overpowering, enrobed in a fruity/herbal/spicy mix of dark plums, licorice, and black pepper. Yummy, and you will want to go back for more. Also, Gewurztraminer deserves mention as a very enjoyable wine from this corner of the United States, sometimes produced dry or almost dry, other times left with a little sweetness to make it a bright, fruity summer white or an equally bright partner with Thai, Vietnamese, or Korean dishes.

CLIMATE

Washington State is more than Seattle, that vital but rainy birthplace of grunge. There is an AVA called Puget Sound in the Seattle area, but it's a very small player; less than 1% of Washington's wine grapes are grown here. The hub of Washington State wine activity is eastward, inland, on the desert side of the Cascade Mountain range, where the other 99% can be found.

The Columbia River Basin has a sunny disposition, with a good two hours of sunlight more per day than the average California vineyard. But that does not make the region unrelentingly hot. Like most deserts, the entire area enjoys relatively cool nighttime temperatures, an essential element in quality wine production. Sun and heat may seem like advantages for ripening, but too much heat can produce both high sugars and low

acids far too quickly in grapes that have not had enough time to fully develop all of their ripe flavor characteristics. They are like a young gymnast or violinist who shows precocious promise but never matures to an accomplished athlete or musician. Cool nighttime temperatures are an advantage, slowing down the vines' and grapes' development and allowing those grapes to enjoy every minute of the long daylight hours that are the blessing of the extreme northwestern United States.

We have to say it: size matters. The huge geographic area covered by Washington's AVAs means that there are many different, varied terrains in many different climatic pockets, with south-facing slopes offering more direct sun and heat for red grapes such as Cabernet Sauvignon, and cooler, north-facing slopes more suited to the delicate varieties such as Riesling. In many other grape-growing regions we might scoff at the possibility of several different grape varietals in the vineyards as a lack of direction. But in Washington State we applaud the growing of a broad variety of grapes, with each one taking advantage of different climatic conditions. Variety can be the spice of Washington wine, and we love spice!

WINEWISE WASHINGTON AVAS

Currently, there are 13 AVAs in Washington State. You very rarely see any wine labeled as simply "Washington State," mostly because almost all of the land that could possibly be planted to vineyards is covered by the huge Columbia Valley AVA, which accounts for 99% of vineyard acreage in the state, with 43,300 acres of vineyards (17,320 hectares) and the AVAs that lie within it: Yakima Valley (13,450 acres [5,800 hectares]), Walla Walla Valley (1,300 acres [520 hectares]), Horse Heaven Hills (10,580 acres [4,235 hectares]), Rattlesnake Hills (1,600 acres [640 hectares]), Red Mountain (1,270 acres [508 hectares]), Lake Chelan (250 acres [100 hectares]), Snipes Mountain (700 acres [280 hectares]), Ancient Lakes of Columbia Valley

(1,400 acres [560 hectares]), Naches Heights (40 acres [16 hectares]), and Wahluke Slope (6,645 acres [2660 hectares]). Adjacent to the Columbia Valley, on the Columbia River, which separates Washington from Oregon, is the much smaller AVA of Columbia Gorge (500 acres [200 hectares]), and toward the west is the Puget Sound AVA (178 acres [72 hectares]), which includes the cities of Olympia and Seattle.

COLUMBIA VALLEY

This is the big one, the AVA you are most likely to see on a bottle of Washington wine, simply because Columbia Valley and its 11 sub-AVAs produce almost all of the wine in the state. This set of AVAs also grows a very broad array of different grape types from a seemingly endless variety of climatic conditions. Columbia Valley is almost the "anti-appellation," representing everything that appellations are not supposed to be. It is too big and too diverse for anybody to make the claim that there is a Columbia Valley style. Since the creation of the Columbia Valley AVA in 1984, we have seen the 11 other sub-AVAs created within its boundaries, a sure—and welcome—sign that grape growers and wine producers are identifying and acting on geographic, topographic, and climatic differences.

That said, we would never suggest that you shy away from Columbia Valley wines. They are too plentiful and too good to avoid. By now, the savvy *WineWise* reader realizes that there are three main grape types that have captured attention in Columbia Valley—Riesling, Cabernet Sauvignon, and Merlot. And if you just cannot get enough Chardonnay, then by all means try the Chardonnay, too. With the immense size of the AVA, it is impossible to give specific information about climatic conditions, but if you read on the back label that the Cab or Merlot benefited from south-facing slopes that get the full impact of the sun, then go for it—it is unlikely you will be disappointed. In addition to being the state's largest wine producer and one of the top 10 wine producers in the nation, Chateau Ste. Michelle is also a

Columbia Valley label. Courtesy of Novelty Hill.

leader in high-quality sparkling wine production at very reasonable prices under the Domaine Ste. Michelle label, and in the development of single-vineyard varietal red and white still wines. Indeed, it is no exaggeration to say that Ste. Michelle is a sort of mini-Washington unto itself. Having tirelessly promoted the state's wines with attractively priced single varietals for many years, the company has been so successful that it was able to branch out into bubbly production and high-end single-vineyard wines. That is essentially what Washington is all about—well-made, affordable wines, plus some very fine top-notch specialties.

Other Columbia Valley wineries that produce fine single-varietal and blends, and whose wines are definitely worth trying include: 14 Hands, Ancestry Cellars, Barnard Griffin, Betz Family, Columbia Crest, Columbia Winery, Covey Run, Elevage, Elevation Cellars, Hogue, Januik/Novelty Hill, Kiona, and Pacific Rim, among several others. Note that wines from these and other quality-conscious Columbia Valley wine producers will most often use the Columbia Valley AVA on the label, but some are just as likely to use any of the 11 sub-AVAs within the Columbia Valley. We're going to discuss five of them right now.

YAKIMA VALLEY

Although Yakima Valley was Washington's first AVA, it is now within the large Columbia Valley AVA. Even so, it has maintained its reputation as a premium site for Chardonnay and Riesling, but

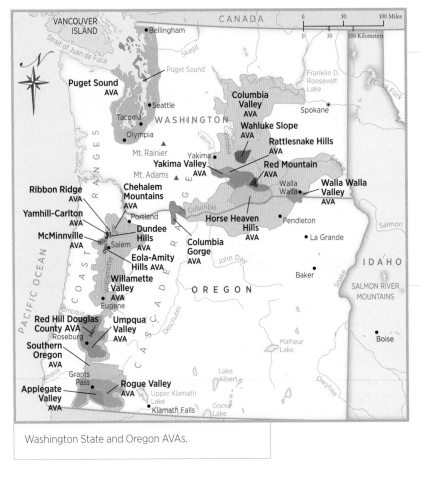

WASHINGTON STATE

- Columbia Gorge AVA (also in Oregon)
- Columbia Valley AVA (also in Oregon)
- Horse Heaven Hills AVA
- Puget Sound AVA
- Rattlesnake Hills AVA
- Red Mountain AVA
- Wahluke Slope AVA
- Walla Walla Valley AVA (also in Oregon)
- Yakima Valley AVA

OREGON

- Applegate Valley AVA
- Chehalem Mountains AVA
- Eola-Amity Hills AVA
- Dundee Hills AVA
- McMinnville AVA
- Ribbon Ridge AVA
- Red Hill Douglas County AVA
- Rogue Valley AVA
- Southern Oregon AVA
- Umpqua Valley AVA
- Willamette Valley AVA
- Yamhill-Carlton AVA

Washington State and Oregon AVAs.

especially for red grape types such as Cabernet Sauvignon, Merlot, and Syrah. This is a reflection of the south-facing slopes situated to the north of the west-to-east-flowing Yakima River. These slopes provide plenty of warm sun during the growing season. They also allow for "air drainage" during the cooler months at the beginning and end of the season—this means that cold air will not sit still long enough to cause a frost that could damage the vines. A number of independent growers have developed excellent reputations for their vineyards, and large and small wineries alike vie for the privilege to buy their grapes. One of the most well-known examples is Red Willow Vineyard, which focuses on Cabernet Sauvignon, Syrah, and Merlot. If you spot this name on a bottle of Yakima Valley wine, you will be in for a treat.

WALLA WALLA VALLEY

This is a special place. Being in the Walla Walla Valley, in the southeast interior of the state, is like being on an island ringed by a circle of mountains, far away from all other civilization. Not that Walla Walla is swank—it's down-country and farmer-friendly. Most of the people who make the wines here actually get their hands dirty and callused in the vineyards.

It's hot and dry most of the time, and, once again, Cabernet, Merlot, and Syrah dominate the red plantings, producing rich and ripe flavors of dark fruit, balanced by a refreshing streak of acidity. Chardonnay is the leading white varietal grown here. The local Blue Mountains provide some higher elevations at which grape varieties such as Gewurztraminer, Sangiovese, and Cabernet Franc do well in the cooler climate. There are small plantings of Grenache, Malbec, and Tempranillo as well. Wineries that produce consistently terrific wines include: Canoe Ridge, Cayuse, Corvus, Figgins/Leonetti, Gramercy Cellars, L'Ecole No. 41, Mark Ryan, Tertulia, and Woodward Canyon.

RED MOUNTAIN

This is Washington's smallest AVA, a modest 4,000 acres (1,600 hectares) in total, which is minuscule compared to most other AVAs in the state. Only about one-third of that area is planted to vineyards, again with Cab, Merlot, and Syrah taking up the most room. This is not at all surprising. Designated as an AVA in 2001, the area had already made a name for itself, with its warm, south-facing slopes, best suited to the fuller-flavored reds. Red Mountain wines can be quite expensive, but worth it. Look for the AVA to appear on wines produced by Col Solare, Cooper, Fidelitas, Hightower, Kiona, Portrait, Tapteil, Terra Blanca, and Upchurch.

HORSE HEAVEN HILLS

Approved as an AVA in 2005, Horse Heaven Hills is best known for Cabernet Sauvignon, Merlot, and Syrah for red wines, Riesling and Chardonnay for whites. Bordered by the Yakima Valley to the north and the Columbia River to the south, Horse Heaven Hills is a very windy area that benefits from well-drained sandy-loam soils. Oustanding producers of red wines include: Alder Ridge, Canyon's Edge, Champoux, Columbia Crest, Heaven's Cave, McKinley Springs, and Red Diamond.

RATTLESNAKE HILLS

An AVA since 2006, Rattlesnake Hills grows mostly red grapes: Cabernet Sauvignon, Malbec, Merlot, and Syrah are the big four; Chardonnay and Riesling are also planted. Most vineyards are located on high ridges and terraces that provide good air circulation to avoid late spring frosts. Interestingly, quite a few wines are produced from under-the-radar grapes, such as Petit Verdot,

Plowing the Horsepower Vineyard at Cayuse, Walla Walla's first winery to fully implement biodynamic farming in its vineyards. Photo by Tyson Kopfer; courtesy of Cayuse Vineyards.

Tempranillo, Grenache, and Mourvedre. A lot of the grapes here will end up in wines sporting the Columbia Valley or Yakima Valley AVA on their label, but resident Rattlesnake Hills wineries that proudly display their own sub-AVA include award winners Bonair, Hyatt, Knight Hill, Maison de Padgett, Portteus, Silver Lake, Steppe, and Tefft. Many of these wines are not distributed nationally, but take a look at www.rattlesnakehills.org to get more info.

The other AVAs of Washington State do not yet have major visibility in the wine world. They all add to the white and red (and sparkling) palette that composes the full portrait of Washington State wines.

For updated information about Washington State's AVAs, their wineries, and wines, check out www.washingtonwine.org.

Oregon

IN THE LATE 1960s AND EARLY 1970s, a number of disillusioned young men and women, unhappy about the mainstreaming and consumerization of their alternative, hippie lifestyle, left California. With no place farther west to move to, they headed north to Oregon and found new idyllic places to drop out. Among this happy band of wanderers were some California winemakers who had become similarly discontent with what they saw as too much emphasis on grape types and not enough consideration of soil and climate combinations.

Fortunately for us and for our *WineWise* readers, the wine industry has its fair share of mavericks and independents. The world benefits from their pioneer spirit in the form of new adventures and better wine. California had been concentrating on Cabernet Sauvignon and Chardonnay. These people wanted something else, and in Oregon they found the near perfect climate and soil conditions for Pinot Noir and related varieties. As a result of their efforts, the world now has another dimension of Pinot to consider, and all Pinot lovers are grateful for it. They have also raised the bar in terms of what is meant by quality Pinot Noir, not just for America but for the world. With Oregon as a model, Carneros was able to come into its own, New Zealand has developed its Pinot mecca in Central Otago, and way back in 2005 the actors and producers of the movie *Sideways* took us along on a road trip in Santa Barbara's Pinot Noir country.

CLIMATE

Unlike Washington State, Oregon's vineyards are located on the ocean side of the Cascade Mountains, so moisture picked up by westerly winds over the Pacific is dropped as the air currents rise and cool when they hit the mountains. This classifies the Oregon vineyard climate as distinctly cool and maritime, especially in the northern part of the state. In that fairly uniform climate, the range of grapes that can be grown is limited mostly to cool-climate varieties such as Pinot Noir, Riesling, Chardonnay, and Pinot Gris.

As you move southward toward the border with California, temperatures are warmer on average, and cloud cover and rainfall diminish, allowing warmer-climate grape varieties to fare well, including Cabernet Sauvignon, Merlot, Syrah, and Viognier.

GRAPE TYPES

Oregon is Pinot Noir country for most growers, winemakers, and wine lovers. Good Oregon Pinot delivers the kind of red fruit character that is associated with the grape, but it tends to be more in the cherry zone than raspberry or cranberry. It is a little denser and fuller than the average red Burgundy from France (see page 174) and is beautifully enhanced by clean, crisp acidity and firm tannins that take the wine a little beyond medium-bodied. Oregon's wine gurus obviously know how to grow the grapes to achieve full, ripe character and how to make those grapes into world-class wines. Broadly speaking, Pinot Noir is the most food-friendly wine on earth, pairing beautifully with intense fish preparations, just about all white meats, game, and leaner cuts of red meat. Oregon's much-heralded chefs and restaurateurs understand the versatility of Pinot Noir with Oregon's food bounty, matching the wine effortlessly with planked wild salmon or with lamb kebabs.

But there are other dimensions to the Oregon wine scene. The natural partner to Pinot Noir everywhere else in the world is Chardonnay, as evidenced in Champagne, Burgundy, and Carneros. But Oregon Chardonnay has had a hard time making a name for itself. Maybe that is simply because there is already an ocean of Chardonnay in the world. But that is not the whole story. The Chardonnay vines that were originally planted in Oregon were brought directly from California, where they worked well in the warm climate. Transplanted to cooler Oregon, they did not fare well, producing

Willamette Valley vineyards resting after a hard day's work.

wines that lacked the lemony zip that makes Chardonnay interesting. In the meantime, the fascination with Oregon Pinot Noir soared. Over the last 20 years, the vineyard acreage of Pinot has dramatically increased while plantings of Chardonnay have fallen. But the faithful still believe. They have researched strains of Chardonnay better suited to Oregon's cooler climate and longer growing season, and they are convinced they can make Chardonnay with verve and zip. Given the emphasis on Pinot Noir and the presence of Chardonnay, sparkling wine could be a good choice for Oregon, and sure enough, the Argyle winery has chosen to do just that, and very successfully, offering a line of high-quality bubblies made by the Champagne method.

Looking for a viable white wine to partner with their benchmark red, Pinot Noir, the Oregon growers and their diehard fans embraced a most unlikely candidate that has now become a real winner—Pinot Gris. Undoubtedly, Oregon Pinot Gris benefits from its association with the Italian version, Pinot Grigio (a small number of Oregon producers now use the Italian varietal name on their labels), but its star began to ascend long before the popularity of Pinot Grigio. Today, compared to Chardonnay, there are almost three times as many acres of Pinot Gris in Oregon; obviously a grape and wine that growers, winemakers, and consumers believe in. But believe this: Oregon Pinot Gris is not your average Pinot Grigio. Good Oregon Pinot Gris

will almost always display considerably more body and structure, with ripe melon flavors and a hint of orange scent. It is a beautiful wine to pair with freshly caught wild salmon, any other grilled firm-fleshed fish with pineapple-and-melon salsa, or spice-rubbed pork.

Riesling is a grape with great potential in Oregon, and certainly the climate seems to be conducive to great Riesling that displays ripe citrus fruit and zingy acidity with floral overtones. Recently, we have seen more wines in the national market, but Oregon Riesling is still a work in progress, and we continue to search for wines that demonstrate the delicacy and finesse that make Riesling special.

Moving away from the cool-climate grape types of the north, the southern part of Oregon tends to be far more varied in its plantings, with everything from Cabernet Sauvignon, Merlot, and Syrah, and even a few hundred acres of Tempranillo inland to Riesling and Gewurztraminer nearer the coast.

LANGUAGE OF THE LABEL

With the early and modern history of Oregon being concentrated on single-variety wines such as Pinot Noir, Chardonnay, and Pinot Gris, it is no surprise that the local wine industry pushed for stiffer regulations concerning varietal labels. For most Oregon wines, including Pinot Noir, Pinot Gris, Chardonnay, and Riesling—the "big

Oregon Pinot Noir, made from grapes grown in the Dundee Hills AVA. Courtesy of Domaine Drouhin Oregon.

Willamette Valley Pinot Gris.

four"—if a grape type is mentioned on a label, the wine must contain at least 90% of that grape, as compared to 75% in the federal regulations. The exceptions to the minimum percentage are wines made from grapes that are traditionally blended and can benefit from blending—such as blends of Cabernet Sauvignon, Merlot, and Cabernet Franc, or Syrah and Grenache, or Sauvignon Blanc and Semillon—which remain at 75% for a varietal-labeled wine. So, an Oregon Cabernet Sauvignon can have up to 25% Merlot and/or other grapes, but an Oregon Pinot Noir can only contain 10% other grapes. This approach is pretty consistent with the best traditional practices around the world. Blended wines represent a very small percentage of Oregon's total wine output.

In addition, Oregon requires a minimum of 95% for any place name that appears on the label, such as an AVA. This is 10% higher than the 85% for AVA mandated by the federal government. Finally, like its neighbor Washington, Oregon has banned the use of all generic terms on its wine labels, such as "Champagne" and "Burgundy." We'll drink to that.

AVAS

Oregon now has a total of 17 AVAs, though 10 of those have a brief history. Four of the 17 are relatively insignificant, including small portions

of the Columbia Valley, Walla Walla Valley, and Columbia Gorge AVAs that extend into Oregon from Washington. The Snake River Valley AVA is shared with Idaho. The AVA that garners all the attention and has brought the most fame to Oregon is the Willamette Valley, which begins just south of the city of Portland, on the northern border of the state, and extends to just south of the state capital, Eugene, in the central coastal part of the state. Within the boundaries of the Willamette Valley AVA lie six sub-AVAs: Chehalem Mountain, Dundee Hills, Eola-Amity Hills, McMinnville, Ribbon Ridge, and Yamhill Carlton District.

The other AVA with a lengthy track record is Southern Oregon, an umbrella AVA encompassing the smaller AVAs of Umpqua Valley including Red Hill Douglas County AVA, Rogue Valley, Elkton Oregon, and Applegate Valley.

WILLAMETTE VALLEY AVA

This is Oregon's most famous AVA, the one with all the glitterati of medal-winning winemakers, both maverick and mainstream. We have found that the sub AVAs of the Willamette Valley express their own unique character, their *terroir*. Whether it's the rocky minerality of Yamhill Carlton, the iron and full-bodied style from Dundee and McMinnville, or the lighter fruitiness of Eola, there is something for every Pinot Noir disciple here. Richly textured Pinot Gris excels here as well, and the saints of Chardonnay continue to seek out the right plots that offer the cool climate and mineral-laden soils Chardonnay loves.

There is no "cheap" Oregon Pinot Noir, and that is how it should be. Pinot Noir needs care and attention, and that costs money. For moderately expensive versions of Pinot Noir, Pinot Gris, and Chardonnay, we suggest the following producers—look for their basic line (most will also produce more expensive bottlings) or perhaps the label that carries the appellation "Oregon" rather than "Willamette Valley": King Estate, Acrobat, A to Z, Bridgeview, Eola Hills, Willamette Valley Vineyards, Erath, Sokol Blosser, Archery Summit, Rex Hill, Firesteed, and Cooper Creek (certified biodynamic). Argyle's sparkling wine also fits in here.

For more expensive wines, try these best bottles: Adelsheim, Ponzi, Bergstom, Penner-Ash, Evening Land, Soter, Panther Creek, Eyrie, Chehalem, Beaux Freres, Domaine Drouhin, Ken Wright, Shea, Brick House, Domaine Serene, Anne Amie, Amity, Benton Lane, Bethel Heights, Hamacher, Henry Estate, Panther Creek, St. Innocent, and WillaKenzie Estate.

SOUTHERN OREGON AVA (and Its Smaller AVAs of Umpqua Valley, Red Hill Douglas County, Rogue Valley, Elkton Oregon, and Applegate Valley)

As soon as you leave the Willamette Valley and travel south toward the other AVAs, the hubbub dies down. There is a noticeable absence of the grape patriotism that pervades the northern part of the state. Instead of "All Hail the Mighty Pinot" as anthem, the song is about diversity and differences, caused in large part by a lack of uniform climate. The Willamette Valley AVA in northern Oregon is a relatively compact area, centered around the Willamette River, but the Southern Oregon AVA and its smaller sub AVAs fan out to include protected, warmer inland river valleys as well as cooler coastal regions. You will find almost everything planted here, from Riesling to Syrah, including northern Italian

Willamette Valley vineyards.

varieties such as Dolcetto and Spanish varieties including Albarino and Tempranillo.

Both the Rogue Valley and the Applegate Valley are hemmed in by mountains that make for an overall warm climate favoring Cabernet, Merlot, Syrah, and the like. What will help them on the road to international recognition is a substantial difference between day and nighttime temperatures that keeps acidity levels high in the finished wines, making the flavors seem fresher and longer-lasting in the mouth.

Vineyard land is cheaper in southern Oregon, which makes for a greater probability of finding relative bargains or moderately expensive wines from producers such as Foris, Bridgeview, Hillcrest, Kriselle, Abacela (which specializes in Spanish and Italian varietals), Girardet, Spangler, Reustle Prayer Rock, Marshanne Landing (making "out of this world" Rhone and Bordeaux blends), Schultz, Agate Ridge, Cricket Hill, Del Rio, Cliff Creek, Devitt, Chateau Lorane, and Madrone Mountain (dessert wines).

New York State

BEFORE WE GET TO SINGING the praises of New York's best wines—and there is much to sing about—we need to give you the full picture. Too much New York State wine continues to be made from native varietals, such as Niagara, Catawba, and especially Concord grapes (though most Concords are used for jams, jellies, and juices). We don't recommend these wines unless you like a grapey, jammy wine that really tastes more like overly sweet juice and harsh alcohol and not much else.

New York also produces many wines produced from hybrid varietals—biological crosses of vinifera and native parents. Examples of prominent hybrids in New York State are Seyval Blanc, Traminette, and Vidal (white) and Marechal Foch, Noiret, and Baco Noir (red). The reason for hybrids in New York State: they are resistant to cold weather and plant diseases, and because of their parentage, they give an approximation of vinifera-quality wine. Wines made from these and other hybrid grapes can be tasty, and as a category,

hybrid-based wines are getting better and better. Still, when compared to fine examples of vinifera-based wines, the hybrids often suffer. Most hybrid wines are sold at the producer's winery, with a small amount of wine in wide distribution.

Now for the good news. We are happy to report that we've tasted great Hudson River Region Chardonnay that blows away a lot of California Chardonnay selling for more than twice the price. Many American Rieslings are not worth your time or money, but we believe that fine Finger Lakes Rieslings are among the best in the country. Cabernet Sauvignon, Merlot, and Cabernet Franc from Long Island have all garnered national and international attention, and the quality can be sublime. As with all regions, the reputation of the producer is important when purchasing, but few New York State wine producers are household names, so get ready to become WineWise about the best New York wines. Note that to get some of the best wines from small producers, you may have to visit the winery or make a virtual visit online.

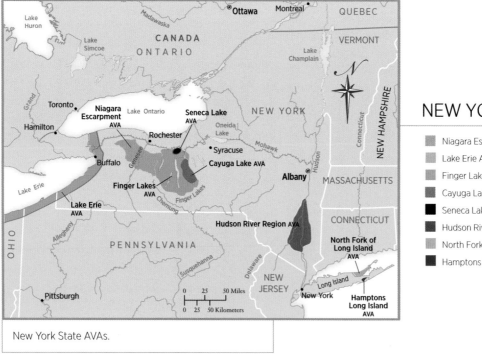

NEW YORK STATE

- Niagara Escarpment AVA
- Lake Erie AVA
- Finger Lakes AVA
- Cayuga Lake AVA
- Seneca Lake AVA
- Hudson River Region AVA
- North Fork of Long Island AVA
- Hamptons Long Island AVA

New York State AVAs.

AVAS

Currently, New York State has a total of nine AVAs.

NIAGARA ESCARPMENT REGION AVA

Bordering Lake Ontario to the north, this AVA contains nine wineries and about 400 acres (150 hectares) of vineyards. This cool region in New York State's "snow belt," hovering around the city of Buffalo, should be an area for Riesling, Chardonnay, and Pinot Noir to shine. Recommended producers are Eveningside Vineyards, Niagara Landing, Schulze, and Warm Lake Estate.

LAKE ERIE AVA

With a sea of Concord grapes covering 20,000 acres (8,000 hectares) in New York State (Lake Erie is a multistate AVA, containing parts of Ohio and Pennsylvania as well), growers in this region sell most of their fruit for jams, jellies, and juices. Exceptions to the rule among the 20 or so resident wineries that produce fruit wines and other novelties, 21 Brix, Woodbury Winery, and Johnson Estate, along with a few others, make some good wines.

THE FINGER LAKES AND TWO SUB-AVAS: CAYUGA LAKE AND SENECA LAKE

With more than 10,000 acres (4,000 hectares) of vineyards and about 90 wineries, the Finger Lakes (with its two sub-AVAs, Cayuga Lake and Seneca Lake) is the most important wine region in New York State, producing close to 90% of New York State's total wine production. Lakeside vineyard soils provide excellent drainage, and the moderating effects of Canandaigua, Keuka, Seneca, and Cayuga lakes control climatic extremes in the winter and summer.

Thanks to the pioneering work of the late Dr. Konstantin Frank (an émigré from Ukraine) and the late Charles Fournier (former president of Veuve Clicquot Champagne in France) in the 1950s, vinifera grapes came to be accepted as

Bully Hill, founded by the eccentric and creative Walter Taylor, produces wines made mostly from hybrid grapes in New York State's Finger Lakes wine region. Bully Hill labels feature Taylor's own humorous and witty artwork. Courtesy of Bully Hill Vineyards.

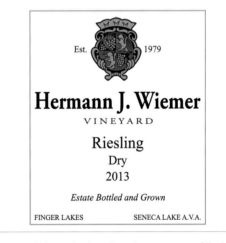

Hermann Wiemer has long been known as one of the best Riesling producers in the Finger Lakes wine region.

commercially viable in the Finger Lakes region. Frank and Fournier forged an alliance that eventually brought the entire New York State wine industry to a new level of quality. Today, Konstantin Frank's legacy is carried on by his grandson, Fred Frank, who continues to produce very fine Riesling, a lovely Rkatsiteli (the most planted white grape in Eastern Europe), extraordinary Gruner Veltliner (the best we've tasted outside of its native Austria), and under the Chateau Frank label, some of the finest vintage-dated Champagne-method sparklers produced anywhere in the United States.

Today, true Riesling lovers go nuts for Riesling wines from any of the Finger Lakes AVAs, especially the dry to semi-dry styles. Chardonnay and Champagne-method sparkling wines are also uniformly good to excellent. The wines are good to great values, especially in whites and bubbly. The wineries of the Finger Lakes welcome hundreds of thousands of visitors every year, and several wineries have tasting rooms, cafés, restaurants, and inns.

The best producers include Anthony Road, Atwater Estates, Billsboro, Chateau Frank (sparkling wines) and Dr. Konstantin Frank's Vinifera Wine Cellars (still wines), Chateau LaFayette Renau, Damiani, Fox Run, Fulkerson, Glenora, Hazlitt 1852, Heron Hill, Hosmer, Hunt Country, Keuka Springs, Knapp, Lamoreaux Landing, McGregor, Rooster Hill, Keuka Overlook, Prejean, Red Newt, Salmon Run (second label for Dr. Frank, extremely good values), Sheldrake Point, Standing Stone, Stony Lonesome, Swedish Hill, Wagner (fourth-generation growers, winery and brewery on site), and Hermann J. Wiemer (extraordinary wines and vinifera vines nursery), among others.

THE HUDSON RIVER REGION AVA

All three *WineWise* authors live in the Hudson Valley, and so we would love to heap praise on all 500 acres (200 hectares) of our local vineyards and the more than 30 local wineries. Unfortunately, we can't. There are some gems, but there is still too much hybrid-based wine, some of it good, some not so good, produced here. The major producer of high-quality wine, especially Chardonnay, Pinot Noir, Cabernet Franc, and the historically Italian varietal Tocai Friulano, is Millbrook Winery (which, in fairness, has an owner with much deeper pockets than the other producers along the Hudson).

Other notable producers include Whitecliff Vineyards (Whitecliff is embarking on a highly promising sparkling wine project), BashaKill Winery (excellent estate-bottled Pinot Noir and Cabernet Franc, aged in their own caves), Hudson-Chatham Winery (excellent estate hybrids, especially Seyval Blanc, Chelois, and Baco Noir), and Clinton Vineyards, which produces the best Seyval Blanc in the region.

Konstantin Frank was a pioneering, quality-minded wine producer in the Finger Lakes; his efforts began in the 1950s. His winery, now run by his grandson Fred Frank, is one of a few American producers of Rkatsiteli, a delicious off-dry wine made from the grape of the same name.

Millbrook Winery is the leading producer of consistently high-quality wines in the Hudson River Region of New York State. Millbrook, whose reputation was established with good Chardonnay, Pinot Noir, and Cabernet Franc, is one of very few producers of the Italian varietal Tocai Friulano (officially known as Friulano in the European Union) in New York State. The wine is crisp, dry, aromatic, delicious, and affordable.

Producers that do a good job with some vinifera, but also hybrids and fruit wines, include Alison, Adair, Baldwin, Benmarl (with some very good red hybrid-based wines), Brimstone Hill, Cascade Mountain, Cereghino Smith (try "Eaten by Bears" red Rhone-style blend), Glorie Farm, Palaia (very good estate Cabernet Franc), Robibero, Stoutbridge, and Tousey wineries.

LONG ISLAND AVA AND THE TWO SUB-AVAS: THE NORTH FORK OF LONG ISLAND AVA AND THE HAMPTONS, LONG ISLAND AVA

Long Island is probably the most sophisticated of all of New York State's wine regions. Long Island vineyards are planted solely to vinifera grapes; no hybrids, no native jam-and-jelly grapes. If you look at a map of the world, you'll see that Long Island is at the same latitude as Bordeaux, so it is no wonder that Merlot, Cabernet Sauvignon, and Cabernet Franc are the focus of the Long Island wine industry.

Long Island does have an inherent problem that it is unlikely to overcome: the cost of land and the small amount of agricultural land available for purchase. Long Island is kind of a "boutique" wine region, with the overwhelming majority of the wines available only at the wineries and in fine restaurants and select retail shops in the New York City metropolitan area.

Considering that the expansion of Long Island's wine industry is limited, it has come a long way over the last 40 years or so (the first winery, Hargrave, was established in 1973). In the early 1980s, when there were fewer than a dozen wineries on Long Island, we can remember going to tastings and spitting out the wine not because it was the professional thing to do but because it was the only thing to do. However, as the vines aged and professional vineyard managers and winemakers came on board, the wines improved quickly.

In addition to the traditional red Bordeaux varietals, Long Island produces good Chardonnay, some nice Gewurztraminer and Riesling, and is beginning to dabble in Sauvignon Blanc and

Lenz is a major Long Island wine producer, and the winery consistently produces very fine white, red, and sparkling wines from grapes grown in its own vineyards.

other white and red varietals. Paumanok winery is the first (and perhaps only) producer of Chenin Blanc in New York State, and the wine is incredibly good. Lenz Merlot is an extremely earthy, balanced, ageworthy wine, able to share a table with the most elegant dinner, and yet it's affordable. Channing Daughters produces some of the most unusual wines in Long Island, featuring a wide variety of both classic varietal-labeled wines and extraordinary off-the-beaten path blends.

The overwhelming majority of Long Island's vineyards and wineries are located in the North Fork AVA (more than 50 wineries), with a smattering in The Hamptons AVA (just six). Recommended producers include Anthony Nappa, Bedell, Channing Daughters, Corey Creek, Duck Walk, Harbes Family, Jamesport, Lenz, Lieb Family, Macari, Martha Clara, McCall, One Woman, Osprey's Dominion, Palmer, Paumanok, Peconic Bay, Pellegrini, Pindar, Pugliese, Raphael, Shinn Estate, Schneider, Sparkling Pointe, The Grapes of Roth, Vineyard 48, and Wölffer Estate.

For more information on New York State wines and wineries, or to buy wines (especially from the small producers without wide distribution), go to Uncork New York at www.newyorkwines.org.

6

WAY DOWN SOUTH

SOUTH AMERICA

WINES FROM CHILE AND ARGENTINA ARE IMMENSELY POPULAR IN THE UNITED STATES WINE MARKET. IN PARTICULAR, Cabernet Sauvignon and Sauvignon Blanc wines from Chile as well as Malbec wines from Argentina have captured our imaginations and palates.

We often think of South American wines as basic wines that provide good value, and that's okay because there is an important place for such budget-based wines. But we need to take another look at the quality of these wines because although we can still find drinkable varietal-labeled wines from Chile or Argentina for under 15 bucks, we can also find memorable, singular, expensive wines—both white and red—that are helping to redefine what it means to be a South American wine.

Let's take a look at the wines of Chile and Argentina. We think you'll find there's a lot to learn and a lot to enjoy about the wines from these two countries. When it comes to South American wines, if you're looking for bargains, you've found your region. If you're looking for a burgeoning quality-based wine region, you'll be glad you're here, too.

Let's start with a trip to Chile . . . *¡Vamos!*

Chile: Bigger, better, and bargains

CHILE, THE FOURTH-LARGEST EXPORTER OF wine to the United States, makes some wonderful wines and has established a solid reputation in the U.S. wine market for good value and quality, producing wines made mostly from internationally known varietals with good track records: Cabernet Sauvignon, Syrah, Merlot, Chardonnay, and Sauvignon Blanc.

Chile has also had success with the Carmenere grape, a varietal with its ancestral roots in Bordeaux, where it is currently just about nonexistent. Chilean winemakers love to work with Carmenere, producing both varietal wines and Carmenere blends, usually partnered with Cabernet Sauvignon.

Chile entered the American market with a bang, providing drinkable wines at highly affordable prices, sometimes less than $5 per bottle. Those days are gone, but WineWise wine shoppers still should have no problem finding many Chilean wines priced under $10. Chile has not confined itself to bargain wines, however. Increasingly, we see quite a few truly expensive wines from Chile on retail shelves and on wine lists. Some of these wines are produced solely by Chilean winemakers, while others are made in partnership with French and American producers.

For Chile to find a toehold in the American luxury wine market, ironically it has to overcome its reputation as a supplier of bargain brands to appreciative and responsive wine consumers looking for value. Think about it: when you're out to dinner and want a special—and expensive—wine, is Chile the first place you think about? In most cases, unless the diner is a patriotic Chilean or has experience with a luxe Chilean import, he or she is thinking California, France, Italy, maybe Spain, or even Oregon Pinot Noir. For most of us, when it comes to expensive wines, Chile is not even on our radar screen.

Chile probably doesn't need *WineWise*'s help to sell its well-made value-driven wines. In the basic "fighting varietal" (fighting for retail shelf space with other $12-and-under wines), Chile is doing perfectly well, thank you. Whether or not Chile will become a major player in luxury wines is currently an unanswered question, but the ultra-premium Chilean wine industry believes it has the goods and will continue to produce these extraordinary wines, hoping to reach a larger audience.

Concha y Toro's Don Melchor vineyard in Chile's Maipo Valley, at the foot of the Andes Mountains. Don Melchor Cabernet Sauvignon is one of the finest wines produced in the Southern Hemisphere, and it's expensive. Photo courtesy of Banfi Vintners.

THE LANGUAGE OF THE LABEL

Chile, like all New World wine producers, uses varietal labels for the overwhelming majority of its wines, which makes it easy for consumers to buy Chilean wines. If a varietal name appears on a label, the wine must be made from at least 85% of that named grape. Other labels are proprietary—fantasy names, just like some of the best-known wines from California ("Opus One," "Insignia," etc.). Here you'll find labels that read "Alpha M," "Almaviva," "Clos Apalta," and so on.

Chile's vineyards cover a vast area of the country and are centered in the country's numerous river valleys. In the past, too many grapes were being harvested in these vineyards, and the overcropping led to diluted flavors. The best producers, realizing that they are in a highly competitive international wine market, have abandoned this practice, and the overall quality of Chile's wines has markedly improved.

In addition to the name of the grape and the name of the producer, you may sometimes find on the label terms such as "*Especial*" (the wine is aged a minimum of two years), "*Reserva*" (at least four years of aging), or rarely "*Gran Vino*" (six years minimum of aging). Beware the term "*Reserva Especial*," a marketing phrase with no legal meaning.

Marques de Casa Concha Cabernet Sauvignon is a single-vineyard estate-bottled red wine from the Puente Alto wine region of Chile. This is an excellent wine, with a moderate price (about $20). Courtesy of Marques de Casa Concha/Concha y Toro.

Of course, the names of Chile's wine regions will appear on wine labels. When a region (*denominacion*) is named, at least 85% of the grapes had to be harvested in that region. On the map of Chile (page 118) are the names of the major wine regions and subregions that you're likely to find on labels.

WINE REGIONS IN CHILE'S VALLE CENTRAL

The Maipo Valley is the most famous wine region here, with a reputation for good to excellent Cabernet Sauvignon, Merlot, and Carmenere. Also look for Puente Alto and Pirque, Maipo subregions with vineyards that produce stellar Cab and Merlot.

The reputation of the Rapel Valley, a reliable source of Cabernet Sauvignon, has been eclipsed by its subregion, the Colchagua Valley, where several boutique wineries and international partnerships have sprung up since the 1990s.

WINE REGIONS IN CHILE'S ACONCAGUA VALLEY

Aconcagua grows a lot of Cabernet Sauvignon, Merlot, Syrah, and Carmenere, and it has also become the focus for several international wine projects, anchored, of course, by Cabernet Sauvignon and blends. The Aconcagua subregion of the Casablanca Valley benefits from the cool breezes and fog generated by the nearby Pacific Ocean and has become the most prized *denominacion* for white wines, in particular Sauvignon Blanc, Chardonnay, and a bit of Gewurztraminer. These whites have up until now been obscured by the Cab-centric nature of the Chilean wine industry and are still good to great values (about $8 and up), but we predict that this will not be the case much longer, so check them out now. The new and promising close-to-the-ocean cool-climate Aconcagua subregions of Leyda

CHILE
Wine Regions and Subregions

■ Elqui Valley
■ Limari Valley
■ Choapa Valley

Aconcagua and Casablanca
▨ Aconcagua Valley
▨ Casablanca Valley

Central Valley
▨ Maipo Valley
▨ San Antonio Valley
▨ Cachapoal Valley
▨ Colchagua Valley
▨ Curico Valley
▨ Maule Valley

Southern Region
▨ Itata Valley
▨ Bio Bio Valley
▨ Malleco Valley

Wine regions of Chile.

and San Antonio are producing fine examples of Sauvignon Blanc, Chardonnay, and—perhaps most important for varietal diversity in Chile's wine industry—Pinot Noir.

CHILEAN WINES: THE CURRENT PICTURE

If it were not for the worldwide popularity of Cabernet Sauvignon, it's quite possible there would be no modern Chilean wine industry. Cab is the grape that defines Chilean wine and represents baseline quality for almost all of Chile's wine producers, especially those who seek export markets.

Most of the bargain-priced Chilean Cabernet Sauvignon is made to satisfy thirsty, price-conscious consumers who like their wines to be fruit-driven, clean, and medium- to full-bodied but without any hint of harsh, bitter tannins. Chile produces these wines in abundance, and we recommend them for informal meals featuring either white or red meat, as well as richer pasta dishes or a meaty pizza. The wines can be enjoyed immediately and will be fine to drink for two or three years after you purchase them. These value-driven wines have a big presence in U.S. retail markets and are likely to show up on wine lists of informal bistros and bars that serve food, as well as a growing number of chain and theme restaurants across the country.

Our field research reveals something you really need to know about Chilean Cab: for a few dollars more—say, between $15 and $25—you can find wonderful, complex, ageworthy, *terroir*-driven Chilean wines that will knock your socks off. Some of the wines are estate-bottled or are made from grapes harvested in a single vineyard. If you love good Cabernet Sauvignon, these wines really deserve your attention.

Merlot has a checkered history in Chile due to misidentification—intentional or otherwise—of the grape, confusing it with Carmenere. All that stuff has come to an end, and Chile is producing some good Merlot, mostly in the international, juicy, touch-of-sweetness style.

Carmenere has become Chile's own grape, and we are seeing more varietal-labeled Carmenere in the market, mostly at attractive prices. We like Carmenere, which is kind of a lighter-style Cab/Merlot blend, but rolled into one grape; it's also a great blender with Cabernet Sauvignon. We encourage you to try varietal-labeled Carmenere, which is tremendously versatile with a wide variety of foods, increasingly easy to find, and a true WineWise value.

Chile has always produced a bit of Syrah, but with this varietal's growing popularity, sometimes under the guise of its other name, Shiraz, more high-quality Chilean Syrah has entered the U.S. market. Be the first in your neighborhood to taste one, especially the expensive but extraordinary Montes "Folly," with label art by Ralph Steadman. Less expensive bottles are also worth a try, especially if you like full-bodied reds. Another WineWise choice.

White wines live in the shadow of Chilean reds, but this is changing, and not all that slowly. As people get off the Cabernet bandwagon, get back on, and then get off once more, Chilean Chardonnay grown in cool-climate regions is beginning to generate international buzz, and we've tasted some good wines at affordable prices. We're happy to report that the buzz generated by Chilean Sauvignon Blanc is even louder, and with good reason: Chile's best Sauvignon Blanc wines are classics, with refreshing lime juice and green fruits, real depth of flavor, lovely texture, and incredible food-friendliness, especially with fish. Right now, prices are still attractive, but they are sure to go up.

OUR FAVORITE PRODUCERS

Much like Australia, many Chilean wine producers make "product lines" of wines that begin with inexpensive entries, include some moderately expensive choices, and go all the way to really costly. We'll identify some of the wines in each of these categories.

> In the category of bargain and super-bargain producers from Chile (under $20) are Alfasi (kosher), Anakena, Apaltagua, Aresti, Caliterra, Canepa, Casa Julia, Casa Lapostolle, Casas Patronales, Casillero del Diablo, Concha y Toro, Cono Sur, Cousino-Macul, Echeverria, Luis Felipe Edwards, Errazuriz, Frontera, Hacienda El Condor, Haras de Pirque, Mapocho, Montes, MontGras, Morande, La Playa, Root:1, Santa Alicia, Santa Ema, Santa Carolina, Santa Rita "120," Sunrise, Tarapaca, Miguel Torres, Undurraga, Los Vascos, Veramonte, Walnut Crest, Xplorador, and Yelcho, among many others.

Aurelio Montes is one of the best winemakers in Chile. He produces wines that sell for well under $10 to well over $100. His "Alpha" series sells for under $20, his "Alpha M" series for more than $50. Courtesy of Montes Wines.

Terrunyo

Carmenere

D.O. Peumo Vineyard
Cachapoal Valley

Vineyard Selection
(Block 27)

Chile

A site-specific unfiltered Carmenere from Chile, from a single block of a single vineyard. Carmenere is an important red grape, both for blending with Cabernet Sauvignon and as the grape for its own varietal-labeled wines. Courtesy of Terrunyo/Concha y Toro.

Many people told Aurelio Montes that it was "folly" to try to make a good Syrah in Chile. He proved them wrong by growing his grapes on a mountain estate in the Apalta Valley and making an extraordinary (and very expensive) wine from those grapes. Label art by Ralph Steadman; courtesy of Montes Wines.

Moving up a notch, to wines that are moderately expensive to expensive (about $15 to $35): Carmen "Reserve," Casa Lapostolle "Cuvee Alexandre," Concha y Toro "Marques de Casa Concha" (fine estate-bottled Cab and Merlot from Puente Alto), Concha y Toro "Terrunyo," Cousino-Macul "Finis Terrae" and "Antiguas Reserva," Luis Felipe Edwards "Dona Bernarda Coleccion Privada," Errazuriz "Grand Selection," Haras de Pirque "Elegance," Matetic, Montes "Alpha," La Playa "Maxima," Santa Ema "Catalina," Santa Rita "Medalla Real," Sincerity (from biodynamic vineyards), Miguel Torres "Cordillera" and "Manso de Velasco," Valdivieso "RSV" and "Single Vineyard," Los Vascos "Reserva," and Veramonte "Primus."

For wines that are truly expensive ($35 and up), try Almaviva, Antiyal (from biodynamic vineyards), Casa Lapostolle "Clos Apalta," Montes "Folly," "Alpha M," and "Purple Angel," Concha y Toro "Don Melchor" and "Amelia," Domaine Paul Bruno, Errazuriz "Don Maximiano," Santa Rita "Casa Real" and "Triple C," Valdivieso "Caballo Loco," and Los Vascos "Le Dix."

Some bubbly is produced by Valdivieso; go for those wines made by the Champagne method: Brut Nature, Extra Brut, Grand Brut, and Grand Demi-Sec.

Argentina: Wines that know how to tango

Argentina is the sixth-largest wine producer in the world, and the largest producer in all of South America, producing far more wine than its neighbor Chile. Until recently, Argentina was a sleeping giant of the wine world. In the last 10 to 15 years, however, Argentina's wine industry has awakened and, at least in the U.S. export market, become as lively as the night life in Buenos Aires. The wines are as delicious as a dish of *churrasco* (barbecued beef on skewers) with *chimichurri* (a garlic/parsley vinaigrette) and as seductive as the tango.

Most of Argentina's vineyards are located in the western part of the country, where the Andes

Mountains (which border Chile) provide cool air currents that benefit the climate in the vineyards. Running north to south, the prime grape-growing regions create a strip of more than 12,000 square miles (19,300 square kilometers). The topography of Argentina's vineyards is varied, encompassing valley floors, mountaintops, and everything in between.

Almost all of Argentina's high-quality red wines and many of the whites that we find in the U.S. market are sourced from the gigantic Mendoza region—60,000 square miles (95,500 square kilometers) with 62,500 acres (25,000 hectares) of vines in central Argentina—the largest wine region in the Southern Hemisphere. Another important wine-growing region for whites is Cafayate, located in the northwest province of Salta. Cafayate's best cool-climate vineyards are sited at about 5,000 feet (1,500 meters) above sea level.

Just about all wines produced in Argentina that are exported to the United States are "*vinos finos*," considered the best wines that the country has to offer. *Vinos finos* represent less than 15% of Argentina's wine production. Despite the fact that these are elite wines, you can find extraordinary values among the many Argentine wines now available in the U.S. market, including very good wines in the $8 to $20 range.

THE LANGUAGE OF THE LABEL

Like wines from other New World producers, the great majority of Argentine wines feature varietal labels. There's nothing to confuse the consumer on the label, and often the only Spanish wording is the name of the wine producer and sometimes the name of the grape.

ARGENTINA
Main Wine Regions

- Salta
- Tucuman
- Catamarca
- La Rioja
- San Juan
- Mendoza
- La Pampa
- Río Negro

Wine regions of Argentina.

GET TO KNOW MALBEC

Argentina produces wines from many of the international varietals (Chardonnay and Cabernet Sauvignon, for example), and because of the country's Hispanic and Italian history and culture, winemakers also produce wines made from Italian varietals, such as Sangiovese and Nebbiolo (see page 192). But Argentina has captured the hearts and taste buds of wine lovers around the world with one red grape: Malbec. A classic blending grape in Bordeaux, Malbec is the primary varietal of Cahors, a red wine produced in the southwest of France. However, more Malbec is grown in Argentina than anywhere else on the planet.

In Argentina, Malbec is produced as a single-varietal wine and also often appears labeled as either Cabernet Sauvignon/Malbec or Malbec/Cabernet Sauvignon, depending on which varietal dominates the wine. These red blends are terrific—full-bodied, balanced, and well-structured, all in a tasty nexus of black fruits. But we are even more enthusiastic about single-varietal Malbec from Argentina, because it is a unique tasting experience. Argentina's best Malbecs are incredibly earthy and powerful, but with a beautiful balance of fruit, acid, and tannins that makes them wonderful accompaniments to a meal.

It has been said, only partly in jest, that Argentina really doesn't have a cuisine; it has beef. Like so many jokes, this one is grounded in

Malbec, a blending grape in Bordeaux, has found its true home in Argentina, where it is the most important varietal. Quality is good to excellent at all price levels. This Trapiche Malbec sells for under $12 and is a good wine and a very good value.

reality. Argentines consume more beef per capita than anyone else on the face of the earth, and the quality of the meat from their grass-fed cattle is legendary. We can't think of too many wines that enhance the flavors, textures, and aromas of a perfectly prepared beef dish as well as or better than Malbec from Argentina. As with so many other Argentine wines, you can find Malbec at different price points, but don't shy away from entry-level wines that cost less than $10, especially if you're new to the varietal; they can be really enjoyable.

A WONDERFUL WHITE: TORRONTES IS TERRIFIC

Although Argentina has made its current international reputation largely on its success with the red Malbec wine, it also produces wonderful white wines from the Torrontes grape. Still little known by all but the WineWise, Torrontes is beginning to gain a stellar reputation by word of mouth. We love the unique flavor of Torrontes: the zippy green apple acidity of Sauvignon Blanc coupled with the exotic spice of Gewurztraminer. What Malbec is to beef, Torrontes is to fish and white meats. This is a wine that can handle spicy food, too; jerk chicken comes to mind, or stir-fried tofu Szechuan-style.

The best sites in Argentina to plant Torrontes are found in the high-elevation, cool-climate vineyards of Cafayate. Luckily, you don't have to climb mountains to enjoy this wine, and you don't have to pay for the trip, either. Most Torrontes is currently priced in the $7 to $20 range, but when word gets out about this luscious wine, expect the price to go up—we hope not as high as its vineyards in the Andes.

Some of the best Argentine producers are Alamos, Alta Vista, Altos Las Hormigas, Balbi, Susana Balbo, BenMarco, Valentin Bianchi, Bodini, Broquel, Catena Zapata, Crios, Finca

Susana Balbo is one of the leading winemakers of Argentina; her name on the label is a virtual guarantee of quality. Her Torrontes is fresh, fruity, off-dry, affordable, and delicious. Courtesy of Dominio del Plata.

Flichman, Funky Llama, Gusto, Huarpe, Kaiken, Hermanos La Posta, Lurton, Melipal, Monte Lomas, Montes, Navarro Correas, Norton, Paqual Toso, Peñaflor, Don Rodolfo, Familia Rutini, Salentein, Santa Julia, Ricardo Santos, Tango Sur, Terrazas de los Andes, Trapiche, Trivento, Trumpeter, Weinert, and Zuccardi.

7

WAY DOWN SOUTH

AUSTRALIA, NEW ZEALAND, SOUTH AFRICA

IN ADDITION TO SOUTH AMERICA, THE SOUTHERN HEMISPHERE IS VERY WELL REPRESENTED IN THE WINE WORLD by the nations of Australia, New Zealand, and South Africa. Of those, New Zealand's wine industry is relatively young compared with the other two, which boast grape-growing and winemaking records back to the 1700s. Our organization of these three nations into the same chapter is not meant to suggest that their wines are similar—each nation has its own idiosyncratic style. However, there are some common factors that are worth pointing out. In the Southern Hemisphere, the climate gets cooler as you head south, away from the equator. Also, the harvesting season for Southern Hemisphere grape growers is early March to late April, depending on exactly how warm or cool the location is. This means that the new wine from the most recent vintage in the Southern Hemisphere will appear on shelves about six months before the Northern Hemisphere versions. You should bear this in mind if you are looking for freshness and youthful vivacity in a wine, especially a white wine—a 2014 wine from the Southern Hemisphere is "older" than a 2014 wine from the Northern Hemisphere.

Australia

WHAT MAKES AUSTRALIAN WINE SO popular and so appealing? It is warm, friendly, inviting, full of ripe fruit, and so easy to drink, but before you get the impression that Australian wine is all about casual drinking or that Australia does not make serious wine, we'd like to set the record straight. Yes, it is true that Australia does dominate the casual segment of the market—[yellow tail]® wines currently sell more bottles than any other imported varietal-labeled wine—but the Australians have been in the winemaking game for hundreds of years, and in that time they have developed some very special vineyard sites that produce extraordinary wines.

Australians seem to have the best of all worlds. They figured out several decades ago what the average modern wine consumer wants—affordable, flavorful wines that suit a twenty-first-century casual lifestyle—and they have the land and the technology to do just that. That same land and winemaking knowledge have also allowed Australian winemakers to use specific plots of land with ideal climates to create wines of incredible depth, nuance, and complexity—wines to meditate on, not just consume. In addition, it's not all about Shiraz. Australia has a wealth of grape varieties and styles to offer: from straightforward, fruity Verdelho and Riesling whites to yummy, luscious Cabernet Sauvignon and Grenache; from clean, lean, refreshing sparklers to complex, ageworthy reds; even "stickies"—what the Aussies call their gorgeous late harvest or fortified sweet wines.

LANGUAGE OF THE LABEL

WINE NAME

Like all New World wine-producing nations, Australia uses varietal labels for most of its wines, as well as a few proprietary labels. The use of varietal labels has certainly been a major factor in Australia's rise to prominence in wine markets all around the world—the consumer recognizes what is in the bottle.

PLACE NAME

All Australian wine labels also give what's called a "geographic indication," telling the consumer where the grapes were grown. The place names range from the unbelievably large to the very small, including the monster area of South Eastern Australia and the individual state names, such as South Australia or New South Wales. Within each state, the Australian system then identifies wine "zones," "regions," and "subregions." Don't worry—this is essentially equivalent to the AVA system in the United States, with smaller areas identified within larger ones, and higher price tags on wines from the smaller areas.

The umbrella area of South Eastern Australia, which accounts for about 90% of the grapes grown in the entire country, includes the states of Tasmania, Victoria, and New South Wales, plus the southern part of South Australia and the southern part of Queensland. It is indeed a massive area of land, and the creation of this catch-all name allows for grapes to be grown and harvested anywhere within that region and then trucked to a major winemaking facility, where the resulting wine will be blended with other wines from elsewhere in the region. It is this practice that has allowed Australia to continuously produce their affordable and attractive midrange wines that have so dominated the market. They are well represented by brands such as [yellow tail]®, Little Penguin, Banrock Station, Greg Norman, Jacob's Creek, Alice White, Leasingham, Oxford Landing, Black Opal, and others, as well as by major producer names such as Orlando, Hardys, Wynns, Lindemans, Penfolds, Rosemount, Wolf Blass, McWilliam's, and Yalumba. Later in this chapter, we will highlight the most important regions in the states of South Australia, New South Wales, Victoria, Tasmania, and Western Australia.

LEGAL REQUIREMENTS

Like other nations, Australia requires minimum percentages to be met if certain terms, such as the grape variety, appear on the label. The principal requirements are:

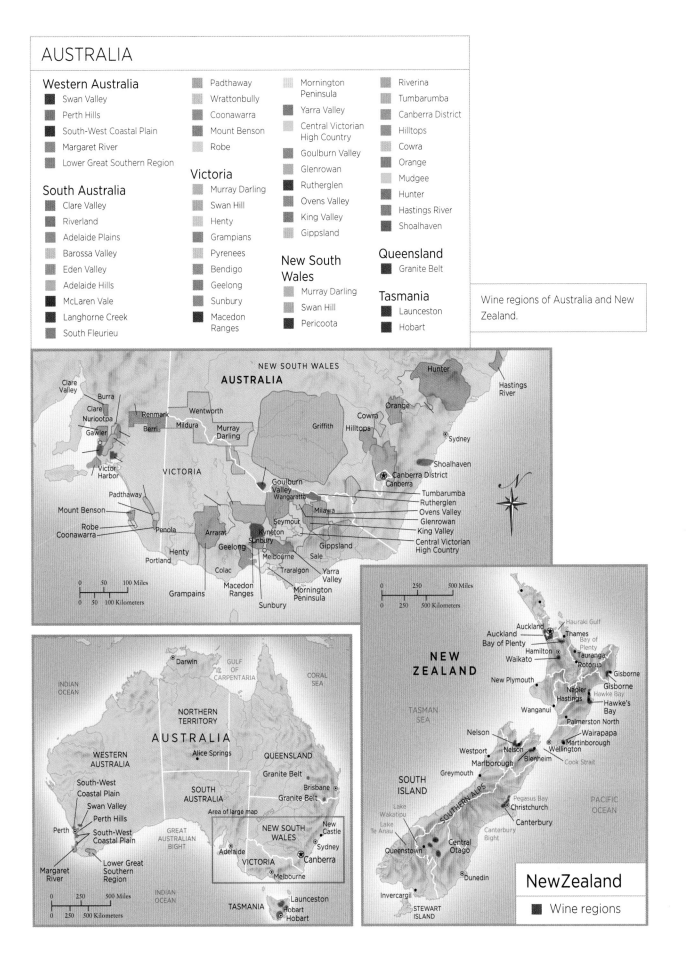

AUSTRALIA

Western Australia
- Swan Valley
- Perth Hills
- South-West Coastal Plain
- Margaret River
- Lower Great Southern Region

South Australia
- Clare Valley
- Riverland
- Adelaide Plains
- Barossa Valley
- Eden Valley
- Adelaide Hills
- McLaren Vale
- Langhorne Creek
- South Fleurieu
- Padthaway
- Wrattonbully
- Coonawarra
- Mount Benson
- Robe

Victoria
- Murray Darling
- Swan Hill
- Henty
- Grampians
- Pyrenees
- Bendigo
- Geelong
- Sunbury
- Macedon Ranges
- Mornington Peninsula
- Yarra Valley
- Central Victorian High Country
- Goulburn Valley
- Glenrowan
- Rutherglen
- Ovens Valley
- King Valley
- Gippsland

New South Wales
- Murray Darling
- Swan Hill
- Pericoota
- Riverina
- Tumbarumba
- Canberra District
- Hilltops
- Cowra
- Orange
- Mudgee
- Hunter
- Hastings River
- Shoalhaven

Queensland
- Granite Belt

Tasmania
- Launceston
- Hobart

Wine regions of Australia and New Zealand.

GRAPE TYPE: a minimum of 85% of any named grape variety must be used in the wine; if two grape types are listed, such as Cabernet/Shiraz, the first listed variety must be the dominant partner

PLACE NAME: a minimum of 85% of the grapes must come from any named place

VINTAGE: a minimum of 95% of the wine must come from grapes grown in the year stated

SPECIAL TERMS

Australia has a history of using certain label terms such as "Bin 25" or "Show Reserve," so these terms are defined. To claim "Show Reserve," the wine must have been a medal winner at a major wine competition, of which there are many in Australia. "Reserve Bin" may be used to denote a wine of demonstrably better quality than the ordinary version of the same wine, while some producers will use different bin numbers to identify different styles or origins of the same grape variety.

GRAPE TYPES

In general, three grape types rule in Australia—Chardonnay in whites and Shiraz and Cabernet Sauvignon in reds. The prominence of Chardonnay and Cabernet Sauvignon is not at all surprising—that is the route that most non-European nations followed when pursuing their own wine path, at least in the late 1900s. But the recognition that Shiraz enjoys all around the world derives from Australia's production and promotion of this wine, which is made in a distinctly Australian style. Shiraz is another name for Syrah. Vines were shipped from France's Rhone Valley to Australia to be planted in the 1700s. To be sure, Shiraz has taken on its own characteristics in its new environment in much the same way that Australia's original immigrants developed their own national character in their new homeland. Compared to Rhone Valley Syrah, Australian Shiraz usually shows riper black fruit character, with a warm, sensual, mouth-filling softness and roundness, something that the entire world has come to appreciate.

Standard Aussie Chardonnay and Cab are made in much the same style as Californian versions—big flavors, ripe fruit, medium to high use of oak, lower acidity, and higher alcohol than European versions. That is the general picture; there are some differences from state to state, usually related to climatic variations. Just as Cabernet Sauvignon is often blended with Merlot in other parts of the world, in Australia it's Shiraz that most often partners with Cab. In fact, historically there was not much Merlot planted and produced in Australia, though the last decade has seen an increase in plantings, bringing it to the third-most-planted red variety after Shiraz and Cabernet Sauvignon.

A nod of recognition, even reverence, should be given to Australian Riesling. Good Riesling needs specific growing conditions to show off its best profile; Riesling has developed a particular Australian style—not as "green" as New Zealand, not "minerally," as in Germany, but definitely ripe, even a little headstrong, with enough emphasis on freshness and acidity to show a bright vivacity. Most often made in the dry to semi-dry style, Aussie Riesling at its best is redolent of both tropical and green fruits, and is a marvelous accompaniment to spicy foods, lighter pork dishes, and especially Asian cuisines: Thai, Vietnamese, Cambodian, to name just three.

In many parts of this book, we encourage you to wander off the beaten path, to venture into unknown or unusual territory, because we believe it is there that you will find the best bargains and the best value. Just like the Tin Man, the Scarecrow, the Cowardly Lion, and Dorothy, you may even find your heart, your brain, your courage, and your home! The land of Oz offers many opportunities to do that with grapes such as Semillon and Verdelho, made as very different but equally fascinating styles of wine (see the "New South Wales" section, page 131, for more details). Also, maybe you've never tasted "Old Bush Vine" Grenache, but you should. These wines, most of them only moderately expensive, are earthy, driven by both dark and red fruits.

They are balanced and ageworthy foils for braised meats and game. And don't forget to look for Australian Champagne-method sparklers, made from Chardonnay and Pinot Noir in any of the cool-climate regions of Oz.

REGIONS

If you have been an occasional and/or bargain-focused Aussie wine drinker, you have probably been drinking mostly wines from South Eastern Australia. As you continue to explore, all of the states and regions within the enormous South Eastern Australia appellation offer plenty of opportunity to branch out and try other wines.

SOUTH AUSTRALIA

This state produces more wine than any other, and it is renowned for some world-class wines from specific regions such as Barossa Valley, Eden Valley, Clare Valley, Langhorne Creek, McLaren Vale, Adelaide Hills, Coonawarra, and Padthaway.

Barossa Valley and Eden Valley. Situated just to the northeast of the city of Adelaide, the Barossa Valley and the Eden Valley are partners

Dark, ripe fruit flavors are typical in Barossa Valley Shiraz.

in producing very fine versions of both Shiraz and Riesling, an unlikely combination that is explained only by the planting of the Riesling vines at higher elevations to ensure crisper acidity. What makes these wines unique in the world of Riesling is a very attractive fully ripe citrus quality, replacing the German delicacy and floral aroma with more fruitiness. They are still obviously Riesling, but a very Australian interpretation of the grape. Grab some yabbies (Australian freshwater crayfish) or Louisiana crawfish and a bottle of Eden Valley Riesling, and the world begins to look a whole lot sunnier.

To talk about the potential of Shiraz in this area, all one need do is remember two names:

The sun-blessed vineyards of the Barossa Valley.

Clare Valley Riesling vines.

Penfolds Grange and Henschke Hill of Grace. If you have never tasted these two wines, trust us—they represent the pinnacle of Aussie Shiraz. When you decide to climb to the top of the Shiraz price mountain, you will be amply rewarded with wines of ripe black fruit, structure, complexity, a suave smoothness, and a long, balanced finish that will keep you well satisfied long after every mouthful. It's worth remembering as well that whenever Shiraz does well in any region, its Rhone Valley partner Grenache will probably do well, too. Look out especially for the old-vine versions of Grenache and Shiraz, either as individual wines or blended. If another Rhone Valley player, Mourvedre (the Aussies call it Mataro), is included, the wine may be given the easy name of GSM—now that's keeping wine simple! These wines are really autumn and winter wines, warming and comforting, and their dark, ripe fruit flavors and fuller body work extremely well with comfort foods such as bean-and-chorizo stews and potpies.

For relative bargains from these areas, look for Wolf Blass, Peter Lehmann, Black Swan, Jacob's Creek, Pewsey Vale, Yalumba, McWilliam's, Angove's, Penfolds, Paringa, and Rosemount Estate, among others.

Moderately expensive versions come from Saltram, Grant Burge, and St Hallett.

Clare Valley. Farther north, the Clare Valley also showcases the two extremes of Riesling and Shiraz, with a substantial dose of Cabernet Sauvignon thrown in for good measure. There seems to be a Clare Valley characteristic, though, and that is a graceful silkiness to the wines, especially on the reds after a bit of age. Clare Valley is best known for its Riesling, however, and with good reason. Most are medium-bodied, fresh, and fruity, with a pleasant dose of minerals for a hint of complexity on the palate. For Riesling lovers, reputable producers of relative bargains include Annie's Lane, McWilliam's, and Leasingham. Moderately expensive to very expensive versions include Mitchell, Jim Barry, Petaluma, and the highly esteemed Grosset, whose Polish Hill Riesling is incredibly delicious and even ageworthy.

McLaren Vale and Langhorne Creek.

McLaren Vale and Langhorne Creek are just to the south and southeast of the city of Adelaide, respectively, and they both have a giant reputation for Shiraz and Cab wines that combine ripe black fruit character with a spiciness of black pepper and a solid core of tannins, though the fruit is so abundant that the tannins never seem to get in the way. Moderately expensive versions come from Metala, Wirra Wirra, d'Arenberg,

Andrew Garrett, McWilliam's/Mount Pleasant, and Ingoldby. Even if the label does not show McLaren Vale or Langhorne as the place of origin, but gives only the state name of South Australia, it is a fair bet that the wines from these producers contain a large percentage of grapes from those areas. Any of the above Shiraz and Cab wines are good partners with grilled 'roo— yes, the Australians do eat kangaroo (most often farmed, not wild), usually the loin section that runs down the center of the back. It is a tasty red meat, slightly gamy, and anything similar in flavor would be a good substitute. Note: a rare and expensive treat from McLaren Vale: the single-vineyard bottlings of Clarendon Hills Old Vines Grenache; they are amazingly powerful and yet subtle on the palate, with an extraordinarily long and complex finish.

Adelaide Hills. Directly to the east of the city of Adelaide are the Adelaide Hills, which have become well known for their versions of Chardonnay, particularly from the Piccadilly Valley subregion, where the Petaluma winery has proven that Australia can make world-class Chard, with muted wood treatment, ripe flavors of apple and citrus, and an elegant, smooth finish. In addition, Brian Croser, the founder of Petaluma, handcrafts a very fine sparkling wine from this area under his own Croser label, using Chardonnay and Pinot Noir. The cool climate of the Adelaide Hills is also conducive to good development of clean flavors in Sauvignon Blanc, with moderately expensive versions offered by Shaw + Smith as well as by Leland Estate. Truly expensive wines—sublime examples of Sauvignon Blanc, Chardonnay, Pinot Gris, and Riesling for whites, and exciting Pinot Noir and Merlot for reds—are produced by the famous Henschke family winery in the Adelaide Hills.

Coonawarra and Padthaway. Much farther south of all these regions, and closer to the south coast of South Australia, lie the regions of Coonawarra and Padthaway. Coonawarra has been hailed for many years as Australia's rival to

Bordeaux based on the excellence of its ageworthy Cabernet Sauvignon wines. Their distinctive black currant fruit with dried leaf and eucalyptus aromas certainly make Coonawarra Cabs stand out: they also age very well if that is your thing— a 20-year-old version tasted recently still surprised us with fresh, dense black fruit alongside cigar box aromas and an earthy mineral character. The wines are very capable partners with leg of lamb, a dish frequently seen in the region. The reputation of Coonawarra puts most of its wines in the moderately expensive to very expensive category, with good versions from Hollick, Lindemans, Mildara, Haselgrove, Brand's of Coonawarra/McWilliam's, and Wynns Coonawarra Estate.

Padthaway is well-suited to Chardonnay. Padthaway Chardonnay tends to show riper, more tropical, pineapple fruit than the Piccadilly Valley versions, but with acidity. Moderately expensive versions are produced by Browns, Lindemans, and Padthaway Estate.

NEW SOUTH WALES

While South Australia has always been home to a broad range of grape types and their wines, the state of New South Wales has tended to favor white grapes and wines, a curious fact since the state generally experiences a warm, humid climate that would not normally lend itself to grape growing of any kind, certainly not white-grape growing. But careful vineyard management has produced some excellent results over the centuries, especially from the state's primary region, Hunter Valley.

Hunter Valley. Chardonnay and Semillon dominate the entire region, though in the lower part of the valley, closer to the ocean, Shiraz and Cabernet also cover significant acreage and produce some outstanding wines. Hunter Valley wines are famous for their rich lusciousness, a quality that comes across in the whites as tropical fruit, so Hunter Valley Chardonnay is more about pineapple and ripe melon than apple and citrus.

If you have never tried a Semillon wine, a Hunter Valley version would be a thrilling initiation. The genius of Semillon is a natural ripeness and high acidity, so you are likely to find ripe melon and orange notes, with crisp citrus acidity when the wine is young. Semillon is one of those wines that collectors love to age, so turn yourself into a collector and let a couple of bottles of Semillon sit around for five years or so—then try one of them. You will be struck by a honey and marmalade aroma with a background of lanolin and ground nuts. On the palate, the wine comes across as distinctly dry, with notes of dried fruits and a silky smoothness—a terrific accompaniment to a blue cheese, walnut, and pear salad.

Hunter Valley Shiraz and Cabernet Sauvignon wines display typical ripe fruit character of dark plums and black currant, offset by some sturdy tannins that diminish with age, when the wines take on a more complex aroma of leather and dried leaves. For a refreshing and novel change, treat yourself to a glass of Verdelho from Hunter Valley and discover a bright, aromatic wine full of citrus character—very refreshing on a warm, humid day, and the perfect foil to blood-orange salad.

Moderately priced Hunter Valley wines include those produced by Rothbury Estate, Brokenwood, Tyrell's, McWilliam's, and De Bortoli.

VICTORIA

Victoria has more wineries than any other Australian state, about 300, and the state remains a strong contender for recognition, embracing its glorious past and an exciting future. That past is well represented by the ongoing presence of Goulburn Valley's Chateau Tahbilk, active since the 1860s and still making world-class Cabernet Sauvignon, and by the mysteries of Rutherglen "stickies," made from Muscat and Muscadelle. Meanwhile, the future seems safe in the hands of cool-climate Pinot Noir, Chardonnay, and sparkling wines from Yarra Valley and Mornington Peninsula.

Goulburn Valley. Despite some very favorable agricultural land, today there are really only two major producers here. Chateau Tahbilk is steeped in tradition, making incredibly complex Cabernet Sauvignon wines in the same way they did a hundred years ago—simple but amazingly effective methods. An aged Chateau Tahbilk Cabernet Sauvignon will raise your spirits and your hope for humanity—if we can make wines like this, surely we can save the planet! The other major producer is a relative newcomer. Mitchelton originally gained fame for an impressive version of Marsanne—impressive because very few other producers in the world make a single-variety version of this white Rhone Valley grape, and because it hits the drinker with a wonderfully scented, floral nose and a tropical fruit salad flavor. Mitchelton's Chardonnay is very good, and their GSM blend can be outstanding.

Rutherglen and Glenrowan. Wine regions may get tired of always being associated with one style of wine, but that is the nature of successful appellations: they do what they do best, and any attempt to make the land and the climate do something else is likely to result in lukewarm reception. Such is the case with both Rutherglen and Glenrowan, which have become inexorably linked with "stickies," deliciously sweet but nimble fortified wines made from late harvest Muscat or Muscadelle grapes, labeled according to the grape used.

These are spiritual wines, made for reflection and designed to reveal the wonders of the world. In small quantities as dessert or at the end of a grueling day, they reward the drinker with wondrously succinct flavors of dried apricots, white grapes, and peaches—the Muscat also reveals a noticeable raisin and prune dimension. By nature of their limited quantity, these wines can appear to be very expensive, but what they offer in return may in fact mean that they are relative bargains, as evidenced by the wines of Stanton & Killeen, Brown Brothers, Rutherglen Estates, and All Saints.

Yarra Valley vineyards.

Yarra Valley. Long hailed as one of Australia's most promising wine regions, Yarra basks in the luxury of a cool climate and mineral-rich soils that seem well suited to a variety of grape types, but particularly to Pinot Noir and Chardonnay. That means, of course, that those grapes are made into single-variety wines and are also used in the production of Champagne-method sparkling wines. The Pinots and Chardonnays are less about weight and oak and more about clean, bright fruit, balanced with high acidity (and light tannins in the Pinot). These are wines of finesse and elegance. A number of Yarra producers also make Shiraz and Cabernet Sauvignon (usually blended with Cabernet Franc or Merlot), but in a noticeably more restrained style than some of the warmer, more northerly regions, emphasizing clean berry fruit, higher acidity for freshness, and a leaner finish, rather than mouth-filling richness. Moderately expensive to very expensive versions are offered by Coldstream Hills, De Bortoli, Mount Mary, St. Hubert's, Yarra Ridge, Yarra Yering, and Yeringberg.

Mornington Peninsula. Like the Yarra Valley, this is a noticeably cool climate—chilly mornings and evenings, even in the summer growing season—and, once again, Pinot Noir and Chardonnay reign, almost supreme. These are *not* overripe and overoaked Chardonnays. Mornington and Yarra Chardonnays do emphasize fruit, but just-ripe fruit that has reached its pinnacle of flavor over a long, cool growing season. The wines are balanced by fresh acidity and enhanced by skilled winemaking that produces a peaches-and-cream softness of texture.

For Pinot Noir, ripe raspberry and cherry notes are matched by an earthy mineral character, while vibrant acidity and tannins seem to "lift" the wine in the mouth as it heads toward a long, give-me-some-more finish.

Given the peninsula's cool to moderate climate, it is perhaps no surprise that Pinot Gris/Pinot Grigio is also grown here in fairly large quantity and with success, producing wines with the kind of structure and flavors found in Oregon's versions of the same grape—leaning toward some fullness and roundness in the mouth, with distinctly ripe apple, pear, and melon flavors, countered by refreshing acidity. Moderately expensive versions come from Tuck's Ridge, Massoni, and Dromana Estate.

TASMANIA

The island state of Tasmania is about one thing—cold growing seasons that demand cool-climate grape varieties, especially Chardonnay, Pinot Noir, and Riesling. For consumers, that means some scintillating single-variety versions of these wines, plus some very exciting Champagne-method sparklers produced from Chardonnay and Pinot Noir. The combination of long hours of sunlight and cooler temperatures means the opportunity for the grapes to develop fully ripe flavor profiles while maintaining fresh, vibrant acidity—just perfect for those varieties. The sparkling wines of Tasmania are among some of the best we have ever tasted, with finely defined flavors and a crisp acidity matched by a reassuring richness on the tongue. These wines may be hard to find but are well worth the search.

Relative bargains can be found from Ninth Island (a second label of Pipers Brook), and Jacob's Creek produces a sparkler for less than $20, while moderately expensive versions come from Dalrymple, Lalla Gully, Heemskerk, Bream Creek, Clover Hill, and Elsewhere (yes, that's the winery name). The very expensive Jansz sparkler is worth every penny.

WESTERN AUSTRALIA

Not only are the wines of Western Australia a continent away from their southeastern counterparts in terms of distance, but there is a major shift in style as well, with the generally cooler climates of the southern tip of Western Australia providing very different growing conditions from most of South Eastern Australia. The exposed corner of the continent and the cooling winds from the Indian Ocean are major players in those cooler conditions. The two big regional names here are Margaret River and Great Southern, with its subregion of Mount Barker.

Margaret River. By any measure, Cabernet Sauvignon is the number-one grape and wine here, often blended with Cabernet Franc and/or Merlot. Margaret River Cabs are not rich and opulent, more modest perhaps, but are interesting; firm and lean, they also feature an elegant smoothness to counter tannins and feature off ripe black currant fruit. That same leaner style is also apparent in the small quantities of Shiraz made here, with more peppery and gamy qualities, rather than being awash in abundant fruit.

In the white wines, Chardonnay certainly benefits from the cool ocean winds and produces some fine lean versions, but this region also does wonderful things with Riesling, Semillon, and Sauvignon Blanc. The last two are frequently blended, in the traditional Bordeaux style. Moderately expensive offerings come from Cape Mentelle, Cullen, Evans & Tate, and Leeuwin Estate.

Great Southern. Again, Cabernet Sauvignon and Chardonnay are the most planted grapes, followed by Riesling, Shiraz, and Merlot (for blending with Cab). For something more exotic, some Great Southern wineries have found good vineyard sites for cool-climate Pinot Noir and Sauvignon Blanc. The wines are unmistakably ripe, but with fresh, lively acidity for freshness. Even more exotic and fun are the Verdelho wines with their seductive fruitiness, a simple indulgence in naive charm. The relative rarity of Great Southern wines makes them moderately expensive, but good versions can be found from Jingalla, Mad Fish, Ferngrove, Fonty's Pool, Goundrey, and Plantagenet.

New Zealand

AT THE VERY LEAST, New Zealand deserves fame and recognition for focusing attention away from Chardonnay in the 1980s and early 1990s when the world most needed that diversion. This was accomplished by the wild and ebullient style that New Zealand winemakers gave to their Sauvignon Blanc, which was boldly different—loads of fresh green fruit, but obviously ripe, backed up by mouthwatering acidity that kept the flavors lingering forever. Like a fruit salad in a glass, really.

But New Zealand winemakers have shown no sign of resting on their Sauvignon Blanc laurels—they want to prove to themselves and the world that their vineyards produce world-class wines from several places and a range of grape types. Certainly, if you love New Zealand's unique Sauvignon Blanc style, and a lot of people do, there is plenty of it to keep you happy. But there is much more to discover.

As the world's southernmost grape-growing area, New Zealand enjoys a combination of climate and sunlight similar to that found in the far northern wine-growing lands of Germany and Washington State. The growing season is cool and long, with extended hours of daylight well into the latter part of the growing season, meaning that the grapes have the chance to reach full physiological ripeness without the sudden rush of sugars that push growers to harvest early in warmer climates. Another characteristic of being far from the equator has an especially beneficial effect: the temperature swing between day and night is more exaggerated, with warm to hot temperatures during the day and cool, even cold temperatures at night. It is the low nighttime temperatures that keep the freshness and liveliness in New Zealand wines, with acidity levels in the grapes actually boosted overnight to counter the acid loss during the day. Add to this New Zealand's unique feature—it is a long, thin two-island nation where the climatic features already mentioned are emphasized—and you have a recipe for success in the modern wine world.

LANGUAGE OF THE LABEL

WINE NAME

New Zealand fits right in with other New World wine producers in that it labels most wines by varietal. All varietally labeled wines must contain a minimum of 75% of the named variety, but in practice most single-varietal wines are made from 100% of the named variety. If two or more grape varieties are named on the label, they must appear in decreasing order of the percentage used—if a wine is labeled as Cabernet/Merlot, there must be more Cabernet than Merlot. Some wines carry a proprietary or brand name, especially when the wine is a blend of two or more grapes, but the grape variety mix is usually included somewhere on the label. Blended wines from New Zealand are most frequently made from the traditional Bordeaux grape mix of Cabernet Sauvignon and Merlot, or maybe Cabernet Franc and Malbec.

PLACE NAME

New Zealand winemakers include place names on labels to indicate the origin of the grapes used in the wine. There are 10 designated grape-growing regions, though in some cases the official name has changed over time. The 10 regions are:

NORTH ISLAND	SOUTH ISLAND
Northland	Nelson
Auckland	Marlborough
Waikato/Bay of Plenty	Canterbury
Gisborne	Central Otago
Hawke's Bay	
Wairarapa/Martinborough	

GRAPES

Like a familiar Agatha Christie mystery, New Zealand assembles the usual cast of characters, so there really is no mystery—although the lead role in this case is Sauvignon Blanc, and Chardonnay is relegated to a supporting role. Over the last 20 years, acreage of Chardonnay has increased incrementally, but Sauvignon Blanc now occupies at least seven times more acreage than in 1997. It was Sauvignon Blanc that blazed the trail for the Kiwis, and they were quick to recognize its potential. Almost all New Zealand Sauvignon Blanc is made in the style discussed in Chapter 2, though some are more minerally than others.

Having developed a forthright, fresh, zingy, and recognizable style for Sauvignon Blanc,

MARLBOROUGH
SAVIGNON BLANC

WINE OF NEW ZEALAND

Marlborough Sauvignon Blanc has become New Zealand's flagship wine.

winemakers were quick to realize that they could apply a similar philosophy to other white varieties. Enter the vibrant yet graceful starlet Riesling, which in New Zealand has fresh fruit nuances of kiwi in the aroma along with ripe citrus. The grace comes from a well-defined streak of acidity that allows some of the very best examples to show off distinct mineral notes to great effect— a core of firmness inside the ripe fruit.

That philosophy is adapted to Chardonnay and Pinot Gris by concentrating on retained acidity and restrained use of oak, allowing the natural apple and lemon flavors of Chardonnay and the rich sensual, almost oily texture of Pinot Gris to shine through.

In red grape varieties, the surprise star is Pinot Noir, with a staggering tenfold increase in acreage in 10 years, and that is attributable not just to fashion or to pigheaded winemakers who will make Pinot Noir or die trying. No, the increase here is valid. It is because New Zealand really does have pockets of climate, topography, and soil structures that favor Pinot. Based on tastings we've attended recently, it appears that winemakers in New Zealand want to make Pinot Noir their signature red grape, just as they have made Sauvignon Blanc their signature white.

REGIONS

We have listed some producers at the end of each regional section. Remember that many wineries will often bring fruit in from other regions, and will always label the wine according to where the grapes were grown. In that model, Giesen, for example, is listed as a Canterbury winery, but its most available wine in the United States is Marlborough Sauvignon Blanc.

NORTH ISLAND

The regions of Northland, Auckland, and Waikato/Bay of Plenty rarely show up on our shelves, so we will concentrate on the other regions.

Gisborne. The real gem in Gisborne's tiara is Chardonnay, especially when made in the style that many more consumers seem to want— bright, fresh, simple, and fruity, with little oak influence. That said, there are a few producers, such as Corbans, who know how to use high-quality fruit from prime vineyard locations to make wines that will age well and gracefully for 10 years or more.

In addition to Corbans, Millton is a highly reputable producer.

Hawke's Bay. Hawke's Bay boasts sunshine— lots of it. And yet it is not that hot, the majority of the vineyard areas being cooled by sea breezes through most of the growing season. As one more testament to its adaptability, Chardonnay also does well here, though a Hawke's Bay Chard usually shows a lot more depth and "oomph" than a Gisborne version, kind of like comparing a sliced chicken breast on romaine lettuce with a spit-roasted chicken with all the trimmings.

Hawke's Bay can produce good Cabernet Sauvignon, though some growers believe that the region is not consistently warm enough to ripen Cab fully every year. There are some select vineyard sites that do achieve success, and the region continues to receive praise for its Bordeaux-style blends, with Merlot playing an increasingly important role, along with Cabernet Franc. The Te Mata red blends are especially noteworthy, and expensive.

There are plenty of other grapes being grown here, and we are likely to see more and more successful attempts at Pinot Noir and even Syrah from Hawke's Bay.

Notable producers include Te Mata, Kim Crawford, Trinity Hill, and Ngatarawa.

Wairarapa. This region includes the smaller district of Martinborough, which will also show up as a geographic indication on labels and is probably better known in wine circles than Wairarapa. Whether we are talking Wairarapa or Martinborough, the topic is likely to be Pinot Noir, Sauvignon Blanc, or Chardonnay. The Martinborough district was one of the first in New Zealand to be recognized as having Pinot potential, and that potential has been delivered in wines that show well-developed dark red fruit character and some of the warm, earthy undertones that Pinot drinkers love. Martinborough Sauvignon Blanc has won over admirers with its extra suggestion of ripe stone fruit underneath the zippy acidity and citrus notes. Wines to look out for come from Craggy Range, Ata Rangi, Kusuda, Palliser Estates, Big Sky, Martinborough Vineyard, and Dry River Wines.

SOUTH ISLAND

Nelson. It is difficult to pick any particular grape variety as the star of Nelson, but the region does an excellent job of producing the cool-climate array of Sauvignon Blanc, Chardonnay, and Riesling, all of which display the cleanness and greenness we have come to expect of New Zealand wines. Notable producers include Seifried, Denton, and Neudorf.

Marlborough. This is the place that started it all in terms of the world's acceptance of Sauvignon Blanc, with a style that is instantly recognizable as bracing acidity behind ripe fruit with an undertone of grassiness and gooseberry flavors. Back in the day, Sauvignon Blanc lovers thought first and foremost of Sancerre in the Loire Valley of France, but today New Zealand is the touchstone, and the truly experienced will not just reference New Zealand, but Marlborough as the place that makes the magic.

Of New Zealand's Sauvignon Blanc vineyards, 90% are planted here, but as good as the Sauvignons are, we should not limit our consideration of Marlborough only to that variety. There are some equally outstanding Rieslings with a finesse and elegance that are rarely seen from other Southern Hemisphere versions of that grape. Equally interesting are the Chardonnays, with a lean edge and an understated use of wood, and the future holds promise for some leanly structured Pinot Noir that will offer a different emphasis than most boldly fruity New World versions.

Marlborough wines are mostly highly affordable, with a few producers making some relatively expensive wines. You should take the opportunity to try any of these wines, especially the Sauvignon Blanc, and especially from producers such as Matua, Montana, Allan Scott, Brancott, Cloudy Bay, Selaks, Nobilo, Villa Maria, Babich, Corbans, Saint Clair, Spy Valley, Coopers Creek, Framingham, Giesen, Nautilus, Monkey Bay, Mud House, Oyster Bay, Seresin, The Crossings, and Vavasour.

The Marlborough region is also enormously important for growing Chardonnay and Pinot Noir that are used in Champagne-method sparkling wine production. Prominent labels of high-quality sparklers include Deutz, Chandon, Lindauer, Pelorus, and Amadeus.

Canterbury. By now our savvy *WineWise* reader will have figured out that as we continue to head southward we will see a continuing concentration on familiar cool-climate varieties. That's certainly the case with Canterbury, where Chardonnay, Riesling, and Pinot Noir are all major players, along with a good smattering of Pinot Gris. Some of the Chardonnay and Pinot

Noir head off to sparkling wine production, but there are also some very fine versions of those wines in their own right. From the right vineyard location and in the right winemaker's hands, Riesling and Pinot Gris from here can reach stellar quality, with an astounding depth and purity. Canterbury producers to watch include Pegasus Bay, Giesen, and Waipara Springs.

Central Otago. To date, all the attention here is focused on Pinot Noir, with much critical acclaim heaped on these wines from wine writers all around the world. The Pinots from Central Otago tend to show riper, denser dark red or even black fruit than many French Burgundies, but there is a meaty, chewy quality to the wines, without excessive intensity. That is something that many people love about Pinot Noir—authority without power. You like it because it suggests rather than dictates. Among the good and great producers are Amisfield, Two Paddocks, Felton Road, Mt. Difficulty, and Rippon Vineyard.

South Africa

SOUTH AFRICA IS A LAND of contrasts, especially within the hundred miles from the east, south, and west coastlines that define this wine land. It is situated at a crossroads of climatic and cultural influences that have helped to define South African history and its wines. Climatically, both the Atlantic and Indian oceans impact the region, bringing dry or moist, hot or cold air, depending on the season and the prevailing winds.

It is easy to make the assumption that South Africa's location at the southern tip of the continental mass of Africa makes it a cool grape-growing area. But the general picture is a warmer climate. Cape Town itself sits at 34 degrees latitude, which is only just within the accepted northerly limit of grape growing in the Southern Hemisphere. However, the varied landscape also provides for contrasts in climate, with pockets of cool, even cold grape-growing areas provided by elevation, proximity to the ocean, or shelter from warm winds. That wide variety of climatic conditions allows South Africa to make a broad range of wine styles, from cool-climate Sauvignon Blanc to warmer Rhone-style wines such as Syrah and Grenache.

GRAPE TYPES

In addition to the usual gathering of international grape types, South Africa has two unusual claims to fame—Chenin Blanc and Pinotage. Chenin Blanc is South Africa's most widely planted grape type, a claim that can be made by no other wine nation. In fact, South Africa is the number one producer of Chenin Blanc in the world. Although South African Chenin Blanc is relatively unknown in the United States, we consider it a true WineWise choice. Our intrepid readers need not be slaves to the fashions of the masses and the uninitiated. Relatively inexpensive South African Chenin Blanc produced in a dry style can be a fascinating wine and is extremely food-friendly. Its flavors of melon, pear, and hazelnut and its naturally high acidity make it a very useful wine to have on hand. Try it with lobster or smoked trout and you will wonder why more places around the world do not make this wine. Watch for the word "Steen" on some labels: it is a South African synonym for Chenin Blanc.

Pinotage is South Africa's own wine grape. It was created by a South African settler by crossing Pinot Noir with the southern French variety called Cinsaut. The *WineWise* reader may immediately recognize that Pinot Noir is a cool-climate grape type. Cinsaut, on the other hand, is a warm-climate variety, originating in the southern Rhone Valley of France. What the intrepid settler seems to have attempted was the creation of a grape type suited to South Africa's climate and growing conditions. Certainly, no other place in the world has adopted this unusual variety as a mainstay of its wine industry, and that should tell you something. Even today, with a strong revitalization of the post-apartheid South African wine industry well under way, Pinotage wines themselves remain something of a mystery and a glassful of contrast, capable of greatness but more often disappointing.

In addition to those two unusual characters, the usual range of international grapes is found in South Africa. Chardonnay is made in an attractive cool-climate style when the right growing conditions can be found, producing a crisp wine with just a hint of oak and flavors of apple and citrus. Occasionally a producer will also go toward a fuller, more tropical style.

Sauvignon Blanc has earned a good reputation here and in export markets thanks to its treatment at the hands of the right growers and winemakers. With an overall warm climate, it is not hard to find sites that will produce Sauvignon Blanc grapes with ripe citrus flavors, but the truly exceptional wines come from areas where there are cool influences that lengthen the growing season and keep acidity levels high. The result is not only a bright lime and gooseberry character, but also an element of green leaf or nettle. Try a glass with blanched asparagus and a drizzle of butter and fresh lemon juice—your day will look brighter.

Cabernet Sauvignon has long claimed its rightful place in South Africa as a grape capable of producing some superb wines, and Merlot has more recently been adopted both as a blender with Cabernet and as a single-varietal wine in its own right. The style of these red wines tends to be warmly ripe, but with attenuating acidity and tannins that seem to make the wines more complete. Cabernet Franc is also frequently used in blends with Cabernet Sauvignon and Merlot.

Many producers of South African wine have won great acclaim for their Syrah/Shiraz and Grenache wines, and with good reason. These grapes and their wines are ideally suited to the general growing conditions in South Africa, and they seem to easily reach full ripeness, which translates into warm, dark fruit flavors with a touch of spice in the glass—a wonderful accompaniment to lamb stew on a cool autumnal evening.

LANGUAGE OF THE LABEL

WINE NAME

Like the other Southern Hemisphere wine nations, South Africa realized a long time ago the advantages of using grape variety names on wine labels to make their wines easily recognizable in the international marketplace. Some producers choose a proprietary name that can become well known as a brand: a good example from South Africa is the Goats Do Roam label—a cute play on the French wine name Cotes du Rhone—produced as a Rhone-style blend by Charles Back of Fairview wines. It has been a great success, attributable to the playfulness of the label and the quality of the wine. By the way, Fairview's farms also produce goat's-milk cheeses, so there really are goats on the property that do roam!

PLACE NAME

Again, like all other wine-producing nations, South Africa has a place name system equivalent to the United States' AVA system or Australia's geographic indicator system. In the South African model there are four main grape-growing regions that contain 21 districts. Occasionally you might also find the name of one of the country's 53 wards on a label. The wards are smaller areas, and most of them lie within the 21 districts. The four large regions are Coastal Region, Breede River Valley, Klein Karoo, and Olifants River. The wines from the Coastal Region and Breede River Valley, along with their better districts and wards, deserve some close attention.

CERTIFICATION

South African wines may carry a neck strip on the bottle indicating that the wine has been certified by the Wine & Spirit Board as authentic

Simonsberg Mountain rises majestically over Stellenbosch vineyards.

with regard to any information on the label such as grape variety, place name, and any specific claims. The certification is awarded only after rigorous tests, including tasting, have been administered. The presence of the certification strip confirms for the consumer that:

> If a grape variety is named on the label, the wine has been made using at least 85% of that variety.
>
> If a vintage year is indicated, at least 85% of the wine originated from grapes harvested in the stated year.
>
> If a place name appears on the label, together with the phrase "Wine of Origin" or the abbreviation "W.O.," 100% of the grapes must have originated in that place.
>
> If the phrase "Estate Grown" appears on the label, the estate must be a single contiguous property, and all of the production processes must occur on the estate.

REGIONS

COASTAL REGION

The defined grape-growing area of the Coastal Region stretches along the west coast of South Africa northward from Cape Town and inland to the towns of Paarl and Tulbagh, a distance of more than 30 miles. The area is undoubtedly warm, though there are pockets that are cooled by ocean breezes, depending on the time of year and the presence or absence of the impressive mountains that can channel cool air inland.

Within this region, the most familiar districts are Paarl and Stellenbosch, and those two place names, especially Stellenbosch, can frequently be found on bottles of South African wine in the American market. That should be reassuring, since both of these districts have a solid reputation for producing very good-quality wines. The districts of Darling and Tygerberg are also beginning to be players in the international market.

Paarl. This district contains four wards, three of which are becoming important as recognizable place names on labels: Franschhoek Valley, Wellington, and Simonsberg-Paarl. As reflected in its name and in the names of some of its wineries (such as L'Ormarins, La Motte, Dieu Donné), Franschhoek has a particularly strong historical French influence, and this can sometimes be seen in the profile of the wines, emphasizing a more reserved style instead of all upfront fruit. Whatever the ward, Paarl's mostly warm climate lends itself to the production of some fine Cabernet Sauvignon wines and Cab blends, as well as Syrah/Shiraz and Rhone blends. This is especially true from producers such as Fairview, Boekenhoutskloof (pronounced book-N-howedskloof; say it five times fast!), and Glen Carlou. At the southeastern end of the Paarl district rises the majestic Simonsberg hill, which provides elevation and cooler sites for Chardonnay, also produced by Glen Carlou.

Stellenbosch. Of all the districts in South Africa, this one contains some of the greatest

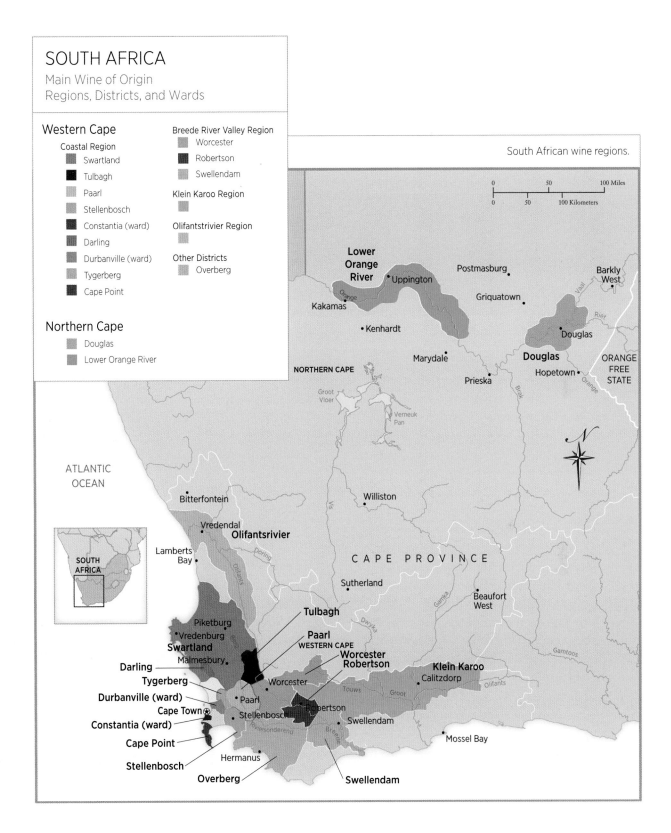

SOUTH AFRICA
Main Wine of Origin
Regions, Districts, and Wards

Western Cape

Coastal Region
- Swartland
- Tulbagh
- Paarl
- Stellenbosch
- Constantia (ward)
- Darling
- Durbanville (ward)
- Tygerberg
- Cape Point

Northern Cape
- Douglas
- Lower Orange River

Breede River Valley Region
- Worcester
- Robertson
- Swellendam

Klein Karoo Region

Olifantsrivier Region

Other Districts
- Overberg

South African wine regions.

estates, renowned for a few exquisite wines. This is because of the extremely diverse soil types and the varying climatic conditions that exist throughout the district, all made possible by the flow of cool ocean air from the south through mountain passes created by such ranges as the Simonsberg and Drakenstein hills. The single estates mentioned in the "Certification" section earlier are particularly prevalent here and include some famous and very reliable names, such as Simonsig, Rustenberg, Rust en Vrede, Meerlust, Uitkyk, Warwick, and Kanonkop. Wines from

The vineyards of the Durbanville Hills.

those producers are all moderately to very expensive. Other very good producers making moderately expensive wines include Delaire, Mulderbosch, Ken Forrester, and Thelema.

Given the variety of climates and soils, you could spend many weeks working your way through the broad range of grapes and wines represented here, from the unrelenting integrity of Ken Forrester's Chenin Blancs to Mulderbosch's lean and austere Sauvignon Blanc and the complex conundrum of Rustenberg's Cabernet Sauvignons. Time well spent!

Darling. This cool area is situated fairly close to the Atlantic Ocean, just to the north of Cape Town, making the Darling district a favorite tourist destination. That alone could bring it fame and fortune, but the good news is that Darling can also produce some outstanding cool-climate versions of Sauvignon Blanc, especially from the Groenekloof ward. Darling Cellars is a representative producer of moderately expensive wines.

Tygerberg. The most important thing about Tygerberg is the Durbanville ward, a series of hills just to the northeast of Cape Town with a staggering view of the city and the ocean in the distance. This is another place where vineyards compete with developers who wish to build high-end residential housing for wealthy suburbanites, and we are happy to report that a few hardy souls have mounted a tough resistance against further encroachment into vineyard territory. The very large Durbanville Hills winery along with smaller players such as Nitida and Biesjes Craal are doing an outstanding job producing fresh, vibrant, ripe versions of Sauvignon Blanc with distinct mineral elements, in addition to some well-structured and elegant Bordeaux-style wines from Cabernet Sauvignon and Merlot.

Constantia. This very famous and historic ward lies within the Coastal Region, just to the south of Cape Town, but is not situated in any district. It is an entity unto itself, and deservedly so, since much of the reputation of South African wines stands on the shoulders of Constantia. Historically famous for its dessert Muscat wines, the area is now recognized as a major producer of Cabernet Sauvignon wines and blends. Chardonnay also does well in the cooler vineyard sites. The three major producers of moderately expensive wines are Groot Constantia, Klein Constantia, and Buitenverwachting.

BREEDE RIVER VALLEY

The Breede River Valley wine region runs from the town of Worcester, about 60 miles inland from the Atlantic Ocean, in a southeasterly direction until the Breede River empties into the Indian Ocean on the south coast. It is sandwiched between the occasional mountains of the western Cape (such as Simonsberg and Drakenstein) and the far greater mass of the inland mountain range. The region contains an unlikely but very promising district, Robertson—unlikely because the relatively flat inland river valley is certainly warm if not hot, but promising because a few renegades have staked their future on the existence of cool climate pockets created by cold air that is sucked all the way from the Atlantic Ocean down through the valley toward the Indian Ocean.

Robertson. In the very heart of the broad sweep of the hot but fertile Breede River Valley, there are a few unique pockets such as Robertson, cool enough to create amazingly complex and mineral-laden Sauvignon Blanc wines, as reflected in Springfield Estate's top-ranking "Life from Stone," a brilliant and very expensive wine with fine apricot notes and the bright flash of flint aromas—a truly remarkable achievement. Down the road from Springfield, an equally adventurous maverick, Danie de Wet, has created the De Wetshof label, offering bright, fresh flavors of Chardonnay and Sauvignon Blanc through careful vineyard management and cold fermentation in stainless-steel vats. The wines of Van Loveren are equally impressive.

OTHER IMPORTANT AREAS TO WATCH FOR

Outside the four principal regions there are a few districts and freestanding wards of note, of interest mostly because the "Cape crusaders" who have developed them have moved into nontraditional areas to exploit specific climatic or territorial conditions. The following areas are particularly worthy of attention.

Overberg District (with Elgin Ward). One of several areas that have expanded the traditional vineyard area much farther southward, the Elgin ward has produced some ripe and flavorful Sauvignon Blancs with vibrant fresh acidity, reflective of the cooler climate here. Paul Cluver is a good example.

The Life from Stone vineyard in Robertson.

Walker Bay. A little farther south from Overberg, this area is snuggled into the southwestern tip of the Cape, with a wide ocean perspective making it particularly cool from the ocean breezes. In this environment, there is ample opportunity to produce truly cool-climate versions of Riesling, Gewurztraminer, Sauvignon Blanc, and Chardonnay. Great work has already been done by pioneers such as the Hamilton Russell winery, and their moderately expensive wines are well worth looking for. Other fine producers include Bouchard Finlayson, Beaumont Wines, Southern Right, and Whalehaven.

Cape Agulhas (with Elim Ward). At the very southern tip of Africa, where the mighty Atlantic and Indian oceans meet, this area is making waves of its own with some remarkable cool-climate winemaking, especially with its lean but vibrant Sauvignon Blanc. The Flagstone Winery version from the Elim ward is particularly impressive.

There is a world of pleasure to be found in the wines of South Africa, and the pleasure should be yours. It certainly continues to be ours.

8

LE VIN ET L'AMOUR

FRANCE

FRENCH WINES. JUST THOSE TWO WORDS ARE ENOUGH TO SEND A WINE LOVER INTO A REVERIE OF FOND MEMORIES. "Back in the day" our first exposure to the diversity of French wines was daunting, but our confidence increased the more we tasted. In France, there is a logical system in place that classifies French wines in terms of quality and flavor profiles. For example, Chardonnay is the authorized grape for white Burgundy wines, while Pinot Noir and Gamay are the grape for red Burgundies. White Bordeaux are based on Sauvignon Blanc and Semillon grapes, reds on the trio of Cabernet Sauvignon, Merlot, and Cabernet Franc.

Once we got the basics of French wine styles down, we began to appreciate the wines with classic food pairings. Enjoying rack of lamb with red Bordeaux or Coq au Vin with red Burgundy certainly enhanced our appreciation of French wines. The next step was to figure out which wineries we liked best.

In this chapter we will take you through these steps and demystify French wines. *WineWise* readers will be able to decipher a wine label and learn about the flavor profiles of the wines and the foods that pair with those flavors, and we'll suggest producers you can trust, because the most important piece of information on any wine label is the reputation of the people who make the wine.

Let's compare the French system of wine labels with wines from the New World. When we purchase a California, Chilean, or Australian white wine we are not always sure if the winery made the wine bone dry or if it has a little sweetness to it. We're also not sure if the wine is light or heavy in body. In France, most fine wines feature the name of the place the grapes are grown on the label, and consumers can be assured that those wines will follow a "recipe." Federal and local governing bodies monitor both the methods of production and the grapes used to make the wines. There is a follow-up tasting panel to confirm the wines fit the flavor profile representative of that place. For example, Sauternes is always sweet and Brut Champagne is always dry.

Once you grasp the basics of which grapes grow in which wine region of France, you will acquire a level of confidence that will be rewarded with wonderful wines with traditional flavors. When you choose French wines with confidence you demonstrate a high level of basic wine knowledge, and you will become more WineWise with every choice you make.

Why do French wines attract so much attention and respect from wine professionals and consumers? In France, wine is one part of an interlocking puzzle that includes cheeses, vegetables, vinegars, meats, and other foods whose origin and production is monitored by the government. For centuries French cuisine has been held in high regard; in 2011, UNESCO recognized French gastronomy as an "intangible cultural heritage of humanity."

More than a thousand years ago, French monks began to identify the best areas to plant vineyards and subsequent evaluations of those vineyards and the wines they produced are still important today. We wish we could take our *WineWise* readers on a journey to Burgundy to see for themselves the inconspicuous property in the middle of a hill that is the Montrachet vineyard. It produces a Chardonnay wine that can cost $1,000 or more. No other country in the world produces white wines that cost that much. As a bonus, wines such as Montrachet can improve when aged five, 10, or 20 years.

But often-unattainable luxury is not all you get with French wines. The same nation that makes fabulously expensive special occasion wines also produces pleasant, inexpensive wines for informal meals and get-togethers. In this chapter and our "Got Cash?" best-bargains buying guide (page 359), we will turn our readers on to some great French wines that we enjoy at home.

While it's been a very long and profitable run for the French wine industry, their dominant position in the wine world has been jostled. Certainly, the "crème de la crème," or top 10% of the finest wines, still sell out to the wealthiest people around the globe. But the French are having a hard time selling the other 90% of the wine. In addition, Italian food is much more popular than French food today and we are enjoying the benefits of improvements in the overall quality of Italian food and wines.

A further threat to French wines is increased interest in and availability of foods and wines from Spain and foods and wines from New World nations, particularly the nations of Latin America. Some Spanish wines and most wines from the New World, including Chile and Argentina, but also the United States, Australia, New Zealand, etc., prominently display the name of the grape on the label. Since most consumers shop for wine by grape rather than place name, this labeling system makes New World wines more approachable and has led to the demise of many a French vineyard and/or winery. At the same time, the widespread use of the "varietal label" has provided opportunities for other players in the global wine market.

In France itself, winemakers are confronted with dwindling sales as a new generation of young French people have turned their backs on the habits of previous generations. One recent survey estimates that in the past decade the amount of time spent on the average French dinner has gone from 88 minutes to 38. If you add to that a vigorous anti-drinking campaign in the French media, it is no surprise that French people are consuming less wine. But French wine woes do not stop there.

Some French wine producers have complained that they are hamstrung by archaic regulations that require them to follow specific growing practices and to plant only certain grape varieties within a defined wine region (the red Bordeaux appellation, for example, that requires the use of mostly Cabernet blends but forbids the use of Syrah). These producers complain that such restrictions leave them with very little room for experimentation and innovation in a world that thrives on the new and different. Despite numerous calls to overhaul impractical rules and too many layers of bureaucracy, little has changed, and French wine producers continue to lose market share worldwide.

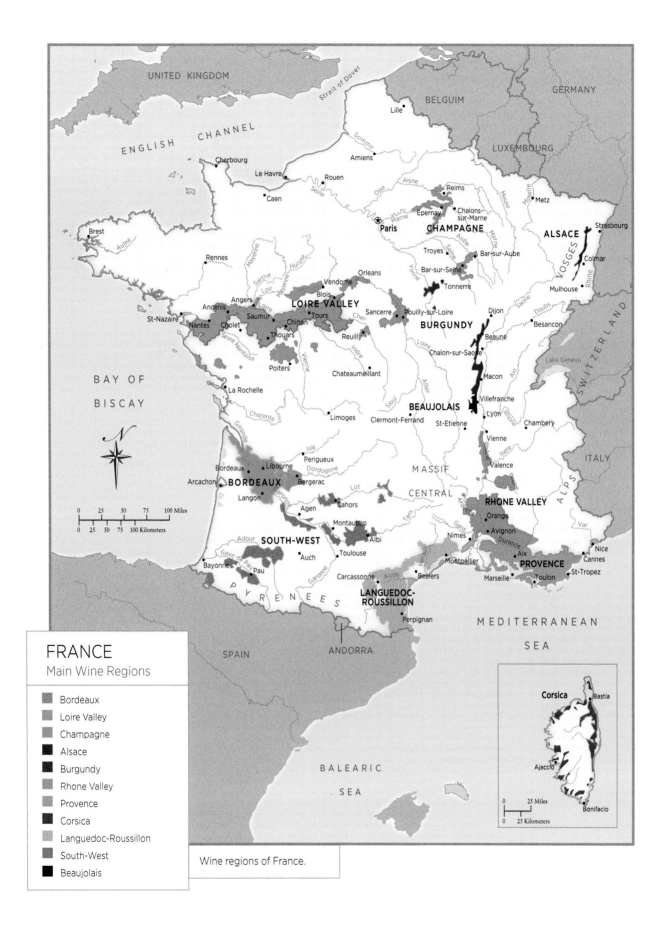

Wine regions of France.

Still, there is good news for *WineWise* readers. There are more and more French farmers using organic and biodynamic growing methods, and in general there are less chemicals being used in the vineyards of France than in the past. Also, because of global competition there are now many wines being exported to North America that deliver "old world" flavors at prices from $10 to $30. Some of those wines are from well known regions and others are from lesser known areas and/or grapes. In this chapter, we will share with you some of those "off the beaten path" gems. French wines are made in every style possible and at different price levels.

The overall picture

FRANCE IS THE WORLD'S LARGEST wine-producing nation, with a total of close to 2.5 million acres (1 million hectares) of vines turning out anywhere from seven to eight billion bottles a year. France's vineyards span climatic ranges from cool to hot, producing everything from crisp, dry whites, charming rosés, light- to full-bodied reds, and sweet, fortified, and sparkling wines as well.

There are seven famous and classic wine regions in France: Alsace, Beaujolais, Bordeaux, Burgundy, Champagne, Loire, and Rhone. In addition, there are several lesser-known regions within the broad sweep of vineyards across southern France in the areas of Languedoc, Roussillon, and Provence.

In the pages that follow, we will introduce you to the more important white, rosé, red, and sparkling wines of each of these regions, as well as the landscapes and people behind them. But first we'll provide some helpful information on understanding French wine labels.

Language of the label

FRENCH WINE LABELS PRESENT INFORMATION that is meant to instill confidence in the consumer about the authenticity of the product. This chapter's simple approach to understanding French wine labels will give our readers the confidence to buy more French wines. Perhaps more important, we will guide you on how to enjoy them on their own, and especially with food.

COMPANY OR PRODUCER'S NAME

All wines labels include a company name, which is the producer of the wine. It might be a grape-growing estate such as Chateau Mouton-Rothschild in Bordeaux, or a family name such as Louis Jadot in Burgundy, or a company name such as Veuve Clicquot in Champagne. Since the reputation of the producer is often synonymous with the wine's quality, the name is prominently displayed on the main label, or perhaps on a neck label.

WINE NAME

The company name and the wine name are the two most important pieces of information on any label. There are three broad possibilities for labels: the place name (such as Bordeaux), the grape name (mostly used in the Alsace region) such as Riesling, or for Champagne, the level of sweetness (such as Brut).

In some cases, the name of a grape-growing estate with a house (or *chateau*) on it is also the name of the wine. This is especially true in Bordeaux, with names such as Chateau Latour or Chateau Bonnet. Sometimes a brand or proprietary name such as "Mouton Cadet" will be in bigger letters on the label than the place name (Bordeaux) or the producer (Baron

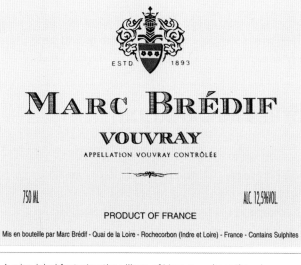

ESTD 1893

MARC BRÉDIF

VOUVRAY

APPELLATION VOUVRAY CONTRÔLÉE

750 ML   ALC 12,5%VOL

PRODUCT OF FRANCE

Mis en bouteille par Marc Brédif - Quai de la Loire - Rochecorbon (Indre et Loire) - France - Contains Sulphites

A wine label featuring the village of Vouvray, where the wines are based on the Chenin Blanc grape.

de Rothschild). Another example of this is "La Grande Dame," which is as prominently featured on the label as the region (Champagne) or producer (Veuve Clicquot). The wine name may also include some variation of the quality of the wine, using the term "*cru*," or it may include an indication of sweetness such as "*selection de grains nobles*," or the fact that old vines—"*vieilles vignes*"—were used to make the wine.

PLACE OF ORIGIN: APPELLATION

No matter what the size of the place of origin, it will always be identified on every French wine label. It could be as large as the entire nation, in which case the label will offer information such as the phrase *vin de France,* or it could be as small as a single vineyard (La Romanee, for example), in which case the French *appellation* system will come into play. By the way, from the modern consumer's perspective, the phrases *appellation d'origine controlee (AOC)* and *appellation d'origine protegee* (AOP) are the same thing. We will take the easy way out and use the current acronym, AOP.

In most wine markets around the world, two levels of wine visibly represent France:

Indication Geographique Protegee (IGP; formerly *vins de pays),* wines from several large, defined regions, with few regulations about what grape types can be used and liberal limits to yields of grapes in the vineyards

AOP wines from both large and small defined areas, with very specific restrictions on which grape types can be used and maximum allowable vineyard yields.

French producers want to capture a share of the New World wine market, so many IGP wines are labeled with a grape variety name. Chardonnay, Merlot, and Syrah, among others, are especially popular in the international market. Whatever the name of the wine, all of these wines will be identified by the inclusion of the phrase *Indication Geographique Protegee* on the label, plus the name of the region where the grapes were grown. Prominent examples of IGP regions are *Pays d'Oc, des Collines Rhodaniennes, l'Ardeche, Gard, l'Herault,* and *pays Cotes de Gascogne.*

The vast majority of AOP wines in France are named after the place where the grapes grow (Vouvray, a village in the Loire Valley, is just one of hundreds of examples), and that place name is prominently displayed on the label (so the actual name of the wine is Vouvray). Underneath that place name, the phrase *appellation controlee* or *appellation protegee* usually appears. That is a consumer's legal guarantee that the wine has been made according to the specific regulations for that place.

The major French exceptions to place-named wines are the wonderful wines of Alsace, named for the grape variety that is used to make the wine. So we can enjoy Alsace Riesling and Alsace Pinot Gris, just two examples of the varietal-labeled wines of Alsace. Those wines are still made according to AOC/AOP regulations and will carry the phrase *appellation controlee* or *appellation protegee* on the label. If the grapes used to make the wine all came from a single vineyard, the name of that vineyard may appear on the label as well.

INDICATIONS OF STATUS

Five of France's classic wine regions (Alsace, Bordeaux, Burgundy, Champagne, and Loire Valley) have adopted a system of indicating on the label the legal status of some of their best vineyards. Though the exact wording varies from region to region, the general picture looks like this: over time, certain vineyards have developed a reputation for consistently producing better grapes, and better wines from those grapes, than their neighbors. These vineyards have earned the title *premier cru* (first growth). In addition, of the several thousand vineyards in France, only a few hundred have earned the extraordinary status of *grand cru* (great growth). (In Bordeaux, things get a little tricky; the equivalent phrase is *grand cru classe*—classified great growth—with the highest level being *premier grand cru classe*—first classified great growth; see "Bordeaux," page 165.)

If all the grapes used to make a wine came from a *premier cru* or *grand cru* vineyard, that phrase will show up on the label. Still, the consumer needs to be WineWise. *Premier cru* or *grand cru* is a sign that the wine might be great, truly memorable. Certainly it will carry a great, truly memorable price tag. But quality, as always, comes from the producer who has a reputation to uphold. In the regional sections that follow, we will be highlighting French producers that we think are consistent purveyors of high quality and whose wines can readily be found in most markets.

OTHER INFORMATION

In addition to the three major signposts of company name, wine name, and place name, wine labels often include other bits of information, such as the legal name and address of the producer and importer, and the alcohol content. Sometimes descriptive phrases that are meant to tell us more about the wine can be found, such as *reserve* or *vieilles vignes* (old vines). As far as we can tell, those particular phrases do not convey any specific legal meaning in France and can be used randomly and arbitrarily by producers.

Much like other wine producing countries such as the U.S.A., French wines sourced from smaller zones of production usually are more expensive than those from larger areas. For example, a wine from the Napa Valley normally sells for much more than one that just says "North Coast" or "California." This relates not only to supply and demand, but also to the idea that a wine lover may more easily define the style of a wine from a smaller area. Continuing with a California example, within the Napa Valley is the Howell Mountain sub-AVA. A Cabernet Sauvignon wine produced by the Cakebread winery and made from a Howell Mountain single vineyard, such as the Dancing Bear Vineyard, would be the smallest place of origin, or as they say in French, "*appellation.*"

Here is a French example: Within the AOP (*appellation*) region of Burgundy is the Cote de Nuits subregion, and within that is the town of Vosne-Romanee. The most expensive wines from that town are the single vineyards that are officially classified as *premier cru* or *grand cru* (more about the "*cru*" system of classification later).

Think of AOP as a recipe that can provide our *WineWise* readers with a dependable flavor. We know that Caesar Salad will have romaine lettuce, cheese, croutons, and yummy

Brut nonvintage Champagne is a dry wine made from a blend of several harvest years, known as "vintages." Veuve Clicquot "Yellow Label" is a popular example.

garlic-anchovy dressing. Similarly, when a consumer sees a label bearing the Medoc or Pauillac AOP designation he will know he has a dry, full-bodied red wine based mostly on Cabernet Sauvignon with some other permitted grapes like Merlot blended in. Since Chateau Mouton-Rothschild is in the village of Pauillac it will follow the same recipe of approved grapes and style.

French producers want to recapture a share of the New World wine market, so while many IGP wines have been labeled with a grape variety name, new laws are now permitting the grape name to appear more often on some AOP labels (for example, Chardonnay may be identified on the label of basic Bourgogne—French for Burgundy—AOP wine).

Olivier Leflaive is the producer/negociant for this regional Burgundy wine, which features the name of the grape—Chardonnay—on the label.

IN FRANCE, THE LOCATION OF THE VINEYARDS IS ON THE LABEL

No matter what the size of the place of origin, it will always be identified on every French wine label.

Visualize a pyramid with the least expensive wines labeled simply as "*Vin*" (wine) at the base of the pyramid. Wines in the "vin" category could come from anywhere in France.

The middle tier offers wines from regions within France that are labeled as *Indication Geographique Protegee* (IGP). An example is the Pays d'Oc, which stretches eastward from around the city of Perpignan near Spain and encompasses 700,000 acres (283,280 hectares) of land. About a third of all French wines fall into the IGP category, in which permitted yields of grapes at harvest are higher than those from the top category of AOP.

At the pinnacle of the quality pyramid are the wines that were traditionally known as AOC, but are now labeled as AOP. The phrases *appellation controlee* or *appellation d'origine controlee* (AOC) have been updated to *appellation d'origine protegee* (AOP), and mean the same thing. We will take the easy way out, sparing you the history of AOC, and use the more recently adopted term AOP.

Generally speaking, consumers will find the finest wines at the AOP (formerly AOC) top level of the quality pyramid. Within the large AOP regions such as Burgundy or Bordeaux the most expensive wines will come from single vineyards or an estate (*chateau*). IGP wines often feature the grape name on the label and are from large zones of wine production. *Vin* are wines that can come from anywhere in France and have the fewest restrictions in terms of grape types used and methods of production.

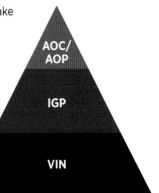

PULIGNY-MONTRACHET
FOLATIÈRES
PREMIER CRU

APPELLATION D'ORIGINE CONTRÔLÉE
MIS EN BOUTEILLE PAR JOSEPH DROUHIN A BEAUNE, FRANCE
AUX CELLIERS DES ROIS DE FRANCE ET DES DUCS DE BOURGOGNE
13,5% vol.   PRODUIT DE FRANCE   750 ml

Folatieres is a *premier cru* vineyard in the village of Puligny-Montrachet.

Unfortunately for the modern French wine industry and for consumers who do not have the patience or the desire to decipher the complicated code about which grapes correspond to which place name, the majority of AOP wines in France are still named after the place where the grapes grow. Also, they may or may not provide the name of the grapes used on the back label.

Remember that the phrase *appellation controlee* or *appellation protegee* is a guarantee of authenticity, not a guarantee of quality. High-quality wines are made by the hard work of conscientious producers, not through some set of rigid regulations. Just as a chef can overcook

and ruin wild salmon, so can high-quality grapes mutate into an undistinguished wine.

Our mantra is "the most important piece of information on any wine label is the name of the people who make the wine." To that end, in this chapter we will list some of our "go-to" producers in some of the most important wine regions. Again, to keep this book in a manageable size we apologize we cannot include all the worthy wineries in each section.

Regions

CHAMPAGNE

Ah, Champagne! A luxury wine in the minds of most people, but the savvy *WineWise* reader will soon come to understand that there are many more daily uses for this wonderful beverage other than celebrations. After all, what would brunch be without sparkling wine? Or the Super Bowl, the World Cup of Soccer, or the Stanley Cup finals, eh? Or, best of all, watching the sunset with someone you love. We're not suggesting that

REAL ESTATE AND THE CRU SYSTEM

As mentioned earlier, Alsace, Bordeaux, Burgundy, Champagne, and Loire have adopted a system to indicate on the label the legal status of some of their best vineyards. The vineyards that have developed a reputation for consistently producing better wines have earned the right to use the word *"cru"* or some variation such as *"premier cru"* (first growth), or *"grand cru"* (great growth). Grapes from a single vineyard may be sold to wineries, or *negociants*. Since the *negociants* who purchase these grapes have to pay a premium price for them, expect wines with a *"cru"* designation to be more interesting and more expensive than the standard wines from a place.

In the case of Bordeaux Chateaux, the vineyards and the house on the site are officially classified and their wines are only sourced from their own estate (estate bottled). Terms such as *grand cru classe* (great classified growth) or *premier grand cru classe* (first great classified growth) may appear on a label. More about the Bordeaux classification will be found in that section of this chapter.

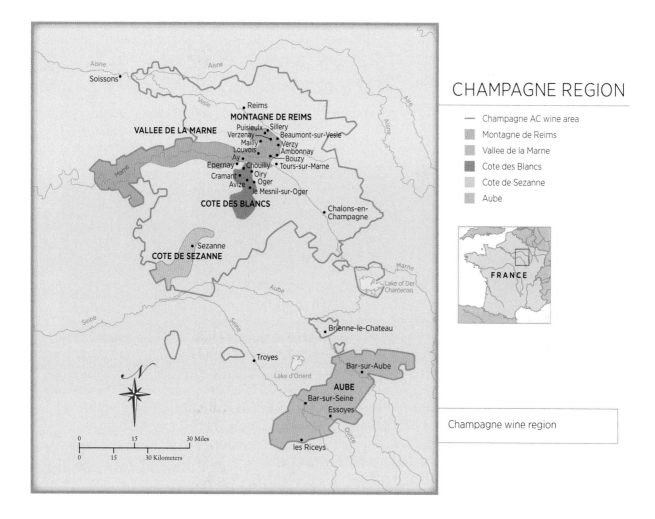

CHAMPAGNE REGION

— Champagne AC wine area
▨ Montagne de Reims
▨ Vallee de la Marne
▨ Cote des Blancs
▨ Cote de Sezanne
▨ Aube

FRANCE

Champagne wine region

you use the finest $250 Champagne to make a mimosa, but Champagne with breakfast, lunch, dinner, or midnight snacks is energizing!

First of all, a distinction: real Champagne comes from the region called Champagne in northern France, and all other sparkling wines are just that—sparkling wines—though some of them are very fine. Sparkling wines made in the Champagne region of France must be produced by the Champagne method (see page 3), and the wine must be made from one or more of the following grapes: the red Pinot Noir and Pinot Meunier, and the white Chardonnay.

Even though two of those grapes are red, the reason most Champagnes are white is because most often the grapes are pressed near the vineyards and only the clear juice is brought to the winery. When a winery wants to make a rosé wine they allow some skin contact. The skins are the source of color for the pale pink or watermelon-colored rosé Champagnes.

Good Champagne is not only bubbly—it has a distinctive flavor profile with slight variations depending on the house style of the producer and on what percentage of red or white grapes are used to make the wine. Many producers like to create a wine with a little yeasty aroma and flavor, something that comes across as (not surprisingly) bread- or dough-like, or toasty, even like brioche. That may seem weird in a wine, but in some ways it's sort of comforting, like the warmth of the kitchen associated with baking. Recall that Champagne gets its bubbles into the wine through a second fermentation in the bottle. After the fermentation has finished, Champagne producers leave the wine aging on the yeast cells in the bottle for at least 15 months (in fact, they are required to do this), and often longer. That is when the wine picks up these yeast aromas.

In terms of flavor profile, you can find anything from green apple and citrus to red berries as an aroma and on the palate, depending on

A cool start to the day in a Champagne vineyard.

whether there was more Chardonnay (apples, citrus) used to make the wine or more of the Pinots (red fruits). Variations of style also derive from techniques used to make the wines, the vineyards the grapes are sourced from, whether the grapes are fermented in stainless-steel or oak barrels, and how much sugar is added to the wines before they are sold. For example, within the most popular category of Brut Champagne there is a permitted range of sugar that can be added.

Seriously, what is so special about Champagne compared to other sparkling wines? In one word, *chalk*. Chalk soil gives Champagne that unique smell that many describe as crushed oyster shells or stones from a river. The vineyards of Champagne contain fossilized oyster shells as well as many other influences from the time that this area was part of an ocean. The mineral qualities of the soils, coupled with the aging process in the bottle, impart complex flavors to the wine. Some Champagne producers ferment their wines in oak barrels, and that too can add flavors and structure to a wine.

Just as you cannot improve someone's personality through cosmetic surgery, you cannot simply add chalk to the vineyard soils of other sparkling wine–producing regions and expect a fantastic result. It just won't happen. Simply put,

Champagnes have a truly unique flavor profile and consumers are willing to pay a premium price to experience it.

THE CHAMPAGNE LABEL

A Champagne label will not ordinarily tell you how long the wine has aged in the bottle after the second fermentation. So getting to know which producers invest the time and money to make more complex aged wines and which producers rush their simple wines to market will require some research. However, there is a style of Champagne that is labeled "recently disgorged"

Blanc de blancs in Champagne indicates a wine that is pure Chardonnay and light in body. Ruinart makes a fine example.

or "RD," a sure indication that the wine stayed aging on the yeast cells for many, many years and will be very toasty (and very expensive). In between the simpler nonvintage style and the recently disgorged style are the vintage-dated wines, which by law are aged a minimum of three years; the best are aged longer than that.

As to grape varieties used, except for some specific styles, there will be no indication on most labels. Most producers make their standard Champagne by blending wines from all three grape varieties, and the proportion of each grape used depends on the producer. But sometimes you will see a label with the words "*blanc de blancs*," which tells you that the wine was made entirely from white (Chardonnay) grapes. If you are drinking Champagne without food, the *blanc de blancs* style is wonderful as an aperitif, a before-dinner drink.

AN IMPORTANT *WINEWISE* TIP: The exclusive association of Chardonnay with *blanc de blancs* is true only for Champagne. Other wine-producing areas all around the world may use the term "*blanc de blancs*," but they may be allowed to use white grapes other than Chardonnay.

The term "*blanc de noirs*" tells us that only Pinot Noir and Pinot Meunier have been used.

Perhaps more important than which grapes have been used is that the *blanc de blancs* style will always be light in body and the *blanc de noirs* style are medium-full to full in body. This is important when balancing the "weight" of the wine with the delicacy or richness of the food with which it will be paired.

So, what does the label always tell us? If the wine is truly Champagne, that term will show up on the label as its appellation.

In addition, the label will always provide an indication of the final sweetness level of the wine, ranging from bone dry to very sweet. These terms allow for a small range of sweetness within the category so one producer's extra-dry Champagne may be a little sweeter than another producer's.

Ultra Brut and Extra Brut are the driest styles of Champagne.

WINEWISE TIP: In terms of wine and food pairing we like to think of extra-dry Champagne as being similar to Riesling or Chenin Blanc, because they all have a hint of sweetness. So any time a touch of sweetness seems appropriate in a wine and food pairing, consider using an extra-dry Champagne instead of a still wine. Or better yet, try both wines with the same foods. With spicy food the bubbles seem to first elevate and then dissipate the heat of a dish. Check out our wine and food pairing chapter, beginning on page 293, for more information about pairing sparkling wine with food.

The terms used have evolved over time, as the fashion for sweetness in Champagne has declined, and the English-language equivalent of the French phrases may appear misleading. However, we assure the *WineWise* reader that the following applications are accurate.

These wines are best for savory foods:

EXTRA BRUT, ULTRA BRUT, OR BRUT SAUVAGE are the driest wines.

BRUT is dry, and by far the most popular style of Champagne.

EXTRA DRY is off-dry or semi-dry.

These wines are for desserts or a cheese course:

SEC is lightly sweet.

DEMI SEC is sweet and easy to find in North America.

DOUX is the sweetest style of Champagne.

Another important label term is the use of the phrase *grand cru* or *premier cru*, meaning that the grapes have come from vineyards that have been classified as such. In fact, both of these quality designations are given to entire villages, so the grapes need only come from vineyards in a village or villages that have been rated *grand cru* or *premier cru*. Not surprisingly, a village name may also appear on the label, such as Ambonnay, Bouzy, or Cramant, if the grapes were sourced in only one village.

WHITE AND ROSÉ /VINTAGE AND NONVINTAGE STYLES OF CHAMPAGNE

The vast majority of all Champagne is white, but many producers also make a rosé version. Rosé Champagne can be made by making rosé base wines from contact with the grape skins before the second fermentation takes place in the bottle. Another way to make rosé Champagne is to use a little local red wine as the final *dosage* that is added to top off the bottle after the sediment is removed from the second fermentation (see page 4).

Whether the wine is white or rosé, Champagne comes in two versions—nonvintage (the norm) or vintage (the exception).

Nonvintage Champagne, especially nonvintage brut Champagne, is the bread and butter of all Champagne producers—it's what pays the bills. But that doesn't mean to say it's second-class stuff. In many ways it is a vastly more remarkable product than vintage Champagne.

To make nonvintage Champagne, the winemaker has to balance several acts of blending on several different levels. He or she is blending different grape varieties, from different locations, to produce a base blend from the current harvest year. Then the winemaker has to blend in small portions of different wines from previous harvests so that the final finished product will taste exactly the same as the previous bottling from that producer—the producer's "house style." That is a remarkable achievement—consistency of style and flavor from year to year despite dramatic swings in growing conditions from one year to the next.

In comparison, making vintage Champagne is relatively easy. Vintage Champagne is not made every year: it is made only in those years when the quality of the grapes makes base wines that the winemaker believes can stand on their own, representative of the growing conditions that year. Even then, it is usually a blended wine, made from different grape varieties grown in different locations, but all in the same year. From all of that fuss you could rightly conclude that discerning Champagne producers make vintage Champagne relatively rarely, and when they do, it is only a small percentage of their total output. Even if they make vintage Champagne, they still have to keep up their regular output of nonvintage wines, produced in much higher volume than vintage Champagnes.

Thus each Champagne producer usually makes at least two versions of Champagne (nonvintage and vintage), perhaps also rosé versions of those, maybe a *blanc de blancs,* perhaps a recently disgorged, and very often a top-of-the-line (usually vintage) product, their *cuvee de prestige* wine. The product line of a company such as Taittinger is fairly typical: nonvintage brut "La Française," vintage brut (produced only in some years), nonvintage sec "Nocturne," and vintage brut *blanc de blancs* "Comtes de Champagne" and "Comtes de Champagne" brut rosé, which are their *cuvee de prestige* premium products.

If nonvintage Brut is the basic breadwinner for most Champagne producers, it follows that those wines are usually the least expensive in any producer's range, often under $50 per bottle. At the truly expensive end of the range are Salon (only available in vintage *blanc de blancs* "Le Mesnil" at about $350) and Krug (*cuvee de prestige* "Clos du Mesnil Blanc de Blancs" at $800 and "Clos d'Ambonnay Blanc de Noirs" at a breathtaking $2,600).

Suggested producers include Charles Heidsieck, Deutz, Pol Roger, Veuve Clicquot, Aubry et Fils, Pierre Gimonnet, Paul Goerg, Egly-Ouriet, Alfred Gratien, Duval-Leroy, Henriot, Jacquart, Philipponnat, Pommery, Laurent-Perrier, Jacques Selosse, Jacquesson, Vilmart, Jean Milan,

Gosset, Perrier Jouet, Billecart-Salmon, Drappier, Pierre Peters, Lasalle, Delamotte, Larmandier-Bernier, Bruno Paillard, Rene Geoffroy, Louis Roederer, Besserat de Bellefon, Charles Ellner, Salon, Ayala, Mumm, Taittinger, Krug, Moet et Chandon, Ruinart, and Bollinger.

ALSACE

Considering the modern international wine market, Alsace might hold a unique competitive advantage over other classic French AOP wine regions because the overwhelming majority of its wines display varietal labels.

Alsace is a region that is unique in many other ways, as well. The gastronomy, which of course includes wines, is an expression of the melding of French and German culture that represents the region's history. With the exception of their exciting but restrained Riesling wines, the other, mainly white grape varieties are presented in a rich, full-bodied style, tempered by refreshing acidity. While Alsace focuses on white wine (90%), its full range of wines includes good value sparkling Cremant d'Alsace and a small amount of red and rosé wines, made from Pinot Noir.

The Alsace region is about 62 miles (100 kilometers) long and the Vosges Mountains and Rhine River help moderate the cold

Alsace wine region.

temperature so grapes can achieve full ripeness. Vineyards are planted as high as 1,300 feet (400 meters) facing south and southwest to receive the morning and afternoon sunshine. The protection from rain by the Vosges Mountains, high acidity from the cool temperature, ripe grapes, and the skill of the winemakers enables Alsace producers to make some of the most full-bodied and long-lived white wines in the world.

Alsace has about 50 *grand cru* vineyards. If all the grapes used to make a wine came from one such vineyard, the phrase *grand cru* and the name of the vineyard may appear on the label. Some wineries have long preferred to use a proprietary name on their labels ("Cuvee Frederic Emile" Riesling, for example, from the Trimbach winery) instead of the term *grand cru*. One reason that some wineries do not use *grand cru* or other vineyard terms is that the place names within Alsace are mostly German, and not so easy to pronounce for French speakers. Also, several producers believe that they make a better wine when it is the product of several fine vineyards, even if some of them are not classified as *grand cru*. In order to have sufficient quantity to market their wines some producers may blend, for example, Riesling grapes

from five or 10 different vineyards and feature *grand cru* on the label without designating which vineyards have been sourced for the wine.

Some wineries take yet another approach to promote a superior vineyard site. The word "*clos*" means an enclosed or walled vineyard and some of the finest wines from Alsace, such as Clos Ste. Hune, Clos des Capucins, or Clos Saint Landelin, feature those names prominently on the label along with the name of the grape type.

The four white grapes considered the most "noble" in Alsace are Riesling, Gewurztraminer, Pinot Gris, and Muscat. If they are planted in a *grand cru* vineyard site that vineyard name can appear on the wine label along with the name of the grape variety.

WHITE WINES

Gewurztraminer and Pinot Gris. Alsatian
wine producers are proud of a couple of wines they like to make in an opulent, almost decadent style: Gewurztraminer and Pinot Gris. Their rich, smooth texture is immediately appealing, in a sensual, gratifying way, but there is just enough

Riesling vines among the roses at Domaine Weinbach in Alsace.

restraint in the fresh acidity and underlying mineral quality that they do not become blatant or overwhelming.

The assertive flavors and supple texture of Gewurztraminer and Pinot Gris make them delightful companions with the intense flavors of Alsatian cuisine, such as onion tart, cured pork dishes with cabbage (the famous *choucroute alsacienne*), braised game birds such as duck and goose, and foie gras. Their light sweetness, full fruitiness, and smooth texture also make them excellent accompaniments to Thai and Korean cuisine with their underlying heat and spice.

Riesling. And then there is Riesling. Alsace offers a unique style of Riesling that must be savored to be understood. If Alsatian "Gewurz" and Pinot Gris are pushed in one direction, toward richness and opulence, Riesling is often pushed in the opposite direction, toward restraint and subtlety. Alsace winemakers are creating delicious wines that show the extraordinary capabilities of all these grapes to their fullest potential.

There is a Riesling renaissance in America and we, along with our professional colleagues and friends, are seriously addicted to Riesling. Riesling may just be the most adaptable, some might say the most tolerant, white wine to pair with food. And Alsace makes some of the best Rieslings in the world. Each producer expresses the grape differently. Some Alsace Rieslings are delicate, lean wines with an emphasis on mineral flavors and just the slightest hint of sweetness. Other wines come at you like a sumo wrestler, with a big attack on the palate of many fruits, spices, flowers, as well as other flavors.

In Alsace, different *negociants*/producers offer different styles of Riesling in terms of "weight" on the palate and the amount of residual sugar in the wine. This is true not only for Riesling but also for Gewurztraminer, Pinot Gris, and Muscat (see next). Remember our mantra: the most important piece of information on the label is the name of the family or company that makes the wine. Just to get *WineWise* readers started, we consider the wines of Trimbach

to be more reserved and refined on the palate and those from Zind Humbrecht to be hedonistically voluptuous and richer in texture. Lighter, less assertive styles of Alsace Riesling lend themselves to pairing with salads, lightly poached or sautéed fish, or sautéed chicken with a light butter and wine sauce. It is also grand with smoked salmon or trout, oysters on the half shell, and ceviche. Richer styles of Riesling can be paired with pork chops, oyster stew, or turkey sandwich leftovers from Thanksgiving.

Muscat. "Isn't Muscat a sweet wine?" you ask. In this world, usually it is. But Alsatian winemakers have their own world, and it has always included dry Muscat, a wonderful, intriguing concept since it combines the aromatic delicacy of ripe and almost tropical flavors with the sharp directness of a dry wine. Alsace Muscat is a beautiful accompaniment to sushi and sashimi and will shine when paired with a dry, crumbly cheese such as aged Cantal or the sharp tanginess of Comté or Emmental.

Pinot Blanc and Sylvaner. With the grape types already discussed, the superlatives are easy to roll out. Pinot Blanc and Sylvaner may not be as showy as the "fabulous four," but that does not mean you should avoid them. They are great choices—and often great values—when you want something like Chardonnay but cannot face the overt oak that is so frequently a part of the Chardonnay scene. Although Pinot Blanc may never shine, it is always a very well-made wine with ripe apple and pear characteristics. We enjoy the racy acidity of Sylvaner. Pair Pinot Blanc with pasta with a cream sauce or a BLT sandwich. Sylvaner can be paired with a weisswurst or hotdog with mustard and sauerkraut or a hearts of palm salad with a citrus dressing.

WineWise tip: Although Alsace is famous for its dry and off-dry wines, the region's wine producers also make rare and expensive sweet wines. Look for the words *"selection de grains nobles"* on the varietal label, which indicates that the grapes have been affected by botrytis, the "noble rot."

Interestingly, Alsace also produces late harvest wines (look for "*vendange tardive*" on the label), which may also be sweet, but just as often the wines are produced in a dry style, with just about all of the residual sugar converted to alcohol.

SPARKLING WINES

Like the sparkling wines of other French regions (except Champagne), the bubblies of Alsace are called *cremant* wines, in this case Cremant d'Alsace.

They are made by the classic Champagne method (see page 3), using any one or a blend of Pinot Blanc, Pinot Gris, Pinot Noir, Riesling, and Chardonnay. Some of the finer examples take on the standard toasty notes that come with prolonged aging in contact with the yeast cells (see page 4), while others are more straightforwardly fruity. Try these delicious wines with potato latkes and sour cream or with spicy pad thai—you will be surprised. While they may never scale the heights of great Champagne, they are an excellent alternative. They may be affordable, even inexpensive, but they are never cheap.

WINEWISE TIP: Cremant d'Alsace is the most popular style of sparkling wine consumed in France and is a *WineWise* best buy. About 20 million bottles are made each year so it should be fairly easy to find.

Suggested producers include Trimbach, Zind Humbrecht, Marcel Deiss, Hugel, Pierre Sparr, Albert Mann, Josmeyer, Kuentz-Bas, Blanck, Leon Beyer, Domaine Mittnacht, Schlumberger, Mure, Dopff au Moulin, Dopff et Irion, Bott-Geyl, Zink, Kreydenweiss, Albert Boxler, Lucien Albrecht, and Domaine Weinbach.

LOIRE VALLEY

Situated in the northwestern quadrant of the nation, the Loire Valley is a huge wine region, radiating out from the banks of the Loire River,

producing every type of wine imaginable, from several different grape types. But when we think of Loire wines the first thing that pops into our heads are the refreshing light white wines of the region. With such an abundance of seafood and fish sourced from the Atlantic Ocean and the river itself, it seems only natural that the area's farmers would plant white grapes to pair with the local cuisine.

We believe that Chenin Blanc is one of the world's finest grape varieties, and the best expressions of that grape come from the Loire Valley. The locals must agree with us as it is the only grape variety to merit "*grand cru*" status and is produced as dry, semi-dry, or sweet still wines and also as dry sparkling wines. In addition to a tiny percentage of *grand cru* wines, Chenin Blanc–based wines from AOP villages such as Vouvray or Montlouis make exciting wines that you can afford to drink whenever you like.

Muscadet is one of our best-value wines in the world and we love to drink it when it's fresh, crisp, and young, but some producers make age-worthy Muscadets that actually improve in the bottle over five or eight years.

Affordable sparkling wines made in the Loire Valley by the Champagne method are known as Cremant de la Loire, and they are delicious bubbly. Completing the color palette of Loire wines are the little-known and often undervalued

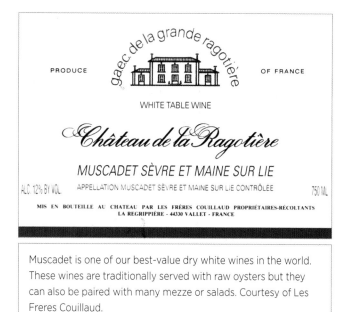

Muscadet is one of our best-value dry white wines in the world. These wines are traditionally served with raw oysters but they can also be paired with many mezze or salads. Courtesy of Les Freres Couillaud.

rosés and reds, especially those wines made from Cabernet Franc and Pinot Noir.

We suggest that the *WineWise* reader think of the Loire Valley as a group of three wine zones—the West End, the Center, and the East End. For each of these areas we will discuss the principal wines and the grape types used.

WEST END

This part of the Loire Valley is closest to the Atlantic Ocean. The climatic and culinary influences are all part of the wine heritage here. Here one wine dominates—the dry still white Muscadet. For those who love wine trivia, the official name of the grape type used is Melon de Bourgogne. But that will not help you in the

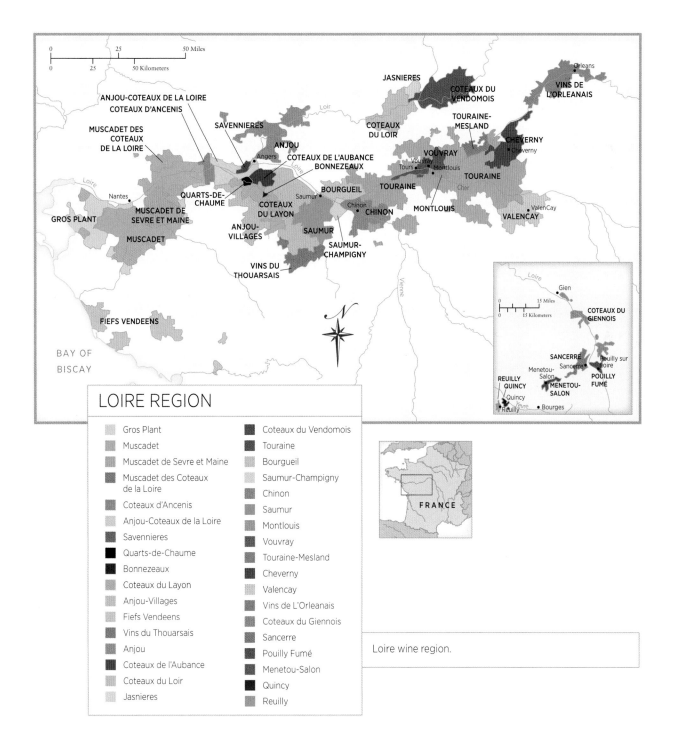

LOIRE REGION

- Gros Plant
- Muscadet
- Muscadet de Sevre et Maine
- Muscadet des Coteaux de la Loire
- Coteaux d'Ancenis
- Anjou-Coteaux de la Loire
- Savennieres
- Quarts-de-Chaume
- Bonnezeaux
- Coteaux du Layon
- Anjou-Villages
- Fiefs Vendeens
- Vins du Thouarsais
- Anjou
- Coteaux de l'Aubance
- Coteaux du Loir
- Jasnieres

- Coteaux du Vendomois
- Touraine
- Bourgueil
- Saumur-Champigny
- Chinon
- Saumur
- Montlouis
- Vouvray
- Touraine-Mesland
- Cheverny
- Valencay
- Vins de L'Orleanais
- Coteaux du Giennois
- Sancerre
- Pouilly Fumé
- Menetou-Salon
- Quincy
- Reuilly

Loire wine region.

least, since you will never see it on a label. The wine is called Muscadet because that is how the local growers refer to the wine.

Whether you find Muscadet, Muscadet Cotes de Grandlieu, Muscadet des Coteaux de la Loire, or the ubiquitous Muscadet Sevre-et-Maine, the wine's characteristics are essentially the same—a high-acid, dry wine with green fruit, a stone-like mineral character, and a sense of smoothness on the middle palate. That smoothness comes from the practice of leaving the wine on the lees—the yeast sediment—in stainless-steel tanks after fermentation (the label will carry the phrase "*sur lie*"). This imparts a smooth texture to the wine, along with perhaps a bit of spritz—a gentle sparkle.

Muscadet is the archetypal seafood wine, shining with oysters on the half shell, but also very good with ceviche, cured herring, fish tacos, Vietnamese spring rolls, or a Greek salad.

Some of our favorite picks for Muscadet in the bargain category (about $15 or less) include Marquis de Goulaine, Les Vergers, Domaine Luneau-Papin, Domaine de L'Ecu, Domaine de la Quilla, Domaine de la Pepiere, Domaine Sauvion, Chateau de la Chesnaie, La Forcine, Domaine de la Louvetrie, and Chateau de la Ragotiere. Brejeon, Guy Bossard, Mark Olivier, Domaine des Dorices, Bonnet Huteau, Domaine la Haute Fevrie, and Chereau Carre are respected producers whose ageworthy wines are in the moderate price range (up to $35, sometimes less).

CENTER

There is a whole lot happening in this part of the Loire Valley. The Center makes every type of wine, from sparkling to white, rosé, and red. For white wines, Chenin Blanc is the star here, with Sauvignon Blanc playing a supporting role. Cabernet Franc is the main grape for reds.

Chenin Blanc is not as widely known as it should be in the wine world, but it has found a home for centuries in this part of the Loire Valley, where it can produce sublime dry and sweet versions in different places, such as Vouvray and Anjou (see the map of the Loire Valley on page 161). Good Chenin Blanc will always display a touch of the aroma of honey, quince, and nuts on the nose and palate. In addition, there is an attractive floral aroma and the flavor of melons. As with all Loire Valley wines, the Chenins from this area retain a high level of refreshing acidity, adding to their charm as summer wines. Chenin Blanc is one of our "go-to" wines when we are doing a tasting menu of many courses, whether the food is poached or sautéed fish dishes, Korean/French fusion, Caribbean, or classic French (we feel the same way about Riesling, a grape featured in the Alsace section of this chapter).

In Bordeaux, Cabernet Franc is often thought of as a minor component in Cabernet Sauvignon or Merlot blended red wines, but here in the Center of the Loire Valley, it is the first violin, while grapes such as Cabernet Sauvignon or Gamay play second fiddle in a blend. Wines such as Chinon, Bourgueil, and Saumur-Champigny, some of them 100% Cabernet Franc, some of them blends, are seen more and more frequently in the U.S. market, and the viability of Cab Franc as a stand-alone wine is reflected in the copycat versions that can now be found from Napa Valley to New York State. Loire Valley Cab Francs have the typically high acidity of the area, balanced nicely by aromas and flavors of ripe red berry fruits such as strawberry and raspberry.

Dry and Semi-Dry White Wines. In the Center there are four major villages that produce various styles of Chenin Blanc wines and two place names associated with Sauvignon Blanc. The Sauvignon Blanc areas are Touraine (the countryside surrounding the city of Tours) and Cheverny. As the *WineWise* reader might by now suspect, these dry whites are refreshingly high in acidity but also bright with the green ripeness of kiwis and limes. The Touraine wines are usually labeled as Sauvignon de Touraine, while the Cheverny wines retain that village name as the name of the wine.

As for the Chenin Blanc AOP villages, they are Anjou, Saumur, Savennieres, Jasnieres, Montlouis, Reuilly, and Vouvray. Of those, Vouvray may be the best known in the U.S. market, but the others are now finding increasing space on store shelves and wine lists. We welcome that development, since the wines from these villages can be truly fine—they are the benchmark of great Chenin Blanc.

However, you will still have some sorting out to do in terms of the styles of these wines. Anjou Blanc is usually dry, as are Saumur and Savennieres (perhaps the most elegant expression of Chenin Blanc in the world). Most Vouvray would fall into a category called "off-dry," showing a hint of sweetness. But in the end it is all up to the producer. Some make their wines bone dry, while others prefer a medium-sweet style. The only hint you might get on the label comes from a few French terms that may appear. *Sec* is dry. *Sec-tendre* indicates an off-dry style, while *moelleux* suggests a fuller sweetness, but not sticky sweet like late harvest wines.

From Vouvray fine producers include Domaine des Aubuisieres, Francois Pinon, Domaine Allias, Domaine Pichot, Domaine Bourillon, Marc Bredif, Domaine de Clos Naudin, and Domaine Huet. Although some of these wines can be expensive they are relative values compared to the great white wines of Burgundy and Bordeaux.

From Savennieres we suggest Domaine des Baumard, Clos du Papillon, and Domaine de Closel. Two expensive but very special wines from within Savennieres are the *grands crus* Roche aux Moines and Coulée de Serrant. The latter is a *monopole* or single owner vineyard made by the famous promoter of biodynamic farming, Nicolas Joly.

WINEWISE tip: Although we adore the wines of Vouvray, as bargain seekers we also suggest the Chenin Blanc still wines from the lesser known Jasnieres AOP and the still and sparkling versions from Montlouis. Francois Chidaine is a very respected producer of both Vouvray and Montlouis.

Distinctly Sweet White Wines. Some areas of the Center specialize in sweeter Chenin Blanc wines, the result of either late harvest and/or botrytis (see page 9). A broad regional appellation is Coteaux du Layon. The much smaller appellations of Bonnezeaux and Quarts de Chaume scale greater heights of intensity and balance and have been honored with *grand cru* status. In quality, these wines are certainly equal to fine Sauternes from Bordeaux or good late harvest and botrytis-affected wines from California or Australia. Yet they are distinctly lighter and less syrupy, with a very high natural acidity that leaves the mouth feeling fresh and clean—a welcome relief after all that sweetness.

Here we get into the territory of moderately expensive to very expensive wines, with Domaine des Baumards, Chateau de Fesles, and Domaine de Closel leading the pack.

Rosé Wines. At one time, rosé wines from the Loire Valley were the White Zinfandels of the wine world in terms of their popularity and widespread consumption. But things change, and now they are the alternative. They come in dry to medium-sweet versions and always display the kind of bright, fresh red berry fruit character that is so attractive in a good rosé. The key to the sweetness level is in sly nuances of labeling, so pay attention: the dry versions are called Rosé de la Loire, while the semi-sweet versions are called Rosé d'Anjou or Cabernet d'Anjou. You don't have to pay quite so much attention to price, as these rosé wines are all good bargains.

Sparkling Wines. Made by the Champagne method, the sparkling wines of the Loire Valley offer excellent quality at competitive prices. Based on the Chenin Blanc grape type, they are distinctly different from Champagne and Champagne lookalikes but are well worth trying. A few different appellations and names are permitted, some regional and some village-specific. Sparkling appellations are Anjou Mousseux, Saumur Mousseux, Vouvray Mousseux, Montlouis Mousseux, and Cremant de la Loire, and they all fall within the relative bargain or moderately expensive category.

Red Wines. Cabernet Franc is the dominant grape here with permitted support from the Cabernet Sauvignon for the best known wines of Chinon and Bourgueil. These medium- to full-bodied dry red wines are very often pure expressions of Cabernet Franc and they offer a bouquet and flavors of spices, flowers, nuts, and red and black fruit. Fine examples of Chinon from wineries such as Charles Joguet or Bourgueil from Yannick Amirault can improve at the table by decanting (see page 358) or in the cellar for a decade or more.

WineWise TIP: Saumur-Champigny is a good value red wine based on Cabernet Franc blended with a bit of Cabernet Sauvignon in a lighter style that can be enjoyed younger than Chinon and Bourgueil.

EAST END

Separated completely from the other Loire Valley wine areas, and situated almost in the geographic center of France, the extraordinary "island" of Sancerre and Pouilly-Fumé produces dry white wines from the Sauvignon Blanc grape, usually unencumbered by oak. The best wines from this area offer a layered complexity that includes a bracing level of acidity, with aromas and flavors of ripe citrus fruits, gooseberry, freshly mowed grass, and an intriguing minerality.

The Loire Valley is also home to some very fine goat cheeses such as Crotin and Chavignol; these cheeses are classically paired with the tart Sauvignon Blanc–based wines from the "East End."

Moderately priced wines from Sancerre are made by Fournier, Jolivet, Domaine des Berthiers, and Domaine de la Perriere. Relative bargains from Pouilly-Fumé are well represented by Michel Redde, Jean Pabiot, and Domaine Chatelain, among others.

In the moderately expensive category for Sancerre we recommend the wines of Henri Bourgeois, Bailly-Riverdy, Lucien Crochet, and Domaine Thomas. For Pouilly-Fumé we suggest Ladoucette and Serge Dagueneau.

A number of East End wines are getting increasingly expensive, but they are well worth trying. In the very expensive category we include Alphonse Mellot, Clos de la Poussie, Vacheron, and Cotat for Sancerre, and Didier Dagueneau for Pouilly-Fumé.

The hilltop town of Sancerre.

BORDEAUX

Almost everything to do with Bordeaux wine is big. The appellation area covers 275,000 acres (111,000 hectares), more than five times the size of Burgundy and eight times the size of Napa Valley. Making a living from grape growing in the region are 1,200 growers whose grapes produce about 850 million bottles of AOP wines each year. That's one big wine cellar.

The sheer size of everything means that Bordeaux has a finger in every pie—or a nose in every glass—of the wine business. They make white, red, rosé, sparkling, and even fortified wines. They can be sweet or dry, expensive or affordable. They boast some of the greatest wine names ever to grace a table, wines that show up on most people's top-ten list. They make excellent, very good, good, and occasionally even mediocre wines.

The region is most famous for its expensive dry red and white wines as well as sweet white wines from the Sauternes and Barsac areas. The world's wealthiest people may have the good fortune to purchase the truly elite wines but the truth of the matter is that there are Bordeaux wines to fit every budget.

One of the reasons we can find very good and good, often from the same producer, is that Bordeaux chateaux (wine-producing estates) often have access to grapes from older, mature vines as well as grapes from recently planted vines. Most vineyards are in a constant state of flux, with older vines being replaced by younger ones on a regular basis. In general, grapes from young vines make wines that are less complex and have a sense of immaturity about them—they are less refined, less polished. Even the finest chateau will use grapes from younger vines to produce a "second-label" wine. For example, Chateau Lagrange produces a second-label Les Fiefs de Lagrange, which sells for about half the price of Chateau Lagrange, the "first-label" wine. Even though the raw material for the second-label wine may be less prestigious, it benefits from being sourced from the same esteemed vineyard and all of the expertise and experience that go into making Chateau Lagrange a fine wine. In this way, second-label wines from Bordeaux chateaux represent excellent value, and most of them can be enjoyed sooner, as they don't require as much aging as a chateau's flagship wine.

Another consideration for the range of qualities and prices is the diversity of the appellations. As in everything, the famous and the perceived best receive 90% of all the attention. In this way, the appellations of Medoc, Haut-Medoc, Pessac-Leognan, St-Emilion, and Pomerol receive the lion's share of publicity and media glare for dry wines. Wines from those appellations are also the most expensive. But if we venture into the outlying appellations, the Bordeaux "satellites" of Premieres Cotes de Bordeaux, Cotes de Bourg, Cotes de Blaye, Fronsac, and Canon Fronsac, we can frequently find very good dry wines at very fair prices. Sauternes and Barsac are the media darlings for sweet wines but the AOPs of Cadillac, Cerons, Cotes de Bordeaux-St. Macaire, and Loupiac also offer sweet wines at much more reasonable prices.

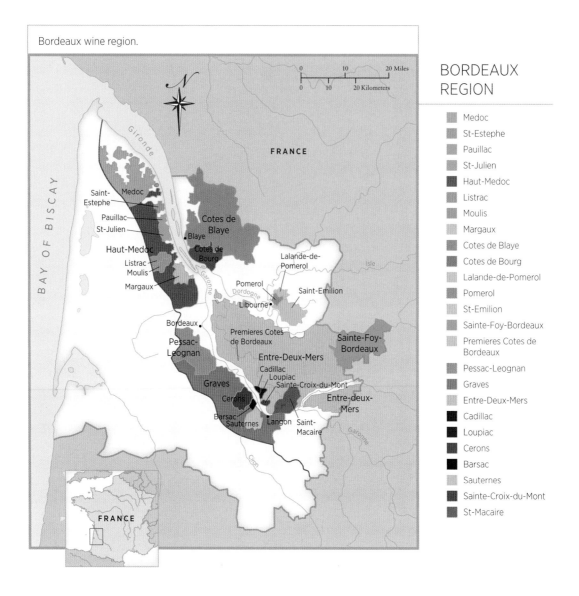

Bordeaux wine region.

BORDEAUX REGION

- Medoc
- St-Estephe
- Pauillac
- St-Julien
- Haut-Medoc
- Listrac
- Moulis
- Margaux
- Cotes de Blaye
- Cotes de Bourg
- Lalande-de-Pomerol
- Pomerol
- St-Emilion
- Sainte-Foy-Bordeaux
- Premieres Cotes de Bordeaux
- Pessac-Leognan
- Graves
- Entre-Deux-Mers
- Cadillac
- Loupiac
- Cerons
- Barsac
- Sauternes
- Sainte-Croix-du-Mont
- St-Macaire

Bordeaux offers 57 distinct appellations, AOPs whose official place names will appear on the label. There are nine permitted grape types and four different classification systems that afford the status of *premier grand cru classe* or *grand cru classe* to a total of about 170 chateaux. To beat a clear and easily navigable path through all of this, we will break down Bordeaux wines in the following manner:

grape types

appellations/AOPs associated with white or red wine production

comments on the status symbols of *premier grand cru classe* and *grand cru classe*

descriptions of each appellation and some of its wines in more detail

GRAPE TYPES

The heart and soul of Bordeaux wines rest on two major white grapes and three dominant reds. For both dry and sweet white wines, Bordeaux winemakers often blend Sauvignon Blanc and Semillon and may include a small amount of Muscadelle.

All the Bordeaux red wines are blends made mostly from two or more of the three major grape types—Cabernet Sauvignon, Merlot, and Cabernet Franc. Petit Verdot and Malbec play supporting roles in the blended red wines. Semillon is the most planted white grape of Bordeaux and Merlot is the most planted red grape of Bordeaux as well as all of France.

MAKING WINE FROM A BLEND OF GRAPE TYPES

When wines are a blend of grape types, usually each grape variety is harvested separately and made into a single-varietal wine. If any oak aging is required, that also is done separately for each single varietal. After each wine has begun to show its potential character, blending begins. The different wines are blended to produce the best possible sum of their parts. This usually means that the exact blend is rarely the same from year to year—it is close, but there are variations. This allows the winemaker to take advantage of any single grape type that excelled during the growing season, using more of that grape type than usual. After the wines from each grape type have been blended, the final product is allowed to age in order to marry together the various flavor and aroma components.

MAJOR APPELLATIONS IN BORDEAUX

Most appellation systems work on the basis of larger, more general appellations that contain smaller ones, and Bordeaux is no exception. The most general appellation here is Bordeaux. If a chateau's vineyards do not fall within a smaller appellation, the wine will be identified with the phrase Appellation Bordeaux Protegee (AOP).

One very attractive feature of the basic AOP Bordeaux wines is that larger, internationally minded producers have begun using these wines as a testing ground for including the grape variety on the label. For now, this is true only for proprietary named wines, many of which have been made as single-variety wines, but the trend may eventually embrace the chateau wines.

Among the smaller appellations, the main dry white wine areas are bargain priced Entre-Deux-Mers, Graves (not as inexpensive as Entre-Deux-Mers, but worth it) and its sub-appellation of Pessac-Leognan. Expect to pay the highest prices and receive the greatest complexity from the chateau wines of Pessac-Leognan.

The best-known and most expensive sweet white wine appellations are Sauternes and Barsac. For dry red wines, the main appellations are Medoc, Haut-Medoc, Graves and Pessac-Leognan (which also have great dry whites), St-Emilion, and Pomerol.

STATUS OR "CRU" CLASSIFICATIONS

Four of the appellations of the Bordeaux region have classification systems. Of these, two date from 1855 and apply to the numerous dry red wines of Haut-Medoc (plus just one red from Graves—the French never make it easy) and a small selection of the sweet white wines of Sauternes and Barsac. Back in those days, the wines listed in these classifications were considered to be the top-quality wines of those districts, and we would argue that, on balance, the classifications are still largely relevant today. Even if there are some new contenders, most of the elite wines included on the original lists still deserve their exalted place.

In 1959, the Graves district classification was introduced. The complete listings of these classifications can be found in *Exploring Wine* (it's written by us, too), or in any other good reference book on Bordeaux. The simple fact about all of these classifications is this: a Bordeaux wine that carries the phrase *grand cru classe* or *premier grand cru classe* on the label is considered to be a premium wine, and it will have a *premium* price tag (in France, "*cru*" means that a vineyard or estate has been officially classified as a superior vineyard). But (there's always a "but") some words of warning:

Chateau Palmer is a grand cru classe red wine from the village of Margaux in the Medoc district of Bordeaux. Courtesy of Chateau Palmer.

Alter Ego is the "second label" wine of Chateau Palmer. Bordeaux's "second label" wines are less expensive and can be enjoyed with less bottle aging. Courtesy of Chateau Palmer.

Bordeaux's Pomerol district has no classification system, and the magic phrase *grand cru classe* will never appear on a Pomerol label, but that does not mean they do not make superb wine there.

Some unclassified chateaux happily use the unrestricted phrase *grand vin de Bordeaux* on their label, but they have never been classified.

Comparing a *grand cru classe* wine from one appellation to a *grand cru classe* wine from another may not be comparing apples to apples (or grapes to grapes), since the grape blend will be different, as will the growing conditions and climate. And remember, some of Bordeaux's *grand cru classe* wines are not as grand as others, and neither are their prices.

The St-Emilion classification is revised every 10 years. The recent version survived a lengthy legal challenge from some unhappy producers who were not included or were demoted.

APPELLATIONS AND THEIR WINES

WHITE WINES

Entre-Deux-Mers. Wines from this appellation are all dry white wines made from Sauvignon Blanc, sometimes blended with Semillon. They will be labeled simply with the appellation name (Entre-Deux-Mers), or they may carry a chateau name if the grapes all came from one grape-growing estate. The area consists mostly of rolling uplands between the two major rivers Dordogne and Garonne. In recent years, most of the wines from this appellation have moved toward a fresh, simple, fruity style, often 100% Sauvignon Blanc with no wood aging. This makes them brightly attractive and appealing wines, great for light lunches and simple seafood dishes. When Semillon is included, the wines take on a riper tropical quality and fuller body; a small amount of Muscadelle lends floral and stone fruit notes. Our long-standing best value wine is Chateau Bonnet. It has a screwcap! Chateau Bonnet is certainly not a Bordeaux for wine snobs, but it works quite well with Asian, Latin, and Mediterranean foods.

Aging cellar at Chateau Palmer.

Graves. The Graves appellation lies on the west side of the Garonne River. Its dry white wines are indeed more serious—more grave, if you will—than their counterparts in Entre-Deux-Mers, but the name "Graves" refers to the gravelly soil that is typical of the area. The weightier style often comes from a higher proportion of Semillon blended with Sauvignon Blanc and a greater reliance on oak barrel fermentation or aging. The two white grapes are good partners, with the Sauvignon Blanc offering crisp acidity and fresh citrus or apricot aromas and flavors, while the Semillon provides greater roundness in the mouth and more tropical fruit flavors. The fuller expression makes the wines good partners with pork, chicken, or turkey dishes, as well as with heavier seafoods with cream sauces.

Some of the respected moderately expensive chateaux include Chateau Berger, Domaine La Grave, Clos Lamothe, Chateau Landiras, Chateau Rahoul, and Chateau Haut La Croix.

Pessac-Leognan. For many, this is the aristocracy of dry white Bordeaux wines, representing the fullest embodiment of the Semillon and Sauvignon Blanc blend. The reverence paid to some of these wines is a reflection of why the French have historically claimed to produce superior wines. There's no denying that there are certain parcels of land where soil type, climate, daylight hours, grape variety, and the winemaker's hard work come together to produce something very special, something impressive and memorable. Situated in the northernmost tip of the Graves appellation, Pessac-Leognan is one of those places. A higher proportion of gravelly quartzite in the soil and the slope and lie of the land bring out a mineral quality in the wine, tropical but clean and vibrant fruit with a depth and complexity that is simply absent in most Entre-Deux-Mers wines.

Chateau wines from Pessac-Leognan offer flowers, citrus, and other tropical fruits in a medium to full body with sufficient acidity to age for a decade or more. The relatively full body of these wines makes them good partners with grilled halibut or swordfish steak, lobster, or Salade Landaise (duck breast and wild mushroom salad).

These wines have become quite expensive, with retail prices starting at about $40 and easily topping out at more than $100. Some of the best producers include: Chateau Carbonnieux, Chateau Bouscaut, Chateau Olivier, Chateau Couhins, and Chateau Smith-Haut-Lafitte. More expensive versions come from Domaine de Chevalier, Chateau Laville Haut-Brion, and the very rare (read *very* expensive) Chateau Haut-Brion.

Sauternes and Barsac. These sweet white wine appellations are at the southern tip of Graves, extending southward from the Garonne River. Indeed, the proximity to the river accounts for much of the success of these places as premium producers of sweet wines. The mists that typically sit on the river in the fall months move through the vineyards and encourage the settlement of the botrytis mold on the grapes as they near the end of the ripening stage. While most molds are ruinous to agricultural crops, the botrytis mold helps to create some of the most sought-after sweet wines in the world.

The wines exhibit a distinctly honeyed aroma, with backgrounds of dried apricots, peaches, and pears. On the palate, they are richly textured and extremely sweet, but they are always balanced by an elevated acidity that leaves the mouth feeling fresh and clean, rather than sticky and cloying. The wines of Sauternes and Barsac were classified in 1855, with Chateau d'Yquem ranked above all others as Premier Cru Superieur. It is still highly respected and is the world's most expensive dessert wine. A bottle of the 1811 vintage recently sold for $117,000. Special occasion coming up? A half bottle of a current vintage will cost about $200 retail. Wines that are still very good but easier on the bank account include the moderately expensive wines of Chateau Suduiraut, Chateau Climens, Chateau Coutet, and Chateau Rieussec as fairly intense versions. Lighter but still impressive (and still moderately expensive) styles come from Chateau Rayne-Vigneau, Chateau Doisy-Vedrines, Chateau Filhot, Chateau Broustet, Chateau Nairac, and Chateau Lafon.

RED WINES

Left Bank: Medoc and Haut-Medoc. Along with the wines of Graves, Medoc and Haut-Medoc wines are often referred to as Left Bank wines since the vineyards are situated on the left (west) side of the Gironde estuary and the Garonne River (see Bordeaux map, page 166). The words "Left Bank" do not appear on wine labels. But the Left Bank moniker does give a clue as to the style of the wines, since the majority of them are produced with Cabernet Sauvignon as the dominant grape in the blend, with Merlot playing second fiddle. The moderating effect of the Atlantic Ocean allows Cabernet Sauvignon to ripen well on the left bank of the Gironde River. Cabernet Franc's importance is waning because it takes quite a bit to lend its personality to a wine, while Petit Verdot can contribute significant color,

Vineyards at Chateau Pichon Longueville.

tannins, and flavors even when accounting for only about 5% of a blended wine. It is the percentage of each of these grapes in a blend, the "*terroir*" of the soil, the exposure of the vineyard, and the winemaker's skill that accounts for the many different styles of wines produced within the Medoc. The estate-bottled chateau wines are the most important and expensive examples.

In their youth Medoc wines tend to be tannic and full-bodied, with a depth and complexity of aroma and flavor. They offer the promise of becoming softer and mellower with age. But exactly how complex, full-bodied, and ageworthy the wines are depends largely on where they came from within the appellation.

The Medoc and Haut-Medoc appellations (often informally referred to collectively as the Medoc) make up a long but narrow strip of land stretching from north of the city of Bordeaux along the west bank of the Gironde estuary toward the Atlantic Ocean. As you move northward from Bordeaux toward the ocean, the soil becomes more sandy and silty; this is the land of the official Medoc appellation. Closer to the city of Bordeaux, in the official Haut-Medoc appellation, there are pockets of the famed gravel soil that makes certain vineyards shine. This is especially true around the villages of Margaux, St-Julien, Pauillac, and St-Estephe, and to a lesser extent in the villages of Moulis and Listrac. It is in these villages that most of the famed chateaux of the 1855 classification are found.

The 1855 classification of the Medoc wines ranked the very best wines as *premier grand cru classe* (first great growth); several other wines were ranked as second, third, fourth, and fifth great growths. During the past century and a half some of the lower ranked chateau have improved while others, including some ranked second or third, have gone down in quality. Indeed, some of these classified chateaux have been caught cheating—breaking the rules of their appellations, sometimes blatantly. But the legal entanglements of the system have allowed for only one change in all these years. Chateau Mouton-Rothschild was elevated from a second growth to a first growth in 1973 after proving their exclusion from the top level was based solely on the fact that the Rothschilds were and are Jewish.

W*INE*W*ISE* TIP: The great and expensive wines of Medoc and Haut-Medoc are easy to identify; they are listed in the 1855 classification. But how can you find good wines to enjoy without pawning your *Star Trek* memorabilia or cashing in your 401(k)?

We believe there are some fine wines that are not *grand cru classe* from these Chateaux at more modest prices: Chateau Labegorce-Zede, Chateau Chasse-Spleen, Chateau Larose-Trintaudon, Chateau Fourcas-Hosten, Chateau Gloria, and Chateau Lanessan produce very good wines. Some "second labels" from classified chateaux we suggest (with the name of the chateau in parentheses) are: Les Pagodes de Cos (Chateau Cos d'Estournel), Reserve de la Comtesse (Chateau Pichon Longueville-Comtesse de Lalande), Echo de Lynch-Bages, (Chateau Lynch Bages), Clos de Marquis (Chateau Leoville-Las-Cases), Alter Ego (Chateau Palmer), and La Dame de Montrose (Chateau Montrose).

For great value, try some of the *cru bourgeois* chateau wines, which offer enjoyment at reasonable prices and can be drunk young.

Left Bank: Graves. Like the red wines of Medoc and Haut-Medoc, red Graves wines are generally dominated by Cabernet Sauvignon, but Graves offers something distinctly different. Medoc usually

Vineyards of the commune of St-Julien.

Vineyards in the village of Pomerol.

offers blackcurrant fruit and firm tannins, but a Graves wine always seems to entice with a note of delicacy and charm, which may be attributable to a higher percentage of Cabernet Franc in the blend, and/or a higher presence of sand in the gravel-rich soil. There are also several estates that concentrate more on Merlot than Cabernet Sauvignon.

Graves wines tend to be underrepresented outside of France; if you find them, they provide an exciting glimpse of what else can be achieved in the world of Cabernet blends. That glimpse can be found in relative bargains from chateaux such as d'Archambeau, Le Bonnat, Haut-Mayne, de Landiras, Rahoul, and de Respide.

Left Bank: Pessac-Leognan. All of the best estates for red are clustered in this sub-appellation at the northern end of Graves, where there is a heavier concentration of the gravel and quartzite pebbles that seem to signify excellence in this region. Compared to the general Graves red wines, these wines offer more substance with riper, deeper, richer fruit as well as a bouquet of violets, tobacco, chocolate, smoke, and licorice.

The renowned red wines of Pessac-Leognan (all of them expensive) will be labeled as *cru classe*, while the following chateaux offer relative bargains: Brown, de Cruzeau, La Garde, La Louviere, and de Rochemorin.

"Special occasion wines" at higher prices and higher concentration levels include these *cru classes*: Domaine de Chevalier (second label is L' Esprit de Chevalier), Chateau La Tour Martillac, Martillac-Lagraviere, Chateau Smith Haut-Lafitte, Chateau Laville Haut Brion, Chateau La Mission Haut Brion, and Chateau Haut Brion (second label is Le Clarence de Haut Brion).

Right Bank: Pomerol. In direct contrast to the Left Bank wines, where Cabernet Sauvignon generally dominates the blend, Right Bank wines are mostly about the soft, juicy Merlot supported by the aromatic and more corpulent Cabernet Franc. Pomerol is capable of producing some thought-provoking versions of extraordinary depth and attraction. Perhaps to the dismay of the Medocians who have traditionally ruled the roost and run the market, the Merlot-based wines of the Right Bank have found great favor among knowledgeable and wealthy New World consumers. Despite the fact that Pomerol has no *grand cru* or *premier cru* designations, its most famous wine, Chateau Petrus, regularly out-prices all of the other wines in Bordeaux. Undoubtedly, the attraction of Right Bank Merlot wines is their rounder, more approachable style with softer tannins, particularly when young. The ripening season on the Right Bank is long and hot enough

Vineyard work in St-Emilion.

to ripen Merlot to perfection most years, though in Pomerol that forward fruit character in the wine is held in check by a mineral note. That means the wines are not all buoyant, one-dimensional black fruit; instead you will find an intriguing palette of color and weight with nuances of vanilla, violets, red fruit, and earthiness.

If you can afford them, it is hard to go wrong with a Pomerol wine. Perennial crowd pleasers include these expensive selections: Beauregard, Certan de May, la Conseillante, La Fleur Petrus, Gazin, Lafleur, Plince, and de Sales.

As one of Pomerol's satellite appellations, Lalande de Pomerol often produces wines that approach the fruitiness and elegance of Pomerol itself, and usually at far more reasonable prices. True WineWise choices, these are some of the chateaux worth seeking out for relative bargains: Belles Graves, La Chenade, Les Cruzelles, La Fleur de Bouard, La Croix-Bellevue, La Fleur St-Georges, Haut-Chaigneau, Moulin de Sales, and La Sergue.

Right Bank: St-Emilion. Again, Merlot is dominant here, with Cabernet Franc playing a stronger role in the blends than Cabernet Sauvignon. In the generally warm, sunny conditions of this region, Merlot ripens gracefully to its full potential, and St-Emilion wines offer spice, coffee, mineral, and red plum on both the nose and the palate.

If you want to go straight for the very expensive wines it's a no-brainer—the most highly revered *premier grand cru classe* "A" chateaux in St-Emilion are Chateau Ausone, Chateau Angelus, Chateau Pavie, and Chateau Cheval Blanc. The moderately expensive second labels of those three chateaux are La Chapelle d'Ausone, Carillon de l'Angelus, Les Aromes de Pavie, and Petit Cheval. Relative bargains are offered by Chateau Simard, Chateau Tertre du Moulin, and Chateau Fonplegade.

Wonderful St-Emilion lookalike wines that are relative bargains and are well worth searching out come from the four satellite appellations of Lussac-St-Emilion (Chateau Bel Air, Chateau des Rochers), Montagne-St-Emilion (Chateau Plaisance, Chateau Les Bardes), Puisseguin-St-Emilion (Chateau de l'Anglais, Chateau Lafaurie), and St-Georges-St-Emilion (Chateau St-Georges).

Right Bank: Cotes de Blaye, Cotes de Bourg, Cotes de Francs, and Premieres Cotes de Bordeaux. For the real money-saving bargains in Bordeaux reds, these are the areas to look for. On occasion you will be rewarded with a wine that begins to approach the weight and elegance of a wine from a more "aristocratic" appellation. The majority grape is Merlot, providing ripe, supple fruitiness, and the varying depths of limestone soils will sometimes combine with the ripe Merlot fruit to produce a wine of distinction and class. There are no classification lists to worry about, so feel free to shop around and experiment—for less than $20 you will sometimes hit the jackpot.

BURGUNDY

Just as Bordeaux is big, Burgundy is small, with only 65,000 acres (26,000 hectares) in the entire appellation. Ironically, the Burgundy vineyards are owned and operated by nearly as many growers as Bordeaux, but that only underscores the small size of the plots worked by the Burgundy growers. Since most individual landholdings are so small, many growers do not make their own wine, so they often sell their grapes to *negociants,* companies that buy raw material from several sources, make the wines, and label them with the most appropriate appellation according to the origin of the grapes. In Burgundy, as anywhere else, ultimate quality is in the hands of the producer/*negociant*, whose name is on the label.

We will follow the same format with Burgundy as we did with Bordeaux, starting with grape types, then moving on to a list of the major appellations with a discussion of any *premier cru* or *grand cru* designations, and concluding with a more in-depth look at each appellation and its wines.

GRAPE TYPES

Nothing is more simple than the major Burgundy grape types—Chardonnay for white wines, Pinot Noir for red. Everybody can remember that. Chardonnay is the most important grape type for white wines and many connoisseurs would argue that the best come from Burgundy. While we enjoy Chardonnay from other cool climate regions throughout the world, we have rarely found Chardonnay wines that have the finesse that white Burgundy has. We enjoy regional wines labeled as Bourgogne for under $15 or $20 retail; these wines often display the grape name on their labels. But Burgundy also produces some of the rarest and most elegant Chardonnay wines in the world. *Grand cru* white Burgundies, such as Corton-Charlemagne or Le Montrachet, can sell for hundreds of dollars, or even more than $1,000 if they are older wines from superior vintage years.

Pinot Noir is known as the "heartbreak grape" to farmers and winemakers because it is difficult to tame in the vineyard and in the bottle, but when all the planets align, Pinot Noir creates perhaps the most sublime, the most satisfying red wine on Earth. When that happens it becomes our heartbreak grape, only because we wish we could afford to enjoy great Pinot Noir on a daily basis. Ask 20 wine professionals what their favorite red wine is and we'll bet more than half will say Pinot Noir.

There are two minor grapes of Burgundy that can also make good wines. Gamay is not the prima donna that Pinot Noir is and in Burgundy's Cote Chalonnaise district can produce some very drinkable and affordable wines, most often as part of a Pinot Noir blend. Note that Gamay is the only red grape of the Beaujolais subregion; more about Beaujolais later.

Aligote, another lesser-known grape, makes lightweight white wines that can be delightful on their own, or in the local *kir* cocktail, which includes a splash of blackcurrant Cassis liqueur.

WINEWISE TIP: Affordable sparkling wines made in the Champagne method—*Cremant de Bourgogne*—are produced in Burgundy as well.

MAJOR APPELLATIONS

Burgundy (in French, *Bourgogne*) has several AOP appellation levels, starting with the umbrella regional appellation of Bourgogne itself. Within that large region, there are smaller regional and village-level appellations, and within the villages there are sometimes individual vineyard appellations of *premier cru* or *grand cru* status. As you progress from the large regional appellations down to the tiny single-vineyard appellations, the permitted yield of grapes from the vineyards in the appellation is smaller and the grapes must have a higher level of ripeness. Fewer grapes from each vine and a correspondingly smaller quantity of wine should translate into a higher-quality wine. It will certainly translate into a higher price.

Here's a summary of the structure of Burgundy appellations:

REGIONAL APPELLATIONS:

The umbrella regional appellation, Bourgogne, is used for basic whites and reds from anywhere within the appellation.

Chablis (whites only). Wines are labeled as Chablis if the grapes came from anywhere within the regional appellation; *premier cru* or *grand cru* may be added if the grapes came from a vineyard or group of vineyards with that status. Wines may carry the name of a single *premier cru* or *grand cru* vineyard if the grapes are all from that vineyard.

Cote de Nuits-Villages and Cote de Beaune-Villages produce red wines only. Macon-Villages produces white wines. When the name of the Burgundy subregion is followed by the word "*villages,*" the yields are lower and the ripeness requirement is higher. With these wines we're moving up in quality but at very little additional cost.

Village or *commune* appellations use the name of the town as the name of the wine. These individual villages fall within the areas of Cote de Nuits, Cote de Beaune, Chalon (officially called Cote Chalonnaise), and Macon (officially called Maconnais). We just want to make it simple to understand how these wines are labeled; you can locate these areas and some of the villages within them on the Burgundy map on page 176. Note: *The name of the village is the name of the wine.*

Single-vineyard appellations of *premier cru* or *grand cru* status. With the exception of Macon, every area has vineyards of *premier cru* status—in the Cote de Nuits and Cote de Beaune subregions of Burgundy *premier cru* vineyards are sited in several villages. The words *premier cru* and the name of both the village (e.g., Vosne-Romanee) and the vineyard (Aux Malconsorts) will appear on the label. In Cote de Nuits and Cote de Beaune there are *grand cru* vineyards; on wines from these vineyards, the words *grand cru* and the name of the vineyard (e.g., Richebourg Grand Cru) will appear on the label, but the village that contains the *grand cru* vineyard will *not* appear (in this case that village is Vosne-Romanee, but its name will not be included on the label).

APPELLATIONS AND THEIR WINES

WHITE WINES

Bourgogne. Any wine that carries the AOP Bourgogne is the most basic type of Burgundy and there are some relative bargains available. Olivier Leflaive's white Bourgogne "Les Setilles" is particularly attractive. Joseph Drouhin produces consistently reliable wines carrying the "Bourgogne" designation, as do Louis Jadot, Vincent Girardin and Bernard Morey.

Chablis. Since Chablis is a white wine, and since Chablis is in the Burgundy region, the grape variety for the wine is Chardonnay. But Chablis is like no other Chardonnay you have ever tasted. The standard approach for Chablis is to avoid the smell and taste of wood, especially new wood, and to limit if not avoid malolactic fermentation (see page 7) to retain the natural acidity of the wine. If the producers do use oak barrels, they tend to

DOMAINE CHRISTIAN MOREAU
PÈRE & FILS

CHABLIS 1ER CRU
VAILLON
APPELLATION CHABLIS 1ER CRU VAILLON CONTRÔLÉE

MIS EN BOUTEILLE AU DOMAINE PAR
CHRISTIAN MOREAU PÈRE & FILS · CHABLIS · FRANCE
PRODUCT OF FRANCE

Chablis label showing Vaillon as a *premier cru* vineyard.

be large old casks that do not impart the smell and taste of wood but allow the wine to breathe through the oak staves. That oxygen makes the wines more complex compared to wines made in concrete vats or stainless steel. The result is a lean, light-bodied wine with green fruit and a pleasant tartness, very much like Granny Smith apples. For riper, richer, more mineral and complex versions of Chablis, you should look for the wines labeled *premier cru* or *grand cru*. The name of an individual vineyard, such as Vaudesir or Les Clos, will also appear on the label. These wines are much more interesting and longer lived than standard Chablis. Compared to their oak-rich cousins from the Cote de Beaune Chablis prices are quite reasonable, starting at about $20-$25, and going progressively higher for *premier cru* and *grand cru* wines.

Some of our favorite producers of Chablis include Christian Moreau, Verget, Dauvissat, Jean-Marc Brocard, Albert Bichot, William Fevre, Domaine Laroche, Raveneau, Louis Michel, and A. Regnard et Fils.

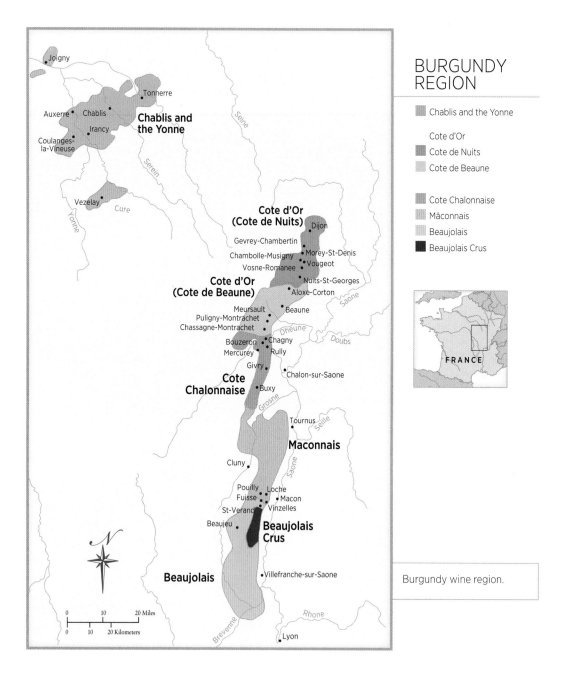

BURGUNDY REGION

- Chablis and the Yonne
- Cote d'Or
- Cote de Nuits
- Cote de Beaune
- Cote Chalonnaise
- Mâconnais
- Beaujolais
- Beaujolais Crus

FRANCE

Burgundy wine region.

Joseph Drouhin

PROPRIÉTÉS DE LA FAMILLE DROUHIN

CHAMBOLLE-MUSIGNY
AMOUREUSES
PREMIER CRU

APPELLATION D'ORIGINE CONTRÔLÉE
MIS EN BOUTEILLE PAR JOSEPH DROUHIN A BEAUNE, FRANCE
AUX CELLIERS DES ROIS DE FRANCE ET DES DUCS DE BOURGOGNE

13% vol.   PRODUIT DE FRANCE   750 ml

Label showing the *premier cru* vineyard Amoureuses in the village of Chambolle-Musigny.

One of the gated entrances to the Montrachet *grand cru* vineyard.

Cote de Beaune. In contrast to Chablis, the white (Chardonnay) wines of the Cote de Beaune appellation are more like what might be considered mainstream Chardonnay. Yet they are still a world away from standard New World offerings. The usual Burgundian approach is to highlight the characteristics of the grape from a specific place—wood and malolactic fermentation are secondary. White Burgundy, then, is more typically a full-bodied wine with noticeable acidity to highlight ripe apple, white pepper, nutty, and white floral flavors.

The Cote de Beaune and Cote de Beaune-Villages appellations are used only for red wines, so the majority of Cote de Beaune white wines carry a village appellation and name, such as Meursault, with a small percentage coming from individual *premier cru* or *grand cru* vineyards.

Meursault, Puligny-Montrachet, and Chassagne-Montrachet are the most famous white-wine-producing villages of Cote de Beaune, and the most frequently seen on the U.S. market. Meursault wines have a distinctive hazelnut and almond butter aroma, and a rich texture. The Puligny-Montrachet and Chassagne-Montrachet wines offer the smell of white flowers, apples, pears, pineapple, other fruits like quince, mineral notes, and a hint of honey. When you want that special Chardonnay, a wine from any of those villages will be a good WineWise purchase but be prepared to pay about $50 retail for these wines and much more for the *premier cru* and *grand cru* wines.

For special occasions or if you're feeling flush, try any of the *premier cru* vineyard wines from Meursault, such as Les Gouttes d'Or, Les Perrieres, or Les Charmes. A pair of Puligny-Montrachet's better *premier cru* sites are Les Folatieres and Les Pucelles, while Chassagne-Montrachet's best includes Les Caillerets and Les Champs-Gains.

For *grand cru* vineyards, the villages of Puligny-Montrachet and Chassagne-Montrachet are the lucky guardians of the most famous and perhaps the finest Chardonnay vineyards in the world—a cluster of five plots that all include "Montrachet" in the name. They are Montrachet, Batard-Montrachet, Bienvenue-Batard-Montrachet, Criots-Batard-Montrachet and Chevalier-Montrachet.

Corton-Charlemagne is another *grand cru* white wine that can be truly inspirational and will improve after aging for eight years or more.

Some of the better Cote de Beaune producers include Vincent Girardin, Louis Jadot, Bouchard Aine et Fils, Bouchard Pere et Fils, Joseph Drouhin, Louis Latour, Olivier Leflaive,

AGING WHITE WINES FROM BURGUNDY

The standard notion is that white wines should be drunk within a year or two from the year they were harvested, but with fine white wines from France and elsewhere, aging can actually improve the quality of your experience. Even if you have the good fortune to enjoy a Chassagne-Montrachet *premier cru* wine from the Champ Gains vineyard or a Montrachet *grand cru* wine, these gems really do not begin to express their full potential for at least three to five years after the harvest. They may be best after eight or 10 years. We have enjoyed 30-year-old white Burgundy wines that were sublime.

Buy some of the great white wines of the Cote de Beaune or the *premier cru* or *grand cru* wines of Chablis on the year of your child's birth, or wedding, or really any occasion. Let these wines slowly age in a cool cellar. After ample time has passed, perhaps on an anniversary, or a twenty-first birthday, or any other landmark celebration, break it out and share with your loved ones. Now that's how you drink an ageworthy Burgundy!

Domaine Leflaive, Domaine des Comtes Lafont, Coche-Dury, Chateau de Pommard, Michel Gay, Alex Gambal, Chanson, and Sauzet.

WINEWISE TIP: For real value and high quality in white Burgundy, and Chardonnay in general, go off the beaten path and try the white wines from these lesser-known villages in the Cote de Beaune: Savigny-Les-Beaunes, Auxey-Duresses, St.-Aubin, St.-Romain, and Santenay. As we mentioned before, the name of the village will be the name of the wine; the word "Chardonnay" will not appear on the label.

Chalon. The white wines of the Chalon area are generally less elegant and less complex than the elite wines from the Cote de Beaune, but some good expressions of French Chardonnay are available at modest prices. While the better wines of the Cote de Beaune might sing out, Chalon wines might just hum, but they carry a very pleasant tune. The wines from here have village names: for white wines the two main villages are Montagny and Rully. Occasionally you will find a Rully *premier cru* with a vineyard name such as Les Cloux on the label.

Vineyards around the village of Chassagne-Montrachet.

Chambolle-Musigny is a village in the Burgundy region that makes charming red wines based on the Pinot Noir grape. Courtesy of Kobrand Corporation.

Musigny is the *grand cru* vineyard within the town of Chambolle-Musigny. Louis Jadot is the negociant who makes the wine. Courtesy of Kobrand Corporation.

White wines from Chalon are worth seeking out and represent great value when you want Burgundian Chardonnay but cannot stretch your budget too far. Reliable producers offering relative bargains include Faiveley, Joseph Drouhin, Louis Latour, Andre Delorme, Antonin Rodet, Jaffelin, and Olivier Leflaive.

Macon. The whites of the Macon area are refreshing, light- or medium-bodied Chardonnays, ideal reminders of how straightforward and simply enjoyable Chardonnay can be. Many wines are sold under the collective appellation of Macon-Villages, while some of the villages prefer to attach their own village name to Macon, such as Macon-Lugny or Macon-Vire. They are all attractively priced bargains.

Within the region, two villages have earned fame as stand-alone names on the label: St-Veran and Pouilly-Fuisse. St-Veran is much lighter in style and is best enjoyed soon after bottling. Pouilly-Fuisse should be a fuller, firmer wine, with ripe apple, white flowers, and wood notes. Some examples may also have tropical fruit aromas and flavors. Pouilly-Fuisse has been a popular French chardonnay on the wine lists of fine-dining restaurants for decades, and although it is not as complex or long-lived as the fine whites of the Cote de Beaune, Pouilly Fuisse can improve in the bottle for about five years or so.

Good producers of Macon wines include J.J. Vincent, Jean Thevenet, Joseph Drouhin,

Louis Jadot, Georges Duboeuf, and Bouchard Aine et Fils.

Red Wines

Bourgogne. As with white wines labeled simply as Bourgogne (see page 175), the reds are good values; good basic drinkable, light- to medium-bodied Pinot Noir, and sometimes a cut above that baseline. The same producers who make good white Bourgogne also make good reds.

Cote de Nuits. Cote de Nuits is all about Pinot Noir from the regional appellation of Cote de Nuits-Villages to village-named wines, and individual vineyards at *premier cru* and *grand cru* level. For many wine lovers the Cote de Nuits is the spiritual home of Pinot Noir, a place worthy of a pilgrimage to worship the heavenly qualities of "The Grape."

At the entrance to these holy gates are the basic Cote de Nuits-Villages wines, which are pleasant Pinot Noir–based wines, and traditional by being less opulent and fruity than New World Pinots. It is, however, the village-level or *premier cru* and *grand cru* wines that are the most rewarding. A very fine red Burgundy offers a delicate balance of red fruit notes, flowers, spices and herbs, fresh acidity to keep the wine lively, light to medium tannins, and a noticeable woodsy character that might remind you of mushrooms, potting soil, or dried leaves. Think outdoorsy. It's what the French call *sousbois*, or "under wood."

The great villages or communes of Cote de Nuits are Gevrey-Chambertin, Morey-St-Denis, Chambolle-Musigny, Vosne-Romanee, Nuits-St.-Georges, Vougeot, and Flagey-Echezeaux. The vineyards of each village provide a different expression of Pinot Noir—each village, each vineyard expresses its different *terroir* in the wine. Gevrey-Chambertin produces a wine that is virile and rich, sourced from soils with more clay than the delicate wines of Chambolle-Musigny, where there is more limestone/chalk in the soils. The perfume of a Chambolle-Musigny *premier cru* such as Les Amoureuses ("the lovers") or the *grand cru* Le Musigny is redolent of violets, cherries, raspberries, even gingerbread. Grand Echezeaux and Echezeaux are *grand cru* wines from the village of Flagey-Echezeaux that offer red cherry and berry flavors and aromas of those fruits as well as wild flowers. These wines are not defined merely by the amount of clay or chalk in the soils of their vineyards, but those soils are part of the explanation for the many expressions of Pinot Noir in Burgundy.

Obviously, the *premier cru* and *grand cru* vineyards in the villages of the Cote de Nuits produce the marquee wines of the region, and although some of these wines are close-to-reasonably priced, there is almost no limit to what you can spend for the absolute best wines. For example, the village of Vosne-Romanee contains many gems available from its *premier cru* or *grand cru* vineyards. Want the best of the best? Consider buying one bottle of the well-aged Romanee-Conti *grand cru* from the 4-acre (1.6-hectare) vineyard owned by the Domaine de la Romane-Conti. For the same money you could buy a used Porsche or put a down payment on a modest house! Your call.

But let's put things into a more-reasonable perspective. A typical village-named wine from Cote de Nuits certainly falls into the moderately expensive category, starting at about $45 to $50, while a *premier cru* version will push you into the very expensive category ($60 and up), and a *grand cru* wine will be double that and beyond, sometimes way beyond.

But hold on. There's some good news for the WineWise bargain hunter, too. Reward yourself by seeking out less well-known village-named wines from the Cote de Nuits, such as Marsannay (also good dry rosé) or Fixin.

Just some of the top producers of Cote de Nuits wines include Louis Jadot, Dujac, Roumier, Bouchard Aine et Fils, Bouchard Pere et Fils, Mugnier, Ghislaine Barthod, Potel, Alex Gambal, Jean Grivot, Boillot, Jessiaume, Bruno Clair, Lucien Le Moine, Bonneau du Martray, Louis Latour, Domaine Leroy, and the legendary Domaine de la Romanee-Conti. Domaine Clair Dau makes good rosé in Marsannay.

Cote de Beaune. Best-known for its famous white wines, Cote de Beaune actually produces far more red wine. The style of Pinot Noir in Cote de Beaune is a little lighter, less sturdy, and more delicate than that of Cote de Nuits. The Cote de Beaune-Villages appellation wines tend to be relatively light, with just-ripe red fruit flavors. The village-level wines and the *premier cru* and *grand cru* wines are another story.

The prominent red-wine-producing villages are Aloxe-Corton, Beaune, Pommard, Volnay, and Chassagne-Montrachet. Aloxe-Corton offers smells of cherries, while mushrooms and leather reflect age. Pommard is the most tannic and full-bodied of these wines and has a gamey, musky, spicy, and black fruit character coupled with great acidity. Beaune and Volnay offer a more floral and perfumed character in addition to the standard red berry qualities of Pinot Noir. Chassagne-Montrachet red, living in the shadow of its more famous white counterpart, is a much-overlooked wine, worthy of attention for its depth of flavor and sense of completeness.

The only red *grand cru* in Cote de Beaune is Le Corton, in the village of Aloxe-Corton. The wine may be labeled simply as Le Corton *grand cru* or have the name of a vineyard after it such as Corton Clos de Roi or Corton Bressandes. Some of the fine *premier cru* sites from the above villages include: Les Greves and Les Bressandes in the village of Beaune; Les Caillerets and Clos des Chenes in Volnay; and Clos St-Jean and La Boudriotte from Chassagne-Montrachet.

Chateau des Jacques is a biodynamic vineyard within the town of Moulin A Vent. This wine, produced from Gamay grapes, is a very fine cru Beaujolais made by Louis Jadot. Courtesy of Korbrand Corporation.

As with white wines from Cote de Beaune, village-named red wines from this region of Burgundy fall into the moderately expensive category, starting at about $40. For *premier cru* vineyards, think very expensive (beginning at about $60), and for *grand cru,* double that at least. Unlike the Cote de Nuits region, Cote de Beaune doesn't produce any red wines that require a second mortgage.

For our money, some of the real gems of Cote de Beaune come from the underappreciated villages of Auxey-Duresses, Pernand-Vergelesses, Savigny-Les-Beaune, Santenay, St.-Aubin, St.-Romain, Maranges, and Chorey-Les-Beaune, where for about $35 (a relative bargain) you can find the delicate sensuality of Pinot Noir that makes life worth living.

Chalon. Chalon's vineyards produce highly acceptable versions of Old World Pinot at highly acceptable prices, around $20 to $30—moderately expensive perhaps, but a relative bargain for good red Burgundy. The wines will carry a village name, and the principal red-wine-producing villages are Rully, Givry, and Mercurey, with *premier cru* vineyards in all three. Our favorite red from Chalon is the Mercurey *premier cru*, Clos des Myglands, produced by Faiveley, featuring ripe red fruits, earth, and herbal notes in the nose with a medium body, lively acidity, and a long aftertaste.

Reliable producers offering relative bargains include Joseph Drouhin, Faiveley, Louis Latour, Andre Delorme, Antonin Rodet, Jaffelin, Debray, and Olivier Leflaive.

Sparkling Wines. Known as *Cremant de Bourgogne,* this is an important category for Burgundy producers. These are good wines, all made by the Champagne method. The favored grapes used by the better producers include the Burgundy mainstays of Pinot Noir and Chardonnay, with Pinot Blanc also used by some. The finished wines are well balanced, with fresh, lively fruit notes and good balancing acidity. At one-third to one-half the cost of Champagne, they are a worthy alternative.

BEAUJOLAIS

Beaujolais and its wines are easy to understand, easy to buy, and easy to love. A huge amount of red Beaujolais is produced, all of it made solely from the Gamay grape. A small quantity of white wine is also produced from Chardonnay.

The region of Beaujolais is situated between Burgundy and the Rhone Valley, marked by rolling granite hills and a warm climate that allows grapes to ripen easily just about every year (see Burgundy map, page 176). The friendliness and fruitiness of the wines are enhanced by a winemaking method that pushes fruitiness to the max. It is called carbonic maceration, which entails placing whole, unbroken grapes into a large stainless-steel vat and then enveloping them with carbon dioxide gas. In this "hostile" environment, the whole grapes use their own internal enzymes to try to consume the sugars. In the process they create alcohol, just as yeasts would. Basically, the grapes ferment from the inside out. Because this process involves very little movement or violent activity, the wines are lower in color and tannin levels, making them light and easy to drink.

In addition to the huge quantity of simple, fruity red wines, there are also some more intense red styles of Beaujolais, made by traditional winemaking methods, and well worth seeking out.

In fact, high quality Beaujolais wines are enjoying a surge in popularity. Thanks to the efforts of the best producers to coax the most they can from their vineyards of Gamay grapes, these are wines to be taken seriously. Compare the prices of the best Beaujolais wines with any of the *premiers crus* from the Cote de Beaune or Cote de Nuits and you will be happily surprised that you can drink good Burgundy on a regular basis. Some of the wines may even be made from organically farmed grapes.

RED WINES

Beaujolais is all about red wines, from the fresh *nouveau* wine to ageworthy *cru* wines with greater depth and more complex flavors. Here are the basic styles of Beaujolais and the names to look for on their labels.

Beaujolais Nouveau. Every year, Beaujolais producers launch their *nouveau* or *primeur* wines on a "show me the money" schedule: grapes are harvested in September, the wine is made in October, and the bottles are sold on retail shelves starting the third Thursday of November, with cash in the bank by December. Although international excitement about Beaujolais Nouveau has faded, this wine may appeal to those who dislike the astringency of red wines. Beaujolais Nouveau has been called "the whitest of red wines," and although it is released just in time for Thanksgiving, it really lacks the "stuffing" to marry with the traditional holiday dinner.

Beaujolais and Beaujolais-Villages. The Beaujolais label indicates the wine can come from anywhere in the region, while the Beaujolais-Villages label tells you that the grapes came from vineyards within any or all of 38 select villages, all located in the northern part of Beaujolais. Here, in vineyards rich in granite-based soils, the grapes tend to ripen more than elsewhere in the region. A good Beaujolais-Villages wine should be bright, ripe, and full of fruit in its aroma, and should have a smooth texture on your palate. In warm weather, chill the bottle for a half hour before pouring to help bring out the essential fruit of the wine and

ramp up its acidity. Beaujolais-Villages is a good choice for a wide variety of foods, and is particularly comfortable pairing itself with picnics and backyard cookouts.

The Best of Beaujolais: The "*Crus*." Wines labeled as Beaujolais Nouveau or Beaujolais-Villages are usually juicy, enjoyable, inexpensive, and fun, perfect with a burger or a pizza. But we want to share our true excitement for some *WineWise* favorites, the "*Cru* Beaujolais" wines. These wines come from any one of 10 villages in the Beaujolais region and are labeled with the village name. The vineyards within these villages are recognized as premium sites, and the depth of flavors, pigments, and tannins in the grapes respond very well to more traditional winemaking methods, producing full-flavored, structured wines with darker colors and a more assertive, more complex set of characteristics. In many ways, they approach their Pinot Noir cousins to the north in Burgundy with red berry, cherry, and plum flavors, and a touch of earthiness to add interest. The 10 villages that have earned the privilege to use their name on the label are Brouilly, Chenas, Chiroubles, Cote de Brouilly, Fleurie, Julienas, Morgon, Moulin-a-Vent, Regnie, and St-Amour. Moulin-a-Vent and Morgon are usually the longest-lived of the 10 *crus*, meaning that they can age about five years or more. The other wines are meant for early enjoyment. Producers of Beaujolais and Beaujolais-Villages also produce the *Cru* wines.

Although *Cru* Beaujolais wines are more expensive than Beaujolais-Villages (which often sell for $10 or less), they still represent some of the greatest bargains in delicious red wine (priced from $15 to about $35). One of the reasons? Many wine consumers have never heard of them, and for those who have, these wines have zero snob appeal. *Cru* Beaujolais is a secret hidden in plain sight, a largely undiscovered tiny gem, a true WineWise wine.

WINEWISE TIP: A bottle of St-Amour might be a good way to impress your lover on Valentine's Day, while Fleurie is the equivalent of a bouquet of flowers in a bottle. Good luck!

Morgon may be the most powerful and complex of the *cru* wines and from a good vintage and fine *negociant* it can stand shoulder to shoulder with many of the Pinot Noir wines from areas north of Beaujolais.

Suggested Beaujolais producers include Chateau des Jacques and Chateau des Lumieres by Louis Jadot, Marcel Lapierre, Michel Tete, Paul Beaudet, J.-P. Brun, Chateau de la Chaize, Cheysson, Jean Descombes, Domaine des Ducs, Joseph Drouhin, Georges Duboeuf (by far the largest producer in the Beaujolais region), Henry Fessy, Sylvain Fessy, Foillard, Chateau Grand Cochard, Thorin, Georges Descombes, Jean Claude Debeaune, Trinel, and Vincent Girardin.

RHONE VALLEY

Geographically and stylistically, the Rhone Valley is divided in two. The northern Rhone concentrates on Syrah for reds and Viognier, Marsanne, and Roussanne for whites. The southern Rhone blends numerous grape types for their dry white, rosé, and red wines. In both parts of the Rhone Valley, appellations range in size from regional, such as Cotes du Rhone, to village, such as Cornas or Gigondas. The climate of the entire valley is usually thought of as at least warm if not hot, resulting in ripe, full-bodied wines. Between the south and the north some pleasant, inexpensive sparkling wines known as Clairette de Die are produced.

Both traditional AOP and IGP wines labeled as "des Collines Rhodaniennes" are sourced from vineyards within the Rhone Valley. IGP wines usually feature the name of the grape variety, such as Syrah or Viognier.

THE NORTHERN RHONE

Many of the vineyards here are sited on terraces and face south or southeast to get the full blessing of the sun. Yields from the vineyards are lower than in the south and the wines are concentrated and rich in flavors, and the finest Syrah-based red wines of the Northern Rhone often rival the more expensive reds of Burgundy and Bordeaux. While New World Syrah have the intrinsic stamp of black pepper combined with chocolate-covered cherries and black fruits, Northern Rhone wines are "wilder," with notes of game meats, dark earth, mushrooms, a horse barn, minerality, and herbs. We also like to describe them as inky and stinky, which is a good thing. These massive northern Rhone red wines can be drunk when released, preferably with hearty food, but we believe they are worthy of long aging, perhaps as much as 20 years, when they deliver pure pleasure.

WHITE WINES OF THE NORTHERN RHONE

The wines of the north are only about 5% of the Rhone's total production and although Syrah is "King," the whites can also be fabulous. Condrieu and Chateau Grillet are pure expressions of the Viognier grape with all the ripe stone fruit notes associated with that varietal. The wines are dry with great structure and sufficient acidity to balance their richness. While they can be paired with rich seafood such as lobster they could also "cross over" to be paired with poultry or simply grilled meats.

St-Joseph, Crozes-Hermitage, and Hermitage dry white wines are based on Marsanne and Roussanne and they can be complex, full-bodied wines with intriguing bouquets. The St-Joseph wines are the most affordable of the three.

St-Peray wines are also based on Marsanne and Roussanne and come in both still and sparkling versions.

WINEWISE TIP: Since the great *negociants*/producers want to protect their reputations, when they have a younger vineyard or a barrel of wine they feel is not up to their standards, they may declassify a white wine such as Condrieu or St-Joseph to the simpler Cotes du Rhone appellation, which is always a great buy.

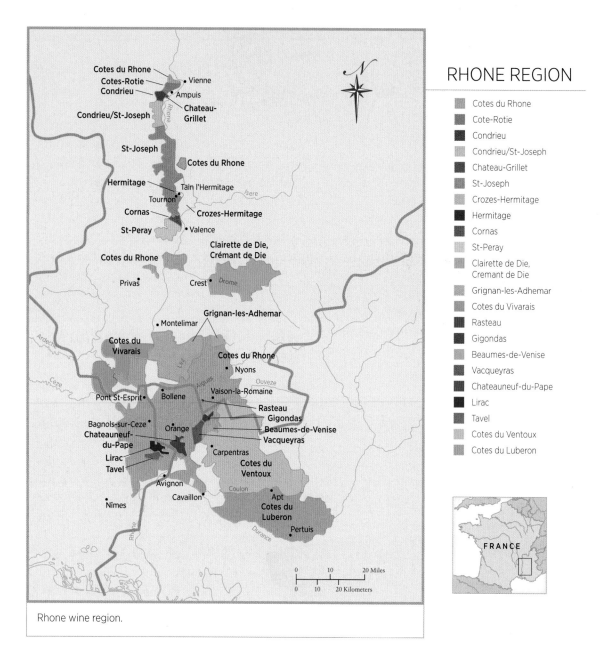

Rhone wine region.

RHONE REGION

- Cotes du Rhone
- Cote-Rotie
- Condrieu
- Condrieu/St-Joseph
- Chateau-Grillet
- St-Joseph
- Crozes-Hermitage
- Hermitage
- Cornas
- St-Peray
- Clairette de Die, Cremant de Die
- Grignan-les-Adhemar
- Cotes du Vivarais
- Rasteau
- Gigondas
- Beaumes-de-Venise
- Vacqueyras
- Chateauneuf-du-Pape
- Lirac
- Tavel
- Cotes du Ventoux
- Cotes du Luberon

FRANCE

Red Wines of the Northern Rhone. The Hermitage and Crozes-Hermitage appellations produce outstanding red wines based on the Syrah grape (the only permitted red grape in the northern Rhone). As mentioned earlier in this section, we believe these wines are among the world's finest reds. Considering the overall quality of the Hermitage wines they are certainly not inexpensive, yet they are undervalued when compared with the prices of the finest Bordeaux and Burgundy wines. At even more affordable prices are the wines produced from the vineyards surrounding Hermitage, known as Crozes-Hermitage. Again, they are based on Syrah but they are less concentrated than AOP Hermitage wines. However, Crozes-Hermitage

from a great producer such as Combier or the "Thalabert" version by Paul Jaboulet can still be cellared for a decade and provide great Rhone Syrah flavors at a reasonable price. Other suggested producers of Hermitage or Crozes-Hermitage include Chave, Chapoutier, Delas, Guigal, Grippat, Graillot, and Sorrel.

Cornas. This is pure Syrah in its darkest and richest form, with a wild and rustic nature that is unleashed by some producers and polished by others. Dark purple in color and redolent of black pepper, licorice, black fruits, flowers, nuts, and mushrooms, it is unapologetically demanding of all the senses. Jean-Luc Colombo

Vineyards in the village of Cornas.

makes some of the richest, yet most elegant wines of Cornas. His wines offer black pepper, violets, black fruits, and licorice notes with fine tannins and acidity. Other respected producers include Clape, Verget, Tardieu Laurent, Durand, Jaboulet, Delas, and Courbis.

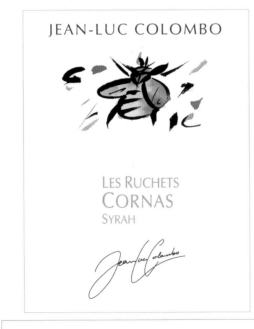

Jean-Luc Colombo is one of the top producers of wines from the Rhone and his Cornas "Les Ruchets" is an elegant example of an "Old World" Syrah.

Cote-Rotie. Producers such as Guigal and Jean Michel Gerin have elevated Cote-Rotie to such a level that many wine lovers consider this to be the Rhone's finest jewel. The Cote de Brune portion is known as such because of clay-based soils with iron while the Cote de Blonde portion is more limestone and granite-laced sand. While most wineries blend from those two sections and elsewhere within this "roasted slope" for consistency, consumers may find a wine that singles out the Blonde or Brune sections. These red wines have a bouquet and flavors of the roasted character in the name as well as black fruits, olives, spices, and truffles. In addition to Guigal, other suggested producers include Rostaing, Jasmin, Bernard, Gaillard, and Ogier.

St-Joseph. These Syrah-based wines are not as full-bodied as the other appellations but there are some good examples from reputable producers that are well worth trying. Floral, black pepper, licorice, and black fruits are typical St-Joseph aromas and flavors. We suggest the wines of Louis Cheze, Chapoutier, Courbis, Gripa, and Chave.

NOTE: Overall, for moderately expensive but very good wines from the northern Rhone we have suggested some trustworthy producers. Bear in mind that the exact cost will depend on the exact appellation—Hermitage and Cote Rotie will push you into the very expensive range.

RED WINES OF THE SOUTHERN RHONE

Cote du Rhone and Cote du Rhone-Villages.

The south relies on blends of numerous grapes, most notably Grenache, Syrah, and Mourvedre for its red wines. Again, these wines are not your average "GSM" blend from anywhere else. Yes, they have delicious, mouth-filling ripe flavors, but there is also a sense of structure and poise gained from the tautness of tannins and a streak of acidity.

Almost all of the red wines from the regional appellations of Cote du Rhone and Cote du Rhone-Villages come from southern Rhone vineyards (with a handful of Cote du Rhone producers in the North), and are made from the standard GSM blend, possibly with the addition of other less well-known varieties, such as Cinsaut and Carignan. These southern reds tend to be rounder, softer and smoother and juicier on the palate than the darker, richer Syrah wines of the northern Rhone. They are wines of exceptional value: sound, reliable, and enjoyable. No worries, you will always find a pleasant experience here—a true WineWise choice.

In the south you will also find the relatively unknown AOP wines of Cotes du Ventoux, Cotes du Luberon, Grignan-les-Adhemar, Cotes du Vivarais, and Costieres de Nimes. Usually reds made in a very light and fruity style, they are at the lower end of the price scale but the upper end of the satisfaction scale, especially if you enjoy clean, straightforward red fruit flavors without the power and persistence of more concentrated wines.

All relative bargains, the Cotes du Rhone and Cotes du Rhone Villages appellations are very well represented by the following producers. For Cotes du Rhone and Cotes du Rhone-Villages (from the south, dominated by Grenache): La Chasse du Pape, Coudelet de Beaucastel, Caves des Papes, Chapoutier, Clos du Caillou, Alary, Louis Bernard, Andre Brunel, Cave de Cairanne, Chateau du Trignon, Domaine de Coste Chaude, Domaine Santa Duc, Domaine St-Luc, Domaines de la Guicharde, Domaines Perrin, Guigal, Gabriel Meffre Laurus, Mas de Boislauzon, Les Garrigues, Domaine Gramenon, Domaine de l'Ameillaud, Domaine du Pesquier, Perrin Reserve, Patrick Lesec, Mont-Redon, Les Monticauts, St-Cosme, and Tardieu Laurent.

For Cotes du Rhone (from the north, dominated by Syrah): Jean-Luc Colombo "Les Abeilles," "Guigal," "Domaine de la Solitude," and Jaboulet "Parallele 45".

Chateauneuf-du-Pape, Gigondas, Vacqueyras, and Rasteau.

In effect, these are village names, and the name on the label reflects the fact that the grapes came from vineyards in and around the named village. The exact blend used depends on the village, but also on the producer. When French guidelines list a number of grapes approved for use in an appellation, the producer can use any number of the grapes in whatever proportion he or she sees fit. In general, most of the wines from these areas are dominated by Grenache, supported by Syrah and Mourvedre.

For example, red Chateauneuf-du-Pape may include as many as 13 grapes including Grenache, Mourvedre, Syrah, Cinsaut, Counoise, Muscardin, Vaccarese, Picpoul Noir, and Terret, plus the white grapes Grenache Blanc, Clairette, Bourboulenc, Roussanne, Picpoul Gris, and Picardin. Phew! Some wineries use all the permitted grapes to make their wine while others opt to only use three of them, or two, or only red Grenache. If you count the same grape such as Grenache for both white and red versions you get over 13 permitted grapes. The percentage of each grape used does not matter as much as whether or not you enjoy the wine.

Chateauneuf-du-Pape is the most famous of this group and usually the most expensive. Expect aromas and flavors of cinnamon, coffee, leather, *herbes de Provence* (green herbs and lavender), cedar, and red fruits in these reds.

Chateauneuf-du-Pape vineyards.

WINEWISE TIP: Although best known for their red wines, the white wines of Hermitage and Chateauneuf-du-Pape are full-bodied, complex wines that can be paired with dishes such as white truffle risotto, halibut steak with roast endive and fennel, squash blossoms stuffed with lobster mousseline, or Saint-Marcellin, a cow's-milk cheese.

Within the Rasteau area there are some sweet fortified red Grenache wines in addition to dry red wines. They are known as "*Vins Doux Naturels*" that can be paired with desserts such as Creme Caramel or with aged cheeses. Another sweet wine from the southern Rhone is the white Muscat Beaumes de Venise, which is delightful to drink well chilled and within about three years of the harvest date.

Tavel is France's only 100% rosé wine AOP. These dry wines are based mostly on Grenache and Cinsaut grapes, but seven other grapes can be included. Fresh red fruit aromas and flavors with medium weight and soft tannins make this a very adaptable wine for many foods. Read more about how well rosés work with a wide variety of foods in our chapter on wine and food (starting on page 294).

The popularity of the southern Rhone style, partially encouraged by the American wine media, has meant that prices have risen from merely moderately expensive to very expensive for wines such as Chateauneuf-du-Pape. Even so, you may want to bite the bullet and break out your credit card to find out what the fuss is all about. If you do, try wines from some of the following producers: Chateau de Beaucastel, Chateau La Nerthe, Chateau Fortia, Domaine de Mont-Redon, Clos des Papes, and Chateau Rayas. If you choose to stay moderately expensive, then head for Gigondas, while Vacqueyras may afford you the occasional relative bargain (look for Chateau de Montmirail in both Gigondas and Vacqueyras).

LANGUEDOC, ROUSSILLON, AND PROVENCE

Situated in the south of France, Languedoc, Roussillon, and Provence bathe in sunshine for much of the summer. Cinsaut and Carignan grapes are important players in the production of red and rosé wines, with the reliable GSM trio offering support. For white wines, Grenache Blanc, Bourboulenc, and Clairette are the likely candidates. Some lovely wines can be found both within the broad regional appellations such as Coteaux du Languedoc and in the smaller appellations such as Les Baux de Provence, Bandol, Minervois, and Collioure. Whatever the appellation, red wines dominate, and rosé wines are gaining popularity because of their price point, charm, and potential for pairing with a diversity of foods.

For the *WineWise* reader, the comfort zone might be the IGP category, since producers are labeling their wines with grape variety names known all around the world, allowing the consumer to buy with ease and confidence.

In some cases, wine producers from other regions have purchased old run-down vineyards in this area that had been planted with the high-yielding varieties such as Carignan and Cinsaut, and they have replanted with the much more marketable varieties such as Merlot, Syrah, Chardonnay, and so on. The resulting wines have international appeal at everyday, even bargain basement prices. Reliable producers of IGP wines include Georges Duboeuf, Reserve St-Martin, Fortant, and Val d'Orbieu.

THREE FOR THE ROAD

Our intention as authors is not to cover every wine region in the world but to turn our *WineWise* readers on to the most important wine regions, while offering some off-the-beaten-path wine values. Here are three suggestions that do not fit into the major French wine regions we've written about in this chapter:

The first AOP, located at the foothills of the Alps, produces a delightful light-bodied crisp dry white called Vin de Savoie, based on the Jacquere grape variety; when a village name appears on the label the white grapes Roussette or Chasselas may be used.

The second AOP we hope you will try is Cahors from Southwest France, which is a very dark, rich, sometimes complex, dry red wine based on the Malbec grape. Black fruits, flowers, licorice, graphite, mineral, and cocoa are just some of the smells and flavors of Cahors wines.

Finally, there is a range of white and red wines at different price points from Mas de Daumas Gassac winery, wines that do not fall within the AOP or IGP system because the producers use unapproved grape varieties in their blended wines. For example, they make a white wine based on mostly Viognier, Chardonnay, and Petit Manseng with minor support from the Muscat, Marsanne, and Roussanne grapes. That is certainly not a traditional mix, which is why the wines do not conform to the AOP or IGP rules.

LANGUEDOC

Dry white wines in the Languedoc are usually based on the white version of Grenache, Bourboulenc and Clairette grapes and there are some sweet *vin doux naturels* made from the Muscat grape. The Muscat St-Jean-de-Minervois is a good example of an inexpensive sweet white wine from the south.

Within the large Coteaux du Languedoc appellation, the villages of St-Saturnin, Montpeyroux, Pic St-Loup, Cabrieres, and La Clape may add their own name to the regional Coteaux du Languedoc appellation. Grenache, Syrah, and Mourvedre dominate here with Cinsaut and Carignan filling out the blended rosé and red wines.

The appellation of Minervois also offers some exciting possibilities, especially from producers such as Chateau Helene. Of all the up-and-coming appellations in the south of France, Minervois would be our *WineWise* pick for value in the relative bargain category. Slightly less intense versions can also be found in the neighboring appellation of St-Chinian, especially from producers such as Chateau Coujan and Clos Bagatelle.

ROUSSILLON

The most likely finds here will fall under the regional appellations of Cotes du Roussillon and Cotes du Roussillon-Villages. The fruity, slightly peppery reds are generally enjoyable quaffers, but producers such as Domaine Gauby, Chateau Mosse, and Chateau La Casenove make wines of denser fruit character and sturdier structure. The villages of Caramony, Tautavel, Lesquerde, and Latour de France may add their own name to the label to indicate more emphasis on the expression of their location for the Syrah, Mourvedre, Grenache, Carignan, and Cinsault grapes grown there.

Corbieres and the Fitou appellation within it can offer some good value medium-bodied red wines with the interesting smell of the "garrigue"—a wild herb and floral character—as well as ripe red and black fruits.

Collioure wines are an interesting blend of Grenache, Syrah, Mourvedre, Cinsault, and Carignan that results in full-bodied, complex dry wines. The same vineyards also make a sweet fortified *vins doux naturel* counterpart, Banyuls, which must contain at least 50% Grenache grapes in the blend. Ask a French sommelier for a perfect pairing for chocolate and his or her response will most likely be Banyuls.

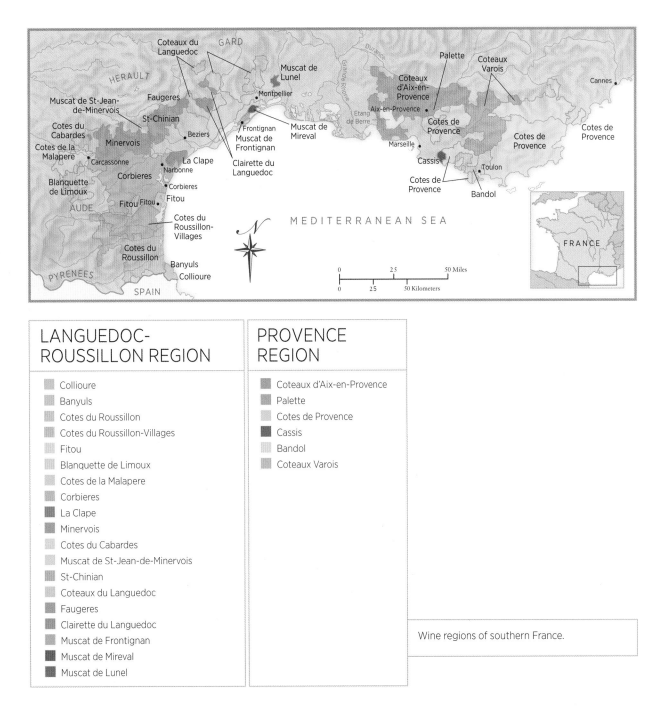

LANGUEDOC-ROUSSILLON REGION

- Collioure
- Banyuls
- Cotes du Roussillon
- Cotes du Roussillon-Villages
- Fitou
- Blanquette de Limoux
- Cotes de la Malapere
- Corbieres
- La Clape
- Minervois
- Cotes du Cabardes
- Muscat de St-Jean-de-Minervois
- St-Chinian
- Coteaux du Languedoc
- Faugeres
- Clairette du Languedoc
- Muscat de Frontignan
- Muscat de Mireval
- Muscat de Lunel

PROVENCE REGION

- Coteaux d'Aix-en-Provence
- Palette
- Cotes de Provence
- Cassis
- Bandol
- Coteaux Varois

Wine regions of southern France.

Maury and Rivesaltes are best known for sweet fortified wines based mostly on Grenache.

PROVENCE

The red and rosé wines of Provence are often blends including grapes such as Grenache, Syrah, Mourvedre, Cinsault, Counoise, Tibouren, Calitor, and Cabernet Sauvignon. Within the Cotes de Provence appellation, Domaine Ott and Chateau Vignelaure are important and reputable producers, while from Les Baux de Provence try the rosé and red wines of Anne Poniatowski from the estate Mas de la Dame. Some equally impressive rosé and red wines come from the Bandol appellation with Domaine Tempier, Domaine Bunan, and Chateau Pradeaux among the leading producers. Peter Fischer at Chateau Revelette makes outstanding Coteaux d'Aix en Provence red and white wines. The grapes used to make dry white wines in Provence include Sauvignon Blanc, Semillon, Clairette, Bourboulenc, and Ugni Blanc.

9

ANDIAMO

ITALY

THE WINES OF ITALY HAVE NEVER BEEN BETTER, AND THE PRESENCE OF ITALY IN THE WORLD WINE MARKET, ESPECIALLY the United States, has never been stronger. And yet Italian wines continue to be among the least understood of all European wines, perhaps because there are so many of them, possibly because their labels can be challenging to consumers, or maybe because of the introduction over the last two decades of extraordinary wines from almost every one of Italy's 20 provinces.

Classic red wines produced in Tuscany's wine regions are exciting, delicious, and food-friendly. At the same time, Italy's "Super Tuscan" wines, a sometimes paradoxical mix of ultra-classic wines made from traditional Italian grapes and ultra-modern wines produced from international varietals, have taken the wine world, especially fine restaurants, by storm.

The Piedmont region in northwest Italy has built a solid and universal reputation on traditional wines produced in a modern world. There is a virtual revolution in quality taking place in the vineyards and wineries of Italy's southern and island provinces of Sicily, Sardinia, Puglia, and Campania. The white and red wines from the multicultural provinces of Italy's northeast—Alto Adige and Friuli–Venezia Giulia, with their German, Austrian, and Slavic heritages—have helped to redefine what it is to be an "Italian wine."

While much of Italy is enjoying a rebirth of wine quality and wine diversity, the anchors—classic wines of the Piedmont, Tuscany, Veneto, and Umbria regions—create a sense of historical and cultural continuity. Improvements and innovations in both vineyards and wineries in these regions allow producers who have embraced a new paradigm based on quality wine that's made to compete in a global market. Both large producers and artisans are working to create a new portrait of Italian wines, a work of art that may be grounded in classic techniques but with an image whose sensibility is postmodern.

Welcome to the new world of the Old World: Italian wines!

The grapes of Italy: A bit of a challenge, but so much fun

ITALY PRODUCES WINES FROM HUNDREDS of different grape varietals, some of which you've heard of, many of which you haven't. While Italy makes oodles of good wine from international varietals—the usual suspects of Chardonnay, Merlot, Cabernet Sauvignon, and so on—the backbone of Italian wine production is the country's own collection of vines. Here's our list of Italy's most important grapes, alphabetically arranged, with a few notes on each.

RED GRAPES

Of the 10 grapes listed here, the two most heralded, the most "noble" of all Italian red wine grapes, are Sangiovese and Nebbiolo. As you become more familiar with Italian wines, you may want to learn a little bit more about some of the others, too.

Aglianico: Grown mostly in the southern regions of Campania and Basilicata, this vine was brought to Italy by the ancient Greeks. Produces mostly powerful reds, with high levels of both tannin and acid, making Aglianico-based wines quite ageworthy.

Barbera: The second-most frequently planted grape in Italy, it shines in the Piedmont region, where it produces a wide variety of wine styles, from light and simple to medium-bodied, even full-bodied, wines, complex and capable of serious aging. In all styles, the wines are delicious, with refreshing—sometimes searing—acidity.

Cannonau (Italy's name for Grenache; see page 58): The most important red grape for the quality red wines of Sardinia, its earthy, medium- to full-bodied flavors have begun to catch on in the United States.

Corvina: From the Veneto region, Corvina is the most important grape in the blend that makes two of Italy's best-known lighter reds, Bardolino and Valpolicella, and ironically Italy's most full-bodied red, Amarone, made from dried grapes. Also, a lovely rosé—*chiaretto*—is produced in the Bardolino region.

Dolcetto: Grown mostly in the Piedmont region, this grape produces fruit-forward, easy-to-drink wines, but with deep red color.

Nebbiolo: Considered one of Italy's two most "noble" grapes (the other is Sangiovese, below), Nebbiolo reaches its powerful zenith in the Piedmont region, where it is represented by extraordinary wines, particularly Barolo and Barbaresco. It is also an important grape in Lombardy, where it ends up in delectable wines such as Inferno and Grumello. The beauty of Nebbiolo is found in its best wines: a compelling balance of high acidity, firm tannins, and black fruits.

Negroamaro: Grown throughout southern Italy and islands, it is represented best by deep, rich, earthy red wines from Puglia.

Nero d'Avola: The "Syrah of the south," this grape shines in Sicily, where its wines can be dark, dense, and wild, great with hearty food.

Primitivo (it's really Zinfandel—see page 55): Along with Negroamaro, Primitivo is one of the two most important grapes in Puglia, making now-popular wines that are fruity, balanced, and full of sunshine.

Sangiovese: With Nebbiolo, one of the two most "noble" red grapes; Sangiovese is also the most-planted red grape in Italy. It achieves its full potential in the Tuscany region, where it is the backbone of every traditional (and some nontraditional) reds. Styles of wines made from Sangiovese can range from a simple, light-bodied Chianti to a memorable, complex, deep "meditation wine" called Brunello di Montalcino that is capable of long aging. As with Nebbiolo, the noble Sangiovese displays high acidity, coupled with supple tannins.

ITALY
Main DOC/DOCG Wine Areas

Valle d'Aosta

Piedmont
1. Gattinara
2. Barbera d'Asti
3. Roero, Arneis de Roero
4. Barbaresco
5. Dolcetto d'Alba
6. Barolo
7. Asti, Moscato d'Asti
8. Gavi, Cortese di Gavi

Liguria

Lombardy
9. Oltrepò Pavese
10. Franciacorta
11. Lugana
12. Valtellina Superiore

Veneto
13. Bardolino
14. Bianco di Custoza
15. Valpolicella
16. Soave/Recioto di Soave
17. Prosecco di Conegliano-Valdobbiadene
18. Piave

Trentino-Alto Adige
19. Alto Adige
20. Lago de Caldaro
21. Santa Maddalena

Friuli-Venezia Giulia
22. Colli Orientali del Friuli
23. Collio

Emilia-Romagna
24. Lambrusco
25. Albana di Romagna

Tuscany
26. Vernaccia di San Gimignano
27. Chianti, Chianti Classico
28. Brunello di Montalcino
29. Vino Nobile di Montepukciano

Umbria
30. Orvieto
31. Torgiano Rosso Riserva
32. Sagrantino di Montefalco

Marche
33. Verdicchio dei Castellli di Jesi
34. Rosso Conero

Abruzzo
35. Montepulciano d'Abruzzo

Lazio
36. Frascati

Molise

Campania
37. Taurasi

Basilicata
38. Aglianico del Vulture

Puglia
39. Locorotondo

Calabria

Sicily
40. Alcamo, Bianco d'Alcamo
41. Marsala

Sardinia
42. Cannonau di Sardegna, Vermentino di Sardegna
43. Vermentino di Gallura

Wine regions of Italy.

WHITE GRAPES

Although Italy produces some killer whites, it is still known mostly for its red wines. Of the white grapes listed below, the one that almost everybody knows is Pinot Grigio. The other grapes on the list either are really important to broad-based Italian winemaking or are grapes you should get to know.

Falanghina, Fiano, and Greco: Luckily, these three wonderful grapes maintain our alphabetical approach. They also grow in the same district of Campania province, where they end up in beautiful, soulful whites that feature their names: Falanghina, Fiano di Avellino, and Greco di Tufo.

Friulano (formerly Tocai Friulano): Capable of rendering some of the best wines in Friuli, it offers earthy minerality in a medium- to full-bodied swirl of apples and pears.

Malvasia: Widely planted, it serves many uses and exhibits several names. Malvasia is an important constituent of many white wines, both dry and sweet, from just drinkable to exquisite.

Moscato: Italy produces extraordinary examples of wines from this grape, most of them sweet with irresistible peach overtones. Some of the best examples are from the Piedmont region: Moscato d'Asti (a bit bubbly) and fully bubbly Asti.

Pinot Bianco and Pinot Grigio (Italy's name for Pinot Blanc and Pinot Gris; see Chapter 2, page 33): Pinot Grigio is grown and produced almost everywhere, with the best examples produced in the cool northeastern regions, especially Friuli and Alto Adige. Pinot Bianco can be crisper and leaner, but often with more character, especially the wines from Alto Adige.

Prosecco (aka Glera): This grape lends its name to the popular, charmingly refreshing, and highly affordable sparkler. In Italy, especially in the Veneto region, Glera has become the preferred name for the grape.

Trebbiano: When you take into account all of its variants, Trebbiano trumps Malvasia for the status of Italy's most-planted white grape. In the Soave region of Veneto and in Tuscan whites, Trebbiano can really add character to blended wines. In other regions, it grows like crazy (sometimes referred to as a "weed," it's so prolific) and is used as a largely anonymous blender.

Verdicchio: Grown in the Marche province, Verdicchio lends its name to wines that can be stupendous: full-bodied, with exotic aromas and crisp acidity, an often overlooked gem that shines when paired with rustic fish dishes.

Vermentino: An important grape in Tuscany and Sardinia, Vermentino, a coastal grape, produces fish-friendly wine, with high acids to refresh the palate and pleasant hints of green grasses in the nose.

Vernaccia: The best-known example of wine from this grape is Vernaccia di San Gimignano from Tuscany, a white that is delicate yet so satisfying with shellfish and seafood.

The language of the label

WE OFTEN HEAR FOLKS COMPLAIN about Italian wine labels, saying that they're hard to decipher. True enough. But with a bit of *WineWise* coaching, we can simplify these labels and help to remove any stress in choosing a good Italian wine.

Whatever info the label conveys, remember that when it comes to Italian wines, the reputation of the producer is paramount. In Italy, that name on the label is often a family name, and it is not difficult to find producers whose families have been making wine for hundreds of years, or at least for several generations. At the same time, there's a new wave of Italian winemakers whose families might have just grown grapes up until recently, or whose wine previously ended up as part of the anonymous

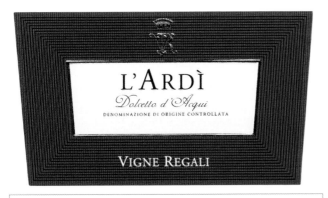

Vigne Regali is the wine producer; "L'Ardì" means "bright and brave"; Dolcetto is the grape; Acqui is the place where the grapes are grown. A DOC wine (see page 198).

blend of a regional wine co-op. These "new wave" winemakers are doing some pretty exciting things and establishing good reputations in Italy and in the world's export markets.

Once you're aware that the producer's good name is important, what are some other *WineWise* shortcuts to understanding an Italian wine label? Well, first off, you should know that there are three basic ways to label an Italian wine:

1. GRAPE AND PLACE NAME

This is a common label format, and what's easy to remember is that it's almost always the name of the grape first, the name of the place second. The grape and place name will be separated by a form of the Italian word for "from." Here are some examples:

DOLCETTO D'ACQUI: Dolcetto is a red grape, and the grapes grew in the Acqui district of the Piedmont region.

SANGIOVESE DI ROMAGNA: Sangiovese is a red grape, and the grapes grew in the Romagna subregion of the Emilia-Romagna region.

VERNACCIA DI SAN GIMIGNANO: Vernaccia is a white grape, and the grapes grew in or around the town of San Gimignano in Tuscany.

2. PLACE NAME ONLY

The label features just the name of the place where the grapes are grown. That place can be very small—perhaps the name of a small town—or huge—maybe the name of an entire region—and everything in between. Some examples:

CHIANTI is a red wine made from grapes grown anywhere in the Chianti region of Tuscany. Chianti Classico is made from grapes grown only within the Classico subregion.

SOAVE is a white wine made from grapes grown in the Soave district of the Veneto region. Soave Classico is also produced.

BAROLO is a red wine made from grapes grown only in the Barolo appellation in the Piedmont region.

FRANCIACORTA is a sparkling wine made from grapes grown in the Franciacorta district of the Lombardy region.

3. PROPRIETARY NAME

A fantasy name chosen by the producer to represent the "story" or "soul" of the wine. Sometimes these are names of a vineyard or some other piece of land, but just as often a wine is named for a person or an idea. There are dozens of these wines in the American market. Many, though not all, are produced in Tuscany (and

Spalletti is the producer; Chianti is the place where the grapes (mostly Sangiovese, in this case) are grown. A DOCG wine (see page 198). Courtesy of Kobrand Corporation.

these wines are collectively known as "Super Tuscans"). They include label names such as Ornellaia, SummuS, Excelsus, Le Pergole Torte, Solaia, Tignanello, Cepparello, Oreno, and Lupicaia, among many, many others.

The origin of the wine

JUST AS FRANCE HAS ITS own set of wine regions regulated by the government under its AOC (also known as AOP) laws (see page 149), so does Italy, but under its DOC laws. DOC is shorthand for *denominazione di origine controllata* (controlled denomination of origin). Under these laws you'll find four official levels of quality:

Vino da Tavola (VdT): We see a minuscule amount of this wine in the U.S. export market, and when we do it is a perverse commentary on Italy's wine laws. VdT is the most basic wine in Italy, wine made for the family or for the rural village with few official rules, or wine you might drink with a straw from a juice box at an Italian McDonald's. It is supposed to be dirt cheap and usually is.

What we might see in this country are older vintages of very expensive wines, mostly the "Super Tuscans," that had no place to go but to the *Vino da Tavola* category because they were made with perhaps some Merlot, Syrah, Chardonnay, or some other foreign interloper grape not permitted by DOC regulations. Go buy a 1990 Tignanello, a humble little VdT blend of Sangiovese and Cabernet, for $200 a bottle at retail, or $500 a bottle on a wine list. Crazy, huh?

Indicazione Geografica Tipica (IGT): As the nontraditional wines of Italy caught on in the international markets, demanding high prices at retail and in restaurants, the Italian government realized that to keep these wines in the low-class VdT category was a bad idea, and they changed the law to accommodate these new Italian wines.

The producers were kind of getting into this idea of being outlaws—making great wines essentially free of government regulation—so to convince them to play along, the government declared that VdT wines could no longer carry a vintage year on the label. Well, the truth is you can't sell a nonvintage wine for big bucks. Starting around 1996, most of the producers of the expensive VdT wines changed their wine's quality classification to this new official category, IGT, in order to continue to produce fine, vintage-dated wines. So while that 1990 Tignanello is a VdT, the 2000-and-beyond Tignanello is an IGT. Note: with a change in the European Union wine laws that began in 2011, "IGT" may transition to "IGP" (*Indicazione Geografica Protetta*).

THE EVOLUTION (OR INTELLIGENT DESIGN?) OF AN ITALIAN WINE LABEL

Once you get the hang of an Italian wine label, you can decipher its "code words" with ease. Here, we're going to give some examples of how a simple label can become more elaborate. You'll notice that with every layer of added information, the origin and/or style of the wine becomes clearer, allowing you to make an informed, WineWise choice. Here are some examples:

Chianti: The general name of the DOCG wine region in Tuscany; a red wine with little aging.

Chianti Classico: The term "Classico" indicates the traditional heartland of the region, usually with the best vineyard sites.

Chianti Classico Riserva: A wine from the traditional heartland with the best vineyards, and aged in accordance with Italy's wine laws. In Chianti Classico the term "Riserva" on the label indicates a minimum aging time of two years in a barrel and three months in the bottle before the wine is released. Note that there is no federal Italian standard for riserva. Aging minimums vary widely, depending on provincial laws for each wine zone.

Barbaresco: The name of the DOCG wine region, located in the Piedmont province.

Barbaresco Riserva: For riserva wines from Barbaresco, the minimum aging time is four years before the wine is released.

Barbaresco Riserva "Asili": A Barbaresco Riserva from the single vineyard (vigneti) Asili. This is a wine with a unique terroir, made in a seriously limited quantity. It will be more expensive than a Barbaresco Riserva and much more expensive than a Barbaresco.

Two excellent single-vineyard (Paje and Asili) Barbaresco riserva wines from the highly regarded cooperative Produttori del Barbaresco. Barbaresco is a DOCG wine zone within Italy's Piedmont region.

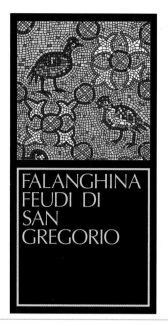

Falanghina, a delicious dry white wine from the Campania region of southern Italy. Courtesy of Feudi di San Gregorio.

Denominazione di Origine Controllata **(DOC):** The majority of Italian wine that you'll encounter falls into this category. There are hundreds of DOC zones, the equivalent of the French AOC (now AOP) (page 149), and they are not so different from a United States AVA (see page 66). In essence, they are place names (sometimes grape and place names in Italy) that appear on the label. The DOC is a defined geographic area, and for each DOC the government approves which grapes can be grown there and specifies approved vineyard and winery practices. While this is an outward sign of quality, remember that the DOC is awarded to a geographical zone (Valpolicella, for example), not to a particular producer. In Italy, as in the rest of the world, each producer's reputation is far more important than the designated DOC. Note: Again, with the new European Union wine laws, we may begin to see this category transition to DOP (*Denominazione di Origine Protetta*).

Denominazione di Origine Controllata e Garantita **(DOCG):** This is a category of Italian wines that have been elevated from DOC because the regions in which they are produced are considered special and unique. The criteria for elevation include quality, history, improvement, and, frankly, contribution to Italy's wine economy. Legally, just like the current DOC wines, DOCG producers may transition to "DOP," but at least in the short term we consider this unlikely. Currently, there are at least 73 DOCG zones; we're certain that there are more to follow. Wikipedia is the best source for a full listing of Italy's DOCG wines: http://en.wikipedia.org/wiki/List_of_Italian_DOCG_wines.

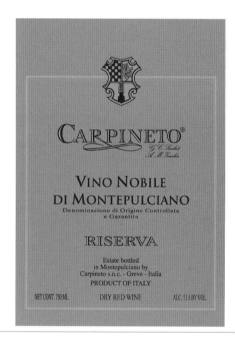

Vino Nobile di Montepulciano is a DOCG red wine from Tuscany, a Sangiovese-dominated blend. This wine, made by Carpineto, is a *riserva*, meaning that the wine has been aged longer in barrel and bottle than a wine that is not designated as *riserva*. Courtesy of Carpineto.

The major wine regions of Italy

WHEN IT COMES TO WINE, it's been said that Italy is not so much a country as it is one big vineyard. This cliché is only a slight exaggeration. Wine abounds from all 20 provinces that constitute Italy (and the twenty-first, the Vatican, makes wine, too, although not from water as far as we know). The export market is chock-a-block with fine Italian wines, many from wine regions that not so long ago were written off as suppliers of vapid, bitter, thin wines, with no hope that they would enter the export market to stellar reviews and consumer acceptance.

Following the lead of the classic regions that have always had an important presence in the U.S. market, the "new" wines of Italy may not really be new at all, but rather the product of better vineyard management and better wine-making. Many of the wines that have caught fire here are made from ancient grapes, but winemakers, both young and old, have adopted modern methods to make their wines technically and aesthetically better; in other words, the wine tastes good. At the same time, an increasing number of producers in just about all of Italy's wine regions have been successful with both white and red wines made from popular international varietals, or blends of Italian and international grapes.

So gaze upon our *WineWise* gazetteer of Italy's most famous—and most promising—wine regions, complete with the names of some of the best producers. (Note: We have intentionally left out the wine regions of Liguria, Molise, and Valle d'Aosta, none of which currently have a significant presence in the U.S. export market.)

WINEWISE TIP: When you see the actual labels of these wines, some of the producers' names may be preceded by certain words or phrases, such as "Azienda Agricola" (a wine estate), "Cantina" or "Cantine" (a winery), "Castello" (a wine estate with a feudal castle on site), "Fattoria" (a name for a winery, often connected to traditional and historic wine estates), "Podere" (a small, historic farm estate), and "Tenuta" or "Tenute" (a large wine estate).

CENTRAL ITALY

TUSCANY

CLASSIC DOCG WINE REGIONS

Brunello di Montalcino

Carmignano

Chianti

Chianti Classico

Morellino di Scansano

Vernaccia di San Gimignano

Vino Nobile di Montepulciano

IMPORTANT DOC WINE REGIONS

Bolgheri

Bolgheri Sassicaia

Pomino

Rosso di Montalcino

Rosso di Montepulciano

Sant'Antimo

Once you are bitten by the Tuscan wine bug, you'll want to taste more and more of the region's wines.

Over the last 30 years, Tuscan winemakers have revolutionized Italian wines, and this revolution has spread throughout the wine world. The best Tuscan winemakers have set out to dramatically improve their traditional wines, and at the same time turn tradition on its ear. Some traditionalists feel that many producers have gone too far in rejecting Tuscan wine history, ritual, and custom, but it's undeniable that the revolution has become an exciting and vibrant movement.

Back to tradition for a moment. Even the most revolutionary Tuscan winemaker would agree that without the Sangiovese grape there is no Tuscan wine industry. Tuscany's most famous red wines— the wines that brought the revolutionaries to the party—rely on Sangiovese. All of Tuscany's most famous red wines are based on Sangiovese, and many of the region's "new" red wines—"Super Tuscans," a term with no deep meaning, invented by wine writers—are either 100% Sangiovese or

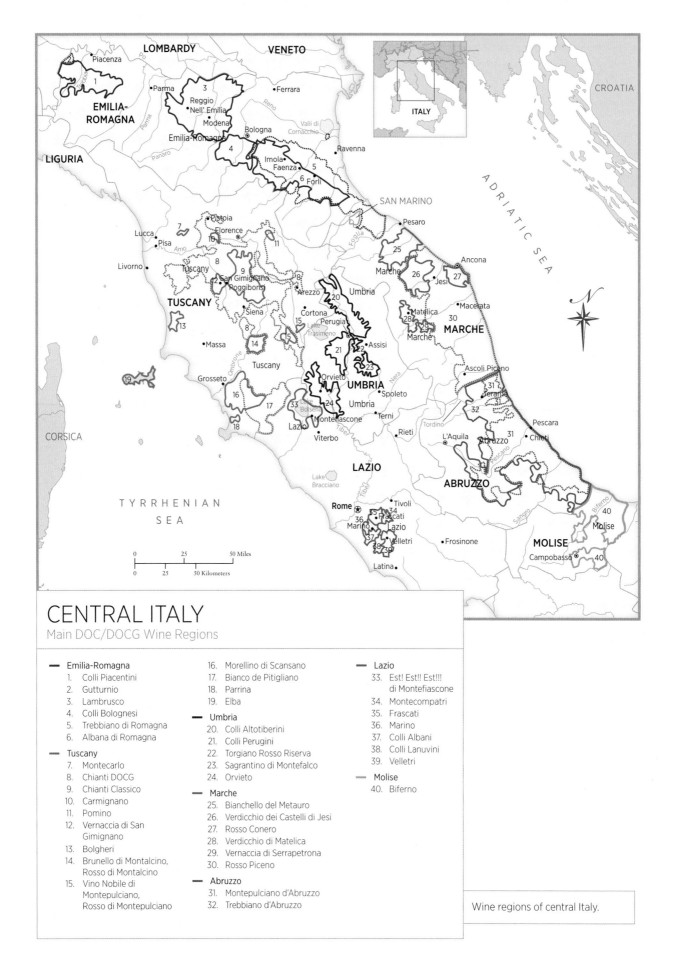

CENTRAL ITALY
Main DOC/DOCG Wine Regions

Emilia-Romagna
1. Colli Piacentini
2. Gutturnio
3. Lambrusco
4. Colli Bolognesi
5. Trebbiano di Romagna
6. Albana di Romagna

Tuscany
7. Montecarlo
8. Chianti DOCG
9. Chianti Classico
10. Carmignano
11. Pomino
12. Vernaccia di San Gimignano
13. Bolgheri
14. Brunello di Montalcino, Rosso di Montalcino
15. Vino Nobile di Montepulciano, Rosso di Montepulciano
16. Morellino di Scansano
17. Bianco de Pitigliano
18. Parrina
19. Elba

Umbria
20. Colli Altotiberini
21. Colli Perugini
22. Torgiano Rosso Riserva
23. Sagrantino di Montefalco
24. Orvieto

Marche
25. Bianchello del Metauro
26. Verdicchio dei Castelli di Jesi
27. Rosso Conero
28. Verdicchio di Matelica
29. Vernaccia di Serrapetrona
30. Rosso Piceno

Abruzzo
31. Montepulciano d'Abruzzo
32. Trebbiano d'Abruzzo

Lazio
33. Est! Est!! Est!!! di Montefiascone
34. Montecompatri
35. Frascati
36. Marino
37. Colli Albani
38. Colli Lanuvini
39. Velletri

Molise
40. Biferno

Wine regions of central Italy.

The rolling hills of Tuscany.

often use it as part of a blend with international varietals such as Cabernet Sauvignon, Cabernet Franc, Merlot, and Syrah. (White "Super Tuscans" often employ Chardonnay and Sauvignon Blanc, either as single varietals or blended with Italy's indigenous varietals.)

Let's take a look at the wines that have made Tuscany famous.

Chianti. At one time the image of this wine was so bad that the name for the traditional wicker basket wrapped around the Chianti bottle, *fiasco*, entered the English language as a term meaning something that's all screwed up. Those days are gone. You can still find the old style of Chianti in the old *fiasco*, but you're far more likely to find a wine in a bottle reminiscent of red Bordeaux or California Cabernet Sauvignon. And the changes are not just cosmetic. Today's Chianti is delicious and food-friendly. You can buy a fruit-forward wine labeled as simply "Chianti" from a good producer for about $10 to $20 (good with veggies, fish, or meats); Chianti Classico, which we consider a true *WineWise* value, starts at about $15 and stops before $30 (a little more power, acidity, and complexity in this wine; food can be a bit heartier), and Chianti Classico Riserva starts at about $25 and climbs to about $45, depending on vintage and producer (a powerful and

complex wine, great with braised and grilled meats). Also look for Chianti Rufina, Chianti Colli Senesi, Chianti Colli Fiorentino, and other wines featuring the name of any of the eight Chianti subregions—great wines with extremely reasonable prices.

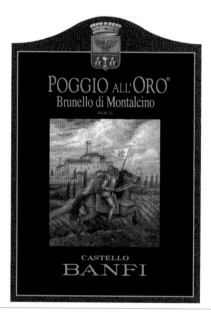

A single-vineyard Brunello di Montalcino (Poggio all'Oro is the vineyard), which must, by law, age a minimum of four years before release. This expensive wine is made from 100% Sangiovese grapes. Tuscany's Castello Banfi is an astoundingly beautiful and historic estate of more than 1,000 acres (400 hectares).

Vino Nobile di Montepulciano. It's a mouthful to say, but Vino Nobile di Montepulciano is also a mouthful of delicious wine at an affordable price, often under $30 at retail. For that money, you get a world-class wine from a small collection of vineyards that is not as well known as the other red DOCG wines of Tuscany (that's good for consumers) but is irrepressibly delicious. The full-bodied wine is fragrant, with herbal and spice notes, moderate acidity, and mature black and red fruits on the palate.

Carmignano. With Sangiovese as its base, Carmignano, a wine from the vineyards surrounding Florence, can include as much as 20% Cabernet Sauvignon or Cabernet Franc in the finished wine. This is a limited-production, elegant wine, with the aroma of rose petals and black currants, as well as wild black fruit flavors and high acidity. If you've never tasted

Carmignano, it can be a revelation. Priced about the same as Chianti Classico Riserva (usually under $30).

Brunello di Montalcino. We've saved the biggest, baddest, boldest, and arguably the best wine for last; it is also the most expensive. Many people believe that Brunello di Montalcino is consistently the finest red wine produced in Italy. It is an extraordinary wine, certainly the most powerful example of wine made from Sangiovese grapes; this is a wine that can and should age for years, and some of the *riserva* wines for a lifetime. Big and brawny but at the same time delicately balanced, Brunello di Montalcino is definitely a special-occasion wine, with retail prices starting at more than $60 and rising to the heavens for older, sought-after wines. On restaurant wine lists it is not uncommon for these wines to sell for $200 and up—way up. For those who can afford it, the experience of tasting a great Brunello di Montalcino is priceless.

Wine regions of Tuscany.

TUSCANY
Main DOC/DOCG
Wine Regions

— Chianti boundary

Central Hills

— Chianti Classico

— Val d'Arbia

— Bianco della Valdinievole

— Bianco dell'Empolese

— Carmignano

— Vernaccia di San Gimignano

— Bianco Vergine Valdichiana

— Brunello di Montalcino
Rosso di Montalcino
Moscadello di Montalcino

— Vino Nobile di Montepulciano
Rosso di Montepulciano

Coastal Flank

— Colli di Luni

— Elba

— Candia dei Colli Apuani

— Colline Lucchesi

— Montecarlo

— Bianco Pisano di San Torpe

— Montescudaio

— Bolgheri

— Morellino di Scansano

— Bianco di Pitigliano

— Parrina

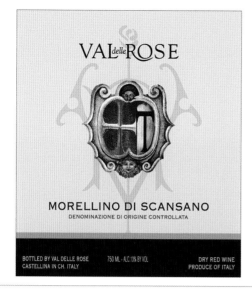

Morellino di Scansano is a Sangiovese-based wine made from grapes that grow in the coastal Maremma region of Tuscany. Val delle Rose is a leading producer of this wine.

Vernaccia di San Gimignano is a moderately priced white wine that pairs well with fish dishes. Courtesy of Kobrand Corporation.

WineWise TIP: There is good news for those of us who can afford only a "baby Brunello": Rosso di Montalcino. Like Brunello, Rosso is made from 100% Sangiovese picked in and around the same vineyards as the more esteemed wine, and made mostly by Brunello di Montalcino producers. For less than $30 at retail, you can enjoy some hints of Brunello in a wine that is enjoyable right out of the bottle, or within a few years—your choice. DOC Rosso di Montalcino is among our top *WineWise* choices for value and quality.

Morellino di Scansano.
From southern, coastal Tuscany, this is an earthy, rich, and complex yet fresh red. Morellino (one of dozens of alternative names for Sangiovese) is often priced under $30 and worth almost double the price. The *riserva* wines are more expensive (about $40) and are glorious.

Vernaccia di San Gimignano.
A popular dry white wine of historical significance, produced in the vineyards surrounding San Gimignano, a medieval town perched on top of a hill. A light- to medium-bodied wine, Vernaccia di San Gimignano marries well with seafood and shellfish.

SOME OF THE BEST WINE PRODUCERS

CHIANTI: Badiolo, Bellini, Borgo Salce, Cal del Vispo, Castellani, Geografico, Ghizzano, Parri e Figio, Petrolo, Spalletti, Villa La Selva; Malenchini and Le Querce in Chianti Colli Fiorentini; Frescobaldi in Chianti Rufina, especially their "Nipozzano" Riserva.

CHIANTI CLASSICO: Antinori, Badia a Coltibuono, Banfi, Barbi, Borgo Scopeto, Brolio/Barone Ricasoli, Carpineto, Casa Emma, Castellare, Castello di Ama, Cecchi, Felsina, Fonterutoli, Fontodi, Gabbiano, Grevepesa, Isole e Olena, Machiavelli, Melini, Monsanto, Nozzole, Poggerino, Querciabella, Querceto, Rampolla, Ruffino, San Felice, Verrazano, Vicchiomaggio, Villa Cafaggio, and Volpaia.

BRUNELLO DI MONTALCINO AND ROSSO DI MONTALCINO: Altesino, Antinori, Argiano, Castello Banfi, Barbi, Biondi-Santi, Campogiovanni, Caparzo, Casa Basse di Soldera, Casanova di Neri, Castelgiocondo/ Frescobaldi, Castello Banfi, Col d'Orcia, Corte Pavoni, Fanti, Fattoi, Fuligni, Gaja,

Lisini, La Magla, Mastrojanni, Nardi, Pacenti, Poggio Antico, Il Poggione, Salvioni, Solaria, Uccelliera, and Val di Suga.

VINO NOBILE DI MONTEPULCIANO AND ROSSO DI MONTEPULCIANO: Avignonesi, Boscarelli, Contucci, Fassati, Poliziano, Redi, Salcheto, and Valdipiatta.

CARMIGNANO: Capezzana, also Ambra, Artimino, and Cantagallo.

VERNACCIA DI SAN GIMIGNANO: Falchini, San Quirico, Spalletti, Strozzi, and Teruzzi e Puthod.

UMBRIA

CLASSIC DOCG WINE REGIONS
Sagrantino di Montefalco

Torgiano Rosso Riserva

IMPORTANT DOC WINE REGIONS
Montefalco

Orvieto

Torgiano

Although landlocked Umbria lives in the shadow of its neighbor Tuscany, Umbria produces excellent wines of its own, the best of which are still a secret to the American wine public.

One white wine from Umbria has had great success in the United States: Orvieto. Look for Orvieto Classico; easy to find, a bargain—about $12 to $15—and a great wine for delicate fish dishes.

Lungarotti is a producer who has had great success with its Rubesco, a reasonably priced Sangiovese-based red blend from the Torgiano wine district. Rubesco is a hearty, complex, and food-friendly red. Lungarotti also produces a more expensive version of this wine, made from a single vineyard site, "Vigna Monticchio," a Torgiano Rosso Riserva (DOCG) aged for five years in the bottle before release.

LUNGAROTTI

Lungarotti has long been Umbria's most famous wine producer in the U.S. market. Rubesco is a brand name for Lungarotti's Rosso di Torgiano, a Sangiovese-based blend that is both ageworthy and affordable.

Sagrantino di Montefalco is an extraordinary red, unique thanks to its singular grape, Sagrantino. Inky, full, and rich, with just the right acidity, it is one of the world's great wines. It is expensive and can be found mostly on fine Italian restaurant wine lists.

SOME OF THE BEST WINE PRODUCERS

RUBESCO AND TORGIANO ROSSO RISERVA FROM LUNGAROTTI; SAGRANTINO DI MONTEFALCO: Arnaldo Caprai and also Adante, Colpetrone, Fongoli, and Tiburzi.

ORVIETO CLASSICO: Antinori, Barberani-Vallesanta, Barbi, Barone Ricasoli, Bigi, Cecchi, Fontana-Candida, Melini, Palazzone, Picini, Ruffino, Salviano, Straccali, and Le Velette.

ABRUZZO

CLASSIC DOCG WINE REGION
Montepulciano d'Abruzzo Colline Terramane

IMPORTANT DOC WINE REGION
Montepulciano d'Abruzzo

Montepulciano d'Abruzzo is an enjoyable, affordable, food-friendly, medium-bodied red. Zaccagnini is a leading producer.

Verdicchio from Le Marche has long been a popular Italian white wine in the United States and at its best can be medium- to full-bodied and complex. Fazi Battaglia is one of the best-known producers of estate-bottled Verdicchio dei Castelli di Jesi.

Montepulciano d'Abruzzo is a red wine that is enjoyable in its youth; it's quite fruity and easy to drink. Widely available in the United States, this wine is developing a good reputation among wine drinkers who enjoy a good, food-friendly wine (especially with pizza, barbecue, and roasts) at a very reasonable price, often under $20. It's really not necessary to go out of your way to find the DOCG version from the Colline Terramane district.

Some of the Best Wine Producers

Bove, Casal Thaulero, Cataldi Madonna, Citra, Contesa, Marina Cvetic, Gru, Masciarelli, Umani Ronchi, Valentini, Valori, and Zaccagnini

LE MARCHE

CLASSIC DOCG WINE REGIONS

Conero

Verdicchio dei Castelli di Jesi Riserva

Verdicchio di Matelica Riserva

IMPORTANT DOC WINE REGION

Rosso Piceno

The most famous wine in Marche is Verdicchio. This wine is so accessible, so reasonably priced, and of such high quality that it qualifies as a true *WineWise* bargain. A medium-bodied dry white with an herbaceous nose and green apple acidity to refresh the palate, Verdicchio at its best shows off a bit of hazelnut in the finish to add some complexity. A great match for fish and poultry, styles of Verdicchio range from clean and crisp to versions that are more about minerals and earth.

Two reds from Marche have made some small inroads in the United States. Rosso Conero and Rosso Piceno, both Montepulciano/Sangiovese blends, are appealing, medium-bodied wines meant to be drunk young, within three to five years of vintage. These are great pasta wines that would also be just as happy accompanying a grilled salmon as marrying with white or red meat dishes.

Some of the Best Wine Producers

VERDICCHIO DEI CASTELLI DI JESI AND VERDICCHIO DI MATELICA: Belisario, Bisci, Bucci, Colonnara, Fazi Battaglia, Garofoli, Luchetti, Martinetti, Mecella, La Monacesca, Montalto, San Lorenzo, Sartarelli, Tavignano, Umani Ronchi, and Zaccagnini.

ROSSO CONERO AND ROSSO PICENO:
Le Caniette, Colonnara, Ercole Velenosi, Grifoni, Lanari, Montecappone, Moroder, Saladini Pilastri, Serenelli, Le Terraze, Tavignano, and Velenosi.

LAZIO

CLASSIC DOCG WINE REGION

Frascati Superiore

IMPORTANT DOC WINE REGION

Est! Est!! Est!!! di Montefiascone

In the American market, just as it is in the Italian capital city of Rome, Lazio is all about Frascati, an affordable, fruity, fragrant, simple, crisp, light, and dry wine. Frascati, which is produced with mostly Malvasia and/or Trebbiano grapes, works well as an accompaniment to light, simple dishes, especially fish, or deep-fried artichokes, a historic staple of Rome's Jewish ghetto. Often overlooked, Frascati is one of our favorite wines for warm weather, when you want to sip something that does not demand your attention but is tasty, especially when dining al fresco.

Est! Est!! Est!!! di Montefiascone, another light, crisp white that features Trebbiano and Malvasia, has zippy acidity and lovely aromatics,

Orvieto is a medium-bodied, refreshing dry white wine that can be sourced from vineyards in both the Lazio and Umbria regions of Italy. Orvieto, a good match with seafood, is a *WineWise* bargain.

and those found in the American market are pleasant, especially with fried foods.

SOME OF THE BEST WINE PRODUCERS

FRASCATI: Casale Mattia, Castel de Paolis, Colli di Catone, Conte Zandotti, Fontana Candida, Gotto d'Oro, San Marco, and Villa Simone.

EST! EST!! EST!!! DI MONTEFIASCONE:
Cerveteri, Falesco, Mazziotti, and Mottura.

NORTHWEST ITALY

PIEDMONT

CLASSIC DOCG WINE REGIONS

Asti/Moscato d'Asti

Barbaresco, Barbera d'Asti

Barbera del Monferrato Superiore

Barolo

Brachetto d'Acqui

Dolcetto di Diano d'Alba

Dolcetto di Dogliani Superiore

Gattinara

Gavi/Cortese di Gavi

Ghemme

Roero

IMPORTANT DOC WINE REGIONS

Barbera d'Alba

Dolcetto d'Acqui

Dolcetto d'Alba

Dolcetto d'Asti

Grignolino d'Asti

Grignolino del Monferrato

Lovers of Italian wine who don't think that Brunello di Montalcino (see "Tuscany," page 202) is Italy's finest wine usually come down on the

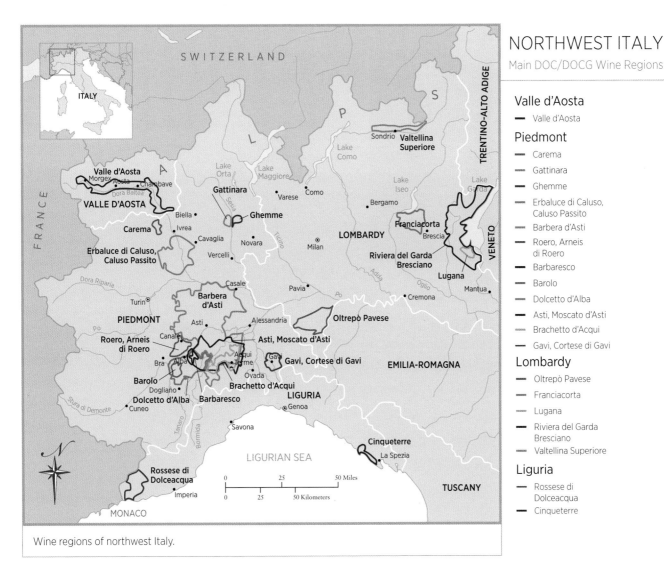

Wine regions of northwest Italy.

side of one of two famous DOCG reds from the Piedmont region as their first choice: Barolo or Barbaresco. While we will never settle this argument among these three big wines, we can say without fear of contradiction that Barolo and Barbaresco are extraordinary wines that beautifully represent the traditions of Piedmontese winemaking. But Piedmont is about more than two great red wines.

Piedmont (*Piemonte* in Italian) is steeped in a tradition of *terroir* in the vineyards and production of officially classified DOC and DOCG wines made from Italian varietals (there are no newfangled IGT wines from Piedmont, the only wine region other than its teeny-tiny neighbor Valle d'Aosta not to have any). Piedmont is considered by many to be the true home of classic Italian wines, yet it is a region that is not standing still.

It is with their native varietals—Nebbiolo, Barbera, and Dolcetto among the reds, Cortese, Arneis, and Moscato among the whites—that Piedmont's wines shine, creating a brilliant luster to attract the wine world.

Piedmont borders France and Switzerland; the views of the Alps from Piedmontese vineyards are majestic. This is one of the coolest wine regions of Italy, and Piedmont's best wines exhibit searing acidity to refresh the palate in its whites, sparklers, and lighter reds, and balance the complex structure and tannins of its biggest reds.

There is an old Piedmontese expression: *Il vino e rosso* ("Wine is red"). That belief certainly doesn't allow much wiggle room. Of course Piedmont winemakers do produce white wines, but most of them live in the shadow of the region's famous reds. Let's look at those reds and then survey the most popular whites.

Barbaresco vineyards in Piedmont.

Barolo and Barbaresco. These are red wines produced from 100% Nebbiolo grapes grown in the vineyards surrounding the small city of Alba: Barolo to the south of the city, Barbaresco to the north. In the old days, Barolo, known as the "king of Piedmont's wines," was almost always the more powerful wine that needed more time to age to tame the rustic, wild, sometimes harsh tannins in the wine. Barbaresco, the "queen," was in those days the more delicate of the two wines, although it still needed plenty of aging to achieve balance. Today, these wines are largely gender-neutral, with Barolo sometimes more delicate than a Barbaresco, and a Barbaresco likely to be as powerful as a Barolo.

Barolo and Barbaresco call into question much of what we think we know about powerful, tannic wines. We usually assume that such blockbusters must be deeply colored, bordering on black, especially when young. Yet both of these wines, because they are made from the thin-skinned Nebbiolo grape, start life as medium-red in color, losing some of that color and taking on orange highlights as the wine ages. What a pleasant surprise it is to taste Barolo or Barbaresco for the first time. The tannins grab you and hold on, but soon give way to background flavors of spiced and dried red fruits, especially dried cherries. The nose of Nebbiolo is also pronounced: spices, roses, tar, and the earthy and exotic aromas of *tartufo bianco*, the white truffles that grow wild in Piedmont. These are wines that call for hearty foods without elaborate sauces or complicated, competing flavors. Keep it simple—grilled steak, roast duck, or braised lamb shanks served with potatoes or polenta—and the wine will rapidly emerge as another flavor and texture component of the dish.

Barbaresco and especially Barolo are very expensive wines, and worth it. Best value: Produttori del Barbaresco (starting at under $40 retail, a bit more for some very special single-vineyard wines). Also look for the DOC wines Nebbiolo d'Alba and Langhe Nebbiolo, which

A single-vineyard (Rocche) Barolo from Renato Ratti, a leading quality-driven producer. Marcenasco is a subdistrict within Barolo. Renato Ratti's son, Pietro, is in charge of the vineyards, the ultra-modern winery, and making the wines.

Barbera d'Alba from the Gepin single vineyard, made by Albino Rocca, one of Piedmont's best producers. Barbera from Piedmont, with forward fruit and high acidity, is an excellent wine for a wide variety of foods.

are great bargains (starting at about $20 to $25). They are a bit softer on the palate, a bit fruitier, and ready to drink within a few years of vintage.

Gattinara and Ghemme. Also based in Nebbiolo, Gattinara and Ghemme (occasionally labeled as "Spanna") are both DOCG red wines from the north of Piedmont. Cooler than the southern region that is home to Barolo and Barbaresco, these wines are produced from grapes with higher acid levels. It is difficult to ripen Nebbiolo here, so these wines are normally lighter than Barolo or Barbaresco, unless the growing season has been peppered with many dry, hot days. These wines are pretty: floral, perfumed, and delicate but substantive. They are normally less expensive than Barolo or Barbaresco.

Barbera d'Alba, Barbera d'Asti, Barbera del Monferrato. Barbera is the most-planted grape in Piedmont and the second-most-planted red grape in all of Italy (after Sangiovese). Barbera is planted in other parts of the world, but Piedmont is its ancestral home, and the region produces some of the world's best wines made from this grape.

Unlike wines made from Nebbiolo grapes, Barbera wines from Piedmont are anywhere from cherry red to moderately dark in color. They are generally medium-bodied and fruit-forward and always show off bright, sometimes searingly high

acidity. These are fine examples of "crossover" wines, equally at home in the company of grilled fish, white meats, red meats, pasta, pizza, or roasted vegetables. Barbera is considered a signature wine of Piedmont, so a good producer won't put his or her name on an inferior wine. These wines usually range from under $20 to about $30, with some more powerful wines that are produced and aged in small oak barrels and/or from single vineyards priced significantly higher. Compare, for example, the charming, refreshing, and affordable medium-bodied Barbera d'Asti from Cascina Castlet (featuring an adorable hand-tinted family photo of the winemaker and her three sisters when they were children, all posed on a Vespa motor scooter) with the full-bodied, ageworthy, single-vineyard Barbera d'Asti Superiore "Stradivario" produced by the Bava family. "Stradivario" needs at least 10 years of age to fully express the unique *terroir* of the vineyard and vintage; a truly singular wine, which could cost anywhere from $70 to $100 at retail.

Dolcetto d'Acqui, Dolcetto d'Alba, Dolcetto d'Asti, Dolcetto di Diano d'Alba, Dolcetto di Dogliani. Dolcetto is a light- to medium-bodied dry red, with juicy berry flavors and high acidity. Often compared to Beaujolais from France because of its simplicity, Dolcetto is in fact a bit more complex. Still, this is a great "crossover"

B A R B A R E S C O
DENOMINAZIONE DI ORIGINE CONTROLLATA E GARANTITA

O V E L L O

2009

A single-vineyard (Ovello) Barbaresco from Cantine del Pino, owned by Renato Vacca, a Piedmontese winemaker.

Dolcetto is a great "crossover" red, a fine accompaniment to grilled fish, white meats, leaner red meats, and roasted or grilled veggies. Gigi Rosso makes a very good Dolcetto d'Alba.

wine for a wide variety of dishes and can take a bit of chilling to bring out its fruit, especially in warm weather—a great wine for a picnic or old-fashioned family cookout. Dolcetto d'Alba, often produced by leading Barolo and Barbaresco producers, is widely available in the American market, but try Dolcetto from any of Piedmont's wine districts. An excellent value, with prices ranging from about $18 to under $30.

Brachetto d'Acqui. This is a sweet, pale-red, almost-rosé wine, mostly produced in a light, sparkling style, that is a lot of fun, from its red berry color and frothing foam to its low alcohol content (8% to 10%) and flavors of fresh red fruits. Sometimes labeled as simply "Acqui," it's the perfect match for dark chocolate and fresh-fruit-based desserts, and a good summer sipper. From $20 to $30 per bottle.

Gavi/Cortese di Gavi. Made from 100% Cortese grapes, this light-bodied DOCG dry white with refreshing, almost minty green, acidity can actually be called by three possible names: Gavi, Cortese di Gavi, and Gavi di Gavi. Well-chilled Gavi is an excellent match with seafood and shellfish, including cold dishes, such as a Nicoise salad. Usually produced as a still wine, we also recommend the slightly sparkling

version, Principessa Gavia Perlante, produced by Banfi. Retail prices for Gavi start at about $15 and will rarely exceed $25.

Roero Arneis. Red wines are made from Nebbiolo grapes in the Roero DOCG, located between the cities of Alba and Asti. However, the region is best known in the United States for its white wines made from Arneis. With its aromas of flowers and hazelnuts, Arneis is an appealing light- to medium-bodied white with moderately high acidity. Produced commercially only since the early 1980s, Roero Arneis is still a little-known "insider wine" but is high on our list of *WineWise* recommendations, and it's a very good value, with retail prices beginning at about $20.

Asti/Moscato d'Asti. The name of this shared DOCG actually represents two different styles of wine, both peachy-sweet and both made from 100% Moscato grapes. Asti used to be called Asti Spumante; the Italian word *spumante* means "sparkling." Because the wine is always presented in a Champagne-style bottle, allowing the consumer to easily figure out that it's got a lot of bubbles, it is now simply called "Asti." Moscato d'Asti is essentially the same wine, but with far less sparkle; it's made in the *frizzantino* style, which means "a little fizzy." Both wines are

Gavi is a light- to medium-bodied white. Perfect for fish, the wine is light, refreshing, and fun. Gavi is made only from Cortese grapes.

Moscato d'Asti is a light, frothy, refreshing, moderately sweet, low-alcohol wine, perfect to accompany cookies, cheesecake, or fruit-based desserts. Ceretto's "Santo Stefano" Moscato d'Asti is an elegant wine in an elegant bottle. Asti is basically the same wine—but with more bubbles—in a Champagne bottle. Courtesy of Ceretto Winery.

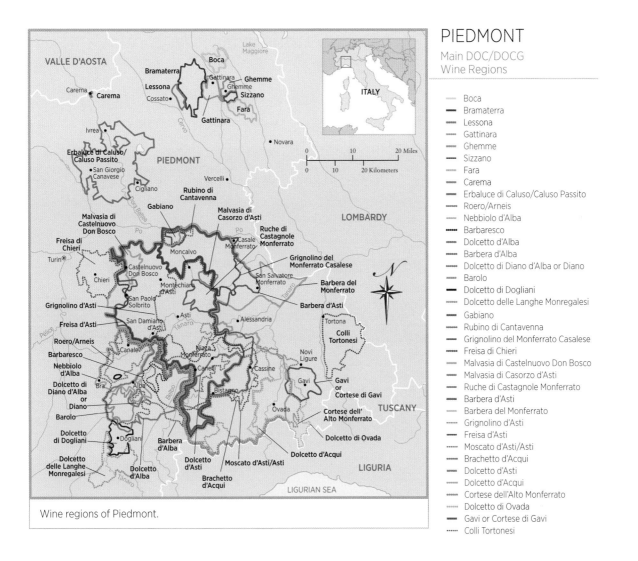

PIEDMONT
Main DOC/DOCG
Wine Regions

- Boca
- Bramaterra
- Lessona
- Gattinara
- Ghemme
- Sizzano
- Fara
- Carema
- Erbaluce di Caluso/Caluso Passito
- Roero/Arneis
- Nebbiolo d'Alba
- Barbaresco
- Dolcetto d'Alba
- Barbera d'Alba
- Dolcetto di Diano d'Alba or Diano
- Barolo
- Dolcetto di Dogliani
- Dolcetto delle Langhe Monregalesi
- Gabiano
- Rubino di Cantavenna
- Grignolino del Monferrato Casalese
- Freisa di Chieri
- Malvasia di Castelnuovo Don Bosco
- Malvasia di Casorzo d'Asti
- Ruche di Castagnole Monferrato
- Barbera d'Asti
- Barbera del Monferrato
- Grignolino d'Asti
- Freisa d'Asti
- Moscato d'Asti/Asti
- Brachetto d'Acqui
- Dolcetto d'Asti
- Dolcetto d'Acqui
- Cortese dell'Alto Monferrato
- Dolcetto di Ovada
- Gavi or Cortese di Gavi
- Colli Tortonesi

Wine regions of Piedmont.

charming, fun, and low in alcohol, from 5% to 7%. They're cheesecake wines, wines for fruit-based desserts, wines to sip and enjoy in warm weather, maybe by the pool or in the garden on a hot and muggy day when the only thought in your head involves cooling down.

SOME OF THE BEST WINE PRODUCERS

BARBARESCO: Albino Rocca, Aldo Conterno, Ca' Rome', Cantina del Pino, Ceretto, Gaja, Bruno Giacosa, Fratelli Giacosa, I Paglieri, Marchese di Gresy, Mascarello e Figlio, Moccagatta, Pio Cesare, Produttori del Barbaresco, Prunotto, and Vietti.

BAROLO: Abbona, Alessandria, Elio Altare, Batasiolo, Borgogno, Boroli, Ceretto, Chiarlo, Clerico, Aldo Conterno, Giacomo Conterno, Einaudi, Fontanafredda, Gaja, Bruno Giacosa, Grasso, Manzone, Manzoni, Marcarini, Marchese di Barolo, Mascarello, Pio Cesare, Prunotto, Ratti, Revello, Rinaldi, Sandrone, Scavino, Sottimano, La Spinetta, Vietti, and Voerzio.

GATTINARA AND GHEMME: Antoniolo, Bianchi, Cantalupo, Le Colline, Nervi, and Travaglini.

Ca' del Bosco is a fine producer of Franciacorta, one of the best Champagne-method sparkling wines in the world. Courtesy of Ca'del Bosco.

BARBERA D'ALBA DOC AND BARBERA D'ASTI DOC: Batasiolo, Bava, Bricco Mandolino, Giacomo Bologna/Braida, Boroli, Cascina Castelet, Chiarlo, Conterno, Gaja, Negro, Olim Bauda, Pio Cesare, and Ratti.

DOLCETTO D'ALBA, DOLCETTO D'ASTI, DOLCETTO DI DIANO D'ALBA, DOLCETTO DI DOGLIANI: Elio Altare, Azelia, Ceretto, Conterno, Einaudi, Gaja, Giacosa, L'Ardi, Mascarello, Pecchenino, Ratti, Sandrone, San Romano, and Vietti.

GAVI/CORTESE DI GAVI DOCG: Banfi, Bava, Bersano, Chiarlo, Fontanafredda, Pio Cesare, Gigi Rosso, La Scolca, Villa Sparina, and Volpi.

ROERO (WHITES USING THE ARNEIS GRAPE): Bongiovanni, Broglia, Ceretto, Corregia, Bruno Giacosa, Pio Cesare, Porello, and Vietti.

ASTI/MOSCATO D'ASTI AND BRACHETTO D'ACQUI: Banfi, Giacomo Bologna/Braida, Bosca, Cascina Giovinale, Ceretto, Chiarlo, Cinzano, Contratto, Coppo, Costello del Poggio, Marenco, Martini e Rossi, Olim Bauda, Palazzacci, Santini, Saracco, Tosti, and Vallebelbo.

LOMBARDY

Franciacorta

Valtellina Superiore (which includes four subregions: Inferno, Grumello, Sassella, and Valgella)

IMPORTANT DOC WINE REGION

Oltrepo Pavese

Lombardy is often defined by its cosmopolitan capital, Milan, and its best wines are still a bit of a secret, except to the neighboring Swiss, who tend to think of these wines as their own and consume copious amounts of *vino di Lombardia*. Franciacorta, the famous sparkler made by the *methode champenoise* (*metodo classico* or *metodo tradizionale* in Italian) is produced here, with spectacular—and expensive—results.

The umbrella DOCG of Valtellina Superiore refers to four red wines sourced from vineyards located on the steep banks of the Adda River: Inferno, Grumello, Sassella, and Valgella. These wines are made almost entirely from the Nebbiolo grape, here called Chiavennasca. A *WineWise* favorite is Grumello ($25 to $35) because it consistently delivers the pleasure of a complex mélange of both black and red fruits with balanced tannins.

SOME OF THE BEST WINE PRODUCERS

FRANCIACORTA: Bellavista, Berlucchi, Ca' del Bosco, Contado Castaldi, Cavalleri, Lantieri, Majolini, and Ronco Calino.

VALTELLINA SUPERIORE (INFERNO, GRUMELLO, SASSELLA, AND VALGELLA): Nino Negri and Rainoldi.

EMILIA-ROMAGNA

CLASSIC DOCG WINE REGION

Albana di Romagna

IMPORTANT DOC WINE REGIONS

Lambrusco di Sorbara

Lambrusco Grasparossa di Castelvetro

Lambrusco Salamino di Santa Croce

Sangiovese di Romagna

Sweet tooth? Lambrusco is the mainstay of Emilia-Romagna's wine industry. In the United States we see mostly sweeter Lambruscos. Riunite, the category's brand leader, is made in many different styles and is exported throughout the world. Most Lambrusco wines are inexpensive and fun to drink.

In the American market, Emilia-Romagna is widely represented by one wine, Lambrusco, made from a red grape of the same name. Lambrusco can be made as a white, rosé, or red wine, and is often *frizzante* (semi-sparkling). A small amount of fine dry red Lambrusco is available in the American market, but you really have to search for it.

While wine snobs mock the simplicity and popularity of fizzy Lambrusco, the original screwcap wine, we have found few wines that are a happier match for the famous foods of Emilia-Romagna: a lunch of Prosciutto di Parma cured ham and Parmigiano-Reggiano cheese. Try all three—the wine, the ham, and the cheese—with some good bread and see if you don't agree.

Albana di Romagna is a white DOCG wine, most often dry when sold in the United States. There is nothing truly special about this wine on the palate, but it is a reliable, medium-bodied, tasty sip. We much prefer Sangiovese di Romagna, a well-made, fruit-forward, medium-bodied red that is extremely food-friendly and extremely well priced—a true *WineWise* value.

Some of the Best Wine Producers

ALBANA DI ROMAGNA AND SANGIOVESE DI ROMAGNA: Castelluccio, Celli, Umberto Cesari, Dantello, Ferrucci, La Macolina, Paradiso, Poggio Pollino, San Patrignano, Tre Monte, and La Zerbina.

WIDELY AVAILABLE LAMBRUSCO PRODUCERS: Caprari, Cella, Giacobazzi, Grasparossa, Riunite, Villa di Corlo, and Zonin.

NORTHEAST ITALY

VENETO

CLASSIC DOCG WINE REGIONS

Amarone della Valpolicella

Bardolino Superiore

Conegliano-Valdobbiadene Prosecco Superiore

Recioto di Soave

Soave Superiore

IMPORTANT DOC WINE REGIONS

Bardolino

Soave

Valpolicella

Veneto produces more DOC wines than any other Italian wine region, but it is best known in the United States for the white wine Soave, the sparkling wine Prosecco, and the reds Bardolino, Valpolicella, and Amarone. These are all classic Veneto wines that are made largely from classic Italian grapes. Veneto also produces plenty of Pinot Grigio, as well as reds and whites based on international varietals, especially Merlot.

Soave is a refreshing, pretty, straightforward quaffing white, and can easily become a go-to

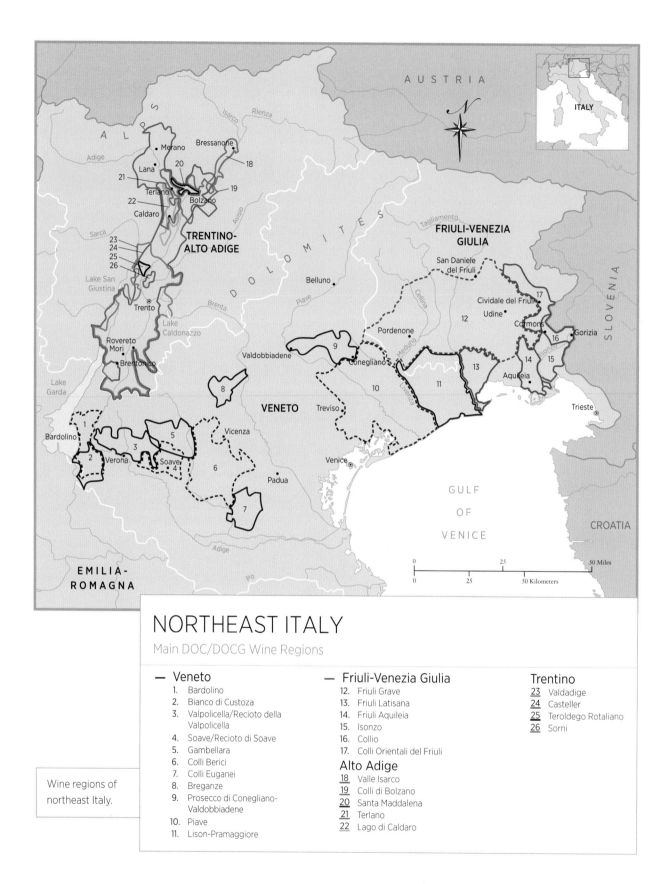

NORTHEAST ITALY

Main DOC/DOCG Wine Regions

— Veneto
1. Bardolino
2. Bianco di Custoza
3. Valpolicella/Recioto della Valpolicella
4. Soave/Recioto di Soave
5. Gambellara
6. Colli Berici
7. Colli Euganei
8. Breganze
9. Prosecco di Conegliano-Valdobbiadene
10. Piave
11. Lison-Pramaggiore

— Friuli-Venezia Giulia
12. Friuli Grave
13. Friuli Latisana
14. Friuli Aquileia
15. Isonzo
16. Collio
17. Colli Orientali del Friuli

Alto Adige
18. Valle Isarco
19. Colli di Bolzano
20. Santa Maddalena
21. Terlano
22. Lago di Caldaro

Trentino
23. Valdadige
24. Casteller
25. Teroldego Rotaliano
26. Sorni

Wine regions of northeast Italy.

wine with fish, vegetables, and rice dishes. We recommend Soave Classico for just a few bucks more, which can be more complex and provocative. Soave Superiore is hard to find, but we prefer good Soave or Soave Classico from a great producer anyway. Recioto di Soave is a sweet version made from dried grapes, is hard to find, and relatively expensive.

Prosecco is a widely available, charming, and lively sparkler that's highly affordable (often in the $10 to $20 range)—a refreshing drink before a meal, or fun when paired with light, simple foods. Not long ago, Prosecco from the regions of Conegliano and Valdobbiadene was awarded DOCG status. The wine, made principally from the Glera grape (also known as Prosecco, but the local producers are firm in using Glera as the name), is not hard to find and highly recommended. There is a lot of wine labeled "Prosecco" in the market of questionable provenance and low quality; some of it not even made in Italy, much less Veneto. Go with the real deal, and look for Prosecco di Valdobbiadene or Prosecco di Conegliano-Valdobbiadene. For truly special Prosecco, look for the relatively rare and expensive "Cartizze" wines, produced from vineyards on a very steep hillside.

Bardolino and Valpolicella are both made from the same grapes; Corvina is the dominant varietal. Both of these reds are some of our favorite highly affordable "crossover" reds, equally at home with meat, fish, pasta, and pizza. Look for wines from the Classico districts, and don't forget

Bardolino Chiaretto—a light- to medium-bodied dry rosé that pairs beautifully with the lighter, often cold foods of summer picnics.

Ironically, Italy's most powerful wine, Amarone, is made from grapes grown in the same vineyards as the light- to medium-bodied Valpolicella. The difference is that Amarone is made from *passito* grapes dried in the sun and then indoors over the winter. The grapes shrivel, becoming virtual raisins, and the resulting dry red wine is well above 15% alcohol. There is a less-known sweet version (somewhat lower in alcohol, but still potent stuff) called Recioto della Valpolicella.

WINEWISE TIP: Look for the *ripasso* style of Valpolicella. In this style, Valpolicella juice is "re-passed" over the lees—the spent yeast cells—of Amarone and then fermented, creating a medium- to full-bodied wine with luscious and complex flavors. The best known *ripasso* in the American market is the affordable Campofiorin, produced by Masi.

SOME OF THE BEST WINE PRODUCERS

BARDOLINO: Bertani, Bolla, Boscaini, Guerrieri-Rizzardi, and Lamberti.

VALPOLICELLA, VALPOLICELLA RIPASSO, AND AMARONE: Accordini, Aldegheri, Serego Alighieri, Allegrini, Aneri, Arano, Begali, Bertani, Bolla, Boscaini, Brigaldara, Bussola, Castellani, Cesari, Fabiano, Farina, Masi, Musella, Quintarelli, Righetti, Speri, Tedeschi, Tommasi, Trabucchi, Zenato, and Zonin.

Prosecco is a refreshing, fruity, sparkling wine, most often produced in a dry to semi-dry style, with moderate alcohol. It is wildly popular in the United States and makes a great aperitif before dinner, as well as a good partner with oysters, clams, and lighter seafood in general. Maschio dei Cavalieri produces an excellent Prosecco di Valdobbiadene.

Soave is one of the most popular Italian white wines in the U.S. market. The "Sereole" Soave is a high-quality single-vineyard bottling from Bertani, a well-known producer in the Veneto region. Courtesy of Bertani.

SOAVE: Allegrini, Anselmi, Bertani, Bolla, La Cappuccina, Ca' Rugate, Gini, Graziano Pa, Fratelli Pasqua, Inama, Pieropan, Portinari, Pra, Santi, Sartori, and Zonin.

PROSECCO DI CONEGLIANO-VALDOBBIADENE: Adami, Aneri, Bellenda, Bisol, Canevel, Collalbrigio, Desiderio Bisol, Nino Franco, Maschio dei Cavalieri, Mionetto, Ruggeri, Santa Margherita, Valdo, Val d'Oca, and Zardetto.

TRENTINO-ALTO ADIGE

IMPORTANT DOC WINE REGIONS

Alto Adige

Teroldego Rotaliano

Trentino

Trento

Valdadige

This region borders Austria and Switzerland and combines two cultures: Alto Adige is officially bilingual (Italian and German). In fact, Italy's official alternate name for Alto Adige is Sudtirol. There is a real divide in the styles of many of the wines produced here as well. The entire region is, however, known for producing Italy's finest examples of Pinot Grigio.

Unlike the watery or merely serviceable wines that have flooded the American markets, fine Pinot Grigio from Alto Adige is sublime: a medium-bodied wine with a nose of tropical fruits wrapped in cashews and hazelnuts and a refreshing, mouthwatering flavor that is not at all simple, but lively and complex.

Alto Adige has made its reputation in the United States on Pinot Grigio, as well as whites and reds made mostly from popular market-driven varietals. Raise the bar for Pinot Grigio by tasting a great one from Alto Adige. Trentino (the traditionally Italian sector of this multi-cultural region) is best known for its excellent *metodo tradizionale* sparkling wines, as well as Teroldego Rotaliano, a wine that can be made as a rosé, as a light, accessible red, or as a full-bodied, hearty, ageworthy red.

A single-vineyard Valpolicella Classico Superiore from Veneto. Valpolicella is one of our favorite light- to medium-bodied reds, easy-drinking, food-friendly, and affordable.

One of the best examples of a fine Italian Pinot Bianco is made by Alois Lageder, made from grapes sourced in the vineyards of the Dolomiti (Dolomites), a mountain range in Northeast Italy. Courtesy of Alois Lageder.

SOME OF THE BEST WINE PRODUCERS

ALTO ADIGE (SUDTIROL) AND VALDADIGE:
Kettmeir, Lageder, Santa Magdalena, Santa Margherita, Tiefenbrunner, and Tolloy.

TRENTINO, TRENTO, AND TEROLDEGO ROTALIANO: Cavit, Concilio, Ferrari, Foradori, Rotari, Pojer e Sandri, San Leonardo, La Vis, and Zeni.

FRIULI–VENEZIA GIULIA

CLASSIC DOCG WINE REGIONS

Colli Orientali del Friuli Picolit

Ramondolo

IMPORTANT DOC WINE REGIONS

Colli Orientali del Friuli

Collio

Friuli Grave

Lison-Pramaggiore

Commonly called simply Friuli, this region borders Austria and Slovenia, and its wines, especially its whites, display that influence. Since the 1970s, when Friuli began to embrace low yields in its vineyards and high-tech methods for its wine production, the region's reputation for clean, delicious, food-friendly, varietally correct wine began to spread.

With the exception of its obscure DOCG sweet white, Ramondolo, which very few Americans (and even Italians) have tasted, internationally recognized varietals rule in Friuli, especially Pinot Grigio, Pinot Bianco, Riesling, and Chardonnay, and Merlot among reds. A fine medium- to full-bodied white made from the native varietal Friulano (formerly Tocai Friulano) has a healthy presence in the American market, as does the native red varietal wine, Refosco. The classic wine made from the Refosco grape is Refosco dal Peduncolo Rosso, a full-bodied, fruit-driven, violet-red wine, with flavors of damson plums and moderate tannins that create

a pleasant, slightly bitter aftertaste, something akin to a hint of anise or black licorice. Refosco can easily age for five years. As it ages, its bouquet develops and features violets and dried fruits in the nose.

Today, Friulian whites and reds are major players in the international market. Prices vary, with some true values still available from larger producers, along with quite a few expensive artisan wines.

SOME OF THE BEST WINE PRODUCERS

Antonutti, Bastianich, Bollini, Borgo San Daniele, Castelvecchio, Colluta Friuli, Livio Felluga, Marco Felluga, Eno Friulia, Jermann, Lis Neris, Livon, Luisa, Luna di Luna, Pighin, Plozner, Rocca Bernarda, Ronchi di Manzano, Russiz Superiore, Mario Schiopetto, Tere di Ger, Vie di Romans, Villa Russiz, and Zamo.

SOUTHERN ITALY AND ISLANDS

CAMPANIA

CLASSIC DOCG WINE REGIONS

Fiano di Avellino

Greco di Tufo

Taurasi

Campania, with a population of about six million people and famous for Mount Vesuvius and the cities of Pompeii and Naples, produces only about 3% of Italy's wines, but what beautiful wines they are. Taurasi, the first red DOCG wine in southern Italy, made from the Aglianico grape, is sometimes known as the "Barolo of the South" for its power and complexity (and perhaps for its high price). The two white DOCGs, Greco di Tufo and Fiano di Avellino, are full-bodied white wines with moderate acidity levels. Both wines marry well with fish stews, shellfish, and white meats, and are moderately expensive. Also look for varietal-labeled Falanghina, a wonderfully refreshing and mineral-driven medium-bodied fish-friendly white that is quite reasonably priced. Other affordable and enjoyable choices from Campania include the white, rosé, and red wines of the Lacryma Christi del Vesuvio DOC. The white and rosé pair beautifully with fresh fish dishes and the local pasta *puttanesca*; the red is an ideal match for pizza. There is nothing like eating a classic pizza in its birthplace of Campania with an accessible, pizza-friendly local wine, and that's Lacryma Christa *rosso*.

SOME OF THE BEST WINE PRODUCERS

Caggiano, De Lucia, Feudi di San Gregorio, Mastroberardino, Mustilli, Ocone, Terredora, Villa Matilde, and Villa San Michele.

PUGLIA

IMPORTANT DOC WINE REGIONS

Primitivo di Manduria

Salice Salentino

Another southern region that not long ago was known as Italy's largest producer of bulk, characterless wine, Puglia has gone through a sea change in the way it thinks about and produces wine for the international market. Puglia's two best-known DOC reds are Salice Salentino and Primitivo di Manduria, the former made mostly from Negroamaro grapes, the latter from Primitivo (same DNA as Zinfandel). But Puglia produces not only medium- to full-bodied red wines from Italian varietals grown in the red clay soils of the region but also whites made from Chardonnay, Sauvignon Blanc, and other international varietals. Almost all of Puglia's export wines offer tremendous value and quality.

A *WineWise* best buy from "off the beaten path" is Salice Salentino, a medium- to

Taurasi is a full-bodied, ageworthy powerhouse that needs assertive foods such as roasts and stews. Feudi di San Gregorio produces excellent wines in the Campania region of Italy. Courtesy of Feudi de San Gregorio.

full-bodied red based largely on the Negroamaro grape. This affordable red is terrific with grilled meats and pastas with meat sauces. Next time you fire up the grill, try Salice Salentino, and it might just become a healthy habit. Taurino is a widely available producer.

The appeal of Puglia has not been lost on Italian wine producers from other, more famous wine regions. Several have purchased large tracts of vineyard land and have built wineries in Puglia, including Piero Antinori, possibly the most famous wine producer in Tuscany, if not all of Italy.

SOME OF THE BEST WINE PRODUCERS

A Mano, Bortomagno, Candido, Cantele, Cantine Due Palme, Felline, Flaio, Leone de Castris, Li Veli, Masseria Pepe, Mocavero, Monaci, Pervini, La Pusara, Rivera, Rosa del Golfo, Salento, Sinfarosa, Taurino, Tormaresca (Antinori), and Vallone.

BASILICATA

IMPORTANT DOCG WINE REGION

Aglianico del Vulture Superiore

Basilicata, a region that produces only 1% of Italy's wine, is known in the United States solely for one wine made solely from one grape, produced solely in one region. That wine is Aglianico del Vulture, grown on the steep slopes of Monte Vulture. A full-flavored, deeply colored, often ageworthy red, this earthy wine can be a powerhouse, but it's always food-friendly with hearty dishes. Many producers currently offer American wine consumers great value, because the wine is not yet widely appreciated in the American market. Aglianico del Vulture, which is often priced under $20, is a true *WineWise* choice.

SOME OF THE BEST WINE PRODUCERS

Ars Poetica, Basilim, Cantina di Palma, Cantina di Venosa, Cantine Sasso, Consorzio Viticoltori del Vulture, d'Angelo, Eubea, Manfredi, Paternoster, Le Querce, Rosa del Golfo.

SARDINIA

CLASSIC DOCG WINE REGION

Vermentino di Gallura

IMPORTANT DOC WINE REGIONS

Cannonau di Sardegna

Vermentino di Sardegna

Sardinia, an island of about a million inhabitants, lies about 150 miles (241 kilometers) from mainland Italy. Sardinia's most highly regarded white wine is Vermentino di Gallura, a dry wine from the far north that is the perfect accompaniment to the local *pesce alla griglia*, grilled fish in olive oil with fresh herbs. Vermentino di Sardegna is just a bit less expensive and easier to

Cannonau is the Italian name for the Grenache grape, and the best producers in Sardinia, such as Sella e Mosca, are working wonders with this varietal to make truly exciting and delicious reds. Courtesy of Sella & Mosca.

find. Both wines, like most Italian dry whites, are best consumed within two or three years of their vintage year.

Earthy, fruit-driven, full-bodied Sardinian red wines often feature the Cannonau (Grenache) grape. Cannonau di Sardegna and other Cannonau-based reds, sometimes blended with 15% to 20% Merlot or Cabernet Sauvignon, are now widely available in the United States. These are great wines to enjoy with pasta, pizza, and meat-based dishes.

With steady improvement in whites and reds for the export market, Sardinia is now on the wine world's map as a region to watch for quality and for excellent value.

SOME OF THE BEST WINE PRODUCERS

Argiolas, Cantine Sociale del Vermentino, Cantine Sociale Gallura, Cantine Sociale Santadi, Capichera, Contini, Gabbas, Mancini, Meloni, and Sella e Mosca.

SOUTHERN ITALY AND SARDINIA

Main DOC/DOCG Wine Regions

Campania
- Falerno del Massico
- Solopaca
- Greco di Tufo
- Taurasi
- Fiano di Avellino
- Ischia
- Capri

Puglia
- Aleatico di Puglia (covers all DOC zones in the region)
- San Severo
- Moscato di Trani
- Castel del Monte
- Locorotondo
- Primitivo di Manduria

Basilicata
- Aglianico del Vulture

Calabria
- Ciro
- Donnici
- Savuto

Sicily
- Faro
- Etna
- Moscato di Siracusa
- Moscato di Noto
- Cerasuolo di Vittoria
- Alcamo
- Marsala
- Malvasia delle Lipari
- Moscato di Pantelleria and Passito di Pantelleria

Sardinia
- Vermentino di Gallura
- Moscato di Sorso-Sennori
- Oliena
- 1 Malvasia di Bosa
- 2 Vernaccia di Oristano
- 3 Arborea
- Mandrolisai
- 4 Campidano di Terralba
- Nuragus di Cagliari
- 5 Giro di Cagliari
- 5 Malvasia di Cagliari
- 5 Monica di Cagliari
- 5 Moscato di Cagliari
- 5 Nasco di Cagliari
- Carignano del Sulcis

Wine regions of southern Italy and Sardinia.

SICILY

CLASSIC DOCG WINE REGION

Cerasuolo di Vittoria

IMPORTANT DOC WINE REGIONS

Etna

Faro

Malvasia delle Lipari

Marsala

Sicily, perhaps the largest producer of wine in Italy, still produces too much indifferent wine for local and regional consumption, but it is also one of its most exciting wine regions. This contradiction resolves itself when we examine examples made from Sicily's own varieties—not only Nero d'Avola, Nerello Mascalese, and Frappato, but also Catarratto, Inzolia, and Grillo, among many others—as well as fine examples of wines made from popular international varietals, including Chardonnay, Syrah, Cabernet Sauvignon, and Merlot. Some very good wines are produced from blends of traditional grapes, or from blends of those traditional varietals with the international grape varieties.

The reds of Sicily are rustic: earthy, full-bodied, and excellent when paired with red meats and hearty pasta dishes. Sicily's best whites are usually medium-bodied and display a distinctive seaside minerality that makes for an attractive match with fish stews and many other soulful seafood dishes. The region is famous for its fortified wine, Marsala, available in a wide range of styles. Sicily's best Marsalas can be almost impossible to find in the U.S. export market, which is a shame as the wines can be extraordinary.

The reds produced from Nerello Mascalese vineyards on Mount Etna have caught the attention of wine lovers in the U.S. market, as have wines made from the Nero d'Avola grape, and it's easy to see why. A big, earthy, inky, food-friendly red that reflects the sunshine of Sicily in its ripe flavors, Nero d'Avola is a perfect match for hearty dishes such as rich stews. One of the best quality-driven values in Sicilian reds is the island's first DOCG wine, Cersuolo di Vittoria, made from Nero d'Avola and Frappato. This medium-bodied wine is quite earthy and dry, but driven by the taste of red fruits. The wine usually sells for less than $25, which is an affordable "sweet spot" for most of the wines available from Sicily.

SOME OF THE BEST WINE PRODUCERS

Alvis-Rallo, Benanti, Colosi, Corvo/Duca di Salaparuta, COS, de Bertoli, Donnafugata, Fazio, Firriato Paceco, Florio, Hauner, Melia, Miceli, Palari, Pellegrino, Planeta, Settesoli, Spadafora, Tasca d'Almerita, and Torrevecchia.

Planeta, run by a brother-sister team in Sicily, makes some of the island's best wines, both from traditional grapes and international varietals. Planeta's full-bodied red Cerasuolo di Vittoria is a blend of Nero d'Avola and Frappato. Courtesy of Planeta.

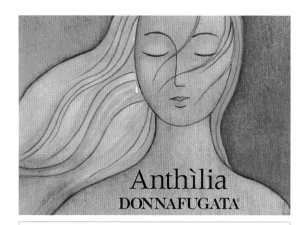

Donnafugata is an excellent Sicilian producer. Its "Anthilia" is a refreshing white, a 50/50 blend of Ansonica and Catarratto grapes that's great with fish and other seafood.

10

OLÉ

SPAIN

SPANISH WINES ARE HOT, ESPECIALLY IN THE AMERICAN WINE MARKET. SALES OF THESE WINES HAVE INCREASED, almost exponentially, as American wine lovers have discovered and embraced their favorite *vinos de España*. We love the wines of Spain and we want to share the love by turning you on to some of our favorites Spanish wine grapes, regions, and producers.

Spain's winemakers are creating exciting wines from historical and established vineyards in classic wine regions, but they're also pioneering new areas. *WineWise* readers can savor sophisticated traditional Spanish wines or roll the dice and go off the time-honored track to discover the "new" wines of Spain. Some of these wines have been hiding in plain sight, but are only recently planting their flags in the American export market. Add to this the fact that Spain produces some of the best quality- and value-driven wines in the world, and exploring the wines of Spain becomes almost irresistible.

In this chapter we will try to convey to *WineWise* readers what makes Spanish wine so special, and how these special wines pair with some of our favorite dishes. We are fascinated by Spanish wines and we're happy to share that fascination with *WineWise* readers. Try the wines of Spain and see if you don't catch the fever!

The success story of Spanish wines

FROM THE REVOLUTIONARY CULINARY CONCEPTS of chef Ferran Adria, to the films of Pedro Almodovar, to Picasso's paintings, to the architectural genius of Antoni Gaudi, to the passion of flamenco guitarist Paco de Lucia, all things Spanish have penetrated American culture. Spanish wines are no exception.

Spanish wines seem to be everywhere, and in such volume that Spain is now a major wine exporter to the United States and the rest of the world. We have done our fair share to contribute to this phenomenon, and we hope you will join us. Our refrigerators are always stocked with at least one bottle of Cava sparkling wine, as well as a Spanish white. We love a cool, dry Fino or Manzanilla Sherry with everything from tapas to Chinese takeout. An inexpensive Spanish red is always close to our kitchens, and when we dine out, the reds are often a good choice because of their reasonable prices and their affinity with the foods we choose. How did Spanish wine producers succeed in making Spanish wine a part of our everyday life?

Until the 1970s, most Spanish wineries—with the exception of those in the highly acclaimed Rioja region (see page 231)—made large quantities of rough and ready, inexpensive reds. An expanding Spanish middle class and Spain's subsequent entry into the European Union brought a more sophisticated approach to wine, and today wineries throughout the country are focused on making and exporting quality wines.

Spain has more acres of vineyards than any other nation in the world but ranks third in wine production after France and Italy. Why? Yields in the finest vineyards are kept low to concentrate flavors in the grapes and in the finished wines.

Clearly, this country is home to some very warm regions that produce big, concentrated wines with lots of ripe fruit and a high alcohol content. Thoughts of Spain may conjure up images of proud bullfighters in a hot, dusty arena, or exotic flamenco dancers on warm, sultry evenings. But Spain is not just about sun and heat. There are plenty of cooler locations at higher elevations and in coastal regions and river valleys, and they are turning out gorgeous wines with balanced acidity and without an overabundance of alcohol. Also, many farmers pick their vineyards early, when the grapes have more acidity and less sweetness. The result is fresh, crisp wines with balanced acidity, rather than stronger alcohol wines that could be dubbed "flabby" because of their lower acid levels.

It is this attention to quality that allows Spanish winemakers to quietly build a reputation as producers of world-class wines, and that burgeoning international reputation is good news for *WineWise* readers. With a selection that includes refreshing bubblies and crisp whites, deliciously dry rosés, an amazingly broad range of reds, and Spain's famous fortified Sherries, this nation has a wine to suit every preference, occasion, and budget. Spanish wines are particularly enticing for two reasons:

Value. Spanish wines offer some of the best quality for the price anywhere in the world. Most Spanish table wines are bargain priced (some are less than $10 a bottle for simple, fruity, everyday wines) to moderately priced (from about $15, with many of the more complex versions under $35); more expensive wines are available for special occasions.

Quality. Spain is home to many delicious, distinctive wines from both traditional and revolutionary winemakers who emphasize quality over quantity. More important to us than any label jargon is the integrity of the folks who make the wine, and so our most valuable (and oft-repeated) advice to *WineWise* readers is to buy wine based on the integrity of the producer. The best wineries will offer good wines at fair prices.

Our personal journey on the road to a love affair with Spanish wines began with our introduction to red wines, which were often released after aging and were less aggressive than the more powerful New World Cabernets and French Bordeaux that dominated most wine lists in the past. The first reds we embraced were "Coronas" and "Sangre de Toro," inexpensive wines produced by the Torres winery in Catalonia. Torres offered helpful information on their back labels (see label on page 233) about how the wines were made, how to pair them with food, the flavor profile of the wine, and at what temperature to serve them. We wish more wineries would offer such information on their back labels.

Next we fell for Rioja wines. The Rioja region has long been Spain's most respected producer of fine wine. Although it was their red wines that put Rioja in that preeminent position, their dry white wines are well worth trying. Plus, their delicious rosés are a steal.

Over the years, we have come to love a wide variety of Spanish wines, and "variety" is the operative word. While some wineries honor their native grapes and techniques to make traditional wines, others are experimenting with both local and international grapes (such as Cabernet Sauvignon or Syrah) to create alternative expressions, often from the same vineyards. Another shift in the winery has been the increased use of French oak barrels; traditionally Spanish producers have favored American oak for aging their wines. Regardless of the type of oak, the grape blend, or the methods used in the vineyards and the wineries, we are happiest when we taste a wine and recognize it as "being Spanish."

So, the good news for *WineWise* readers is that there are many more styles of Spanish wine to choose from than ever before and at every possible price point, from under $10 for easy drinking and up to $350 or more for a small number of wines for very special occasions. If you winced or shuddered at the thought of $350 (we saw you), check out some of the prices for the top wines of France, Italy, or California. Spain produces wines of the highest quality, and their best wines, like the best wines everywhere, can be expensive.

In general, red wines that cost $30 and up will be more full-bodied, and will have more concentrated flavors and aromatics to discover than wines under $15 or $20 from the same region and/or grape types. However, remember that the inexpensive wines may be more adaptable to "global cuisine"—foods filled with the flavors of spice and herbs, for example—or a better choice for easy sipping than pricy versions.

Both easy-sipping and substantial reds from Spain are irresistible. Tempranillo and Garnacha are the nation's premier red grapes. Today, Tempranillo and Garnacha may be blended with international varieties such as Cabernet Sauvignon, or bottled on their own as single-varietal wines. Spain's best winemakers allow the location of their plantings to be expressed in their wines. For example, we expect a Tempranillo-based wine from the Ribera del Duero wine region to be a heftier or more muscular wine than one from the Rioja region. Understanding the connection between the place name on the label and the style of wine is important in Spain, just as it is in other "Old World" wine producing nations.

We love bubbles and we believe that sparkling Cava, Spain's Champagne method wines, are the world's best value in bubbly, with prices starting at about $10 and rarely exceeding $20; you'll pay a bit more for vintage-dated Cava. We're also delighted by the range of fortified Sherries and crisp dry white and rosé wines of Spain. Many of these are inexpensive and reliable wines for everyday drinking.

While you cannot go wrong buying inexpensive reds from the Rioja region or the Tempranillo grape from almost any Spanish wine region, we urge our *WineWise* readers to go off the beaten path and experiment with wines from lesser known regions and grape types. We get excited by out-of-the-way wines of great value, because that's when wine becomes fun. *Salud*!

The grapes of Spain

SPANISH WINES INCORPORATE MANY NOW-FAMILIAR international grapes, whose presence can be explained by simple geography. With one look at Spain's neighbor to the north-east, France, you'll understand the abundance of predominantly French varietals: Cabernet Sauvignon, Merlot, Syrah, Chardonnay, and Sauvignon Blanc are all represented in Spain. Its neighbor to the west, Portugal, is home to some of the same grape varieties as Spain, although they may have a slightly different spelling. For example, Spain's finest white grape, the Albarino, is known as Alvarinho in Portugal. The finest red grape, the Tempranillo, is known as Tinta Roriz or Aragonez, while the Mencia is called Jaen in Portugal. The most celebrated wines of Spain are either single-variety versions or blends made from indigenous grapes. While some nations can claim dozens of important grape varieties, there are only a dozen major Spanish types to learn about. Of course, where they are grown and how they are made can make a world of difference in the wines they produce.

RED GRAPES

The three most important red grapes are Tempranillo, Garnacha, and Monastrell.

TEMPRANILLO

Tempranillo is Spain's most famous and most planted red grape, with over 500,000 acres (200,000 hectares) planted there. *WineWise* readers can find simple fruit-forward Tempranillo-based wines at bargain prices, or opt for the more complex wines at moderate to expensive prices. This thick-skinned, black-colored grape ripens early (*temprano* in Spanish) and displays an array of flavors including red cherry, blackberry, licorice, aged balsamic vinegar, and spices. It produces wines relatively low in alcohol (10.5% to 13%) and acidity. Tempranillo-based wines can age well, especially when blended with Garnacha, Graciano, and Mazuelo (at right and next page). Today, there are full-bodied "beefcake" wines: Tempranillo blended with Cabernet Sauvignon and/or Syrah. Indeed, there is a straight-up Tempranillo or Tempranillo blend ranging from light to full-bodied and being made at every price point.

GARNACHA

Known as Grenache in other countries, this is the second-most widely planted red grape in Spain, and one of the most planted in the world. Unlike Tempranillo, which is harvested early in the growing season, Garnacha needs to bask in the sun for a long time to ripen. Garnacha's popularity may be partially explained by its ability to ripen well in warm climates. Another reason is that Garnacha produces so many different styles of wine. It is our "jack-in-the-box" grape, popping out of the bottle to say surprise! We have tasted light-bodied Garnacha as well as full-bodied versions; both displayed the grape's characteristic strawberry and raspberry flavors. Delicious dry rosé wines are made with this grape in Spain as well. But what really turns us on are the old "inky," "stinky" (in a nice earthy, leathery kind of way) Garnachas that are dark in color and full in body.

Some of the finest wines are made from vines that are more than 40 years old. Some Garnacha-based wines are made for simple quaffing, while others are destined for greatness.

MONASTRELL

Known as Mourvedre in other countries, Monastrell is Spain's third-most widely planted red grape. On its own, this grape produces medium- to full-bodied wines with black fruit flavors. It also contributes high levels of alcohol, deep color, and good aging potential to blended wines. If you want more bang for your buck, seek out Spanish Monastrells from regions such as Jumilla.

Other red grapes native to Spain that you will encounter in the coming pages include:

MENCIA: Both bright red and black fruit flavors can be detected in Mencia-based wines, which come in lighter-weight styles with moderate acidity, and full-bodied styles with less acidity. The success story of the Mencia based wines in the Bierzo region has prompted other regions to plant this variety.

GRACIANO: Most commonly used as a blending grape, Graciano makes wines that are low in alcohol and high in acidity with spicy aromas. It may also be found as a charming single-variety wine.

MAZUELO OR CARINENA (ALSO KNOWN AS CARIGNAN IN OTHER COUNTRIES): Another blending grape particularly prominent in Rioja and Priorat, Mazuelo bumps up the wine's color, acidity, and tannins. It too is now available as a single-variety wine.

WHITE GRAPES

ALBARINO

Spain's most important white varietal, this grape produces medium- to full-bodied wines with complex aromas and flavors such as peach, citrus, cinnamon, and melon. Albarino wines from Spain's Rias Baixas wine region are delicious, especially with seafood.

VERDEJO

This high-acid grape displays aromas of apricots, citrus, melon, pears, and flowers. Verdejo wines from the Rueda wine region are exciting and affordable.

GODELLO

We love Godello wines! Is it the minerality, floral aromatics, and citrus notes that seduce us? Or is it about mouthfeel?

There is a rich texture to Godello wines, sometimes due to the use of oak barrels. We hope Spanish farmers plant more of this gem. Most Godello is sourced from the wine regions within the province of Galicia: Ribeiro, Valdeorras, Monterrei, and Ribeira Sacra.

MACABEO/VIURA

Macabeo, also known as Viura, produces light, fruity wines with subtle floral aromas and flavors. Whether on its own or blended, Macabeo is the grape used in more than 90% of Rioja's white wines. Macabeo is a key component in sparkling Cava, along with Parellada and Xarel-lo.

PARELLADA

Parellada produces wines with floral and citrusy aromas, high acidity, and low alcohol.

XAREL-LO

Xarel-lo produces wines with earthy, apple, spice and citrus aromas and flavors, and it gives richness to sparkling Cava blends.

The language of the label

As in most European nations, the table wines of Spain may be sold by place name (e.g., Rioja), by varietal (e.g., Albarino), or by a fantasy name (e.g., Gran Vina Sol—"great wine of the sun"). Sparkling wines will feature the level of sweetness such as "Brut" or "Extra Dry." Sherry label terms, such as "Fino" or "Amontillado," will be explained toward the end of this chapter.

Albarino by Morgadio is an example of a varietal-labeled wine. Courtesy of Adegas Morgadio s.l.

Rioja, Lorinon by Bodegas (winery) Breton is an example of a wine labeled by place name. Courtesy of B. y. V. Breton

GRATAVINUM

GV5

2003

PRIORAT
Denominació d'origen qualificada

14,7%vol   750ml

EMBOTELLAT PER GRATAVINUM S.L.
Nº Embotellador 29.025.01 CAT
43.737 GRATALLOPS - PRIORAT - SPAIN

GV5 is a proprietary label by the winery Gratavinum in the Priorat region. It is a full-bodied and elegant blend of Carignan, Grenache, Cabernet Sauvignon, and Syrah grapes. Courtesy of Gratavinum.

THE ORIGIN OF THE WINE

Spanish wines are labeled according to government-controlled designations of origin, the *Denominacion de Origen* system.

The model is based on the French appellation system with restrictions such as grape types permitted, maximum yield of grapes during harvest, methods in the vineyard and winery, etc.

DO and DOC wines, traditionally the top tiers of Spain's designations of origin system, should offer a consistent and traditional style of wine from the area named on the label, just as a classic dish such as seafood paella should have shellfish, meats, vegetables, and saffron-flavored rice baked in a pan. If you structure a pyramid of wine quality, DO and DOC wines would sit at the top of the pyramid because the appellations guarantee authenticity of the wines. However, creative winemakers may want the freedom to make a wine that breaks with tradition. They may opt to declassify their wines to "lower" levels such as "*vino de mesa*" or "*vino de la tierra,*" but these nontraditional wines may, in fact, be extraordinarily good.

What all this means to *WineWise* readers is that there are good wines at every level, be they classics from historical regions or "new" wines that break all the traditional rules.

Listed in order of increasing quality when the appellation system was put into place, the designations are:

VINO DE MESA (TABLE WINE): These basic table wines are often blends of various grapes and regions, but today fine wines can be found as well. The basic wines are inexpensive and mostly consumed in Spain.

VINO DE LA TIERRA (WINE OF THE LAND): These wines express the character of a particular district. Both inexpensive and expensive wines are made in this category.

VINOS DE CALIDAD CON INDICACION GEOGRAFICA: Quality wines with an indicated geographical area. After five years, these wines may be promoted to DO status (see below).

DENOMINACION DE ORIGEN (DO) (DENOMINATION OF ORIGIN): The equivalent of the French AOC/AOP and Italian DOC/DOP, this designation covers nearly 80 wine-producing regions. Penedes, Rias Baixas, and Ribera del Duero are just some examples of DOs whose name will appear on a label.

Pares Balta has been producing Cavas and table wines for more than two centuries. The Blanc de Pacs crisp white wine made from organic indigenous grapes is a great value at $12. Courtesy of Pares Balta.

Red *reserva* wines develop complex flavors from aging in the barrel and the bottle. Alejandro Fernandez produces a *reserva* version of his Pesquera wine. Courtesy of Bodegas Alejandro Fernanadez Tinto Pesquera s.l.

DENOMINACION DE ORIGEN CALIFICADA (DOC) (QUALIFIED DENOMINATION OF ORIGIN): Similar to Italy's DOCG designation, this is reserved for truly superior wine regions. So far, the only DOCs are Rioja and Priorat.

VINO DE PAGO: Introduced in 2003, *Vino de Pago* officially recognizes a single vineyard or a wine estate of high quality. *Vino de Pago* wines must express the *terroir* of the estate and must be estate-bottled. Each *Vino de Pago* has its own DO, much like the *grand cru* wines of Burgundy, France have their own AOC/AOP (see Chapter 8, page 149). These wines are considered to be among Spain's finest. As of 2014, there were 14 official *Vinos de Pago*, all of them in the provinces of Castilla-La Mancha, Navarra, and Valencia. Surely, there are more *Vinos de Pago* to come.

THE AGE OF THE WINE

Spanish label terms may also include terms that refer to aging the wine in barrel and in bottle.

The benefit of aging is twofold. Most important, the harsh tannins that may be present in a young wine diminish over time, so an aged wine develops a silky texture. In addition, aged wines develop more complex aromas; one can usually detect notes of earth, spice, or even vegetable alongside the primary fruit or floral aromas.

Aged wines may be considered more traditional by some wineries. If producers want to make a more modern or international style of wine, they may utilize a proprietary name and not include a legally defined term of aging such as "*reserva*" for their wines. An example of this is GV5 by Gratavinum (see label, opposite).

Terms you may find on the front or back labels of DO and DOC wines to indicate age include:

COSECHA: Vintage wine. At least 85% of the wine is made from grapes harvested in the stated vintage. The unoaked "*joven*" (young) wine is, as the name implies, sold immediately and not aged in the bottle.

ROBLE: Wines with just a kiss of oak and less age than a *crianza* (see next).

CRIANZA: For most regions, *crianza* indicates a wine that is aged for a minimum of two years, including at least six months in small oak casks. In Rioja, Ribera del Duero, and Navarra *crianza* wines must have a minimum of a year in oak.

RESERVA: Red wines aged at least three years, including one year in barrel. Producers of the finest reds will always exceed the minimum aging requirements. White *reserva* wines, aged at least two years, are not as popular as the red versions.

GRAN RESERVA: Made only in exceptional vintages, *gran reserva* reds are aged at least five years (two of these years in barrel), although the finest wines may not appear on the market for eight to 10 years. White *gran reserva* wines are rare and must be aged a minimum of four years. These whites can be pricy and complex. We consider them special-occasion wines.

WINEWISE TIP: Many *bodegas* (wineries) label each of their wines with different proprietary names to differentiate their styles. For example, La Rioja Alta winery (in—you guessed it—the Rioja region) offers a *crianza* called "Vina Alberdi," while its *reservas* are named "Vina Ardanza" and "Vina Arana." Its *gran reservas* are labeled "904" and "890."

Spanish wines: What's hot now

WHAT IS NEW AND HOT in the world of Spanish wines? On the white front, most winemakers have replaced their heavy, golden-colored whites with appealing, modern, lighter versions. Crisp, dry white wines produced in the Rias Baixas, Rueda, Ribeiro, Valdeorras, and Txacolina de Guetaria wine regions have been embraced by American sommeliers and consumers alike.

The wines are fresh and fruity, with a zingy acidity that pairs easily with a wide variety of foods. Spanish whites also tend to be lighter in texture and lower in alcohol than most New World Chardonnays, so they coexist with food rather than compete with it. In addition, most are inexpensive (under $15) to moderately priced (under $30).

Spain—most notably the region of Penedes—is also known for its inexpensive sparkling wines, or Cavas. Made using the quality-driven Champagne method, Cavas are ideal for casual sipping, Sunday brunch, or even a day at the beach. New vineyards of Chardonnay and Pinot Noir are being planted alongside the indigenous Macabeo, Parellada, Xarel-lo, and Trepat grapes to make Cava wines. Since the finest Champagnes in the world are based on mostly Chardonnay and Pinot Noir, the potential for Cava producers to make even more elegant wines in the future is great. Some Cava wineries are now offering both young, fresh versions as well as more complex wines that are a result of extending aging on the lees—the expired yeast cells—of the wine in the bottle. Gramona, Josep Raventos, and Pares Balta are some of the wineries that offer aged sparkling wines that compete with French Champagnes in quality, yet are more modestly priced.

Spanish whites, rosés, Cavas, and Sherries are pleasant partners to food or just great to savor on their own. But the inspiration for poets, musicians, and other romantics are the nation's reds, which are increasingly regarded as some of the most interesting and delicious in the world. Our survey of Spanish reds includes wines that range from the simple to the inspirational, from the bargain-priced to the very expensive. And while most whites and Cavas should be drunk within three years of their harvest, the best reds continue to improve over one or two decades.

Two regions long recognized for producing some of Spain's hottest, most sought-after reds are Rioja—the nation's oldest recognized wine region—and the newer Ribera del Duero, located in the province of Castilla y Leon. The esteemed

Tempranillo grape is the dominant varietal in both regions. The wines of Rioja are most often Tempranillo-dominated blends of indigenous grapes, while Ribera del Duero reds tend to be pure Tempranillo or blends with international grapes such as Cabernet Sauvignon and Merlot. Simple red wines from Rioja or Ribera del Duero retail for about $10, with many fine wines priced under $25, but some of the extraordinary wines command prices starting at $50, with a select few topping out at more than $350. Ouch! Talk about hot!

Perhaps slightly less well known (though not for long), Bierzo, which features the Mencia grape, and Priorat, where Garnacha and Carinena are featured, are setting trends of their own. These wine regions have garnered international acclaim by resurrecting old vineyards and planting new vines in the best locations, producing some of Spain's most sensuous (and sometimes most expensive) reds. Their success has encouraged grape growers and winemakers throughout the nation to coax the best quality from their vineyards.

Today many newcomers are issuing challenges to the supremacy of Spain's most celebrated wine regions. Many hot new red wines creating a buzz are from the lesser-known areas of Toro, Calatayud, Campo de Borja, Navarra, Valdeorras, and Jumilla; their non-star status is reflected in their bargain to moderate prices, at least for now. Remember, some of the best values are waiting for WineWise adventurers who experiment with lesser-known grape varieties or venture to regions off the beaten path. More important to us than any label jargon is the integrity of the folks who make the wine, and so our most valuable (and oft-repeated) advice to *WineWise* readers is to buy wine based on the integrity of the producer. The best wineries will offer good wines at fair prices. We suggest some of our favorites in the following pages.

The major wine regions of Spain

AS THEY SAY IN REAL estate and in the restaurant biz, it's all about location. Spain is divided into a number of provinces; specific DO (or DOC) areas fall under the umbrella of each province. In the following pages, we will explore the better-known wine-producing DOs and DOCs, and some notable value-driven up-and-comers.

NORTHERN SPAIN

PROVINCE OF LA RIOJA

DOC REGION

Rioja

Rioja has the distinction of being Spain's oldest and most important fine-wine-producing region. There are 120,000 vineyards managed by over 17,000 farmers, so the average size of a vineyard is only 1.3 acres (0.5 hectare). Although this is an area with a long history of making high-quality wine, wineries are still researching how to take advantage of the unique flavors each of these vineyards can provide, either on their own or in a blend of multiple vineyards.

Tempranillo is the star varietal here, and a typical red Rioja contains about 70% to 90% of that grape. Garnacha, Graciano, and Mazuelo complete the blend, producing wines that are truly unique and ageworthy. Some winemakers are now going beyond the native grapes, adding such international varietals as Cabernet Sauvignon and Merlot.

Rioja is blessed with protection from winds and excessive rain by 150 square miles (40,000 hectares) of mountains that surround the region. The Ebro River provides a moderating influence on temperature extremes in the region. The cooler Rioja Alta and Rioja Alavesa subregions are best suited to the early ripening Tempranillo

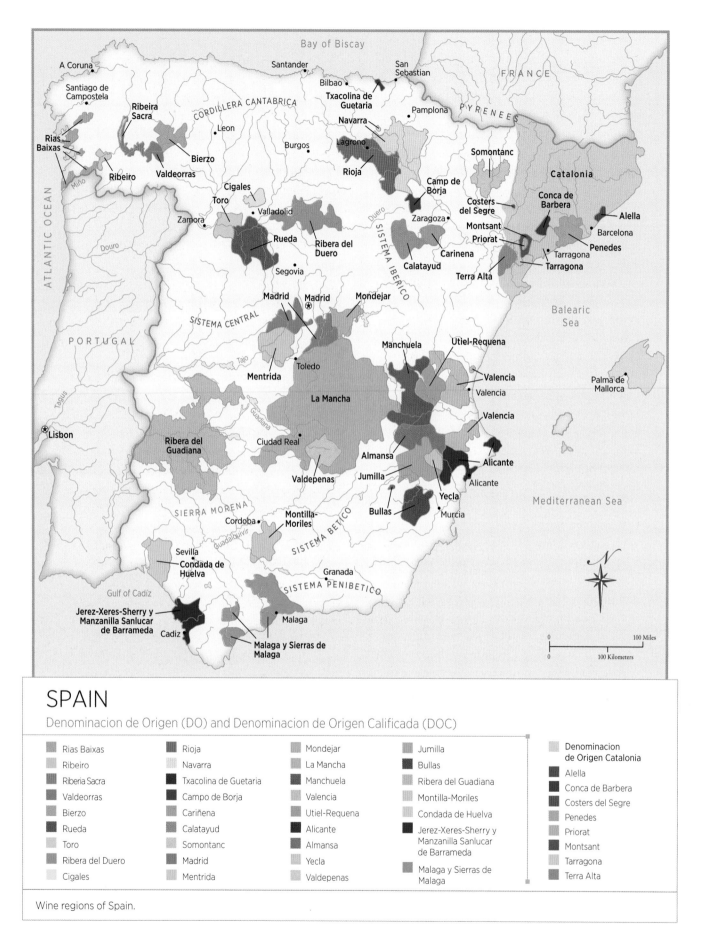

SPAIN

Denominacion de Origen (DO) and Denominacion de Origen Calificada (DOC)

Rias Baixas	Rioja	Mondejar	Jumilla
Ribeiro	Navarra	La Mancha	Bullas
Riberia Sacra	Txacolina de Guetaria	Manchuela	Ribera del Guadiana
Valdeorras	Campo de Borja	Valencia	Montilla-Moriles
Bierzo	Cariñena	Utiel-Requena	Condada de Huelva
Rueda	Calatayud	Alicante	Jerez-Xeres-Sherry y Manzanilla Sanlucar de Barrameda
Toro	Somontanc	Almansa	
Ribera del Duero	Madrid	Yecla	Malaga y Sierras de Malaga
Cigales	Mentrida	Valdepenas	

Denominacion de Origen Catalonia
Alella
Conca de Barbera
Costers del Segre
Penedes
Priorat
Montsant
Tarragona
Terra Alta

Wine regions of Spain.

while in the warmer Rioja Baja in the south, Garnacha thrives. Graciano and Mazuelo complete the blend for red wines, the former providing spice notes and freshness, and the latter dark color, tannins, and acidity.

Cabernet Sauvignon and Merlot have had a presence in Rioja since the nineteenth century. The use of these varieties may not be revolutionary, but there are now wineries in Rioja whose aim is to emulate an international Cabernet wine style. These lush wines are chock-full of ripe, rich fruit flavors and tend to be full-bodied with a heaping helping of oak influence. The modern style wines are often labeled with proprietary names and can be more pricy than the traditional aged *reserva* or *gran reserva* wines.

WineWise readers who love New World Cabernet Sauvignon, such as those from California or Australia, can sample similar wines from Rioja. This international style of Rioja is brasher, more aggressive; kind of like thrash metal, hardcore rap, or salsa music. Alternately, the reader can savor a 20-year-old Rioja Gran Reserva, which is similar to listening to a serene piece of classical or bossa nova music; it's a mellow experience. To be honest, we much prefer the classic Rioja wines, and on a daily basis we prefer the bargain-priced to relatively inexpensive bottlings that stay true to their regional roots.

Clearly the red wines of Rioja garner the most attention, and with good reason. There are affordable *cosecha*, *robles*, and *crianza* wines that can be found for well under $20 a bottle. Blueberries, red fruits, and soft tannins in a light- to medium-bodied package make these wines easy for sipping or pairing with a wider range of foods than their more noble brethren or elegant older sisters. Experiment with ethnic foods, such as lamb biryani, burritos, or a gyro sandwich. *Reserva*, *gran reserva*, and pricy proprietary-labeled reds are best paired with simple dishes that do not compete with their complex flavors, such as a wild mushroom risotto, roast suckling pig, or grilled lamb chops. Some of these wines cost up to $300.

Color is often an indicator of style as well as age, and this holds true especially for the red wines of Rioja. Young wines tend to be a red cherry color and display black cherry and spice notes. Aged wines become a reddish brown and take on more complex aromas and flavors of earth, spice, leather, and mushroom.

Rioja's dry whites and rosés are beginning to see an increase in popularity, mostly due to their accessibility: the wines are fresh, fruity, floral, and inexpensive. White Riojas shine as an aperitif or as an accompaniment to such *tapas* (little plates) as cold octopus salad, chickpea salad, or fresh sardines. Today most of the region's whites are made in a lighter style without oak. But lovers of oaky Chardonnays can still find some barrel-fermented versions based on local white grapes, such as the superb example made by the Muga winery.

The dry rosé wines of Rioja have undergone a similar makeover. They are dry, light- to medium-bodied wines with strawberry and red cherry flavors and bright, refreshing acidity. Marques de Caceres, Muga, and El Coto are three producers we suggest for bargain-priced rosés; each retails for about $10. These rosés shine when paired with a ham and Swiss or pastrami sandwich; they are also ideal partners for the local *lomo* (cured ham loin) or a spicy seafood gumbo.

Today there are so many styles of Rioja to choose from that a multicourse meal or a brunch buffet could be served with a variety of these wines. We hope we've piqued your curiosity

Spain's Tempranillo grape is blended with some Cabernet Sauvignon in the medium-bodied Coronas wine from Torres. This is consistently one of our best-value red wines from Spain. Note the helpful information on the back label.

CHILLIN' WITH TXACOLINA

WineWise tip: Getariako Txacolina (also known as Txacoli in the Basque language Euskara, or as Chacoli in Castilian) is a refreshing, low-alcohol, pleasantly spritzy Basque wine.

About 90% of the wine is based on the tongue-twisting Hondarribi Zuri white grape, and the balance is from the red version, Hondarribi Beltza.

The Basque region of northern Spain is known for its gastronomy, which ranges from "*pintxos*," the local version of tapas, to both traditional and modern foods. But don't limit yourself to Basque cuisine when you refresh your palate with Getariako Txacolina. Anytime you are enjoying a wide variety of lighter dishes, some with a bit of spicy heat, less can be more: light, fruity, spritzy Txacolina is an ideal wine when you are ordering takeout from an Asian or Latin American restaurant, enjoying a Scandinavian smorgasbord, or going to a BYOB (bring your own bottle) restaurant. Serve Txacolina cold!

Amaztoi, Talai Berri, Txomin Etxaniz, Elzaguirre, Aizpura, Ulacia Txacolina, and Zudugarai are all producers of Getariako Txacolina that we can recommend.

---

about this historical and much lauded region and that you're excited to taste what all the fuss is about. About two million bottles are produced annually so there is plenty of Rioja to enjoy! Where do you want to start?

Some of the Best Wine Producers

Artadi, Baron de Ley, Bilbainas, Ramon Bilbao, Bodegas Breton, Campillo, Campo Viejo, Castillo Labistada, Conde de Valdemar, Contino, Contador, Cortijo, CVNE, El Coto, Criadores, Dinastia Vivanco, Faustino, Hacienda de Susar, Izadi, La Rioja Alta, Lan, Marques de Arienzo, Marques de Caceres, Marques de Grinon, Marques de Murrieta, Marques de Riscal, Martinez Bujanda, Montecillo, Muga, Pujanza, Palacios Remondo, Rafael Lopez de Heredia, Remelluri, Remirez de Ganuza, Roda, Sierra Cantabria, Senorio de San Vicente, Valenciso, Vina Real, and Ysios.

There are many other reputable Rioja producers to seek out; this is a mere fraction of that list. Young white, rosé, and red Rioja *crianzas* are bargains or relatively inexpensive (from under $10 to about $18); *reservas* for $15 to $30; *gran reserva* and other top wines start at about $30 and can go up to as much as $350.

PROVINCE OF CATALONIA

DOC REGION
Priorat

IMPORTANT DO REGIONS
Penedes
Montsant
Cava

Located in the northeast corner of Spain and including the city of Barcelona, this province is famous for artists Pablo Picasso and Salvador Dali, architectural genius Antoni Gaudi, musical inspiration Pablo Casals, and many celebrated chefs. The artistic temperament and creativity of the Catalans have resulted in fine food and wine that can rival those of any wine region in the world.

Together with the DOC region of Priorat, the eight DO regions produce everything from simple quaffing table wines and sparklers to some of the most expensive and sublime wines in the world. You may be able to source some good-value wines from the lesser-known DOs, but they may be harder to find. So, we will focus mostly on the four most important regions of Penedes, Priorat, Montsant, and Cava (see "Cava," page 236), all well represented in the American market.

Penedes. Penedes is home to many fine table wines as well as the majority of sparkling Cavas. The region's inexpensive dry white wines are pale, green, and fairly low in alcohol with an apple-skin bouquet. The featured local white grapes, used to produce both table wines and sparklers, are Macabeo (also known as Viura in the Rioja region), Parellada, and Xarel-lo. Xarel-lo can also be found as a single-variety wine that could be a great choice for fans of oaked Chardonnay wines. "Electio" by Balta is a great example of a white Xarel-lo based wine, while their "Blanc de Pacs" is an inexpensive best buy ($12) sourced from a blend of organic local grapes. The Can Feixes winery is a top pick for its relatively inexpensive tart, dry white blend, Blanc Seleccio (about $17).

French and German white varietals also pop up here: Chardonnay, Gewurztraminer, Riesling, Sauvignon Blanc, and Muscat may be used on their own or in blends.

Penedes reds may be based on single varietals, or blended with international varieties; they take well to oak aging. Prices range from inexpensive to moderate, with a small selection of expensive wines. The Torres family was instrumental in bringing modern grape-growing and winemaking methods to Penedes. Their skillful use of both indigenous grapes such as Tempranillo and international varietals such as Cabernet Sauvignon helped to put Penedes wines on restaurant lists and at tables all over the world. Jean Leon is another Penedes producer who pioneered the use of varietal labeling and the planting of Chardonnay, Merlot, and Cabernet Sauvignon in the region's vineyards; prices for his wines range from about $25 to $35. Pares Balta produces proprietary wines made from organic grapes such as the "Mas Petit" (about $12), a blend of Cabernet Sauvignon and Garnacha, or the "Indigena" pure Garnacha (about $20).

Reliable Penedes producers include Torres, Huguet Can Feixes, Jean Leon, Albet i Noya, Rene Barbier, Ferrer Bobet, Gramona, Mascaro, Masia L'Hereu, Josep Raventos I Blanc, Juve y Camps, Masia Bach, Naveran, Sarda, Pares Balta, and Valformosa. Most Penedes reds can be found at relatively inexpensive prices (under $20) to moderate prices (under $30), but some expensive wines are available as well.

Priorat (also known as Priorato).

Speaking of Catalonian reds, does the name Priorat sound familiar? While it may not be as well known as California's Napa Valley, this DOC region is the source for many of Spain's most expensive and exotic wine treasures. The Catalans' pride in their own language and culture has encouraged them to use the local name for their region and drop the "o" off Priorato. So you will most likely see "Priorat" on wine labels.

Historically the wines produced in this region were rich reds with a hint of sweetness, full body, and high alcohol. The quality revolution that began in the 1980s has proven successful, and today, in the pursuit of elegant and extraordinary wines, the grape varieties and winemaking techniques used in the region often break from that tradition.

Priorat is a remote and magical place to visit. Unlike many other well-traveled wine destinations, the journey to Priorat is a true wine pilgrimage.

The volcanic soils here, known as *"licorella,"* contain slate and quartz that imbue the red wines from this area with mineral, earthy, and graphite smells that speak of the Old World. These soils allow the roots of the vines to go deep into the subsoil and source trace minerals that are transmitted to the wine's flavors.

Many of the region's vineyards are on precipitous slopes that make harvesting difficult, but oh so rewarding. Grapes grown at higher elevations contain a high level of acidity, which adds freshness to the wine, and strong tannins, which helps to produce long-lived wines.

Most Spanish wines made with Garnacha use the standard red or *"Tinta"* variety, but in Priorat, farmers grow Garnacha Peluda, which has more acidity, deeper color, more floral and mineral aromatics, and slightly lower alcohol than Garnacha Tinta. Think of this as

CAVA

The secret is out: Cava is the best value sparkling wine in the world! Just as the word "Champagne" refers to the method used to make the wine, the grape types permitted, and the location of the vineyards, so "Cava" indicates the traditional Champagne method and the grape types used.

More than 90% of all Cava comes from the Penedes region, although it may also be produced in other provinces such as Rioja or Navarra. The majority of white Cava from Penedes is made from the local white grapes Macabeo, Parellada, and Xarel-lo and may also include Chardonnay. Red grapes include the indigenous Garnacha, Monastrell, and Trepat, as well as Pinot Noir. There are more than 250 wineries that produce about 130,000,000 (that's 130 million!) bottles of this bubbly annually. About two-thirds of Cava is exported.

Like those of its Champagne cousins, Cava labels will display their level of dryness. From driest to sweetest, Cava will be labeled in the U.S. market as *extra brut*, *brut*, *extra dry*, *seco*, *semi-seco*, *semi-dulce*, or *dulce*, although most imported wines in the American market are brut or extra dry. Serve extra brut, brut, and extra dry with savory foods. The sweeter wines are best with fruits and desserts.

Cava labels will also bear the term "*Reserva*" or "*Gran Reserva*" to indicate more age and complexity. *Reservas* must be aged at least 18 months before release; *gran reservas* are aged at least two years. Some wineries today are extending the aging process and those wines are much richer in flavors and more ageworthy than their less expensive wines.

Tasting fine Brut Cavas with more age, such as those from Gramona, Pares Balta, Recaredo, and Raventos I Blanc is a great experience. The wines offer aromas of flowers, dried herbs, white fruits, nuts, and mushrooms and on the palate they should have a silky texture from their extended contact in the bottle with their own lees, their expired yeast cells.

The extra aging adds earthy flavors and brioche or toasty notes to the fruit flavors of the wine. Aficionados of bubbly who find themselves in Spain should check out Barcelona's Cavateria restaurants, where many wines are available by the glass.

With prices starting under $10 a bottle, Cava may be served on its own or in a wide variety of what are popularly known as "champagne" cocktails. But remember, it's not Champagne, it's Cava.

Producers whose wines we recommend include Gramona, Pares Balta, Segura Viudas, Raventos i Blanc, Juve y Camps, Castellblanch, Cavas Masachs, Paul Cheneau, El Cep, Codorniu Jaume Serra (Cristalino), Ferret, Castelroig, Freixenet, Gran Sarao, Llopart, Vilarnau, Mont Marcal, Albet i Noya, Parxet, Vega Barcelona, Giro Ribot, Naveran, Recaredo, Sarda, and Torello.

Brut Cava by Pares Balta is a dry, Champagne-method wine that is aged for 18 months before it's sold. It is a delicious food-friendly wine and a bargain at about $16 retail. Courtesy of Pares Balta.

comparing a superb heirloom tomato to a widely available commercial tomato. While simple Garnacha wines from other regions tend toward the one-dimensional, tasting merely of bright red fruit, fine Priorat versions deliver dark fruit, floral, and spice flavors in a rich package.

Carinena (also known as Mazuelo in other parts of Spain) is the other most important red grape of Priorat, and we believe this is the best place in the world for the variety. In France, where the grape is known as Carignan, most wineries have used it for quantity rather than quality. In

Priorat, old-vine Carinena can make wines with dark color and high acidity with flavors of ripe black fruits, tobacco, dark chocolate, and spices.

Red blends from this area may also include Syrah, Cabernet Sauvignon, Merlot, or Pinot Noir. Fine Priorat reds deliver dark fruit, floral, and spice flavors in a rich package.

Time in costly new oak barrels adds to the body—and the price—of the more concentrated, ageworthy wines. In fact, the best reds can and should be aged for five to 25 years to allow their tannins to soften and bouquet to develop. Priorat reds range in price from moderate to expensive, from about $20 to a select few priced at more than $300. Enjoying a great Priorat is like digging through a treasure chest, finding more jewels the deeper you dig. Grilled meats, simply seasoned squab, and pasta with sautéed mushrooms are fabulous food partners for these wines.

Some white wines are produced in Priorat, but its stellar reputation is strongly linked to its reds. About half of Priorat's production is exported, so the secret is out that these wines are helping to define the growing category of Spain's elite wines.

Some of the Best Wine Producers

Alvaro Palacios, Rene Barbier, Buil i Gine, Cellers Scala Dei, Cartoixa, Clos Berenguer, Clos Erasmus, Clos i Terraces, Clos de l'Obac, Clos Mogador, Combier-Fischer-Gerin, Domini de la Cartoixa, Ferrer-Bobet, Gratavinum, Mas Martinet, Mas d'en Gil, Mas Igneus, Onix, Pasenau, Vall Llach, Valsotillo, and Torres Priorat.

Montsant. The grapes used in this DO are similar to those found in Priorat, as are the flavors of the wines themselves. Overall, the wines may not be as powerful as their Priorat cousins, but Montsant is still a bit of a hidden gem and some great-value wines are produced in this region. From the Els Guiamets winery, you can't go wrong with the inexpensive, medium-bodied "Les Tallades," made with native grapes and boasting fresh strawberry flavors, or the richer and more complex "Isis," with black pepper and raspberry flavors.

Another winner from the region is "Fra Guerau" by Vinas del Montsant. This blend of primarily Syrah, Grenache, and Carinena is jam-packed with blackberry and earth flavors. Some other recommended wines include "Baboix" by Buil I Gine, "Sola Fred" by Celler El Masroig, and "Karma de Drac" by Celler Los Trovadores.

For a special occasion, you may want to treat yourself to the complex and memorable "Peraj Ha'abib Flor de Primavera" made by the Capcanes winery from about one third each of Garnacha, Carinena, and Cabernet Sauvignon. It is one of the finest red wines made in this region, and it sells in the $40 to $50 range at retail. (As an added bonus, it's kosher!)

PROVINCE OF CASTILLA Y LEON

IMPORTANT DO REGIONS

Bierzo

Toro

Ribera del Duero

Cigales, Rueda

Jumilla (part of the Jumilla DO is in Castilla y Leon, and the rest is in Murcia province; we will cover Jumilla in this section)

Bierzo. In this northwest corner of Castilla y Leon, grape pickers really earn their money, working at high elevations in the steep mountainside vineyards. Cool nighttime temperatures provide acidity to the supple red wines made from the local Mencia grape. The elevation of the vineyards, along with adequate rainfall and cooling winds from the Atlantic Ocean, allow this region to produce balanced, delicious wines with refreshing acidity even in very hot years.

In general, Bierzo wines are marked by floral and fresh red cherry flavors and a medium to full body. Mencia may also be blended with Garnacha to add raspberry and strawberry flavors and ripeness. You do not have to break the bank to buy quality Bierzo wines; many fine examples sell for under $20 a bottle, although several truly stellar wines are available for $100 or more. For an off-the-beaten-path, delicious dry white from Bierzo, try a Godello-based wine such as Dom Abad.

SOME OF THE BEST WINE PRODUCERS

Adria, Akilia, Godelia, Cassar de Burbia, Descendientes de J. Palacios, Dom Abad, Dominio de Tares, El Castro de Valtuille, Losados Vino de Finaca, Estefania, Luna Beberide, Pago de Valdoneje, Perez Carames, Pittacum, and Joaquin Rebolledo.

Toro. Toro is best known for its powerful, dry red wines made mostly from the Tempranillo grape, here known as Tinta de Toro. Garnacha plays second fiddle to Tinta de Toro and is never more than a quarter of the blend. Vineyards planted at high altitudes provide a nice level of acidity to balance out the tannins in the red wines.

Toro reds tend to exhibit flavors of licorice, leather, and blackberries. The high tannins are best tamed by rich foods such as rack of lamb or vegetarian lasagna. As with most full-bodied special occasion reds, Toro wines open up and are easier to enjoy after being aerated for an hour. Prices range from inexpensive (under $15) to expensive for the finest wines from producers such as Pintia, Elias Mora, Farina, Gil Luna, Numanthia, and Rejadorada. Try a few Toro wines and you'll see why we think this is a region to watch.

Ribera del Duero. The refined red wines of Ribera del Duero should be on every wine lover's wish list. Most fine Ribera del Duero reds are full-bodied and in their youth exhibit flavors of dark berries, plums, licorice, coffee, and dark spices. The best examples also offer mineral and earthy smells and flavor that we crave in Old World wines. After a decade of aging they become incredibly rich and complex, with a bouquet that includes black tobacco, licorice, and forest undergrowth. Enticing flavors of black plums, herbs, spices, aged balsamic vinegar, dark coffee, and grilled bell peppers can be detected in these wines.

What makes these wines so special is the location or "*terroir*" of the vineyards, the dedication of local growers to produce world-class wines, and the type of Tempranillo grape: Tinto Fino and Tinto del Pais are the local names for Tempranillo, which comprises over 80% of plantings.

The Duero River moderates the temperature in this region. Warm days during the growing season ensure ripeness in the grapes and the cool nights extend the growing season and contribute good levels of acidity to the wines. Here, as in Toro, the local versions of Tempranillo contribute more color and tannins than Tempranillo-based wines from most other regions of Spain. Some blends contain Cabernet Sauvignon, Merlot, Malbec, and Syrah, lending the wines the darker color and black fruit flavors associated with those grapes.

Aside from very special occasion wines such as Vega Sicilia "Unico," Dominio de Pingus "T," or Alejandro Fernandez "Pesquera Reserva," there are plenty of moderately priced Ribera del Duero wines to enjoy. Some use traditional label terms such as "*Crianza*" and "*Reserva*" while many others opt for a proprietary name such as "Camino" by Dominio Romano, "Alfa Spiga" by Ortega Fournier, "Disco" by Neo, "Vina Mayor" from Hijos de Antonio Barcelo, or "Tomas Esteban" by Valderiz. The overall high quality of these wines means that they are easy to find in retail shops and restaurants that sell Spanish wines. Retail prices range anywhere from $15 to $800, with older vintages of the region's finest checking in at exorbitant prices (over $1,000 a bottle). But don't worry, you can find excellent wines from Ribera del Duero at all price points.

The bold wines of Ribera del Duero are traditionally served with lamb or suckling pig roasted in a wood-fired oven or Morcillo blood sausages, although a hunk of aged Manchego cheese is another appealing option. The richness of the cheese lessens the tannins in the wine while providing a pleasant contrast between salty (the cheese) and fruity (the wine). The wines of Ribera del Duero are certainly not limited to local dishes. We recommend them with some international fare in our chapter on wine and food pairing.

In addition to those wineries already mentioned, some other suggested wine producers include:

Dominio de Autauta, Hacienda Montasterio, Arzuaga, Astrales, Balbas, Dehesa de Los Canonigos, Fuentespina, Lleirosa, Matarommera, Emilio Moro, Pago de los Capellanes, Pagos de Quintana, Prado Rey, Protos, Telmo Rodriguez, Secreto, and Senorio de Nava.

Cigales. This region produces mostly dry rosé wines from Tempranillo and Garnacha grapes, though some dry red and white wines are made here as well. We really enjoy the medium-bodied rosés of Cigales. Typically a beautiful pale pink with tastes of ripe red berries and cherries, these refreshing wines are a perfect match for picnic food. Try one with a tomato salad, cold cuts, or fried chicken and you'll never look back.

Rueda. In Rueda, white wine rules, and the queen bee is the Verdejo grape. Verdejo's sting lies in its high acidity, which makes it a lovely partner to acidic foods such as ceviche. Modern Ruedas are light and fresh with moderate alcohol. While Verdejo dominates, the wines may be blended with the native Viura, or internationally popular Sauvignon Blanc.

Rueda wines sell in the inexpensive (under $15) to moderate ($30) price range. Try the inexpensive ones with a Greek salad: the wine's light body will not overwhelm the greens, and its acidity will complement the acidity of the tomatoes, feta cheese, and citrus dressing. By contrast, moderately priced Ruedas are more full-bodied due to oak aging. These can stand up to grilled sausages and yellow peppers, or grilled octopus as well as soft ripened cheeses. We suggest "Naia" by Aldial, "Martinsancho" by Angel Rodriguez, Verdejo by Protos, and the Rueda by Marques de Riscal, which are all inexpensive and widely available.

Jumilla. There are some great jewels to be mined from the lesser-known wine regions, and Jumilla in particular is a bargain seeker's paradise. If you are looking for an affordable red that is not wimpy, the wines of this region should be on your radar. Jumilla wines are most often blends. The featured grape here is Monastrell (also known as Mourvedre), with Merlot, Syrah, Cabernet Sauvignon, and/or Garnacha commonly added to the mix.

Agapito Rico laid the foundation for other wineries in the region with its Monastrell-based "Carchelo." This bargain-priced wine is medium-bodied with lots of rich black fruit flavors. The winery's "Altico," a Monastrell and Syrah blend loaded with blackberry and black pepper flavors, has a little more body and is worth seeking out. Another of our favorite local wineries is Casa de la Ermita. We enjoy its inexpensive Monastrell-based "Monasterio." For a treat, look no further than its pure Petit Verdot (about $32), a grape commonly found in Bordeaux blends. Another wine we enjoy is the Caracol Serrano. This Monastrell, Syrah, and Cabernet Sauvignon blend is medium-bodied with lovely blueberry, black currant, and black fig flavors and is bargain priced.

Other Jumilla producers we suggest include:

Finca Luzon and Casa Castillo. El Nido winery makes expensive, complex blends of Jumilla based on Monastrell and Cabernet Sauvignon. If you think that's too much information, you are Wrongo Dongo! Sorry, that's just a playful local wine made by the winery Juan Gil. We love wine producers that don't take themselves too seriously.

VINO DE LA TIERRA DE CASTILLA Y LEON

Vino de la Tierra de Castilla y Leon wines come in both inexpensive, easy-drinking, light-bodied versions as well as complex full-bodied wines that range from the simple to the spectacular. The Vino de La Tierra Castilla-Leon designation allows wineries more creative freedom to experiment and go beyond the stringent DO rules of permitted grape types and methods.

For bargain seekers, there are some lively, easy-drinking wines available under $10, such as the white Verdejo and Viura blend by Fuente Milano, or the red Tempranillo by Penascal. For a walk on the wild side, check out the red and rosé wines of the Tierra de Leon. These unique wines are delicious, with the reds offering notes of black fruits, black pepper, warm spices and some mineral notes. Preto and Flor de Paramo offer good examples of these off-the-beaten-path wines.

Abadia de Retuerta is a state-of-the-art winery situated very close to the esteemed Ribera del Duero DO, producing an entry-level "Rivola" red wine for $15, as well as a more complex "Cuvee Palomar" for $50. Both wines are oak-aged Tempranillo and Cabernet Sauvignon blends that offer floral and spice aromas and black fruit flavors. We also enjoy their Seleccion Especial ($20), a blend of Tempranillo, Cabernet Sauvignon, and Merlot.

Other Castilla y Leon producers we suggest include Hijos de Antonio Barcelo, Mauro, Dominio de Eguren, Ledas Vinas Viejas, Triton, and Femal. Prices range from bargain to expensive.

PROVINCE OF GALICIA

IMPORTANT DO REGIONS

Rias Baixas

Ribeira Sacra

Ribeiro

Valdeorras

The province of Galicia—especially the DOs of Rias Baixas, Valdeorras, Ribeira Sacra, and Ribeiro—produces some of the best white wines in all of Spain. The Galician coastline attracted many Celtic immigrants, whose cultural influence is evident in the local music, where the *gaita*, or bagpipes, are prominent. The proximity of the Portuguese border is reflected in the similarity of the white grapes grown in each country, especially Albarino, Loureiro, Treixadura, and Godello. The local seafood is among the most celebrated in all of Europe, and the white wines of Galicia have evolved to be in perfect balance with the local seafood-based dishes. Unlike many over-oaked Chardonnays produced around the world, the discreet use of oak barrels in the production of most of these wines allows them to happily coexist with (rather than dominate) the food.

The white wines of Galicia really shine when paired with foods such as sashimi, Indian dosa with yellow dal, lobster, linguine with white clam sauce, falafel, or a seaweed salad. Some delicious medium- to full-bodied red wines are also made in Galicia. We encourage you to take advantage of the excellent quality and value offered by these off-the-beaten-path wines.

Rias Baixas. Rias Baixas is home to the Iberian Peninsula's premier white grape, Albarino. Though the grape is difficult to grow and the wine painstaking to produce, pure Albarino wines have achieved international acclaim. They are complex, medium-bodied, and redolent of white flowers, white peach, apple, citrus, spices such as cinnamon, and herbs. Wines labeled "Albarino" contain 100% of the grape, while those labeled "Rias Baixas" contain a minimum of 70%, with Treixadura and Loureiro added to the blend. Either way, the region's whites are a perfect match with fresh seafood dishes. Rias Baixas blends are inexpensive (under $15), while pure Albarinos are moderately priced (most are well under $30). Looking for a bargain? Try the Martin Codax, Nora, or Vionta Albarino for $15 to $20.

Some of the Best Wine Producers

Agro de Bazan, Burgans, Martin Codax, Condes de Albarei, Palacio de Fefinanes, Fillaboa, Lusco, Mar de Frades, Morgadio, Bodegas Vina Nora, Pazo de Barrantes, Pazo de Senorans, Pazo de Lusco, Pazo San Mauro, Valdamor, and Vionta.

Ribeiro and Valdeorras. These two regions produce crisp white wines made from a blend of Treixadura, Loureiro, and Godello or feature Godello on its own. We recommend the "Reboreda" blend by Campante. This dry, medium-bodied wine is typical of the Ribeiro region with its lemon, mineral, and nectarine flavors. Pure Godello can be savored for under $15 from the wineries Godeval, Telmo Rodriguez, and Rafael Palacios. Some fine Mencia-based red wines and blends are also produced in these regions.

Ribeira Sacra is an up and coming area offering dry whites based on Albarino and Godello as well as complex red wines based on the Mencia grape. Two wineries we suggest are Adega Moura and Ponte de Boga.

PROVINCE OF ARAGON

IMPORTANT DO REGIONS

Calatayud
Campo de Borja

The wineries of these fast-improving, lesser-known wine regions are shooting for success and offering wonderful wines of tremendous quality at great prices. The red wines offer several different expressions of native grape varieties such as Garnacha and Monastrell, but may also include international varieties such as Cabernet Sauvignon.

A perfect example of a great value is "Borsao" (about $10), a red from the Campo de Borja DO. A dry, light- to medium-bodied blend of Garnacha and Tempranillo, this wine features appealing red fruit flavors and low tannins, making it an ideal wine to sip on its own, or to serve at a buffet.

From the Calatayud DO, try Vina Alarba by Bodegas Castillo de Maluenda. This pure Garnacha has a similar character and price as the basic Borsao red wine described above. It is light- to medium-bodied with bright red fruit flavors and can complement a pizza topped with roasted red peppers. The limestone soils here are ideal for dry white wines, which are based mostly on Macabeo and Malvasia grapes.

WINEWISE TIP: On a hot summer day, we serve inexpensive lighter reds, such as those from Campo de Borja or Calatayud, with a bit of a chill to bring out their fruit flavors. Or we throw in a few ice cubes and add about one-third soda or sparkling water and a slice of lemon for a red spritzer. Don't try this with tannic red wines such as Cabernet Sauvignon as the cold temperature would make them more astringent.

PROVINCE OF NAVARRA

IMPORTANT DO REGION

Navarra

The Navarra wine region is perhaps best known for the dry, inexpensive rosé wines it produces; these wines feature characteristic strawberry flavors and are medium in body. Rosés have a chameleon-like ability to adapt to a wide range of foods, and the wines of Navarra are a good example of this: seafood gumbo, jambalaya, and *jamon* (ham) all show off the best of the region. Garnacha is currently the dominant grape, although many new vineyards have been planted with Tempranillo, Cabernet Sauvignon, and

Merlot. Prices for these rosés are typically under $15; you can also find some dry, medium-weight reds and whites at comparable prices.

Our go-to producer in Navarra is Bodegas Julian Chivite, which was founded in 1647. Under their name are the Vino de Pago (Senorio de Arinzano) and estate wines (Coleccion 125) and they also make the accessible, reasonably priced "Gran Feudo" line of wines. Bodegas Julian Chivite make white wines from Chardonnay and Moscatel, rosé and red from Garnacha, as well as Garnacha blends with Cabernet Sauvignon and Tempranillo.

SOME OF THE BEST WINE PRODUCERS

Agramont, Castillo de Monjardin, Julian Chivite, de Sarria, Inurreta, Nekeas, Julian Ochoa, Palacio de la Vega, and Vinicola Navarra

CENTRAL SPAIN

PROVINCE OF CASTILLA–LA MANCHA

IMPORTANT DO REGIONS

La Mancha

Valdepenas

The largest DO in all of Spain, La Mancha has been a source for the good, the bad, and the ugly of Spanish wines. Lucky for us, only the good are worth exporting to the Americas. Most of these Tempranillo-based wines are medium-bodied with red- and black-cherry flavors. Their simplicity makes them good candidates for pub grub; a Chicago pizza stuffed with sausage and pepperoni, or a Philadelphia cheesesteak are cozy pairings. Try the Tempranillo wine by Bodegas Campos Reales (about $10); a dry, medium-bodied red with the red cherry flavors typical of Tempranillo. And if you're looking for a refreshing dry rosé, try the Condesa de Leganza for under $10. Volver winery makes a lovely Verdejo dry white wine as well as red Tempranillos that are delicious and undervalued.

Airen, which is actually the most planted grape in the world, is the workhorse white grape here. Tempranillo, Garnacha, and Monastrell as well as international red grapes can also be found in this area.

Based in Rioja, the respected Martinez Bujanda family also owns the Finca Antigua winery in La Mancha. The soils are rich in limestone and the vineyards are planted at high altitudes, allowing for slow ripening of the Viura, Viognier, Tempranillo, Garnacha, Merlot, Syrah, Petit Verdot, and Cabernet Sauvignon grapes. Experienced owners dedicated to excellence combined with the right soils and altitude creates a wine trifecta! The reds are produced as single varietal wines, and as a bonus the Finca Antigua wines are under $20 retail.

SOME OF THE BEST WINE PRODUCERS

Campos Reales, Condeza de Leganza, Dominio de Eguren, Alejandro Fernandez, Finca Antigua, Fontana, Marques de Grinon, Santa Quiteria, and Vinedos y Crianza.

SOUTHERN SPAIN

REGION OF ANDALUCIA

IMPORTANT DO REGIONS

**Jerez/Xeres/Sherry and
Manzanilla Sanlucar de Barrameda**

Jerez/Xeres/Sherry. Sherry is the unique fortified wine of Spain, and true Sherry is produced only from the vineyards of Jerez. The nation's southernmost region is named after the capital of the province, Jerez (or Xeres) de la Frontera; "Sherry" is its bastardized English form. In 1996 the European Union formalized laws that prohibit other European nations from making imitations and calling them Sherry; now the fight is on to convince other countries outside Europe (such as the United States) to refrain from producing imitations under the name.

Sherry is one of the "insider wines" that most wine professionals love. Whether you are sipping a dry Fino to pique your appetite or kicking back with some sweet Pedro Ximenez at the end of the day, we urge you to explore the wines of Jerez.

GROWING THE GRAPES, MAKING THE WINE

Farmers can count on producing ripe grapes every year in the sun-baked region of Jerez. More than 90% of the region's vineyards are planted with the Palomino grape, which serves as the base for dry Sherries. Sun-dried Pedro Ximenez ("PX") and Moscatel can provide sweetness and color to the base Palomino wine or they may also be bottled as single-variety dessert wines (see labels).

Sherry is a fortified wine, which simply means that clear brandy is added to the base wine. The fortification process also determines the presence or absence of the influential *flor* yeast, which affects the color and style of the wine. This native yeast is either encouraged to enter the barrel by keeping the alcohol level of the wine under 15.5% or avoided by fortifying the wine to a higher alcohol level.

STYLES OF SHERRY

There are three basic styles of Sherry: Fino, Amontillado, and Oloroso. Fino wines spend their life protected from oxidation by the *flor* yeast and therefore have a pale yellow color. Olorosos receive no *flor* protection, and the resulting exposure to oxygen results in mahogany or dark-chocolate-colored wines. Between these two extremes are Sherries that are protected by *flor* in their youth but then are subjected to oxygen in later years. This process results in an amber-colored Sherry known as Amontillado.

The pale colored and delicate Fino is the most popular style of Sherry. A glass of Fino is a great way to whet your appetite before a meal; it also makes a perfect accompaniment to tapas, the assortment of "little plates" of appetizers served in the region. We wish we could take all our *WineWise* readers to Andulucia to hop from one tapas bar to the next for another cool glass of Fino Sherry and another delicious morsel. Fortunately, you can still experience Fino's flexibility by dining at one of the many exciting tapas bars and restaurants in North America.

MANZANILLAS ARE FINO SHERRIES that originate in the salt marshes of the Sanlucar de Barrameda subregion of Jerez. The driest of all basic Sherries, Manzanillas have a briny aroma

Fino and Manzanilla are dry styles of Sherry that are excellent as a before-dinner drink or with a wide variety of savory foods. Pedro Ximinez is a great wine to drink with Fig Newtons or dark chocolate brownies, or to pour over vanilla ice cream. La Gitana label courtesy of Bodegas Hidalgo La Gitana. Puerto Fino and PX courtesy of Bodegas Emilio Lustau (Jerez, Spain).

The *flor* yeast affects the color of Sherry wines. It forms a protective layer over Fino and Manzanilla wines, allowing them to preserve their pale color.

because they are aged close to the ocean, and the oak barrels in which they are stored are influenced by salty sea breezes. Fino and Manzanilla Sherries are always dry and are light to medium in body with no more than 15.5% alcohol. The pale color of Fino and Manzanilla wines that are released after five to 10 years in barrels can be explained by the protective effect of the *flor* yeast. These wines usually taste of salted almonds, with other common aromas and flavors (cashew, banana, apple, pear, and dough) reminiscent of a trip to a bakery. Wines labeled "En Rama" are lightly filtered.

AMONTILLADO SHERRIES are amber colored and medium-bodied, a bit fuller-bodied than Finos. Because they receive the benefits of both *flor* protection and exposure to oxygen, amontillados often develop to be the most complex of all styles of Sherry. Their signature aromas and flavors are varied and exotic, from nuts (hazelnut, Brazil nut, macadamia nut) to spice (clove, nutmeg, cinnamon) to fruit (quince paste, orange peel, papaya, yellow plum), not to mention cocoa powder, caramel, butter toffee, and even soy/miso. These wines register an alcohol content of 16% to 18%. On a cold winter night, try them with a wild mushroom soup, or classic French onion soup. That'll warm you up, body and soul! And Amontillados are also a great choice for a summer picnic with cold cuts and cheeses.

OLOROSO SHERRIES are full-bodied and rich, with up to 20% alcohol. Whether dry or sweet, they are intensely aromatic and flavored. Dry Olorosos, with aromas and flavors of mocha, orange, clove, ginger, and salted pecans, are considered the finest. They can age for decades. The more common sweet Olorosos offer flavors of black figs, Christmas fruitcake, molasses, cola, coffee, licorice, chocolate-covered raisins, beef consommé, mushrooms, pecans, and tamarind. Sweet Olorosos are amazing over ice cream, though they are also wonderful served chilled in the summertime, as a dessert of their own.

OTHER TYPES OF SHERRY

CREAM SHERRIES are sweetened by adding a rich sweet juice, wine, or paste to a base wine. Pale, medium, and rich cream Sherries are popular but are usually not as fine in quality as the Olorosos made exclusively from dried Pedro Ximenez or Moscatel grapes.

PALO CORTADO SHERRIES have the nose of an Amontillado and the flavor and color of an Oloroso. They could also be described as dry wines having the delicacy of an Amontillado and the generosity of an Oloroso.

DESIGNATED-AGE SHERRIES of 12, 15, or 18 years have been aged a minimum of the years stated before they are sold.

VERY OLD SHERRIES (VOS) are aged a minimum of 20 years and due to long aging are quite complex and more expensive than standard Sherries.

VERY OLD RESERVE SHERRIES (VORS) are aged a minimum of 30 years. Both VOS and VORS are special-occasion wines offering generous richness on the palate and a truly memorable array of flavors.

SERVING SHERRY

Sherry is traditionally served in a small glass the locals call a "*copita*" (cup), although any small wine glass will do.

THE SOLERA SYSTEM

Once the Sherries are classified by type and style, they are placed in a "solera," a fractional blending and aging system. Because the system consists of blending younger and older wines together, Sherries are, by definition, nonvintage wines.

The *solera* system involves transferring wines through a series of several rows of barrels stored in tiers. Usually they are stacked three to four barrels high.

Over time, about a third of the wine in each barrel is progressively transferred to a lower tier in its stack. Each time wine is transferred to a lower row in the *solera*, it is replenished with younger wine from the row above. This labor-intensive system moves the wines toward the bottom row of barrels in the original row. The *suelo* (floor level) contains the oldest blend of wines in the system, and by law, only a fraction of the wine in each of these barrels may be drawn off for sale each year.

The new wine of each vintage is introduced to the blend by placing it in the row farthest from the *suelo*. The beauty of the *solera* system is that over time, the younger wines contribute freshness to the older wines, and the older wines lend complexity to the younger wines. This blending of young and old enables winemakers to achieve a consistency of quality and flavor in each of their Sherries. As you can see, producing Sherry is an exacting process, truly a labor of love.

A standard Sherry pour is 2 to 2½ ounces (60 to 75 milliliters). Fino, Manzanilla, and pale cream styles should be served well chilled from a refrigerated bottle. Amontillado, Palo Cortado, Pedro Ximenez, Moscatel and dry Oloroso are usually not chilled unless you are drinking them outdoors on a hot day.

The wide range of styles of Sherries means they can be served from the beginning to the end of a meal. Typically, the lighter-bodied dry Finos and Manzanillas are served before the medium- to full-bodied dry Amontillados. Tapas such as codfish-stuffed piquillo peppers, marinated octopus, grilled sardines, tortilla of egg and potato, slices of *jamon*, or a stew of chickpeas, sausage, and spinach are just a few dishes that locals have enjoyed with dry Sherry for centuries. However, *WineWise* readers should not limit their enjoyment of Sherry to Spanish foods, as we have enjoyed these wines with foods from around the world. Finos and Manzanillas are nothing short of amazing with sushi or ceviche, or oysters, not to mention a whole roasted fish with fresh herbs. Amontillados can be enjoyed with kung pao chicken, roast veal chops, or fried tempeh in a salad with a sesame-based dressing.

Sherry is a bargain, with some of the best producers offering their wines at prices starting well under $20 per bottle. Special bottlings can go as high as $60, but these are rare. We encourage *WineWise* readers new to this category to try them with food. You may just be amazed by the unique flavor profiles created by the mingling of Sherry with your favorite dishes.

Some of the Best Wine Producers

Argueza, Barbadillo, Cesar Florido, Dios Bacos, El Maestro, Equipo Navazos, Gonzalez Byass (famous for dry Fino "Tio Pepe" and sweet "Noe"), Pedro Domecq (famous for dry Fino "La Ina"), Fernando de Castilla, Hartley & Gibson, Harvey's, Hidalgo (famous for dry Manzanilla "La Gitana"), La Cigarrea, Lustau (famous for dry Fino "Puerto Solera Reserva," dry Amontillado "Los Arcos," and sweet Pedro Ximenez "San Emilio"), Osborne, Orleans Borbon, Pedro Romero, Sacristia aB, Sanchez Romate, Sandeman (famous for medium-dry "Character"), Savory & James, Tradicion, Valdespino (famous for dry Fino "Inocente"), Williams & Humbert (famous for medium-dry "Dry Sack" and "15-Year-Old Dry Sack"), and Wisdom & Warter.

APAIXONADO POR PORTUGAL

TAKE THE FIRST STEP ON A JOURNEY TO DISCOVER SOME OF THE TASTIEST WINES ON THE PLANET, THE WINES OF PORTUGAL. Portuguese wines offer great value, distinctive flavors, and some unique food pairing possibilities. Portugal has more than 300,000 farmers carrying on a tradition of growing grapes to make wines for both a thirsty local market and for export markets. Until the 1990s, only a handful of truly exceptional table wines were being produced in Portugal; today, many fine wines are being made from both indigenous and international grapes. Portuguese winemakers, who offer wines in both traditional styles and modern blends, are experimenting with different techniques and grape types to compete in the global wine market.

Not only do Portuguese wines provide great quality and value, but also the diversity of wine styles is truly exciting: more than 200 indigenous grape types are used to make everything from sparkling wines to whites, rosés, and reds as well as fortified wines. Portugal is a treasure trove waiting to be discovered.

If you have never drunk Portuguese wines, we suggest that your first glass should be a low-alcohol, dry, crisp, white Vinho Verde wine. Many of these charming wines cost under $10 a bottle. If a glass of Vinho Verde piques your palate and your interest, then try some of the easy-sipping light-bodied rosé and red wines, also bargain priced.

Once you are comfortable with the value wines of Portugal, take a step up to the complex, sinewy red wines. Remember our WineWise advice: undervalued gems can often be discovered from wine-growing regions that are off the beaten path. And try some of the classic fortified wines of Portugal: Moscatel de Setubal, Madeira, and of course, Port, or Porto (remember that true Port must come from Portugal, just as true Champagne comes from France).

In this chapter, we will take you on a tour through the best-known wine-producing regions, describe the styles of wines made there, and mention some specific producers we respect. We will also suggest some wine and food pairing possibilities, taking advantage of the wide range of wine styles in Portugal.

The grapes of Portugal

MULTIPLE PERSONALITIES AND NAMES

For a fairly small nation, Portugal grows an amazing diversity of grape types. Portugal's vineyards are home to numerous international grapes: Chardonnay, Muscat, Cabernet Sauvignon, Merlot, Alicante Bouschet, and Syrah are all grown here. Yet, as is often the case around the world, it's the indigenous grapes that are instrumental in producing the most famous (and perhaps soon to be famous) wines of Portugal.

A quick review of some of the nation's native grape varieties reads like a mystery novel: there's Esgana Cao, the "dog strangler," and Borrado das Moscas, "fly droppings." One grape suffering from an identity crisis has a masculine name, Fernao Pires, in one province and a feminine name, Maria Gomes, in another.

Humor aside, Portugal is host to a number of "serious" grapes, such as the red varieties Touriga Nacional, Baga, and Trincadeira, that are used to produce some of the country's finest—and most famous—wines.

RED GRAPES

Touriga Nacional. This important grape produces dark-colored, tannic wines with good acidity. Mulberries, plums, violets, bergamot (slightly bitter orange), and spice notes are just some of the many flavors found in the wines from this noble grape. Some of the spice notes we often detect are cardamom, clove, rosemary, and cinnamon. Although Touriga Nacional's springboard to fame has been the Douro region, where it is a major component of both red wine and fortified Port, today it is grown in most of the major wine-growing regions of Portugal, where it produces outstanding single-variety wines as well as delicious blends. Touriga Nacional is regarded as the nation's premier wine grape.

Baga. The thin-skinned Baga grape is the premier grape of the Bairrada region and can produce some of the greatest wines of Portugal. The wines are high in acidity and tannins, two ingredients necessary to make long-lived wines. Flavors of the wines are of black fruit such as plums, as well as olives, herbs, and spices. Baga is also used to make delicious sparkling wines.

Alfrocheiro Preto. Lends aromas of spice, berries, and flowers to the red blends of the Dao region. Also produced as a single-variety wine with a medium body.

Jaen. This grape, with scents of black pepper, blueberry, and raspberry, is a popular component in the blends of the Dao region, and it is also produced as a single-variety wine with medium body. Jaen is known as Mencia in Spain.

Castelao. This grape, also known as Periquita, is the most-planted variety in Portugal. Wines based on Castelao have charming flavors of raspberries and strawberries and are light- to medium-bodied. Sparkling, rosé, red, and fortified wines can all contain some Castelao grapes.

Trincadeira. This grape is a major component of the blended wines of central and southern Portugal. As a single-variety wine or in a blend, it offers black fruit aromas and flavors, as well as warm spice flavors (such as clove and cinnamon), acidity, and tannins. It is also used in the northern region of the Douro where it is known as the Tinta Amarela.

Tinta Roriz. Tinta Roriz (as it is known in the north of the country; Aragones in the south) is actually Spain's finest red variety, Tempranillo. As in Spain, the grape is used to make single-variety wines as well as blends. Affordable wines based on this grape will have flavors of strawberries and cherries. They will be light- to medium-bodied. Moderate to expensive wines have aromas of black fruits, dark spices, and licorice and are medium- to full-bodied. If you are one of the many fans of Spanish wines, Tinta Roriz/Aragones wines are a no-brainer introduction to the pleasures of Portuguese red wines.

Alicante Bouschet. This is a grape with dark colored juice, used to add deep color and black fruit flavors to a blended wine. Some excellent wines of the Alentejo region are based on this grape.

WHITE GRAPES

Alvarinho. Known as Albarino in Spain, this is considered by many to be the finest white grape variety in Portugal. Wines made from this grape are medium- to full-bodied with a great balance of acidity and a seductive, aromatic bouquet of white flowers, peaches, and mango. Notable examples come from Vinho Verde in the Minho region. Wines made from Alvarinho are some of the most versatile wines for food pairing. In Portugal, Alvarinho-based wines are often served with grilled sardines, bacalhau (one of many seafood dishes based on codfish), the soup known as *caldo verde*, and local cheeses.

Arinto. Common to the Bucelas region, it is grown in other areas, and is also known as "Pederna." This grape is most prized for its vibrant acidity and has aromas and flavors of apples and lemons, as well as mineral notes. It is available in both lightweight versions made in stainless steel, and richer barrel-aged versions. Arinto is used to make both still wine and "*espumante*" (sparkling wine).

Encruzado. This queen bee white grape of the Dao region is often anointed with expensive new oak. If you like full-bodied whites and want a break from Chardonnay, this is the Portuguese white wine you have been looking for. When used in blended wines from the Dao region, the grape contributes citrus, yellow plum, mineral, violets, and nutty flavors.

Fernao Pires (also known as Maria Gomes). This grape makes wines with trademark aromas of orange zest, flowers, and white pepper. It is the most-planted white variety in Portugal, is low in acidity, and is used to make still and sparkling wines.

Trajadura. Known for its citrus, stone fruit, and apple aromas, it may be found as a single-variety wine or in Vinho Verde blends.

Avesso. Adds structure to the blends of Vinho Verde. It also produces fine single-variety wines with citrus and stone fruit flavors with good levels of acidity.

Loureiro. Named for its aroma of bay laurel, it also offers scents of orange, peach, apple, and flowers. Loureiro is made as a single-variety wine and also found in Vinho Verde blends.

Malvasia Fina. Grown in Douro, Dao, and other areas for table wines and for the fortified wine Madeira. Whether this grape is used as part of a blended table wine or produced as a fortified wine, there are usually flavors of white flowers, kiwi, and pineapple.

Moscatel. We admit it—we cannot resist the orange blossom and honey aromas of Muscat grape varieties. In Portugal, this grape is used to make pleasant semi-dry still wines as well as the sensational sweet aged fortified wine, Moscatel de Setubal.

Language of the label

AS IS TRUE OF MOST European nations, once you have a basic familiarity with Portugal's wine regions and grape types, reading their wine labels will be a piece of cake. Common to all labels is, of course, the producer, and a few terms will help you out here:

QUINTA, PALACIO, CASA, HERDADE, OR SOLAR: a wine estate, similar to a French chateau.

ADEGA: a winery.

MARQUES: as in Spain, denotes a wine producer of noble heritage.

A few additional terms you may encounter on Portuguese wine labels include:

GARRAFEIRA, used by some wineries to indicate additional aging before a table wine is released.

VELHO literally means "old" and indicates that white wines have been aged at least two years and reds three years before they can be sold.

COLHEITA means "vintage."

SUPERIOR indicates higher minimum ripeness than the standard wines of a region, but they don't have to be from a single vintage.

RESERVA also indicates riper grapes, producing wines with a little more alcohol to supply richness on the palate. In some areas such as the Dao region, it indicates more aging before the wine can be sold.

GRANDE ESCOLHA (GRAND SELECTION) OR ESCOLHA (SELECTION): terms a winery may put on the bottles it believes represent its best efforts.

ENGARRAFADO NA ORIGEM: estate-bottled by the grower.

ESPUMANTE: sparkling.

Next, Portuguese wine labels will include either the name of the grape, the place where the grapes were grown, both the grape and place name, or a proprietary name. The name of the grape is easy: Alvarinho or Touriga Nacional. When a place name is used, *WineWise* readers will have to depend on the "recipe" or blend of grapes permitted in the area just as they would with other Old World wines; helpful information is often found on the back label of the wine bottle. Proprietary names such as "Warrior" or "Incognito" can also be used.

THE ORIGIN OF THE WINE

The following terms are used to indicate the origin of the wine.

DENOMINACAO DE ORIGEM PROTEGIDA/DOP (FORMERLY DOC)

Think of DOP wines as classic recipes to ensure a consistent style, similar to AOP in France. Just as we suggested in the French chapter, AOP is a guarantee of authenticity, not quality. DOP wines must conform to the strictest rules concerning permitted grape types and production methods. The most important DOP regions include:

An example of a wine labeled by place name (Douro), produced by the winery Quinta do Vale Meao. A blend of red grapes is used for this superb dry red DOP wine. Courtesy of Quinta do Vale Meao/Deutsch Family Wine & Spirits.

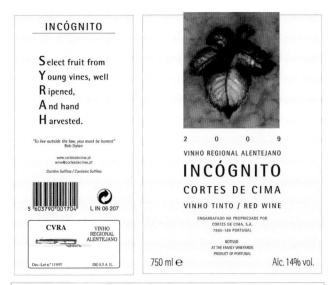

INCÓGNITO

Select fruit from
Young vines, well
Ripened,
And hand
Harvested.

"To live outside the law, you must be honest"
Bob Dylan

www.cortesdecima.pt
wine@cortesdecima.pt

Contém Sulfitos / Contains Sulfites

5 603790 001704   L IN 06 207

CVRA   VINHO
REGIONAL
ALENTEJANO

Dec.-Lei n.º 119/97   DE 0,5 A 1L

2   0   0   9

VINHO REGIONAL ALENTEJANO
INCÓGNITO
CORTES DE CIMA
VINHO TINTO / RED WINE

ENGARRAFADO NA PROPRIEDADE POR
CORTES DE CIMA, S.A.
7960-189 PORTUGAL

BOTTLED
AT THE FAMILY VINEYARDS
PRODUCT OF PORTUGAL

750 ml e   Alc. 14% vol.

Cortes de Cima is an innovative winery based in the Alentejo DOP. Their "Incognito" wine, which features a Bob Dylan quote and the word "Syrah" hidden on the back label, is a playful reference to the hesitancy of the local authorities to permit the use of Syrah grapes in the Alentejo DOP. Courtesy of Cortes de Cima.

VINHO VERDE, BUCELAS: best known for dry white wines.

DOURO, ALENTEJO, BAIRRADA, DAO: best known for dry reds, though rosé, white, and sparkling wines are also made in most of these areas.

MOSCATEL DE SETUBAL, PORTO, MADEIRA: best known for fortified wines. Most of them are sweet. In Madeira, the styles known as Sercial and Verdelho are dry exceptions.

INDICACAO GEOGRAFICA PROTEGIDA/ IGP (FORMERLY VINHO REGIONAL OR VR)

Winemakers are allowed more freedom to use nontraditional grapes or blends in this category than at the DOP level. The three largest production areas for IGP wines are Alentejano, Lisboa, and Peninsula de Setubal.

VINHO

These are the least expensive of Portugal's table wines; a vintage year will not appear on the label. About two thirds of exported wine from Portugal is from this basic Vinho level. The finer IGP and DOP wines make up most of the balance in a near-50/50 split. What we gather from this information is that while Portugal is still selling a lot of cheap wine, in the fine wine category, customers are equally divided between the DOP traditional style of Portuguese wines and the more modern, often more international IGP wine category.

The overall picture: Some of the best wines

WE HAVE SUGGESTED TIME AND again in *WineWise* to go off the beaten path for the best wine values. Portugal is no exception. The Portuguese can boast of having a wide diversity of wine styles, including sparkling, still, and fortified wines. If you're looking for alternatives to the world's most popular grapes or wine regions, we recommend exploring the unique wines of Portugal.

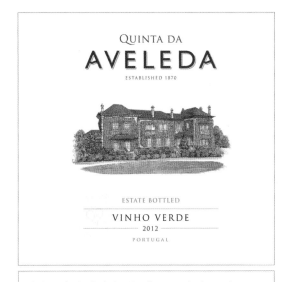

QUINTA DA
AVELEDA
ESTABLISHED 1870

ESTATE BOTTLED
VINHO VERDE
— 2012 —
PORTUGAL

Quinta da Aveleda is a family-owned winery that produces delicious blended and single-variety wines at great value prices. Courtesy of Aveleda.

The major wine regions of Portugal

FOR A SMALL COUNTRY—ROUGHLY 520 miles (837 kilometers) long and 120 miles (193 kilometers) wide—Portugal features numerous geographic and climatic conditions, which have played a major role in determining the styles of wines best suited to each area. In general, the vineyards in the west are closer to the ocean and have a more moderate climate and more rainfall than the torrid areas in the east. In the west, farmers can expect about 40 inches of rainfall a year, while some areas in the east only get a tenth of that. As a result the drier, hotter eastern vineyards are mostly devoted to red grapes, while vineyards to the west are more diverse. Mountains also play a major role in the wines of Portugal by offering protection from rain and winds for some vineyards as well as cooler temperatures for those at higher elevations. Cooler temperatures are indicators of higher acidity levels, which gives balance and freshness to the wines produced from those vineyards.

In each Portuguese wine region we will offer *WineWise* readers suggestions for bargain and moderately priced to expensive wines. Note that the finest (and often the most expensive) examples will usually bear the label terms *reserva*, *garrafeira*, or *grande escolha*, or they may have the name of a single grape variety and/or single vineyard.

WINEWISE TIP: Since so many of the red wines of Portugal are blended, you should know that the versions costing $15 and under will be lighter in body than wines from the same region at higher prices. Moderately priced and expensive versions from a region should have more complexity compared to the bargain-priced wines. In some situations, such as wine for easy consumption or with certain foods, the less expensive wines could be the better choice.

NORTHERN PORTUGAL

MINHO

IMPORTANT DOP REGION

Vinho Verde

One of the easiest and least expensive Portuguese wines to find and drink is Vinho Verde ("green wine"). This wine is fruity, affordable, and plentiful. The Minho is Portugal's largest DOP wine region, with most of the vines devoted to making these dry, crisp white blends. A number of varietals can contribute to the mix; the most typical are Alvarinho, Loureiro, Trajadura, Azal, Pederna, and Avesso.

Vinho Verde wines are usually light-bodied and low in alcohol (8.5% to 11%). At a time when the alcohol level of many international wines has surged beyond 15%, Vinho Verde's lighter style makes it perfect for hot summer days. So unlike brawny Chardonnays, Vinho Verde will not increase the heat of fiery dishes such as hot chicken wings, spicy Thai seafood, or blackened catfish. Likewise, their acidity makes a refreshing backdrop for steamed seafood or a salad with a citrus dressing. Many of the less expensive versions have a pronounced effervescence that can cleanse the palate from the richness of fried codfish fritters, falafel, or arepas. The popular "Gazela" wine by Sogrape is a good example of a spritzy, simple white wine blend priced under $6. The finest of the single-variety wines is Alvarinho and for $13 Quinta da Aveleda makes an amazing example. Wines based solely on this grape are richer in texture than inexpensive Vinho Verde blends, so they can handle grilled sardines, saffron risotto, or a roast chicken. For a pure expression of the Loureiro grape, we suggest the organically farmed Quinta do Ameal which offers stone fruit and citrus flavors. Anselmo Mendes may be the finest winemaker of the region and we suggest his pure Alvarinho "Muros Antigos Escolha" as well as his "Parcela Unica" and "Passaros" wines. Other top

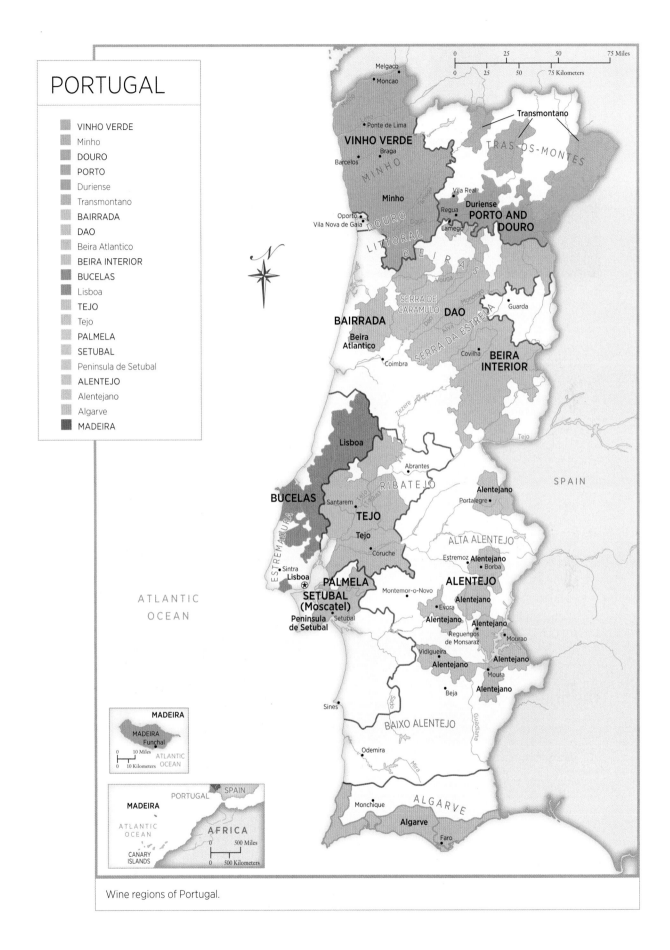

PORTUGAL

- VINHO VERDE
- Minho
- DOURO
- PORTO
- Duriense
- Transmontano
- BAIRRADA
- DAO
- Beira Atlantico
- BEIRA INTERIOR
- BUCELAS
- Lisboa
- TEJO
- Tejo
- PALMELA
- SETUBAL
- Peninsula de Setubal
- ALENTEJO
- Alentejano
- Algarve
- MADEIRA

Melgaco
Moncao
Ponte de Lima
VINHO VERDE
Braga
Barcelos
MINHO
Minho
Vila Real
Oporto
Vila Nova de Gaia
DOURO
Regua
Duriense
Lamego
PORTO AND DOURO
Transmontano
TRAS-OS-MONTES
LITTORAL
BEIRA
Vouga
SERRA DE CARAMULO
Dao
DAO
Guarda
BAIRRADA
Beira Atlantico
SERRA DA ESTREDA
Covilha
BEIRA INTERIOR
Coimbra
Mondego
Alva
Tejo
Lisboa
Abrantes
RIBATEJO
Alentejano
Portalegre
SPAIN
BUCELAS
Santarem
TEJO
Tejo
ALTA ALENTEJO
Coruche
Estremoz
Alentejano
Borba
ESTREMADURA
Sintra
Lisboa
PALMELA
Montemor-o-Novo
ALENTEJO
SETUBAL (Moscatel)
Peninsula de Setubal
Setubal
Evora
Alentejano
Alentejano
ATLANTIC OCEAN
Reguengos de Monsaraz
Mourao
Vidigueira
Alentejano
Moura
Alentejano
Sines
Beja
Sado
BAIXO ALENTEJO
Guadiana
Odemira
Mira
ALGARVE
Monchique
Algarve
Faro

MADEIRA

MADEIRA
Funchal
0   10 Miles
0   10 Kilometers
ATLANTIC OCEAN

MADEIRA
PORTUGAL
SPAIN
ATLANTIC OCEAN
AFRICA
CANARY ISLANDS
0   500 Miles
0   500 Kilometers

0   25   50   75 Miles
0   25   50   75 Kilometers

Wine regions of Portugal.

QUINTA DO CRASTO
Touriga Nacional

Quinta do Crasto makes a single-variety Touriga Nacional, single-vineyard wines, and blended dry red wines as well as fortified Ports. Evident in all the Quinta do Crasto wines are the scent of rose petals, spices, and both red and black fruit flavors. Courtesy of Quinta do Crasto.

producers we highly recommend are Soalheiro and the Cooperative of Moncao.

SUGGESTED WINES AND PRODUCERS

Solar das Boucas, Quinta da Lixa, Quinta do Ameal, Niepoort, "Gatao" by Borges, Broadbent, Famega, Adega Cooperative Regional de Moncao, Casa de Cello, Quinta de Carapecos, Soalheiro, "Portal do Fidalgo" by Provam, Quinta da Azevedo, Casa de Vila Verde, Quinta do Melgacao, Palacio da Brejoeira.

THE DOURO VALLEY

IMPORTANT DOP REGIONS

Douro, Porto

WINEWISE TIP: If you see "Douro" on a label you will be buying a dry wine, while the word "Port" will indicate a sweet, high-alcohol, fortified red wine (a small amount of White Port is produced). Both Douro and Port wines are sourced from the same grape types and vineyards.

Douro. The Douro is one of the most beautiful wine regions in the world. What looks like a crazy patchwork quilt of vineyards is the result of various planting strategies on the precipitous slopes of the region. The Douro River (the Duero in Spain) moderates the area's climate. In an area where daytime temperatures can reach 115°F (46°C), achieving a balance of fruit, tannins, alcohol, and acidity proves a constant challenge to the area's winemakers.

Historically, the Douro was best known by collectors for expensive Porto fortified wines and only one fine dry red, Barca Velha by Ferreira. There were no challengers to its elite status until the 1990s, when competition appeared in the form of single-variety wines and blends, mostly of Touriga Nacional or Tinta Roriz. While many wineries hold on to certain traditions—some still tread their grapes by foot in *lagares* to get the maximum extraction of flavors, tannins, and color—others have taken modernization quite far, using robots to crush the grapes and extract the juice. Today, the lush, full-bodied dry red wines of the Douro are among the world's finest, and have proved their nobility in many international competitions.

Douro reds range in price from inexpensive (about $15; mostly medium-bodied) to expensive (up to $200; full-bodied), but don't be disheartened by the high ceiling: you can sample some wonderful examples of the region without emptying your wallet. Douro red wines offer scents and flavors of flowers, earth, cured meats, mineral, and spice notes as well as a range of red and black fruits. The Douro's dramatic and supple wines are ideal with game birds, *cabrito* (goat roasted in a wood-fired oven), and many Indian vegetarian and meat dishes.

Although the Douro region is best known for its dry red wines and sweet Portos sourced from the same region, there has been an important increase in the quality of the dry white wines of the area. Gouveio (Godello in Spain), Viosinho, and Rabigato are just some of the grapes used to make these exotic wines.

A view of the terraced vineyards of the Douro Valley that flank the river. The Quinta do Crasto winery is in the foreground. Photo courtesy of Quinta do Crasto.

We adore the red wines of the Douro. The extensive list of suggested wines is our testimony to how excited we are for *WineWise* readers to try wines from this region.

Many of our favorite producers make a basic entry-level wine as well as more expensive *reservas* or single-vineyard wines. If there is a "brand name," it is followed by the producer's name.

SOME OF THE BEST WINES AND THEIR PRODUCERS

INEXPENSIVE: "Adriano" by Ramos Pinto, "Altano" by Symington, "Charamba" by Quinta da Aveleda, "Foral" by Aliança, "Vila Regia" by Sogrape, "Esteva" by Ferreira, "Twisted" by Niepoort, "Meandro" by Quinta do Vale de Meao, Quinta do Portal, Quinta do Ventozelo, and Quinta do Cotto.

MODERATE TO EXPENSIVE: Touriga Nacional and Reserva by Quinta do Crasto, Quinta do Vale de Meao, "Quinta da Leda" and "Barca Velha" by Ferreira, "Redoma" and "Batuta" by Niepoort, "Pintas" by Wine and Soul, Muxagat, Quinta do Vale do Dona Maria, Quinta do Vallado,

Quinta do Ventozelo, Quinta de la Rosa, "Abandonado," "Quinta do Vale da Raposa," and "Quinta da Gaivosa" by Alves de Sousa, "Quinta dos Quatros Ventos" by Alianca, "Post Scriptum" and "Chryseia" by Prats and Symington, "Poeira" by J. Moreira, "Xisto" by Roquette e Cazes, "Quinta das Pias" by Lavadores de Feitora, "Duas Quintas Reserva" and "Collection" by Ramos Pinto.

Porto. The one and only true Port. California, Australia, and South Africa make some decent "Ports," but as the song goes, "ain't nothing like the real thing, baby." Just as true Champagne and Sherry are wines of a specific place that must be produced in a traditional way, true Porto (often labeled as "Port") has its own DOP and must come from the Douro Valley. Each bottle of Porto wine must pass rigorous quality tests before receiving the seal of authenticity.

The process of making Porto is fairly simple. Before the fermentation proceeds to the point where all the sugar is converted to alcohol, the wine is transferred to casks containing clear grape brandy. The brandy's high alcohol kills off the yeast, resulting in a wine that is sweet, full-bodied, dark in color, and high in alcohol. The amount of time the wine spends in oak casks before it is bottled has a lot to do with the naming and styles of Porto.

Wines that are bottled young are known as Ruby or Vintage Portos, and those that are aged longer in wood are known as Tawny Portos.

THE POWERFUL YOUNG WINES

Ruby Portos are fruity blends from young, nonvintage wines. At under $20, they are a good introduction to the pleasures of Porto.

Ruby Reserve Portos (formerly known as vintage character) are blended Portos with a little more age than Rubies. They have proprietary names such as Fonseca Bin 27, Taylor Fladgate First Estate, Sandeman's Founders Reserve, Warre's Warrior, or Graham's 6 Grapes. A simple Ruby or Reserve Porto is all you need to pair with Cherry Garcia ice cream or a fudge brownie, as the complexities of a more expensive wine would be lost alongside such rich desserts. Reserves are great value wines, costing under $30.

Ruby Reserve wines, such as the Bin 27 by Fonseca, are an affordable alternative to Vintage Porto. Courtesy of Kobrand Corporation.

Crusted Porto is a wine made from a blend of years. The wine spends time in oak casks and then in bottle, where it throws a "crust" or deposit of sediment. Churchill and Smith Woodhouse are good examples that sell for moderate prices.

Late-Bottled Vintage (LBV) Portos are sourced from a single vintage and spend more time in cask and bottle than Vintage Portos (see next). "Unfiltered" or "Traditional" on a label indicates a wine that is ageworthy. Most often, they are moderately priced and can be a delicious alternative to the more pricy Vintage Portos.

Vintage Portos are sourced from the finest vineyards and are declared by a winery only when the harvest is of superb quality. On average, only three years in 10 are declared vintage years. In their youth, Vintage Portos are packed with intense black fruit and floral flavors and have lots of richness and power on the palate. The first taste on the palate is sweet but the aftertaste is dry. The wine mellows with age, becoming softer and more harmonious. These wines are moderately to expensively priced ($50 to hundreds of dollars for older vintages). (See "Act Your Age!," page 258.)

Single-Quinta Portos are made from the grapes of one vineyard, and may be vintage or nonvintage wines. After spending less time in cask and bottle than Tawny Portos (see opposite), the wines of an individual estate may be sold. This

Workers are foot-treading the grapes at Quinta do Vesuvio to get the maximum extraction of color, tannins, and flavors before fermentation. Photo by Joao Pedro Marnoto, courtesy of Symington Family Estates.

category is a bit confusing, as the wineries have the option of making these wines from a mediocre harvest or from a very fine harvest. Unlike Vintage Portos, which are released in the third year following the vintage, wineries may wait longer to release these wines to allow more time to develop harmonious flavors. We recommend Quinta do Vesuvio, Quinta do Noval, Quinta dos Canais by Cockburn, Quinta da Foz by Calem, Quinta do Crasto, Quinta do Bonfim by Dow's, Quinta do Gaivosa, Quinta do Seixo by Ferreira, and for a very special occasion Taylor's Quinta de Vargellas *Vinha Velha* (old vines).

THE GRACEFUL AGED WINES

Tawny Porto is aged for at least six years in cask. Some Tawnies are made by blending white and red Porto, or by aging and blending Ruby Portos; these can be found at bargain prices, and quality is generally good.

Indicated-Age Tawny Portos are available in 10-, 20-, 30-, and 40-year versions. These are based on an average minimum age of the blend of vintages in the bottle; the oxidation of the wines as they age allows them to develop a tawny color. Prices for Indicated-Age Tawnies range from moderate to expensive based on age (about $30 for the 10-year to over $100 for the 40-year). We believe the 20-year versions are good values at $40 to $60. They are some of the most wonderful sweet wines in the world, adored for their exotic bouquet, flavors, and balance. Since the wines are not as tannic as the Vintage style, it is a lot easier to enjoy a second glass, or even a third over time. Some of our favorite producers of Indicated-Age Tawny Porto are Adriano Ramos Pinto, Barros, Calem, Delaforce, Ferreira, Quinta do Portal, Pocas, Taylor-Fladgate, Fonseca, Rozes, Offley, Graham's, Dow's, Warre's, Wine and Soul, and Cockburn.

Indicated-Age Single-Vineyard/Quinta Tawnies contain the name of an estate vineyard. Fine examples include Adriano Ramos Pinto's 10-year tawny from its Quinta da Ervamoira vineyard and its 20-year tawny from the Quinta do Bom Retiro estate. Both are moderately priced.

Colheita Vintage Tawny Portos (very old single harvest) are from a single harvest and spend a long time in barrels before they are bottled. We recommend those of Niepoort, Calem, Royal Oporto, Graham's, and Barros. They can be found at moderate to expensive prices.

WINEWISE TIP: When pairing Portos with chocolate, match their intensities. Milk chocolate has an affinity with Tawny Portos, while dark chocolate complements the darker flavors of Vintage Porto or Late-Bottled Vintage Porto. We enjoy pairing chocolate brownies accompanied by cherry or strawberry ice cream with Ruby Reserve Ports. Portos certainly have an affinity with chocolate, but the cooling effect of ice cream in your mouth before a sip of Porto lessens the heat of its alcohol content and extends the rush of intermingling flavors.

CENTRAL AND SOUTHERN PORTUGAL

BEIRA ATLANTICO AND BEIRA INTERIOR

IMPORTANT DOP WINE REGION
Bairrada

As the names indicate, the Beira Atlantico is situated by the Atlantic Ocean while the Beira Interior is further east where conditions are hotter and drier. The Beira Atlantico contains the DOP region of Bairrada.

Bairrada. The Bairrada DOP produces sparkling, white, red, and rosé wines. The Baga grape dominates the vineyards of Bairrada. Bairrada wines are generous in body and acidity with delicious black fig, blueberry, licorice, and floral

ACT YOUR AGE!

Age is an issue in Porto for two reasons. First, older vines result in lower yields of grapes, which in turn results in more concentrated wine. Second, the amount of time the wine spends in cask and bottle before it is sold directly affects the naming of the wine and its character.

Vintage Portos, for example, are released between the second and third year after the grapes were harvested. Late-Bottled Vintage (LBV) Portos are released between the fourth and sixth years. Because they are bottled young and not exposed to very much oxygen, both vintage and LBV Portos deteriorate quicker in an open bottle than the Tawny style of wines, which are more resistant to the effects of oxygen.

Although tannic and full-bodied in their youth, Vintage Portos become suave and complex as they age, developing an opaque black cherry or deep purple color and flavors of black plum, blueberries, black figs, fruit, flowers, chocolate, and spices. You can cellar a great vintage Porto for 15, 30, or even 50 years. Those from 1945, 1963, 1970, 1977, and 1994 are still delicious, while the 2000, 2003, 2004, 2007 and 2011 vintages all promise to be great wines when they mature.

Most Late-Bottled Vintage Portos employ a modified twist-off cork (with a short cork, called a stopper cork) and are meant for drinking within three years. Versions from Dow's and Taylor Fladgate fall into this category. The LBVs labeled "Traditional" or "Unfiltered," with driven corks—such as those of Ramos Pinto, Fonseca, and Niepoort—can be aged for at least 20 years. The flavors of these LBV Portos are quite similar to Vintage Portos, with black fruits, wildflowers, spices, and chocolate.

Ten-, 20-, 30-, and 40-year-old Tawny Portos are chestnut in color and display aromas and flavors of dried white fruits, flowers, and spices. They have medium tannins and are lighter in body than Vintage Portos. Portos are usually reserved for after dinner, but we suggest pairing a foie gras terrine or duck pate with pistachios appetizer with a fine Designated-Age Tawny. This may seem like an unusual combination, but trust us, it works. While we would not serve these wines too cold, they can be enjoyed cooler than the Ruby or Vintage style.

Another bonus of Tawny Portos: they can be stored in a cellar for a decade, and once opened they will retain their basic flavors for a couple of weeks.

Some well-known producers of ageworthy Portos include: Adriano Ramos Pinto, Barros, Burmester, Calem, Churchill, Croft, Cockburn, Delaforce, Dow's, Ferreira, Fonseca, Graham's, Kopke, Niepoort, Offley-Forester, Pocas, Quinta do Crasto, Quinta da Gaivosa, Quinta do Noval, Quinta do Vale do Dona Maria, Quinta de la Rosa, Quinta do Vallado, Quinta do Vale Meao, Quinta do Vesuvio, Rozes, Sandeman, Smith-Woodhouse, Taylor Fladgate, and Warre's.

Tawny Porto wines are lighter in body and lower in tannins than Vintage Portos. We enjoy these complex wines as an after-dinner drink or with a platter of aged cheeses, dried fruits, and nuts. Courtesy of Ramos Pinto.

TAYLOR FLADGATE®

LATE BOTTLED VINTAGE PORTO

TAYLOR FLADGATE & YEATMAN

Bottled in 2012 by Quinta and Vineyard Bottlers Vinhos SA, Oporto

Product of Portugal

ALC 20% BY VOL   THE LBV FROM PORTO   750ML

Late-Bottled Vintage Porto has flavors similar to Vintage Porto but is more affordable. This example from the well-respected producer Taylor Fladgate has a modified twist-off cork that makes it easy to open and serve.

notes. How can you tame the assertive tannins of Bairrada red wines? They pair well with hearty foods such as rack of lamb, ribs with chimichurri sauce, roast duck, or steak. Vegetarians might consider a hearty black bean stew.

Bairrada red wines must be aged at least a year and a half before they are sold to allow the wine to become more harmonious. We believe that you can cellar their fine *garrafeira*, *reserva*, or single-vineyard wines for at least a decade and they will become even more balanced and complex. Our top Bairrada wines come from Quinta das Bageiras (the Garrafeira is sensational), Campolargo (try the "Termao"), Caves Messias, Alianca, Foz de Arouce, and Marques de Marialva. The "Follies" line of wines by Quinta da Aveleda includes a medium-weight Touriga Nacional we recommend.

Fernao Pires (also called Maria Gomes) accounts for the majority of the white grapes grown in the Bairrada region, but there is also Bical, Arinto, and Cerceal. Whether used for dry table whites or *espumante* bubbly, these wines often have a pleasant floral aroma and bright acidity. They are a good match for one of the 365 Portuguese recipes for codfish.

The "power couple" of the Beiras wine regions are the father and daughter Luis Pato and Filipa Pato and their eponymous wineries. Luis was the first winemaker in the region of Bairrada to achieve international acclaim for his wines. His single-vineyard wine, Vigna Pan, tastes of red and black berries and the acidity balances the tannins imparted by the Baga grape. His "Rebel Red" is mostly Baga with a little Touriga Nacional and a drop of Bical, while his "Joao Pato" wine uses the Touriga Nacional as the dominant grape in the blend. Luis' "Vinhas Velhas" are deliciously crisp, dry white wines. He even makes a luscious dessert white wine by freezing the grapes after harvest.

Filipa Pato's Baga "Nossa Calcario" from the Bairrada DOP and her IGP Beira Atlantico crisp dry white blended wines are both worth trying with a range of foods. We are equally enamored of her sparkling wines such as the "Metodo Tradicional 3B," a full-bodied blend of

Baga and Arinto grapes. The bubbles of this wine can cleanse the richness of the local specialty, *leitao* (roasted young suckling pig). The bright red berry flavors of the wine will complement a tapa of piquillo peppers with codfish, or contrast spicy, smoked, and salty flavors.

TERRAS DO DAO

IMPORTANT DOP WINE REGION

Dao

Red grapes thrive in this mountainous region, and in fact two-thirds of Dao's production is red wine. The dominant grape is Touriga Nacional, Portugal's finest red grape. Alfrocheiro Preto and Jaen usually comprise the balance of a Touriga Nacional-dominated blend, but single variety versions are also available. Most Dao reds tend to be medium to medium-full in body, with moderately soft tannins. They can coexist with a wide range of foods, from borscht soup to tandoori chicken to mushroom risotto.

On the white front in Dao, blended wines are dry, medium-bodied, and usually inexpensive. The exceptional wines made from 100% Encruzado grapes are wonderful alternatives to oaked Chardonnay. They are usually pricier than the blended wines of the Dao but well worth the money. The bouquet and flavors of Encruzado include citrus, minerality, flowers, and hazelnuts. Quinta dos Roques makes a wonderful Encruzado that can stand up to Bacalhau Espiritual (baked codfish with béchamel sauce and cheese).

Favorite producers include Quinta da Pellada and Quinta de Saes by Alvaro Castro, Quinta dos Roques, Quinta da Cabriz, Quinta da Garrida, Quinta dos Carvalhais by Sogrape, Casa de Santar, Fontes de Cunha, Quinta da Perdigao, and Pedra Cancela by Lusovini.

TEJO

Confusingly, Tejo is the name for both the IGP and DOP wine regions. The Tejo DOP used to be called Ribatejo, and older wines from the area may bear that name.

Fernao Pires is the major grape used for the inexpensive dry white blended wines of the region and we drink them young. Our favorite dry whites from the region are the pure Arinto made by Quinta da Alorna and the Alvarinho/Sauvignon Blanc/Verdelho blend from Quinta da Lagoalva de Cima.

Casa Cadaval, Conde de Vimioso, Quinta do Casal Branco, and Quinta da Lagoalva de Cima wineries produce fine medium- to full-bodied red wines made with indigenous and international grape varieties. For a pure expression of the local Trincadeira grape, we suggest Casa Cadaval's tasty red wine.

LISBOA (FORMERLY ESTREMADURA)

IMPORTANT DOP WINE REGION
Bucelas

We are off the beaten path here so we've entered a bargain zone. There are also extraordinary wines to discover, and *WineWise* readers can buy both traditional and modern wines from this region.

One of our favorite bargain-priced producers in Lisboa is Casa Santos Lima. Try their inexpensive blended wines such as "Bon Ventos," "Lab," or "Cigarra," a Shiraz-Tinta Barocca blend. Or if you want a full-bodied red wine with blackberry flavors, check out their varietal Tinta Barocca. Another fine producer using indigenous and international grape varieties such as Viognier and Syrah is Quinta do Monte d'Oiro. Quinta da Chocopalha is the family winery of Sandra Tavares, who also makes "Wine and Soul" wines with her husband, Jorge, in the Douro region. Sandra works her magic with Chardonnay, Arinto, Sauvignon Blanc, Viosinho and Vital white grapes. When it comes to red wines, she also makes a great Touriga Nacional, Tinta Roriz, and Syrah blend.

BUCELAS DOP

A region of note for the *WineWise* reader is Bucelas, which produces only white wines. These are mostly crisp whites based on the tart Arinto grape. To highlight the lemon flavors characteristic of Arinto, try serving them with a citrusy ceviche or salad with goat cheese and lemon vinaigrette. Quinta da Romeira's wine is a great bargain at about $12.

PENINSULA DE SETUBAL

IMPORTANT DOP WINE REGIONS
Setubal

Palmela

Peninsula de Setubal wines are often blends of native and international varieties. The Jose Maria de Fonseca winery was the first to export a dry red wine known as "Periquita" in the nineteenth century. Today the red wine is based on the Castelao grape and the dry white version is a blend of local grapes and Muscat. These inexpensive wines can be paired with a wide range of foods. Try the red wine with a burger or pepperoni pizza and the white with salads or codfish fritters.

Moscatel de Setubal is a full-bodied, fortified wine produced from the white Moscatel grape in Portugal's Setubal region. Moscatel is the local name for the Muscat grape. It can be labeled as five, 20, or 25 years and typically exhibits orange blossom and stone fruit flavors. Vintage-dated Moscatel de Setubal is complex, long-lived, and one of our "off the beaten path" undervalued wines. These luscious sweet whites can be paired with aged hard cheeses, fresh peaches, crepes Suzette, or a flan. J. M. Fonseca produces an entry-level, five-year-old wine called Alambre, as well as a 20-year-old Moscatel de Setubal. Other producers include Adega Cooperativa de Palmela, Quinta da Bacalhoa, and Horacio Simoes.

ALENTEJANO

IMPORTANT DOP WINE REGION

Alentejo

Alentejo is a very large DOP region and is home to some of the nation's finest, most complex, and most expensive red wines. The area also produces easy drinking rosés, interesting white wine blends and affordable reds. Alentejo is also the largest source of corks in the world.

Vineyards in the Alentejo are planted with both indigenous and international white and red grape types. Trincadeira, Aragones, Castelao, and Alicante Bouschet are the most important native red grapes featured here. This is where Alicante Bouschet does best, and it was the Herdade de Mouchao winery that first planted it in the 1950s. Their wines such as the "Dom Rafael," a blend of Trincadeira and Aragones, are worth seeking out.

Winemaker David Baverstock of Esporao winery makes delicious wines at all price points for Herdade de Esporao winery.

A bargain-priced dry white wine we suggest is their Monte Velho. This wine features fresh white fruit flavors and is about $10. Serve it well chilled as a refreshing lunchtime accompaniment to the region's most famous dish, *carne de porco alentejano* (a stew of clams, linguica sausage, and pork topped with potato and onions). We also suggest Herdade de Esporao's pure Touriga Nacional wine and their blended Reserva red wines.

A fine wine "pioneer" of the Alentejo is Joao Portugal Ramos. He has been a consultant for more than a dozen wineries and makes fine wines at his own property in Alentejo, as well as in the Tejo and Douro regions. His basic easy-drinking, light-bodied, inexpensive red wine is Marques de Borba; Ramos also makes excellent single-variety and *reserva* wines. Another winemaker we respect in the Alentejo region is Luis Duarte of Herdade dos Grous; their "Moon Harvested" is a romantic red to seek out.

Some wineries in Alentejo epitomize the traditional wine styles, and others produce international style wines. For a traditional-style wine with leather and earthy flavors, try the "Cartuxa" by Fundacao Eugenio de Almeida. Or try the more international style wines made by the Cortes da Quinta do Carmo, Alianca, and Cortes de Cima wineries. Cortes de Cima makes fine single-variety wines; look for a Syrah called "Incognito."

In Alentejo, wineries may use the most modern stainless-steel fermenting tanks as well as old school clay pots or amphorae known as *talhas*.

We have suggested just a few producers whose wines we enjoy and there are certainly many others to sample in this huge region, which occupies about a third of the landmass of mainland Portugal. The red wines may not have as much acidity as wines from cooler growing areas to the north, but they have appealing ripe fruit flavors. They also offer some exciting food pairing possibilities.

The Alentejo is known within Portugal for its delicious charcuterie products, whose smoky and salty flavors are a wonderful contrast to the region's fruity rosés and inexpensive reds. The moderately priced to expensive red wines of the Alentejo partner well with traditional wild game dishes and aged hard cheeses, among many other dishes.

MADEIRA DOP

The island of Madeira is located off the coast of Africa. This DOP region is best known for the fortified wines labeled as Madeira. One of the reasons we enjoy these wines so much is their high levels of refreshing acidity. High acidity is an unusual trait of a wine sourced from an island just 466 miles (750 kilometers) off the coast of Morocco. The acidity is due to the high elevation of vineyard plantings (up to 2,625 feet [800 meters]), the volcanic soils of those vineyards, and sometimes the type of grape variety used.

Another attractive attribute of Madeira wines is their nutty smells and flavors, which can be explained by how these wines are made. The process of making Madeira is unique. Most of

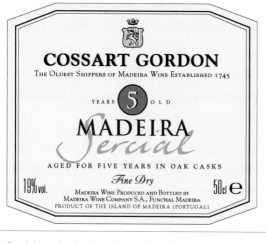

Sercial is a dry fortified wine with high acidity. Serve about 2½ ounces chilled in a small wine glass.

the wines are heated to 130°F (55°C) in concrete vats or stainless-steel tanks. This process is known as the *estufa method*. The best Vintage Madeira wines are an exception; these are slowly warmed in *canteiros*, or oak casks, for 20 years. This extended period of aging and oxidation gives them their signature nuttiness as well as other complex scents and flavors. Then Vintage wines must be aged an additional two years in bottle before they are sold. It boggles our minds to consider that Madeira winery owners must be patient and wait 22 years to be able to sell their vintage wines. Perhaps that is why the "Colheita" category of single-vintage wines aged for five years was created.

The fortification of the sweet wines—known as Bual and Malmsey—is completed before the sugar in the grapes can be converted to alcohol. This process retains natural sweetness. With the dry styles—known as Sercial and Verdelho— most of the sugar in the grapes is fermented out first and then the grape spirit is added. Wineries who want a little sweetness in the Sercial or Verdelho styles of wine are permitted to sweeten them afterwards.

The range of finer Madeira wines begins with the "Five Year" or "Reserve" category followed by the "Ten Year" or "Old Reserve," then "Fifteen Year" or "Extra Reserve." True Vintage, aged a minimum of 22 years before it can be sold, is the ultimate expression of Madeira.

We have sampled Vintage Madeira wines that were over a hundred years old and still lively. Vintage Madeira is a special occasion wine, but Five or Ten Year are affordable wines that we enjoy on a regular basis.

Unlike most wines, which can be harmed by too much air, Madeira wines are purposely exposed to oxygen. So an open bottle will last much longer than a traditional table wine.

A standard pour of Madeira is about 2½ ounces (75 milliliters). Sercial and Verdelho are excellent partners for savory foods. Their refreshing nature serves to cleanse the palate after rich foods such as seared foie gras or codfish fritters. Their nutty flavor is a perfect complement to foods with nuts, such as duck terrine with pistachios, chicken satay, or vegetable dumplings with a peanut sauce. We usually chill the Sercial and Verdelho wines unless they are accompanying a hot soup. Serve the Bual and Malmsey at cellar temperature (about 55°F [13°C] or slightly warmer in the winter months) with nut-based desserts such as pecan pie, baklava, or chestnut and chocolate cake.

Some of the Best Madeira Producers

Blandy's, Leacock, Cossart Gordon, D'Olivares, and Henriques & Henriques are the major wineries that export to America. Prices range from inexpensive to very expensive for older vintage wines.

ESSEN UND TRINKEN

GERMANY AND AUSTRIA

FINE WINES PERFORM A BALANCING ACT WITH THEIR ACIDITY, ALCOHOL LEVELS, TANNINS, AND FLAVORS. WE LOVE WHITE wines with high acidity and low alcohol. While it is possible to have a 15% alcohol Chardonnay that is balanced, most often they are overwhelming as a beverage, and will compete with, rather than enhance, foods. Even worse, the heat from their alcohol spikes dramatically when paired with spicy foods. *WineWise* readers who love white wines that are refreshing, not too aggressive, and truly food-friendly will benefit from tasting German and Austrian wines.

We choose Riesling more often than Chardonnay when it comes to pairings with Asian, Cajun, and Indian foods or as a drink before dinner. Here is the good news about Rieslings: they offer high acidity, minerality, fairly low alcohol levels, and range from light to medium body and from off-dry to lusciously sweet. *WineWise* readers can plan an entire dinner party using Rieslings, from appetizers through dessert. We are not alone in our love of Riesling wines and there is a true Riesling renaissance in the United States, with many more wine bars and restaurants creating Riesling-paired dinners and promotional events.

Austria's native grapes, particularly the white Gruner Veltliner, are especially expressive and individualistic. Indeed, German and Austrian winemakers offer wine lovers the full range of wine styles, except for the heavy-handed use of oak. For a glimpse of the new and exciting possibilities from a new wave of winemakers in these countries, we will present a survey of their grape types and major growing regions. An important point that we want to emphasize most about the wines of Germany and Austria is that they are not all sweet. Yes, these countries make beautifully structured, even mesmerizing sweet wines, but their dry and off-dry wines are fine expressions of their environment and just as worthy of your consideration.

Austrian and German wine labels use similar terminology. For a better understanding of both wine nations, we suggest that you read the section on Germany before moving on to Austria.

Germany

CLIMATE

As the northern partner in this duo, Germany has always been considered a cool, even cold grape-growing climate. Because of that, Germany has always been associated with lighter, lower-alcohol, more delicate white wines, with very little attention given to red grapes. As we have pointed out in other places in this book, an extreme latitude away from the equator may mean cooler temperatures overall, but it also means longer hours of daylight during the growing season. And it is not just heat that ripens grapes. As long as there is daylight, the vine is working and the grapes are ripening. In the attentive hands of an understanding grape grower, the result is often a more balanced ripeness that will translate into a more harmonious, if delicate, wine. From that simple truth, we move to an inconvenient truth: the world is hotter, and that is affecting climate patterns, including Germany's. It is impossible to say right now what the long-term effects of climate change will be. Ironically, there is the possibility of colder winters that may cause devastating damage to some of the vineyards. But if it is simply a matter of warmer springs, summers, and falls, then we may see a long streak of riper, more alcoholic wines from Germany, as well as the establishment of a serious red wine industry where previously such an idea was unthinkable.

LANGUAGE OF THE LABEL

Historically, German wine labels have been a nightmare for many wine consumers, including Germans. We will not even try to explain the various systems that have been established over the years. We can only encourage astute *WineWise* readers to retain a few German label words and their interpretation.

S. A. Prum uses the brand name Essence for one of its Riesling wines.

Grans-Fassian produces a Riesling from the town of Trittenheim. Courtesy of Grans-Fassian.

WINE NAME

Like all other wine-producing nations, Germany has its fair share of brand-name wines, many of which will be familiar to consumers. Those brands include Clean Slate, Urban, Twisted River, and Saint M still wines. Labels on these wines will always provide regional information, and many will also give the grape variety used.

Away from the safety net of brand names, it is easy to develop a fear of falling when it comes to German wine names. Essentially, they are place names—either a village name, a vineyard name, or a combination of both. As with some other European wine-naming systems, it is sometimes impossible to tell from the label whether the name is a village or a vineyard, but here are a couple hints.

1. If the wine name is two German words, and the first word ends in the letters -*er,* the wine is almost certainly named after a village *and* a vineyard, with the first word being the village reference and the second word being the vineyard. For example, a wine named Piesporter Goldtropfchen comes from a vineyard called Goldtropfchen in the village of Piesport. The wine is a Piesporter just like you might be a New Yorker.

2. If the wine name is one single German-looking word, there is no way from the label to tell if the wine is named for a village (in which case several vineyards might be the source of the grapes) or for one single vineyard. If it is from a single vineyard, probably your only indication will be the higher price.

From the perspective of the consumer, especially the adventurous consumer, the actual village and/or vineyard may be the last details to come to grips with. What are more important are the grape variety and the region, since those bits of information will directly open the window into the soul of the wine.

GRAPE VARIETY

Ninety-nine percent of German wine labels name the grape variety. As mentioned already, Germany has always concentrated on white grape varieties, and of those, the most revered is Riesling. When the climate cooperates, Germany makes superlative Riesling in many different styles, from bone dry through off-dry to lightly sweet and very sweet.

A little rarer are Germany's examples of Gewurztraminer, Pinot Blanc (*Weissburgunder*), Silvaner, and Pinot Gris (*Grauburgunder* or *Rulander*), each providing greater impact of flavors and more body and substance in the wines. If warmer climates do become a fact of life, we can expect to see more of these varieties in the future. The same is true of Pinot Noir (*Spatburgunder*), which is becoming increasingly important in Germany.

DRYNESS AND SWEETNESS LEVELS

Many German producers try to help the consumer by including on the label a notation of the relative dryness or sweetness of the wine. The two possible indications are:

> **TROCKEN**, meaning dry
>
> **HALBTROCKEN**, suggesting off-dry, or a little sweet

A spatlese semi-dry wine produced by Schloss Johannisberg using Riesling grapes grown in the Rheingau region. Courtesy of Schloss Johannisberg.

However, if neither term is on the label, you cannot infer that the wine is sweet; you will just have to try it to find out. That can't be too painful, can it? Special *WineWise* hint: check the alcohol level on the label; if it is over 12.5%, it is probably a dry wine. Lower alcohol levels will indicate that the winemaker or the cold temperature in the cellar stopped the fermentation, leaving residual sugar in the finished wine.

DESIGNATED "QUALITY" LEVELS

WineWise TIP: We describe these quality terms so our readers will be able to decipher a German wine label, but to be honest with you, we just look for German wines labeled "Riesling" and make sure it is a dry or semi-dry wine if it's for sipping or pairing with savory foods. When we have a sweet tooth we can satisfy that with sweet German Rieslings. We think these basic terms provide sufficient information for *WineWise* readers to buy German wines and start enjoying them.

Germany has two levels of "quality" wines:

> **QUALITATSWEIN**, which means "quality wine"
>
> **PRADIKATSWEIN**, usually translated as "quality wine with special attributes."

Pradikat rankings (the "special attributes") are based on sugar levels in the grapes at harvest, not an assessment of the wines after they have been made.

Within the *Pradikatswein* category, the rankings are:

KABINETT, suggesting ripe grapes, based on sugar content; the wine should show ripe but not overripe flavors—there may still be some greenness to the flavors. This is the least sweet style of *Pradikatswein* and these wines can be paired with savory foods.

SPATLESE, suggesting slightly overripe grapes, with fuller fruit flavors. These are semi-dry wines that can be paired with savory foods, and are great choices for lighter spicy, salty, or smoked foods.

AUSLESE, indicating a wine made from specially selected, obviously ripe bunches, giving a wine of solid flavors, complexity, and length. Generally, these are sweet wines that are best paired with dessert.

Note that any of the *Pradikat* designations might also include the label indication of *Trocken* or *Halbtrocken*, which signifies a dry or semi-dry wine. With the subsequent rankings of *Pradikat* listed below, there is so much sugar in the grapes at harvest that the wines will always be sweet.

EISWEIN (ICEWINE), made from grapes frozen on the vine (see page 9).

BEERENAUSLESE, rare and expensive, indicating a concentrated, sweet dessert wine made from very ripe or botrytized grapes.

TROCKENBEERENAUSLESE, extremely rare and expensive, indicating all the grapes were botrytized to make a sinfully rich and decadent dessert wine.

And just to make things a bit more complicated, the following are terms you might look for in some of the best German wines. We include these in the spirit of the best and current information, but we understand these labels take a while to get used to, and if you don't speak German, some of these labels can be exhausting!

SPECIAL *WINEWISE* INSIGHT INTO GERMAN "QUALITY" LEVELS

If you have been wondering why we often put the word quality within quotation marks, you are WineWise beyond your years. Our reason is that the method behind the system is not really about quality at all.

It is true that the grapes for *Qualitatswein* and *Pradikatswein* must be grown within specially designated "quality" wine regions—that is, the grapes cannot be grown just anywhere. But the whole system is really based on sugar levels in the grapes at harvest. In other words, the system is about how ripe (based on sugar content) the grapes are. As we have said all along, true, balanced ripeness is not just about sugar. And just because grapes come to the winemaker with high sugar levels does not mean that the result will be good-quality wine! So with that major caveat in mind, the WineWise consumer needs to interpret the other words that appear on the label.

"GROSSE LAGE" means the finest vineyard site. If the wine is dry and from one of these superb vineyards, it may also include the term *"Grosses Gewachs."*

"ERSTE LAGE" is a fine vineyard site, second-best to a *Grosse Lage* vineyard.

"ORTSWEIN" is a wine from a single village.

"GUTSWEIN" is from a single wine region.

If we were to compare these terms to French Burgundy wines, *Grosse Lage* would be a *grand cru* wine such as Musigny; *Erste Lage* would be a *premier cru* wine such as Chambolle-Musigny "Les Amoureuses," *Ortswein* would be the village of Chambolle-Musigny; *Gutswein* would be the region of Burgundy (see the Burgundy section of the France chapter, page 174).

REGION NAME

For all *Qualitatswein* and *Pradikatswein* products, the label will indicate which region the grapes came from. There are 13 official grape-growing regions for "quality" wine in Germany, but don't fret, the U.S. market rarely sees wines from more than five. The five, in order of presence on the U.S. market, are:

> Mosel (formerly Mosel-Saar-Ruwer)
> Rheinhessen
> Pfalz
> Rheingau
> Nahe

PRICE LEVELS

The relative prices of German wines are certainly a reflection of availability and the integrity of the producer. Within any one category of wine, there will be price variation. But for the most part, the relative bargains are to be found in the brand-name wines and at the *Qualitatswein* and

Kabinett levels. *Spatlese* and *Auslese* wines will be moderately expensive to expensive, while the truly expensive group includes the three dessert wine rankings (*Beerenauslese*, *Eiswein*, and *Trockenbeerenauslese*).

Since any one producer will often make a range of wines covering several rankings from the same region, even from the same village or vineyard, our comments in the regional section will include listings of reputable producers without any indication of expense, unless there is something particularly noteworthy.

REGIONS

MOSEL

For decades this region has produced the archetypal German Rieslings—floral, delicate, lightly perfumed wines that walk a razor-thin line between acidity and sweetness while providing vibrant, fresh citric fruit flavors like a burst of lime sorbet. These wines are so well balanced that we never really notice that they are sweet or searingly high in acidity. Like a magnificent monarch butterfly, they bring great pleasure, and yet they are elusive, hard to pin down.

What makes all this possible is the sacred combination of climate, soil, and topography in the three river valleys that contain the Mosel, Saar, and Ruwer rivers. The rest of the magic lies in the steep river valleys that provide dramatic examples of south-facing slopes with slate as a major component of the soil. In many places, even the topsoil is slate. The delicacy of such wines makes them perfect as an aperitif, a before-dinner drink to whet the appetite. However, do not dismiss them as food wines. The foods would have to be delicately prepared, but Mosel wines work particularly well with lightly poached or lightly smoked seafood items. They are also the perfect choice for moderately spicy foods, especially Indian, Thai, Vietnamese, and Szechuan or Hunan Chinese dishes.

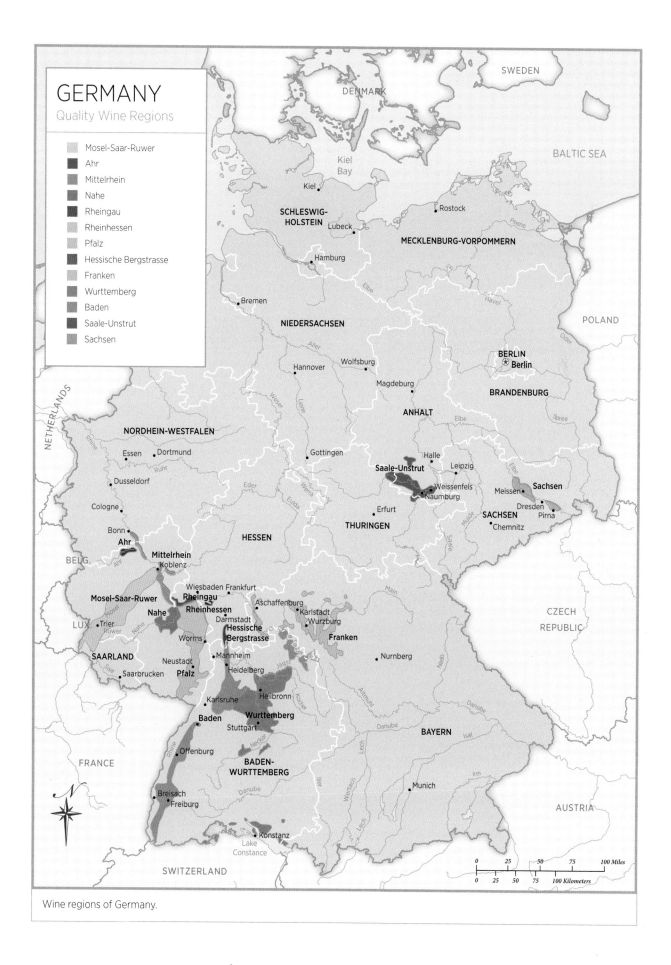

Wine regions of Germany.

The village of Trittenheim on the Mosel River is surrounded on all sides by vineyards.

NOTABLE PRODUCERS ARE NUMEROUS. WE PARTICULARLY RECOMMEND THE FOLLOWING

Fritz Haag, Willi Haag, Reinhold Haart, Johannishof, Keller, Reichsgraf von Kesselstatt, Kuhling-Gillot, Schloss-Lieser, Dr. Loosen, Egon Muller, von Othegraven, J. J. Prum, Dr. Lipphold, Selbach-Oster, Dr. H. Thanisch, and St. Urbans-Hof.

As we have mentioned before, the relatively light, green nature of wines from this region is reflected in the tradition of using green bottles. The wines from the regions discussed below have traditionally been marketed in brown bottles, reflecting their fuller body and riper fruit flavors.

RHEINHESSEN

The region of Rheinhessen has been making noise lately, and a very pleasant noise it is, created by the hard work and creative dynamism of a new generation of winemakers.

First, it has to be said that there has always been a handful of highly reputable producers of very fine wines from vineyards around the village of Nierstein in the northeast corner of the region. Perched high above the Rhine River on east- and southeast-facing slopes, the wines from these vineyards project the ripeness of apricots and peaches as well as the minerality of the red sandstone that is clearly visible in that sacred enclave. Our advice would be never pass up the opportunity to taste or buy a Niersteiner (that's a wine from Nierstein, right?), especially if the vineyards involved are Holle, Hipping, Pettenthal, Paterberg, or Bruckchen.

But in the rest of this very large region, it is the sheer determination of the new mavericks who have turned their back on the ubiquitous and easy Muller-Thurgau and sought out special pockets of vineyard land suited to particular grapes. In addition, they are farming the vineyards completely with an eye to quality, restricting the yield per vine. The results, in some cases, have been nothing short of astounding—with Riesling, to be sure, but also with the underappreciated Silvaner grape and the previously untried Sauvignon Blanc.

NOTABLE PRODUCERS INCLUDE

Bruder Dr. Becker, Groebe, Gunderloch, Heyl Zu Herrnsheim, Keller, Kuhling-Gillot, Villa Sachsen, Geschwister Scuch, Wagner-Stempel, Schloss Westerhaus, Winter, and Wittman.

PFALZ

Of the five regions we discuss here, Pfalz is the warmest on a regular basis, as evidenced by the frequent sightings of lemons and figs growing in various places throughout the region. Consequently, the wines show a good deal more ripe fruit character, even tropical fruit, creating a warm glow in the drinker, balanced by a good zip of acidity to bring us back to reality. Riesling is the most important grape here, especially in the more favored vineyard locations, but other grapes such as Gewurztraminer and the *drei* Pinots (Blanc, Gris, and Noir) have gained some ground and are drawing increased attention.

The solid mouthfeel that these wines present, along with their fuller, clean flavors and high acidity, all make them especially well suited to the table. They make excellent accompaniments to whole roasted or fried fish or roast chicken, turkey, or pork, especially if those dishes include a spicy fruit note. But they are also very versatile, working well with the milder spice notes of biryani or masala dishes from India or the spicy peanut cuisine from Thailand or Korea.

SOME OF OUR FAVORITE PRODUCERS INCLUDE

Basserman-Jordan, Burklin-Wolf, von Buhl, and Pfeffingen-Fuhrmann-Eymael.

RHEINGAU

Mosel wines perform their incredibly delicate balancing act that always makes them attractive; Pfalz wines can be deeply satisfying; but there is something spiritual, almost religious, about a good Rheingau—an exquisite marriage of clean, lean, laser-like fruit with a stony, mineral edge that is simply uplifting. The Rheingau area specializes almost completely in Riesling, made in a dry, austere style that is definitely a reflection of south-facing slopes and the red slate, sandstone, and schist soils. Fine Rheingau Riesling, whether dry or slightly sweet, is such a classically elegant wine that it really demands a classic dish such as perfectly

A cliff of Riesling vineyards at the western end of the Rheingau region.

cooked Dover sole, lobster thermidor, or roast goose (often served on holidays in Germany).

The Schloss Vollrads estate has been making fine Riesling wines since 1211; Schloss Johannisberg estate for more than 900 years, and uses colored capsules on their bottle necks to indicate the level of sweetness in their wines. The color code is yellow for Qualitatswein, red for Kabinett, green for Spatlese, pink for Auslese, pink-gold for Beerenauslese, gold for Trockenbeerenauslese, and blue for Eiswein. Wines from both these estates are complex, long lived, expensive, and well worth seeking out.

PRIME PRODUCERS IN RHEINGAU INCLUDE

Robert Weil, Georg Breuer, Verwaltung der Staatsweinguter Eltville (whose vineyards include the historic Kloster Eberbach), Schloss Johannisberg, Weingut Johannishof Eser, Freiherr zu Knyphausen, Balthasar Ress, Schloss Vollrads, and Domdechant Werner.

NAHE

Until recently, Nahe wines have not been much admired in the United States, perhaps because Mosel, Rheinhessen, Pfalz, and Rheingau are so

The messenger whose tardiness resulted in rotten grapes at the Johannisberg estate (see below).

much more famous and thus more marketable. But there are gems to be had here, especially if you can find some Riesling from the villages of Bad Kreuznach, Schlossbockelheim, or their nearby neighbors. These villages lie about midpoint on the Nahe River as it winds its way in a particularly snaky slither northeastward to Bad Kreuznach. Here the volcanic soils give Riesling from the best (south-facing) vineyards a healthy dose of hard minerality that seems to perfectly set off the riper apricot and peach notes of this noble grape.

Farther north, the landscape begins to flatten out as the Nahe flows toward its confluence with the Rhine at the city of Bingen. Although not as well known as the wines of the central Nahe, increased plantings of the tricolor of Pinot grape varieties (Noir, Blanc, and Gris) may bring greater fame in the future.

PREFERRED NAHE PRODUCERS INCLUDE

Dr. Crusius, Diel, Emrich-Schonleber, Donnhoff, Kruger-Rumpf, Prinz zu Salm-Dalberg, and Tesch.

THE "DISCOVERY" OF THE JOYS OF ROT

Today, botrytis-affected grapes produce luscious dessert wines in Germany *(trockenbeerenauslese)*, France (Sauternes), Hungary (Tokaji), and many other wine regions. In particular, Schloss Johannisberg in Germany has a unique story describing the origin of these distinctively delicious wines. According to Johannisberg legend, back in the eighteenth century the beginning of the grape harvest had to be approved by the local bishop, a prominent lord and landowner. Although the customary courier was sent off to the bishop's domain as usual, his return was somehow delayed, and the polite but puzzled grape growers refused to pick without permission. With the delayed return of the messenger, the grapes began to rot, much to the dismay of the growers, but still they held off. On the return of the courier, harvesting of the rotten grapes began, and the hapless growers let the fermentation proceed, only to "discover" the glories of wine made from grapes that had shriveled due to the onset of the mold.

Austria

AUSTRIA HAS EMERGED AS A scintillating wine personality of the twenty-first century, based primarily on its commitment to quality and its unabashed promotion of some unusual grape varieties. Some of the intriguing newcomers on the wine scene are first and foremost Gruner Veltliner (white) and Zweigelt, Blaufrankisch, and St. Laurent (reds). If you have not tried these gems so far, we encourage you warmly and heartily to get out there and do so. Riesling as well as some lesser-known grape varieties also produce delightful Austrian wines.

The Austrian grape-growing regions boast a variety of climates that allow for the full expression of these grape varieties and in a dry style, as well as some of the most highly sought-after sweet dessert Rieslings in the world.

LANGUAGE OF THE LABEL

Like German wine labels, Austrian versions are immediately consumer-friendly because they specify the grape type prominently. They also provide information about which growing region the grapes are from, and they use a very similar system of "quality" designation (note the quotation marks again) based on sugar levels at harvest. Occasionally there are also dryness or sweetness descriptions.

WINE NAME

Some Austrian producers stress the grape variety as the wine name, while others use the village and/or vineyard method that is also used in Germany (see pages 265–266). Even if the wine is named for the place (region, village, or vineyard), the grape variety will also be indicated.

GRAPE VARIETY

Currently the two most frequently seen Austrian wines in the U.S. market are both white: Riesling and Gruner Veltliner. In a broad sense, Austrian

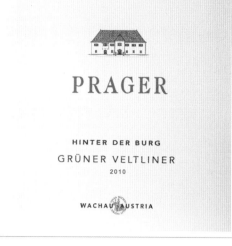

Label showing the district name of Wachau. Courtesy of Weingut Prager.

Riesling has some similarities to the various German versions, ranging from steely, nervy minerality with green citrus fruit to rich, luscious, and very sweet—there really is something for everybody. But Gruner Veltliner is a world unto itself, like stumbling into an exotic Moroccan market in the middle of Fifth Avenue—slightly musky, perfumed, but always fresh, even prickly, with an Asian pear flavor and background of spicy white pepper.

The three Pinots—Pinot Noir (Spatburgunder), Pinot Blanc (Weissburgunder), and Pinot Gris (Grauburgunder or Rulander)—are making something of a splash here, and may even win acclaim as the climate picture continues to change. And there are a few old faithfuls in the guise of Chardonnay (Morillon), Sauvignon Blanc, Cabernet Sauvignon, and Merlot. As always, the latter two are sometimes made as single-varietal wines, but more often they are blended. Significantly, about one-third of Austria's wine production is now dedicated to red wine, and some of the real excitement lies in the well-made but little-known reds that Austria has embraced as its own—Saint Laurent, Blaufrankisch, and Zweigelt.

DRYNESS AND SWEETNESS LEVELS

The use of the terms *Trocken* and *Halbtrocken* have the same meaning as in Germany, dry and semi-dry, while the additional term *Halbsuss* will indicate semi-sweet, which would be noticeably sweeter than *Halbtrocken.*

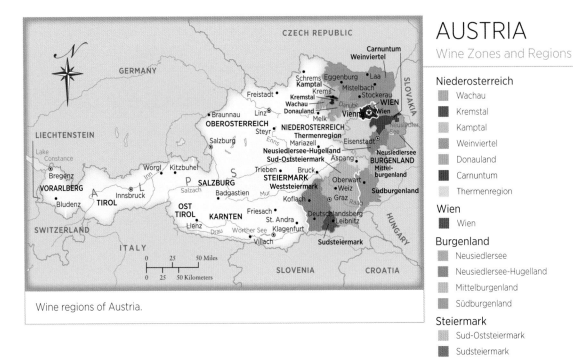

AUSTRIA
Wine Zones and Regions

Niederosterreich
- Wachau
- Kremstal
- Kamptal
- Weinviertel
- Donauland
- Carnuntum
- Thermenregion

Wien
- Wien

Burgenland
- Neusiedlersee
- Neusiedlersee-Hugelland
- Mittelburgenland
- Südburgenland

Steiermark
- Sud-Oststeiermark
- Sudsteiermark
- Weststeiermark

Wine regions of Austria.

DESIGNATED "QUALITY" LEVELS

Once again we are dealing with words on the label that convey an indication of "quality," though the words themselves are a direct reflection of sugar levels in the grapes at harvest. The system is the same as the German (see pages 266–267), with these two differences:

KABINETT: In Austria, *Kabinett* is not a ranking within the *Pradikat* system but is its own category, above *Qualitatswein* but below the *Pradikat* level.

AUSBRUCH: This is an additional ranking of sugar ripeness between *Beerenauslese* and *Trockenbeerenauslese*.

PLACE NAME

Austrian labels are almost obsessive about indicating the place where the grapes were grown. There are three large regions (Niederosterreich, Burgenland, and Styria), and each of these has smaller districts within them. If all of the grapes came from one of these smaller districts, that name will be indicated on the label. The most important and most frequently seen district names are Kamptal, Kremstal, and Wachau, all contained within the Niederosterreich region.

PRICE LEVELS

Given the quality and discovery factor surrounding Austrian wines, they are remarkably affordable. In addition to the *Qualitatswein* level, the Austrian *Kabinett* wines and some of the *Pradikatswein* will easily qualify as only moderately expensive if not relative bargains. As always, once you ascend to the dizzy heights of limited-production Icewine or botrytis-affected wines, the price will soar to the truly expensive level. There are some producers whose wines are rare and highly sought after and are therefore very expensive across the board.

REGIONS

NIEDEROSTERREICH (LOWER AUSTRIA)

With its holy trinity of the subdistricts Kamptal, Kremstal, and Wachau, this region commands a lot of attention around the world, especially for its dry versions of Riesling and Gruner Veltliner. The aromatic emphases of stone fruits and hard mineral edge are truly revelatory, and any one of the dry wines would be a valid candidate for some serious aging. Don't pass by any opportunity to try a dry version from any one of these districts, especially if the wine is from a single vineyard such as Heiligenstein. Be prepared to be transported.

If you would like food to enter that ethereal picture, imagine the Riesling with poached turbot or a dish with white asparagus and crawfish, and the Gruner Veltliner with pork medallions with spaetzle in a light tarragon cream sauce, or a Thai green curry scallop or tofu dish—equally out of this world.

We should also point out that when climatic conditions permit, the prized vineyards of these districts produce extraordinary dessert styles of Riesling that exhibit a purity of flavor that is hard to comprehend. It's like having a lifetime of good Riesling in a single glass.

One note about label terminology: the Wachau district retains slightly different terms on its labels, as indicated here:

Qualitatswein = *Steinfeder*
Kabinett = *Federspiel*
Spatlese = *Smaragd*

Further south, in the district of Thermenregion, there is a greater concentration on the red varieties of Pinot Noir and St. Laurent, the new *noir* in Austrian wine, and, for some, a viable alternative to Pinot Noir with similar characteristics. Of the two, St. Laurent tends to be a little fuller in body if treated well in the vineyard and winery, but both display what might be thought of as a New World profile—bright red to dark red fruit character, a little spiciness of black pepper, and an edge of earthy exotica. As such, they work well with dishes such as lamb kebabs or mushroom risotto.

Well-respected producers in this region include F. X. Pichler, Prager (both producers of some very expensive wines, but they are well worth it), Brundlmayer, Nigl, Lenz Moser, Weinrieder, Loimer, and Alzinger.

BURGENLAND

As a much warmer region, Burgenland concentrates more on red wines and white dessert wines—indeed, many authorities would cite the village of Rust in Burgenland as the mecca for sweet dessert white wine. The vineyards here seem to have no problem producing fully ripe grapes that have elevated sugar levels but also retain high levels of acidity to provide balance in the finished wines.

For reds, the plantings include Zweigelt and Blaufrankisch (known as Limberger or Lemberger in other places, including Washington State), as well as the international varieties of Cabernet Sauvignon, Merlot, and Syrah. Of the two native varieties, the Blaufrankisch produces a fuller, darker wine with firm tannins and high acidity, a bit like the Barbera wines of Piedmont in Italy (see page 209), while the Zweigelt is closer to the Beaujolais wines of France (see pages 181–183). Reputable producers in Burgenland include Kracher, Opitz (both almost entirely sweet wine production, very expensive and very much worth it), Wenzel, Tremmel, Umathum, Krutzler, Braunstein, Schrock, and Igler.

STEIERMARK (STYRIA)

This most southerly of the regions is home mostly to white grapes, especially Sauvignon Blanc, Chardonnay (sometimes labeled as Morillon), Pinot Blanc (Weissburgunder), and Pinot Gris (Grauburgunder). In that regard, this is an area to look for if you have been invited to a tasting or dinner and asked to bring a Sauvignon Blanc or Chardonnay. How much more fun to show up with a Styrian version rather than the too familiar New World regulars! Look for them and try them—you may find a winner. Some of these will likely come from one of the following producers: Polz, Domane Muller, Wohlmuth, Sattler, Koller, and Platzer.

13

UP AND COMING

CANADA AND GREECE

WHILE THERE ARE MANY COUNTRIES AND WINE REGIONS THAT MAKE SOME VERY GOOD WINES, NOT ALL OF THEM HAVE an important presence in the U.S. market. For example, the wines of Israel, Lebanon, Hungary, Mexico, and Uruguay are all available, but on a nationwide basis, representation on store shelves and wine lists can be spotty. Likewise, good wines from Michigan, Idaho, Texas, and Pennsylvania, among many other U.S. states, are not always available outside of local or regional markets.

There are several potentially "up-and-coming" wine regions that are drawing attention in the wine world. China is now the world's fifth-largest wine producer, while the Eastern European nations of Slovenia, Croatia, and Hungary offer distinctive wines that are often undervalued.

As climate change begins to impact the global wine industry, cooler regions such as southern England are producing fine wines—especially sparkling wines.

Mexico, India, Thailand, and Japan all have growing wine industries. Clearly, the global wine market is ripe for exploration.

We've identified two countries—Canada and Greece—as up and coming in the U.S. wine markets. We like these wines a lot and encourage you to give them a try. The quality is good to great, they are a pleasure to drink with a good meal, and the prices are reasonable.

Canada: cool wines with finesse

QUALITY CANADIAN WINES FIRST CAME on the scene in the 1970s. Today, there are more than 300 wineries making fine wines. With so many wine-producing nations competing for your attention and affection, Canada is probably not the first country that comes to mind. But if you believe the maxim that "less is more," then you should be checking out Canadian wines, eh?

First, a clarification: when we say "less is more," we are referring to the fact that most Canadian wines are neither high in alcohol nor full-bodied and heavily oaked. This means that when it comes to wine and food pairing, the wines coexist with rather than dominate a dish. Just like most Canadian people, the nation's wines can finesse difficult situations with equanimity. *WineWise* readers will also discover that there are many Canadian wines that offer great value.

Due to cool growing conditions in Canada, wine grapes retain a high level of acidity, which translates to mouthwatering, food-friendly wines with bright fruit flavors. Still and sparkling Rieslings—whether dry, semi-dry, or sweet—are racy and luscious. Graceful Chardonnays and elegant Pinot Gris wines round out our list of best bets. You'll note that these are the same grapes found in the Burgundy, Alsace, and Champagne regions of northern France, but the Canadian vineyards are blessed with more sunshine hours than those European regions. Most of the vineyards are planted close to bodies of water, which helps to moderate any extremes in temperature.

Chardonnay, Pinot Gris, Pinot Blanc, Sauvignon Blanc, Semillon, and Gewurztraminer are the principal white varieties planted in Canada's vineyards, while most of the red wines are based on Pinot Noir, Gamay, Syrah, Merlot, Cabernet Sauvignon, and Cabernet Franc. In this chapter we will suggest several of our favorite producers of these grape types. Some of these wines are easy-drinking examples for every day; others have that special something that merits your attention.

In this latter category, look no further than the pinnacle of Canadian wines, Icewine. Icewine may be the greatest dessert wine around, and Canada is the world's largest producer of it. It is made by gently pressing grapes that have been naturally frozen on the vine. The frozen water remains behind, yielding a few drops of concentrated nectar from each grape. Icewines have a mouthwatering acidity that balances out their sweetness; as a result, they are never cloying and always alluring. They are usually sold in half bottles for $40 to $75 retail—pretty reasonable considering how little juice is taken from each berry.

LANGUAGE OF THE LABEL

Hooray! You do not have to take a wine course to understand Canadian wine labels. Most are labeled by varietal, which means that, by Canadian law, the wine contains at least 85% of the grape type named on the label. You may also encounter some fantasy- or proprietary-named wines, such as "Oculus" by Mission Hill winery.

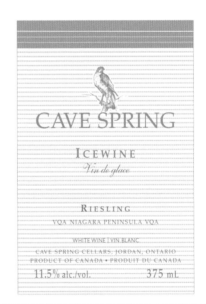

Icewine is truly a treasure. These low-alcohol wines offer bright acidity and layers of white fruit flavors. Enjoy a glass as a refreshing end to a meal or with simple desserts such as a pear tart. Courtesy of Cave Spring Cellars.

Estate Bottled

CAVE SPRING

RIESLING
VQA BEAMSVILLE BENCH VQA
CAVE SPRING VINEYARD
CAVE SPRING CELLARS, JORDAN, ONTARIO, CANADA

Riesling may be our favorite white grape. Cave Spring makes a lean, clean, fruity wine we enjoy on its own or with a variety of ethnic foods (see "Eat/Drink/Man/Woman: Wine and Food," pages 294–324). The grapes for this wine were grown in the Beamsville Bench subregion of the Niagara Peninsula DVA. Courtesy of Cave Spring Cellars.

ORIGIN OF THE WINE

If a Designated Viticultural Area, or DVA (such as Niagara Peninsula), appears on the label, a minimum of 85% of the grapes must come from that area. Aside from the hybrid white grape Vidal, which is used for some Icewines, all DVA wines must be made exclusively from *Vitis vinifera* grapes (the good stuff) planted within that DVA. The label term "Estate-Bottled" guarantees that the grapes for the wine were grown in vineyards owned or controlled by the winery and that the grapes are 100% vinifera.

NOTE: Look for the Vintners Quality Alliance (VQA) sticker on the labels of Canadian wines. It's your assurance that 100% of the wine comes from the province listed on the label.

THE MAJOR WINE REGIONS OF CANADA

Although a small amount of wine (as well as some delicious dessert ice apple ciders) is produced in Quebec and other provinces, in this chapter we will focus on the two provinces that produce the most wine, Ontario and British Columbia.

ONTARIO

IMPORTANT DVA WINE REGIONS

Lake Erie North Shore

Pelee Island

Niagara Peninsula (subregions such as "Beamsville Bench," within the Niagara Peninsula, may also be listed on labels)

About 80% of Canadian wines come from the province of Ontario; the vineyards that produce grapes for fine wine are in the southern portion of the province. Perhaps you have a mental picture of vast, snowy fields. In actuality, this is not the frozen tundra. It is part of a temperate zone known as the Carolinian Forest that stretches south to the Carolinas in the United States.

The climate in Ontario is comparable to that of Oregon or New Zealand; in fact, the Chianti vineyards of central Italy and those of the Niagara region are at the same latitude, the forty-third parallel. Here, the ambient temperature of the vineyards is impacted by their proximity to Lake Ontario and Lake Erie. In the spring, warm air rises from the land, drawing in cool air from the lakes. In the winter, the reverse is true: warm air from the lake rises, drawing in cool air from the land. This natural circulation system protects the vines from extreme temperatures.

The cool conditions allow the wineries to produce pure varietal wines that offer a direct expression of the vineyards' personality or *terroir*. Another benefit of the cool temperatures is high acidity levels, which extend the life of the wines.

It is this acidity that makes Canadian wines such good food wines. Consider Ontario Chardonnays, with their characteristic flavors of green apple and pear. Though medium-bodied when unadorned by oak, they become full-bodied when fermented or aged in oak. Try one with grilled swordfish with lemon butter and capers or even corn on the cob. What about fruity, light- to medium-bodied wines with a hint of sweetness?

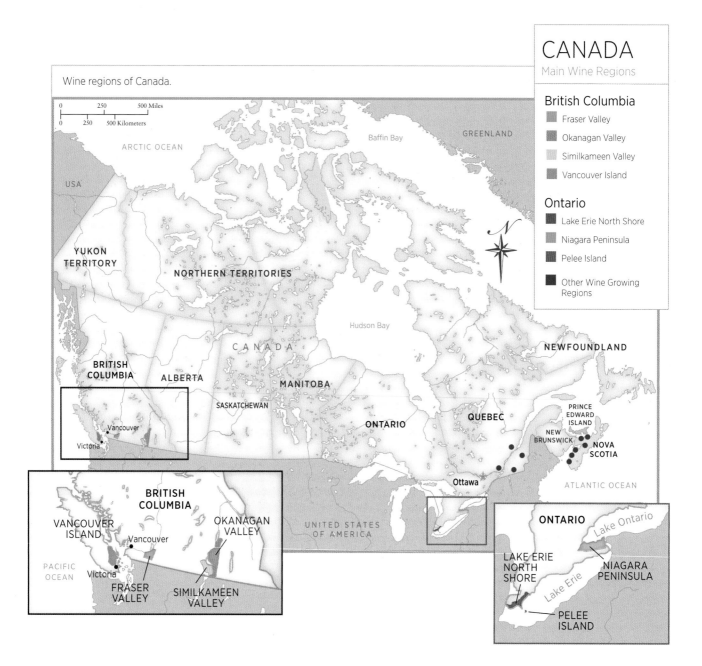

Wine regions of Canada.

CANADA
Main Wine Regions

British Columbia
Fraser Valley
Okanagan Valley
Similkameen Valley
Vancouver Island

Ontario
Lake Erie North Shore
Niagara Peninsula
Pelee Island

Other Wine Growing Regions

Chenin Blanc, Gewurztraminer, and semi-dry Riesling wines may be used to contrast spicy, smoked, or salty foods. The hint of sweetness in these wines may also be used as a complement for dishes such as potato latkes or pork chops with apple sauce or a green papaya salad. The late harvest and Icewine versions of Riesling are even richer and more complex. Flavors of honey, lychee nut, pineapple, and tropical fruits such as guava are retained by pairing these wines with a simple pound cake or apple pie. Of course, Icewines also can be enjoyed solo, as a "liquid dessert."

This province also produces a number of lovely reds. Elegant Pinot Noirs show all the bright red cherry, strawberry, and raspberry flavors you expect in their youth, taking on additional notes of mushrooms and tea with age. A perfectly grilled salmon steak with chopped tomatoes makes a lovely complement. The Beaujolais grape, Gamay, does well in Niagara, producing light-bodied, cherry-flavored wines with less complexity than Pinot Noir but at more affordable prices. Gamays are a good match for Prince Edward Island mussels marinara. Cabernet Franc, a better choice for the climate than Cabernet Sauvignon, is also worth seeking out. The wine is medium to full in body, with charming red and/or black cherry flavors that showcase simply seasoned grilled red meats.

The Niagara Escarpment protects many of Ontario's vineyards from cold northern winds. Courtesy of Cave Spring Cellars.

In 1974, Inniskillin was the first Canadian winery to be established since Prohibition. From the beginning, the founding team of Donald Ziraldo and Karl Kaiser focused on high quality rather than quantity. When their 1989 Vidal Icewine won a prestigious Grand Prize of Honor in a 1991 competition in France, it caught the attention of wine lovers around the world. Inniskillin continues to be one of the nation's finest wineries, and we recommend its full line of wines. Another pioneer winery of the region is Cave Spring. Owned by the Penachetti family, Cave Spring was the first Canadian winery to emphasize gastronomy by opening a fine-dining restaurant, the Inn on the Twenty, at the winery. We enjoy its entire range of wines, especially when accompanied by food.

Most of Ontario's dry and semi-dry wines are inexpensive to moderately priced; some of the finer reds cost more, and the dessert-style late harvest and Icewines are always expensive.

In general, we believe Ontario excels with its white wines and lighter-style reds. If you are searching for full-bodied Canadian reds, then British Columbia can fill that bill.

We trust *WineWise* readers to be adventurous and seek out some of these flavorful wines. If you are traveling to Canada's largest city (Toronto) or to nearby Buffalo in New York State, you are within striking distance of the country's scenic wine regions.

UNTIL THEN, HERE ARE SOME WINERIES WE SUGGEST:

Cave Spring, Inniskillin, Le Clos Jordanne, Thirty Bench, Vineland Estates, Chateau des Charmes, Angel's Gate, Featherstone, Charles Baker, 2027 Cellars, Fielding, Flat Rock, Hillebrand Trius, Henry of Pelham, Hinterland, Creekside, Birchwood, Magnotta, Konzelmann Estate, Lailey, Peller, Thomas and Vaughan, 13th Street, Bachelder, Pearl Morissette, Norman Hardie, Malivoire, Peninsula Ridge, Southbrook, Tawse, Hidden Bench, Five Rows, and Vineland Estates.

BRITISH COLUMBIA

IMPORTANT DVA WINE REGIONS

Okanagan Valley

Similkameen Valley

Fraser Valley

Gulf Islands

Vancouver Island

The scenic beauty of the Coastal Mountains, Pacific Ocean, and verdant valleys make British Columbia an ideal place to live or tour. In fact, some of Canada's finest wines are produced in this province's vineyards. As in Ontario, it is the temperature-moderating effect of nearby water—in this case, the Pacific Ocean or Lake Okanagan—that aids the vines in achieving balanced ripeness in the grapes. Similar to their southern neighbor Washington, this province's diverse temperature zones and soils allows wineries the opportunity to plant a great diversity of grape varieties.

The wine scene in British Columbia is vibrant. New investments have brought more competition and wines to choose from, and as a result, the number of wineries has grown from 14 in 1980 to more than 100 today. As established wineries gain wisdom from working their land and the vines mature, quality will continue to improve. The diversity of restaurants and the high quality of local foods offers opportunities for wineries to offer more than just "vanilla" and "chocolate" (Chardonnay and Cabernet) to accompany the foods.

The region's vineyards are about equally split with white and red grapes. Ninety-seven percent are planted with the finest *Vitis vinifera* varieties; the balance is planted with hybrids. The comment "elegant" continually pops up in our tasting notes of BC wines. Leading the pack of our favorite whites are Pinot Gris and Chardonnay, followed by Pinot Blanc, Riesling, Gewurztraminer, and Sauvignon Blanc. Dry, medium- to full-bodied Pinot Gris has the structure to showcase roasted chicken, lobster, or mushroom risotto. Or try a tart, juicy Sauvignon Blanc with raw oysters, another wonderful—and classic—pairing. Want to try something off the beaten path? Ehrenfelser, a Riesling cross, is made in semi-dry to sweet styles. Our go-to red is the cool-climate-friendly Pinot Noir; we also like the Cabernet Sauvignon, Merlot, and (as in the United States) Bordeaux-style "Meritage" blends of the two. Syrah, which most folks consider to be a warm-region grape, also does very well in British Columbia. Pair one of the region's Pinot Noirs with a gorgeous, meaty piece of fish—tuna, black cod, or salmon are all good choices. The full-bodied "Meritage" Bordeaux-style blends have the weight to stand up to wild game such as venison. Finally, full-bodied, peppery Syrah is a perfect complement for peppercorn-crusted steak—or, if you're slightly more adventurous, venison chops or a wild game stew.

Within the five DVAs of British Columbia there are subregions, each with its own distinct character. The Okanagan Valley, for example, is sheltered from rain by mountains. The low rainfall forces the vines to dig deep into the soil for moisture, and the resulting wines have an attractive mineral flavor.

As in Ontario, prices of British Columbia wines range from inexpensive to moderate, with some of the noble red wines costing more and the dessert wines being the most expensive selections.

SOME SUGGESTED WINERIES:

Sumac Ridge, Osoyoos Larose, Gehringer Brothers, Jackson-Triggs, Nk'Mip, Burrowing Owl, Cedar Creek, Mission Hill, Calona Vineyard, Laughing Stock, Stag's Hollow, Tinhorn Creek, Township 7, Joie, Mount Boucherie, Quails' Gate, Road 13, Dirty Laundry, Kettle Valley, Gray Monk, Thornhaven, Wild Goose, Blue Mountain, Lake Breeze, Mystic River, Blasted Church, Red Rooster, Sandhill, Stoneboat, Tantalas, Orofino, Herder, Pentage, Black Hill, Hawthorne Mountain, Poplar Grove, Quinta Ferreira, Synchromesh, 8th Generation, Fort Beerens, La Frenz, Cassini, Hester Creek, Nichol, Therapy, Bella, Sumerhill, See Ya Later, Meyer Family, Le Vieux Pin, Painted Rock, and Marichel.

Greece: wines of antiquity and wines for today

WINE HAS ALWAYS BEEN IMPORTANT to Greek culture. The Greeks have been getting together to drink wine, party, and exchange opinions at symposia since the seventh century B.C. They were also the first to develop and record organized vineyard strategies and fermentation methods, and in fact their farming, winemaking, and storage methods were adopted by the

Romans. Wine was integral to the country's religious ceremonies, whether Christian, Jewish, or pagan. And perhaps most telling of all, the Greeks named a god after the wonderful liquid: Dionysus, the god of wine and merriment. Throughout Greek culture, wine was and is food for the body, mind, and soul.

This chapter will take *WineWise* readers beyond the world of Retsina and other rustic wines served in *tavernas*. We want to turn you on to the pleasures of sharing food and Greek wines with friends and loved ones.

Are *you* ready to break free and venture outside the mainstream? Because here's the skinny: Greece is making some killer wines! A host of ambitious winemakers, many of whom studied and/or worked overseas, have brought back knowledge and techniques that have allowed the country to take giant steps forward. Advances in vineyard management and winemaking have resulted in wines of good value and distinction. Today, both traditional and "new wave" wines are being made from indigenous and international grape varieties.

THE GRAPES OF GREECE

Are you ready to go off the beaten path and taste wines made from uniquely Greek grapes? We give a *WineWise* thumbs up to the five native grape types most easy to find and the most exciting to drink. Ask for Assyrtiko, Malagousia, and Moschofilero for white wines and Xinomavro and Agiorgitiko for red wines and you are well on your way to being a Greek wine expert (don't worry about pronunciation; just give them a try)! With these five grapes you'll be on your way to drinking sparkling, white, rosé, and red Greek wines that will inspire you to turn your friends on to distinctive wines that are sensibly priced. Now that you are in the comfort zone with these grapes, there are a few others indigenous varieties we can suggest as well. If you are comfy with Chard and Cab, no worries. You can find those grapes and other international varieties being made in Greece as well.

Here are descriptions of some of the most important grape varieties of Greece:

THE REDS

Xinomavro. The finest grape of northern Greece. The name translates as "acid black," which is also a good indication of the grape's tart and tannic nature. Wines based on this grape have aromas and flavors of black pepper, blackberries, black olives, nuts, spices, and tobacco. When Xinomavro is aged there are smells and flavors of sun-dried tomato, mushrooms, and olives. In the Naoussa and Amyndeo regions producers make single-variety wines. In Rapsani and Goumenissa, Xinomavro is the dominant grape in blended wines. Wines from any of these four regions are worth seeking out.

Agiorgitiko. The most-planted red grape in Greece, it produces dry wines than can be anywhere from light- to full-bodied. Moderately priced versions offer aromas and flavors of black currant, strawberry, cherry, and plum. Some delightful dry rosé wines are based on Agiorgitiko as well.

Mavrodaphne. This "black laurel" grape is used in blended dry wines to contribute dark color and blackberry flavors. When used to make sweet wines such as Mavrodaphne of Patras, it has a rich flavor of raisins, honey, and walnuts.

Mandelaria. Supplies lots of color and tannins as well as some acidity to blended wines. The blackberry-scented grape is used in the rosés and reds of such regions as Rhodes and Santorini.

Mavrotagano. The name translates as "black and crisp" as a reference to its color, tannins, and high acidity. As a single-variety dry red wine from the island of Santorini it offers mineral, spice, and black fruits smells and flavors.

GREECE
Wine Regions

1 Côtes de Meliton
2 Naoussa
3 Amyndeo
4 Goumenissa
5 Rapsani
6 Aghialos
7 Zitsa
8 Messenikolas
9 Nemea
10 Mantinia
11 Patra
12 Cephalonia
13 Limnos
14 Samos
15 Paros
16 Santorini
17 Rhodos
18 Peza
19 Dafnes
20 Archanes
21 Sitia

Wine regions of Greece.

THE WHITES

Assyrtiko. This is the principal grape grown on the island of Santorini, where it is used to make dry, ageworthy wines and sweet Vinsantos, both of which are high in acidity. Pure, young wines fermented in stainless steel have discreet aromas of white pepper, ocean, mineral, citrus, and pear and are light in body. Barrel-aged versions will be medium- to full-bodied. Wine lovers who cherish minerality in their white wines need to try Assyrtiko! On its own or with food, Assyrtiko will get you hooked on Greek wines.

Moschofilero. Seductive rose petal, honey, and ginger aromas are typically followed by tropical fruit flavors and a good balance of acidity. Sparkling, white, and rosé versions are available.

Malagousia. This white grape has similar floral and tropical fruit flavors as Moschofilero but can also offer citrus, celery, and basil aromas as well.

Muscat. If Greece is the birthplace of wine, this might be considered a native variety. Many historians suggest that Muscat was *the* original vinifera and that all of the fine grape varieties used today are its descendants. Regardless of its history, this grape produces highly aromatic wines that are more often sweet than dry. The heady smell of orange blossoms and honey is usually followed by richness on the palate.

Robola. Produces wines with notes of lemon, green melon, and minerality on the island of Cephalonia.

Savatiano. The most widely planted white grape in Greece is a major component of Retsina wines. Savatiano is occasionally used to make good, medium-bodied wines with orange aromas, but it needs a blending partner to supply acidity.

Vilana. Grown in Crete, it produces crisp, dry wines with green apple flavors.

THE LANGUAGE OF THE LABEL

Greek table wines may be labeled in a variety of ways:

> by grape name, such as Assyrtiko
>
> by place name, such as Nemea (a dry red) or Santorini (a dry white)
>
> by grape and place name
>
> by fantasy or proprietary name

Sparkling wines use the ubiquitous terms to denote dryness or sweetness, such as brut. Some wineries label their sparkling wines with a fantasy or proprietary name, such as "Ode Panos" by Domaine Spiropoulos.

Currently, Greek wine bottles will carry either the designation PDO (Protected Designation of Origin) or PGI (Protected Geographic Indication) with the name of the location of the wine region. In addition, some table wines may have a varietal label or a traditional name such as "Retsina" (a historic wine made with the addition of pine resin).

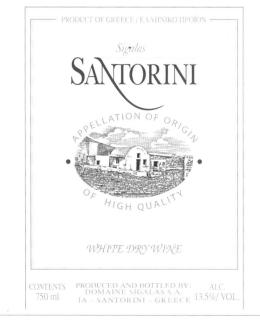

Santorini produces some of the best dry white wines in the world, produced from Assyrtiko and Athiri grapes. Courtesy of Domaine Sigalas.

Protected Geographic Indication (PGI) wines are divided into three concentric circles, starting with the regional wines from the largest areas, scaling down to the districts within them, and then to the smaller areas within those districts. This is similar to the model used in many parts of the world with the smaller calling of origin having a more defined growing condition than a large area.

The highest echelon in Greek wines is Protected Designation of Origin, modeled on the French AOP and meant to guarantee authenticity and maintain traditional "recipes" of grape content for the wines. We will refer to these wines as "PDO" when we discuss wine regions.

The label terms "Reserve" and "Grand Reserve" on PDO wines carry a legal responsibility to age the wines longer. White wines are aged a minimum of one year for reserve and two for grand reserve, while reds must be aged three years for reserve and four years for grand reserve. "Cava" is another legal term for aging (it has no connection with the sparkling wines of Spain). Greek Cava rules for aging are one year for white and rosé wines and three years for red wines.

A wine label may also contain the term "*Ktima*," which refers to a wine estate that produces wine from its own vineyards.

The wine regions of Greece

WHEREVER YOU TRAVEL IN GREECE, vineyards are part of the landscape. From the sun-soaked islands in the south to the cooler mountainous areas in the north, the nation's vineyards grow grapes for eating as well as for wine and brandy production.

Unlike most other European wine-growing nations, many of the Greek vineyards are planted with a northern exposure to avoid too much heat and to maintain acidity in their grapes (and ultimately their wines). Planting vineyards at higher elevations or by bodies of water is another tactic used by farmers to produce balanced wines.

In this chapter we will briefly discuss the regions, but our aim is to turn you on to our favorite wines so you can share our appreciation for the "new wines" of ancient Greece.

Prices are referred to as inexpensive (under $15), moderate (under $25), and moderate to expensive (over $25).

NORTHERN GREECE

MACEDONIA

IMPORTANT PDO REGIONS

Naoussa
Slopes of Meliton
Amyndeo
Goumenissa

IMPORTANT PGI REGIONS

Epanomi
Pangeon
Drama
Agioritikos

The vineyards of Macedonia benefit from enough rainfall to nurture the grapes so they are not "stressed out." The elegant and complex character of red Xinomavro wines can be explored in the examples from this region. Tart dry whites feature native grapes such as the Malagousia, Athiri, and Assyrtiko as well as international varieties such as Sauvignon Blanc. Two bargain priced wines we suggest are the Athiri dry white (about $10) and the Xinomavro and Cabernet Sauvignon "Cava" blended red (about $16) by Tsantali.

Naoussa PDO. We begin our survey of Macedonia with the most famous PDO of northern Greece, where the Xinomavro grape is grown on the foothills of Mount Vermio. Here the grape's natural acidity is heightened by being grown at such a high altitude. Just as Barolo is referred to as the "king of Italian reds," Naoussa is referred to as the "king of Greek reds." A typical Naoussa wine has flavors of spices, red fruit, black olives, and features high acidity. The wines are aged a minimum of one year in oak while reserve wines mature for two or more years in oak before they can be sold. Naoussa wines can age gracefully for a decade or more. Older Naoussa wines have soft tannins, earthy minerals, tomato, red fruit, and spice notes, and refreshing acidity. We have served high quality, aged Xinomavro-based wines to our friends, who often mistake them for the highly regarded wines of Burgundy from France or Barolo from Italy. Locals enjoy this red with lamb chops, and the black olive flavors make it a good complement to rabbit or duck stew with kalamata olives. Prices range from inexpensive for medium-bodied versions to moderate for wines that are some of Greece's finest red wines. The Boutari Grande Reserve (about $30) and the Kir Yanni Ramnista (about $27) are both fine examples of Naoussa wines.

SUGGESTED WINE PRODUCERS

Kir Yianni, Boutari, Domaine Karydas, Katogi, Strofilia, Dalamaras, Foundis, Tsantali, and Thymiopoulus.

Naoussa is a medium- to full-bodied dry red wine with high acidity, based on the Xinomavro grape. The Boutari winery makes ageworthy Naoussa and also produces fine wines from many other regions of Greece. Courtesy of Boutari.

Slopes of Meliton PDO.

This region produces medium-bodied, crisp whites from the Assyrtiko, Malagousia, Roditis, and Athiri grapes. The medium- to full-bodied red wines are based on the local Limnio grape partnered with French varieties such as Cabernet Sauvignon or Cabernet Franc. Limnio is an ancient variety that has herbal and red fruit aromas and soft tannins. The wines are inexpensive to moderately priced. We suggest the full-bodied red wine by Chateau Porto Carras.

Epanomi and Pangeon PGI.

Domaine Gerovassiliou is one of Greece's finest wineries. Check out its dry Malagousia white from Epanomi for its charming flavor of ripe apricots. If red's your thing, the winery's full-bodied Syrah offers characteristic aromas of black pepper combined with earthy and gamy scents, followed by lots of black fruit flavors and richness on the palate. Biblia Chora in Pangeon offers a crisp Assyrtiko and Sauvignon Blanc blend as well as a more opulent "Ovilos" blend of Assyrtiko and Semillon. Pair the light-bodied white with ceviche and move up to halibut steaks, roast turkey, or a mighty calzone with "Ovilos."

Drama PGI.

The vineyards of Drama benefit from cool breezes from the nearby Aegean Sea. Acidity is a key component in white wines and there is a healthy dose of it in the "Thema" blend of Assyrtiko and Sauvignon Blanc by Ktima Pavlidis. For purists, they make "Emphasis," a single variety Assyrtiko as well. "Amethystos" is a crisp blend of Sauvignon Blanc, Semillon, and Assyrtiko by Domaine Costas Lazaridi, while Wine Art Estate makes "Techni Alipias" a dramatic blend of Agiorgitiko, Cabernet Sauvignon, and Merlot featuring black fruit and herbal flavors.

Amyndeo PDO.

Xinomavro may be Greece's finest red grape and in this area there is an additional attractive floral note to the usual flavors of the variety. Alpha Estate is producing the type of wines that prompt people to ask, "Where is this from, and how do I buy some?" This winery makes sumptuous world-class red wines. Try the Xinomavro ($35), which is bursting with bright red berry flavors; the peppery Syrah ($35); or for a special occasion, the expensive blackberry-rich Alpha "One." Grilled lamb chops, a Moroccan lamb tagine, or vegetarian stuffed red peppers are some suggested pairings. Alpha also makes a crisp Sauvignon Blanc for $24. Amyndeo is also home to delicious dry rosé wines based on the Xinomavro grape. Our favorite is by Kir Yanni and it sells for under $15. It is essential to have dry rosé wines in your fridge for summer sipping or to pair with foods.

Agioritikos PGI.

From the hillside vineyards of the monastery of Mount Athos are two wines, produced by Tsantali, that we recommend. The Metoxi dry white is a tart white blend of Assyrtiko with Sauvignon Blanc and Athiri that can be paired with a mezze of Mediterranean appetizers, fish tacos, or whole roasted red snapper with fresh herbs. The Metoxi X Chromista single-vineyard red is a blend of Xinomavro, Limnio, and Cabernet Sauvignon, a complex full-bodied red wine with mineral, black fruit, and spice flavors that is a perfect partner for lamb chops.

CENTRAL GREECE

IMPORTANT PDO REGION

Rapsani

IMPORTANT PGI REGION

Attica

Rapsani PDO. The iron and schist soils on the slopes of Mount Olympus give extra power, richness, and complexity to the wines produced here. Vineyards planted as high as 2,300 feet (700 meters) allow the grapes to ripen slowly and provide high levels of acidity to balance the tannins in the wines made from a blend of Xinomavro, Stavroto, and Krassato grapes. We recommend the Reserve by Tsantali ($24), which features a deep purple color and aromas and flavors of black pepper and black plums in a full-bodied package. Try Rapsani Reserve red wines with richer foods such as a vegetarian seitan stroganoff, *pastitsio* (a Greek version of meat lasagna), or, to focus in on the wine, a simple grilled steak.

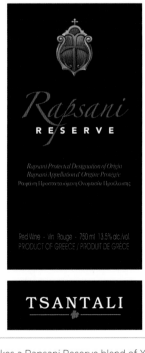

Tsantali makes a Rapsani Reserve blend of Xinomavro, Stavroto, and Krassato grapes that is full-bodied and complex. Courtesy of Tsantali.

Attica PGI. Dionysus' original stomping grounds were in this part of central Greece. Today both local and international grape varieties are grown here; unfortunately, the proximity to Athens has led to urban expansion and the uprooting of some of the ancient vineyards. Try the bargain-priced Savatiano or Moschofilero dry white wines by Papagiannakos winery.

SOUTHERN GREECE

PELOPONNESE

IMPORTANT PDO REGIONS

Nemea

Mantinia

Patras

In his epic poem *The Iliad*, Homer made the first written reference to the Peloponnese vineyards, calling them "*ampeloessa*" or full of vines. The description is still true today. Tourists visiting Olympia, site of the original Olympic Games, should experience the magnificent Mercouri estate. Walking in their beautiful gardens while sipping their Roditis-based "Foloi" (about $11) or their Assyrtiko and Robola

The Gaia Estate winery produces an excellent example of Nemea, based on the Agiorgitiko grape. The Koutsi subregion of Nemea is also featured on this label. Courtesy of Gaia Wines.

The vineyards of Nemea produce some of the Greece's finest red wines. Courtesy of All About Greek Wines.

"Kallisto" ($16) dry white blend is a magical experience. "Zoe" by Skouras is another bargain-priced dry white Peloponnese wine at about $10.

Nemea PDO. Tourists flock to Nemea, which boasts the largest vineyard area in Greece. Just outside of Nemea is the city of Nafplio—the first capital of modern Greece. Wine and mezze flow at the outdoor restaurants in this charming town. In fact, the region's red wine is referred to by the locals as the "blood of Hercules" because it was here that he killed the lion.

The Agiorgitiko grape rules in this region, and it is used to produce dry rosés and red wines that are medium to full in body. Vineyards are planted in the valley as well as on hillsides. Nemea wines possess aromas and flavors of black cherry, black currant, black licorice, tobacco, and black fig. Some wineries, such as Gaia, will feature the name of the cool subregion "Koutsi" on their wine labels as an indication of a finer wine from that smaller area. Koutsi is featured on the label of Gaia Estate's most full-bodied and complex red wine (see label on opposite page). They also produce a medium-bodied varietal wine and a lighter style called "Notios." Yiannis Paraskevopoulus is the winemaker of Gaia, and *WineWise* readers who want to try

something unique should try his noble version of the dry white wine Retsina. Other noteworthy winemakers of Nemea include Yiannis Tselepos, George Papaioannou, and Georges Skouras, whose namesake wineries offer wines that speak of sunshine and elegance.

Suggested Wine Producers

Gaia, Boutari, Domaine Skouras, Domaine Tselepos, Aivalis Family, Papaioannou, Palivos, Nasiakos, Harflatis, Greek Wine Cellars, and Nemeion Estate.

Mantinia PDO. Here the Moschofilero grape is planted at high altitudes, where the cool temperatures and sunshine result in wines with ripe fruit flavors balanced by high acidity. Expect flavors such as orange blossoms, clove, nutmeg, tangerine, rose water, and lemon. The sparkling and still white wines produced from this grape are delightful. Our two favorite Greek sparkling wines come from the Mantinia AOC. "Ode Panos" is a fine dry bubbly made by Domaine Spiropoulos that offers rose petal and orange zest flavors. The medium-bodied "Amalia" by Domaine Tselepos is also a standout, with notes of allspice, ginger, grapefruit, and pear. At under $30 retail these wines offer a flavorful and affordable alternative to Champagne. For a dry rosé, look no further than the Domaine Spiropoulos "Meliasto," with its unusual notes of rose petal, lychee, cherry tomatoes, and paprika. Moschofilero-based wines are well suited to the salty-sweet profile of many Asian seafood or chicken dishes. Prices range from inexpensive to moderate.

Patras PDO. You'll find both dry and sweet wines in this lively, culture-rich region, almost all of which are inexpensive. Dry whites are labeled as Patras PDO; we suggest the lemon-and-grapefruit-flavored "Asprolithi" by Oenoforos Winery. Parparoussis makes a sweet white Muscat of Patras as well as a dry red Mavrodaphne named "Taos," both recommended. We also suggest the Mercouri, Antonopoulos, and Parparoussis wineries for their sweet Mavrodaphe wines.

THE ISLANDS

IMPORTANT PDO REGIONS

Cephalonia

Samos

Rhodes

Crete

Santorini

IMPORTANT PGI REGION

Crete

Cephalonia PDO (Ionian Islands). One of the most beautiful and hospitable islands in Greece is Cephalonia. Here the most significant winery is Gentilini. The limestone soil, which produces many of the world's finest white wines, imparts a mineral flavor to the winery's Robola-based dry white wine. We also suggest the "San Gerassimo" Robola made by the Robola Cooperative of Cephalonia. Sashimi, crab, and lobster are good choices to highlight the lemon curd, green melon, nectarine, and mineral flavors of these dry white wines.

Samos PDO (Aegean Islands). Sweet Muscat of Samos may be the nation's finest dessert wine. The local cooperative makes "Anthemis," which is aged five years in oak before it is sold ($28). With its decadent caramel, honeysuckle, and brown sugar flavors, this wine makes a wonderful dessert unto itself or marries well with cheesecake, flan, or apple pie with vanilla ice cream. Muscat of Samos wines are inexpensive to moderately priced.

Crete PGI. Our favorite Boutari red wine is the full-bodied and complex "Skalani" blend of Syrah and Kotsifali grapes. For dry white wines we suggest the wineries Domaine Economou, Lyrarakis, and Alexakis. The Vidiano grape produces dry white wines with rich tropical fruit flavors and refreshing acidity. We also recommend the Douloufakis winery for their white as well as their red, made from Liatiko grapes. Two great values from Crete are the "Mirambelo," a blend of Mandelaria and Kotsifali red grapes by Mediterra winery, and the pure Kotsifali by Lyrarakis.

Rhodes PDO (Dodecanese Islands). This island's vineyards receive lots of sunshine and enough rainfall to prevent the vines from becoming parched. Athiri is the principal grape for the region's dry whites. Young Athiri wines taste of lemon and grapefruit, while older versions develop notes of honeycomb, aloe, and sesame. Muscat of Rhodes are sweet wines for desserts or they may be served as an after-dinner drink on their own.

Santorini PDO (Cyclades Islands). Santorini is an odd mix of ancient culture combined with the demands of the tourist trade. The lost world of Atlantis is said to be under the water near Santorini. Ruins and museums of antiquity on this island speak of the Minoan culture, with evidence of wine production dating back to the second century B.C. (Actually, the oldest wine press in the world, circa 1600 B.C., was found on the island of Crete.)

It's telling that this region is home to what many believe to be Greece's finest white wine. Santorini's dry whites must be made from at least 70% Assyrtiko, which supplies lots of acidity to the blend, while the Athiri grape contributes fruit and vegetal aromas. In addition, while 90% of the world's whites are better when drunk within three years of their harvest date, these wines, which are charming and flavorful when young, can improve with age—a decade for the dry whites and even longer for the sweet wines.

It is amazing that the grapes can survive—and thrive—in this hot, arid climate. There is little rainfall, so the grapes receive water via the moisture brought by sea breezes. As a result, the vineyards and the wines they produce are truly unique.

DRY WHITE WINES

A top producer in the region, Sigalas, makes both a stainless-steel-aged white and one aged in oak; we prefer the clean flavors of the stainless-steel version. Aromas and flavors of lemon, cucumber, and green melon are enveloped in a medium-bodied wine with a long finish. One of the largest wineries on the island is the Santo Wines cooperative. Their lineup of wines includes a pure Assyrtiko with aromas of lime, almond paste, and minerality from the volcanic soils. Flavors of nectarine, kumquat, lemon, and "wet stones" can be enjoyed in this delightful, dry wine.

The word "Nykteri" on a label indicates a few months of oak aging before the wine is sold. Nykteri Reserve and Grand Reserve are barrel fermented and aged even longer. So wine consumers can choose from the lightest-bodied stainless-steel versions or enjoy a more full-bodied, richer Nykteri Reserve or Grand Reserve wine. In all these wines you'll find the trademark minerality and acidity of Santorini wines.

For a walk on the wild side, check out the wild-ferment Santorini by Gaia. Other fine wines from this island are made by Argyros, Boutari, Gavalas, Hatzidakis, Koutsoyannopoulos, Roussos, and Athina Tsoli. Dry white wines range in price from inexpensive to moderate.

DRY RED WINES

While Santorini is best known for its crisp white wines, there has been new interest in the red wines based on blends of Mavrotagano, Mandelaria, and Voudomato, as well as pure expression of each of the native red grapes. Mavrotagano as a single variety has flavors of black plum, black cherry, black licorice, minerality, and spices such as caraway. For a special occasion, the pure Mavrotagano by Sigalas at $60 retail does deliver the wow factor we expect at that price level. The Santo Wines co-op also makes a pure Mavrotagano as well as a pure Mandelaria that is chock-full of bright red-fruit flavors, with a medium body.

SWEET WINES

Historically, Santorini was famous for its sweet wines. Vinsanto is a dessert wine made from a minimum of 51% Assyrtiko with Athiri, Aidani, and other local grapes making up the balance. The grapes are dried on mats to concentrate their sugars. The wines must be aged at least two years in oak barrels before they may be sold.

Aromas and flavors typically include dried apricots, figs, cinnamon, nutmeg, clove, chestnut cream, and tangerine. These are luscious wines with lively acidity to balance their sweetness.

Vinsanto is lovely as an after-dinner drink or paired with cheese and desserts. Honey, cinnamon, nutmeg, praline, and dried fruits are just some of the flavors of this luscious wine.

Vinsanto is wonderful as an after-dinner drink, or try it with a dessert such as *galaktaboureko* (a semolina-based custard wrapped in phyllo dough) or a *baklava* pastry with nuts and honey. Vinsanto prices are moderate to expensive, but still undervalued compared to some of the world's other better-known dessert wines.

DRY SANTORINI WHITE WINE PAIRINGS

On the island of Santorini you'll find excellent *tavernas* serving traditional dishes as well as cutting-edge restaurants where creative chefs offer some of the best foods in Greece. Seafood reigns supreme in the region's restaurants and provides an ideal accompaniment to Santorini's white wines. Since the wines are tart, dishes such as ceviche or trout *grenobloise* (lemon and caper sauce) will really amplify the flavors of both the wine and the food. Fried sardines or anchovies, young red mullet served with lemon (*barbouni*), and grilled swordfish steaks are just some of the seafood dishes that pair with the local white wines. Craving veggies? Try a cool puree of local split peas, olive oil, and garlic known locally as "*fava*" or a salad with tomatoes and capers. Although it may seem to break the rules, on a hot summer day the acidity and minerality of these wines, served chilled, provide an ideal foil for lamb kebabs.

In Santorini there is a unique method of growing grapes. Vines are planted close to the ground and protected from direct sunshine by a wreath of branches and leaves. This technique is known locally as "*ampelia*." Wines labeled as "Santorini" are crisp, dry white wines. "Vinsanto" is the term used for the sweet whites, which may be enjoyed as an after-dinner drink or paired with pastries such as baklava. Photos courtesy of All About Greek Wines.

EAT/DRINK/
MAN/WOMAN

WINE AND FOOD

WE COULD CONSIDER IT A DUTY, BUT IT REALLY IS A PLEASURE TO HELP OUR *WineWise* READERS DEMYSTIFY THE subject of wine and food pairing. Although there are no set rules, the "right" wine can elevate a humble meal into something truly memorable. We will provide some simple guidelines for achieving successful food and wine marriages, and wine recommendations for a myriad of ethnic and American foods.

As you read this chapter, remember that pairing wine and food is fun, requiring only an adventurous spirit and a little common sense. You may just discover the next perfect combination, such as the classic examples of Sancerre (Sauvignon Blanc from France) white wine and goat cheese, Ribera del Duero (Tempranillo from Spain) with oven roasted lamb, or Chianti Classico Riserva (Sangiovese from Italy) with Bistecca Fiorentina.

In this chapter we will provide *WineWise* readers with some terminology to explain the logical reasons for their delightful response to a wine and food pairing. But why limit our lives to logic? Some of our most rewarding wine and food pairings were the results of happenstance. So relax! Be experimental. After all, how bad can it be when your body and spirit are being nourished by wine and food? Let's begin with some basic principles for pairing wine and food.

Basic principles

COMPLEMENT OR CONTRAST FLAVORS

Wine is simply a product made from grapes that are fermented. Grape types used to make wine have intrinsic flavors, and great winemakers allow the grapes to speak for themselves. Similarly, a great chef should not obscure the natural flavors of a just-picked, sun-ripened tomato. Working from these principles, we can emphasize specific flavors or play them off one another.

COMPLEMENTING FLAVORS

When we complement flavors, we are simply highlighting specific flavor characteristics in the wine by pairing it with foods that have similar flavors. For example, Cabernet Sauvignon typically features aromas and flavors of black currants and black olives. Syrah has distinct black pepper notes, and Zinfandel is known for its ripe berry flavors. Of course, these smells and flavors are affected by where the grapes are grown. Wines from the warmer New World regions (United States, Australia, Chile) usually have more forward fruit flavors than wines from the Old World (Western Europe). So an Aussie Shiraz will be chock-full of ripe fruit flavors, while a French Syrah will have less pronounced fruit along with notes of earth, game, or leather.

The key in complementing flavors is simply to play up these attributes. An unoaked Chardonnay-based Chablis from the Burgundy region of France, with its aromas and flavors of green apple, may be ideal for pork with a tart apple sauce or apple stuffing, while an oaky California Chardonnay is better suited to a cedar-planked salmon.

The ultimate complement is to "bridge" the wine with the food by using the wine in cooking, to create an "echo" of flavors.

For example, after roasting a chicken over some onions, sliced fennel, and carrots, you can bridge the wine by adding an ounce or two of the same wine you intend to serve with the chicken, creating a complementary sauce. A classic chicken dish, coq au vin, actually uses the wine—traditionally either red or white wine from Burgundy—as the braising liquid, and is best served with the same wine.

A fun tasting for a dinner party is to try a New World and an Old World wine with two preparations of duck. A California Cabernet Sauvignon/Merlot blend, with its fruit-forward flavors, should complement a duck with hoisin sauce, a fruit glaze, or a barbecue sauce that is not too sweet. Try an Old World Bordeaux

Courtesy of Culinary Institute of America, Hyde Park, New York.

(Cabernet Sauvignon/Merlot blend) with a duck dish with olives or mushrooms. Consider adding a splash of the Bordeaux to the duck with olives and the California Cab to the duck dish with the fruit flavors.

CONTRASTING FLAVORS

Another way to highlight a flavor characteristic in the wine is to play it off the food to contrast flavors. For example, smoked, spicy, gamy, and salty foods pair beautifully with wines that are semi-dry or dry yet fruity. Our mind can play tricks on us when it comes to discerning fruity from sweet. If every experience you had smelling a strawberry was followed by sweetness on the palate, then the smell of strawberries will cause you to expect a sweet taste. But certain red grape types that smell of strawberries, such as Grenache, Gamay, Pinot Noir, and Zinfandel, usually make dry wines that are fruity (as opposed to sweet wines). Here again, place plays a role, as New World examples of Grenache are more obviously fruity than their Old World counterparts. (An obvious exception is the "blush" wine, White Zinfandel, which usually has a hint of sweetness.)

So how do you contrast spice and fruit? The classic combination of prosciutto and melon is a good food example of this attraction of opposites. The juxtaposition of salty meat with the sweet melon is very appealing, and you'll notice this principle followed in many ethnic dishes. It is also why semi-dry wines such as Riesling, Gewürztraminer, and Chenin Blanc are often suggested in the "global" food pairings found later in this chapter.

THE BEST OF BOTH WORLDS: COMPLEMENT AND CONTRAST

It may sound contrarian, but it is possible for a wine to both complement and contrast a dish. For example, staying with our prosciutto and melon appetizer, consider a Riesling from the Finger Lakes of New York or the Canadian province of Ontario. The semi-dry wine complements the sweetness of the melon while providing a contrast

to the salt of the prosciutto. Or partner a German Riesling from Mosel with a spicy shrimp curry with mango chutney. The hint of sweetness in the wine offsets the heat of the curry, while playing up the sweetness of the chutney and hint of sweetness of the shellfish. The cold serving temperature of the Riesling also serves as a physical contrast to the heat of the dish and helps alleviate the spicy "buzz" on your lips.

MATCH INTENSITIES

Simply put, the principle here is to match the body of the wine with the "body" (texture or richness) of the dish, ensuring that the flavor intensity of the wine and food are more or less equal. You should be able to taste the food and the wine without either one overwhelming the other.

When enjoying wine with our meal, we want to be able to taste both the food and the wine and not sacrifice one to appreciate the other. For example, if you serve a big, oaky Chardonnay with a delicate poached sole, the flavor of the fish will be lost. Likewise, if you pair a light-bodied red such as Beaujolais with a hearty dish such as short ribs, the flavor of the wine will be lost. A harmonious pairing is based on balance. Most of the time, flavor intensity parallels the body of a wine: a lightly flavored wine tends to be light-bodied and delicate, while a full-flavored wine usually feels heavier in the mouth and is full-bodied.

White wines tend to be lighter than red wines, with those that are fermented and/or aged in oak barrels being more full-bodied than those that are fermented in stainless steel. Pinot Noir is a thin-skinned red grape that usually makes medium-bodied wines that are equal in power to full-bodied whites, such as barrel-fermented Chardonnays. Cabernet Sauvignon is a thick-skinned red grape that produces wines with a fuller body than Pinot Noir.

Another point to consider when evaluating a wine's intensity is price. Within the world of Cabernet Sauvignon, for example, inexpensive

"CROSSOVER" WINES: WHITES FOR RED MEATS AND REDS FOR SEAFOOD

WineWise readers will notice in our "Tower of Power" grids that follow that full-bodied white wines are equivalent to medium-bodied red wines. This "crossover" zone allows us to pair richer preparations of vegetables, seafood, or white meats as well as lean red meats with either a white or a red wine or half portions of both. Rosé still and sparkling wines can also be used for lighter preparations of red meats or duck and heartier vegetarian, fish, and poultry or pork dishes. We truly enjoy serving two wines at the same time throughout a meal. Get started with an American or French barrel-aged Chardonnay and a Pinot Noir, then try a Greco di Tufo and a Rosso di Montalcino from Italy, or a Godello and a Rosé Cava from Spain. How about a New World and Old World tasting of Grenache from Australia and an Agiorgitiko from Greece? These are fun pairings and it will be interesting to taste how different components of a dish will work better with each of the wines.

versions that retail for under $15 are generally not as rich or complex as moderately priced or expensive Cabs from the same growing region. For example, we enjoy the inexpensive Cabernet Sauvignon/Merlot blend by Concha y Toro from Chile. This wine is a great value, though not as full-bodied or as complex as the winery's moderately priced "Marques de Casa Concha" Cab or its expensive "Don Melchor" Cabernet Sauvignon. The same is true for wines from many other countries. Dry red wines from the Douro region of Portugal, Penedes region of Spain, and wines made from the Barbera grape in Italy can range from light- to medium-bodied for the inexpensive wines while the pricier versions will be more full-bodied.

THE TOWER OF POWER

The Tower of Power (see pages 301–302) classifies many of the world's most important wines by body. For ease of reference, the first tower lists wines by grape type; the second tower, by European place name.

There are a few things you should be aware of when reading the towers:

Generally speaking, bargain-priced wines tend to be easy-drinking and lighter in body than moderately priced to expensive versions of the same grape or regional wine. Thus, a higher price tag often corresponds to more complex flavors and a more full-bodied example of the wine.

You'll notice that some red and white wines overlap. In the table that follows, the medium-bodied reds line up next to the full-bodied whites, and the light-bodied reds correspond with the medium- to full-bodied whites. In these cases, feel free to choose either red, rosé, or white, or serve half portions of each wine. For example, pair a grilled salmon and Provencal sauce with a barrel-fermented Chardonnay or a Pinot Noir (or try both). Or try a lamb or beef carpaccio with a medium-bodied rosé sparkling or still wine and/or a Gamay.

Now that you know how to evaluate a wine's flavor intensity or body, how do you apply that to food? You're probably familiar with the age-old rule that dictates having only white wine with seafood and poultry and red wine with red meats. Although this maxim works, it limits the amount of fun you can have by experimenting with other choices. Consider how vast the world of seafood or red meats really is. Just as Cabernet Sauvignon comes in different levels of intensity, so do proteins. Let's look at them according to intensity or body.

Seafood/Fish

MOST DELICATE: clams, crab, mussels, oysters, sole

DELICATE: bay scallops, shrimp, perch, pike, trout, turbot

MODERATELY RICH: diver scallops, sea bass, cod, cuttlefish, flounder, grouper, halibut, lobster, sea urchin, skate, snapper, squid, halibut filet

RICH: black cod (sable), cobia, marlin, monkfish, octopus, sturgeon, halibut steak

VERY RICH: bluefish, eel, herring, mackerel, salmon, sardines, tuna

In assessing a food's level of intensity, texture is very important. Small bay scallops do not have as rich a mouthfeel as the larger diver scallops. A sashimi or filet of halibut would fall under the moderately rich category, while halibut steak would be considered rich. Likewise, smoked salmon or sashimi of salmon would be moderately rich, while a salmon steak would be very rich. Notice how the pink to red color of salmon, tuna, or bluefish are visual clues to their affinity to rosé or light- to medium-bodied red wines.

THE BOTTOM LINE
Serve the lightest styles of white wines with the most delicate seafood.

Pair medium- to full-bodied whites with seafood in the moderately rich, rich, and very rich categories.

Light- to medium-bodied reds can be served with rich or very rich seafoods.

Rosé and sparkling wines are another alternative for moderately rich or rich seafoods.

For example, light-bodied whites (such as Sauvignon Blanc or Riesling) will not overwhelm delicate oysters on the half shell, while seared tuna can be served with either a full-bodied white (barrel-fermented Chardonnay) or a light to medium red (Pinot Noir).

Poultry/Game Birds

MOST DELICATE: chicken or turkey breast without skin

DELICATE: chicken or turkey breast with skin

MODERATELY RICH: chunks of chicken for stews, tacos, or stir-fries; chicken or turkey wings, thighs, or drumsticks; Cornish game hen; duck breast without skin; quail

RICH: chicken livers and gizzards, morsels of duck for stews or pastas, pheasant, partridge

VERY RICH: whole duck, goose

THE BOTTOM LINE
Pair the most delicate and delicate birds with light whites.

Serve moderately rich or rich poultry preparations with full-bodied whites, rosés, or light- to medium-bodied reds.

Pair the very rich examples with full-bodied reds.

Veal/Pork

DELICATE: thin medallions of veal or pork, sliced boiled ham

MODERATELY RICH: chunks of veal for stews, chunks of pork for dishes such as souvlaki, loin of pork for roast

RICH: veal or pork chops, pork knuckles or trotters

VERY RICH: veal breast, veal shank (*osso buco*), pork ribs, *cocinella* (Spanish roast suckling baby pig)

THE BOTTOM LINE
Serve delicate preparations with light whites.

Try moderately rich veal and pork dishes with medium- to full-bodied whites and rosés.

Pair rich and very rich foods with medium- to full-bodied whites, rosés, or medium- to medium-full-bodied red wines.

Lamb/Beef

DELICATE: carpaccio of lamb or beef, thinly sliced roast beef

MODERATELY RICH: medallions of lamb or beef or filet mignon; slices of beef for tacos, fajitas, or subs (such as cheesesteak sandwiches)

RICH: leg or loin of lamb, lamb chops, hamburger, lamb burger, skirt steak

VERY RICH: rack of lamb, lamb ribs, New York strip, T-bone or porterhouse steak, short ribs

Two important considerations when pairing red meats with wine are the amount of marbling (internal fat) the meat has and how rare it is served. The more fat it has and the rarer it is, the richer it is—and the more full-bodied the wine required.

THE BOTTOM LINE
A filet mignon is leaner than a sirloin steak, so it can be paired with a full-bodied white, a rosé, or a medium-bodied red.

A lean burger cooked well done needs a light-bodied red or a rosé.

A rare T-bone steak is best with a full-bodied red.

A rare to medium-rare rack of lamb with a powerful, full-bodied red is a classic marriage we adore.

So far it's pretty straightforward, right? Just to make it interesting, there are other factors you would do well to take into account besides the intensity and richness of the food. The first consideration is the cooking method, then the sauce, the grain or starch served with the protein, and the vegetables—they all contribute to the overall "weight" of the finished dish. If a lean hamburger is topped with some mushrooms or bacon and a thick slice of cheddar cheese it would raise the Tower of Power and could be paired with a full-bodied red wine.

Cooking Method

DELICATE: poaching, marinating (e.g., ceviche), steaming

MODERATELY RICH: baking, sautéing, pan frying, smoking, stir-frying

RICH TO VERY RICH: deep-frying, grilling, searing

Sauce

DELICATE: tomato water, lemon and capers, or lemongrass broth, as well as soy, tamari, and fish sauces used to accompany Asian foods

MODERATELY RICH: mango salsa, lemon butter, butter and garlic, yellow pumpkin seed molé

RICH: bechamel, chimichurri, coconut-milk-based sauces, cream-based sauces, hollandaise, bearnaise, ketchup, bolognese, mayonnaise, pesto, satay, ranch dressing

VERY RICH: beef gravy, demiglace-based sauces, Provencal, Eastern European sauces with sour cream such as paprikash or stroganoff

Grain or Starch

VERY DELICATE: angel hair pasta, boiled potato, white rice

DELICATE: baked potato, couscous, cellophane noodles, linguine, yellow rice

MODERATELY RICH: barley, fettuccine or egg noodle pasta, hominy, kasha, mashed potato or roasted red potato, quinoa, teff, soba noodles

RICH: cheese grits, gnocchi, home-fried potatoes, lasagna noodles

VERY RICH: french-fried potatoes, polenta, poutine (a Quebec specialty of french fries with cheese and gravy), potato knishes, latkes, kugel, *mofongo* (smashed plantains cooked with pork fat and used in place of a starch)

Vegetables

MOST DELICATE: celery, endive, iceberg lettuce, grape leaves, radishes, squash blossoms

DELICATE: arugula, bean sprouts, bell peppers, bok choy, cabbage, hen-of-the-woods mushrooms, kale, oyster mushrooms, romaine or red leaf lettuce, radicchio, salsify, spinach, Swiss chard, water chestnuts, yellow squash, zucchini, collard greens

MODERATELY RICH: black-eyed peas, broccoli, carrots, cauliflower, chickpeas (garbanzo beans), corn, edamame, fennel, green peas, oyster mushrooms, pigeon peas, string beans, turnips, wood ear mushrooms

RICH: Brussels sprouts, butternut squash, turnips, chanterelle mushrooms, chayote squash (mirliton), green olives, okra, red beans, spaghetti squash, tomatoes, yucca

VERY RICH: beets, black beans, brown or black olives, eggplant, porcini mushrooms, portobello mushrooms, shiitake mushrooms

THE BOTTOM LINE—VEGGIES

Whether the vegetables are the side dish or the focal point of the meal, their textural richness is the most important consideration when balancing the vegetables' power with the wine.

You'll notice that the majority of the more delicate vegetables are pale in color, and as the colors increase in intensity, so do the flavors. In this way, the color of the vegetables often provides a clue as to whether a white or a red wine is appropriate. We love yellow beet salad with white wine and red beet salad with red wine. Red peppers, tomatoes, beets, and radicchio, especially when they are cooked, are all excellent examples of veggies to pair with red wines.

The cooking technique you employ can affect the delicacy or richness of the vegetables. Red peppers, zucchini, and tomatoes all will taste richer when they are grilled, roasted, or fried. Brussels sprouts and cauliflower pair well with

The richness of salmon Provencal is balanced by a full-bodied white such as an oak-aged Chardonnay, a medium-bodied rosé, or a medium-bodied "crossover" red wine such as Pinot Noir.

a light-bodied white when steamed but require a full-bodied white or rosé (or even a red) when stir-fried, deep-fried, or sautéed.

As with fish and meats, the sauce can have a profound influence on the intensity of the vegetable and the wine needed to balance it. Adding red peppers to your cauliflower stir-fry or serving the cauliflower with a tomato-based sauce may encourage you to enjoy a red wine with this white vegetable.

For vegetarian proteins, apply the same principles you would for vegetables. Tofu, tempeh, and seitan are strongly influenced by cooking technique and the garnish or sauce that accompanies them. When butter, oils, or other fats are included in the preparation of vegetarian dishes, they raise the level of richness of that dish. The use of seeds and nuts—a vegan alternative to butter or dairy—also adds richness. Depending on the preparation, everything from light-bodied whites to rosés and even the heaviest reds can be served with vegetarian dishes.

TOWER OF POWER BY GRAPE TYPE

	RED WINES	WHITE WINES
NEW WORLD		
Full-bodied red wines	Cabernet Sauvignon, Syrah/Shiraz, Petite Sirah, Mourvedre	
Medium- to full-bodied red wines	Zinfandel (moderate to pricy versions), Malbec (Argentina), Grenache, Tannat (Uruguay), Merlot, Cabernet Franc, Pinotage (South Africa)	
Medium-bodied red wines are equivalent to full-bodied white wines	Pinot Noir, Carmenere (Chile)	Chardonnay (barrel fermented), Viognier, Pinot Gris (barrel fermented)
Light-bodied red wines are equivalent to medium-bodied white and rosé wines	Gamay and rosé or "blush" wines	Fumé Blanc (barrel-fermented Sauvignon Blanc), Semillon, Marsanne, Torrontes (Argentina), Gewurztraminer
Light-bodied white wines		Riesling, Chenin Blanc, stainless-steel fermented Sauvignon Blanc, Pinot Grigio

TOWER OF POWER BY EUROPEAN WINE NAME

Here we offer some of the best-known wines; for others, we suggest you look in other chapters of WineWise.

	RED WINES	WHITE WINES
ITALY		
Full-bodied red wines	Amarone, Barolo, Barbaresco, Brunello di Montalcino, Carmignano, Sagrantino de Montefalco, Vino Nobile di Montepulciano, Aglianico del Vulture, Taurasi	
Medium- to full-bodied red wines	Chianti Classico Riserva, Salice Salentino, Barbera d'Asti or Barbera d'Alba, Cannonau di Sardegna, Teroldego Rotliano, Lagrein	
Medium-bodied red wines are equivalent to full-bodied white wines	Chianti Classico, Nero d'Avola, Primitivo, Dolcetto d'Alba or Dolcetto d'Asti, Rosso di Montalcino	Barrel fermented Chardonnay, Greco di Tufo, Fiano di Avellino
Light-bodied red wines are equivalent to medium-bodied white and rosé wines	Chianti, Valpolicella, Bardolino, Grignolino, and rosé wines	Gavi, Arneis, Vermentino, Vernaccia di San Gimignano, Verdicchio, Friulano
Light-bodied white wines		Galestro, Soave, Frascati, Orvieto

	RED WINES	WHITE WINES
FRANCE		
Full-bodied red wines	Cornas, Cote Rotie, Hermitage, Chateauneuf du Pape, Cahors; Bordeaux wines from Pauillac, Pessac-Leognan/Graves, St-Estephe, St-Julien, and Margaux	
Medium- to full-bodied red wines	Pomerol, St-Emilion, St-Joseph, Crozes-Hermitage, Chinon, Minervois, Bandol, Cotes du Bourg, Cotes du Roussillon Villages	
Medium-bodied red wines are equivalent to full-bodied sparkling and white wines	Chambolle-Musigny, Vosne-Romanee, Gevrey-Chambertin, Volnay, Morey-St-Denis, Beaune, Morgon, Moulin-a-Vent, Cote de Beaune-Villages, Cote de Nuits-Villages, Bourgogne, Mercurey, rosé or *blanc de noirs* Champagne or Cremant	Alsace Gewurztraminer, Pinot Gris, Muscat, or Riesling; Meursault, Puligny-Montrachet, Condrieu, Chassagne-Montrachet, Savigny-Les-Beaunes, chateau-level wines from Pessac-Leognan/Graves
Light-bodied red wines are equivalent to medium-bodied rosé and white wines	Fleurie, Brouilly, Beaujolais-Villages, and rosé wines from Provence	Pouilly-Fuisse, Pouilly-Fumé, Sancerre, Quincy, Chablis *premier cru* and Chablis *grand cru*, Vouvray, Savennieres
Light-bodied white wines		Entre-Deux-Mers, Muscadet Sevre et Maine, Macon-Villages, Savoie, Chablis, Sylvaner
SPAIN		
Full-bodied red wines	Ribera del Duero, Toro, Priorat, Montsant, Penedes blends with Cabernet Sauvignon and/or Syrah	
Medium- to full-bodied red wines	Rioja *gran reserva* or *reserva*, moderately to expensively priced Jumilla or Bierzo	
Medium-bodied red wines are equivalent to full-bodied sparkling and white wines	Rioja Crianza, Campo de Borja, Navarra, Cigales, Yecla, Calatayud; inexpensive Penedes, Jumilla, or Bierzo	Godello from Valdeorras, Bierzo, or Ribeiro; Rioja (barrel fermented); Penedes Chardonnay or Xarel-lo (barrel fermented); Rioja *gran reserva*
Light-bodied red wines are equivalent to medium-bodied rosé and white wines	Young Rioja red and Rioja or Navarra rosé	Albarino, Rias Baixas, Rueda, Penedes, Rioja
Light-bodied white wines		Getariako Txacolina

PRIORITIZE! WHAT IS THE DOMINANT FLAVOR OF THE DISH?

We've looked at how to choose a wine for a single element of a dish—the protein, sauce, or vegetable, for example. But consider a typical dish or course: you have a moderately rich protein, a light sauce, a rich vegetable, a very rich starch. How do you decide what the overriding component is and what approach to take when choosing a wine to accompany it? Sometimes one element of the dish, perhaps the sauce, is the most important factor to consider when choosing a wine. Complementing or contrasting that sauce—or matching its power—becomes a priority and trumps the pairing of the grain or protein on the plate. Other times, a special or unique component of the dish warrants the spotlight—for example, wild game, chipotle peppers, tamarind, chanterelle mushrooms, or just-picked blueberries.

USE ACIDITY AND BUBBLES TO CLEANSE THE PALATE

There's a kind of wacky mathematics involved here, where 1 + 1 = 1. When acidic wines are paired with acidic foods, the total impression of acidity is lowered and the other components of the dish are highlighted. Of course, it helps to know which grapes are naturally high in acidity. As a side note: high acidity in wine also lowers the impression of sweetness and of salt in foods.

WHITE WINES

Rieslings from cool growing regions (such as Germany, New York, and Canada) have a refreshing acidity that can reinvigorate the palate. The international varieties of Sauvignon Blanc and Chenin Blanc are always high in acidity, as are certain indigenous white grapes, including Assyrtiko (Greece) and Arinto (Portugal).

Since acidic wines in combination with acidic foods lower the impression of acidity on the palate, the wines from these grapes are delicious accompaniments to ceviche or dishes with acidic sauces. Citrus-based sauces or sauces with rice vinegar, Sherry vinegar, or balsamic vinegar are preferred. White, apple cider, white wine, and red wine vinegars are too aggressive and make the wine taste sour, so if you must use them in a recipe, do so sparingly.

RED WINES

Always high in acidity is the Pinot Noir grape, which makes it such a wonderfully versatile food wine. Additionally, Italy boasts a number of high-acid red grapes, including Barbera, Sangiovese, and Nebbiolo. Just think of all those tomato-based sauces: the combination of fruit and acid in the tomatoes is a perfect match with the region's fruity, acidic red wines. A slice of pizza and a glass of Chianti demonstrate how the acidity of the wine complements the tomato and cleanses the palate from the richness of the cheese.

WINEWISE TIP: If you're looking for an "off the beaten path" red wine with high acidity, try the exciting wines made with the Xinomavro grape from northern Greece.

SPARKLING WINES

Good sparkling wines are usually sourced from cool growing regions that also produce high-acid table wines. Because of this, they have a remarkable effect when paired with food. Not only are they wonderful for heightening and then cooling down the flavors of hot, spicy dishes, but their effervescence cleanses the palate from fatty or rich foods.

Some of our favorite food-and-bubbly pairings include an egg salad sandwich or fish and chips with a Spanish brut Cava, linguine with pesto or Parmigiano cheese with an Italian Franciacorta or Prosecco, and chili dogs or a pastrami sandwich with a New World Blanc

FORGET BEER, SPARKLING WINES RULE!

Pinot Noir sits right in the middle of the Tower of Power and is a great red wine choice when some people are enjoying a rich fish dish, while others have ordered meat or vegetarian dishes. The problem is that it's hard to find good Pinot Noir at affordable prices. Solution? Drink bubbly!

Pinot Noir is often used to make good sparkling wines that can be found at inexpensive to moderate prices. Rosé sparklers are normally the most full-bodied and will work whenever you find yourself in the "crossover" section of these Tower of Power grids. They have a similar "weight" to Pinot Noir and barrel-fermented Chardonnay wines. *Blanc de noirs* bubbly is usually a bit lighter than rosé, with about the same body as wines made from Gamay (the grape of Beaujolais in France). If you want to match intensities with fish, poultry, or vegetarian foods that are not very rich, the popular dry brut style will serve you well. *Blanc de blancs*—made only from white grapes—is the most delicate of sparkling wines and will not overwhelm raw oysters, steamed vegetables with a miso broth, or stuffed grape leaves, among other lighter dishes.

de Noirs. Sparkling Shiraz from Australia can be paired with hearty meat stews or cheeseburgers. Sparkling rosés from North America or Champagne are perfect pairings for grilled salmon, cioppino (seafood stew with tomato broth), Philly cheesesteak sandwiches, or lamb chops. We enjoy stone crabs, cold lobster, or caviar with a light-bodied *blanc de blancs*.

For spicy-hot dishes such as blackened fish, jerk chicken, or a Thai seafood curry, you may want a hint of sweetness in your wine; go for extra dry sparklers (not as dry as wines labeled "Brut"). Inexpensive fruity brut rosé Cava wines from Spain are fantastic with spicy beef tacos or Korean beef ribs with spicy kimchee.

THE DEFAULT WINES

Now that selecting a glass of wine to accompany your own dinner is a snap, what do you do if you're ordering a bottle for the table and everyone is eating something different? How do you please so many different tastes?

First, you can order sparkling wine (see above). Not only is it festive, but its acidity makes it a great companion to a range of foods, and the bubbles reinvigorate the palate. Brut sparkling wines and Champagnes tend to be medium-bodied and the most versatile. If you're eating heartier fare such as salmon, tuna, lamb, beef, or even rich vegetarian dishes, order a full-bodied sparkling rosé or *blanc de noirs*. On the other hand, if the cuisine tends toward more delicate foods such as sushi, raw oysters, steamed vegetables, or tabouleh salad, go for the light-bodied *blanc de blancs*.

We understand that not everyone is a bubblehead, so great alternatives to sparkling wines are medium-bodied still wines, which are unlikely to overwhelm (or be overwhelmed by) most foods. Our tried-and-true choices: for the whites, a dry Sauvignon Blanc or semi-dry Riesling, and for the reds, Pinot Noir as well as some Sangiovese or Grenache-based wines. (For a more complete list of medium-bodied wines, consult the Tower of Power charts earlier in the chapter.) If there are four or more in your party, we suggest ordering both a bottle of white and a medium-bodied red.

THE PROGRESSION OF INTENSITIES: HORIZONTAL AND VERTICAL PAIRINGS

Although we enjoy popcorn and Champagne in bed, that is not what we mean when we refer to a horizontal pairing. Rather, we're talking about matching one plate of food with one wine. A vertical pairing involves matching a series of wines with a succession of dishes. It is exciting to climb a ladder of intensities in both the foods and the wines served with them.

When planning a multicourse meal, you do not want to serve powerful foods and wines early on. The idea is to serve low-alcohol wines before fuller-bodied, high-alcohol wines, simple young wines before complex old ones, and dry or semi-dry wines before sweet ones. An expensive oaky Chardonnay or Cabernet Sauvignon early in the meal will overwhelm not only the palate but delicate appetizers or salads. Instead, we prefer to start with lighter-style wines of good value and revel in the anticipation of the more complex wines to come.

Red alert! Possible pitfalls

BEWARE OF SWEETNESS

Pop a grape in your mouth and then taste a dry Chardonnay. Or try some chocolate ice cream with Cabernet Sauvignon. Trust us, it's gross! The sweetness of the food robs the wine of its fruit, making it taste really awful. So how can we manage to pair dry Cabernet Sauvignon or Zinfandel with chocolate? The trick is to serve wines with obvious fruit flavors and fairly high alcohol levels, which contribute some sweetness. Also, the desserts should contain dark chocolate, which is richer and more bitter than the sweeter milk chocolate. The rule overall is that the wine must be at least equal in sweetness to the food.

This caveat doesn't apply just to desserts. These days we enjoy chicken fingers with honey mustard, fish with fruit salsas, honey-baked hams, coconut shrimp with chutney... the list goes on. You know to avoid most dry wines with these sweeter dishes, but what does that leave? You have several options.

MAGIC MUSHROOMS!

Mushrooms are one of our favorite foods to pair with wines. The meatiness of mushrooms such as shiitake, porcini, portobello, chanterelles, or morels often allows them to be paired with medium- to full-bodied red wines. *WineWise* readers can choose to substitute mushrooms for red meats on "meatless Mondays" (or any day) and have a burger or steak with 'shrooms another day. Aside from their rich texture, the earthy flavors of mushrooms bring out the fruit flavors in red wines. We think of Old World wines as being more earthy and a great complement to the earthiness of mushrooms, but we have also had many exciting dinners pairing New World wines such as Pinot Noir with 'shrooms, where the fruit-driven wine and the earthy, funky mushrooms create a compelling and delicious interplay of flavors.

Dining al fresco on a hot summer day and in the mood for a special wine? We suggest vintage Champagne or an older fine dry white wine to pair with mushrooms. As white wines and Champagnes age, their fruitiness is diminished and earthy, mushroom-like flavors evolve.

SEMI-DRY WHITES

The wine should be as sweet or sweeter than the food or the food robs the wine of its fruit flavors. Riesling, Chenin Blanc, and Gewurztraminer, among other whites, all have a hint of sweetness so they can hold their own against these sweeter foods. Extra-dry Prosecco bubbly from Italy or extra-dry French Champagnes have a hint of sweetness and work as well as a Riesling, Chenin Blanc or Gewurztraminer with similar foods. The fruit-forward style of New Zealand Sauvignon Blanc can sometimes be substituted for semi-dry wines in pairings.

ROSÉS

Don't be a wine snob! In the semi-dry category, check out the "blush" wines of America: White Zinfandel, White Grenache, or White Merlot. Or experiment with dry yet fruity rosé table or sparkling wines from around the globe. We enjoy the dry rosés from the Navarra, Cigales, and Rioja regions of Spain. From Portugal, try a bone-dry rosé from the Alentejo. Australia makes some great dry rosés, and so do Italy and Greece. Most of these wines have the added benefit of bargain to inexpensive prices.

B.Y.O.B STRATEGY—A PERFECT CASE

Many cities have a vibrant B.Y.O.B (bring your own bottle) restaurant scene. With many years of fun experimentation under our loosened belts, we have figured out that some wines are the most versatile with food and are also great values.

If we are a group of six people we usually bring three bottles (about two and a half glasses for each of us). For a couple we suggest bringing two half bottles or one bottle that you both love. We have two basic strategies for our wine choices:

1. For Asian, Indian, Mexican, Middle Eastern, African, Caribbean, or Cajun restaurants with exotic flavors we suggest a white Riesling (U.S. or Canada), rosé sparkling (U.S., Cava from Spain, or cremant from France), and a red Zinfandel (California). We find Zinfandel never disappoints us. It's the most playful red wine with flavorful dishes. OK. We know that not everyone shares our love for semi-dry Rieslings so our best choices for a light, dry white are either Muscadet (France) or Vinho Verde (Portugal).

2. For classic Continental food (France, Italy, etc.) or American bistros our choices are dry white Sauvignon Blanc (Santorini from Greece will work very nicely, but you may not find this at the corner wine shop) or brut sparkling wine from the New World. For a red our go-to choices are either the medium-bodied Rosso di Montalcino (Italy) or the full-bodied Crozes-Hermitage (France). If you think some people in your group may be having veggies or fish, bring the Rosso. If you are going to a steakhouse or know your friends love monster reds, bring the Crozes.

Here is a recap of our short list of 12 best-buy B.Y.O.B wines (so you can buy a case today!):

DRY SPARKLING: Brut or Rosé Brut (U.S.), Cava (Spain), Cremant (France)

DRY WHITE: Muscadet (France), Vinho Verde (Portugal), Santorini (Greece), Sauvignon Blanc (New World or Old World)

SEMI-DRY WHITE: Riesling (New World or Old World)

DRY RED: Zinfandel (California), Rosso di Montalcino (Italy), Crozes-Hermitage (France)

For a wee bit more money we buy the more complex Tavel, Bandol, or Les Baux de Provence rosé wines from southern France.

DRY, FRUITY, LIGHT-BODIED REDS

Look for California Gamay by Beringer or Edmunds St. John, or New York State Gamay by Whitecliff; Grenache by Bonny Doon; fun, inexpensive proprietary reds such as Francis Coppola's Rosso; or inexpensive Zinfandel by Sutter Home, Barefoot Cellars, Mondavi/Woodbridge, Peachy Canyon, Bogle, or Parducci, among others.

French Beaujolais, based on the Gamay grape, is also a nice option (and a lot easier to find than New World Gamay). Try the lightest, simplest Beaujolais or Nouveau style served with a light chill, or a finer *cru* Beaujolais, such as Morgon, Fleurie, or Moulin-a-Vent, at room temperature. In this category, Georges Duboeuf wines are good quality, relatively inexpensive, and not difficult to find.

Italian wines that are dry and fruity include Valpolicella by Masi, Allegrini, or Sartori, or Bardolino by Bertani or Folonari. Dry versions of Lambrusco such as Lambrusco Grasparossa di Castelvetro are fruity and can be enjoyed chilled.

"Periquita" from Setubal and other inexpensive wines from the Alentejo region of Portugal fit in this category as do less expensive Greek reds made from the Agiorgitiko grape.

Bargain-priced Australian Shiraz or "GSM" (Grenache/Shiraz/Mourvedre) blends are also appropriate, but the moderately priced to expensive versions of these grape types will usually be richer and too tannic.

BEWARE OF VERY SPICY AND SALTY FOODS

The only time you should not match the power or intensity of wine and food is when the food is spicy-hot (rather than rich) or very salty. The high tannins of a full-bodied wine and high alcohol only exacerbate the heat. So forget your favorite oaky Chardonnay, Cabernet, or Shiraz and opt for lighter-bodied wines and/or wines with lower alcohol. The idea is similar to not getting caught up in another person's fiery words. Shouting back just fuels the fire; it's much better to take a step back and chill out. Instead of meeting fiery hot foods head-on with a big wine, take the road of less resistance with a light-bodied (or low-alcohol) wine, such as Vinho Verde (Portugal), Riesling (Canada, United States, Germany, Austria), Moschofilero (Greece), Chenin Blanc (New World), or Getariako Txacolina (Spain), among many other light, fruity whites.

Another unpleasant combination is very salty foods with full-bodied or high-alcohol wines. Sparkling wines or tart (high-acid) whites such as Sauvignon Blanc cleanse the palate from saltiness; the "briny" flavor of Manzanilla Sherry from Spain also can complement salty dishes. Although it has a fairly high alcohol level (15%), its almost-salty flavors and high acidity work wonders with foods such as salt cod or sardines.

You can also contrast spicy, smoked, or salty foods with semi-dry or fruity wines, as mentioned earlier in the chapter (see "Complement or Contrast Flavors," page 295). Chenin Blanc, Gewurztraminer, and Riesling, for example, are semi-dry whites that are usually lower in alcohol than Chardonnay. However, if you really love Chardonnay, choose one from a cooler climate such as New York, Oregon, or Canada. They usually have less alcohol than wines from warmer growing regions. And try to choose a Chardonnay with little obvious oak-driven flavors; too much oak with spicy, smoked, or salty foods will also amp up the "shouting match" you're trying to avoid.

Semi-dry, light-bodied reds are another option. The wine police aren't watching you, so admit it—you like a little sweetness if you are just having a glass of wine instead of beer or a cocktail. Perhaps you are hanging out with friends after work and need the perfect wine to pair with pigs in a blanket, spicy chicken wings, smoked almonds, or jalapeño poppers. Choose light-bodied reds using the Tower of Power charts, and don't be afraid to chill them. The cool temperature is a great contrast to the heat on your lips.

RESIST THE URGE TO OVERCOMPLICATE

Expensive foods or complicated fusion dishes are often best paired with simple wines.

Special or expensive ingredients such as caviar or truffles deserve to take center stage, and a moderately priced simple wine can act as a good canvas or backdrop for the food. The same holds true for "fusion" dishes, where a complex wine would only compete with the complex flavors of the dish, leading to confusion. In these cases, brut sparkling wine is a perfect choice. As we mentioned before, bubbles renew the palate and the spirit.

BEWARE OF PROBLEM CHILDREN

Several foods are notoriously hard to pair with wine. Here are some of the most common wine antagonists.

ASPARAGUS AND ARTICHOKES

These items may cause your wine to taste sweeter than it is. The solution is to serve the asparagus with a sauce that has some richness. For example, we serve steamed asparagus with a little butter and lemon, then partner it with a light- to medium-bodied dry white such as a Sancerre from France or a good *blanc de blancs* sparkling wine from anywhere. However, when we get a char on the asparagus and top it with a rich sauce, we can serve a full-bodied Chardonnay, Greco di Tufo from Italy, or Godello from Spain. If we top the asparagus with a mild red curry sauce, we opt for Beaujolais, Chianti, or Pinot Noir.

As for the artichokes, we adore oyster and artichoke stuffing on Thanksgiving Day. A dry rosé will not compete with the flavor of the artichokes; it also complements the sweet-tart cranberry sauce and is in balance with the flavor

and intensity of the turkey. Fried artichokes (a historic Jewish Roman specialty) diminish the taste of the ingredient that causes wine problems. Try this artichoke dish with a Frascati white wine produced near Rome, or other crisp white wines.

Another option for asparagus and artichokes are sparkling wines or dry Manzanilla or Fino Sherries from Spain. Honestly, quite often when we are confronted with wine antagonists we find our best choices are rosé, Sherry, or sparkling wines.

SPINACH/OTHER LEAFY GREENS

This is the top vegetable side dish served at steakhouses, where most people order a full-bodied red such as a California Cabernet, French Bordeaux, Italian Barolo, or Spanish Ribera del Duero to match the intensity of the juicy steak. However, the tannic nature of such brawny wines will clash with the spinach, producing a very unappealing metallic flavor. To combat this reaction, order creamed spinach or a spinach timbale. The added fat will turn a negative combination into a positive one. Employ a similar technique for broccoli rabe, kale, Swiss chard, or collard greens by sautéing these vegetables with olive oil or butter and garlic, or toss in some bacon or pancetta, which will contribute fat to the dish.

GARLIC

The stinky bulb is much more wine-friendly when it is sautéed or roasted than when it is raw. It has a mineral flavor that can complement mineral flavors in a wine (such as Sauvignon Blanc, Riesling, or Assyrtiko) as well as some sweetness that can complement fruity or off-dry wines.

TAMARIND

The acidity and bitterness of tamarind can destroy the flavors of a fine wine. Try instead a dry rosé still or sparkling wine with dishes that have a strong tamarind flavor.

EGGS

Eggs have a protein-based richness that can wreak havoc with many wines. What does work with omelettes, frittatas, and quiches are Fino or Manzanilla Sherries, brut sparkling wines, or tart, semi-dry Rieslings, as well as dry, medium- to full-bodied whites from Alsace, France.

CHEESE: FRIEND OR FOE?

You might think pairing wine and cheese is a no-brainer, hard to mess up. If only it were that simple. Once again, the possibilities for ambrosial combinations—and legendary disasters—are endless. After years of experimentation (and dieting), we have come to a few conclusions about pairing wine with cheese. The following is a simple guide and does not go into the myriad possible options.

Dry or semi-dry white wines and sparklers are usually the best choice to showcase the flavors of cheese. If the cheese is tart, such as a fresh domestic goat cheese or Greek feta, a tart (high-acid) dry white wine such as Sauvignon Blanc or a tart semi-dry white such as Riesling is ideal. Remember our wacky math (1 + 1 = 1)? The acids in the wine and cheese negate each other, allowing the creamy flavors of the cheese to shine through. Semi-dry whites can also be used to contrast a smoked or spicy cheese. Try a smoked Edam or goat cheese with peppercorns with a Riesling, Chenin Blanc, or Gewurztraminer wine.

An aged cheese such as Manchego (sheep's milk) or Reblochon (cow's milk) can handle medium- to heavy-bodied whites such as an Albarino from Spain or Alvarinho from Portugal. This Iberian grape is also a good middle-of-the-road choice when serving an assortment of cheeses, as it tends to coexist with a variety of cheeses rather than dominate them.

Where does Chardonnay, the most popular dry white of all, fit into the equation? Chardonnay can work with cheese as well, but it is a grape with multiple personalities. The wine's style is largely dictated by where it is grown and how it is made,

and this in turn affects the kinds of cheeses suited to the wine. In the Burgundy region of France, for example, the unoaked versions from Chablis are rather austere with a distinct mineral flavor, while the oaky Chardonnays from villages such as Meursault or Puligny-Montrachet are more complex and full-bodied. The same holds true for California and Australia, where price is often an indicator of style. There is a plethora of popular, pleasant, simple Chardonnays that are dry and light- to medium-bodied. After that, the more you spend—generally speaking—the more complex the wine and the more "weight" on the palate. Try milder cheeses such as Edam, Swiss, or mozzarella with the lighter versions of Chardonnay (or try a Pinot Blanc from Alsace).

Aged cheeses such as Jack, Emmentaler, or cheddar have more pronounced flavors and are better balanced by fuller-bodied Chardonnays or medium-bodied reds.

Sparkling wines have a natural affinity with cheese. A glass of delicate *blanc de blancs* or a medium-bodied brut with mild Mascarpone, gooey Camembert, smoked Gouda, or nutty Parmigiano is a beautiful thing. Demi-sec Champagnes are equally versatile. Their sweetness provides a great foil to a pungent peppercorn goat cheese or jalapeño Jack, yet complements a Spanish or Portuguese cheese served with a sweet quince paste. In addition, demi-sec bubblies can hold their own against the sweet fresh fruits that accompany the cheese course, maintaining their fruit flavors.

As cheese ages, it loses moisture and becomes richer and saltier. This is where red wines come into play. Convention held that the tannins in red wine tame the fattiness of the cheese, and the fruit of the wine will contrast the saltiness of the cheese. Reds with high acidity, such as Pinot Noir, have the added bonus of cleansing the palate. We have seen many classic still-life paintings depicting a table with cheese, bread, and a big glass of red wine. Indeed, red wine has been enjoyed with cheese for centuries. However, recent scientific research has found that cheese destroys the flavor of most red wines. Whom do we believe?

It's a good thing we never read that report until this year. We have been enjoying pizza, cheeseburgers, and Gruyere-topped onion soup with red wines for a long time. Combined, the three of us have probably drunk 100,000 glasses of the "wrong" wine without knowing it! We have also been fortunate enough to travel to many wine regions where the local cheese is usually an ideal pairing with the local wine, which may be red. In Portugal's Douro Valley, for example, we savored a Portuguese Serra mountain cheese with a dry, full-bodied, tannic red and a sweet, fortified Porto. Both were fabulous. Why did these pairings work so well? Was it the amazing scenery of the region? The emotional connection from drinking wine at the site it was created? The excellent company at the table? Whatever the reason, we know it was a positive experience.

You can decide for yourselves where you fall on the red-wine-with-cheese debate by having a wine and cheese tasting. For the wines, start with a sparkler, a white, a light- to medium-bodied red, and a full-bodied red. Then try them with three different styles of cheese, such as cow's milk, goat's milk, and sheep's milk. Or select cheeses of different ages and different textures— for example, a fresh, soft, ripened cheese such as Brie, a semi-hard aged Fontina, and a young hard cheese such as a Pecorino Romano. Or for a cold winter day, compare an open-faced sandwich of Swiss raclette heated underneath the broiler with an American grilled cheese sandwich, saganaki (fried Greek Kasseri cheese), and a cheese calzone.

Another option is to pair regional wines with regional cheeses. Serve fresh mozzarella, Bel Paese, and Parmigiano Reggiano from Italy with a Prosecco (Italian sparkling wine), Vernaccia di San Gimignano (white), Chianti (medium-bodied red), and Barolo Riserva (full-bodied red). Or you can mix it up and sample those same Italian cheeses with affordable American wines, such as a brut sparkling wine, a Riesling, a red Zinfandel, and a Cabernet Sauvignon. Do not limit yourself to four types of wine or three cheeses: the more

combinations you have, the more opportunities for a successful pairing and a fun experience with friends that you'll want to repeat.

"If it grows together it goes together" is one way to approach wine and food pairings, and especially wine and cheese. Try Epoisses from Burgundy, France with a Chardonnay from the region. A great value would be a simple regional "Bourgogne Blanc," or for a moderately priced village-level wine try Chardonnay from the village of Savigny Les Beaune. Special occasion? A *premier cru* Meursault, Puligny-Montrachet, or Chassagne-Montrachet with Epoisses could blow your mind!

The most difficult cheeses to pair with wine are the blue-veined cheeses. They are very salty and thus can clash with tannic red wines. Traditionally, blue cheeses are best paired with sweet table wines or fortified wines. Classic examples include French Roquefort with Sauternes or English Stilton with a vintage Porto from Portugal. Other matches we recommend are a Cabrales blue from Spain with a dry, salty-flavored Manzanilla Sherry, or an American Maytag or Point Reyes Blue with a Napa Valley Cabernet Sauvignon or Barossa Valley Shiraz from Australia.

A world of flavors: some magical matches from around the globe

WITH THE INCREASING PRESENCE OF the "global village"—fusion dishes and ethnic foods—and the myriad flavors they offer—comes the chance to experiment with a diversity of wines. While some play it safe and just drink beer with ethnic foods, we prefer sparkling wines over beer, and you'll notice that many of our suggestions in this section include bubbly. Table wines can be a

THE LOW-DOWN, NITTY-GRITTY CHEAT SHEET

When selecting a wine to pair with a meal, assess the wine using the following simple guidelines:

1. Temperature at which you will serve the wine: chilled, cool, or room temperature. Chilled wines can relieve and contrast the heat of spicy foods. Also, hot outside temperatures (or a day at the beach) may suggest a chilled glass of wine, whereas cold damp weather (or a day on the slopes) may have you thirsting for a big dry red or even a mug of glogg (a hot spiced-wine cocktail).

2. Body of the wine: very light, light, medium, medium-full, or full. Use the body of the wine to balance a dish's power, its delicacy or richness.

3. Level of sweetness: dry, semi-dry, semi-sweet, or sweet. The wine should be at least as sweet as the food.

4. Level of acidity: low, medium, or so tart you drool with pleasure. Acidic wines cleanse your palate of richness; they also pair well with tart foods.

5. Level of alcohol: low, medium, or high. Lower alcohol is best for spicy foods or salty foods.

6. Level of bitterness: Bitter wines are better than semi-sweet wines with earthy foods.

7. Level of oak influence: none, a hint, or so high you taste bark. Very oaky wines complement smoky flavors or grilled fish and meats.

8. Level of complexity: simple, interesting, or amazing. Truly complex wines shine when paired with simple foods, and vice versa.

9. Major flavor(s) and aroma(s) of the wine:

    FRUITY stone fruit, citrus, red or black fruit? Dried or fresh fruit?

    FLORAL violets, lilacs, or roses?

    SPICY dark savory spices (cumin, coriander), dark sweet spices (cinnamon, clove, ginger, nutmeg, allspice), or green herbs (rosemary, sage, marjoram, thyme)?

    PEPPERY white pepper, black pepper, or bell pepper?

    SMOKY embers in a fireplace or smoked meat?

    OTHER gamy or leather aromas? Mineral?

    Pair wines with foods that have complementary flavors. For example, Syrah/Shiraz almost always smells and tastes of black peppercorn, making it a nice match for pepper-crusted New York strip steak. Likewise, the salted almond flavor of Manzanilla Sherry comes shining through when served with trout amandine (trout with almonds) or kung pao chicken (made with peanuts, a soy-sesame sauce, and hot chili paste).

10. Wow factor: Does the wine put a big smile on your face? If so, it's a keeper—experiment with a variety of foods. Part of the fun of pairing food and wine is that potential rush of excitement that comes from discovering an unorthodox but magnificent combination.

little more hit-or-miss, but we are willing to roll the dice and take some chances in pursuit of a heavenly pairing. When wine and food exalt each other, it's magic!

First, a couple of reminders about pairing wine with ethnic foods:

Temperature of the wine is very important. Make sure your sparkling, white, and rosé wines are well chilled to refresh your palate.

Here are some suggestions for proper temperatures:

SIMPLE INEXPENSIVE DRY WHITES, ROSÉS, AND SPARKLERS:
41° to 47°F (5° to 8°C)

MORE COMPLEX WHITES, SPARKLERS, AND LIGHT-BODIED REDS:
50° to 54°F (10° to 12°C)

MEDIUM-BODIED REDS: about 55°F (13°C)

FULL-BODIED REDS: 59° to 64°F (15° to 18°C)

SWEET STILL AND SPARKLING WINES:
41° to 47°F (5° to 8°C)

SWEET FORTIFIED WINES, such as Ruby or Vintage Port, are usually served at room temperature; **TAWNY PORT** can be served cooler; **SWEET PEDRO XIMENEZ SHERRY** can be served at room temperature, but if you're outdoors on a hot day and intend to pour some on your ice cream, go ahead and chill that Sherry.

In each of these categories, serve the simpler wines at the lower range of the temperature spectrum and the more complex ones at the higher end.

Simpler, often inexpensive to moderately priced table wines are the best backdrop for complex dishes, as very powerful, complex, expensive wines will create a tug-of-war for your attention.

If the dish has a hint of sweetness, you're often better off with the riper fruit flavors of New World wines. If the dish has a more earthy profile, Old World wines with their vegetal or herbal notes are better complements.

We apologize that we cannot feature all the nations of the world or all the foods we enjoy in this section. However, our goal is to provide a general approach to pairing styles of wines with different regional or ethnic foods. Use these guidelines as a starting point, then go wild and experiment on your own. Substitute wines of equal intensity from other countries (refer to the Tower of Power charts), keeping in mind the wine antagonists we listed earlier in this chapter. And remember, when in doubt, you can rarely go wrong choosing a regional wine to accompany food from the same region.

ASIA

VIETNAM

SPRING ROLLS: dry, light-bodied whites such as Soave or Pinot Grigio (Italy), Sauvignon Blanc (New Zealand) or Entre-Deux-Mers (France); light sparkling wines such as *blanc de blancs* (United States) or Prosecco (Italy)

PHO WITH BEEF: in the summer, medium-full-bodied whites such as Chardonnay or Viognier (United States); in the winter, light- to medium-bodied reds such as Beaujolais-Villages (France), Gamay, or Cabernet Franc (New York, other parts of the United States, or Canada), Rosso di Montalcino, Chianti Classico (Italy)

KOREA

BEEF SHORT RIBS, TRADITIONAL OR "LA STYLE," WITH SPICY KIMCHEE: dry rosé sparkling wines from United States or Spain (Cava); light- to medium-bodied reds such as inexpensive Zinfandel (United States), Valpolicella, Dolcetto, or dry Lambrusco (Italy)

THAILAND

PAD THAI NOODLES WITH SEAFOOD: light- to medium-bodied, semi-dry whites such as Riesling, Muscat, or Gewurztraminer (Alsace, France); Chenin Blanc (United States or Canada); or Vouvray (France). If you prefer dry whites we suggest Albarino/ Alvarinho (Spain/Portugal), Moschofilero, or Malagousia (Greece)

COCONUT-MILK-BASED SEAFOOD CURRY WITH LEMONGRASS: dry, tart, herbal whites such as Sauvignon/Fumé Blanc (United States); Sancerre, Pouilly-Fumé, Menetou-Salon, or Graves (France). If it's spicy, Chenin Blanc (United States or Canada), or Vouvray (France)

INDONESIA

CHICKEN SATAY: dry fortified wines such as Amontillado Sherry (Spain) or Sercial Madeira (Portugal); semi-dry white such as Riesling or Gewurztraminer (California, Washington, or Alsace, France)

NASI GORENG (FRIED RICE WITH SHRIMP, CHICKEN, AND VEGETABLES): crisp whites such as Vermentino di Gallura (Italy); Rueda (Spain); richer whites such as Marsanne and Roussanne (United States, France), Semillon (Washington or Australia), Godello (Spain); Dao, Alentejo, or Douro (Portugal)

BHUTAN

EMA DATSHI (AGED CHEESE WITH SPICY PEPPERS, TOMATOES, ONIONS, AND CILANTRO SERVED OVER RICE): semi-dry low alcohol whites such as Riesling; dry, low alcohol whites such as Vinho Verde (Portugal), Getariako Txacolina (Spain), or Moschofilero (Greece)

MOMO (DUMPLINGS FILLED WITH POTATO AND WILD CHIVE OR WITH MEAT): dry (brut) sparkling wines from New World or Old World; dry medium-bodied whites such as Chardonnay or Albarino/Alvarinho (Spain/ Portugal); on a cold winter day medium-bodied reds such as Morgon or Cote de Beaune-Villages (France), Chianti Classico (Italy)

SINGAPORE

SAMBAL STING RAY OR CHILI CRAB: semi-dry whites such as Riesling, Chenin Blanc, or Gewurztraminer (New York, Washington, Canada, or Australia); low-alcohol whites such as Vinho Verde (Portugal); dry rosé sparkling

CHICKEN RICE (POACHED CHICKEN, VEGETABLES AND RICE WITH DIPPING SAUCES): crisp dry white such as Sauvignon Blanc (New Zealand), Santorini (Greece), Entre-Deux-Mers (France)

CHINA

EGG ROLLS: sparkling Prosecco (Italy); semi-dry whites such as Riesling (New York, Canada, or Australia)

MU SHU PORK: semi-dry whites such as Riesling (New York, Canada, or Australia); medium- to medium-full-bodied reds such as Cabernet Franc (New York), Merlot (Washington), Zinfandel (California), Carmenere (Chile), or Malbec and Bonarda (Argentina); or for a walk on the wild side, Amontillado Sherry (Spain)

EGGPLANT IN BLACK BEAN SAUCE: full-bodied reds such as Ribera del Duero, Montsant, Toro (Spain), Douro, Bairrada and Beiras (Portugal), Nemea, Naoussa, or Rapsani (Greece), or Syrah and Petite Sirah (California)

SZECHUAN SCALLOPS: semi-dry white such as Riesling (New York, Canada, or Australia); low-alcohol dry whites such as Vinho Verde (Portugal); Moschofilero (Greece); extra-dry sparkling Prosecco (Italy)

JAPAN

SUSHI/SASHIMI: Sparkling brut or *blanc de blancs* (United States); dry Fino or Manzanilla Sherry (Spain); dry light- to medium-bodied whites such as Verdelho (Australia); Graves (France); Rueda (Spain); Santorini or Robola of Cephalonia (Greece); Gruner Veltliner (Austria); semi-dry whites such as Riesling, Chenin Blanc, or Gewurztraminer (New World)

TEMPURA: dry, tart white such as Sauvignon Blanc (Chile or New Zealand); Entre-Deux-Mers, Quincy, or Sancerre (France); sparkling brut (New World or Old World)

CHICKEN OR BEEF TERIYAKI: fruity, light-bodied reds such as Gamay (United States or Beaujolais, France); Valpolicella (Italy); rosé still wine from Rioja or Navarra, or sparkling Cava (Spain)

BLACK COD WITH YUZU MISO SAUCE: Sparkling Brut or medium- to full-bodied whites such as Godello or Albarino (Spain) Alvarinho or Encruzado (Portugal)

INDIA

SAMOSA: sparkling brut (United States) or extra dry (Champagne, France), or dry, medium- to full-bodied whites such as Marsanne (Australia or United States), white Cotes du Rhone (France), Alentejo, Dao (Portugal)

SHRIMP OR LOBSTER WITH MILD CURRY SAUCE: full-bodied dry whites with forward fruit flavors such as a New World Chardonnay from Oregon, Washington, Australia or New Zealand; Godello or Albarino (Spain); Encruzado, Alvarinho, Lisboa, Alentejo, or Douro (Portugal)

SHRIMP OR LOBSTER WITH SPICY CURRY SAUCE AND CHUTNEY: light-bodied, fairly low-alcohol dry white wines such as Vinho Verde from Portugal, or semi-dry white wines such as Riesling from Germany, the United States, or Canada; Vouvray, Montlouis, or Jasnieres (France)

VEGETARIAN DHOSA WITH YELLOW DAL: light- to medium-bodied dry whites such as Viognier, Marsanne, Roussanne (United States, Australia, or France); Gavi, Vernaccia di San Gimignano, Friulano (Italy), Godello (Spain); Alvarinho, Dao, Douro, Alentejo, or Beiras Atlantico (Portugal)

TANDOORI LAMB WITH RED LENTIL DAL: dry, full-bodied red wines such as Petite Sirah or moderate to expensive Zinfandel (United States); "GSM" (Grenache/Syrah/Mourvedre) blend (Australia); Gigondas, Les Baux de Provence, or Bandol (France); Ribera del Duero, Jumilla, Toro (Spain); Amyndeo, Drama, Epanomi, Rapsani Reserve, Nemea (Greece); Douro, Dao, Beiras, Alentejo, or Lisboa red (Portugal)

EUROPE

ITALY

Since Italian is often cited as the most popular style of food in America, we will feature a more comprehensive list of pairings than for other nations.

LINGUINE WITH PESTO: dry, tart whites such as Sauvignon Blanc (United States, Chile, South Africa); Sancerre, Quincy, Menetou-Salon, Pouilly-Fumé (France); Vermentino, Gavi (Italy); dry sparkling brut

FETTUCCINE ALFREDO: dry sparkling brut (Franciacorta, Italy) to break through the richness or Chardonnay (Tuscany or California) to complement it. Another tactic: balance the richness of the dish with medium-full-bodied wines such as Greco di Tufo or Fiano di Avellino (Italy)

SPAGHETTI WITH WHITE CLAM SAUCE: dry, medium-bodied Italian whites such as Vernaccia di San Gimignano, Orvieto Classico, Frascati, or Falanghina (Italy); dry sparkling Cava (Spain); Prosecco; sparkling brut from the New World

SPAGHETTI WITH MEAT SAUCE: dry, medium- to full-bodied Italian reds such as moderately priced Zinfandel (United States); Primitivo, Chianti Classico Riserva, Ghemme, or Barbera Superiore (Italy)

MEAT LASAGNA: gutsy, dry, full-bodied reds such as Cabernet Sauvignon, Petite Sirah, or Syrah/Shiraz (United States or Australia); Amarone, Salice Salentino, Gattinara, Inferno, or Aglianico del Vulture (Italy), Cahors, Marcillac, or Crozes-Hermitage (France), Toro, Jumilla, or Ribera del Duero (Spain)

VEGGIE PIZZA: light- to medium-bodied reds such as Valpolicella, Freisa, Bardolino, or Dolcetto (Italy) or Merlot (United States). If it is a white pie, medium- to full-bodied whites such as Chardonnay (Old or New World), Albarino/Alvarinho (Spain/Portugal). If it is goat cheese instead of mozzarella, try crisp Sauvignon Blanc (United States, Canada New Zealand); Entre-Deux-Mers (France); Santorini (Greece)

EVERYTHING PIZZA (LOADED WITH MEATS AND VEGGIES): full-bodied reds such as Shiraz (Australia), moderate to expensive Zinfandel (United States), Cabernet Sauvignon (United States, Chile, Argentina, Australia), Malbec (Argentina) or Aglianico del Vulture, Nero D'Avola, Carmignano, Salice Salentino, Barbera d'Asti or Barbera d'Alba Superiore (Italy). On a hot summer day rosé sparkling or still wine is a great option.

CALZONE: dry, full-bodied whites such as Chardonnay (California), Semillon (Australia), or Greco di Tufo or Fiano di Avellino (Italy)

FRIED CALAMARI WITH MARINARA SAUCE, OR ZUPPA DI PESCE (SEAFOOD SOUP): dry rosé table or sparkling wine from Franciacorta (Italy); light- to medium-bodied reds such as Chianti Classico, Sangiovese di Romagna, Morellino di Scansano, Freisa, or Grignolino (Italy), Pinot Noir (New Zealand or Oregon), or an inexpensive Zinfandel (California)

CHICKEN PICCATA: dry, light- to medium-bodied whites such as Soave Classico, Arneis, Frascati, or Gavi (Italy); Savoie, Sylvaner, or Muscadet Sevre et Maine (France)

VEAL CHOP WITH WILD MUSHROOMS: dry, full-bodied, complex reds with at least five years' aging, such as Barolo, Barbaresco, or Brunello di Montalcino (Italy) or Pinot Noir (Oregon or France); dining al fresco on a warm day: a full-bodied white or if your budget permits, aged vintage brut Champagne; Chardonnay with some age (New World or Old World); chateau-level Pessac-Leognan Bordeaux (France)

OSSO BUCO SERVED WITH A SAFFRON RISOTTO: full-bodied Chardonnay, Greco di Tufo or Fiano di Avellino (Italy); white Cotes du Rhone, Condrieu (France); Godello (Spain); Moschofilero or Malagousia (Greece); medium- to full-bodied Sangiovese-based reds such as Chianti Classico Riserva, Morellino di Scansano, Vino Nobile di Montepulciano (Italy)

BEEFSTEAK FIORENTINA: big Italian reds such as Brunello di Montalcino, Sagrantino di Montefalco, Barolo, Barbaresco, Taurasi, Inferno, or Amarone or any other "big red" from our Tower of Power charts at the beginning of this chapter

FRANCE

PATE DE CAMPAGNE: dry, medium- to full-bodied reds such as Gigondas, Canon-Fronsac, Vacqueyras, Marcillac, or Collioure (France); dry, medium- to full-bodied whites from Alsace (France). For a daring pairing try Amontillado Sherry (Spain) or the Sercial and Verdelho styles of Madeira (Portugal)

CHOUCROUTE (CABBAGE AND CHARCUTERIE): dry or semi-dry, medium- to full-bodied whites such as Muscat, Riesling, Pinot Gris,

Gewurztraminer, or sparkling Cremant (Alsace, France); semi-dry table or sparkling cold-climate Riesling or Gewurztraminer (Germany, Austria, Canada, or New York)

CASSOULET (WHITE BEANS WITH PORK AND DUCK): in the summer, dry, full-bodied whites such as Marsanne (California or Australia), white Cotes du Rhone or Coteaux d'Aix-en-Provence (France), dry French rosé (Bandol, Les Baux de Provence, or Tavel); in the winter medium- to full-bodied reds from France (such as Corbieres, Cotes du Ventoux, Coteaux du Languedoc, Cotes de Provence, Chateauneuf du Pape, St-Emilion, or Pomerol; Zinfandel or "GSM" blends (California, Washington)

SALADE NIÇOISE: dry, Grenache-based rosés from California, Bandol (France), or Navarra or Cigales (Spain); dry, crisp white such as Sauvignon/Fumé Blanc (California), dry white from Cote de Provence (France)

BOUILLABAISE: dry rosés, *blanc de noirs* or brut sparklers, such as Cremant de Bourgogne or Champagne (France); full-bodied French whites such as white Condrieu or Coteaux d'Aix en Provence; medium-bodied French reds (Pinot Noir from the Burgundy villages of Marsannay, Pernand-Vergelesses, or Chorey-les-Beaune, or a regional Bourgogne)

DUCK CONFIT IN A SALAD (AS AN APPETIZER) AT ROOM TEMPERATURE: medium-bodied dry whites such as the Chardonnay-based Macon, St-Veran, or Pouilly-Fuisse (Burgundy, France), or a Pinot Gris (Oregon or Alsace, France); semi-dry white such as Riesling from Alsace or Vouvray from the Loire Valley (France)

DUCK CONFIT AS A MAIN COURSE, SERVED HOT: bold French reds such as chateau wines from Graves, St-Estephe Pauillac, Margaux, or St-Emilion (Bordeaux) or Cornas, St-Joseph, Cote Rotie, Crozes-Hermitage (Rhone Valley);

full-bodied versions of Zinfandel, "GSM" blends, Cabernet Sauvignon, or Syrah (United States); Bierzo or Toro (Spain); Douro, Bairrada, or Dao (Portugal); Naoussa, Amyndeo, or Nemea (Greece)

Spain

CLASSIC PAELLA (WITH CHICKEN AND SEA-FOOD): dry, medium- to full-bodied whites such as Albarino, Ribeiro, Valdeorras, Penedes blends, or Rueda (Spain); fortified dry Manzanilla or Fino Sherry (Spain); Chardonnay, Viognier, Marsanne (California); Semillon (Australia)

COCHINILLO (ROAST SUCKLING PIG): in the summer, dry, medium- to full-bodied white such as Albarino and Godello (Spain); in the winter, medium- to full-bodied Spanish reds such as Rioja Reserva, Ribera del Duero Reserva, Toro, Valdeorras, Calatayud, Priorat, Montsant, or Bierzo

TAPAS OR PINTXOS (AN ASSORTMENT OF LITTLE PLATES OR TASTES): sparkling Cava; dry, fortified Fino or Manzanilla Sherry; dry white Getariako Txacolina, Rueda, Rioja, Penedes, Rias Baixas, or rosé from Navarra (all Spain all the time).

Portugal

CALDO VERDE (KALE SOUP WITH LINGUICA SAUSAGE): dry, medium- to full-bodied whites from the Dao, Beiras Atlantico, Bairrada, Dao, Peninsula de Setubal, Lisboa, or Bucelas regions (Portugal); light-bodied, low-alcohol dry whites such as Vinho Verde (Portugal); dry sparkling brut "Espumante" (Portugal)

CABRITO (BABY GOAT COOKED IN A WOOD-FIRED OVEN): dry, full-bodied noble reds from the Douro, Dao, Bairrada, Beiras Atlantico, or Alentejo regions (Portugal); Cabernet Sauvignon, Zinfandel, Petite Sirah, "GSM" blends (California). Outdoors on a hot summer day, rosé still or sparkling wine is a great option

CARNE DE PORCO ALENTEJANO (PORK AND CLAMS WITH POTATOES): in the summer, dry, medium-bodied Portuguese whites from the Alentejo, Tejo, Lisboa, Peninsula de Setubal, or Dao regions; in the winter, light- to medium-bodied inexpensive reds from the same regions

GREECE

MOUSSAKA: dry, full-bodied Greek reds based on the Xinomavro grape such as Naoussa or Amyndeo; red wine blends from Rapsani, Epanomi, Drama, or Peloponnese; Agiorgitiko from Nemea

GYRO OR SOUVLAKI SANDWICH: in the summer, dry or semi-dry Greek rosé wines based on the Moschofilero, Agiorgitiko, or Xinomavro grapes, or a dry rosé from California; in the winter, medium-bodied Greek reds such as inexpensive to moderately priced Nemea, Rapsani, Drama, Amyndeo, Peloponnese, and Naoussa

SPANAKOPITA WITH TZATZIKI, OR GREEK SALAD WITH FETA: dry, tart, local wines based on the Roditis, Robola or Assyrtiko grape or a blend such as a Santorini based on Assyrtiko and Athiri; tart Sauvignon Blanc (United States, New Zealand, Australia, South Africa, or a white Bordeaux blend)

GRILLED OCTOPUS, MULLET, OR SWORDFISH WITH OLIVE OIL: dry, floral local whites based on the Moschofilero or Malagousia grape or dry whites such as Santorini or Assyrtiko and Sauvignon blends from northern Greece

GREAT BRITAIN

FISH AND CHIPS (WATCH OUT FOR THE VIN-EGAR, IT CAN MAKE THE WINE TASTE SOUR SO TRY FRESH LEMON JUICE INSTEAD): tart, dry, medium-bodied fruity whites such as Sauvignon Blanc (New Zealand, Canada, or California); Graves or regional Bordeaux (France); sparkling brut from England or Cava (Spain); Vinho Verde (Portugal)

ROAST BEEF WITH YORKSHIRE PUDDING: dry, full-bodied reds such as chateau wines from Graves, Pauillac, or Margaux (Bordeaux, France) or Cabernet Sauvignon and "Meritage" blends from California; Cabernet Sauvignon or Syrah from Washington or Canada; Australian Cabernet Sauvignon or Shiraz, Rioja, or Ribera del Duero Gran Reserva (Spain), Douro or Dao (Portugal)

BELGIUM

MOULES FRITES (STEAMED MUSSELS WITH BELGIAN FRIES): dry, light-bodied whites such as Muscadet, Sylvaner, or Savoie (France); Vinho Verde (Portugal); dry sparkling Cremant d'Alsace or Cremant de Bourgogne (France)

WAFFLES WITH STRAWBERRIES AND WHIPPED CREAM: in the summer, sweet, sparkling (and low-alcohol) Brachetto d'Acqui or Moscato d'Asti (Italy); in the winter, the sweet, higher-alcohol Ruby Reserve or Late Bottled Vintage Port (Portugal)

SWEDEN/NORWAY

GRAVLAX : semi-dry, light-bodied whites such as cold-climate Riesling (New York, Canada, or Germany); Chenin Blanc (South Africa, Canada, or Vouvray from France); dry light-bodied fruity whites such as Sauvignon Blanc (New Zealand); dry rosé sparkling wine

EASTERN EUROPE

BORSCHT (WHO KNEW THAT BEETS AND WINE COULD BE SO MARVELOUS TOGETHER, AS LONG AS THE SOUP IS NOT SWEET): medium- to full-bodied reds such as Grenache or Grenache blends (California; Washington, Australia; Cannonau di Sardegna, Italy; Gigondas, France); Zinfandel (California); outdoors on a warm day, dry still or sparkling rosé

CHICKEN SOUP WITH MATZOH BALLS: dry, full-bodied white such as Chardonnay (kosher versions are available from many nations); Pinot Gris (Oregon or Canada); Semillon (Australia), Xarel-lo (Spain), Encruzado (Portugal), sparkling brut (Israel or United States)

WIENER SCHNITZEL: dry, medium- to full-bodied whites such as Chardonnay (New World or Old World); Pinot Gris (Oregon, British Columbia, or Alsace, France), Falanghina (Italy), Godello (Spain), Furmint (Hungary), Gruner Veltliner (Austria); or on a cold winter day a light- to medium-bodied red such as Morgon, Moulin-a-Vent, Minervois, Faugeres (France); Rioja Crianza (Spain), Zweigelt or Blaufrankisch (Austria)

VEAL OR BEEF GULYAS (GOULASH): dry, medium- to full-bodied reds such as moderate to expensive Zinfandel or Merlot (California), *cru* Beaujolais such as Morgon or Moulin-a-Vent (France), Egri Bikaver (Hungary), Lisboa, Alentejo (Portugal), Barbera d'Alba, Lagrein, or Montepulciano d'Abruzzo (Italy); Nemea, Naoussa (Greece)

CHICKEN PAPRIKASH: medium- to full-bodied whites such as Furmint (Hungary), Marsanne (California or Australia) or a white Cotes du Rhone (France); medium-bodied reds such as Torgiano Rosso or Rosso di Montalcino (Italy), Pinot Noir (New World or Old World), Merlot (Israel)

DUCK WITH RED CABBAGE: dry, medium- to full-bodied reds such as Mourvedre (California, or the Spanish version known as Monastrell), Zinfandel (California or the Italian version, Primitivo); "GSM" (New World or Old World)

BEEF STROGANOFF: full-bodied reds such as Cabernet Sauvignon (New World or Old World); Chateauneuf-du-Pape, Gigondas, or Vacqueyras (France), Grumello or Sforzato (Italy), Calatayud, Somontano, Navarra, Montsant (Spain); Dao (Portugal); Naoussa, Rapsani Reserve (Greece)

PIEROGIS: dry, full-bodied white such as Chardonnay (California, Israel, or a French version such as Pouilly-Fuisse or Rully), Pinot Gris (France); brut sparkling wine

TURKEY

KARNIYARIK (EGGPLANT STUFFED WITH MINCED MEAT): medium-full-bodied reds such as "GSM" blends (New World or Old World), Chinon, Pomerol, Minervois (France), Rosso di Montalcino (Italy)

LAMACUN/LAHMAJAHN (THIN BAKED DOUGH WITH GROUND MEAT AND DICED VEGETA-BLES): in the summer dry still or sparkling rosé or medium-full-bodied white such as Greco di Tufo (Italy); in the winter light- to medium-bodied reds such as inexpensive blends from Penedes (Spain) or Alentejo (Portugal); Zinfandel (United States)

AFRICA

MOROCCO/ALGERIA

VEGETABLE COUSCOUS: dry, medium- to full-bodied white such as Chardonnay (California); if you prefer a lot of spicy harissa, then a dry, light-bodied, low-alcohol Getariako Txacolina (Spain); Vinho Verde (Portugal); Moschofilero (Greece); or semi-dry, low-alcohol Riesling

LAMB TAGINE: dry, fruity, medium-bodied red such as an inexpensive to moderately priced Zinfandel or "GSM" blend (California); semi-dry rosé such as white Zinfandel (California); dry rosé still wine from Rioja or Navarra, or sparkling rosé Cava (Spain)

ETHIOPIA

INJERA AND WAT (THIN PANCAKES MADE OF THE GRAIN TEFF, SERVED WITH A SPICY MEAT STEW): dry, light-bodied reds that can be served with a light chill, such as Gamay (United States or Beaujolais, France), Bardolino or Valpolicella (Italy); dry and semi-dry rosés

MIDDLE EAST

Israel, Lebanon, Syria

VEGETARIAN MEZZE OF TABOULEH, FATOUCHE, BABA GHANOUSH, AND HUMMUS: dry, light-bodied whites such as Sauvignon Blanc (Israel) or a Lebanese blend such as Chateau Musar from the Bekaa Valley; brut sparkling wine; fruity, floral dry white such as Moschofilero or Malagousia (Greece)

KEFTA KEBABS OR SHAWARMA: dry rosé table or sparkling wines; medium- to full-bodied reds such as Cabernet Sauvignon blends (Israel, Lebanon, California, Australia, or Chile); Zinfandel or Primitivo (California or Italy); Malbec (Argentina); Lisboa, Alentejo (Portugal); Nemea or Rapsani (Greece)

AMERICAS AND THE CARIBBEAN

Brazil

FEIJOADA: full-bodied reds such as Cabernet Sauvignon or Syrah (Chile); Malbec (Argentina); Cahors, Fitou, Cotes du Roussillon-Villages (France); Tannat (Uruguay); Douro, Dao, Beiras Atlantico, Bairrada, Tejo, Lisboa, Alentejo (Portugal)

Argentina

BEEF CHIMICHURRI: full-bodied reds such as Malbec, Syrah, or Bonarda (Argentina), Cabernet Sauvignon and "Meritage" blends, moderate to expensive Zinfandel (California); Priorat, Montsant, Bierzo, Jumilla, Rioja Reserva (Spain); Douro, Dao, Beiras Atlantico, Bairrada, Alentejo, (Portugal)

Venezuela

AREPAS WITH CHORIZO AND QUESO FRESCO: medium-bodied dry whites such as Torrontes (Argentina), Sauvignon Blanc (Chile), Rueda, Rias Baixas, Albarino, Valdeorras, sparkling Brut Cava; light- to medium-bodied reds such as inexpensive Garnacha or Tempranillo from Castilla La Mancha (Spain)

Peru

TIRADITO (RAW FISH CARPACCIO WITH AJI AMARILLO PASTE [SPICY PEPPERS, LIME JUICE, AND GINGER]): light-bodied low alcohol white wines such as Riesling, Getariako Txakolina (Spain), or Vinho Verde (Portugal); semi-dry sparkling wines, such as extra-dry Prosecco

POLLO A LA BRASA: medium- to full-bodied white wines such as Chardonnay; Godello, Xarel-lo, or Albarino (Spain); light-bodied inexpensive reds that can be served with a light chill such as Garnacha or Moristel (Spain), Lambrusco Grasparossa di Castelvetro, Grignolino, Freisa, or Bardolino (Italy)

Puerto Rico

PERNIL OF PORK: in the summer, dry, medium-bodied whites such as Albarino/ Alvarinho (Spain/Portugal) or Torrontes (Argentina); in the winter, medium- to medium-full-bodied reds such as Merlot (New World or Old World); Bonarda (Argentina); Rosso di Montalcino or Cerasuolo di Vittoria (Italy); Rioja Crianza, Prieto Picudo, Campo de Borja, or Penedes blends (Spain)

Mexico

POZOLE: if green pozole, dry, tart Sauvignon Blanc (Mexico, Chile, or United States); if red pozole, light-bodied reds such as Gamay (California or Beaujolais, France) or Moristel (Spain)

RED SNAPPER VERACRUZ: dry, light- to medium-bodied whites such as Sauvignon Blanc (Mexico or Chile); Torrontes (Argentina); sparkling *blanc de blancs* or brut Cava (Spain)

GUACAMOLE: rich, full-bodied Chardonnay (Mexico or California) to balance the avocado's richness; tart Sauvignon Blanc (New Zealand or South Africa); sparkling Cava (Spain) to cleanse the richness

CHILES RELLENOS: semi-dry whites such as Riesling (New York, Washington, or Ontario, Canada); dry, fruity whites such as Torrontes (Argentina); Moschofilero or Malagousia (Greece)

BEEF OR TONGUE TACOS: dry rosé table or sparkling wines such as Cava (Spain); medium-bodied reds such as Merlot (Mexico or Chile) or inexpensive Tempranillo, Garnacha, or Monastrell (Spain)

LOBSTER WITH HUITLACOCHE (CORN TRUFFLE) CREAM SAUCE: older vintage brut Champagne (France); fine white Burgundy such as Chassagne-Montrachet or Meursault; white Rhone wines such as Chateauneuf-du-Pape Blanc, Condrieu, or St-Joseph Blanc (France); Godello, Xarel-lo, or Albarino (Spain)

BEEF CHIMICHANGAS, ENCHILADAS, OR FAJITAS: for mild preparations, medium-full to full-bodied reds such as moderate to expensive Zinfandel or Mourvedre (California); for spicy-hot versions, rosé table or sparkling wines such as Cava (Spain) or a light-bodied red served chilled, such as Beaujolais (France) and Bardolino or Valpolicella (Italy)

JAMAICA

CURRY GOAT: if served by itself, dry, light- to medium-bodied reds such as an inexpensive Zinfandel (California); if served with a jicama salad or fruity slaw (as is customary), semi-dry whites such as Chenin Blanc, Gewurztraminer, or Riesling

ACKEE: dry floral white with some richness such as Torrontes (Argentina), Moschofilero or Malagousia (Greece), or sparkling Prosecco (Italy)

UNITED STATES

DOWN-HOME AMERICAN COOKING

After all those exciting ethnic foods, it seems appropriate to end this section with American comfort food. Following are some of the traditional foods we grew up with and the wines we enjoy with them.

HAMBURGER WITH ALL THE FIXINGS: Cabernet Sauvignon or Cabernet blend (California, Australia, or Chile), Zinfandel or "GSM" blend from California; outdoors on a hot summer day, *blanc de noirs* or rosé bubbly

HOT DOG: with mustard, Pinot Blanc (New World or Old World); semi-dry Riesling from Washington, New York State, or Canada; Gewurztraminer (New World or France); for a chili dog with onions and cheese, inexpensive Zinfandel/Primitivo (California/Italy); still or sparkling rosé

CHILE CON CARNE: for mild versions, inexpensive Zinfandel (California); if spicy, semi-dry white Zinfandel (California) or a light red served chilled such as Beaujolais (France); Bardolino or Valpolicella (Italy); sparkling rosé (New Mexico or California); Cava from Spain, or Lambrusco from Italy

NEW YORK PASTRAMI OR MONTREAL (CANADA) SMOKED MEAT SANDWICH: *blanc de noirs* or sparkling rosé (Oregon, New Mexico, or California); a dry rosé such as Cigales or Navarra (Spain); a semi-dry Riesling or Chenin Blanc (New York, Washington, Ontario, British Columbia); Dr. Brown's Cel-Ray

MAC AND CHEESE: Chardonnay to balance the richness, or Sauvignon Blanc to cleanse the palate (California); white Cotes du Rhone (France); Falanghina, Vernaccia di San Gimignano (Italy); Albarino (Spain)

FRIED CHICKEN: dry, medium- to medium-full-bodied California white such as Viognier, Marsanne, or Chardonnay; sparkling brut from New Mexico, California, or a Cava (Spain), dry American rosé; on a cold winter day, Zinfandel (California), Morgon or Montpeyroux (France), Valgella, Inferno, or Grumello (Italy), Rioja Crianza (Spain); Dao or "Periquita" (Portugal); Nemea or Rapsani (Greece)

WHOLE DEEP-FRIED TURKEY, SPICY CAJUN STYLE: Riesling or Gewurztraminer (New World); extra-dry sparkling wine from California or Prosecco (Italy); Chenin Blanc, still or sparkling, from Vouvray or Montlouis (France); White Zinfandel or dry rosé (New World or Old World); if you love spicy hot, red Zinfandel can amp it up!

BARBECUED RIBS: dry, full-bodied reds such as Zinfandel (California), Shiraz, or "GSM" blend; Sforzato or Amarone (Italy); outdoors on a hot day: semi-dry white Gewurztraminer from Washington or California, sparkling rosé from New Mexico or California, or Cava from Spain

NEW ENGLAND CLAM CHOWDER: New York Chardonnay, Viognier, brut sparkling wine

MANHATTAN CLAM CHOWDER OR CALIFORNIA CIOPPINO: cool-climate Pinot Noir (New York or Oregon); cool-climate California Pinot Noir (Russian River Valley, Carneros, Anderson Valley, Santa Maria Valley, Sta. Rita Hills, among others); Fleurie, Chiroubles, Julienas (France); outdoors in the summer: rosé sparkling wines

Cajun/Creole

SEAFOOD GUMBO: dry or semi-dry rosé table or sparkling wine, such as Cava (Spain) or Cremant de Bourgogne (France)

CRAWFISH ÉTOUFFÉE: medium- to full-bodied white such as Chardonnay (Burgundy, France); sparkling *blanc de noirs* (California); Pinot Blanc or Gewurztraminer (France); Godello or Albarino (Spain)

JAMBALAYA: Riesling or Chenin Blanc; dry or semi-dry Grenache-based rosé such as Tavel or Bandol (France) or versions from Navarra, Spain or California; medium-bodied reds such as Chianti Classico (Italy), Garnacha (Spain)

CRAWFISH BOIL: dry, light-bodied sparkling such as *blanc de blancs* from New York, Washington, or California; Prosecco (Italy); semi-dry whites such as Gewurztraminer, Riesling, or Chenin Blanc (United States, Canada); low-alcohol dry whites such as Getariako Txacolina (Spain) or Vinho Verde (Portugal)

RED BEANS AND RICE WITH SAUSAGE: medium- to full-bodied reds with ripe fruit flavors such as Zinfandel, Petite Sirah, "GSM" blends (California); Shiraz (Australia); Bierzo, Cigales, Penedes, Carinena, Calatayud (Spain); Douro, Dao, Alentejo (Portugal)

MUFFALETTA SANDWICH: in the summer, dry, light- to medium-bodied whites such as Vermentino, Arneis, or Ribolla Gialla (Italy); semi-dry white wines such as Riesling; in the winter, medium-bodied reds such as inexpensive Zinfandel or Merlot (California); Carmenere (Chile); Bonarda (Argentina); Rosso di Montalcino or Teroldego Rotaliano (Italy); Penedes blends or Campo de Borja, (Spain); Nemea (Greece)

Pairing sweet wines with food

WHAT BETTER WAY TO END a meal than with wine? There are two views of pairing sweet wines with food: You can treat the wine as the dessert, or you can serve it with fruit, cheese, or dessert. The ideal serving for sweet wine is 2 to 3 ounces (60 to 90 milliliters)—about half of the standard serving for table wine.

First, a quick lesson in identifying sweet wines and reading their labels. Whether table (still), sparkling, or fortified, sweet wines have their own vocabulary. Once you know a few key terms, however, decoding them is a snap.

SWEET TABLE WINES

These wines may be labeled by varietal, proprietary name, place name, or a combination of varietal and place name.

VARIETAL LABELS

These include the grape name along with country-specific terms that indicate the wine is made in a sweet style. For example:

IN ENGLISH-SPEAKING NATIONS: Late Harvest, Botrytis, or Icewine

IN FRANCE: *Vendange Tardive* (usually sweet but some producers ferment out the sugars to make a dry or semi-dry style) or *selection de grains nobles* (guaranteed these are sweet!)

IN GERMANY: *Auslese, Beerenauslese, Trockenbeerenauslese,* or *Eiswein*

IN AUSTRIA: *Ausbruch*, as well as the German terms above

IN ITALY: *Recioto, Dolce,* or Vin Santo

The most common grapes to be made into sweet wines include Riesling, Gewurztraminer, Chenin Blanc, Semillon, and Muscat. In fact, the Muscat grape is used so often that the label may not include a term such as "Late Harvest." (Portugal and the Alsace region of France do make some dry versions of this grape, so ask your wine shop or server to confirm it is sweet before buying the wine.)

PROPRIETARY NAMES

These may also be used to label sweet wines: Quady's "Electra" (California) and Maculan's "Torcolato" (Italy) are examples.

LABELS BY PLACE NAME

Just like their dry counterparts, many sweet wines from Old World regions especially are labeled according to place. The place will often provide the key to the grape type used. In Bordeaux, France, the wines of Barsac, Loupiac, Ste-Croix-de-Mont, Cadillac, and Sauternes are based mostly on the Semillon grape. These wines are all full-bodied, with the most expensive versions from individual chateaux. In the Loire Valley, Vouvray Moelleux, Coteaux du Layon, Bonnezeaux, and Quarts de Chaume are based on the Chenin Blanc grape. Italian sweet wines that honor their birthplace include Recioto di Soave (white) and Recioto della Valpolicella (red). Vinsanto comes from the island of Santorini in Greece. (The Italian version, Vino Santo or Vin Santo, translates as "holy wine.")

LABELS WITH GRAPE NAME FOLLOWED BY PLACE NAME

Sometimes the grape name will be followed by a word meaning "of" (de, d', di, etc.) and the place name, as is the case with a sweet Muscat from the Rhone Valley (Muscat de Beaumes-de-Venise) and the Cotes de Roussillon (Muscat de Rivesaltes) of France. Greece makes a delicious sweet white wine called Muscat of Samos and a red Mavrodaphne of Patras. From Italy, there is Moscato d'Asti, a charming, low-alcohol, spritzy white, as well as the medium-bodied Malvasia di Lipari.

SWEET SPARKLING WINES

The terms "*sec*," "*demi-sec*," and "*doux*," used in the Champagne region of France to denote whether the wine is dry, off-dry, or sweet, respectively, are commonly employed in other nations as well. Demi-sec is the easiest to find. A proprietary name such as "Nectar Imperiale," a demi-sec Champagne by Moet et Chandon, may also be used.

SWEET FORTIFIED WINES

These wines are made by the addition of brandy, so they can pack a wallop of power and flavor. Although not all fortified wines are sweet, below are some of our favorite sweet fortified wines from around the world.

ITALY: Marsala Dolce

SPAIN: sweet Sherries, including the varietal-labeled Pedro Ximenez and Moscatel, as well as the blended Cream-style wines

PORTUGAL: true Porto can only come from Portugal's Douro Valley, although California, Australia, and South Africa are all producing very good wines in the style of Porto; Portugal is also home to Moscatel de Setubal and sweet Bual and Malmsey Madeiras.

UNITED STATES/CALIFORNIA: some good Port-style wines

AUSTRALIA: famous for its "stickies"—sweet wines based on the Muscat grape—as well as some Port-style wines

CYPRUS: Commandaria (an off-the-beaten-path delicious bargain-priced sweet wine)

DESSERT PAIRING GUIDELINES

Just because a wine is sweet does not guarantee a perfect marriage with dessert. We once attended a dessert and wine pairing with 25 different sweet wines, and only by trial and error did we discover our favorite combinations. The lesson is that experimentation is key. Luckily, experimenting is half the fun. Following are some guidelines to get you started.

COLOR COUNTS

As a general rule, we like to pair sweet white wines with desserts that feature white to yellow fruits such as apples, pears, mangoes, peaches, nectarines, apricots, gooseberries, or bananas. Likewise, show off those red dessert wines with red- or black-fruit-based desserts (think blueberries, blackberries, raspberries, strawberries, plums, and cherries). For example, an *Auslese* or *Eiswein* Riesling from Germany is lovely with apple strudel, while blueberry pie is a wonderful partner for the black-fruit flavors of a Late-Bottled Vintage Porto from Portugal.

GO NUTS

Oxidized sweet wines, such as Vin Santo (Italy) and Bual or Malmsey Madeira (Portugal), have a nutty flavor that perfectly complements nut-based cookies, cakes, or other desserts such as pecan pie, baklava (Greek nut pastry), almond biscotti, or even a Nutty Buddy ice cream bar.

EMBRACE THE RICHNESS OR REVIVE YOUR TASTE BUDS

Almost any style of sweet wine works with the following desserts: ice cream, custards, yogurt, crème caramel or flan, tres leches cake, cheesecake, and rice pudding. You just need to decide what you want the wine to do. If the goal is to refresh your palate and contrast with the richness of the dessert, choose a sweet sparkling wine. If you want to play up and extend the richness of the dessert, serve either a sweet table wine or a sweet fortified wine. Some of the same guidelines apply here as for savory pairings: complement the flavor of an apricot cheesecake with a sweet white, such as a Tokaji Aszu from Hungary. You can also match intensities. For a light, fluffy cheesecake, try a sweet, light-bodied white—perhaps a Moscato d'Asti from Italy. A dense and sinful cheesecake, however, calls for a richer wine, such as a Sauternes from France or Vinsanto from Greece.

A WORD ABOUT CHOCOLATE

If a chocolate dessert is more bitter than sweet (i.e., based on dark chocolate), then a rich Cabernet Sauvignon, Shiraz, or Zinfandel is one way to go, though it's not our favorite choice. We prefer powerful sweet fortified wines that will balance the richness of the chocolate, such as true Porto from Portugal or Port-style wines from California or Australia. An alternative is the red, effervescent Brachetto d'Acqui from Italy; the bubbles break through the richness of chocolate.

Perhaps the dessert has a secondary component that can indicate a pairing. Chocolate-dipped strawberries and Black Forest cake have red-fruit flavors in addition to the chocolate—a good match for the Portos and Brachetto mentioned above. Likewise, the orange flavors of fortified Muscats are wonderful play pals for a chocolate-orange mousse.

Another factor when pairing chocolate desserts is texture—how thin or dense are they? The dense texture of a chocolate terrine or gooey chocolate brownies demands an equally powerful wine, so a sweet fortified wine such as a Malmsey Madeira from Portugal or a Pedro Ximenez Sherry

from Spain are our go-to wines of choice. With bittersweet chocolate desserts the sweetness of dessert wines is a contrast to the bitterness and a complement to the sweetness of the dessert.

THE WINE MUST BE AT LEAST AS SWEET AS THE DESSERT

If the wine is less sweet than the dessert, you will be left with a bitter aftertaste. Needless to say, it is best to avoid ending a meal with bitterness. Remember that people's impression of sweetness varies, so if someone recommends a Riesling with dessert, make sure it is a late harvest, botrytis, or Icewine style.

REGIONAL WINES ROCK WITH REGIONAL DESSERTS

Classic examples of regional pairings are hazelnut biscotti with Vin Santo of Italy; another is Vinsanto of Greece with baklava. Over time, certain wines have proven to be fabulous with local desserts. We nominate apple pie and New York State late harvest Riesling as a marriage made in heaven. It's our contribution to a regional sweet ending.

OUR SWEETEST DESSERT EXPERIENCE

A truly incredible combination is Pedro Ximenez Sherry or Montilla Moriles poured over vanilla or rum raisin ice cream—hedonistic heaven! The cold temperature calms down the heat of the alcohol in the fortified wine. The richness of the ice cream balances out the full body of the wine and there are complementary dried fruit (raisins) and sweet flavors. Did we mention they taste soooo yummy together?

15

THE
GOOD
LIFE

WINE IS A GOOD PART, A FUN PART, SOMETIMES EVEN A PROFOUND PART, OF DAILY LIFE. IN THIS CHAPTER, WE'LL BE sharing some thoughts about wine tasting at home, the "seasonality" of some wines—light whites in warm weather, hearty reds in cold—special wines for special occasions, and the evolution of the wine container—screwcaps on bottles and swapping bottles for boxes.

What we hope you'll glean from all of this is that wine fits with the patterns of modern life, whether it's just a glass of wine with dinner, a little bit of a reward at the end of a tough day, or making just another meal a heightened, even special, experience.

And of course, the theme that runs throughout this chapter is that wine is a gift from nature that is meant to be shared with friends and family, expanding our conversations and humor and bringing us closer to one another.

Wine tasting: do try this at home

THE REAL FUN OF TASTING wine is tasting for pleasure, exploring what appeals to you about a particular wine, and sharing that enthusiasm, that pleasure with others. And the best place to do this is at home, with friends, in a relaxed atmosphere of conviviality and generosity. Tasting wine at home is fun coupled with a bit of self-guided education. But don't worry—in this case the education mimics the learning curve that began with the awkward pleasures of your first kiss and grew exponentially into sensual subtlety: the confident strut, the irresistible smile.

How to begin? What wines? How many wines? How expensive are the wines? What glassware? What room? Outside or inside?

Wait! The most important factor is the people. You can taste some of the most glorious wines in the world, but if you taste them with miserable people, guess what? The wines will taste miserable, too. You want to invite friends who enjoy the company of other people, have a sense of humor, don't judge others harshly, and don't want to be the "expert" but have something to say. Finally, invite friends who are moderate drinkers. Wine tastings are not for lushes, who can diminish or even ruin the experience for everyone else. *Tasting* is the operative word.

Once you've put together your guest list, start to think about the wine. Some basics:

Use wine glasses. Don't use clear plastic cups, which make the wine taste like clear plastic cups. Most people don't have enough glasses, so here's a hint: rather than burdening your guests with a request to bring glasses from home, check out the local party rental folks. You'll be surprised how inexpensive it is to rent two or three racks of glasses—not necessarily great glasses, but all of them the same size and shape, and racked together for convenience and to avoid breakage.

Provide spit cups and napkins. Tasting involves four steps: looking (judging the color of the wine), smelling (the "nose" of the wine), tasting (sampling a small amount of wine and swishing it around in the mouth), and spitting. That's right, part of tasting is spitting the wine into a spittoon or spit cup. While you're at the party place renting glasses, pick up a sleeve of 16-ounce (480 milliliter) paper cups, and place one at every setting. You may not be able to enforce spitting at a home wine tasting, but especially if your friends are driving away from the tasting, you can certainly encourage it. A couple of good-quality white paper napkins should be placed at each setting, too.

Bread and water. Water should be plentiful and available. A few bread baskets filled with crisp sliced baguettes and/or individual plates with water crackers should be available for cleansing the palate between wines. Make sure the bread or crackers are as neutral tasting as possible: no brioche, croissants, or flavored crackers because these will have a dramatic impact on the wine's taste.

Tasting mats/tasting sheets. On your home computer you can make a simple or an elaborate and creative tasting mat, or if you're truly inspired, you can design your own.

If you are tasting the wines blind—nobody at the tasting knows which wine is which until the big reveal—obviously the wines will be identified by number only. If you know what wines you are tasting, list them by name. It helps your guests to be consistent in how you list the wine. We recommend listing each wine this way:

1. **PRODUCT**
2. **SPECIAL ATTRIBUTE,** if any
3. **PRODUCER**
4. **SUBREGION,** if any
5. **REGION,** if any
6. **STATE** (U.S.) or **COUNTRY**
7. **VINTAGE,** if any (write "NV" if nonvintage)

Wine tastings may be a prelude to or part of a festive meal, outdoors or indoors, such as shown here at the home of Iron Horse Winery founders Audrey and Barry Sterling. Photos courtesy of Iron Horse Winery.

EXAMPLES

Pinot Noir (1)

Reserve (2)

Robert Sinskey (3)

Carneros (4)

Napa Valley (5)

California (6)

2013 (7)

Chianti Classico (1)

Reserva (2)

Banfi (3)

Tuscany (5)

Italy (6)

2011 (7)

Shiraz (1)

Peter Lehmann (3)

Barossa Valley (4)

South Australia (5 and 6)

2012 (7)

(It would be redundant to write "South Australia, Australia," as most people can figure this one out. If they can't, well, then you probably don't want them at your tasting.)

Chateau Larose-Trintaudon (1 and 3)

Haut-Medoc (4)

Bordeaux (5)

France (6)

2011 (7)

(Note that when it comes to chateau-named wines from Bordeaux, the name of the product [the wine] and the name of the producer [the chateau] are one and the same, as there is only one Chateau Larose-Trintaudon or only one Chateau Blah Blah Blah, *n'est ce pas?*)

On the tasting mat, or better yet (and especially if you are tasting more than four or five wines) on separate sheets of paper, allow each taster to make notes on each wine based on these criteria: color, nose, flavor, body, length of finish on the palate. You might also ask "Did you like it?" and/or "What would be a good dish to pair with this wine?"

Maps of the wine regions represented at your tasting are a nice plus for your guests. Use the maps in this book, or utilize the interactive maps available at Kobrand's website, www.kobrandwine.com. You might want to print these out, but if you've got a large computer monitor, it might be more fun to play with these maps online, highlighting specific areas (for example, the *premier cru* vineyard sites of the Chablis district in Burgundy). Looking at maps gives people a sense of place for the wines.

The tasting can be done indoors or outdoors—the more light, the better to see the true color of the wine—as a prelude to dinner, or as its own little party. You should pour between 1 and 2 ounces (30 and 60 milliliters) per person per wine; 1½ ounces (45 milliliters) is ideal. It's very important to make sure your guests stay for at least a couple of hours after the tasting, and never let a friend drive drunk. If everybody is on the same page with the concept of the tasting, this should not be an issue.

As to what wines to serve, think thematically: New World reds under $15, white wines from the Loire Valley, sparkling wines of the world, American wines not from California, zigging and zagging with Zinfandel. Of course, if money is no object, then feel free to host a tasting of Opus One: 2001 to 2011; the *premier grands crus* of the Haut-Medoc: 1995 to 2010; Barolo versus Barbaresco: the 2009 vintage; and so on. At home, we prefer tasting accessible, affordable wines that our friends can appreciate, enjoy, and can have some fun with, followed by a simple dinner, picnic, or cookout with the "partials," the leftover wines. For an exotic and unexpected twist, have a tasting followed by a dinner of good Chinese takeout, the best pizza in town, or some exciting dishes from that new Lebanese restaurant. You get the picture.

As for us, we'll be busy planning our next blind tasting at home: "$10.99 Rieslings: World-Class, Kick-Ass, or We'll Pass." See you there.

Life is short: Drink (and share) that special bottle!

WHEN IT COMES TO THE SUBJECT of rare and expensive wines that you have been saving for those special occasions, our advice is simple, direct, and concise: drink up!

So many wine lovers are the stewards of rare and wonderful wines that they are saving for a special occasion. In a world where every day we are increasingly reminded how fleeting life can be, we might want to reexamine the concept and definition of "special occasion" to make it more inclusive, more elastic, more fun. Get those bottles out of the dusty cellar, stand them up in the light of day, and bring them to your table to enjoy. Opening and sharing a rare and wonderful wine makes the food taste better, the conversation more sophisticated (or at least the same old stories more bearable), your dining companions more attractive. Even close friends and family realize, perhaps for the first time, that you and your home exude a glowing warmth and generosity.

Yes, we call wine lovers who cellar treasured and rare wines "stewards," not "owners." Unless you get inordinate pleasure from looking at or stroking bottles with labels, you "own" very little until that bottle is opened and that wine is drunk. If you collect wine to resell it, you merely steward that wine from the previous cellar to your cellar to the buyer's cellar, and the only pleasure is profit; you might as well invest in pork bellies or any other commodity. As anyone who has ever tasted truly great wine can attest, it is a magical elixir that provides pleasure so far beyond dollars, pounds, or euros that the *sale* of fine wines and the *enjoyment* of fine wines do not even inhabit the same pleasure universe.

We often wonder if even the most wine-stained among us realize how truly rare is the opportunity to taste great wine. No more than one-tenth of 1% of the wine produced in the world is destined

AT-HOME TASTING SHEET

WINE	COLOR	NOSE
Name of the wine, producer, any special attributes, any subregions and/or regions, state (U.S.) or country (foreign), vintage (if any)	Your perception of depth, hue, and clarity	What the wine smells like to you: aroma and/or bouquet
1.		
2.		
3.		
4.		
5.		
6.		
7.		
8.		

BODY	TASTE	FINISH	FOOD MATCH
Your impression of the wine on the palate: light, medium, or full	Flavor components that you experience on your palate	Duration of flavors after tasting (short, medium, or long); any new flavors?	What would you like to eat with this wine? Why?

to be among the treasured classics. Fortunately, the equivalent of about 15 billion bottles of wine are produced every year, so about 1.5 million bottles from each worldwide vintage might be keepers. This collection is diminished even more by the relative quality of the vintage; the reputation of the producer; the wine futures market, especially in Bordeaux; the auction block; the finest restaurants, who get first dibs on treasured wines; and the generally rich and powerful, who, if they want to, can always get there first.

We the many, who are neither so rich nor so powerful, can afford very few of life's large luxuries. Occasionally, we purchase or perhaps receive as a gift a little luxury: a fine bottle of wine, a wine to be shared with special people at a special time. *Now* is that time, a moment that will never come again, so don't wait for that "special dinner." Make tonight's dinner special: special for the one you love more than any other, special for your kids home from college, special for the friends whose support you rely on and who rely on you, special for the folks who don't always feel so special but you know they are. Sharing your finest wines creates a truly special atmosphere, as the table becomes a place not only for celebration but also for meditation.

With our first look, our first smell, our first sip, we are transported to a place where riches and power run a distant second to pure pleasure, and for that brief shining moment we are as rich as the richest person, as happy as the happiest, and power just doesn't matter.

Warm weather wines: sparklers for summer

WE'RE BUBBLEHEADS. LOVE THOSE BUBBLES. And what better time to enjoy refreshing, thirst-quenching sparkling wines than the summer in multiseason environs or anyplace that's warm

year-round? Please don't expect us to wait for the holiday season (when more than 40% of all sparklers are consumed) or for a birthday, anniversary, or some other holiday. No, we want our bubbles now!

Why should we relegate Champagne and other wonderful sparklers to the rarefied dustbin of special occasion wines? Are we secretly so pleasure-negative that we feel we deserve to feel the sexy exhilaration that bubbles provide only once in a while, and then only on socially acceptable rites and festivals? When did carbonated pleasure become a commodity to be doled out to us at holidays for being good little boys and girls? Enough!

There is just no good excuse for not enjoying sparkling wines year-round, but especially in warm weather, when the exciting combination of acidity and carbonation both satisfies our thirst and refreshes our palate. Just the image of a champagne bottle in a silver or glass ice bucket quickens the pulse, as does the exquisite *perlage* of small bubbles rising in a straight line from a single point of departure in a beautiful flute or tulip glass. If ever form followed function, it does so in a crystal flute of bubbly.

The first taste of the wine! So refreshing, so heady, so romantic. The bubbles, sustained as if by magic, dance on your tongue well after the initial sip. By the second glass, we truly sing the body electric, and all is right with the world.

And please don't consign good sparkling wines to the realm of aperitifs and hors d'oeuvres. You can have great fun planning an all-bubbly dinner: a light *blanc de blancs* with poached fish in lemongrass broth, followed by a medium-bodied brut with a mushroom risotto and a full-bodied rosé reserved for a perfectly roasted chicken or grilled filet mignon served with roasted new potatoes and ratatouille. A toast to the health of the all those sharing the pleasures of the table with a *blanc de noirs* sparkler is followed by a delightful dessert of coconut, mango, and blackberry sorbets served on a banana waffle with a softly sweet demi-sec sparkler.

Now what's stopping you from indulging in the beauty of the bubbles, the sensuality

Courtesy of Gloria Ferrer Caves and Vineyards.

of the sparkle? Expense? Pish-tosh. What century are you living in? Sparkling wines can be real bargains. The best estate-bottled sparklers made in the United States, Iron Horse (Sonoma/Green Valley) and Roederer Estate (Mendocino/Anderson Valley), are bargains at under $35. Fine wines from Domaine Carneros (Napa Valley/Carneros), Argyle (Oregon/Willamette Valley), the very exciting Gruet (New Mexico), and Chateau Frank (Finger Lakes, New York State) are even less.

Champagne taste with a six-pack budget? Remember just one word...Cava! These Champagne-method sparklers from outside of Barcelona, Spain, are charming, sexy, and satisfying, and most are available at prices starting at less than $10 or $12. A current favorite is Segura Viudas (look for the brut reserva and the rosé) as well as Cristalino, Juve y Camps, Pares Balta, Sumarocca, Paul Cheneau, and the ubiquitous Freixenet and Cordoniu, among many others. For a very special vintage-dated wine at about $30, the Llopart "Leopardi" Gran Reserva Brut Nature (aged 46 to 52 months) is an amazing find in prestige bubbly, as is the Gramona "III Lustros."

And please don't forget Prosecco. This light, frothy, fruity sparkler is a crowd- and budget-pleaser, terrific on a hot day and with spicy foods. Look for Prosecco from Mionetto, Maschio, Adami, Nino Franco, Bisol, Zardetto, Bellussi, Valdo, La Marca, and many other fine producers. While Prosecco is a good budget-based choice, when looking for something truly special from Italy, we suggest Franciacorta, the Champagne-method sparkler from Lombardy.

Franciacorta is a bit of a splurge, with most bottles selling in the $30 to $40 range.

True Champagne, the real deal from that eponymous region of France, while more expensive than other sparklers, can be surprisingly affordable. We love sparkling wines from all over the world, but the one wine that is truly *terroir*-driven is Champagne. Chalk soil (formed by ancient receding oceans) and low temperatures (it is the coldest wine region in France) give Champagne the earthy/yeasty aroma and complex flavor with subtly searing acidity that is unique in the world of sparkling wines.

Expensive vintage-dated and *cuvee de prestige* Champagnes are easy to find, but look a little deeper and you will find some real bargains. Look for Phillipponnat, Jacquart, Gosset, Charbaut, Alfred Gratien, Pol Roger, Montaudon, Lanson, Jacquesson, Ayala, Charles Heidsieck, and Deutz, all of which retail in the $35 to $45 range. Also, try some of the small producers—the "grower Champagnes" that are often less expensive than the nonvintage wines produced by the major Champagne houses. Producers to look for include: Aubry et Fils, Paul Goerg, Pierre Gimonnet, Larmandier-Bernier, Pierre Peters, Vilmart, and Egly-Ouriet.

France produces some very fine sparklers outside of the Champagne region in the $15 to $25 range. Look for Cremant d'Alsace or Cremant de Loire, available from a wide variety of producers.

Finally, for an off the beaten path choice, try Moschofilero-based bubbly from Peloponnese in Greece.

We think we've made the case for sparkling wines to be an important part of your wine regimen, never again to be cast aside until the "right occasion." The truth is this: if we were told that we could drink only one category of wine for the rest of our lives, our choice would be sparkling wine. Why? Because it's sexy and it's fun, and in a world where we're only allowed one kind of wine to drink, we think we'll need all the sexy fun we can get.

Warm weather wines: Whites for summer

IN 1935, GEORGE AND IRA GERSHWIN wrote "Summertime," the most memorable song featured in the American opera classic *Porgy and Bess*. The lyrics begin: "Summertime and the livin' is easy…" This timeless lullaby perfectly describes our approach to eating and drinking during the hot months of summer: slow down, take it easy, bask in the warm sunshine, and enjoy lighter meals with lighter wines. And the wines don't have to lighten your wallet, either.

Summer should be a season for rest, relaxation, and recuperation. We still may work 9 to 5 but it's light when we get up, and it's still daylight when we drive home; that alone should put us in a sunny mood. And most of us can manage to get away or just goof off for at least a couple of long, lazy weekends, while the lucky ones sneak a few weeks. Ah, summer! That cherished time of year that means life in the great outdoors of fun, friends, family, and food.

We are summer-lovers, and so are most of our friends. We live in the beautiful Hudson Valley in shorts and T-shirts whenever we can, and we cook and dine al fresco every chance we get. We love to fire up the grill and then jump in the water to meditate on the menu, which is inevitably based on what's fresh from the garden and what looked good at the fish market or butcher. And, of course, there's the wine . . . .

So many light wines are a pleasure to imbibe in the summertime. Good Pinot Grigio is a great match with rotisserie chicken. New World Sauvignon Blanc—especially those from California and Chile, and "fruit salad in a glass" from New Zealand and South Africa—is terrific with grilled salmon served with spicy fruit salsas. Dry and semi-dry Rieslings are magnificent foils for many spicy Cajun, Thai, or Indian dishes. Vinho Verde from Portugal is a low-alcohol, spritzy wine that is a fabulous match with ceviche and also a wonderful aperitif. A simple summer meal of mussels in saffron broth was made to go with Muscadet from the Loire Valley. Dry- to semi-dry rosé is terrific with North Carolina–style barbecue of pulled-pork sandwiches. And don't forget lighter reds— Beaujolais-Villages or Valpolicella Classico, among others, served with a bit of a chill, for those burgers and steaks hot off the grill.

Summer wines should be full of fruit, cool and refreshing, and as informal and inexpensive as the summer-lovers' dress code. When you're relaxing and talking, playing killer croquet or badass badminton, hard-hearted horseshoes, or simply silently swimming, you don't want to ruminate over ponderous, serious wines full of complexity and depth. When the sun is shining, you want the alcohol to be low, so that you don't become groggy, and you're able to have safe and responsible fun. Save those big reds and oaky whites for sitting by the fireplace in late autumn, winter, and early spring, dining on lamb stews, hearty soups, and scripted meals. Just as food is seasonal— greens, tomatoes, and corn are the cornerstones of the true summer-lover's diet—so is wine. So bring on the wines of summer: light, crisp whites, thirst-quenching dry rosés, and fruity, luscious reds!

VINHO VERDE

In the mood for a salad of fresh greens studded with boiled, steamed, or grilled lobster and drizzled with a dreamy dressing of coarsely puréed watermelon, onion, and ripe peaches? What could be better with this light and simple dish than a Vinho Verde from Portugal, an elegant, dry white wine that is redolent of grapefruit, often with just a bit of spritz for a refreshing cleansing of the palate.

Vinho Verde is the ultimate summer-lover's wine: 8% to 11% alcohol, and it's not afraid of an ice cube or two, or even a little sparkling water for a magnificent wine spritzer. Vinho Verde is the reigning monarch of the land of ABC (anything but Chardonnay), and she is a ruler who favors almost unbelievably progressive taxation. Basic Vinho Verde sells for $6 to $15

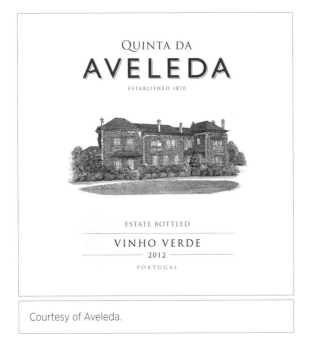

per bottle, a truly great wine value, so buy a case or two for the summer. You want to drink this charming wine as young as possible, so look for the most current vintage or bottling date (found in very small print on the back label).

ENTRE-DEUX-MERS

One of the delights of writing about wine is turning *WineWise* readers on to a wonderful wine that they may never have tried or maybe never even thought about trying. When the wine is also a great value, the delight doubles.

This particular summer white carries a passport from the European Union. No matter: it is at home in the backyards, on the decks, by the seashore or by the pool, and in the hills and mountains of the United States. If you welcome this wine once during the summer, you will beg a case or two to stay as a guest for the entire season.

The wine is Entre-Deux-Mers, a dry white wine from Bordeaux in France. For the record, Entre-Deux-Mers is comprised of a blend of mostly Sauvignon Blanc and Semillon grapes. It is meant for early drinking, is light- to medium-bodied with crisp and refreshing acidity, and is a perfect summer wine.

Entre-Deux-Mers produces a wine with a minimum alcohol content of 10%, but most in the American market are 11% to 12%. The moderate alcohol makes these wines very attractive mates for light and simple foods, especially fish and seafood. Salsas trump sauces with this wine, and there is just nothing better with *caprese*, a tomato and fresh mozzarella salad with fresh basil, good olive oil, and a touch of balsamic vinegar.

Unfortunately, Entre-Deux-Mers can be difficult (but by no means impossible) to find, and here's the reason:

1. Raise your hand if prior to reading *WineWise* you were familiar with a wine labeled "Entre-Deux-Mers."

2. Now raise your hand if prior to reading *WineWise* you were familiar with a wine labeled "Bordeaux."

We're willing to bet that 90% of readers raised their hand only once, and it wasn't for choice number-one. The winemakers in Entre-Deux-Mers realize this problem, and so very often they will label their wine simply as "Bordeaux" because it is easier to sell with the less specific but legally allowed label. This is a fact of life in our increasingly vanilla world, but it is still wrong. "Bordeaux Blanc" usually sells for more money than Entre-Deux-Mers; the reverse should be true.

But what is bad news for the reputation of Entre-Deux-Mers is good news for the consumer. Forty years ago Entre-Deux-Mers sold at retail for $4 per bottle. Today, you can still buy estate-bottled—*mise en bouteilles au chateau*—Entre-Deux-Mers for $10 to $15. In 40-year-old dollars, when you figure the annual rate of inflation, the wine now costs less than nothing. It's like the *vignerons* of Entre-Deux-Mers are paying you to drink their wine!

And there are stellar producers of this lovely summer-perfect wine, including our personal favorite, Chateau Bonnet, which sports a consumer-friendly screwcap. Other very fine Entre-Deux-Mers producers include: Chateau Marjosse, Chateau Fondarzac, Chateau Moulin de Launay, Chateau Roquefort, Chateau Thieuley, and Chateau Turcaud.

Back to the Gershwin brothers and their song that brought us to the party. Entre-Deux-Mers is a perfect accompaniment to "Summertime." It is such an enjoyable warm-weather wine that it is sure to confirm that "your daddy's rich, and your mama's good-lookin'." You can't ask more from any wine.

THE BOUNTY OF THE LOIRE VALLEY

As we mentioned in our chapter on French wines (see pages 145–189), the wines of the Loire are intrinsically linked with summer sun and fun, elegantly simple and coolly refreshing. From the numerous appellations along the Loire Valley comes an almost limitless array of bright whites, dry rosés, and lollipop reds that make any back-yard bash so much more enjoyable. If you were so inclined, you could spend the full three months of summer metaphorically cruising up and down the Loire, sampling all of its wine wares, and never having to repeat one. Add that to your list of "must do before I'm 50" (or 60, or . . .).

Start at the western end of the valley and sample all of Muscadet's simple pleasures, from straightforward, razor-sharp Muscadet *tout court* to the greater complexities of the *sur lie* style with noticeable yeasty, brioche-like aromas and flavors. These wines are terrific relaxation beverages, the best timing mechanism ever invented for making sure that the corn, still in its husk, cooks gently on top of the grill: just reach out every now and then and give the corn a quarter turn. Since we are all concerned about enjoying and appreciating every drop of wine we consume, we also want to be sure that we don't simply load up on alcohol. Take advantage of Muscadet's simplicity and you will never again face a dish of steamed clams, mussels, or raw oysters without Muscadet to wash it all down as a decadent lead-in to a summer feast.

Move inland down the Loire Valley toward the center, tie up at some virtual mooring, and you could spend the next month exploring all that this area has to offer, with dry to semi-dry

Courtesy of Chateau de la Ragotiere.

Chenin Blancs and ripe, juicy, medium-bodied Cabernet Francs. The villages of Saumur and Vouvray produce incomparable Chenin-based white wines, and we have spent many an enjoyable summer evening musing over our next course with the sensual promise provided in a glass of Vouvray or Saumur—especially sparkling Saumur, one of the great undiscovered wonders of the world of sparkling wine. And don't keep those reds from Chinon or Saumur-Champigny locked in the closet or sitting in the sun; dunk them in the ice bucket or let them doze undisturbed in the fridge for a while until they get the lightest chill that will make their Cabernet Franc red berry flavors sing rather than just wilt in the heat.

Put out a sumptuous spread of smoked trout, grilled salmon, egg rolls, prosciutto and melon, baby lamb chops, grilled pork tenderloin, potato salad—and the wines of the central Loire Valley will show you just how well they are suited to summer backyard living.

Of course, like many an errant sailor, you may decide that the central Loire Valley is where you will permanently drop anchor, but if the urge to move on grabs you, you don't have far to go upstream before Sancerre and Pouilly-Fumé call to you as the sirens they are, beguiling you to stop and try the wonders of these Sauvignon Blancs (and don't forget to try Sancerre *rouge* and rosé, each made from Pinot Noir). This is where the grilled tuna, seafood sausage, and asparagus come in. And for those who have really paced themselves well, a classic pairing of fresh goat cheese with a white Sancerre will send us all to sleep happy and sated.

Warm weather wines: Riveting rosés of summer

HERE IS A WARM-WEATHER MANTRA for you to channel your inner sunshine: "Summer-lovers love rosé." During the cool months of the year, rosé wines get little notice and less respect. Rosé is all but forgotten or ignored by wine geeks, but for wine and food lovers who adore fresh, cool flavors of orange and strawberries, dry rosé is a revelation.

Paired with a chilled dry rosé, grilled salmon served medium-rare with "creamers" (tiny roasted red potatoes) and roasted summer garlic alongside a salad of garden greens dressed with extra-virgin olive oil and fresh herbs is nothing short of perfection. A wine that will enhance your food as well as slake your thirst, rosé is to summer as falling leaves are to autumn, an undeniable part of the landscape. Try rosé wines from California, Spain, Italy, or Greece, but especially from Provence, France, where rosé is a regional specialty. Many of these wines start at under $15 and rarely exceed $25.

If we had to choose but one summer wine to accompany a variety of lighter grilled foods, we know what we'd choose in a heartbeat. While we're happy that we don't have to make such a dramatic choice, we honestly believe that we could be happy chilling out and grilling out with a glass of cold rosé.

Rosé gets almost no respect from wine snobs, but it is the perfect drink for the hot, the thirsty, and the hungry.

Like virtually all important and mysterious enigmas, the perfection of rosé lies in those same qualities long identified, often erroneously, as faults in the wine. To wit: rosé has no real character; it's neither white nor red; it's not really sweet, but you can't call it dry; it's so simple to drink; it's a pizza wine; it's a picnic wine; it's a wine for the beach; it's an inexpensive, unsophisticated wine; it's so unhip to drink rosé. Sounds perfect to us.

Rosé is the near-perfect wine to drink with elegant yet simple food: grilled salmon, kabobs, a beautiful burger, a succulent steak, grilled sausages, a salad of grill-roasted sweet corn with grilled tomatoes and ripe peaches. Rosé is a wine that does not dull the senses; it refreshes and reinvigorates them.

A dry to semi-dry rosé is the ultimate wine to serenade a Mediterranean-influenced barbecue, to create fireworks at an all-American cookout on the Fourth of July, to dive in with a "Floribbean" nut-encrusted grilled grouper, or to meditate on the essence of spa-inspired vegetarian fare.

Fresh, crisp rosé will transport you to the world of cool, refreshing, very dry white wines, but with more than a little of the fruitiness and depth of a light red. Even among the driest rosés, a vein of strawberry or citrus fruits will appear out of nowhere. Rosé at its best is a simple, flexible, and affordable accompaniment to all the food we love to cook and eat in the fresh air.

Especially during warm weather, rosé wines deserve a prominent place on your table. Try dry and semi-dry rosé wines and you may find that, because of their affinity with your food as well as their friendly price points, rosé will bring a welcome chill to the grill.

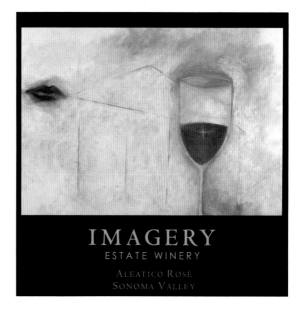

IMAGERY
ESTATE WINERY
ALEATICO ROSÉ
SONOMA VALLEY

Warm weather wines: Fruity reds of summer

THE PERFECTLY GRILLED BURGER, COOKED and served outdoors, is as much a part of summer's iconography as fireworks on the Fourth of July. Serve it with fresh tomatoes, lettuce, onion, salted cucumbers picked that day, a sauce of ketchup, mustard, and mayo, with just a touch of Tabasco or sriracha, all piled on hearth-baked bread, with homemade potato salad on the side, and just ask yourself as you taste this American delicacy, "Does it gets any better than this?"

Yes, it does. Pair that burger with a light, fruity, but dry red, such as Barbera from California's Amador County, Beaujolais-Villages from France, a young red Rioja from Spain, Dao from Portugal, or perhaps best of all some fruity reds from Italy—a Valpolicella Classico from Veneto, a simple Chianti from Tuscany, or a Dolcetto from Piedmont (each of these wines can be found easily for under $20). Now, take a sip and taste a second sauce, a true "secret sauce" for that burger, revealed only to your palate. These wines smell and taste of red summer berries. The fruit of the wine harmonizes with the earthy, sweet flavors of the burger, creating a simultaneous counterpoint and complement for the sensual nexus of flavors going on in this dish.

We say "chill these reds." That's right—serve 'em cool, serve 'em cold. Why? Putting a chill on these simple reds will bring out their fresh flavors and pump up the refreshing acidity that we crave on a hot day to refresh our palates. If you taste these wines warm (made even warmer in the glass by your hand and by the sun), they might taste flat and flabby and lose some of their many charms. So treat these reds like whites or rosés when you enjoy them in the summer sunshine.

The pleasures of summer are many, but fleeting. But for those precious few languorous months of intense warmth and sunshine, let's celebrate the glorious summer season with glorious summer wines.

Winter warmers: Reds for winter

AS AUTUMN TURNS TO WINTER, we begin to eat heartier foods and drink heartier wines. For us, this means enjoying full-bodied wines—especially big reds—with the aromatic and comforting stews, slow-cooked meats, brawny pasta dishes, and roasted vegetables that help to offset the chill of cold weather. When it's cold outside you can warm up inside with a hearty dish and a hearty wine.

"To everything there is a season," and that's true for seasonal foods served with seasonal wines. In the summertime, you might enjoy cold stone crabs in a lemongrass broth with a glass or two of chilled Sauvignon Blanc, but in the winter you are more likely to gravitate to a lamb stew served with garlic-roasted potatoes and a few glasses of Cabernet Sauvignon or Syrah to take away your physical and psychic chill.

These days, winter warmers can be found from all over the wine world and at all different price points. These wines are red, full-bodied, and complex. Think about some of these wines with a plate of Hungarian goulash, a rib-eye steak with creamy mashed potatoes, pasta with sausages, a classic cassoulet of beans, pork, and duck, or its Portuguese and Brazilian cousin, *feijoada*. Slow-roasted root vegetables sprinkled liberally with Parmigiano Reggiano cheese is a robust dish without meat that can support a winter warmer, too.

So what are some of our favorite winter warmers? From the New World—the United States, South America, Australia, New Zealand, and South Africa—look for wines made from Cabernet Sauvignon, Cabernet Franc, and Cab-based blends, as well as Syrah/Shiraz (sometimes blended with Grenache and Mourvedre, the GSM blend). We especially like earthy, stick-to-your-ribs Zinfandels during the winter months.

When we think of robust winter-friendly wines from Europe, the first place we think about is the Rhone Valley of France, where the reds are powerful, earthy, and so satisfying. From the southern Rhone consider the quintessential winter warmer, Chateauneuf-du-Pape, as well as a few of its neighbors, Gigondas and Vacqueyras, where you should find excellent value. From the northern Rhone you'll find pricier but delicious full-bodied Syrah-based wines to warm you up: Hermitage, Cote Rotie, Cornas, St-Joseph. The value wine to look for here is Crozes-Hermitage.

Italy: Where to start, when to stop? We're sure we'll miss more than a few Italian winter warmers, but here are some of our regional favorites:

Piedmont: Barolo, Barbaresco, Gattinara, and Ghemme, all based on the Nebbiolo grape. The value wines here are Nebbiolo d'Alba, or Langhe Nebbiolo.

Tuscany: All driven by the Sangiovese grape, we love Brunello di Montalcino, Chianti Classico Riserva, Vino Nobile di Montepulciano, and Carmignano. The true value here is Rosso di Montalcino. Also, there are literally more than a thousand red "Super Tuscans," based on Sangiovese, Cabernet Sauvignon, and Syrah: many blends, some single varietals, mostly expensive, and all quite powerful.

Southern Italy and islands: Taurasi, an incredibly full-bodied, black-ink wine from Campania; Salice Salentino Riserva from Puglia; Cannonau di Sardegna from Sardinia; Nero d'Avola from Sicily. Values include Aglianico del Vulture from Basilicata and Primitivo (psst . . . it's Zinfandel!) from Puglia.

From Spain, look for Rioja Reserva and Gran Reserva; Ribera del Duero Reserva; red wines from Priorat and Montsant; Cabernet Sauvignon and blends from Penedes. From Portugal, the red wines of Bairrada are real powerhouses, based on the Baga grape, and utilizing Cabernet Sauvignon to *lighten* the blend! Also, the red wines of the Douro Valley are perfect winter wines. Of course, after dinner the chill of the season will be practically erased by fortified Port or Madeira—a cozy fireplace in a glass. Values here include Five-Year-Old Malmsey Madeira, as well as Late-Bottled Vintage and basic Tawny Ports.

Best winter choices from Greece include the reds Naoussa and Nemea, as well as single varietals and blends made from Cabernet Sauvignon and Syrah. Also, try Lebanon's classic powerful red, Chateau Musar. From Israel, look for single-vineyard Cabernet Sauvignon and Shiraz.

Kosher wines: not just for Passover anymore

THE IMAGE OF KOSHER WINES in the United States, at least until recently, has been pretty much abysmal. There is little doubt that the traditional, ceremonial, virtually undrinkable kosher jug made from Concord grapes will always be available for those who, by either habit or desire, choose to drink the stuff on high holy days or with their Friday night Sabbath dinner. We are happy to report, however, that kosher wines do not have to be the product of God in His or Her wrathful phase. The "new" kosher wines can only be described as great wines that just happen to be kosher, and for that all of us, Jewish or not, can only sing out, "Amen!"

Today, good kosher wine is produced all over the world—including the United States, Italy, Spain, France, Australia, Chile, and of course Israel. The differences between these wines and the stereotypical Concord jugs are palpable and pleasurable. We no longer feel as though we might be atoning for what must be some pretty serious sins when we taste kosher wines. Instead, these blessed bottles allow wine lovers of all religious persuasions and permutations—including those who worship only Bacchus—to enjoy, indulge, and luxuriate, without suffering, without guilt (a big step forward for those of us who were raised in a traditional Jewish home, where guilt is a dish best served either hot or cold, but repeatedly).

So what makes a wine kosher? This question is not as easy to answer as it might seem. For example, a majority of Conservative and Reform Jews, many of whom do not eat and drink only kosher food and wine on a daily basis, believe that all wines—like all fruits—are kosher and do not

need any further elaboration. This secular interpretation flies in the face of Orthodox Jewish law and custom. Essentially, the Orthodox approach to kosher wine includes the following rules:

The wine must be certified by a rabbi or rabbinical agency licensed to perform such duties.

All equipment and machinery used to make the wine must be approved to produce kosher wines.

Any commercial yeasts (as opposed to natural yeasts on the grapes, known as "native yeasts"), filtering agents, or clarifying agents must be certified as kosher. No milk or non-kosher gelatin can be used for clarification.

Traditionally, only Sabbath-observant Jews can handle the wine, including during the winemaking process, the service of the wine, and the consumption of the wine, unless the wine has gone through a flash-heating pasteurization process known as *mevushal*.

In the modern kosher wine industry, both non-mevushal wines and mevushal wines are available. *Mevushal*, which in Hebrew means "boiled," is actually a flash heating and cooling process. Throughout history, some rabbis have insisted that all wine must be boiled so that the wines would

not taste good enough to enjoy for pleasure—just barely good enough to drink to observe the sacraments of faith (again with the guilt!).

Wines that undergo *mevushal* are flash-heated either before or immediately after the juice is fermented. The pasteurization process occurs as either the juice or the wine is heated to about 185°F/85°C for a few moments and then cooled very quickly. Alternatively, the grapes themselves can be heated before they are pressed. There is an ongoing debate in the kosher wine community about whether or not the *mevushal* process alters the color, aromatics, and taste of the wine. Research done at the University of California at Davis in 1993 concluded that drinkers of *mevushal* wines do not perceive any difference in color, nose, or taste of the wine. But some producers of non-*mevushal* wines disagree, feeling that flash-pasteurization can result in a profound change in both the aromatics and taste of the wine.

Good kosher wines—both *mevushal* and non-*mevushal*—are increasingly available to the general public in wine shops and restaurants and via the Internet. These wines are worth tasting by all those who enjoy good wine, and also make a thoughtful gift if you're having dinner at the home of a friend who keeps kosher.

The next sections list, by region, some of the exciting kosher wines that we've tasted recently. Kosher wines are a fast-growing consumer category, and all we can do here is just scratch the surface. Retailers and restaurateurs are bound to have some of the wines; the Internet is a good place to start exploring what is available. Go to www.kosherwine.com for a good selection.

CALIFORNIA

Herzog is the major California line of wines produced by the Royal Wine Company. The Herzog winery in Oxnard, California is the largest kosher winery in the world. We have tasted many Herzog wines over the years and have found a steady and impressive improvement in both grape sourcing and winemaking. Today, some of the wines are amongst the best kosher wines available from California. We particularly like the Lodi Old Vine Zinfandel (about $15) and the special-occasion, single-vineyard bottlings of Cabernet Sauvignon ($75 to $100).

At Four Gates Winery, Benyamin Cantz produces estate-bottled wines produced from 3.5 acres (1.4 hectares) of certified organic grapes on dry-farmed vineyards situated on a south-facing slope of California's Santa Cruz Mountains. At a total production of about 4,800 bottles (400 cases), Four Gates is perhaps the smallest kosher winery in the United States; it's a one-man operation. Both the Chardonnay and the Pinot Noir are two of the purest, most balanced, *terroir*-driven wines we've tasted from California in quite some time. Showing beautifully now, both of these wines will improve with a bit of age, especially the Pinot Noir. Four Gates also produces estate-bottled organic Cabernet Franc, Zinfandel, and Merlot. All of the wines sell for $20 to $45 each. These are true artisan wines made by a dedicated *mensch*. To find out more about Four Gates, or to purchase wines, do yourself a *mitzvah* and contact Benyamin Cantz at www.fourgateswine.com.

Other good kosher producers include Hagafen, Weinstock, Shirah, and Agua Dulce. Covenant Winery is a small, high-end producer of very fine Napa Valley Cabernet Sauvignon, Dry Creek Valley Sauvignon Blanc, and Sonoma Mountain Chardonnay.

CHILE

Alfasi is the major kosher producer here, with Cabernet Sauvignon, Merlot, and Malbec/Syrah bottlings all selling for about $15. The wines are well made and true to their varietal types; good values.

AUSTRALIA

Teal Lake is the kosher category leader here, with solid wines at about $15 from the South Eastern Australia mega-appellation. We enjoyed the Teal Lake Shiraz quite a bit. Beckett's Flat in the Margaret River region of Western Australia makes estate-bottled wines. Reds include Shiraz and Shiraz/Cabernet, whites Chardonnay and Sauvignon Blanc/Semillon. The wines range from $25 to $30 each.

ISRAEL

We really enjoyed the Carmel Emerald Riesling/Chenin Blanc from the Shomron region (about $10): a perfect hot-weather fruity off-dry sipper, great for spicy foods, lighter fish dishes, and salads. The Binyamina Chardonnay, also from Shomron (about $20) is well made, with luscious fruit and toasty oak. We also tasted good non-*mevushal* Cabernet Sauvignon and Merlot from Israel, made by Galil from fruit grown in the highly regarded region of Upper Galilee (each under $25). Recanati Cabernet Sauvignon from Galilee is also another fine choice (about $30).

Note that Israel produces both kosher and non-kosher wines; check the label if you are looking for kosher wines only.

FRANCE

Several Champagne producers, including Laurent Perrier and Drappier, produce kosher versions of their wines, as do about 20 Bordeaux chateaux (including Smith Haut-Lafitte, Giscours, Leoville Poyferre, and Fonbadet), as well as inexpensive Bordeaux, such as Mouton-Cadet. Roberto Cohen is a major kosher producer in Burgundy, making everything from inexpensive Beaujolais to moderately expensive Chablis to painfully expensive *grand cru* Burgundy. Kosher wines are available from Alsace (look for Abarbanel), the Loire Valley, and the Rhone Valley as well.

SPAIN

Tio Pepe, the Sherry that even rival Sherry producers bring as a gift, makes a lovely kosher Fino Sherry (about $18). We also very much enjoyed the lively Rioja Cosecha from Ramon Cardova, made from 100% Tempranillo grapes picked from old vines in Haro (about $20). Tierra Salvaje in the Yecla region produces a variety of wines (all under $25, some under $15). In Montsant region, the Capcanes cooperative produces the award-winning red, Pereaj Ha'abib Flor de Primavera in the $50 range.

ITALY

Italy, too, produces some good kosher wines, with Bartenura importing wines to us from Piedmont and Veneto. Rashi makes a good Barolo (under $50), while Borgo Reale focuses on reds from the province of Puglia in the south (under $25).

Living with screwcaps: twist and pour!

FOR SEVERAL YEARS NOW, WE have been supporting the move toward screwcap closures for wines, and we applaud the work and commitment of those producers who have taken this route. If wine truly is a noble beverage, it makes no sense to stopper it with a piece of tree bark that is susceptible to all kinds of mold and bacteria. Add to this the fact that wine with a cork stopper is the only beverage that requires a special tool to open the bottle and you have a recipe for limiting consumption via intimidation ("What if I break the cork?") and encouraging snobbery. And don't forget that it's a terrible thing to be on the right beach with the right sunset, the right person, the right wine—and no corkscrew.

So, for all those who have embraced screwcaps, we say right on! But why stop there? Why not make wine truly accessible by packaging it the way that many other beverages are marketed—boxes, cartons, cans? The naysayers here will argue that screwcaps and boxes take away from the "romance" of wine. Leaving aside the question of what is romantic about a grungy, moldy piece of tree bark, while we would certainly argue that there are some special occasions when we do enjoy the ritual of presentation and pouring, for the most part we want our wine to be practical and accessible so that we can enjoy it with a minimum of fuss. Recent statistics show that for wine consumption at home, Australians (who invented the bag-in-the-box technology) purchase more than 50% of their wine in boxes, and the Scandinavian nations are not far behind. Our guess is that more and more Americans will slowly but surely follow suit (we're now at about 30%).

The most important thing to understand is that screwcaps and boxes do *not* mean low-quality wine—quite the opposite. As closure and container, both the screwcap and the box are safer and better than corks and bottles. The cork

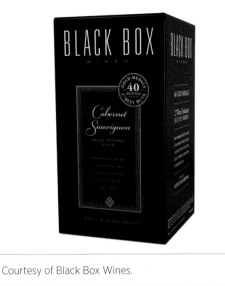

Courtesy of Black Box Wines.

can deteriorate and become infected by mold, and the bottle, after opening, will inevitably allow air to oxidize the wine. But the screwcap is inert and guarantees that the wine will arrive and remain in good condition, and the boxes on the market are designed with a pouch inside that collapses as the wine is poured, ensuring almost no contact with air and minimal oxidation. As a recent experiment, we tried a selection of boxed wines to vet them for style and quality. We kept one of the open boxes in the refrigerator, and three weeks later tried the wine again. It was still fresh and bright, fruity and delicious, with little sign of deterioration.

From our sampling of boxed wines, we come away with the general conclusion that most of them are sound, everyday-drinking wines, and some are quite good. We were particularly impressed by the price, which ranged from the equivalent of under $5 a bottle to about $8 a bottle. You can't beat that for value when the wine is good. Most of the boxes contain 3 liters (a little more than 100 ounces) of wine; some smaller boxes—tetrapaks—are 1 liter (about 34 ounces) or a half liter (about 17 ounces). From California look for Black Box, Three Thieves, Bandit, Bota Box, Clif, Big House, Wine Block, Pepperwood Grove, Monthaven, Turning Leaf; Australia: Hardy's, Banrock Station, De Bortoli, FishEye; France: French Rabbit, dtour, From the

Tank, La Vieille Ferme; Germany: R. Muller, Seeburger; Argentina: Yellow+Blue; South Afrca: Rain Dance. Just a partial listing from a wine category that is blowing up.

We're also happy with the increasingly popular Vino-Seal (in Europe, Vino-Lok) glass wine closure, which is very pretty and 100% recyclable. The closure looks very much like the decorative stoppers in wine decanters and utilizes a sterile and inert O-ring, protecting the wine from oxidation or bacterial spoilage. We expect to see more of these corkscrew-free stoppers in more and more bottles of good wine.

Screwcaps, glass stoppers, and boxes make sense to us, especially in our modern world where convenience and accessibility have become so important. Your boxed white wine can sit in the fridge; all you have to do is take your glass to it, open the spigot, and pour. It's just like having an ice water dispenser as part of your fridge, though (so far) for the wine you will have to open the door. At the very least, all of this convenience will make us appreciate it even more when somebody presents us with that very special bottle and proceeds to dazzle us with their nimble use of that ancient and curious implement, the corkscrew.

Wine gadgets: a necessity or a waste of money?

THESE DAYS IT'S EASY TO find all kinds of gadgets designed to improve your experience with wines. Most of these gadgets work, but they are also mostly unnecessary if your goal is to enjoy wine on a daily or semi-daily basis. Some of these "tools" promise to deliver more flavor and aromatics to young wines, to preserve the wine in open bottles, to quickly chill whites and sparklers. And then there are the wine refrigerators—everything from tabletop fridges to behemoths that are essentially refrigerated cellars.

We are not arguing that these gadgets don't do what they promise to do. But we would rather spend our money on actual wine rather than the accouterments that are designed to accompany the actual experience, but instead sometimes take center stage. For example, we've heard "ooohs" and "aaahs" expressed over wine aerators—nifty devices that sell for $25 to $30 each and allow the wine to "open up" by taking on more oxygen, and delivering a better-balanced wine to the glass. Guess what? You can achieve the same result by swirling the wine in a good wine glass for about a minute, and it will cost you *nada*.

How about specialized wine refrigerators? These are nicely-designed units with racks meant for wine bottles. In fact, we're staring at one right now; its compressor died a few years after we bought it. The unit, all glass and stainless steel, still looks nice, except there are wine books, not wines, inside it. We have a solution for keeping your white and sparkling wines cool. Keep them just above (or in) the vegetable crisper in your fridge. If you have a lot of white wines or bubbly that you always want at the ready, pick up a small refrigerator when it's on sale at a discount retailer, or score one at a yard sale. Reds can be kept in a cool, dark place; a cellar is ideal if you have one, but really any cool dark place will do.

Then you have the portable vacuum pumps that extract air from an open bottle, promising to preserve the wine for about a week. They do work and at less than $20 do not represent a big investment. Except they're really not necessary. If you have about a half-bottle of wine left at the end of the evening just pour it into a clean, empty half bottle (a wine bottle is good, but a soda bottle will work) and seal with the cork or the cap. If the wine features a screwcap, just screw the cap back on the original bottle. These wines, red or white, should be kept in the fridge, which will help to keep them fresh. Honestly, most wines consumed on a daily basis really will be fine in their original bottle for four or five days in the fridge and don't need special preparation. We've found that older, more delicate wines do

not take well to these vacuum pumps. We encourage consuming those wines with friends and family at dinner; save the bottle, but not the wine, as a memento of the occasion.

If you like to drink a glass or two of fine, expensive wine on a regular basis and are worried about spoilage after opening the wine, there is a tool that shows promise, but it does cost $300. The Coravin allows you to insert a very thin needle in the cork, pressurize the bottle with inert argon gas, and then pour the wine. When you remove the needle, the cork reseals itself. Our tests show that the wine remains in near-original condition for weeks. We think the Coravin is a beautiful thing for restaurants that want to offer premium wines by the glass, but its price point may be prohibitive for most consumers and unnecessary for folks who enjoy affordable wines at home. That's most of us.

Clay or marble chillers for white and sparkling wines? They look nice, very decorative. They don't work so well. Keep the wine on ice, preferably in a metal bucket.

Wine glasses can also be included in this section on "gadgets" because there is so much buzz about the "right glass" for the "right wine." We're gonna go old school on this. It may be our age talking, but we like wine glasses with stems even though we understand the appeal of the "destemmed" wine tumbler. On a practical basis, the stem allows you to swirl the glass more easily. Aesthetically, the stem keeps fingerprints off the bowl and looks good, bringing a bit of elegance to even the simplest meal.

You can spend a fortune for wine glasses, but there's no need to do so. You want a clear glass (etched, patterned, or colored glass obscures the true color of the wine) with as thin a bowl as possible in order to better illuminate the wine. You can get by with a set of Champagne glasses and a set of nice, basic all-purpose glasses, or you might want to have a set of white wine glasses (smaller bowl) and a set of red wine glasses (larger bowl). Companies such as Riedel of Austria make specific glasses for specific wines and truth be told these glasses really can make a difference in the aromas and flavors of the wine. The best of these varietal or style-specific glasses can be very expensive, but there are less expensive versions of them as well. We believe in good wine glasses, but never let the "wrong glass" be an impediment to enjoying wine.

Some good news on wine "gadgets." There are some very good, even excellent wine apps available—many of them for free or at very low cost—for your smartphone, tablet, etc. Some of these apps give good basic information about wine, some focus on wines from particular regions throughout the world, some deal with wine and food pairing. There are apps that allow you to take a photo of a wine label and get info about that particular wine, sometimes including tasting notes from other wine consumers. Of course, any wine app is merely a tool to make you a better-informed wine buyer and drinker. By the time you read this there will undoubtedly be new wine apps available to you, and we wouldn't be surprised if some of them are so good that they redefine the category, but we still strongly suggest that the best thing you can do when it comes to learning about and enjoying wine is to trust your own palate and know your own budget.

Buying wine online, tastings, and wine festivals

By now, BUYING WINE ONLINE is old hat. We must admit that some of the wines sold online at bargain prices and featuring free shipping are tempting. Sites such as WinesTilSoldOut (WTSO.com), among many others, offer fine wines at heavily discounted prices. Honestly, our preference for buying wine is a live interaction with a dedicated and knowledgeable wine merchant, but we would be foolish to ignore the appeal of online wine buying.

You can also join online "wine clubs," but in most of these clubs your choices are limited. You might not even know what wines you're getting each month until you receive them on your doorstep. However, many wineries maintain their own wine clubs; this is a good way to ensure first crack at wines that may be in short supply or even unavailable to the general public. We like these single-producer clubs, as they foster a direct and positive relationship between the producer and the consumer.

Tasting wine before you buy it? Impossible, you say. Not true. Many wine merchants hold tastings of selected wines in their shops on a weekly or even daily basis. Establish a good rapport with your local wine shops so that you know when these tastings are being held. Get your name on the shop's e-mail list or follow it on Facebook or Twitter to keep updated about when tastings are happening.

Increasingly, there are wine festivals happening all over North America, and there is a large subset of wine consumers who love to travel to these festivals. You might be surprised that some of these festivals occur close to your home. The best way to find out about wine festivals being held all over the world, but especially the United States and Canada is to check in with the website www.localwineevents.com. Like us, you'll be amazed at the staggering number of wine celebrations held on any given day on Planet Earth.

16

LOVING THE LIST

WINE IN RESTAURANTS

WHEN IT COMES TO RESTAURANT WINE LISTS, WINE LOVERS HAVE LITTLE TO COMPLAIN ABOUT THESE DAYS, BECAUSE it is easy to find excellent formal restaurants with superb wine lists, along with simpler roadhouses, bistros, and trattorias—informal restaurants and wine bars of all kinds—with exciting wine choices. Thanks to the Internet and forward-thinking restaurateurs, we can even peruse many restaurant wine lists and menus online and make some decisions before we arrive at our "wine destination" restaurant.

It takes hard work and passion to maintain, enhance, and improve a restaurant wine list, and kudos to the restaurateurs and wine professionals who do so. Many restaurants have ideal wine programs, some do a very good job, some are just okay, and some definitely need improvement. To build a terrific wine list takes time, energy, money, talent, and attitude, and so most good wine lists are in a constant state of becoming. If a restaurant rests on its laurels (or in this case, its vines), that establishment risks losing customers, because we may perceive the wine list as stale and ho-hum, and in the restaurant business customer perception is reality.

Here are some of the things to look for—and discover—in a great restaurant wine list.

The wine list should be customer-friendly

First, the list should be clean, graphically appealing, and easy to read. We know that restaurants often have subdued, soft lighting, but we shouldn't have to resort to using one of those tiny flashlights to read the list.

Second, the list should be arranged in some logical order: grape varietal, geographical designation, body of the wine, and food pairings are just some of the ways to do it. If the list is organized by varietal, you might want to skip past the Chardonnay and Cabernet in search of something new and different. We love lists that place Chardonnay and Cabernet last instead of first. You'll always find those two grape types no matter where they are on the list, but you might miss an interesting Gewurztraminer, Riesling, Sauvignon Blanc, or even a Torrontes from Argentina among the whites, or a delicious Syrah, Grenache, Tempranillo, or Xinomavro from Greece, especially if they get buried between the vanilla (Chardonnay) and chocolate (Cabernet). If you live in a wine-growing region—and in the United States that means most every state in the Union—it's always nice to have a highlighted section of well-chosen local and regional wines; we love to eat and drink local.

If the list is organized geographically—by country and wine regions—we like to see an easy-to-follow, consistent format. For a small list arranged this way, it's probably best to highlight a country (e.g., Italy) and then include the name of the region in each listing (Chianti Classico Riserva, Badia a Coltibuono, Tuscany 2010). If the list is large, with many wines from many regions, or if the list is dedicated to the wines of just one country (in this case, Italy), then major regions should probably get their own subheads on the list (e.g., Tuscany), and the wine listed above would read Chianti Classico Riserva, Badia a Coltibuono 2010. Above all, we like to see customer-friendly geographical lists, with a wide variety of choices and price points.

Arranging a wine list by the body of the wine (light, light-to-medium, medium, medium-to-full, full, *really* full, etc.) can be a tricky business because it can often be highly subjective. One woman's medium-bodied wine is another's medium- to full-bodied wine. One man's *really* full-bodied wine is another's *just* full-bodied wine. We think that these types of wine lists provide a general road map for the restaurant's approach to wine and wine styles and should be taken with a grain of salt. These "body" lists also assume a degree of familiarity with wine and food pairing that not everybody has (after all, not everyone has read *WineWise* . . . yet), and we think that may be why you don't see too many successful wine lists arranged this way. Likewise, if the list is arranged by food pairings (wines for veggies, wines for fish, wines for meat), we use it as a thumbnail sketch to match the restaurant menu. There can be a world of difference between the wine you choose for salmon poached in lemongrass broth and the one you pick to pair with grilled salmon served with rice and black beans. A wine that foots the bill for a filet mignon may seem a bit light for a well-marbled porterhouse steak.

The computer age is surely a mixed blessing, but it's all good for wine lists. The reason we say this is that computers allow restaurateurs to keep their wine lists current and complete. There is almost no reason why a wine on a computerized list should be suddenly unavailable or would have mysteriously undergone a vintage change. Customers don't want to go to the effort of choosing one wine from many, after choosing one dish from many, and then be told that they can't have that wine, or that the vintage is different. If this happens, most of us will feel rushed to make a second choice and generally uncomfortable, even if we have no idea—*especially* if we have no idea—if the available wine or vintage is better or worse than the one listed and originally chosen. It is a fact of modern life that to stay on top of a wine list, the restaurateur, sommelier, or whoever is in charge may have to tweak the info on the list—updating vintages or prices, adding new wines, removing ones that are sold out—several times per week. A bit of a drag for the restaurant, perhaps, but so easy thanks to fast computers and printers. And so customer-friendly.

The wine list should relate to the menu

CALL US TRADITIONAL, BUT WE still think that it's important that there's an understandable relationship between the restaurant's food and wine. A steakhouse is likely to feature lots of blockbuster red wines and a smaller number of carefully chosen whites. A restaurant known for its fish might do the exact opposite, but with a bit more emphasis on "crossover" reds (Pinot Noir being a near-perfect example of a wine that works with many fish dishes). A vegetarian restaurant? Some of the most exciting vegetarian restaurants have exciting wine lists, often featuring wines made from organically grown or biodynamically grown grapes (biodynamics utilize organic practices, but with a more holistic approach that includes treating soil fertility, plant growth, and even the livestock that live on the land as part of an interconnected system of agriculture). Asian restaurants and pan-American restaurants where the food may be pretty spicy often feature small or large lists of fruit- and spice-driven whites (Riesling, Gewurztraminer, Pinot Grigio, and Southern Hemisphere Sauvignon Blanc are just some examples) and light, fruity reds (Beaujolais, Valpolicella, and lighter examples of Cote du Rhone, Pinot Noir, and Zinfandel come to mind), as well as dry rosés and a nice selection of sparklers. Those bubbles do wonders in putting out the fire of curries and chilies.

If a trattoria or *ristorante* wine list is, say, all Italian, a good selection of affordable wines from many of the 20 wine regions of Italy should be available. Likewise, a Spanish-inspired tapas bar that specializes in the delicious "small plates" of Spain may offer Spanish wines only, including a variety of Sherries, to help create the authentic tapas experience. A Greek restaurant might have a harder time selling the public on a totally Greek list, but Greek wines should be featured (they are great—try 'em!). You get the picture.

Go off the beaten path

IF YOU'VE BEEN READING *WineWise* closely, by now you must realize that we love wines whose origins are off the beaten path. After all, just how much California Cab, Aussie Shiraz, or throw-a-dart-at-the-map Chardonnay can you drink before you want to explore the rest of the world? Bring on the "new" wines of Spain—especially from the lesser known *denominaciones*, such as Rueda, Jumilla, and Toro—Portugal, Greece, Canada, and the 49 American states other than California (fact: all 50 states produce wine, even Alaska). Let's explore the glories of southern Italy as well as the sunny wines of southern France. Skip Chile and fly to Argentina (or even to Uruguay to try a red Tannat). Don't forget the wonderful whites of Alsace and Austria and the redolent reds of Israel and Lebanon.

We don't advise you to go off the beaten path just to be different; we truly enjoy these wines with food and think you will, too. As an added WineWise bonus, these lesser-known, often underappreciated wines are great values and can form the most affordable part of an adventurous wine list. If you don't see wines from some of these places in your favorite restaurants (or retail shops), ask for them. An engaging wine list is often based on two aspects of the same self-fulfilling prophecy: if you request and drink these wines, more of them will appear on the list, but if you don't request and drink them, a restaurant has little or no incentive to offer them. We can hear James Earl Jones now: "If you drink it, they will come." Truly, a creative wine list can be an affordable "field of dreams."

The service staff should know the wine list

HOWEVER THE LIST IS ARRANGED, and whatever wines are featured, in the end it is just a list of wines. But we believe that wine is often a hand-sold item that takes a bit of discussion, a bit of chatting back and forth between the customer and the server. That server might be a waiter, a sommelier, a manager, an owner, or anyone working in the restaurant, as long as he or she can speak intelligently, enthusiastically, and honestly about the wine list. If the server loves a wine that he or she thinks will work well with the foods ordered by the guests, and if it is reasonably priced, we usually welcome that recommendation. We hate it when a server recommends a wine that he or she, or someone whose opinion the server respects, has never tasted, as the customer can see through that BS. If a question arises that a server can't answer due to lack of experience with a particular wine, he or she should quickly fetch someone in the restaurant who can answer the question.

Customers often blame service staff for poor food and wine service, but we know from years of hard experience that most service staff want to please the customer, even if some have not been trained properly to provide professional wine service before "hitting the floor." If the restaurant does not take the time for training, wine service can dissolve into a *Saturday Night Live* or *Fawlty Towers* moment, only without the laughs.

We're also not big fans of wine-speak. We like easy-to-decipher words such as *delicious*, *medium- to full-bodied*, or *refreshing*. The server should always assume the customer is the expert (sometimes that's true) and should never try to intimidate the guest with a bunch of puffed-up but in the end superficial jargon that makes the customer feel small.

The wine on the list should be the wine in the bottle

IF THE LIST IS INCONSISTENT or incorrect, the customer can become confused, and this confusion can bite the restaurant in the glass. Here's an example of inconsistency that comes to mind: Some years ago, we ordered the following featured wine in what appeared to be a "wine destination" restaurant: a Cabernet Sauvignon, Hess Collection, Napa Valley, California 2002 for $47, which seemed like a very fair price for this wine—an astounding bargain, in fact. This wine sold for about $36 at retail.

The wine that was brought to our table was Cabernet Sauvignon, Hess Select, California 2002 for $47, which seemed like a complete rip-off. This wine sold for about $16 at retail.

When we quietly pointed out that we specifically ordered the estate-bottled Napa Valley bottling of the Hess wine—a wine made solely from grapes harvested atop Napa's glorious Mount Veeder, not the anywhere-in-California bottling—we received the following answer, complete with tons of attitude: "Well, the Napa Valley is in California, you know." Anyway, we did not accept the wine, and ordered something else. And what do we remember about the entire dining experience? Nothing, except what we perceived to be a wine rip-off (although it might have just been wine ignorance, but we doubt it), and thinking about how many people had ordered that featured wine, paid for it, never knew the difference, and thought the wine was just okay but definitely overpriced. So the moral of the story is that to ensure a good customer experience, the restaurant should make sure the wine list is consistent, clear, and correct.

Wines by the glass, "quartinos," wine flights, and half bottles

A LIST OF WINES BY the glass and/or by the "quartino" (a small decanter or flask that is usually about 9 or 10 ounces [270 or 300 milliliters] of wine—roughly a glass and a half), a selection of wine "flights" (three or four glasses, 2- to 3-ounce [60- to 90-milliliter] pours in each glass, of wines that are somehow thematically linked), and a list of half bottles (12.7 ounces [375 milliliters], a little more than two glasses) have become increasingly popular with the American wine drinker. Making wines available in these ways customizes the dining experience for guests, allowing them to sample several wines and still stay within their budget (the price budget, but also the alcohol budget; especially if you drive to and from restaurants, a seriously low alcohol budget is necessary for a happy, healthy, and safe dining experience). Sometimes all we want is a glass of Sauvignon Blanc, but a flight of four 2-ounce (60-milliliter) glasses of Sauvignon Blanc—one from France, one from California, one from New Zealand, one from Chile—is hard to resist. Three Zinfandels—one from Mendocino, one from Sonoma, one from Paso Robles—iz a Zinful pleazure. Likewise, a party of four may want a white for two people and a red for two people but desire little more than a glass per person. Half bottles, "quartinos," and/ or a good selection of wines by the glass at different price points is the answer.

The standard "pour" for a single wine by the glass is usually between 5 and 6 ounces (150 and 180 milliliters). You should expect to pay somewhere between 20% and 25% of the price of a bottle for a glass of wine. In other words, a wine that appears on the wine list for $44 per bottle (25.4 ounces [750 milliliters]) should be in the $10 to $12 range per 6-ounce (180-milliliter) glass.

Five ounces (150 milliliters) should be closer to $8 to $10 per glass. Often, wines by the glass don't appear on the by-the-bottle list, but if you simply want a good glass of wine, we suggest you don't spend too much time doing the math; just enjoy your glass of wine with your meal as one of life's affordable pleasures (and drive safely).

BYOB?/What's the corkage fee?

BYOB IS SHORT FOR "BRING your own bottle," and you'd be surprised how many BYOB restaurants there are in both large cities and small towns. Some states limit the amount of wine and liquor licenses available or charge license fees that are prohibitive for small restaurant owners. There are cities where BYOB has become a way of life (Philadelphia and Montreal come to mind), and restaurant customers enjoy bringing their own wines to dinner. Dinner becomes more affordable, and in a simple twist of fate, BYOB restaurants make the customer match the food to the wine, not vice versa. If you don't know the menu of the BYOB place you want to go to, check its website to see if the menu is online, or call ahead to ask about the menu. That should give you some ideas for the wines you want to bring along to the restaurant.

"Corkage" is a great word that describes the fee a restaurant charges to open and serve wines that customers bring with them to the restaurant. Policies vary widely—some restaurants discourage it or completely forbid customers to bring their own wines, while some welcome those same wine-toting folks with open arms. If you're planning on bringing some of your own wines to the restaurant, call ahead to find out what that restaurant's corkage policy is and how much they charge. You may be surprised to learn that some restaurants charge less than $10 per bottle while others charge more than $25, or even more than $50 (this is rare). Some restaurants only allow

PLAYING THE NUMBERS GAME

Although they are sometimes popular, we are not big fans of wine lists that feature the "scores" granted to wines by wine journalists and critics. Maybe it's great for the wine producer if his or her wine gets a score of 94 from *The Wine Advocate* or a 96 from *Wine Spectator*, but what does it really mean to the wine consumer, the restaurant customer? Featuring these scores on wine lists speaks volumes about a kind of insecurity surrounding our own taste, both on the part of the restaurant and the customer. We really believe that when it comes to wine, you should trust your own palate and not follow the pack who think that if they are drinking a wine with a score of 95 they are drinking nectar, but if they are drinking a wine scored a mere 81 they should not let themselves get too excited.

Remember also that the price and/or value of the wine is rarely a factor in the scoring of wines. It will come as no surprise that the highest-scoring wines on a wine list are also often the most expensive. To us, this smacks of subtle intimidation: if you want to sample the best, pay the most. We don't like this, because we believe that good wines should be available to everyone, and we know for a fact that those wines don't have to be expensive to be good.

We'll never forget sitting in a restaurant whose wine list was organized by scores and overhearing a fellow at the next table ordering "the '95 Cabernet Sauvignon." We soon learned that he was ordering not a 1995 Cab but a wine from the 2008 vintage that was listed with a score of 95! We could only shake our old-fashioned heads. Trust your own palate, people!

---

you to bring wines that do not appear on their list, while others will not charge a corkage fee for your own bottle if you also order a wine from their list. Corkage policies and fees are all over the place, so make sure you check with the restaurant before you bring in a bottle of your own wine. Also, remember that in the United States most servers survive on tips. If you bring in a bottle or two of wine and pay a reasonable corkage fee, don't forget to tip your server generously to at least partially make up for the lost income generated by your choice to bring your own wine.

Reasonable wine pricing, please!

RESTAURANT CUSTOMERS WANT TO HAVE a good time when they dine out, and most are not interested in pinching pennies, but neither do they want to feel ripped off when they order a bottle of wine. The perception of value on a wine list is an important consideration for most diners. If they pay $14 in a retail wine shop for one of their favorite wines and they see it on a wine list for $40, they are not going to be happy. Long ago, after more arguments than we care to count, we decided that there is no standard restaurant markup on any bottle of wine. The restaurateur and his or her wine staff must make those decisions, but we still do believe in a useful rule of thumb: the wine should never cost double its retail price on the wine list. In other words, we doubt there would be much consumer resistance to paying $25 (instead of $40) for that same $14 bottle, and it may lead to ordering a second bottle of the same or different wine. A reasonable consumer perception is that $10 or $11 above retail is a fair profit (even though many restaurants, depending on the state in which they're located, can buy wines at wholesale prices, and so the profit on that $25 bottle might actually be as much as $16 or $17). Obviously, on rare and truly hard-to-find bottles of singular pedigree, all bets are off, and the restaurant can charge whatever it wants.

A final word about wine list pricing (a very touchy subject these days, for both consumers and restaurateurs): there is nothing wrong with featuring some expensive wines on the list, as long as there is a good selection of wines at all price points. There is no reason why any restaurant can't offer white or red wines, even sparkling wines (Cava or Prosecco, for example) for less than $25 per bottle. That doesn't mean that all the bottles have to be $25 or less—although there is a place for such lists, and they can be wildly popular—but it does mean that almost any restaurant customer, including those of modest means and/or inclinations, can enjoy a bottle or two of wine with friends and family. The very same restaurant that offers some good wine bargains can also offer wines at any other reasonable price points, well into the hundreds of dollars, as long as each price point is well represented. Intimidating customers with the price of a wine list is a sure way to lose those customers and many of those former customers' friends (potential future customers).

Finding the "sweet spot": how to find good value on the wine list

JUST ABOUT EVERYONE LOVES TO dine out for special occasions—celebrating birthdays, anniversaries, job promotions, a juicy book contract, whatever—and on these occasions we might be in the mood to splurge. We choose a fine and expensive restaurant and expect to blow a small fortune on dinner. For these rare and expensive nights, it's kind of exciting to throw caution to the wind and order that rare and expensive wine: a beautiful Burgundy, a killer Cab, a cool *cuvee de prestige* Champagne, a sexy Syrah. Enough alliteration; you know what we mean—a night of

exotic fun, at least until the credit card statement arrives.

Yup, special-occasion dining, complete with special (and expensive) wines, is a rare and (we hope) memorable treat. But don't you also like to go out to get a bite to eat with friends and/or family at a favorite restaurant, not to celebrate anything special, but simply to reaffirm friendship, to catch up on the latest news (or gossip), or just to hang out and let someone else do the cooking and do the dishes? On days or nights like these, you're looking to relax, and you're certainly not interested in blowing a wad on wine. So how do you drink good wine without spending a lot of money? How can you be WineWise in a restaurant? It's easy.

First, don't pick a fancy, expensive restaurant. Meet your friends at a place where the food and wine are good, the service is bright and friendly, and the price is reasonable. Ask to see the wine list as soon as you sit down, to give you some time to peruse the list. Don't hesitate to ask for a couple of copies of the list if more than one person at the table is interested in choosing wine. (We really like informal restaurants where the wine list is appended to the menu, so that everybody gets a chance to look at the list. Why shouldn't they?)

Don't be afraid to settle on a per-bottle price range for the wines you plan to order. Choosing wine is not an exercise in impressing people with how much money you spend (or think you have to spend). It's about ordering an enjoyable wine to accompany an enjoyable meal. If the wine list seems out of whack—too expensive for the place, or just plain too expensive for you—make a note of this, and carefully consider if you want to come back next time. The solution to this problem: order your wine by the glass and stay within your budget.

We're thankful that the above scenario happens less and less these days, as restaurateurs know that their customers want to enjoy a bottle of wine with dinner, and if the customer is unhappy, he or she doesn't come back. Most good restaurants have good wine lists: a choice of enjoyable wines at various price points. There are low-priced wines, moderately priced wines, expensive wines, and ultra-expensive wines to choose from, but what really constitutes good value in a bottle of wine?

Value is a relative term—relative to how much money you have to spend on a bottle of wine. Ironically, if money is no object, the most expensive wine on the list might be the best value, because that 2007 Brunello di Montalcino is selling for just about the same price as in a good wine shop, with almost a 0% markup. Unfortunately, the price is $250. So if you have the money, this is a great value. But let's stop dreaming and get back to reality.

Most of the time value wine is represented by a moderately priced wine that delivers great pleasure. It underpromises (price) and overdelivers (pleasure). The good news is that there are lots of value wines appearing on wine lists if you just know where to look.

Just as it's unlikely that you are going to choose that $250 Brunello as your value wine, we also would warn you away from choosing the least expensive wines on the list, especially if they are from well-known New World regions, such as California, Chile, and Australia. There is absolutely nothing wrong with these wines, but they might not represent great value. We have seen Chardonnay from California, Cabs from Chile, and Shiraz wines from Australia that retail in supermarkets and shops for less than $10 selling for more than $30 on many restaurant wine lists. Although $30 is usually a reasonable price to pay for a bottle of wine in a restaurant, the markup on these wines can sometimes be as high as 500% (!), based on the wholesale price of the wine. If the restaurant buys the wine for the wholesale price of $6 and charges $30 for the wine, there's your 500% markup. This does not represent good—or even mediocre—value. Plus, wines in these categories can usually be found easily in supermarkets and wine shops, where at $10 to $12 retail they are good values. So we suggest you drink these wines at home, not in restaurants.

We've already mentioned that one place to look for good value is off the beaten path (see page 349): wines that aren't as well known as they should be from regions that are just beginning to gain renown for the quality of their wines. Again, we encourage you to take a serious look at these wines, since they often represent good value, and certainly deliver the goods: the pleasure of a good wine at a good price.

If you're looking at a wine list that is not that creative, a boilerplate list that features well-known producers and "brands," chances are the bottom end of the list is not where you're going to find true value. Likewise, at the top end of the list, the percentage of markup on the wine may be less, but you pay for wine in dollars, not in percentages, and these wines may be just plain unaffordable. You need to find the sweet spot in the wine list: the place where the wine is simultaneously affordable and good, where pleasure is paramount. But how to find the sweet spot? *WineWise* readers should have little trouble finding it if they explore the list just a little.

Let's say you're looking at a wine list whose least expensive wine is $23 and whose *most* expensive wine is $450. Ignore these wines for now, but take an informal survey of where most of the wines are priced. And now let's say after a little bit of detective work you notice that the overwhelming majority of the wines are priced between $29 and $55. Take the average of these wines—$42—and there's your sweet spot. This doesn't mean that you can't spend $36 or $51, but chances are good if you stick close to $42, you'll get a good wine at a good price. Test: find a wine that you've bought in the supermarket or retail shop, a wine that you paid about $20 for and enjoyed. If that wine is under $40 on the wine list, go for it. If the wine is much more than $40, pass it by, because you know that it is not a good value. If this test yields consistent negative results, you can assume you are looking at an overpriced wine list, but if the results are consistently positive, you've found a value-driven, consumer-friendly list.

WINEWISE LIST OF VALUE WINES

Over time, we've found that certain wines deliver excellent value on most wine lists, and we'd like to share those wines with you. While not all of these may be represented on every restaurant's list, some of them will be.

This list is not complete by any means, because by the time you read it we're sure that other value-driven but delicious wines will pop up on lists all over the country. But for now, here are some consistently outstanding WineWise values.

SPARKLING WINES

Cava from Spain

Prosecco from Italy

Cremant d'Alsace and Cremant de Loire

American Champagne-method bubbly from California, Washington State, Oregon, New York State, and New Mexico, among others

WHITE WINES

United States
CALIFORNIA: Sauvignon Blanc, Viognier, Gewurztraminer, Pinot Gris

OREGON: Pinot Gris, Chardonnay

WASHINGTON STATE: Riesling, Gewurztraminer, Chardonnay

NEW YORK STATE: Riesling, Chardonnay

Canada: Riesling, Pinot Gris, Chardonnay

Chile: Sauvignon Blanc, Chardonnay, Viognier

Argentina: Torrontes

Australia: Riesling, Sauvignon Blanc, "Rhone" varietals and blends (Viognier, Marsanne, Rousanne), Verdelho, Semillon

New Zealand: Sauvignon Blanc, Chardonnay, Chenin Blanc

South Africa: Chenin Blanc, Sauvignon Blanc, Chardonnay

France
ALSACE: Gewurztraminer, Riesling, Pinot Gris, Pinot Blanc, Sylvaner

BORDEAUX: Entre-Deux-Mers and Graves

BURGUNDY: Bourgogne, Chablis, Macon-Villages, Rully, Montagny

LOIRE VALLEY: Saumur, Vouvray, Savennieres, Quincy, Menetou-Salon

RHONE VALLEY: Cotes du Rhone

Whites from Cotes de Gascogne

Spain: whites from Rueda, Penedes, and Rioja; Albarino from Rias Baixas; Godello from Ribeiro, Bierzo, and Valdeorras

Italy
PIEDMONT: Gavi, Arneis

TUSCANY: Vernaccia di San Gimignano

UMBRIA: Orvieto Classico

VENETO: Soave Classico, Pinot Grigio

FRIULI AND ALTO ADIGE: Pinot Grigio, Pinot Bianco, Sauvignon Blanc, Chardonnay, Riesling, Gewurztraminer, varietal blends

TRENTINO: Pinot Grigio

MARCHE: Verdicchio dei Castelli di Jesi Classico

CAMPANIA: Falanghina, Fiano di Avellino, Greco di Tufo

SARDINIA: Vermentino di Gallura

SICILY: Ansonica, Chardonnay, and varietal blends

Portugal: Vinho Verde, Arinto

Greece: Assyrtiko-based wines from Santorini; charming whites made from Moschofilero, Malagousia, and Robola grapes, as well as blends with international varietals (Sauvignon Blanc, etc.)

Germany: Riesling from the Rhine and Mosel river valleys

Austria: Gruner Veltliner and Riesling

RED AND ROSÉ WINES

United States

CALIFORNIA: Zinfandel, Syrah, Rhone-varietal wines and blends (Syrah, Grenache, Mourvedre); Sonoma and Mendocino Cabernet Sauvignon

OREGON: a small selection of value-driven Pinot Noir

WASHINGTON STATE: Syrah, Merlot, Cabernet Sauvignon, Lemberger

NEW YORK STATE: Long Island Merlot, Cabernet Sauvignon, Cabernet Franc (and blends of these)

Canada: Cabernet Franc, Pinot Noir, and Gamay

Chile: Carmenere; single-vineyard Cabernet Sauvignon and Merlot

Argentina: Malbec, Bonarda

Australia: Barossa Valley Shiraz and McLaren Vale Grenache

New Zealand: Cabernet Sauvignon, Merlot, and blends

South Africa: Cabernet Sauvignon and blends, Shiraz

France

ALSACE: Pinot Noir

BORDEAUX: "second labels" of the famous chateaux; St-Emilion and satellites (Lussac, Montagne, Puisseguin, and Saint-Georges); Lalande de Pomerol, Fronsac, Cotes de Blaye and Cotes de Bourg

BURGUNDY: Bourgogne, Cote de Nuits-Villages, Cote de Beaune-Villages, Pernand-Vergelesses, Savigny-les-Beaunes, Mercurey, Rully, Givry

BEAUJOLAIS: Moulin-a-Vent, Morgon, Brouilly, Fleurie

LOIRE VALLEY: Chinon, Bourgueil, Saumur-Champigny, Sancerre

RHONE VALLEY: Cotes du Rhone, Rasteau, St-Joseph, Crozes-Hermitage, Vacqueyras, Gigondas; Tavel dry rosé

MIDI AND PROVENCE: excellent dry rosés from Provence and hearty reds such as Minervois, Fitou, Faugeres, Corbieres, Aix-en-Provence, Cotes du Roussillon

Spain

Cosecha, *crianza*, and *reserva* wines from Rioja and Ribera del Duero; reds from Montsant, Bierzo, Toro, Jumilla, Campo de Borja; rosés (*rosados*) from Navarra and Rioja

Italy

PIEDMONT: Nebbiolo d'Alba, Langhe Nebbiolo, Dolcetto, Barbera, Grignolino, Ruche

TUSCANY: Chianti Classico, Rosso di Montalcino, Morellino di Scansano

UMBRIA: Lungarotti's "Rubesco" and Montefalco Rosso

VENETO: Valpolicella Classico Superiore, Valpolicella Classico "Ripasso," Bardolino Classico, Merlot, and proprietary blends

FRIULI AND ALTO ADIGE: Merlot, Cabernet Sauvignon, Pinot Noir, Lagrein, Teroldego Rotliano, proprietary blends

PUGLIA: Salice Salentino and blends based on the Negroamaro grape; Primitivo (Zinfandel)

BASILICATA: Aglianico del Vulture

SARDINIA: Cannonau di Sardegna and Cannonau (Grenache) blends

SICILY: Nero d'Avola and blends; Etna Rosso; Cerasuolo di Vittoria; Frappato and blends

Portugal: crisp, dry rosés and excellent reds from the Douro Valley, Bairrada, Beiras, Alentejo, Tejo, Lisboa, and Dao

Greece: excellent reds made from Xynomaro, such as Naoussa, Amyndeo, and Agiorgitiko grapes, such as Nemea, as well as Rapsani blends; very tasty dry rosés, too

Austria: Zweigelt, Blaufrankisch, and Saint Laurent

DESSERT WINES/SWEET WINES (OFTEN SERVED BY THE GLASS)

United States: sweet white Muscat wines, sweet Rieslings from New York State and the Pacific Northwest

Italy: semi-sparkling Moscato d'Asti and sparkling Asti, and the red sparkler Brachetto d'Acqui; Vin Santo del Chianti Classico

Greece: Muscat of Samos (white), Mavrodaphne (red), Vinsanto

Cyprus: fortified Commandaria St. John

Spain: fortified Pedro Ximenez and Sweet Amontillado Sherry

Portugal: fortified 5- or 10-Year-Old Malmsey Madeira, Late-Bottled Vintage and Ruby Reserve Porto

Proper wine temperature

SPARKLING, WHITE, AND ROSÉ WINES should be served cold, and an ice bucket should be brought to your table. Some restaurants opt to have "ice bucket stations," which is okay, but only if your wine is always visible to you and proper service by your waiter, wine steward, or sommelier is maintained.

Sparkling wines, simple whites, and rosé wines are normally kept in the ice bucket to maintain their cool temperature, which helps to balance the wine's acids and alcohol on your palate; if the wine gets warm, it starts to taste "hot." But when it comes to complex white wines, such as a fine white Burgundy or full-bodied rich California Chardonnay, some of us like the wine to come closer to room temperature. The reason is that if a complex white is served too cold, you may miss the nuances of aroma and flavor; they'll be numbed by the cold. The ice bucket should always be handy for these wines, but don't hesitate to ask your server to take the wine out of the bucket after you taste it, and later ask him or her to place it back in the bucket if the wine starts to get too warm for your liking.

The decanting option

WHEN SHOULD YOU ASK YOUR server to decant your wine? Much of the time decanting is not necessary, especially if you're drinking a wine that is meant to be drunk young and does not exhibit a lot of complexity. There's certainly no reason to decant sparkling wines (it will ruin the bubbles) or rosé wines. We think that there really is no good reason to decant white wines, but we've noticed that some sommeliers are offering to decant complex whites that can age a bit, in order to aerate them and emphasize their volatile elements. There's nothing wrong with this extra touch of service, but we think you'll achieve the same result by pouring the wine in a good wine glass, swirling, smelling, and tasting.

As for decanting red wines, there are two good reasons to do so. The first and best-known reason for decanting a wine is to separate the sediment from the wine, usually an older wine. The proper way to decant an older red is to pour the wine from the bottle into the decanter while illuminating the neck of the bottle with a light source; a candle is the classic tool. When sediment begins to appear in the neck of the bottle, your server will stop pouring. About a half hour later, repeat the decanting procedure; you'll probably get another glass or so out of the bottle once the sediment settles again.

Not everyone believes that older red wines, especially delicate older reds, should be decanted. The reason for this thinking is that when the wine is decanted it takes a big hit of oxygen, and the delicate wine might not be able to handle such dramatic exposure to air all at once. We have witnessed wines that fall apart shortly after decanting, so there is something to this idea. Decanting an older wine, whether at home or in a restaurant, is a personal choice that you should make.

The second good reason to decant a red wine may surprise you, and we actually think it may be more important than decanting old reds as described above. You might want to decant a young red wine that has the potential to age in order to aerate the wine, allowing it to "open up" and demonstrate its potential. We like decanting these younger reds because the air really allows the wine to "breathe," providing another layer of complexity, another layer of enjoyment. A similar outcome can be achieved if you are drinking out of elegant wine glasses with large bowls and you aerate the wine by swirling. And again, decanting is a personal choice.

Good glassware, please!

WE THINK SERVERS SHOULD MAKE sure that the proper glassware is set in advance of the actual wine service. Great wines deserve great glasses, but at the very least the glasses should be aesthetically pleasing, not too thick or heavy, and totally clear (and clean). When held up to the light, ideally the glass should almost disappear, allowing the wine to "float" in midair. If the theme of the restaurant is ultra-informal, the glasses may not be elegant, merely serviceable, but the wines shouldn't be too expensive, either.

Some restaurateurs believe that certain wines deserve better stemware than others, based on the price and pedigree of the wine. We understand that argument, but we also understand the plight of the diner who orders a simple but tasty Chianti served in a modified jelly glass and then looks over to the next table to see a couple drinking an expensive Napa Cabernet out of elegant crystal stemware. Customers should never feel like chopped liver, but treating one customer better than another based on their check totals accomplishes exactly that negative outcome. We say: good glasses for everyone!

GOT CASH?

OUR BARGAIN CHOICES

17

WELL, WE'VE REACHED THE FINAL CHAPTER OF *WineWise*, BUT BY NO MEANS THE FINAL WORD ON WINE. IF you've been reading along faithfully (or at least showing intermittent bursts of enthusiasm and interest), you've probably picked up on the fact that all three of the authors have something in common: when it comes to wine, we love a bargain.

How to define a "bargain"? It's not always the least expensive wine, though price is certainly an issue. We've found that there are many bargain wines available to savvy wine consumers, some priced incredibly low, some moderately priced. What bargain wines have in common, though, is one basic trait: they provide good value for money and often exceed expectations.

In the following pages we are going to present you with our list of bargain wines: hundreds of bargain wines from all over the world at varying price points, starting at under $10 and stepping up to under $25. Most of these wines can be found easily, a few you'll have to search for, but we know from experience that all of these wines will be enjoyable. At the very least, you'll find some exciting choices to accompany your next lunch or dinner, or some interesting components for a home wine tasting. Not all these wines will curl your toes and blow your mind but quite a few will.

Let the bargains begin . . .

Our laundry list: best bargain wines

FOR WINE LOVERS ON A BUDGET, there has never been a better time to buy and enjoy wines. Most of these wines are just plain good and provide tasty foils for your dinner at home. Some of them are truly extraordinary, especially when you figure in how little you pay for them. Some of these wines are likely to be found in supermarkets, big-box stores, and large wine shops, but just as many will show up in specialty stores.

The beauty of these wines is that they are not too hard to find, and if you can't find one, you can find another. Feel free to experiment, and we guarantee you'll find several wines that you return to time and again for the pleasure (and value) they give. We can also guarantee, because taste is subjective, that there will be a few wines on our list that you'll taste once and forget, or maybe not like at all. But isn't it better to find that out by paying about $15 for that bottle rather than $40?

We've tried to create a list of good, accessible wines with a weekly wine budget in mind. Once you start using this list and enjoying these wines, you'll find that you, your friends, and your family can enjoy a different wine several nights per week while spending a total of between $50 and $75. This makes wine fun, not fancy, and makes you WineWise. We want to encourage you to mix and match—a French white one night, a Spanish red the next; a California Sauvignon Blanc on Tuesday, an Argentine Syrah on Thursday. The idea is to enjoy great wines at a great price, to learn a bit about the wines as you go, but more important, to learn more about your own taste.

For many years now, we've prided ourselves on spending relatively little on wines to enjoy every day. We simply cannot bring ourselves to spend more than $15 to $20 per bottle on a regular basis. More often than not, our "house" wines are under $15. We are blessed to be living at a time when there is so much good wine available, with so much of it at reasonable prices.

Of course, not all inexpensive wines are great values (nor are all expensive wines worth the money). If our $25 wine can compete with a wine costing $50 or even more, we consider that to be a great value. An example: one of our favorite reds is Brunello di Montalcino from Tuscany, Italy. Today, prices for this wine start at about $60 and escalate to $200 or more for some single-vineyard and *riserva* versions. On the other hand, the less well-known Rosso di Montalcino (sometimes known as "Baby Brunello") is made from the same grapes, hails from the same region, and importantly, is often made by a great Brunello producer. Yet Rosso di Montalcino often costs less than $25. What's the catch? Rosso di Montalcino is bottled younger and may be sourced from younger vines. In this case, young is good for the value seeker, especially if you plan to drink the wine in the near future as opposed to cellaring it. Trust us: Rosso di Montalcino is delicious.

Another important point: many of the best-bargain wines we suggest are from family-owned wineries that have a sense of integrity not always found in corporate-owned wineries. The best wineries, family-owned or corporate, will put their name only on the bottles they are proud of and will sell you the best wine they can make at a fair price.

We are fortunate to live in New York State's Hudson Valley, where there are four distinct seasons. In spring and summer we tend to drink more rosé and lighter white wines. In fall and winter we like to cozy up at the fireplace with red wines. So, although wine is a bottled product and is available any time of year, that doesn't stop us from approaching our wine choices based, at least in part, on the seasons (and especially the holidays of those seasons). Of course, sparkling wine is a year-round beverage for us. We are unapologetic "bubbleheads."

Especially when we have friends over, we like to try two different wines with dinner; this can make for a memorable dinner and a fun evening. For example, we'll try a tart white wine and a dry still or sparkling rosé wine, or a sparkling wine and an off-the-beaten-path red wine. Remember that whenever you take a chance on lesser-known grape varieties or off-the-beaten-path regions, you will get more bang for your buck than if you had played it safe.

We've decided not to include vintage years in this list, as most of these wines are made to a fairly consistent standard year after year. Some vintages will be better, some worse, but these wines are consistently good, consistently enjoyable. We are confident that any wine listed by us is worth trying. Some of them may not knock your socks off, but they will all be honest, well-made wines.

Within our bargain choices you may find some wines you've already tried, but we hope you'll find some new wines to enjoy.

We've chosen hundreds of wines for your consideration—all of them good, and all at affordable prices. Happily, based on their price-to-quality ratio, these value-driven wines really do underpromise and overdeliver. In other words, they're true WineWise wines.

Of course, all of these wines really come alive when paired with food, and we hope you will experiment with some of the wine and food pairing suggestions we offer in *WineWise* as well as come up with your own combinations. Finally, to get the best value—and most enjoyment—out of these wines, please drink them in good health and in good company.

Cheers!

Note that wines that normally retail for under $15 are marked with an asterisk (*). Some of these wines actually sell for less than $10, but these days pricing of wines at such low price points tends to be fluid depending on where you live and who's selling the wine. We haven't just chosen these wines because they're "cheap"; we really think they deliver good value. These are good wines at very affordable prices.

SPARKLING WINES: DRY AND SEMI-DRY UNDER $25

Brut, *Blanc de Noirs*, and Rosé produced by Handley, Domaine Carneros, Roederer Estate, Domaine Chandon, Schramsberg "Mirabelle," Gloria Ferrer, California

"Celebre," Chateau Frank, New York (semi-dry)

Brut, *Blanc de Blancs*, Domaine Ste. Michelle, Washington

Brut, *Blanc de Noirs*, and Rosé produced by Gruet, New Mexico

Brut, Cave Spring, Canada

Vouvray Mousseux produced by Domaine de Clos de L'Epernay, Marc Bredif, Vincent Raimbault, Phillipe Foreau, Monmousseau, France

Cremant d'Alsace produced by Lucien Albrecht, Pierre Sparr, Willm, France

Cremant de Bourgogne produced by Jaillance, Louis Baillot, Simonnet-Febvre, Bailly-Lapierre, Albert Bichot, Cave de Lugny, France

Brut produced by Banfi, Rotari, Italy

Franciacorta produced by Berlucchi, Contadi Castaldi, Italy

Prosecco produced by Mionetto, La Marca, Nino Franco, Maschio, Bellenda, Bisol, Bortolomiol, Valdo, Zardetto, Italy

Brut and Rosé Cava produced by Juve Y Camps, Pares Balta, Segura Viudas, Leopardi, Cavas Hill, Paul Chenau, Jaume Serra (Cristalino), Spain

Brut Nature Vintage Cava, Freixenet, Jaume Serra (Cristalino), Spain

Baga Brut Rosé, Luis Pato, Portugal

"Metodo Tradicional 3B," Filipa Pato, Portugal

"Ode Panos" produced by Spiropoulos and "Amalia," produced by Tselepos, Greece

WHITE WINES: SEMI-DRY, FRUITY, AND FLORAL UNDER $25

Riesling produced by Trefethen, Jekel, California

Riesling produced by Konstantin Frank, Anthony Road, Wagner, Hermann Wiemer, New York

Riesling produced by Hogue, "Eroica" by Chateau Ste. Michelle, Pacific Rim, Snoqualmie, Columbia Crest*, Covey Run*, Washington

Gewurztraminer produced by Navarro, Handley, Frey, Gundlach Bundschu, Adler Fels, California

Gewurztraminer, Lenz, New York

Chenin Blanc produced by Pacific Rim*, L'Ecole No. 41, Washington

Riesling produced by Cave Spring, Inniskillin, Flat Rock, Gray Monk, Mission Hill, Cedar Creek, Canada

Chenin Blanc, Quail's Gate, Canada

Gewurztraminer produced by Malivoire, Thornhaven, Tinhorn Creek, Wild Goose, Gray Monk, Canada

Riesling produced by Jacob's Creek*, Petaluma, McWilliams*, Wakefield, Kilikanoon, Yalumba "Y"*, Rosemount*, Annie's Lane*, Australia

"Vina Esmeralda," Moscatel-Gewurztraminer, Torres, Spain

Vouvray produced by Domaine des Aubuisieres, Francois Pinon, Marc Bredif, Chateau Moncontour, Saget, Chateau Monfort, France

Jasnieres produced by Domaine de Bellivieres, Pascal Janvier, Domaine de Cezin, France

Riesling and Gewurztraminer produced by Zind-Humbrecht, Trimbach, Hugel, Paul Blanck, Albert Mann, Pierre Sparr, Schlumberger, Leon Beyer, Lucien Albrecht, Willm, Dopff au Moulin, Dopff et Irion, France

Riesling produced by St. Urbans-Hof ("Urban"*), Dr. Loosen ("L"*), Schloss Vollrads, S.A. Prum, Dr. Burklin-Wolf, Bert Simon, Deinhard, Hans Lang, Von Kesselstatt, Monchof, Rudolf Muller; "Wehlener Sonnenuhr" by Richter; "Niersteiner Paterberg" by George Albrecht Steiner, Germany

Riesling produced by Domaine Wachau, Austria

WHITE WINES: DRY UNDER $25

Chardonnay produced by Iron Horse, Dry Creek, Wente, Trefethen, Benziger, Calera, Au Bon Climat, Schug, Fetzer*, Lincourt, Joseph Phelps "Fogdog," Mirrasou*, Pepperwood Grove*, Bogle*, Smoking Loon*, Bonterra, Artesa, Buehler, Beringer, Raymond, Concannon, La Crema, Hartford, Simi, Chalone, Acacia, DeLoach, Pedroncelli, Rued, Jenner, Brutocao, Buena Vista, Coppola "Director's Cut," California

Sauvignon Blanc produced by Benziger*, Preston, Matanzas Creek, Honig, Quivira, Dry Creek, Frog's Leap, St. Supery, Quivira, Smoking Loon*, Barefoot*, Greystone Cellars*, Adler Fels, Geyser Peak, Guenoc, Husch, Provenance, Charles Krug, Wildhurst*, Rodney Strong, Joel Gott, California

Marsanne produced by Qupe, California

Viognier produced by Miner, Zaca Mesa, Bonterra, Smoking Loon*, Cline*, and Viognier–Chenin Blanc Pine Ridge*, California

Albarino produced by Bonny Doon, Lindquist, Mariposa, LaZarre, Martina, Odisea, Ferdinand, Chateau Lettau, Abrente, Martian Ranch, California

Pinot Gris, Pinot Grigio, or Pinot Blanc produced by Au Bon Climat, Benessere, J Vineyards, Montevina*, Big House*, Rex Goliath*, Coppola "Bianco"*, Van Ruiten*, Tamas Estates*, Gnarly Head*, California

Chardonnay produced by Millbrook, Whitecliff, Lenz, Channing Daughters, Paumonok, Konstantin Frank, Lamoreaux Landing, Red Newt, Swedish Hill, Atwater, McGregor, Sheldrake Point, New York

Rkatsiteli, Konstantin Frank, New York

Gruner Veltliner produced by Konstantin Frank, One Woman Winery, New York

Tocai Friulano produced by Millbrook, Channing Daughters, New York

Pinot Gris, Sheldrake Point, New York

Semillon, L'Ecole No. 41, Washington

Pinot Gris produced by Willakenzie, Willamette Valley Vineyards, Schmidt Family, Duck Pond, Firesteed, King Estate, Oregon

Pinot Blanc produced by Eyrie, The Four Graces, Oregon

Chardonnay produced by Cave Spring, Le Clos Jordanne, Mission Hill, Quails Gate, Canada

Pinot Gris produced by Blasted Church, Burrowing Owl, Lake Breeze, Sandhill, Red Rooster, Canada

Marsanne, Mitchelton, Australia

Viognier, Yalumba, Australia

Chardonnay produced by McGuigan, Houghton, De Bortoli, Philp Shaw, Yalumba, Dominique Portet, Australia

Sauvignon Blanc produced by Shaw & Smith, De Bortoli, Philip Shaw, D'Arenberg, Cape Mentelle, Yalumba, Dominique Portet, Katnook Estate, Groom, Australia

Sauvignon Blanc produced by Craggy Range, Giesen, Matua Valley, The Crossings*, Corbans, Milton, Te Mata, Kim Crawford, Ata Rangi, Palliser, Dry River, Brancott, Selaks, Villa Maria, Nautilus, Kumeu River, Babich, New Zealand

Torrontes produced by Trapiche*, Susana Balbo, Argentina

Sauvignon Blanc produced by Terrunyo, Maycas del Limari, Emiliana Natura*, Veramonte*, Montes, Torres, Carmen, Santa Rita*, Cono Sur*, Errazuriz*, Leyda, Kingston Family, Casillero del Diablo*, Viu Manent, Morande*, Los Vascos, MontGras*, Casa Lapostolle, Nimbus, Santa Carolina*, Caliterra*, Chile

Sauvignon Blanc produced by Mulderbosch, Warwick, Boschendal, Klein Constantia, Robertson, Buitenverwachting, Simonsig, Thelema, Brampton, Nederburg, Sebeka, Neil Ellis, South Africa

"Goats do Roam"*, South Africa

Muscadet Sevre et Maine produced by Chateau de la Chesnaie*, Domaine de la Louveterie*, Marquis de Goulaine*, Chateau de la Ragotiere*, Domaine Sauvion*, Domaine de la Quilla*, Les Vergers*, La Forcine*, Pierre Luneau-Papin, Domaine de la Pepiere, Domaine L'Ecu, France

Cotes du Rhone produced by Jean-Luc Colombo*; Guigal*, Louis Bernard, France

Pinot Blanc produced by Schlumberger, Sparr, Hugel, Albrecht*, Blanck*, France

Sylvaner, Domaine Ostertag, France

Chateau Bonnet*, France

Quincy produced by Henri Bourgeois, Joseph Mellot, Phillipe Portier, Domaine Mardon, France

Menetou-Salon produced by Domaine de Chatenoy, H. Pelle, Latour St. Martin, France

Savoie "Jongiuex," Eugene Carrel*, France

Bourgogne (Chardonnay) produced by Joseph Drouhin*, Louis Jadot*, Olivier Leflaive, Bouchard Pere et Fils, Faiveley, France

Rully produced by Vincent Girardin, Champy, Jobard, France

La Vielle Ferme*, France

Gavi produced by La Scolca, Villa Sparina, Pio Cesare, Michele Chiarlo, Marchese di Barolo, Bersano*, "Principessa Gavia" and "Principessa Perlante" by Banfi, Italy

Falanghina produced by Mastroberardinio, Feudi di San Gregorio, Ocone, Italy

Soave and Soave Classico produced by Pieropan, Anselmi, Inama, Bertani*, Allegrini*, Gini, Cantina di Soave, Bolla "Tufaie"*, Italy

Pinot Grigio produced by Bastianich, Tiefenbrunner, Kris, Lageder, Jermann, Livio Felluga, Masi*, Pighin*, Sartori*, Lungarotti, Cavit*, Italy

"Blanc de Pacs"* and "Electio"*, Pares Balta, Spain

"Seleccio"*, Can Feixes-Huguet, Spain

Godello produced by Dom Abad, Alvarez de Toledo, Godelia, Godeval, Valdesil, Telmo Rodriguez, Luna Beberide, Spain

Ribeiro, Vina Costeira, Spain

"Reboreda"*, Campante, Spain

Albarino produced by Nora, Palacio de Fefinanes, Vionta, Martin Codax, Valdamor, Morgadio, Condes de Alberei, Fillaboa, As Laxas, Spain

Rueda produced by Martinsancho, Marques de Riscal, Naia, Protos, Spain

"Fuente Milano Verdejo-Viura"*, Pedro Escudero Platon, Spain

Rioja produced by Baron de Ley*, Marques de Caceres*, Muga, Zuazo Gaston*, Spain

Getariako Txacolina produced by Aizpura, Amaztoi, Talai Berri, Txomin Extxaniz, Elzaguirre, Zudugarai, Spain

Vinho Verde produced by Quinta da Aveleda*, Adega Cooperativa de Moncao*, Quinta do Ameal*, Broadbent*, Caso da Valle*, Quinta da Lixa*, "Gazela" by Sogrape*, Portugal

Alvarinho produced by Anselmo Mendes "Muros Antigos," Soalheiro, Quinta da Aveleda*, Portugal

Bucelas, Quinta da Romeira*, Portugal

Arinto, Quinta da Alorna*, Portugal

Bical and Arinto, and "Nossa Calcario" Filipa Pato, Portugal

Vinhas Velhas, Luis Pato*, Portugal

Encruzado produced by Quinta dos Roques, Perdigao, Portugal

"Monte Velho Reserva"*, "Private Selection" Esporao*, Portugal

Douro produced by Quinta do Crasto, "Redoma" by Niepoort, Quinta de la Rosa, Portugal

Santorini produced by Sigalas, Santo, Gaia, Argyros, Athina Tsoli, Gavalas, Boutari, Hatzidakis, Koutsoyannopoulos, Karamolegos, Greece

Moschofilero produced by Tselepos, Biblia Chora, Boutari, Antonopoulos, Tsantali*, Greece

Malagousia produced by Geravissiliou, Alpha Estate, Boutari, Domaine Zafeirakis, Antonopoulos, Greece

Assyrtiko-Sauvignon Blanc, "Metoxi"*, Tsantali, Greece

"Foloi" and "Kallisto"*, Mercouri, Greece

Robola produced by Gentilini and Robola Cooperative Cephalonia, Greece

Sauvignon Blanc, Alpha Estate, Greece

Malvasia, Alexakis, Greece

"Zoe"*, George Skouras, Greece

Assyrtiko produced by Ktima Pavlidis and "Emphasis" produced by Lyrarakis, Greece

ROSÉ WINES: DRY UNDER $25

Rosé produced by Bonny Doon, J Vineyards, Tablas Creek, Sobon*, Toad Hollow*, MacPhail, California

Rosé produced by Mas de la Dame "Rosé du Mas"*, Mas de Gourgonnier, Domaine Ott, Chateau du Roquefort "Corail"*, Chateau d'Eclans "Whispering Angel," Commanderie de Peyrassol, Domaine de la Foquette, Chateau du Rouet, Jean-Luc Colombo "Cape Bleue"*, Domaine Sainte Lucie, Chateau Guiot*, Chateau Routas, Chateau Miraval, Chateau Coussin, Caves Plaimont "Retrouvees Rosé"*, Domaine Le Galantin, Gueissard, Domaine Tempier, Chateau Pradeaux, Domaine Bunan, Chateau D'Aqueria, Prieure de Montezargues, France

Rosato produced by Banfi "Centine"*, Argiolas, San Giovanni, Maculan, Mastroberardino, La Scolca, Re Manfredi, Falesco, Planeta, Cusumano, Cavalchina, Corte Gardoni, Librandi, Italy

Rosado produced by Julian Chivite "Gran Feudo"*, Marques de Caceres*, Muga*, El Coto*, Capcanes "Mas Donis"*, Las Rocas*, Pares Balta*, Cuatro Pasos*, Ameztoi "Rubentis" Ochoa, Spain

"Akakies" produced by Kir-Yianni, and "Meliasto"* produced by Spiropoulos, Greece

RED WINES: DRY UNDER $25

Zinfandel produced by Dendor Patton, Dry Creek, Edmeades, Seghesio, St. Francis, Buena Vista, Benziger, Frey, Joel Gott, Montevina, Quivira, Bogle*, Gnarly Head*, Dancing Bull*, Cline*, Ravenswood (Lodi)*, Rancho Zabaco*, Pepperwood Grove*, Decoy, Coppola "Diamond Series" and "Director's Cut," Alexander Valley Vineyards, Terra d'Oro, Murphy-Goode*, California

Syrah produced by Qupe, Benziger, Valley of the Moon, Fess Parker, Guenoc, Justin, Bonterra, California

Petite Sirah produced by Foppiano, Bogle*, Castle Rock*, Concannon*, Parducci, Spellbound, California

Cabernet Sauvignon and/or Merlot produced by Benziger, Louis M. Martini, Dry Creek, Geyser Peak, Alexander Valley Vineyards, Ghost Pines, Greystone Cellars*, Buena Vista, Kenwood, Lyeth "L"*, Pepperwood Grove*, J. Lohr, Eberle, Aquinas, Kunde, Hess Select, Merryvale "Starmont," DeLoach*, Coppola "Diamond Series," Cupcake*, Chateau St. Jean, Joel Gott, Frei Brothers, St. Francis, Layer Cake, Rodney

Strong, Smoking Loon*, Guenoc, BV, Avalon, Joseph Carr, Firestone, Bogle*, Raymond "R Collection"*, Wente, Edna Valley Vineyard*, Kendall-Jackson, Joseph Phelps "Fogdog," California

Pinot Noir produced by Kenwood, Wild Horse, Calera (Central Coast), Au Bon Climat, Chamisal, Carmel Road, Echelon*, Concannon, Mark West*, Sanford "Flor de Campo," Geyser Peak, MacMurray Ranch, Cambria, Sebastiani, Byron, DeLoach, Castle Rock*, Rodney Strong, Bernardus, Parducci*, Coppola "Director's," Joseph Phelps "Fogdog," California

"Old Patch Red," Trentadue, California

Pinot Noir produced by Millbrook, Whitecliff, Bashakill, McGregor, Heart in Hands, Ravines, Konstantin Frank, New York

Pinot Noir produced by A to Z, Acrobat, Erath, Ken Wright, Cloudline, Evening Land, Elk Cove, Oregon

Cabernet Sauvignon and/or Merlot produced by Columbia Crest*, Chateau Ste. Michelle, Three Rivers, Charles Smith, Castle Rock*, Red Diamond*, 14 Hands*, Waterbrook, Canoe Ridge, StoneCap*, Washington

Cabernet Sauvignon and Cabernet Blends produced by Cedar Creek, Mission Hill, Sumac Ridge, Canada

Grenache produced by Pirramimma, Layer Cake, D'Arenberg, Yalumba, St Hallett, Ross Estate, Australia

Shiraz and blends produced by Kilikanoon, D'Arenberg, WoopWoop*, Wyndham*, St Hallett, Yalumba, Domaine Terlato and Chapoutier, Penfolds, Oxford Landing*, Yangarra, Tahbilk, Torbreck "Woodcutters," Hardys, Peter Lehmann, Greg Norman, Angove*, Taltarni, Layer Cake, Jim Barry, Evans, Hewitson, Australia

Crozes-Hermitage produced by Guigal, Chapoutier, Yann Chave, Cave de Tain l'Hermitage, Domaine Combier, Paul Jaboulet, Alain Graillot, Jean Luc Colombo, Delas Freres, France

Vacqueyras produced by Vidal-Fleury, Le Colombier, Pierre Amadieu, Arnoux & Fils, la Bouissiere, Font Sarade, Barnier, Prat Sura, la Pigeade, Edmond Berle, Montirius, les Ondines, Roucas Toumba, France

Cotes du Rhone, Cotes du Rhone-Villages, and Cotes de Ventoux produced by Guigal, Jaboulet "Parallele 45"*, Jean-Luc Colombo, Perrin et Fils, Louis Bernard*, Verget*, Andre Brunel*, Chateau de Saint Cosme, Tardieu-Laurent, Vidal Fleury, Alain Jaume et Fils, Delas*, Chateau Mont Redon, La Vieille Ferme*, France

Chinon produced by Joguet, Couly-Dutheil, Guy Saguet, Bernard Baudry, Olga Raffault, Jean-Maurice Raffault, Marc Bredif, France

Bordeaux produced by the following chateaux (all will feature *Chateau* as the first word on the label. An example: Chateau de Macard): Larose Trintaudon, Greysac, Croix Figeac, Chantegrive, La Tour Leognan, Lusseau, Maison Neuve, Leontins, Puy Blanquet, Beaumont, Citran, Cap de Faugeres, Macard, Reynon, Charmail, Marjosse, La Grave, Les Carregades, Bonnet, Malescasse, France

Bourgogne (Pinot Noir) produced by Champy, Nicolas Potel, Louis Jadot, Joseph Drouhin, Olivier Leflaive, Bouchard Pere et Fils, Boisset, Mommesin, France

Moulin-a-Vent, Morgon, Brouilly and other *cru* Beaujolais produced by Georges Dufoeuf, Louis Jadot, Vincent Girardin, Louis Latour, Domaine Diochon, Marcel Lapierre, Trenel, Chateau de la Chaize, Chateau de Pierreux, Jean-Paul Brun, Chaeau Thivin, Michel Tete, Henry Fessy, Jean Descombes, Laurent Martray, Hubert Lapierre, Jean-Marc Bourgaud, Joseph Drouhin, Dominique Piron, Jean-Marc Lafont, Potel-Aviron, Louis-Claude Desvignes, France

Minervois produced by Hecht et Bannier, Gerard Bertrand, Chateau Helene, France

Cahors, Chateau Lagrezette, Domaine la Berangeraie, France

Coteaux d'Aix en Provence by Chateau Revelette, France

Barbera d'Asti and Barbera d'Alba produced by Bava, "Libera," Cascina Castlet, Albina Rocca, Olim Bauda, Beni di Batasiolo*, Pio Cesare, Coppo, Michele Chiarlo, Stefano Farina*, Renato Ratti, Borgogno, Bersano, Icardi, G.D. Vajra, Silvio Grasso, Marchesi di Barolo, Fontanafredda, Carlo Giacosa, Damilano, Rovero*, La Spinetta, Prunotto, Marcarini, Batasiolo, Italy

Langhe Nebbiolo and Nebbiolo d'Alba produced by Produttori del Barbaresco, Renato Ratti, Marcarini, Fontanafredda, Vietti, Pio Cesare, Damilano, Elio Grasso, Giacomo Ascheri, Gigi Rosso, Albino Rocca, Italy

Dolcetto d'Alba, Dolcetto d'Asti, and Dolcetto di Dogliani produced by Lucio Sandrone, Bruno Giacosa, Bersano, Bava, Poderi Luigi, Pio Cesare, Prunotto, Icardi, Elio Altare, Albina Rocca, Aldo Conterno, Stefano Farina, Marchese di Barolo, Renato Ratti, Marcarini, Domenico Clerico, Mascarello, Moccagatta, Punset, Borgogno, Boschis, Voerzio, Italy

"Centine"* and "Col di Sasso"* by Banfi; "Borgoforte," by Villa Pillo, Italy

Chianti and Chianti Classico produced by Badia a Coltibuono, Isole e Olena, Gabbiano, Malenchini, Geografico, Falchini, Antinori, Badia a Passignano, Banfi, Barbi, Barone Ricasoli/Brolio, Carpineto, Castellare, Fonterutoli, Nippozzano, Querceto, Volpaia, Vicchiomaggio, Cecchi, da Vinci, Dievole, Felsina, Fontodi, Marcellina, Melini, Il Molino di Grace, Monsanto, Nozzole, Rocca delle Macie, Rocca di Castagnole, Ruffino, Italy

Rosso di Montalcino produced by Banfi, Il Poggione, Caparzo, Geografico, La Fortuna, Poggio Il Castellare, Fanti, Casanova di Neri, Mastrojanni, San Lorenzo, Col d'Orcia, Italy

Aglianico del Vulture produced by D'Angelo, Paternoster, Tenuta La Querce, Sasso*, Cantina di Venosa, Tenuta del Portale, Notaio, Bisceglia, Basilisco, Italy

Garnacha produced by Los Rocas*, Borsao*, Ochoa*, Torres*, Almez*, Jean Leon*, Ramon Cordova (kosher), Sin-Ley*, Josep Masachs*, Red Guitar*, Spain

Bierzo produced by Luna Beberide, Dominio Tares, Losados Vinos de Finca, "Petalos" by Descendientes de J. Palacios, Spain

Valdeorras, Telmo Rodriguez, Spain

Ribeira Sacra produced by Algueira, Estrella*, Adega Cachin, Spain

Calatayud, Los Rocas*, Honora Vera, Spain

Toro produced by Campina, Rejadorada, Taurus, Spain

Montsant produced by Fra Guerau*, Buil & Gine, Celler Malondro, Spain

Priorat produced by Vall Llachs "Embruix," Alvaro Palacios "Camins del Priorat," Capafons-Osso, Tossalet, Spain

Rioja Crianza produced by Conde de Valdemar*, Montecillo*, Marques de Caceres*, Faustino*, Marques de Grinon, Marques de Riscal, Dinastia Vivanco, Marques de Arienzo, Martinez Bujanda*, Baron de Ley*, Ramon Bilbao*, CVNE, Ostatu, Beronia, Luis Canas, Paternina*, Ontanon*, LAN*, El Coto*, La Rioja Alta, Ramon Cordova (kosher), Spain

"Coronas"* and "Sangre de Toro"*, Torres, Spain

"Mas Petit" and "Indigena," Pares Balta, Spain

Tempranillo produced by Volver*, Penascal*, Marques de Riscal*, Ochoa*, Leganza*, Campo Viejo*, Raimat*, Spain

Monastrell produced by Castano, Agatipo Rico "Carchelo"*, Juan Gil*, Volver*, Casa de la Ermita*, Luzon*, Yellow+Blue*, Luis Martinez*, Spain

"Dehesa La Granja" Alejandro Fernandez, Spain

Ribera del Duero produced by Hijos Antonio de Barcelo "Vina Mayor," Finca El Encinal*, Vina Gormaz*, Cruz de Alba, Cepa 21, Emilio Moro, Prado Rey, Spain

Douro produced by Ramos Pinto "Duas Quintas"* and "Collection," Symington "Altano"*, Quinta do Crasto, Quinta do Vallado, Quinta do Vale do Meao "Meandro," Wine and Soul "Manoella," Quinta do Portal "Mural"*, Ferreirinha "Esteva"*, Lavradores de Feitora "Tres Bagos," Aveleda "Charamba"*, Dow's "Vale do Bonfim Reserva," Lemos and Van Zeller, Poeria, Quinta de la Rosa, Niepoort "Vertente" and "Twisted," Portugal

Dao produced by Alvaro Castro, Casa de Santar, Quinta dos Roques, Sogrape "Callabriga," Alianca "Particular"*, Portugal

"Periquita"*, Jose Maria de Fonseca, Portugal

Trincadeira, "Vila Santa Reserva" and "Marques de Borba"*, Joao Portugal Ramos, Portugal

Touriga Nacional produced by DFJ "Point West"*, Alianca Vista Reserva, Quinta do Pinto, Portugal

Reserva and "Monte Velho"*, Esporao, Portugal

"Chamine" and Alentejano Tinto, Cortes de Cima, Portugal

Baga-Touriga Nacional produced by Luis Pato*, Foz de Arouce, Portugal

Bairrada, produced by Quinta da Bageiras, Campolargo, Portugal

Tinta Barocca*, "Bons Ventos"* and "Lab"*, Casa Santos Lima, Portugal

Tinto, Quinta do Chocopalha, Portugal

Naoussa produced by Boutari, Kir-Yianni, Domaine Karydas, Katogi & Strofilia, Thymiopoulus, Foundis, Argatia, Dalamaras, Tsantali, Greece

Nemea produced by Gaia, Papaioannou, Tselepos, Spiropoulos, Skouras, Greece

Rapsani* and Rapsani Reserve, Tsantali, Greece

"Siatista" Xinomavro, Dio Fili, Greece

"Cava," Mercouri, Greece

"Eclipse" Mavrodaphne, Gentilini, Greece

SWEET WINES UNDER $25

"Electra" Moscato*, Quady, California

Moscato Giallo, Alois Lageder, Italy

Muscat of Samos produced by Tsantali*, Kourtaki*, Cooperative of Samos*, Greece

Mavrodaphne of Patras, produced by Mercouri, Antonopoulos, Greece

"Rosa Regale," Brachetto d'Acqui, Banfi, Italy

Moscato d'Asti produced by Paolo Saracco, Ceretto, Chiarlo, Cascina Castlet, Italy

DRY FORTIFIED WINES UNDER $25

Manzanilla Sherry produced by Hidalgo "La Gitana," Barbadillo, Lustau "Jarana," Osborne, Valdespino "Deliciosa," Pedro Domecq, Spain

Fino Sherry produced by Gonzalez Byass ("Tio Pepe" kosher and non-kosher versions), Lustau "Papirusa"*, Osborne, Barbadillo, Hidalgo, Valdespino "Inocente," Spain

Amontillado Sherry produced by Williams & Humbert ("Dry Sack"), Hidalgo "Napoleon," Lustau "Los Arcos," Barbadillo, Osborne, Hartey & Gibson, Sandeman, Valdespino, Gonzalez-Byass "AB Palomino," Spain

Five-Year Sercial Madeira produced by Justino, Blandy's, Leacock's, Portugal

SWEET FORTIFIED WINES UNDER $25

Pedro Ximenez Sherry produced by Lustau "San Emilio," Dios Baco "Oxford 1970," Valdespino "El Candado," Spain

Fifteen-Year Oloroso Dulce, "Dry Sack," Sherry, Williams & Humbert, Spain

"Alambre," Moscatel de Setubal, Jose Maria de Fonseca, Portugal

Tawny Porto produced by Ramos Pinto, Taylor Fladgate, Dow's*, Graham's, Fonseca, Sandeman, Niepoort, Cockburn's*, Ferreira, Portugal

Ruby Reserve Porto produced by Graham's "Six Grapes," Fonseca "Bin 27," Taylor Fladgate "First Estate," Warre's "Warrior," Sandeman "Founder's Reserve," Cockburn's "Special Reserve," Noval "Black," Kopke "Special Reserve," Portugal

Late-Bottled Vintage Porto produced by Quinta do Crasto, Dow's, Quinto do Noval, Ramos Pinto, Cockburn's, Smith Woodhouse, Taylor Fladgate, Delaforce, Graham's, Quinta do Noval, Offley, Warre's Osborne, Croft, Sandeman, Churchill's, Portugal

Five-Year Bual Madeira, Cossart-Gordon, Blandy's, Portugal

Five-Year Malmsey Madeira, Leacock, Blandy's, Portugal

"St. John," Commandaria, KEO, Cyprus

Index

Campania region (Italy), 217–218, 220m

Campo de Borja DO (Spain), 231, 241

Canada, 23, 30, 33, 278–282, 280m, 355, 356

Cannonau di Sardegna DOC (Italy), 219

Canterbury region (New Zealand), 136, 137–138

Cap, twist-off, 14, 16, 258, 342–343

Cape Agulhas region (South Africa), 143

Carbonic maceration, 181

Carmignano DOCG (Italy), 202, 204

Carneros AVA (Calif.), 50, 52, 69, 79–80, 85, 88, 106

Casablanca Valley (Chile), 23, 26, 52, 117

Castilla-La Mancha province (Spain), 242

Castilla y Leon province (Spain), 237–240

Catalonia province (Spain), 232m, 234–237

Cava (aging term), 285

Cava (sparkling wine), 225, 227, 230, 236, 297, 303–304, 306, 333

Cayuga Lake AVA (N.Y.), 111

Central Coast AVA (Calif.), 72m, 92–94, 92m

Central Otago (New Zealand), 52, 106, 138

Central Valley (Calif.), 43, 48, 72m, 94–95, 95m

Cephalonia PDO (Greece), 285, 290

Cerasuolo di Vittoria DOCG (Italy), 221

Certifications, 139–140

Chablis AOP (France), 175–176, 309

Chalk Hill AVA (Calif.), 13m, 87

Chalon AOP (France), 51, 174, 175, 178–179, 181

Chalone AVA (Calif.), 93

Chambolle-Musigny AOP (France), 50, 177, 179, 180, 268

Champagne. *See also* Sparkling wines: grapes used in, 3, 51, 153, 155; label, 154–156; nonvintage, 150, 156, 333; pairing, with food, 155, 304–306, 309; *perlage,* 15, 332; vintage, 156, 333

Champagne method. See *Methode champenoise*

Champagne region (France), 22, 50, 51, 147m, 152–157, 153m

Chardonnay (grape), 20–24; Argentinean wines, 23; Australian wines, 24, 128, 131–134; Austrian wines, 24, 273, 275; Calif. wines, 22, 79, 93; Canadian wines, 23, 278, 279, 281; Chilean wines, 23, 118, 119; Chinese wines, 24; Eastern European wines, 24; French wines, 21–22, 51, 174–179, 181, 188; German wines, 24; Greek wines, 24; Italian wines, 24, 201, 217, 218, 221; New Zealand wines, 23–24, 135–138; N.Y. wines, 22, 110–113; oak aging, 7, 20, 101, 175–176; Ore. wines, 23, 106–107, 109; pairing, with food, 22, 264, 295, 296, 298, 305, 307–310; Portuguese wines, 24, 248, 260; South African wines, 23, 139, 140, 143; Spanish wines, 24, 226, 230, 235, 236, 242; Swiss wines, 24; U.S. wines, 22–23; Wash. wines, 23, 101, 103–105

Chassagne-Montrachet AOP (France), 177, 178, 180, 310

Chateau Grillet AOP (France), 36, 37, 183

Chateauneuf-du-Pape AOP (France), 58, 59, 186, 187

Cheese, 309–310

Chenas cru Beaujolais (France), 182

Chenin Blanc (grape): Calif. wines, 73, 95; Canadian wines, 280; Loire Valley wines, 160, 162–163; Long Island wines, 113; pairing, with food, 138, 160, 162, 296, 303, 306, 307, 309; South African wines, 138, 142; sweet wines from, 322

Chianti Classico DOCG (Italy), 197, 203

Chianti Classico Riserva (Italy), 197, 201

Chianti DOCG (Italy), 195, 197, 201, 203

Chile, 116–120; kosher wines, 341; labels, 117; regions, 117–118, 118m; value wines from, 119, 355, 356

China, 277

Chiroubles cru Beaujolais (France), 182

Choosing wine, 15. *See also* Wine list; go off the beaten path, 349, 354, 361–362; and scores, 352; Tower of Power, 297, 301–302

Chorey-Les-Beaune AOP (France), 181

Cigales DO (Spain), 239, 306

Clairette de Die AOP (France), 183

Clare Valley region (Australia), 130

Clarification, 9

Clarksburg AVA (Calif.), 95, 96

Cleansing the palate, 16, 262, 303–304, 323

Clubs, wine, 63, 64, 345

Coastal Region (South Africa), 140–142

Colchagua Valley (Chile), 44, 117

Colheita Vintage Madeira (Portugal), 262

Colheita Vintage Tawny Porto (Portugal), 257

Collio DOC (Italy), 217

Colli Orientali del Friuli Picolit DOCG (Italy), 217

Colli Orientali del Friuli DOC (Italy), 217

Collioure AOP (France), 187, 188

Columbia Gorge AVA (Ore.-Wash.), 103, 108

Columbia Valley AVA (Wash.), 44, 48, 55, 100, 103

Commune. See Village AOPs

Condrieu AOP (France), 36, 37, 183

Conegliano-Valdobbiadene Prosecco Superiore DOCG (Italy), 215

Conero DOCG (Italy), 205

Constantia region (South Africa), 142

Cooking method, and choice of wine, 295, 299, 300

Coonawarra region (Australia), 45, 131

Coravin, 344

Corbieres AOP (France), 188

Corkage fees, 351–352

Corked wine, 14, 16

Corks, 4, 14, 258, 261, 342

Cornas AOP (France), 53, 184–185

Corton-Charlemagne grand cru Burgundy, 174, 177

Cosecha (label term), 229

Costieres de Nimes AOP (France), 186

Costs. *See* Market factors; Pricing

Coteaux du Languedoc AOP (France), 188

Coteaux du Layon AOP (France), 163

Cote Chalonnaise (France). *See* Chalon AOP

Cote de Beaune AOP (France), 51, 175, 177–178, 180–181

Cote de Beaune-Villages AOP (France), 175, 177, 180

Cote de Brouilly cru Beaujolais (France), 182

Cote de Nuits AOP (France), 51, 175, 179–180

Cote de Nuits-Villages AOP (France), 175, 179

Cote-Rotie AOP (France), 53, 54, 185

Coteaux d'Aix en Provence AOP (France), 189

Coteaux du Languedoc AOP (France), 187, 188

Cotes de Blaye AOP (France), 173

Cotes de Bourg AOP (France), 173

Cotes de Francs AOP (France), 173

Cotes du Rhone AOP (France), 183, 186

Cotes du Rhone-Villages AOP (France), 186

Cotes du Luberon AOP (France), 186

Cotes du Rousillon AOP (France), 188, 322

Cotes du Rousillon-Villages AOP (France), 188

Cotes du Ventoux AOP (France), 186

Cotes du Vivarais AOP (France), 186

Cream Sherry (Spain), 5, 244

Cremant wines, 157, 160, 174, 181, 306, 333

Crianza (label term), 230

Crozes-Hermitage AOP (France), 53, 54, 183, 184, 306

Cru Beaujolais, 182–183

Cru bourgeois, 171

Cru classe, 172

Crusted Porto (Portugal), 256

Curico region (Chile), 44

Cuvee de prestige, 156

D

Dao DOP (Portugal), 248, 249, 251, 259

Darling region (South Africa), 142

Decanting, 358

Des Collines Rhodaniennes IGP (France), 149, 183

Demi sec (label term), 155

Designated-Age Sherry (Spain), 244

Dessert wines, 291–292, 357. *See also* Icewine

Diamond Mountain District AVA (Calif.), 82, 83

DO (Spain), 228

DOC (Italy), 196, 198

DOC (Spain), 229

DOCG (Italy), 198

Dolcetto d'Acqui DOC (Italy), 195, 209–210

Dolcetto d'Alba DOC (Italy), 209–210, 212